# A TREASURY
# of
# EARLY CHRISTIANITY

# A Treasury of EARLY CHRISTIANITY

EDITED WITH AN INTRODUCTION BY

Anne Fremantle

NEW YORK · MCMLIII

PUBLISHED BY THE VIKING PRESS

For A.J.
who will never read it


PUBLISHED IN NOVEMBER 1953
PUBLISHED ON THE SAME DAY IN THE DOMINION OF CANADA
BY THE MACMILLAN COMPANY OF CANADA LIMITED



LIBRARY OF CONGRESS CATALOG CARD NUMBER: 53-7952

SET IN GRANJON AND CASLON TYPES
BY VAIL-BALLOU PRESS, INC.
PRINTED IN THE UNITED STATES BY HADDON CRAFTSMEN,
SCRANTON, PA.

# Preface

Why do we know so little today about the early Fathers? Few people even know who they are or when they were, and it is easier to get hold of Buddhist or Brahman literature and legend than of the writings of the men who for seven hundred years made all the literature of Christendom. It is true that St Augustine's *Confessions* can be bought entire, unexpurgated, for as little as 35 cents, but most of the Fathers—Greek, Syrian, Armenian, or Latin—are almost inaccessible behind the cliff wall of Migne's* formidable *Patrologia*. The Fathers may also be found, in some theological libraries, unappetizingly set out in double columns on poor paper in the dusty Victorian volumes of ante-Nicene, Nicene, and post-Nicene Fathers, translated and edited by the great men of the Oxford Movement, Pusey, Newman, Keble. It is true that there are two excellent new series being published currently: the one in The Ancient Christian Writers series by the Newman Bookshop, at Westminster, Maryland; the other by The Fathers of the Church, Inc., 475 Fifth Avenue, New York, N.Y. But these are series, not single volumes. And who wants to buy, say, Arnobius's *Case Against the Pagans,* in seven books, or Prosper of Aquitaine on *Grace and Free Will,* before having first sampled them?

Yet if anyone—from lack of opportunity, perforce, or deliberately—passes up the whole first seven hundred years of Christian life and letters, he is neglecting an irreplaceable source of nourishment and delight.

Yes, delight. For the Fathers are as gay as they are great. These men who effected the greatest religious change in the history of mankind, who in the course of some four hundred years applied "the most powerful moral lever that has ever been applied to the affairs of man" (as the rationalist W. E. H. Lecky admitted in his *History*

* The French nineteenth-century priest who assembled and edited 161 volumes of Greek Fathers and 221 volumes of Latin Fathers.

*of European Morals*), were violent, startling, daring writers, quite tremendously vital, and they are still passionately alive today. It is impossible to read Clement of Alexandria's Emily Post-ish account of the Christian etiquette for banquet or baths, or St Gregory Thaumaturgus's commencement address for his beloved Origen's school, without smiling; Sulpicius Severus's naïve attempts to boost his life of St Martin, and his fishing for good reviews of his book, are as absolutely modern as they are authentically antique; St Jerome's dignified attempts to cuff the loutish young Augustine back into his place are only equaled by Augustine's snide needling of the crusty old translator.

Yet it is the serious side of the Fathers that should most appeal to the reader of today. The tremendous sale of inspirational books, of conversion stories, of self-help manuals, shows there is a steady group of readers seeking a *way*. Some of these seekers are more aware of Indian Yoga or Chinese Tao than of the Christian religion. Yet each of these words means exactly the same thing: *yoga,* a yoke; *tao,* a binding (as of a book); *religio,* the thing that binds. And the early Fathers provide essentially just that: a binding, a *religio,* which belongs to all who inherit the Greco-Judaeo-Christian tradition; while to Christians—Catholic, Protestant, or Orthodox—the Fathers are a joint heritage. And in our divided world they should be a binding force, spanning seven hundred splendid years, providing us with great writers and great doers, with teachers, martyrs, and saints in plenty, whom we can unbickeringly and undenominationally admire.

An anthology should be like a good party. When you first look in, you should be able to recognize a few old friends, or you may feel strange and lost and shy; but you don't want to know everyone, or even many people, or you will be bored, for you are hoping to make new friends as well as to rejoice in the old ones. So here are gathered well-known, never-to-be-forgotten passages, such as those from St Augustine's *Confessions;* the story of Thais, which inspired Anatole France; and St Ignatius of Antioch's description of himself as the wheat of God, which the child in Alphonse Daudet's *Letters from My Windmill* spelled aloud. But there are also many less well-known excerpts, and many not published before except in obscure and erudite publications—such as Origen's spirited discussion with some bishops, so like a congressional loyalty hearing of today, and St. Melito's touching second-century Good Friday sermon.

This *Treasury* has been divided into seven sections. The first tries to show the kind of ideal person the Christian had in mind, wanted to be, and often succeeded in becoming. Some of the arguments he advanced, as he had to defend his way against the people among whom he lived—Jewish, pagan, and, later, Saracen—are given in the third section. Then follows a section of descriptions of what he believed: the bare bones, the skeletal structure of dogma and definition, together with accounts of creeds and of councils. The sections on martyrs and monks are frankly human-interest stories: how many there were of both is an astonishment. The Theban Legion, the Phrygian village massacred entire, are but items in the list of that "multitude which none can number" who died during these centuries for their faith: died at the hands of pagans, of Arians or other heretics, or, later, of Saracens. The monks, too, are a sizable crowd: St Jerome (340?–420) writes of fifty thousand in one monastery when he visited the Thebaid; St Serapion (died c. 362) had ten thousand in his; two thousand came to the funeral of St Martin of Tours in 399. Gibbon is sarcastic, and Lecky pained, over the flight from reality which such numbers suggest. Yet, granting that a few fled to the desert to escape persecution or military service, Tertullian is quietly emphatic about the majority of Christians: "We are not Brahmans or Hindus; we fight at your side." And St Macarius, one of the strictest and most famous of the ascetics, is equally positive some time later: "I see that God regards not whether one is virgin or married, whether one is in a monastery or the world: He considers only the disposition of the heart, and gives the Spirit to all who desire to serve Him, whatever their condition may be." Or, as St Augustine put it, "In the beginning was the Word: behold Him to whom Mary hearkened; and the Word was made flesh: behold Him whom Martha served."

For, as the section on the Life of Prayer is intended to show, the water of life continuously irrigates the individual soul and through it flows out into the world. Whether the individual was in the monastery, the arena, the desert, or the barracks, journeying into exile or ruling a nation, the dialogue between man's single soul and its Maker, carried on in countless voices, has been uninterrupted. And all the Fathers, all the martyrs, all the monks, lived only for that conversation, preferred death to its interruption. Indeed, the Incarnation itself only happened, the Church itself only exists, to further it and to bring it to its desired endless continuation in the Beatific Vision.

Finally, there are a few poems—inadequate, as translations of verse always are. But it is hoped they will at least show that the Fathers, from the first to the last—as Thoreau says we all must—*sang* their love.

# Contents



## *The Christian Ideal*

## The Martyrs



## The Arguments: Attacks and Apologies

### THE TESTIMONY OF THE PAGANS



### THE TESTIMONY OF THE CHRISTIANS

## *The Definitions*

### THE CREEDS



### THE COUNCILS



### DEVELOPMENT OF DOGMA



### THE CHRISTIAN REACTION AGAINST HERETICS



## *The Life of Prayer*

## *The Monks*

# Introduction

ANNE FREMANTLE

What is written, they say, remains. From its earliest beginnings the religion of the Word, who himself wrote no word (except one, with His finger, in the dust) was expressed in a literature. Christian literature, which may be said to have begun with Pontius Pilate's superscription over the Cross on Calvary, includes not only the writings of Christians upon Christian subjects, but also the work of Christian authors on profane subjects, such as Celsus's *True Discourse* in the second century, and the anti-Christian writings, such as those of the Emperor Julian in the fourth. Between all these writers and their twentieth-century successors, whether pro- or anti-Christian, the continuity is clear and unbroken.

Jewish in origin, Christianity from the first spread outward, becoming Roman, Greek, Persian, Ethiopian, Egyptian. Historically, at the first, it appeared a pious, reforming Jewish sect. That Rome, not Jerusalem, so early became its headquarters, was due both to the hostility of the persecuting Jews and to the standoffish spirit of the Christian community of Jerusalem, which resented the conversions of pagans and wanted to insist that every catechumen become a Jew before receiving baptism. Twenty years after the Ascension, Jerusalem was a backwater, already outside the strong current of missionary Christianity. The destruction in the year 70 scattered the tiny community, which was further reduced during the last great Jewish revolt in 132. Much later, the few scattered Christian communities grouped themselves around Aelia Capitolina (the purely Roman colony built by Hadrian on the ruins of Jerusalem), but these were recruited from among the pagans. Only at the end of the fourth century was the Bishop of Aelia once more entitled Bishop of Jerusalem. Many of his flock—Nazareans, as they were called—lapsed into heresy and were condemned as Ebionites.

But while the Church of Jerusalem languished, its two vigorous young branches at Antioch and Rome flourished and became the two great centers of the evangelizing activity of the early Church. It was at Antioch that the Christians were first so named, and the modern feasts of the Chair of St Peter in Antioch and the Chair of St Peter in Rome honor the two cities founded by the chief of the Apostles, and honored by the presence of both Peter and Paul. Paul's "seven churches" in Asia Minor were all well established before the end of the first century, as were the churches of Smyrna, Ephesus, the Galician plateau, Bithynia, and Pontus, and that of Cappodocia, with Caesarea its capital. Alexandria, however, in spite of the fact that the Emperor Hadrian mentions having found many Christians there when he visited Egypt at the beginning of the second century, was not to give signs of vigorous life until the end of the third. Edessa in Upper Mesopotamia, however, was converted in 179, when its king, Abgar IX, became a Christian along with his whole family. The Osrhoenian dynasty remained Christian until it was absorbed in the Roman Empire a century later. Persia too was early evangelized (legend has it by St Thomas) though there are no traces of organized Christian communities before the Sassanid dynasty (226). Armenia, thanks to St Gregory Thaumaturgus, was solidly Christianized about the same time, and from thence the Gospel spread north to the plains of Central Russia (Scythia) where St Andrew's presence is as persistent a legend as is St Thomas's in Persia or India.

Thus during the second century the Church acquired in the East a position of considerable importance; in some towns of Syria and Asia Minor a third or even half of the whole population was Christian. In Rome, the persecution of Nero in which St Peter perished checked temporarily the growth of the Christian community, but the presence and death of the two great apostles, Peter and Paul, gave the city, when the Neronian persecution was over, an unequaled glory. St Clement, one of St Peter's earliest successors, already bracketed the two apostles with other Romans whose constancy gave a like example. At about the same date, St Ignatius of Antioch also celebrated the two illustrious martyrs of the Church of Rome.

Strangely enough, the African Church, which used Latin as its language many years earlier than did the Roman Church, had no legends as to its founders. The first memorial of the African Church is the testimony of the martyrdom of the twelve Christians arrested at Scillium in Numidia and executed at Carthage on July 17, 180. This document is the oldest dated Christian document in Latin.

The Church in Gaul comes into recorded history also with an account of martyrdom, that sent by the churches of Lyons and Vienne to the churches of Asia and Phrygia, to tell them (in Greek) of the death in 177 of Pothinus the bishop, and of a certain number of fellow Christians of all ages and both sexes.

Early Christianity, or Christian antiquity, is usually limited by the death of St John Damascene (c. 754) for the Eastern Church, and that of St Isidore of Seville (636) for the Western. Taking the death of Jesus Christ as having occurred between 29 and 33 A.D., and the first authentic writing not included in the Christian Scriptures to be the Epistle of Clement in 95 A.D., early Christian literature covers roughly some six hundred and fifty years.

The study of the life and work of those early Christian ecclesiastical writers who died in the faith and communion of the Christian Church is called Patrology, or the science of the Fathers. The title "Fathers of the Church" was used by writers as early as 400 A.D. to designate the earlier writers. Bishops were called Fathers by the second century; priests were so called by the fourth. Today, only those writers are included among the Fathers of the Church who qualify on four counts: they must have been orthodox in doctrine; they must have been holy in life; they must have received ecclesiastical sanction; they must have lived in antiquity. To be a Doctor of the Church connotes in addition an eminent degree of learning, but a Doctor need not have lived in antiquity; for example, sixteenth-century John of the Cross and seventeenth-century St Francis of Sales are Doctors of the Church. Among the Fathers, seven are known as the Great Doctors: three of the Eastern Church, Saints Basil, Gregory of Nazianzus, and John Chrysostom; and four of the Western, Saints Ambrose, Jerome, Augustine, and Gregory.

The first to compose a history of Christian theological literature was St Jerome (340?–420). He wrote *De Viris Illustribus* (*Of Famous Men*), copying Suetonius's work of the same title in form and style. He followed the Church historian, St Eusebius (260?–340?), so closely that he even repeats the latter's errors and mistakes.

The Church regards the tradition of the Fathers, collectively, as of the most profound importance. Although no single Father is doctrinally infallible, the consensus of *all* the Fathers' interpretations of Scripture is considered infallible by the Church.

At first, Christian literature was mostly letters: either personal letters—such as St Paul's Epistle to Philemon or St John's second Epistle about the freed slave—or collective letters, on a number of subjects, designed to be read aloud to all the faithful. None of the Epistles included in the New Testament is given in this anthology, which begins with the so-called Apostolic Fathers.

This name is given to certain writers, and to certain other anonymous writings, dating from the first century to the middle of the second. These writers are supposed, on as good authority as we are ever likely to have, either to have known personally some of the twelve Apostles or at least to have derived their doctrine and teaching directly from them.

There are six of these Apostolic Fathers: Saints Clement of Rome, Barnabas, Ignatius, Polycarp, Hermas (thought to have been a brother of Pope Pius I), and Papias. The Epistle to Diognetus, the *Didache* or Teachings of the Twelve Apostles, and the Apostles' Creed are the anonymous writings usually included with those of the Apostolic Fathers.

Hard on the heels of the Apostolic Fathers follow the Apologists, a group of second-century writers whose aim was to defend Christianity from the accusations leveled against it. From the first, Christianity was under fire from the Jews, who, when they could not deal directly with the Christians as they did with St Stephen, brought them to the notice of the Roman authorities—as they had done in the case of Jesus Christ. The Romans were completely tolerant of all religions as such but completely intolerant of revolutionaries. Roman civilization was a whole, to be accepted or rejected in its totality. The Christians were not disloyal. They dutifully obeyed the emperor in all lawful things; they prayed for his health and safety. They protested their patriotism in a pathetic series of Apologies, addressed to the various emperors, which the emperors probably never read. For quite early the Christians had run into trouble because they could take no share in public life: "Being inactive, and therefore useless citizens . . . they could not serve on a town-council without being false to their religion, they could not attend festivals, public or private, which began with sacrifice." * Any disturber of the peace was a menace to the Roman Empire, "for the worship of the Emperor's genius was the chief bond of Empire," and the Christians' refusal "caused consternation." At first the Christians were small folk, artisans, tradespeople, illiterates, but as early as 58 A.D. the wife of Aulus Plautius, the conqueror of Britain, was "accused of a foreign superstition," that is, was thought to be a Christian; and in 95 A.D., among the victims of the persecution was Flavius Clemens, an ex-consul descended from the Emperor Vespasian, and his wife Domitilla, Vespasian's own granddaughter.

The first possible allusion to the Christians by Roman authority indicates clearly its attitude. In a letter to the Prefect of Egypt, dated November 10, 41 A.D., the Emperor Claudius first explains that he doesn't want the Alexandrian Greeks to set up statues to him; then he chides both Greeks and Jews, who have been at one another's throats, and tells them they must get together in the interests of public order. Finally he adds, "It is forbidden to the Jews to attract or invite other Jews to come by water from Syria or the rest of Egypt, for that would give me the gravest suspicion about them, *as fomenting a sort of illness common to the whole universe.*"

Now this was written before the travels of St Paul in 45 A.D. Can it refer to the missionary activity of the Christians? Two of the experts, Dr. Francesco De Sanctis and Dr. Salomon Reinach, think it does.

Certainly it is only a very short while later that the rhetor Tertullus

* E. C. E. Owen, *Some Authentic Acts of the Early Martyrs.* Oxford: Clarendon Press, 1927.

called St Paul a "pest," and in 111 A.D. the younger Pliny, timorous and dutiful, wrote to Trajan about "the absurd, extravagant superstition of the Christians," and said "this contagion" had invaded "not only the cities, but also the villages, and even the whole countryside."

But it was not until pagans of some education began to be converted that the apologetical writings begin. The Christians, wrote Lecky, "floated into the Roman Empire on a wave of credulity which brought with it a long train of oriental superstition and legend."

Around 100 A.D., Mithraism, a Persian cult, and various Egyptian beliefs, were all the fashion. The Christian Apologists thus had a double task: to defend Christianity from the rumors surrounding it, and to distinguish what Christians really did believe and teach from the jumble of contemporary prevalent cults, as well as from Judaism.

The first Christian Apologist was a certain Quadratus, perhaps Bishop of Athens, who presented to the Emperor Hadrian (emperor 117–38) an apology of which only one sentence, quoted by the Church historian Eusebius, survives. Next came Aristides, another Athenian, whose *Apology* was long given up for lost but turned up in 1889, first in a Syrian version, later in the revised Greek text of the legend of Saints Barlaam and Joasaph. (This legend, incidentally, is a fictionalized version of the life of Gautama Buddha—which shows what a meeting place of faiths Rome and the Mediterranean cities were, in the first centuries of the Christian era.) Aristides' *Apology* had been addressed to the Emperor Antoninus Pius (138–61); St Justin, a Stoic, Peripatetic, Pythagorean, and Platonistic philosopher before he became a Christian, addressed his two *Apologies* to the same emperor. Athenagoras, another philosopher, an Athenian, became a Christian after reading the Scriptures, and addressed a *Supplication for the Christians* to Marcus Aurelius (161–80). Athenagoras is the first to express the Christian view of virginity. "You will find among us," he wrote, "both men and women growing old unmarried in the hope of living in closer communion with God." Elsewhere he gives another Christian argument for the first time: "the very fetus in the womb is a created being, and so is subject to God's care." Marcus Minucius Felix, a distinguished Roman lawyer; his friend Tertullian, the great fighter, "who had every virtue except moderation"; Tatian, a Syrian from beyond the Tigris; Theophilus of Antioch, who wrote three books *To Autolycus,* are other Apologists whose writings have survived, as have *The Mockery of Heathen Philosophers,* by a second-rate satirist named Hermias, and the elegant and artificial *Apology* of St Melito, bishop of Sardis, also dedicated to Marcus Aurelius.

The Apologists easily disposed of the obviously ridiculous popular charges against Christianity: that the Christians worshiped an ass's head, that they killed and ate newborn babies at their feasts, and that they practiced incest. These charges, absurd as they seem to us, did not seem so preposterous to the Romans. The Egyptians worshiped cat-headed and ape-headed gods and goddesses; both Romans and Greeks exposed newborn babies, so to eat them was an offense against good taste and good manners rather than against good morals; and incest was an obligation upon the Pharaohs, so why not upon the Christians? Scandal was certainly caused by the tremendous secrecy surrounding the Christian Eucharist—at first it might not be spoken of at all, even by the Christians among themselves; later, catechumens were admitted to part of the Mass, but a part only, and the mysteries were veiled, as they still are in Greek and Russian churches—and by the association of the Eucharist with Jewish ritual killings, as well as by the kiss of peace, given at Mass (and not only there), and the habit all Christians had of calling one another "brother" and "sister."

But the charge that underlay all these accusations, the charge upon which the Christians were actually legally convicted by Roman law, was one of which they were guilty and which the Apologists could face only by turning from defensive to offensive. This was the charge of irreligion. For the Roman, religion was a *binding* of the worshiper to the god of his choice, but it specifically included the binding of all other worshipers to the gods of their choice. The Emperor Alexander Severus, for example, had statues in his palace of Abraham, Buddha, Pan, and Jesus, all of which were part of his religion. The Christians made the monstrous claim that there was only *one* God, that He was invisible, and that to recognize Him, to bind oneself to Him, meant not only that the Christian could not recognize, much less worship, any other deity, but that he must try to wean all men from others to the One. This, to the Romans, was not only a threat to their tolerance, it was an atheism, and proved the Christians, as Tacitus put it, to be "enemies of the whole human race." In fact, of course, the Christian Fathers were most tolerant of *people:* St Basil's friendship with Libanius, as that of Synesius with Hypatia, showed that the Christian loved the pagan, while denying his gods. But the idea that Christianity was *a* religion, comparable with the religions of the pagans or the Jews, was not held by any of the early Christians themselves. Christianity as *the* faith has never accepted the position of being *a* faith.

The Church of Rome was traditionally supposed to have been founded by St Peter in 42 A.D. Little more than twenty years later, on July 19, 64, a great fire broke out. The *vigeles,* the Roman fire brigades, did their best to cope with it, tearing down houses to clear a space before the flames, but the fire started up again on the property of Tigellinus, Nero's favorite. It took ten days to bring it under control; of Rome's fourteen districts, three were destroyed and only four remained unscathed. Tacitus, who describes the damage and death roll, implies that Nero gave the order to start the fire, wishing to clear the city in order to build it anew. "To hush the rumors," Tacitus adds, "Nero accused the Christians, first seizing those who confessed, then, on their indication, arresting a considerable number, guilty, not of arson, but of hating humanity. To their agonies, mockery was added: men wrapped in animals' skins were dismembered by dogs, or tied to crosses, and, at dusk, lit as nocturnal torches. Nero lent his gardens for this spectacle, and gave there circus games, mixing with the crowd, disguised as a jockey."

"Nero first bled the nascent church," confirms the historian Eusebius. "Then it was that Peter had his loins girded by another than himself, and both he and Paul were condemned as atheists." Tertullian cries out, "O happy Church of Rome, to which the Apostles left their teaching and their blood, in which Peter suffered a passion like that of the Saviour, and Paul obtained the same coronation as John the Baptist." Casually, describing Nero's reign, Suetonius says it was then that a law "was made forbidding the serving of cooked foods in bars, whereas earlier one could get all sorts of dishes"; then, too, "the Christians, a kind of people addicted to a new and nasty superstition," were persecuted.

After Nero, the Christians were left in peace for twenty-seven years. In 95 A.D. there was a short, sharp persecution, in which St Ignatius was one of the chief victims. Under the "good" emperors—Trajan (98–117), Antoninus Pius (138–61), and Marcus Aurelius (161–80)—Christians were not sought out, but if regularly accused were killed. Those who proved they had never been Christians, or who, by sacrificing, proved they were such no longer, were set free. Those who abjured and then repented were ultimately pardoned by the Church, though many Christians argued against such laxity. Thanks to the Roman passion for making verbatim accounts of trials (Dom John Chapman, O.S.B., insisted there were more shorthand reporters in classical times than in our own), many official accounts of the martyrs' deaths survived. These were sold to the Christians for two hundred denarii (about ten dollars) and were preserved by them with the martyrs' relics. From the procedure in court it is clear that the Christian was persecuted for the Name alone. Tertullian complained of this: "The only thing needed to satisfy the general hatred is not the investigation of a charge, but the confession of the Name." The Christian, in fact, condemned himself. The oath he had to take to the Emperor was coupled with an act of worship. "He had," as Owen points out, "only to offer the pinch of incense and he was free." * Since he would not, he was generally considered antisocial and queer. The general hatred of the Christians was real enough: an earthquake, a flood, a bad harvest, all were blamed on them, and "To the lions" was a truly popular cry in Rome.

With Septimius Severus (emperor 193–211) a new era began. Christians were sought out by the state, and, like the Jews in Hitler's Germany, were hunted down. Decius (emperor 249–51) made a deliberate attempt, says Lecky, "supported by the whole machinery of provincial government, and extended over the entire surface of the empire, to extirpate Christianity from the world. It would be difficult," he concedes, "to find language too strong to paint its horrors."

* Op. cit.

By this time Christianity was well established throughout the empire. "We are but of yesterday," boasted Tertullian, "and we fill all your cities, island, forts, councils, even the camps themselves, the tribes, the decuries, the palaces, the senate and the forum." In a letter, Pope Cornelius (251–53) describes the Church in Rome as possessing one bishop, forty-six priests, seven deacons, seven subdeacons, forty-two acolytes, fifty-two exorcists, and as supporting fifteen hundred widows and other poor persons.

The blood of the martyrs spread the "sort of illness." By 150 A.D. St Justin Martyr could say: "There is no race of man, whether Greek or barbarian, among whom prayers and thanks are not offered up in the name of the Crucified." By this time, too, the Church had ceased to be merely a Mediterranean-centered cult: Persia, Egypt, Gaul, Britain and possibly India, had heard the good news. In the grimmest persecution of all, that under Diocletian, the Christians "longed for death as now they long for bishoprics," as Lactantius (260?–340?) nostalgically wrote. And a village in Phrygia, mentioned by both Lactantius and Eusebius, suffered the fate of later Lidice: it was razed to the ground, and nothing left unburned, because its Christian inhabitants, all of whom were massacred, had refused to sacrifice. Yet Diocletian, savage persecutor, could write from retirement to Galerius, who invited him to resume the purple, "Could you but see the vegetables which I have raised with my own hand, you would perceive at once that I can never be lured from thence." His conscience seems to have been as clear as that of Anatole France's Procurator of Judea, who when reminded of Jesus Christ said, puzzled, "I do not remember him."

Along with Christianity, heresies grew. Inch by inch from earliest days the tares paced the wheat: the Ebionites—Judaeo-Christians—clung to the Law, thought Jesus a human and Israelite Messiah; the Gnostics, from Simon Magus on, whether Syrian, Alexandrian, Marcionite, or Encratite, laid claim to higher powers and profounder knowledge than did the simple faithful of the official Church. Even in the arena, as Eusebius noted, the Catholic martyrs withdrew from the Montanists, lest they should be physically mingled with the heretics in death. The writers of apocryphas and apocalypses pullulated, and the Church's definitions had to be made with ever more minute clarity and increasing frequency.

Although the genius of the Eastern Church was speculative and philosophical and that of the Western practical and administrative, these differences did not crystallize until, in the third century, Latin became the official language of the Western Church. Until then, the important churches had been those of Syria and Asia Minor: Antioch, Jerusalem, Smyrna, had produced such writers as Polycarp, Melito, and Irenaeus. But with the rise of the bridge-church of Alexandria the intellectual center moved west. Clement of Alexandria, Origen, Tertullian, St Cyprian, were first fruits of that African literature which was to provide the Church also with Athanasius, Cyril of Alexandria, and, above all, Augustine.

The golden age of patristic literature was from 313, when, after the battle of the Milvian Bridge, the victorious Emperor Constantine became a Christian, to 461, when St Leo died. During those hundred and fifty years, a spate of great writing and great writers filled the Church: all the "great" Doctors except St Gregory, plus whole groups of others, such as the biographers of the Desert Fathers; the School of Lérins, with its concentration on interior prayer; the followers of St Augustine, who, though they could not match his psychological insight, often equaled his urbane, civilized delight; the historians, Eusebius, Socrates Scholasticus, and the others, who laconically, quizzically, described Attila's arrival in Rome or Hypatia's end in Alexandria with unequaled economy; the translators, like St Jerome, who brought to the cool, ordered clarity of Latin the splendor of Semitic savagery (compare the Vulgate of the Psalms with the banal sentiments flawlessly folded into Horace or Ovid). And, greatest of all, there was St Augustine himself, who today is still as ever old and ever new as the Beauty he so articulately worshiped, who can make us feel how much he cared for the shadow of the Trojan Creusa and how little for the mother of his own son; who has described, as Freud himself could not, a child's greed for its mother, a man's greed for his God.

This glorious century and a half, when the great writers, boxing the compass of the known world, produced by a union of classical form with Christian content a body of literature to set beside that of Periclean Greece or Augustan Rome, in some respects has a glory unparalleled even by these. For when, before or since, have the glory of Greece, the grandeur of Rome, the ingenuity of Egypt, the subtleties of Syria, and the brash humor of Gaul been so combined to delight and to edify the hearts and minds of all the generations of mankind?

The coming together of the great councils brought the personalities into human contact and welded the doctrine; the excellent communications, inherited from Imperial Rome, made traveling easier than for a thousand following years; the mail service was admirable: letters were delivered to Balkan forest, Calabrian mountain, Egyptian desert; not until the nineteenth century, if then, were distances regularly covered on the scale and at the speed to which the early Fathers were accustomed. Travel, indeed, seems to have been continuous. The Church, missionary from her first moments, has always been *mulier peregrina,* the pilgrim woman. But besides missionary journeys and pilgrimages there also were conquests and flights. From St Irenaeus issuing bulletins on his long trek to martyrdom to St John Chrysostom describing to the mourning Olympias the rigors of his journey into an exile that he and she both knew must end in death; from St Athanasius recounting St Anthony's search for solitude, pursued by admirers from cave to cave, to St Patrick confessing how he was carried away into barbarian slavery, literally step by step, "we are treading where the saints have trod."

Of course not all the pilgrims were saints. St Boniface, the Apostle of Germany, writes to Archbishop Cuthbert of Canterbury:

"Moreover I will not conceal from your charity, since you serve God in all things . . . that it would be a good thing and honorable and decent for your church and somewhat a cover for the shame, if the synod and elders of the church would forbid to women and to veiled females to take so frequently to the roads, which they do, coming and going to the city of Rome, so that most are lost on the way, very few remaining virtuous. There are extremely few cities in Lombardy, or in France, or in Gaul, in which there is not an English adulteress or harlot. The which is a scandal and a shame for your whole church."

But there were other, more decorous (but also duller) pilgrims, such as the one who left Bordeaux in May 333, and visited the Holy Land, returning by way of Rome and Milan. He wrote a dry, precise, and proper account. There was also the fourth-century Etheria, that paragon of Spanish sightseers, ladylike but indefatigable, part of whose narrative is included here.

Yet the scandals were constant, always with the Church, like heretics and the poor. St Paul was the first to scold, but the chiding and chastening that is part of the corporal duty of correction sounds in all the Fathers. Salvian is frankly delighted that the nice, good barbarians are coming, because the Christians are so wicked; St Augustine, while admitting it is all the Christians' fault, is sorry for the earthly, beleaguered city; and St Jerome laments that he is "more a Ciceronian than a Christian." But along with the loud tramp of the Church militant can always be heard the steady beating of her heart. Daily communion was the general norm until Constantine; a monk is unable to resist temptation, and the chronicler is not surprised, since he has been absent from the Sacrament five weeks; prayer without ceasing is not a far ideal but a real ambition, not an ascetic discipline but the right breathing of every journeying soul.

After St Leo, the barbarians, a rising tide, further and further submerged what was left of the Roman Empire. Christianity, faced with new foes, had to start all over again, converting, civilizing, incorporating. How successfully and how swiftly this was done, the letters of St Gregory the Great show; how incompletely, such sad documents as St Patrick's letter to Coroticus on the massacre perpetrated by his soldiers—or any of the contemporary papal documents of World War II condemning genocide.

With the welding into one Christendom of what remained of Rome with what had been newly civilized of Goth and Visigoth, Vandal and Saxon and Hun, the age of the Fathers ends, and the Middle Ages begin.

# THE CHRISTIAN IDEAL

# ST CLEMENT I
## (Clement of Rome)

30?–?100

According to the most trustworthy tradition, St Clement was the third successor of St Peter and the fourth bishop of Rome. Modern scholarship has rejected the idea that he was the Clement mentioned by St Paul in writing to the Philippians, or that he was Flavius Clemens, the cousin of Emperor Domitian who, as a Christian, was beheaded by Domitian's orders in 95 or 96. It is very doubtful, indeed, if he was martyred, for the facts of his alleged martyrdom relate to another Clement, a Greek martyr buried at Cherson. The *Epistle,* of which parts follow, is the only authentic work of Pope Clement; it is contained in two fourth-century Greek manuscripts now in the British Museum. Denis of Corinth (fl. 170 A.D.) produced decisive proof that this letter was genuine (Eusebius, *Ecclesiastical History,* IV, 23, 11), and as the letter was written after the end of Domitian's persecution (95–96), and Clement died about 100, it probably dates from 97 or 98. In the early Church the *Epistle* was greatly reverenced, some authors even ranking it with the inspired writings.

## FROM Epistle to the Corinthians

The Church of God which sojourneth in Rome to the Church of God which sojourneth in Corinth, to them which are called and sanctified by the will of God through our Lord Jesus Christ. Grace to you and peace from Almighty God through Jesus Christ be multiplied.

By reason of the sudden and repeated calamities and reverses which have befallen us, brethren, we consider that we have been somewhat tardy in giving heed to the matters of dispute that have arisen among you, dearly beloved, and to the detestable and unholy sedition, so alien and strange to the elect of God, which a few headstrong and self-willed persons have kindled to such a pitch of madness that your name, once revered and renowned and lovely in the sight of all men, hath been greatly reviled. For who that had sojourned among you did not approve your most virtuous and steadfast faith? Who did not admire your sober and forbearing piety in Christ? Who did not publish abroad your magnificent disposition of hospitality? Who did not congratulate you on your perfect and sound knowledge? For ye did all things without respect of persons, and ye walked after the ordinances of God, submitting yourselves to your rulers and rendering to the older men among you the honour which is their due. On the young too ye enjoined modest and seemly thoughts: and the women ye charged to perform all their duties in a blameless and seemly and pure conscience, cherishing their own husbands, as is meet; and ye taught them to keep in the rule of obedience, and to manage the affairs of their household in seemliness, with all discretion.

And ye were all lowly in mind and free from arrogance, yielding rather than claiming submission, more glad to give than to receive, and content with the provisions which God supplieth. And giving heed unto His words, ye laid them up diligently in your hearts, and His sufferings were before your eyes. Thus a profound and rich peace was given to all, and an insatiable desire of doing good. An abundant outpouring also of the Holy Spirit fell upon all; and, being full of holy counsel, in excellent zeal and with a pious confidence ye stretched out your hands to Almighty God, supplicating Him to be propitious, if unwillingly ye had committed any sin. Ye had conflict day and night for all the brotherhood, that the number of His elect might be saved with fearfulness and intentness of mind. Ye were sincere and simple and free from malice one towards another. Every sedition and every schism was abominable to you. Ye mourned over the transgressions of your neighbours: ye judged their shortcomings to be your own. Ye repented not of any well-doing, but were ready unto every good work. Being adorned with a most virtuous and honourable life, ye performed all your duties in the fear of Him. The commandments and the ordinances of the Lord were written on the tables of your hearts.

All glory and enlargement was given unto you, and that was fulfilled which is written. *"My beloved ate and drank and was enlarged and waxed fat and kicked."* Hence come jealousy and envy, strife and sedition, persecution and tumult, war and captivity. So men were stirred up, the mean against the honourable, the ill-reputed against the highly reputed, the foolish against the wise, the young against the elder. For this cause righteousness and peace stand aloof, while each man hath forsaken the fear of the Lord and become purblind in the faith of Him, neither walketh in the ordinances of His commandments nor liveth according to that which becometh Christ, but each goeth after the lusts of his evil heart, seeing that they have conceived an unrighteous and ungodly jealousy, through which also "death entered into the world." . . .

But, to pass from the examples of ancient days, let us come to those champions who lived nearest to our time. Let us set before us the noble examples which belong to our generation. By reason of jealousy and envy the greatest and most righteous pillars of the Church were persecuted, and contended even unto death. Let us set before our eyes the good Apostles. There was Peter who by reason of unrighteous jealousy endured not one nor two but many labours, and thus having borne his testimony went to his appointed place of glory. By reason of jealousy and strife Paul by his example pointed out the prize of patient endurance. After that he had been seven times in bonds, had been driven into exile, had been stoned, had preached in the East and in the West, he won the noble renown which was the reward of his faith, having taught righteousness unto the whole world and having reached the farthest bounds of the West; and when he had borne his testimony before the rulers, so he departed from the world and went unto the holy place, having been found a notable pattern of patient endurance.

Unto these men of holy lives was gathered a vast multitude of the elect, who through many indignities and tortures, being the victims of jealousy, set a brave example among ourselves. By reason of jealousy women being persecuted, after that they had suffered cruel and unholy insults as Danaids and Dircæ, safely reached the goal in the race of faith, and received a noble reward, feeble though they were in body. Jealousy hath estranged wives from their husbands and changed the saying of our father Adam, "This now is bone of my bones and flesh of my flesh." Jealousy and strife have overthrown great cities and uprooted great nations.

These things, dearly beloved, we write, not only as admonishing you, but also as putting ourselves in remembrance. For we are in the same lists, and the same contest awaiteth us. Wherefore let us forsake idle and vain thoughts; and let us conform to the glorious and venerable rule which hath been handed down to us; and let us see what is good and what is pleasant and what is acceptable in the sight of Him that made us. Let us fix our eyes on the blood of Christ and understand how precious it is unto His Father, because being shed for our salvation it won for the whole world the grace of repentance. Let us review all the generations in turn, and learn how from generation to generation the Master hath given a place for repentance unto them that desire to turn to Him. Noah preached repentance, and they that obeyed were saved. Jonah preached destruction unto the men of Nineveh; but they, repenting of their sins, obtained pardon of God by their supplications and received salvation, albeit they were aliens from God. . . .

The humility therefore and the submissiveness of so many and so great men, who have thus obtained a good report, hath through obedience made better not only us but also the generations which were before us, even them that received His oracles in fear and truth. Seeing then that we have been partakers of many great and glorious doings, let us hasten to return unto the goal of peace which hath been handed down to us from the beginning, and let us look steadfastly unto the Father and Maker of the whole world, and cleave unto His splendid and excellent gifts of peace and benefits. Let us behold Him in our mind, and let us look with the eyes of our soul unto His long-suffering will. Let us note how free from anger He is towards all His creatures.

The heavens are moved by His direction and obey Him in peace. Day and night accomplish the course assigned to them by Him, without hindrance one to another. The sun and the moon and the dancing stars according to His appointment circle in harmony within the bounds assigned to them, without any swerving aside. The earth, bearing fruit in fulfilment of His will at her proper seasons, putteth forth the food that supplieth abundantly both men and beasts and all living things which are thereupon, making no dissension, neither altering anything which He hath decreed. Moreover, the inscrutable depths of the abysses and the unutterable statutes of the nether regions are constrained by the same ordinances. The basin of the boundless sea, gathered together by His workmanship into its reservoirs, passeth not the barriers wherewith it is surrounded; but even as He ordered it, so it doeth. For He said, "So far shalt thou come, and thy waves shall be broken within thee." The ocean which is impassable for men, and the worlds beyond it, are directed by the same ordinances of the Master. The seasons of spring and summer and autumn and winter give way in succession one to another in peace. The winds in their several quarters at their proper season fulfil their ministry without disturbance; and the everflowing fountains, created for enjoyment and health, without fail give their breasts which sustain the life for men. Yea, the smallest of living things come together in concord and peace. All these things the great Creator and Master of the universe ordered to be in peace and concord, doing good unto all things, but far beyond the rest unto us, who have taken refuge in His compassionate mercies through our Lord Jesus Christ, to whom be the glory and the majesty for ever and ever. Amen. . . .

Let us consider the marvellous sign which is seen in the regions of the east, that is, in the parts about Arabia. There is a bird, which is named the phœnix. This, being the only one of its kind, liveth for five hundred years; and when it hath now reached the time of its dissolution that it should die, it maketh for itself a coffin of frankincense and myrrh and the other spices, into the which in the fulness of time it entereth, and so it dieth. But, as the flesh rotteth, a certain worm is engendered, which is nurtured from the moisture of the dead creature and putteth forth wings. Then, when it is grown lusty, it taketh up that coffin where are the bones of its parent, and carrying them journeyeth from the country of Arabia even unto Egypt, to the place called the City of the Sun; and in the daytime in the sight of all, flying to the altar of the Sun, it layeth them thereupon; and this done, it setteth forth to return. So the priests examine the registers of the times, and they find that it hath come when the five-hundredth year is completed.

Do we then think it to be a great and marvellous thing, if the Creator of the universe shall bring about the resurrection of them that have served Him with holiness in the assurance of a good faith, seeing that He showeth to us even by a bird the magnificence of His promise? For He saith in a certain place: "And Thou shalt raise me up, and I will praise Thee"; and: "I went to rest and slept, I was awaked, for Thou art with me." And again Job saith: "And Thou shalt raise this my flesh which hath endured all these things." . . .

What then must we do, brethren? Must we idly abstain from doing good, and forsake love? May the Master never allow this to befall us at least; but let us hasten with instancy and zeal to accomplish every good work. For the Creator and Master of the universe Himself rejoiceth in His works. For by His exceeding great might He established the heavens, and in His incomprehensible wisdom He set them in order. And the earth He separated from the water that surroundeth it, and He set it firm on the sure foundation of His own will; and the living creatures which walk upon it He commanded to exist by His ordinance. Having before created the sea and the living creatures therein, He enclosed it by His own power. Above all, as the most excellent and exceeding great work of His intelligence, with His sacred and faultless hands He formed man in the impress of His own image. For thus saith God: "Let us make man after our image and after our likeness. And God made man; male and female made He them." So having finished all these things, He praised them and blessed them and said, "Increase and multiply." We have seen that all the righteous were adorned in good works. Yea, and the Lord Himself, having adorned Himself with works, rejoiced. Seeing then that we have this pattern, let us conform ourselves with all diligence to His will; let us with all our strength work the work of righteousness. . . .

This is the way, dearly beloved, wherein we found our salvation, even Jesus Christ the High Priest of our offerings, the Guardian and Helper of our weakness. Through Him let us look steadfastly unto the heights of the heavens; through Him we behold as in a mirror His faultless and most excellent visage; through Him the eyes of our hearts were opened; through Him our foolish and darkened mind springeth up unto the light; through Him the Master willed that we should taste of the immortal knowledge; "Who, being the brightness of His majesty, is so much greater than angels, as He hath inherited a more excellent name." For so it is written: "Who maketh His angels spirits and His ministers a flame of fire"; but of His Son the Master said thus: "Thou art My Son, I this day have begotten Thee. Ask of Me, and I will give Thee the Gentiles for Thine inheritance, and the ends of the earth for Thy possession." And again He saith unto Him: "Sit Thou on My right hand, until I make Thine enemies a footstool for Thy feet." Who then are these enemies? They that are wicked and resist His will. . . .

Let us therefore enlist ourselves, brethren, with all earnestness in His faultless ordinances. Let us mark the soldiers that are enlisted under our rulers, how exactly, how readily, how submissively, they execute the orders given them. All are not prefects, nor rulers of thousands, nor rulers of hundreds, nor rulers of fifties, and so forth; but each man in his own rank executeth the orders given by the king and the governors. The great without the small cannot exist, neither the small without the great. There is a certain mixture in all things, and therein is utility. Let us take our body as an example. The head without the feet is nothing; so likewise the feet without the head are nothing: even the smallest limbs of our body are necessary and useful for the whole body: but all the members conspire and unite in subjection, that the whole body may be saved.

So in our case let the whole body be saved in Christ Jesus, and let each man be subject unto his neighbour, according as also he was appointed with his special grace. Let not the strong neglect the weak; and let the weak respect the strong. Let the rich minister aid to the poor; and let the poor give thanks to God, because He hath given him one through whom his wants may be supplied. Let the wise display his wisdom, not in words, but in good works. He that is lowly in mind, let him not bear testimony to himself, but leave testimony to be borne to him by his neighbour. He that is pure in the flesh, let him be so, and not boast, knowing that it is Another who bestoweth his continence upon him. Let us consider, brethren, of what matter we were made; who and what manner of beings we were, when we came into the world; from what a sepulchre and what darkness He that moulded and created us brought us into His world, having prepared His benefits aforehand ere ever we were born. Seeing therefore that we have all these things from Him, we ought in all things to give thanks to Him, to whom be the glory for ever and ever. Amen. . . .

The Apostles received the Gospel for us from the Lord Jesus Christ; Jesus Christ was sent forth from God. So then Christ is from God, and the Apostles are from Christ. Both therefore came of the will of God in the appointed order. Having therefore received a charge, and having been fully assured through the resurrection of our Lord Jesus Christ and confirmed in the word of God with full assurance of the Holy Ghost, they went forth with the glad tidings that the kingdom of God should come. So preaching everywhere in country and town, they appointed their first-fruits, when they had proved them by the Spirit, to be bishops and deacons unto them that should believe. And this they did in no new fashion; for indeed it had been written concerning bishops and deacons from very ancient times; for thus saith the Scripture in a certain place, "I will appoint their bishops in righteousness and their deacons in faith." . . .

And our Apostles knew through our Lord Jesus Christ that there would be strife over the name of the bishop's office. For this cause therefore, having received complete foreknowledge, they appointed the aforesaid persons, and afterwards they provided a continuance, that if these should fall asleep, other approved men should succeed to their ministration. Those therefore who were appointed by them, or afterwards by other men of repute with the consent of the whole Church, and have ministered unblameably to the flock of Christ in lowliness of mind, peacefully and with all modesty, and for long time have borne a good report with all—these men we consider to be unjustly thrust out from their ministration. For it will be no light sin for us, if we thrust out those who have offered the gifts of the bishop's office unblameably and holily. Blessed are those presbyters who have gone before, seeing that their departure was fruitful and ripe: for they have no fear lest any one should remove them from their appointed place. For we see that ye have displaced certain persons, though they were living honourably, from the ministration which had been respected by them blamelessly.

Be ye contentious, brethren, and jealous about the things that pertain unto salvation. Ye have searched the Scriptures, which are true, which were given through the Holy Ghost; and ye know that nothing unrighteous or counterfeit is written in them. Ye will not find that righteous persons have been thrust out by holy men. Righteous men were persecuted, but it was by the lawless; they were imprisoned, but it was by the unholy. They were stoned by transgressors: they were slain by those who had conceived a detestable and unrighteous jealousy. Suffering these things, they endured nobly. For what must we say, brethren? Was Daniel cast into the lions' den by them that feared God? Or were Ananias and Azarias and Misael shut up in the furnace of fire by them that professed the excellent and glorious worship of the Most High? Far be this from our thoughts. Who then were they that did these things? Abominable men and full of all wickedness were stirred up to such a pitch of wrath, as to bring cruel suffering upon them that served God in a holy and blameless purpose, not knowing that the Most High is the champion and protector of them that in a pure conscience serve His excellent Name: unto whom be the glory for ever and ever. Amen. But they that endured patiently in confidence inherited glory and honour; they were exalted, and had their names recorded by God in their memorial for ever and ever. Amen. . . .

Take up the epistle of the blessed Paul the Apostle. What wrote he first unto you in the beginning of the Gospel? Of a truth he charged you in the Spirit concerning himself and Cephas and Apollos, because that even then ye had made parties. Yet that making of parties brought less sin upon you; for ye were partisans of Apostles that were highly reputed, and of a man approved in their sight. But now mark ye, who they are that have perverted you and diminished the glory of your renowned love for the brotherhood. It is shameful, dearly beloved, yes, utterly shameful and unworthy of your conduct in Christ, that it should be reported that the very steadfast and ancient Church of the Corinthians, for the sake of one or two persons, maketh sedition against its presbyters. And this report hath reached not only us, but them also which differ from us, so that ye even heap blasphemies on the Name of the Lord by reason of your folly, and moreover create peril for yourselves.

Let us therefore root this out quickly, and let us fall down before the Master and entreat Him with tears, that He may show Himself propitious and be reconciled unto us, and may restore us to the seemly and pure conduct which belongeth to our love of the brethren. For this is a gate of righteousness opened unto life, as it is written: "Open me the gates of righteousness, that I may enter in thereby and praise the Lord. This is the gate of the Lord; the righteous shall enter in thereby." Seeing then that many gates are opened, this is that gate which is in righteousness, even that which is in Christ, whereby all are blessed that have entered in and direct their path in holiness and righteousness, performing all things without confusion. Let a man be faithful, let him be able to expound a deep saying, let him be wise in the discernment of words, let him be strenuous in deeds, let him be pure; for so much the more ought he to be lowly in mind, in proportion as he seemeth to be the greater; and he ought to seek the common advantage of all, and not his own. . . .

Ye therefore that laid the foundation of the sedition, submit yourselves unto the presbyters and receive chastisement unto repentance, bending the knees of your heart. Learn to submit yourselves, laying aside the arrogant and proud stubbornness of your tongue. For it is better for you to be found little in the flock of Christ and to have your name on God's roll, than to be had in exceeding honour and yet be cast out from the hope of Him. . . .

But if certain persons should be disobedient unto the words spoken by Him through us, let them understand that they will entangle themselves in no slight transgression and danger; but we shall be guiltless of this sin. And we will ask, with instancy of prayer and supplication, that the Creator of the universe may guard intact unto the end the number that hath been numbered of His elect throughout the whole world, through His beloved Son Jesus Christ, through whom He called us from darkness to light, from ignorance to the full knowledge of the glory of His Name.

Grant unto us, Lord, that we may set our hope on Thy Name which is the primal source of all creation, and open the eyes of our hearts, that we may know Thee, who alone abidest Highest in the lofty, Holy in the holy; who layest low the insolence of the proud, who scatterest the imaginings of nations; who settest the lowly on high, and bringest the lofty low; who makest rich and makest poor; who killest and makest alive; who alone art the Benefactor of spirits and the God of all flesh; who lookest into the abysses, who scannest the works of man; the Succour of them that are in peril, the Saviour of them that are in despair; the Creator and Overseer of every spirit; who multipliest the nations upon earth, and hast chosen out from all men those that love Thee through Jesus Christ, Thy beloved Son, through whom Thou didst instruct us, didst sanctify us, didst honour us. We beseech Thee, Lord and Master, to be our help and succour. Save those among us who are in tribulation; have mercy on the lowly; lift up the fallen; show Thyself unto the needy; heal the ungodly; convert the wanderers of Thy people; feed the hungry; release our prisoners; raise up the weak; comfort the faint-hearted. Let all the Gentiles know that Thou art God alone, and Jesus Christ is Thy Son, and we are Thy people and the sheep of Thy pasture.

Thou through Thine operations didst make manifest the everlasting fabric of the world. Thou, Lord, didst create the earth. Thou that art faithful throughout all generations, righteous in Thy judgments, marvellous in strength and excellence, Thou that art wise in creating and prudent in establishing that which Thou hast made, that art good in the things which are seen and faithful with them that trust on Thee, pitiful and compassionate, forgive us our iniquities and our unrighteousnesses and our transgressions and shortcomings. Lay not to our account every sin of Thy servants and Thine handmaids, but cleanse us with the cleansing of Thy truth, and guide our steps to walk in holiness and righteousness and singleness of heart and to do such things as are good and well-pleasing in Thy sight and in the sight of our rulers. Yea, Lord, make Thy face to shine upon us in peace for our good, that we may be sheltered by Thy mighty hand *and* delivered from every sin *by* Thine uplifted arm. And deliver us from them that hate us wrongfully. Give concord and peace to us and to all that dwell on the earth, as Thou gavest to our fathers, when they called on Thee in faith and truth with holiness, that we may be saved, while we render obedience to Thine almighty and most excellent Name, and to our rulers and governors upon the earth. . . .

Finally may the All-seeing God and Master of spirits and Lord of all flesh, who chose the Lord Jesus Christ, and us through Him for a peculiar people, grant unto every soul that is called after His excellent and holy Name faith, fear, peace, patience, long-suffering, temperance, chastity and soberness, that they may be well-pleasing unto His Name through our High Priest and Guardian Jesus Christ, through whom unto Him be glory and majesty, might and honour, both now and for ever and ever. Amen.

Now send ye back speedily unto us our messengers Claudius Ephebus and Valerius Bito, together with Fortunatus also, in peace and with joy, to the end that they may the more quickly report the peace and concord which is prayed for and earnestly desired by us, that we also may the more speedily rejoice over your good order.

The grace of our Lord Jesus Christ be with you and with all men in all places who have been called by God and through Him, through whom be glory and honour, power and greatness and eternal dominion, unto Him, from the ages past and for ever and ever. Amen.

# ST IGNATIUS OF ANTIOCH

50?–?109

Ignatius was the third bishop of Antioch. He was probably the only victim of a local persecution. Condemned to fight wild beasts in the Roman amphitheater, on his way thither he passed through Philadelphia, in Lydia, and traveled by land to Smyrna, where St Polycarp met him. While in Smyrna he wrote letters to the Ephesians, Magnesians, Trallians, and Romans. From Smyrna he proceeded to Troas, where he wrote to the Philadelphians, Smyrnans, and also to St Polycarp. He took ship to Neapolis, and finally, via Thessalonica, arrived at Durazzo, on the Adriatic. According to St Jerome, he was martyred in 109. Ernest Renan calls his letter to the Romans "one of the jewels of primitive Christian literature."

## FROM To the Magnesians

. . . It is therefore meet that we not only be called Christians, but also be such; even as some persons have the bishop's name on their lips, but in everything act apart from him. Such men appear to me not to keep a good conscience, forasmuch as they do not assemble themselves together lawfully according to commandment.

Seeing then that all things have an end, and these two—life and death—are set before us together, and each man shall go to his own place; for just as there are two coinages, the one of God and the other of the world, and each of them hath its proper stamp impressed upon it, the unbelievers the stamp of this world, but the faithful in love the stamp of God the Father through Jesus Christ, through whom unless of our own free choice we accept to die unto His passion, His life is not in us. . . .

## FROM To the Trallians

. . . I have many deep thoughts in God: but I take the measure of myself, lest I perish in my boasting. For now I ought to be the more afraid and not to give heed to those that would puff me up: for they that say these things to me are a scourge to me. For though I desire to suffer, yet I know not whether I am worthy: for the envy of the devil is unseen indeed by many, but against me it wages the fiercer war. So then I crave gentleness, whereby the prince of this world is brought to nought.

Am I not able to write to you of heavenly things? But I fear lest I should cause you harm being babes. So bear with me, lest not being able to take them in, ye should be choked. For I myself also, albeit I am in bonds and can comprehend heavenly things and the arrays of the angels and the musterings of the principalities, things visible and things invisible—I myself am not yet by reason of this a disciple. For we lack many things, that God may not be lacking to us.

I exhort you therefore—yet not I, but the love of Jesus Christ—take ye only Christian food, and abstain from strange herbage, which is heresy: for these men do even mingle poison with Jesus Christ, imposing upon others by a show of honesty, like persons administering a deadly drug with honeyed wine, so that one who knoweth it not, fearing nothing, drinketh in death with a baneful delight. . . .

## FROM To the Romans

. . . I write to all the churches, and I bid all men know, that of my own free will I die for God, unless ye should hinder me. I exhort you, be ye not an unseasonable kindness to me. Let me be given to the wild beasts, for through them I can attain unto God. I am God's wheat, and I am ground by the teeth of wild beasts that I may be found pure bread of Christ. Rather entice the wild beasts, that they may become my sepulchre and may leave no part of my body behind, so that I may not, when I am fallen asleep, be burdensome to anyone. Then shall I be truly a disciple of Jesus Christ, when the world shall not so much as see my body. Supplicate the Lord for me, that through these instruments I may be found a sacrifice to God. I do not enjoin you, as Peter and Paul did. They were Apostles, I am a convict; they were free, but I am a slave to this very hour. Yet if I shall suffer, then am I a freedman of Jesus Christ, and I shall rise free in Him. Now I am learning in my bonds to put away every desire.

From Syria even unto Rome I fight with wild beasts, by land and sea, by night and by day, being bound amidst ten leopards, even a company of soldiers, who only wax worse when they are kindly treated. Howbeit through their wrongdoings I become more completely a disciple; yet am I not hereby justified. May I have joy of the beasts that have been prepared for me; and I pray that I may find them prompt; nay I will entice them that they may devour me promptly, not as they have done to some, refusing to touch them through fear. Yea though of themselves they should not be willing while I am ready, I myself will force them to it. Bear with me. I know what is expedient for me. Now am I beginning to be a disciple. May nought of things visible and things invisible envy me; that I may attain unto Jesus Christ. Come fire and cross and grapplings with wild beasts, cuttings and manglings, wrenching of bones, hacking of limbs, crushings of my whole body, come cruel tortures of the devil to assail me. Only be it mine to attain unto Jesus Christ.

The farthest bounds of the universe shall profit me nothing, neither the kingdoms of this world. It is good for me to die for Jesus Christ rather than to reign over the farthest bounds of the earth. Him I seek, who died on our behalf; Him I desire, who rose again for our sake. The pangs of a new birth are upon me. Bear with me, brethren. Do not hinder me from living; do not desire my death. Bestow not on the world one who desireth to be God's, neither allure him with material things. Suffer me to receive the pure light. When I am come thither, then shall I be a man. Permit me to be an imitator of the Passion of my God. If any man hath Him within himself, let him understand what I desire, and let him have fellow-feeling with me, for he knoweth the things which straiten me.

The prince of this world would fain tear me in pieces and corrupt my mind to Godward. Let not any of you therefore who are near abet him. Rather stand ye on my side, that is on God's side. Speak not of Jesus Christ and withal desire the world. Let not envy have a home in you. Even though I myself, when I am with you, should beseech you, obey me not; but rather give credence to these things which I write to you. For I write to you in the midst of life, yet lusting after death. My lust hath been crucified, and there is no fire of material longing in me, but only water living and speaking in me, saying within me, Come to the Father. I have no delight in the food of corruption or in the delights of this life. I desire the bread of God, which is the flesh of Christ who was of the seed of David; and for a draught I desire His blood, which is love incorruptible.

I desire no longer to live after the manner of men; and this shall be, if ye desire it. Desire ye, that ye yourselves also may be desired. In a brief letter I beseech you; believe me. And Jesus Christ shall make manifest unto you these things, that I speak the truth—Jesus Christ, the unerring mouth in whom the Father hath spoken truly. Entreat ye for me, that I may attain through the Holy Spirit. I write not unto you after the flesh, but after the mind of God. If I shall suffer, it was your desire; if I shall be rejected, it was your hatred. . . .

## FROM To the Philadelphians

. . . Abstain from noxious herbs, which are not the husbandry of Jesus Christ, because they are not the planting of the Father. Not that I have found division among you, but filtering. For as many as are of God and of Jesus Christ, they are with the bishop; and as many as shall repent and enter into the unity of the Church, these also shall be of God, that they may be living after Jesus Christ. Be not deceived, my brethren. If any man followeth one that maketh a schism, he doth not inherit the kingdom of God. If any man walketh in strange doctrine, he hath no fellowship with the Passion.

Be ye careful therefore to observe one Eucharist (for there is one flesh of our Lord Jesus Christ and one cup unto union in His blood; there is one altar, as there is one bishop, together with the presbytery and the deacons my fellow-servants), that whatsoever ye do, ye may do it after God.

My brethren, my heart overfloweth altogether in love towards you; and rejoicing above measure I watch over your safety; yet not I, but Jesus Christ, wearing whose bonds I am the more afraid, because I am not yet perfected. But your prayer will make me perfect unto God, that I may attain unto the inheritance wherein I have found mercy, taking refuge in the Gospel as the flesh of Jesus and in the Apostles as the presbytery of the Church. Yea, and we love the prophets also, because they too pointed to the Gospel in their preaching and set their hope on Him and awaited Him; in whom also having faith they were saved in the unity of Jesus Christ, being worthy of all love and admiration as holy men, approved of Jesus Christ and numbered together in the Gospel of our common hope.

---

## FROM To the Smyrnans

. . . For he suffered all these things for our sakes that we might be saved; and He suffered truly, as also He raised Himself truly; not as certain unbelievers say, that He suffered in semblance, being themselves mere semblance. And according as their opinions are, so shall it happen to them, for they are without body and demon-like.

For I know and believe that He was in the flesh even after the Resurrection; and when He came to Peter and his company, He said to them, "Lay hold and handle me, and see that I am not a demon without body." And straightway they touched Him, and they believed, being joined unto His flesh and His blood. Wherefore also they despised death; nay, they were found superior to death. And after His

Resurrection He both ate with them and drank with them as one in the flesh, though spiritually He was united with the Father.

But these things I warn you, dearly beloved, knowing that ye yourselves are so minded. Howbeit I watch over you betimes to protect you from wild beasts in human form—men whom not only should ye not receive, but, if it were possible, not so much as meet them; only pray ye for them, if haply they may repent. This indeed is difficult, but Jesus Christ, our true life, hath power over it.

But certain persons ignorantly deny Him, or rather have been denied by Him, being advocates of death rather than of the truth; and they have not been persuaded by the prophecies nor by the law of Moses, nay nor even to this very hour by the Gospel, nor by the sufferings of each of us severally; for they are of the same mind also concerning us. For what profit is it to me, if a man praiseth me, but blasphemeth my Lord, not confessing that He was a bearer of flesh? Yet he that affirmeth not this, doth thereby deny Him altogether, being himself a bearer of a corpse. But their names, being unbelievers, I have not thought fit to record in writing; nay, far be it from me even to remember them, until they repent and return to the Passion, which is our resurrection. . . .

## FROM Letter to Polycarp

. . . If thou lovest good scholars, this is not thankworthy in thee. Rather bring the more pestilent to submission by gentleness. All wounds are not healed by the same salve. Allay sharp pains by fomentations. Be thou prudent as the serpent in all things and guileless always as the dove. Therefore art thou made of flesh and spirit, that thou mayest humour the things which appear before thine eyes; and as for the invisible things, pray thou that they may be revealed unto thee; that thou mayest be lacking in nothing, but mayest abound in every spiritual gift. The season requireth thee, as pilots require winds or as a storm-tossed mariner a haven, that it may attain unto God. Be sober, as God's athlete. The prize is incorruption and life eternal, concerning which thou also art persuaded. In all things I am devoted to thee—I and my bonds which thou didst cherish. . . .

Let not widows be neglected. After the Lord be thou their protector. Let nothing be done without thy consent; neither do thou anything without the consent of God, as indeed thou doest not. Be steadfast. Let meetings be held more frequently. Seek out all men by name. Despise not slaves, whether men or women. Yet let not these again be puffed up, but let them serve the more faithfully to the glory of God, that they may obtain a better freedom from God. Let them not desire to be set free at the public cost, lest they be found slaves of lust.

Flee evil arts, or rather hold thou discourse about these. Tell my sisters to love the Lord and to be content with their husbands in flesh and in spirit. In like manner also charge my brothers in the name of Jesus Christ to love their wives, as the Lord loved the Church. If anyone is able to abide in chastity to the honour of the flesh of the Lord, let him so abide without boasting. If he boast, he is lost; and if it be known beyond the bishop, he is polluted. It becometh men and women too, when they marry, to unite themselves with the consent of the bishop, that the marriage may be after the Lord and not after concupiscence. Let all things be done to the honour of God.

Give ye heed to the bishop, that God also may give heed to you. I am devoted to those who are subject to the bishop, the presbyters, the deacons. May it be granted me to have my portion with them in the presence of God. Toil together with another, struggle together, run together, suffer together, lie down together, rise up together, as God's stewards and assessors and ministers. Please the Captain in whose army ye serve, from whom also ye will receive your pay. Let none of you be found a deserter. Let your baptism abide with you as your shield; your faith as your helmet; your love as your spear; your patience as your body armour. Let your works be your deposits, that ye may receive your assets due to you. Be ye therefore long-suffering one with another in gentleness, as God is with you. May I have joy of you always. . . .

# HERMAS

fl. 140

*The Shepherd,* written in Rome by one Hermas, was in general circulation both in the Eastern and the Western churches soon after the middle of the second century. There are two ancient traditions as to its origin. One was that the author was the same Hermas who was greeted by St Paul as a member of the Roman Church in 58 A.D. (Romans 16: 14); Origen held this view. The other was that it was written by Hermas, brother of Pope Pius I (140?–?154). This is stated in the Muratorian Canon (c. 180 A.D.). Recent critics suggest about 100 A.D. as the most likely date, since St Clement of Rome is mentioned as a contemporary.

## FROM The Shepherd

### VISION I

The master, who reared me, had sold me to one Rhoda in Rome. After many years, I met her again, and began to love her as a sister. After a certain time I saw her bathing in the river Tiber; and I gave her my hand and led her out of the river. So, seeing her beauty, I reasoned in my heart, saying, "Happy were I, if I had such a one to wife, both in beauty and in character." I merely reflected on this and nothing more. After a certain time, as I was journeying to Cumæ, and glorifying God's creatures for their greatness and splendour and power, as I walked I fell asleep. And a Spirit took me, and bore me away through a pathless tract, through which no man could pass: for the place was precipitous, and broken into clefts by reason of the waters. When then I had crossed the river, I came into the level country, and knelt down, and began to pray to the Lord and to confess my sins. Now, while I prayed, the heaven was opened, and I see the lady whom I had desired, greeting me from heaven, saying, "Good morrow, Hermas." And, looking at her, I said to her, "Lady, what doest *thou* here?" Then she answered me, "I was taken up, that I might convict thee of thy sins before the Lord." I said to her, "Dost thou now convict me?" "Nay, not so," said she, "but hear the words, that I shall say to thee. God, who dwelleth in the heavens, and created out of nothing the things which are, and increased and multiplied them for His holy Church's sake, is wroth with thee, for that thou didst sin against me." I answered her and said, "Sin against thee? In what way? Did I ever speak an unseemly word unto thee? Did I not always regard thee as a goddess? Did I not always respect thee as a sister? How couldst thou falsely charge me, lady, with such villainy and uncleanness?" Laughing she saith unto me, "The desire after evil entered into thine heart. Nay, thinkest thou not that it is an evil deed for a righteous man, if the evil desire should enter into his heart? It is indeed a sin and a great one too," saith she; "for the righteous man entertaineth righteous purposes. While then his purposes are righteous, his repute stands steadfast in the heavens, and he finds the Lord easily propitiated in all that he does. But they that entertain evil purposes in their hearts, bring upon themselves death and captivity, especially they that claim for themselves this present world, and boast in its riches, and cleave not to the good things that are to come. Their souls shall rue it, seeing that they have no hope, but have abandoned themselves and their life. But do thou pray unto God, and He shall heal thine own sins, and those of thy whole house, and of all the saints."

As soon as she had spoken these words the heavens were shut; and I was given over to horror and grief. Then I said within myself, "If this sin is recorded against me, how can I be saved? Or how shall I propitiate God for my sins which are full-blown? Or with what words shall I entreat the Lord that He may be propitious unto me?" While I was advising and discussing these matters in my heart, I see before me a great white chair of snow-white wool; and there came an aged lady in glistening raiment, having a book in her hands, and she sat down alone, and she saluted me, "Good morrow, Hermas." Then I, grieved and weeping, said, "Good morrow, lady." And she said to me, "Why so gloomy, Hermas, thou that art patient and good-tempered, and art always smiling? Why so downcast in thy looks, and far from cheerful?" And I said to her, "Because of an excellent lady's saying that I had sinned against her." Then she said, "Far be this thing from the servant of God! Nevertheless the thought did enter into thy heart concerning her. Now to the servants of God such a purpose bringeth sin. For it is an evil and mad purpose to overtake a devout spirit that hath been already approved, that it should desire an evil deed, and especially if it be Hermas the temperate, who abstaineth from every evil desire, and is full of all simplicity and of great guilelessness.

"Yet it is not for this that God is wroth with thee, but that thou mayest convert thy family, that hath done wrong against the Lord and against you their parents. But out of fondness for thy children thou didst not admonish thy family, but didst suffer it to become fearfully corrupt. Therefore the Lord is wroth with thee. But He will heal all thy past sins, which have been committed in thy family; for by reason of their sins and iniquities thou hast been corrupted by the affairs of this world. But the great mercy of the Lord had pity on thee and thy family, and will strengthen thee, and establish thee in His glory. Only be not thou careless, but take courage, and strengthen thy family. For as the smith hammering his work conquers the task which he wills, so also doth righteous discourse repeated daily conquer all evil. Cease not therefore to reprove thy children; for I know that if they shall repent with all their heart, they shall be written in the books of life with the saints." After these words of hers had ceased, she saith unto me, "Wilt thou listen to me as I read?" Then say I, "Yes, lady." She saith unto me, "Be attentive, and hear the glories of God." I listened with attention and with wonder to that which I had no power to remember; for all the words were terrible, such as man cannot bear. The last words however I remembered, for they were suitable for us and gentle. "Behold, the God of Hosts, who by His invisible and mighty power and by His great wisdom created the world, and by His glorious purpose clothed His creation with comeliness, and by His strong word fixed the heaven, and founded the earth upon the waters, and by His own wisdom and providence formed His holy Church, which also He blessed—behold, He removeth the heavens and the mountains and the hills and the seas, and all things are made level for His elect, that He may fulfil to them the promise which He promised with great glory and rejoicing, if so be that they shall keep the ordinances of God, which they received, with great faith."

When then she finished reading and arose from her chair, there came four young men, and they took away the chair, and departed towards the East. Then she calleth me unto her, and she touched my breast, and saith to me, "Did my reading please thee?" And I say unto her, "Lady, these last words please me, but the former were difficult and hard." Then she spake to me, saying, "These last words are for the righteous, but the former are for the heathen and the rebellious." While she yet spake with me, two men appeared, and took her by the arms, and they departed, whither the chair also had gone, towards the East. And she smiled as she departed and, as she was going, she saith to me, "Play the man, Hermas."

### VISION 2

. . . Now, brethren, a revelation was made unto me in my sleep by a youth of exceeding fair form, who said to me, "Whom thinkest thou the aged woman, from whom thou receivedst the book, to be?" I say, "The Sibyl." "Thou art wrong," saith he, "she is not." "Who then is she?" I say. "The Church," saith he. I said unto him, "Wherefore then is she aged?" "Because," saith he, "she was created before all things; therefore is she aged; and for her sake the world was framed." And afterwards I saw a vision in my house. The aged woman came and asked me if I had already given the book to the elders. I said that I had not given it. "Thou hast done well," she said, "for I have words to add. When then I shall have finished all the words, it shall be made known by thy means to all the elect. Thou shalt therefore write two little books, and shalt send one to Clement, and one to Grapte. So Clement shall send to the foreign cities, for this is his duty; while Grapte shall instruct the widows and the orphans. But thou shalt read the book to this city along with the elders that preside over the Church."

# Epistle to Diognetus

c. 200

The only manuscript which included this epistle was attributed to St Justin; it was destroyed in 1870. The ten chapters were possibly not a letter at all, but a literary fiction. The epistle has always been considered "one of the most perfect literary compositions handed down to us from ancient Christian times," but it is certainly not by St Justin, to whom it was attributed. Among critical authorities, Renan, Zahn, and Harnack place it in the third century; Kuhn, Krüger, and Bardenhewer, in the second.

Since I see, most excellent Diognetus, that thou art exceedingly anxious to understand the religion of the Christians, and that thy inquiries respecting them are distinctly and carefully made, as to what God they trust and how they worship Him, that they all disregard the world and despise death, and take no account of those who are regarded as gods by the Greeks, neither observe the superstition of the Jews, and as to the nature of the affection which they entertain one to another, and of this new development or interest, which has entered into men's lives now and not before: I gladly welcome this zeal in thee, and I ask of God, who supplieth both the speaking and the hearing to us, that it may be granted to myself to speak in such a way that thou mayest be made better by the hearing, and to thee that thou mayest so listen that I the speaker may not be disappointed.

Come then, clear thyself of all the prepossessions which occupy thy mind, and throw off the habit which leadeth thee astray, and become a new man, as it were, from the beginning, as one who would listen to a new story, even as thou thyself didst confess. See not only with thine eyes, but with thine intellect also, of what substance or of what form they chance to be whom ye call and regard as gods. Is not one of them stone, like that which we tread underfoot, and another bronze, no better than the vessels which are forged for our use, and another wood, which has already become rotten, and another silver, which needs a man to guard it lest it be stolen, and another iron, which is corroded with rust, and another earthenware, not a whit more comely than that which is supplied for the most dishonourable service? Are not all these of perishable matter? Are they not forged by iron and fire? Did not the sculptor make one, and the brass-founder another, and the silversmith another, and the potter another? Before they were moulded into this shape by the crafts of these several artificers, was it not possible for each one of them to have been changed in form and made to resemble these several utensils? Might not the vessels which are now made out of the same material, if they met with the same artificers, be made like unto such as these? Could not these things which are now worshipped by you, by human hands again be made vessels like the rest? Are not they all deaf and blind, are they not soul-less, senseless, motionless? Do they not all rot and decay? These things ye call gods, to these ye are slaves, these ye worship; and ye end by becoming altogether like unto them. Therefore ye hate the Christians, because they do not consider these to be gods. For do not ye yourselves, who now regard and worship them, much more despise them? Do ye not much rather mock and insult them, worshipping those that are of stone and earthenware unguarded, but shutting up those that are of silver and gold by night, and setting guards over them by day, to prevent their being stolen? And as for the honours which ye think to offer to them, if they are sensible of them, ye rather punish them thereby, whereas, if they are insensible, ye reproach them by propitiating them with the blood and fat of victims. Let one of yourselves undergo this treatment, let him submit to these things being done to him. Nay, not so much as a single individual will willingly submit to such punishment, for he has sensibility and reason; but a stone submits, because it is insensible. Therefore ye convict his sensibility. Well, I could say much besides concerning Christians not being enslaved to such gods as these; but if anyone should think what has been said insufficient, I hold it superfluous to say more.

In the next place, I fancy that thou art chiefly anxious to hear about their not practising their religion in the same way as the Jews. The Jews then, so far as they abstain from the mode of worship described above, do well in claiming to reverence one God of the universe and to regard Him as Master; but so far as they offer Him this worship in methods similar to those already mentioned, they are altogether at fault. For whereas the Greeks, by offering these things to senseless and deaf images, make an exhibition of stupidity, the Jews, considering that they are presenting them to God, as if He were in need of them, ought in all reason to count it folly and not religious worship. For He that made the heaven and the earth and all things that are therein, and furnisheth us all with what we need, cannot Himself need any of these things which He Himself supplieth to them that imagine they are giving them to Him. But those who think to perform sacrifices to Him with blood and fat and whole burnt offerings, and to honour Him with such honours, seem to me in no way different from those who show the same respect towards deaf images; for the one class think fit to make offerings to things unable to participate in the honour, the other class to One who is in need of nothing. . . .

For Christians are not distinguished from the rest of mankind either in locality or in speech or in customs. For they dwell not somewhere in cities of their own, neither do they use some different language, nor practise an extraordinary kind of life. Nor again do they possess any invention discovered by any intelligence or study of ingenious men, nor are they masters of any human dogma as some are. But while they dwell in cities of Greeks and barbarians as the lot of each is cast, and follow the native customs in dress and food and the other arrangements of life, yet the constitution of their own citizenship, which they set forth, is marvellous, and confessedly contradicts expectation. They dwell in their own countries, but only as sojourners; they bear their share in all things as citizens, and they endure all hardships as strangers. Every foreign country is a fatherland to them, and every fatherland is foreign. They marry like all other men and they beget children; but they do not cast away their offspring. They have their meals in common, but not their wives. They find themselves in the flesh, and yet they live not after the flesh. Their existence is on earth, but their citizenship is in heaven. They obey the established laws, and they surpass the laws in their own lives. They love all men, and they are persecuted by all. They are ignored, and yet they are condemned. They are put to death, and yet they are endued with life. They are in beggary, and yet they make many rich. They are in want of all things, and yet they abound in all things. They are dishonoured, and yet they are glorified in their dishonour. They are evil spoken of, and yet they are vindicated. They are reviled, and they bless; they are insulted, and they respect. Doing good they are punished as evil-doers; being punished they rejoice, as if they were thereby quickened by life. War is waged against them as aliens by the Jews, and persecution is carried on against them by the Greeks, and yet those that hate them cannot tell the reason of their hostility.

In a word, what the soul is in a body, this the Christians are in the world. The soul is spread through all the members of the body, and Christians through the divers cities of the world. The soul hath its abode in the body, and yet it is not of the body. So Christians have their abode in the world, and yet they are not of the world. The soul, which is invisible, is guarded in the body, which is visible: so Christians are recognized as being in the world, and yet their religion remaineth invisible. The flesh hateth the soul and wageth war with it, though it receiveth no wrong, because it is forbidden to indulge in pleasures; so the world hateth Christians, though it receiveth no wrong from them, because they set themselves against its pleasures. The soul loveth the flesh which hateth it, and the members: so Christians love those that hate them. The soul is enclosed in the body, and yet itself holdeth the body together; so Christians are kept in the world as in a prison-house, and yet they themselves hold the world together. The soul, though itself immortal, dwelleth in a mortal tabernacle; so Christians sojourn amidst perishable things, while they look for the imperishability which is in the heavens. The soul when hardly treated in the matter of meats and drinks is improved; and so Christians when punished increase more and more daily. So great is the office for which God hath appointed them, and which it is not lawful for them to decline.

For it is no earthly discovery, as I said, which was committed to them, neither do they care to guard so carefully any mortal invention, nor have they entrusted to them the dispensation of human mysteries. But truly the Almighty Creator of the universe, the Invisible God Himself from heaven planted among men the truth and the holy teaching which surpasseth the wit of man, and fixed it firmly in their hearts, not as any man might imagine, by sending (to mankind) a subaltern, or angel, or ruler, or one of those that direct the affairs of earth, or one of those who have been entrusted with the dispensations in heaven, but the very Artificer and Creator of the universe Himself, by whom He made the heavens, by whom He enclosed the sea in its proper bounds, whose mysteries all the elements faithfully observe, from whom the sun hath received even the measure of the courses of the day to keep them, whom the moon obeys as He bids her shine by night, whom the stars obey as they follow the course of the moon, by whom all things are ordered and bounded and placed in subjection, the heavens and the things that are in the heavens, the earth and the things that are in the earth, the sea and the things that are in the sea, fire, air, abyss, the things that are in the heights, the things that are in the depths, the things that are beween the two. Him He sent unto them. Was He sent, think you, as any man might suppose, to establish a sovereignty, to inspire fear and terror? Not so. But in gentleness and meekness has He sent Him, as a king might send his son who is a king. He sent Him, as sending God; He sent Him, as a man unto men; He sent Him, as Saviour, as using persuasion, not force: for force is no attribute of God. He sent Him, as summoning, not as persecuting; He sent Him, as loving, not as judging. For He will send Him in judgment, and who shall endure His presence? . . . Dost thou not see them thrown to wild beasts that so they may deny the Lord, and yet not overcome? Dost thou not see that the more of them are punished, just so many others abound? These look not like the works of a man; they are the power of God; they are proofs of His presence. . . .

Mine are no strange discourses nor perverse questionings, but, having been a disciple of Apostles, I come forward as a teacher of the Gentiles, ministering worthily to them, as they present themselves disciples of the truth, the lessons which have been handed down. For who that has been rightly taught and has entered into friendship with the Word does not seek to learn distinctly the lessons revealed openly by the Word to the disciples; to whom the Word appeared and declared them, speaking plainly, not perceived by the unbelieving, but relating them to disciples who being reckoned faithful by Him were taught the mysteries of the Father? For which cause He sent forth the Word, that He might appear unto the world, Who being dishonoured by the people, and preached by the Apostles, was believed in by the Gentiles. This Word, who was from the beginning, who appeared as new and yet was proved to be old, and is engendered always young in the hearts of saints, He, I say, Who is eternal, Who to-day was accounted a Son, through Whom the Church is enriched and grace is unfolded and multiplied among the saints, grace which confers understanding, which reveals mysteries, which announces seasons, which rejoices over the faithful, which is bestowed upon those who seek her, even those by whom the pledges of faith are not broken, nor the boundaries of the fathers overstepped. Whereupon the fear of the law is sung, and the grace of the prophets is recognized, and the faith of the Gospels is established, and the tradition of the Apostles is preserved, and the joy of the Church exults. If thou grieve not this grace, thou shalt understand the discourses which the Word holds by the mouth of those whom He desires when He wishes. For in all things, that by the will of the commanding Word we were moved to utter with much pains, we become sharers with you, through love of the things revealed unto us. . . .

# Epitaph of Pectorius

Beginning of 3rd century

This inscription, found at Autun, is one of the longest and best-authenticated of the Christian funerary inscriptions.

Thou, the divine offspring of the heavenly ΙΧΘΥΣ,* keeps a pure heart, while thou receivest the source of God-given waters, immortal gift to mortals. Comfort thy soul, O friend, with the ever-flowing waters of wealth-giving wisdom; and receive the honey-sweet food of the Redeemer of the saints; eat in thy hunger, holding ΙΧΘΥΣ in thy hands. Satisfy thyself with ΙΧΘΥΣ. My desire is to thee, my Saviour; to thee I pray, thou light of the dead. Ascandius, father, my heart's beloved, and with thee my darling mother and my brethren, in the peace of ΙΧΘΥΣ remember thy Pectorius.

* "Fish," in Greek; a symbol frequently written and pictured, since the letters of the Greek word are the initials for "Jesus Christ Son of God, Saviour."

# Epitaph of Abercius

c. 170

Abercius was bishop of Hieropolis in Phrygia in the middle second century. His *Acta* were found in a collection made by Metaphrastes, a ninth-century Byzantine writer; included was an epitaph to be placed on Abercius's tomb. Though the epitaph was regarded with much skepticism, Sir William Ramsay found part of the actual inscription in Phrygia, confirming the accuracy of the copy that had been handed down by Metaphrastes. In 1893 the stones were given to Pope Leo XIII by Sultan Abdul-Hamid II and are now in the Lateran Museum.

I, a citizen of an elect city, made this in my lifetime, that I might, when the time should come, have a place wherein to lay my body. My name is Abercius, a disciple of the Holy Shepherd, who feeds his flocks of sheep on the hills and plains, and who has great eyes that look in every place. For He taught me the faithful letters of life. He sent me to Rome to see a kingdom and to see a queen in a golden robe and golden sandals. And I saw there a people having a splendid seal, and I saw the plain of Syria and many cities and Nisibis. And having crossed the Euphrates, everywhere I had companions. I followed Paul and everywhere Faith was my leader, and she gave me food in every place, the Fish from the fountain, a mighty Fish and pure, which a holy maiden took in her hands and gave to her friends to eat for ever, having goodly wine and giving it mixed with water and also bread. These things, I, Abercius, dictated to be inscribed here while standing by. Truly I was seventy and two years old. Let everyone who understands these things pray for Abercius and everyone who agrees therewith.

Let not, however, anyone place another in my tomb, and if he do so, he shall pay two thousand gold pieces to the treasury of the Romans, and to my goodly fatherland Hieropolis a thousand gold pieces.

# CLEMENT OF ALEXANDRIA
## (Titus Flavius Clemens)

150?–?220

Clement, though born at Athens, is forever associated with the Church of Alexandria; he was one of the first of the great leaders in Africa to whom the Church owes so much. He was born about 150, of pagan parents. He was a great traveler, and throughout southern Italy, Palestine, and Egypt he sought out Christian teachers. In 190 he was ordained a priest and began teaching in Alexandria. In 203 he was forced to interrupt his courses because of the persecution of Septimius Severus, which closed his school. Clement was the first to explore in his writings the relations between faith and reason. His three great treatises, of which *The Instructor* is one, really constitute a whole, a theology apologetical, moral, and dogmatic.

## FROM The Instructor

C. 220

Keeping, then, to our aim, and selecting the Scriptures which bear on the usefulness of training for life, we must now compendiously describe what the man who is called a Christian ought to be during the whole of his life. We must accordingly begin with ourselves, and how we ought to regulate ourselves. We have therefore, preserving a due regard to the symmetry of this work, to say how each of us ought to conduct himself in respect to his body, or rather how to regulate the body itself. For whenever anyone who has been brought away by the Word from external things, and from attention to the body itself to the mind, acquires a clear view of what happens according to nature in man, he will know that he is not to be earnestly occupied about external things, but about what is proper and peculiar to man—to purge the eye of the soul, and to sanctify also his flesh. For he that is clean rid of those things which constitute him still dust, what else has he more serviceable than himself for walking in the way which leads to the comprehension of God?

Some men, in truth, live that they may eat, as the irrational creatures, "whose life is their belly, and nothing else." But the Instructor enjoins us to eat that we may live. For neither is food our business, nor is pleasure our aim; but both are on account of our life here, which the Word is training up to immortality. Wherefore also there is discrimination to be employed in reference to food. And it is to be simple, truly plain, suiting precisely simple and artless children—as ministering to life, not to luxury. And the life to which it conduces consists of two things—health and strength; to which plainness of fare is most suitable, being conducive both to digestion and lightness of body, from which come growth, and health, and right strength, not strength that is wrong or dangerous and wretched, as is that of athletes produced by compulsory feeding.

We must therefore reject different varieties, which engender various mischiefs, such as a depraved habit of body and disorders of the stomach, the taste being vitiated by an unhappy art—that of cookery, and the useless art of making pastry. For people dare to call by the name of food their dabbling in luxuries, which glides into mischievous pleasures. Antiphanes, the Delian physician, said that this variety of viands was the one cause of disease; there being people who dislike the truth, and through various absurd notions abjure moderation of diet, and put themselves to a world of trouble to procure dainties from beyond seas. . . .

We are not, then, to abstain wholly from various kinds of food, but only are not to be taken up about them. We are to partake of what is set before us, as becomes a Christian, out of respect to him who has invited us, by a harmless and moderate participation in the social meeting; regarding the sumptuousness of what is put on the table as a matter of indifference, despising the dainties, as after a little destined to perish. "Let him who eateth, not despise him who eateth not; and let him who eateth not, not judge him who eateth." And a little way on he explains the reason of the command, when he says, "He that eateth, eateth to the Lord, and giveth God thanks; and he that eateth not, to the Lord he eateth not, and giveth God thanks." So that the right food is thanksgiving. And he who gives thanks does not occupy his time in pleasures. And if we would persuade any of our fellow-guests to virtue, we are all the more on this account to abstain from those dainty dishes; and so exhibit ourselves as a bright pattern of virtue, such as we ourselves have in Christ. "For if any of such meats make a brother to stumble, I shall not eat it as long as the world lasts," says he, "that I may not make my brother stumble." I gain the man by a little self-restraint. "Have we not power to eat and to drink?" And "we know"—he says the truth—"that an idol is nothing in the world; but we have only one true God, of whom are all things, and one Lord Jesus. But," he says, "through thy knowledge thy weak brother perishes, for whom Christ died; and they that wound the conscience of the weak brethren sin against Christ." Thus the Apostle, in his solicitude for us, discriminates in the case of entertainments, saying, that "if any one called a brother be found a fornicator, or an adulterer, or an idolater, with such an one not to eat"; neither in discourse or food are we to join, looking with suspicion on the pollution thence proceeding, as on the tables of the demons. "It is good, then, neither to eat flesh nor to drink wine," as both he and the Pythagoreans acknowledge. For this is rather characteristic of a beast; and the fumes arising from them being dense, darken the soul. If one partakes of them, he does not sin. Only let him partake temperately, not dependent on them, nor gaping after fine fare. For a voice will whisper to him, saying, "Destroy not the work of God for the sake of food." For it is the mark of a silly mind to be amazed and stupefied at what is presented at vulgar banquets, after the rich fare which is in the Word; and much sillier to make one's eyes the slaves of the delicacies, so that one's greed is, so to speak, carried round by the servants. And how foolish for people to raise themselves on the couches, all but pitching their faces into the dishes, stretching out from the couch as from a nest, according to the common saying, "that they may catch the wandering steam by breathing it in!" And how senseless, to besmear their hands with the condiments, and to be constantly reaching to the sauce, cramming themselves immoderately and shamelessly, not like people tasting, but ravenously seizing! For you may see such people, liker swine or dogs for gluttony than men, in such a hurry to feed themselves full, that both jaws are stuffed out at once, the veins about the face raised, and besides, the perspiration running all over, as they are tightened with their insatiable greed, and panting with their excess; the food pushed with unsocial eagerness into their stomach, as if they were stowing away their victuals for provision for a journey, not for digestion. Excess, which in all things is an evil, is very highly reprehensible in the matter of food. . . .

From all slavish habits * and excess we must abstain, and touch what is set before us in a decorous way; keeping the hand and couch and chin free of stains; preserving the grace of the countenance undisturbed, and committing no indecorum in the act of swallowing; but stretching out the hand at intervals in an orderly manner. We must guard against speaking anything while eating: for the voice becomes disagreeable and inarticulate when it is confined by full jaws; and the tongue, pressed by the food and impeded in its natural energy, gives forth a compressed utterance. Nor is it suitable to eat and to drink simultaneously. For it is the very extreme of intemperance to confound the times whose uses are discordant. And "whether ye eat or drink, do all to the glory of God," aiming after true frugality, which the Lord also seems to me to have hinted at when He blessed the loaves and the cooked fishes with which He feasted the disciples, introducing a beautiful example of simple food. That fish then which, at the command of the Lord, Peter caught, points to digestible and God-given and moderate food. And by those who rise from the water to the bait of righteousness, He admonishes us to take away luxury and avarice, as the coin from the fish; in order that He might displace vainglory; and by giving the stater to the tax-gatherers, and "rendering to Cæsar the things which are Cæsar's," might preserve "to God the things which are God's." The stater is capable of other explanations not unknown to us, but the present is not a suitable occasion for their treatment. Let the mention we make for our present purpose suffice, as it is not unsuitable to the flowers of the Word; and we have often done this, drawing to the urgent point of the question the most beneficial fountain, in order to water those who have been planted by the Word. "For it is lawful for me to partake of all things, yet all things

* Literally, "slave-manners," the conduct to be expected from slaves.

are not expedient." For those that do all that is lawful, quickly fall into doing what is unlawful. And just as righteousness is not attained by avarice, nor temperance by excess; so neither is the regimen of a Christian formed by indulgence; for the table of truth is far from lascivious dainties. . . .

"Use a little wine," says the Apostle to Timothy, who drank water, "for thy stomach's sake"; most properly applying its aid as a strengthening tonic suitable to a sickly body enfeebled with watery humours; and specifying "a little," lest the remedy should, on account of its quantity, unobserved, create the necessity of other treatment.

The natural, temperate, and necessary beverage, therefore, for the thirsty is water. . . . But towards evening, about supper-time, wine may be used, when we are no longer engaged in more serious readings. Then also the air becomes colder than it is during the day; so that the failing natural warmth requires to be nourished by the introduction of heat. But even then it must only be a little wine that is to be used; for we must not go on to intemperate potations. Those who are already advanced in life may partake more hilariously of the bowl, to warm by the harmless medicine of the vine the chill of age, which the decay of time has produced. For old men's passions are not, for the most part, stirred to such agitation as to drive them to the shipwreck of drunkenness. For being moored by reason and time, as by anchors, they stand with greater ease the storm of passions which rushes down from intemperance. They also may be permitted to indulge in pleasantry at feasts. But to them also let the limit of their potations be the point up to which they keep their reason unwavering, their memory active, and their body unmoved and unshaken by wine. People in such a state are called by those who are skilful in these matters, acrothorakes. It is well, therefore, to leave off betimes, for fear of tripping. . . .

But women, making a profession, forsooth, of aiming at the graceful, that their lips may not be rent apart by stretching them on broad drinking cups, and so widening the mouth, drinking in an unseemly way out of alabastra quite too narrow in the mouth, throw back their heads and bare their necks indecently, as I think; and distending the throat in swallowing, gulp down the liquor as if to make bare all they can to their boon companions; and drawing hiccups like men, or rather like slaves, revel in luxurious riot. For nothing disgraceful is proper for man, who is endowed with reason; much less for woman, to whom it brings shame even to reflect of what nature she is.

"An intoxicated woman is great wrath," it is said, as if a drunken woman were the wrath of God. Why? "Because she will not conceal her shame." For a woman is quickly drawn down to licentiousness, if she only set her choice on pleasures. And we have not prohibited drinking from alabastra; but we forbid studying to drink from them alone, as arrogant; counselling women to use with indifference what comes in the way, and cutting up by the roots the dangerous appetites that are in them. Let the rush of air, then, which regurgitates so as to produce hiccup, be emitted silently. . . .

For in fine, in food, and clothes, and vessels, and everything else belonging to the house, I say comprehensively, that one must follow the institutions of the Christian man, as is serviceable and suitable to one's person, age, pursuits, time of life. For it becomes those that are servants of one God, that their possessions and furniture should exhibit the tokens of one beautiful life; and that each individually should be seen in faith, which shows no difference, practising all other things which are conformable to this uniform mode of life, and harmonious with this one scheme. . . .

On the whole, let young men and young women altogether keep away from such festivals, that they may not make a slip in respect to what is unsuitable. For things to which their ears are unaccustomed, and unseemly sights, inflame the mind, while faith within them is still wavering; and the instability of their age conspires to make them easily carried away by lust. Sometimes also they are the cause of others stumbling, by displaying the dangerous charms of their time of life. For Wisdom appears to enjoin well: "Sit not at all with a married woman, and recline not on the elbow with her"; that is, do not sup nor eat with her frequently. . . .

But if any necessity arises, commanding the presence of married women, let them be well clothed—without by raiment, within by modesty. But as for such as are unmarried, it is the extremest scandal for them to be present at a banquet of men, especially men under the influence of wine. And let the men, fixing their eyes on the couch, and leaning without moving on their elbows, be present with their ears alone; and if they sit, let them not have their feet crossed, nor place one thigh on another, nor apply the hand to the chin. For it is vulgar not to bear one's self without support, and consequently a fault in a young man. And perpetually moving and changing one's position is a sign of frivolousness. It is the part of a temperate man also, in eating and drinking, to take a small portion, and deliberately, not eagerly, both at the beginning and during the courses, and to leave off betimes, and so show his indifference. "Eat," it is said, "like a man what is set before you. Be the first to stop for the sake of regimen; and, if seated in the midst of several people, do not stretch out your hand before them." You must never rush forward under the influence of gluttony; nor must you, though desirous, reach out your hand till some time, inasmuch as by greed one shows an uncontrolled appetite. Nor are you, in the midst of the repast, to exhibit yourselves hugging your food like wild beasts; nor helping yourselves to too much sauce, for man is not by nature a sauce-consumer, but a bread-eater. A temperate man, too, must rise before the general company, and retire quietly from the banquet. . . . We must also check excessive laughter and immoderate tears. For often people under the influence of wine, after laughing immoderately, then are, I know not how, by some impulse of intoxication moved to tears; for both effeminacy and violence are discordant with the Word. And elderly people, looking on the young as children, may, though but very rarely, be playful with them, joking with them to train them in good behaviour. For example, before a bashful and silent youth, one might by way of pleasantry speak thus: "This son of mine (I mean one who is silent) is perpetually talking." For a joke such as this enhances the youth's modesty, by showing the good qualities that belong to him playfully, by censure of the bad qualities, which do not. . . . "For dreadful in his destruction is a loquacious man." And it is with triflers as with old shoes: all the rest is worn away by evil; the tongue only is left for destruction. Wherefore Wisdom gives these most useful exhortations: "Do not talk trifles in the multitude of the elders." Further, eradicating frivolousness, beginning with God, it lays down the law for our regulation somewhat thus: "Do not repeat your words in your prayer." Chirruping and whistling, and sounds made through the fingers, by which domestics are called, being irrational signs, are to be given up by rational men. Frequent spitting, and violent clearing of the throat, and wiping one's nose at an entertainment, are to be shunned. . . .

If anyone is attacked with sneezing, just as in the case of hiccup, he must not startle those near him with the explosion, and so give proof of his bad breeding; but the hiccup is to be quietly transmitted with the expiration of the breath, the mouth being composed becomingly, and not gaping and yawning like the tragic masks. So the disturbance of hiccup may be avoided by making the respirations gently; for thus the threatening symptoms of the ball of wind will be dissipated in the most seemly way, by managing its egress so as also to conceal anything which the air forcibly expelled may bring up with it. To wish to add to the noises, instead of diminishing them, is the sign of arrogance and disorderliness. Those, too, who scrape their teeth, bleeding the wounds, are disagreeable to themselves and detestable to their neighbours. Scratching the ears and the irritation of sneezing are swinish itchings, and attend unbridled fornication. Both shameful sights and shameful conversation about them are to be shunned. Let the look be steady, and the turning and movement of the neck, and the motions of the hands in conversation, be decorous. In a word, the Christian is characterized by composure, tranquillity, calmness, and peace. . . .

But the hiccuping of those who are loaded with wine, and the snortings of those who are stuffed with food, and the snoring rolled in the bed-clothes, and the rumblings of pained stomachs, cover over the clear-seeing eye of the soul, by filling the mind with ten thousand phantasies. And the cause is too much food, which drags the rational part of man down to a condition of stupidity. For much sleep brings advantage neither to our bodies nor our souls; nor is it suitable at all to those processes which have truth for their object, although agreeable to nature. . . .

So those women who wear gold, occupying themselves in curling at their locks, and engaged in anointing their cheeks, painting their eyes, and dyeing their hair, and practising the other pernicious arts of luxury, decking the covering of flesh, in truth, imitate the Egyptians, in order to attract their infatuated lovers.

But if one withdraw the veil of the temple—I mean the headdress, the dye, the clothes, the gold, the paint, the cosmetics—that is, the web consisting of them, the veil, with the view of finding within the true beauty, he will be disgusted, I know well. For he will not find the image of God dwelling within, as is meet; but instead of it a fornicator and adulteress has occupied the shrine of the soul. And the true beast will thus be detected—an ape smeared with white paint. And that deceitful serpent, devouring the understanding part of man through vanity, has the soul as its hole, filling all with deadly poisons; and injecting his own venom of deception, this pander of a dragon has changed women into whores. For love of display is not for a lady, but a courtesan. Such women care little for keeping at home with their husbands; but loosing their husbands' purse-strings, they spend its supplies on their lusts, that they may have many witnesses of their seemingly fair appearance; and, devoting the whole day to their toilet, they spend their time with their bought slaves. Accordingly they season the flesh like a pernicious sauce; and the day they bestow on the toilet shut up in their rooms, so as not to be caught decking themselves. But in the evening this spurious beauty creeps out to candlelight as out of a hole; for drunkenness and the dimness of the light aid what they have put on. The woman who dyes her hair yellow, Menander the comic poet expels from the house:

> Now get out of this house, for no chaste
> Woman ought to make her hair yellow.

Nor, I would add, stain her cheeks, nor paint her eyes. Unawares the poor wretches destroy their own beauty, by the introduction of what is spurious. At the dawn of day, mangling, racking, and plastering themselves over with certain compositions, they chill the skin, furrow the flesh with poisons, and with curiously prepared washes, thus blighting their own beauty. Wherefore they are seen to be yellow from the use of cosmetics, and susceptible to disease, their flesh, which has been shaded with poisons, being now in a melting state. So they dishonour the Creator of men, as if the beauty given by Him were nothing worth. As you might expect, they become lazy in housekeeping, sitting like painted things to be looked at, not as if made for domestic economy. . . .

And these women are carried about over the temples, sacrificing and practising divination day by day, spending their time with fortune-tellers, and begging priests, and disreputable old women; and they keep up old wives' whisperings over their cups, learning charms and incantations from soothsayers, to the ruin of the nuptial bonds. And some men they keep; by others they are kept; and others are promised them by the diviners. They know not that they are cheating themselves, and giving up themselves as a vessel of pleasure to those that wish to indulge in wantonness; and exchanging their purity for the foulest outrage, they think what is the most shameful ruin a great stroke of business. . . .

But these women delight in intercourse with the effeminate. And crowds of abominable creatures flow in, of unbridled tongue, filthy in body, filthy in language; men enough for lewd offices, ministers of adultery, giggling and whispering, and shamelessly making through their noses sounds of lewdness and fornication to provoke lust, endeavouring to please by lewd words and attitudes, inciting to laughter, the precursor of fornication. And sometimes, when inflamed by any provocation, either these fornicators, or those that follow the rabble of abominable creatures to destruction, make a sound in their nose like a frog, as if they had got anger dwelling in their nostrils. But those who are more refined than these keep Indian birds and Median pea-fowls, and recline with peak-headed creatures; playing with satyrs, delighting in monsters. They laugh when they hear Thersites; and these women, purchasing Thersiteses highly valued, pride themselves not in their husbands, but in those wretches which are a burden on the earth, and overlook the chaste widow, who is of far higher value than a Melitæan pup, and look askance at a just old man, who is lovelier in my estimation than a monster purchased for money. And though maintaining parrots and curlews, they do not receive the orphan child; but they expose children that are born at home, and take up the young of birds, and prefer irrational to rational creatures: although they ought to undertake the maintenance of old people with a character for sobriety, who are fairer in my mind than apes, and capable of uttering something better than nightingales . . . But these, on the other hand, prefer ignorance to wisdom, turning their wealth into stone, that is, into pearls and Indian emeralds. And they squander and throw away their wealth on fading dyes, and bought slaves; like crammed fowls scraping the dung of life. . . .

## The Perfect Man

FROM *The Miscellanies*

Here I find perfection apprehended variously in relation to Him who excels in every virtue. Accordingly one is perfected as pious, and as patient, and as continent, and as a worker, and as a martyr, and as a wise man. But I know of no one man perfect in all things at once while still human, though according to the mere letter of the law, except Him alone who for us clothed Himself with humanity. Who then is perfect? He who professes abstinence from what is bad. Well, that is the way to the Gospel and to well-doing. But the acceptance of the Gospel, in the case of the legal man, is knowing perfection, that he after the law may be perfect. And if he conduct himself rightly, and if, further, having made an eminently right confession, he become a martyr out of love, obtaining considerable renown among men, not even thus will he be called perfect in the flesh beforehand; since it is the close of life which claims this appellation, when the wise martyr, having first shown the perfect work, and rightly exhibited it, and having thankfully shed his blood, has yielded up the ghost; blessed then will he be, and truly proclaimed perfect, "that the excellency of the power may be of God and not of us." . . .

# TERTULLIAN

160?–?230

Clement was African by choice, Tertullian by birth. His father, who was a military man, was a pagan. Quintus Septimius Florens Tertullianus, born at Carthage, studied in Rome and was there converted to Christianity, returning to Carthage as a young priest. There he succumbed to the heresy of Montanus, a Phrygian, who made exceptionally severe demands on his followers, especially in connection with fasting, marriage, and martyrdom. Tertullian grew increasingly harsh as his rupture with the Church became more complete. He survived the persecution of Septimius Severus, writing the *De Fuga* against those who had fled. It is known that he broke from the main body of Montanists and founded a sect of his own, the Tertullianists. The date of his death is uncertain; St Jerome says he did not die until 250. Thirty-one of his writings are extant—apologetical, controversial, dogmatic, moral, and disciplinary—all admirably written.

## FROM On Female Dress

My sisters and fellow-servants, handmaids of the living God, the right that ranks me with you in fellow-servantship and brotherhood emboldens me, meanest as I am in that fellowship, to address to you a discourse, not one of affection certainly, but in the service of your salvation taking affection's place. That salvation, in the case of men as well as of women, depends chiefly on the observance of chastity. We are all of us the temple of God as soon as the Holy Spirit has entered into us; but the sacristan and priestess of that temple is Chastity, who must allow nothing unclean or profane to enter, lest God, who dwells within, should be offended and leave the polluted abode. But for the moment we are not speaking of Chastity itself, for the enjoining and exacting of which the urgency of divine precepts is sufficient, but rather of some matters pertaining to it, that is, the fashion in which it behoves you to appear abroad. Very many women—in passing this censure on myself may God allow me to pass it on all—either from simple ignorance or from hypocritical motives have the boldness so to walk in public as though chastity consisted only in the bare integrity of the flesh and in the avoidance of fornication. They seem to think that there is no need of anything further, as regards the manner of their dress, the fashion of their toilet, and the studied graces of form and elegance. In their gait they display the same outward appearance as Gentile women, in whom the sense of true chastity is lacking, inasmuch as in those who know not God, the Guardian and Teacher of truth, there can be nothing that is true. . . .

You, my sisters, in your gait, as in all things, must take a different path from theirs. It is your duty to be perfect, even as your Father is perfect who is in the heavens.

You must know that to perfect, that is Christian, chastity, carnal desire of one's body is a thing not only not to be wished but even utterly to be abhorred. The desire to please by outward charms, which we know naturally invite lust, does not spring from a sound conscience. Why should you rouse an evil passion? Why invite that to which you profess yourself a stranger? . . .

But why should we be a danger to our neighbour? Why should we excite in him lustful desires? In amplifying His law God makes no distinction of penalty between lust and fornication, and it will scarcely be that they escape punishment who have been to another the cause of perdition. That other, as soon as he has lusted after your beauty and in his mind committed the lustful act, perishes; and you have been made the sword of his destruction. Though you be acquitted of actual guilt you will not escape the odium attaching thereto; just as when a highway robbery has been committed on a man's land, the crime itself cannot be laid to the owner's charge, but still the estate gets a bad name, and its owner incurs suspicion. Are we to paint our faces that our neighbours may perish? Where, then, is the command: "Thou shalt love thy neighbour as thyself"? Nay, you must think not only of yourself, but of your neighbour as well. . . .

Someone may say: "Why should we shut out wantonness and only admit chastity? Would it not be permissible then for us to enjoy the praise due to beauty and to glory in our bodily advantages?" Those whose pleasure it is to glory in the flesh must see to that. We have no desire for such "glory," inasmuch as glory is the essence of exaltation, and exaltation suits not those who according to God's precepts are professors of humility. Moreover, if all glorying is vain and foolish, how much more so, especially to us, is glorying in the flesh. Even if glorying is allowable, we ought to wish to give pleasure, not in the flesh, but in the good things of the spirit; for it is of spiritual things that we are suitors. Where our work is, there let our joy be. Let us cull glory where we hope to win salvation. Obviously a Christian may glory sometimes, yea, and glory even in the flesh. But that will be when the flesh has endured laceration for Christ's sake, in order that the spirit thereby may win the crown, not in order that it may draw after it the eyes and sighs of youths. A thing that with you in any case is superfluous you may justly disdain if you have it not and neglect if you have. A holy woman may be beautiful by the gift of nature, but she must not give occasion to lust. If beauty be hers, so far from setting it off she ought rather to obscure it.

As if I were speaking to Gentiles, addressing you with a Gentile precept appropriate to all, I would say: "It is your duty to please your husbands, and your husbands alone." The less you trouble to please other men, the more you will please them. Have no fear, blessed sisters; no wife is ugly to her own husband. She pleased him enough when he chose her, whether it was her character or her looks that were the recommendation. Let none of you think that if she refrains from making the best of herself she will incur her husband's dislike and aversion. Every husband exacts chastity from his wife; but beauty a believing Christian does not require; for we are not attracted by the same charms as the Gentiles. An unbeliever on the other hand will regard your beauty with suspicion, owing to the infamous scandals which the Gentiles attribute to us. For whom is it, then, that you nurse your beauty? If it is for a believer, he does not exact it: if for an unbeliever, he does not believe in it unless it be simple. Why are you eager to please either one who is suspicious or else one who does not want such pleasure?

Of course, you must not infer from these suggestions that we should approve of an uncouth roughness in dress. We do not urge that squalor and slovenliness are good things. We merely set forth the limit and bounds and just measure of bodily adornment. You must not overstep the line to which simple and sufficient elegance limits its desires, the line which is pleasing to God. Against Him those women sin who torment their skin with potions, stain their cheeks with rouge, and extend the line of their eyes with black colouring. Doubtless they are dissatisfied with God's plastic skill. In their own persons they convict and censure the Artificer of all things. . . .

I see that some women change the colour of their hair with saffron dye. They are ashamed even of their own nation, ashamed that they were not born in Germany or Gaul; and so by changing their hair they change their country! Evil, most evil, is the omen of those flame-coloured heads, a defilement imagined to be a charm. Moreover, the force of the cosmetics burns the hair and ruins it; the constant application of any sort of moisture, even though it were undrugged, is harmful to the brain; and there is even danger in the warmth of the sun, so desirable for imparting to the hair vigour and dryness. What has grace to do with injury? What has beauty to do with filth? Shall a Christian woman put saffron upon her head, as the Gentiles lay it upon their altars? A substance which is usually burned in honour of the unclean spirit may be considered part of heathen sacrifice, unless it is used for honest and necessary and salutary purposes, to serve the end for which God's creation was provided.

But God says: "Who of you can make a white hair black or a black white?" And so women prove the Lord wrong! "Behold," they say, "instead of white or black, we make it yellow, a more pleasing and graceful colour." Not but what those who repent of having lived to old age do attempt to change from white to black again! Shame on such temerity! The age which we fervently pray to attain blushes for itself; a theft is accomplished; youth, the period of sin, is sighed after; the opportunity for grave seriousness is wasted. Far from wisdom's daughters be such folly! The more old age strives to conceal itself, the more it will be detected. This, then, is your idea of true eternity, hair that is ever young! This is the incorruptibility which we have to put on for the new house of the Lord, one guaranteed by cosmetics! Well do you hasten to greet the Lord, well do you speed to depart from this iniquitous age, you to whom the near approach of your own end seems unsightly!

Of what service to your salvation, moreover, is all the anxious care you spend in arraying your hair? You will not let it have a moment's rest: one day it is tied back, another day it falls loose; now it is lifted high, now it is pressed flat. Some women set their heart on forcing it into curls; others let it float waving in the air with a simplicity that has nothing of virtue in it. Moreover, you affix huge bundles of false tresses to your heads, making of them, now a bonnet to enclose and cover over the top, now a platform jutting out at the back of your neck. All this striving, be assured, is contrary to our Lord's precepts. . . .

You will say, I suppose, that I am a man and that from sex jealousy I am driving women from their own domain. Are there, then, some things that to men also are not permissible, if we are God-fearing, and have a due regard for gravity? There are, indeed; since in men for the sake of women, just as in women for the sake of men, there is implanted by a defect of nature the wish to please. My own sex recognizes some tricks of beauty which are peculiarly ours—for example, to cut the beard too sharply; to pluck it out in places; to shave round the lips; to arrange the hair and conceal grayness by dyes; to remove the first traces of down from every part of the body; to fix the hair with womanly pigments; to smooth the skin by means of rough powder; to consult the mirror at every opportunity and to gaze anxiously into it. But all these tricks are rejected as being frivolous and hostile to chastity, as soon as the knowledge of God has destroyed the wish to please by opportunities for wantonness. Where God is, there is chastity; there, too, is gravity, her helper and ally. How, then, shall we practise chastity without her effective instrument, that is gravity? Moreover, how shall we make gravity useful in the winning of chastity, unless we made strictness manifest in our face, and in our dress, and in the general aspect of the whole man? . . .

Therefore, blessed sisters, take not to yourself such robes and garments as play the part of pimp and pander; and if there be any of you whom reasons of birth or riches or past dignities compel to appear in public so gorgeously arrayed as not to appear to have attained wisdom, take heed to temper this mischief, lest under the pretext of necessity you should seem to give full rein to licence. . . .

Was it God, forsooth, who showed men how to dye wool with the juices of herbs and the saliva of shellfish? He forgot, perchance, when He was bidding the universe to come to birth, to order purple and scarlet sheep! It was God, too, I suppose, who invented the manufacture of garments, which, light in themselves, are still heavy in price; God who devised the gold settings that encircle and enhance the brightness of jewels; God who introduced the tiny wounds that ear-rings require, regarding it of such importance that His own work should be spoiled and innocent children tortured and made to suffer at once, that from the scars on their body—born, forsooth, for the steel—should hang some or other of those grains which the Parthians, as we see, use for studs upon their very shoes! Why, even the gold itself, whose glory so enthrals you, serves a certain tribe, as Gentile literature tells us, for chains! . . .

Perhaps some women will say: "We fear lest the Holy Name be blasphemed in our case, if we make any changes in our old style and dress." Let us not, then, forsooth, abolish our old vices! Let us cling to the same character, if we must cling to the same outward appearance as of yore! Then truly there will be no fear of the heathen blaspheming! It is a splendid blasphemy that says: "From the day she became a Christian she appears abroad in poorer dress." Will you be afraid to seem poorer, now that you have become more rich; fouler now that you have become more clean? Is it according to the Gentiles' pleasure or according to the pleasure of God that Christians ought to walk? . . .

For Christian chastity it is not enough to be; it wishes also to be seen. So great ought to be its plenitude that it overflows from the mind to the dress and bursts out from the conscience to the outward appearance, from the outside gazing, as it were, upon its furniture designed to hold the faith safe for ever. Such delicacies, then, which can by their softness and effeminacy unman the manliness of faith, must be discarded. The arm that has been wont to wear a bracelet will scarce endure to be benumbed to the rigour of a prisoner's chains. The leg that has rejoiced in a jewelled garter will hardly suffer itself to be squeezed in the stocks. I fear that the neck on which coils of pearls and emeralds have rested will never give a place to the executioner's sword. Therefore, blessed sisters, let us practise hardships now, and we shall not feel them; let us abandon luxuries, and we shall not regret them. Let us stand ready to face any violence, having nothing that we fear to leave behind. These things are but fetters that retard our hopes. Let us cast away earthly ornaments, if we desire heavenly. Love not gold; for it is gold that brands all the sins of the people of Israel. You ought to hate that which brought your fathers to ruin and was adored by them who were forsaking God. Even then gold was food for fire.

It is in iron, not in gold, that Christians always, and now more than ever, pass their days. The stole of martyrdom is today prepared for us. We are waiting for the angels to carry us to heaven. Go forth to meet them arrayed in the cosmetics and adornments of the prophets and apostles. Draw your whiteness from simplicity, your rosy hues from chastity. Paint your eyes with modesty and your lips with silence. Fix in your ears the words of God and fasten on your necks the yoke of Christ. Bow your head before your husbands, and you will be sufficiently adorned. Busy your hands with wool; keep your feet at home; and then you will please more than if you were arrayed in gold. Clothe yourselves with the silk of honesty, the fine linen of righteousness, and the purple of chastity. Thus painted you will have God for your lover.

# ORIGEN

185?–?254

Origen's name means "son of Horus," but he was nicknamed Adamantius because of the power of his reasoning. He was born in Alexandria, perhaps of Christian parents. His father, Leonidus, was martyred in 202 during the persecution by Septimius Severus. Origen, a pupil of Clement, was so brilliant that, at the re-opening of the school at Alexandria, he was chosen, at seventeen, as its headmaster. From 204 to 230 Origen taught at Alexandria. About 230, two friends of his, bishops Theoctistus of Caesarea and Alexander of Jerusalem, ordained him to the priesthood without consulting Bishop Demetrius, which was a violation of the canons. For this Origen was deposed from the school and degraded from the priesthood. He withdrew to Caesarea, in Palestine, where he taught until his death. One of his pupils was St Gregory Thaumaturgus. In his later life he visited Athens once, and made two trips to Arabia to try to bring Beryllus, bishop of Bostra, back to the orthodox faith. During the Decian persecution (250–51) he was imprisoned and tortured, and subsequently died at Tyre, in Phoenicia, from the effects of his sufferings. Origen was the Church's most voluminous writer. St Epiphanius counted six thousand works by him, though Eusebius catalogued only two thousand, and St Jerome only eight hundred.

## Letter to Gregory Thaumaturgus

All hail to thee in God, most excellent and reverend sir, son Gregory, from Origen. A natural quickness of understanding is fitted, as you are well aware, if it be diligently exercised, to produce a work which may bring its owner so far as is possible, if I may so express myself, to the consummation of the art the which he desires to practise, and your natural aptitude is sufficient to make you a consummate Roman lawyer and a Greek philosopher too of the most famous schools. But my desire for you has been that you should direct the whole force of your intelligence to Christianity as your end, and that in the way of production. And I would wish that you should take with you on the one hand those parts of the philosophy of the Greeks which are fit, as it were, to serve as general or preparatory studies for Christianity, and on the other hand so much of Geometry and Astronomy as may be helpful for the interpretation of the Holy Scriptures. The children of the philosophers speak of geometry and music and grammar and rhetoric and astronomy as being ancillary to philosophy; and in the same way we might speak of philosophy itself as being ancillary to Christianity.

It is something of this sort, perhaps, that is enigmatically indicated in the directions God is represented in the Book of Exodus as giving to the children of Israel. They are directed to beg from their neighbours and from those dwelling in their tents vessels of silver and of gold, and raiment; thus they are to spoil the Egyptians, and to obtain materials for making the things they are told to provide in connection with the worship of God. For out of the things of which the children of Israel spoiled the Egyptians the furniture of the Holy of Holies was made, the ark with its cover, and the cherubim and the mercy-seat and the gold jar in which the manna, that bread of angels, was stored. These probably were made from the finest of the gold of the Egyptians, and from a second quality, perhaps, the solid golden candlestick which stood near the inner veil, and the lamps on it, and the golden table on which stood the shewbread, and between these two the golden altar of incense. And if there was gold of a third and of a fourth quality, the sacred vessels were made of it. And of the Egyptian silver, too, other things were made; for it was from their sojourn in Egypt that the children of Israel derived the great advantage of being supplied with such a quantity of precious materials for the use of the service of God. Out of the Egyptian raiment probably were made all those requisites named in Scripture in embroidered work; the embroiderers working with the wisdom of God, such garments for such purposes, to produce the hangings and the inner and outer courts. This is not a suitable opportunity to enlarge on such a theme or to show in how many ways the children of Israel found those things useful which they got from the Egyptians. The Egyptians had not made a proper use of them; but the Hebrews used them, for the wisdom of God was with them, for religious purposes. Holy Scripture knows, however, that it was an evil thing to descend from the land of the children of Israel into Egypt; and in this a great truth is wrapped up. For some it is of evil that they should dwell with the Egyptians, that is to say, with the learning of the world, after they have been enrolled in the law of God and in the Israelite worship of Him. Ader the Edomite, as long as he was in the land of Israel and did not taste the bread of the Egyptians, made no idols; but when he fled from the wise Solomon and went down into Egypt, as one who had fled from the wisdom of God, he becomes connected with Pharaoh, marrying the sister of his wife, and begetting a son who was brought up among the sons of Pharaoh. Therefore, though he did go back to the land of Israel, he came back to it to bring division into the people of God, and to cause them to say to the golden calf, "These are thy gods, O Israel, which brought thee up out of the land of Egypt." I have learned by experience and can tell you that there are few who have taken of the useful things of Egypt and come out of it, and have then prepared what is required for the service of God; but Ader the Edomite on the other hand has many a brother. I mean those who, founding on some piece of Greek learning, have brought forth heretical ideas, and have as it were made golden calves in Bethel, which is, being interpreted, the house of God. This appears to me to be intended to convey that such persons set up their own images in the Scriptures in which the Word of God dwells, and which therefore are tropically called Bethel. The other image is said in the Word to have been set up in Dan. Now the borders of Dan are at the extremities and are contiguous to the country of the heathens, as is plainly recorded in the Book of Jesus, son of Nave. Some of these images, then, are close to the borders of the heathen, which the brothers, as we showed, of Ader have devised.

Do you then, sir, my son, study first of all the divine Scriptures. Study them, I say. For we require to study the divine writings deeply, lest we should speak of them faster than we think; and while you study these divine works with a believing and God-pleasing intention, knock at that which is closed in them, and it shall be opened to thee by the porter, of whom Jesus says, "To him the porter openeth." While you attend to this divine reading seek aright and with unwavering faith in God the hidden sense which is present in most passages of the divine Scriptures. And do not be content with knocking and seeking, for what is most necessary for understanding divine things is prayer, and in urging us to this the Saviour says not only, "Knock, and it shall be opened to you," and "Seek, and ye shall find," but also "Ask, and it shall be given you." So much I have ventured on account of my fatherly love to you. Whether I have ventured well or not, God knows, and His Christ, and he who has part of the Spirit of God and the Spirit of Christ. May you partake in these; may you have an always increasing share of them, so that you may be able to say not only, "We are partakers of Christ," but also "We are partakers of God."

# ST GREGORY THAUMATURGUS
## (Gregory of Neocaesarea)

213?–?270

Gregory was born at Pontus, in Asia Minor, of pagan parents. Having completed his studies in law and literature, he went to Caesarea, where he became very much attached to Origen, under whom he studied for five years. On his return to Pontus, in 240, he was consecrated bishop of Neocaesarea, in spite of his youth. He survived unharmed the Decian persecution (250–51), and in 264 took part in the synod of Antioch. He died about 270, in the reign of Aurelian. Soon after his death numerous miracles were claimed to be due to his intercession.

## FROM Panegyric on Origen

For my earliest upbringing from the time of my birth onwards was under the hand of my parents; and the manner of life in my father's house was one of error, and of a kind from which no one, I imagine, expected that we should be delivered; nor had I myself the hope, boy as I was, and without understanding, and under a superstitious father. Then followed the loss of my father, and my orphanhood, which perchance was also the beginning of the knowledge of the truth to me. For then it was that I was brought over first to the Word of salvation and truth, in what manner I cannot tell, by constraint rather than by voluntary choice. For what power of decision had I then, who was but fourteen years of age? Yet from this very time this sacred Word began somehow to visit me, just at the period when the reason common to all men attained its full function in me; yea, then for the first time did it visit me. And though I thought but little of this in that olden time, yet now at least, as I ponder it, I consider that no small token of the holy and marvellous providence exercised over me is discernible in this concurrence, which was so distinctly marked in the matter of my years, and which provided that all those deeds of error which preceded that age might be ascribed to youth and want of understanding, and that the Holy Word might not be imparted vainly to a soul yet ungifted with the full power of reason; and which secured at the same time that when the soul now became endowed with that power, though not gifted with the divine and pure reason, it might not be devoid at least of that fear which is accordant with this reason, but that the human and the divine reason might begin to act in me at once and together—the one giving help with a power to me at least inexplicable, though proper to itself, and the other receiving help. And when I reflect on this, I am filled at once with gladness and with terror, while I rejoice indeed in the leading of providence, and yet am also awed by the fear lest, after being privileged with such blessings, I should still in any way fail of the end. But indeed I know not how my discourse has dwelt so long on this matter, desirous as I am to give an account of the wonderful arrangement (of God's providence) in the course that brought me to this man, and anxious as nevertheless I formerly was to pass with few words to the matters which follow in their order, not certainly imagining that I could render to him who thus dealt with me that tribute of praise, or gratitude, or piety which is due to him (for, were we to designate our discourse in such terms, while yet we said nothing worthy of the theme, we might seem chargeable with arrogance), but simply with the view of offering what may be called a plain narrative or confession, or whatever other humble title may be given it. It seemed good to the only one of my parents who survived to care for me—my mother, namely—that, being already under instruction in those other branches in which boys not ignobly born and nurtured are usually trained, I should attend also a teacher of public speaking, in the hope that I too should become a public speaker. And accordingly I did attend such a teacher; and those who could judge in that department then declared that I should in a short period be a public speaker. I for my own part know not how to pronounce on that, neither should I desire to do so; for there was no apparent ground for that gift then, nor was there as yet any foundation for those forces which were capable of bringing me to it. But that divine conductor and true curator, ever so watchful, when my friends were not thinking of such a step, and when I was not myself desirous of it, came and suggested an extension of my studies to one of my teachers under whose charge I had been put, with a view to instruction in the Roman tongue, not in the expectation that I was to reach the completest mastery of that tongue, but only that I might not be absolutely ignorant of it; and this person happened also to be not altogether unversed in laws. Putting the idea, therefore, into this teacher's mind, he set me to learn in a thorough way the laws of the Romans by his help. And that man took up this charge zealously with me; and I, on my side, gave myself to it—more, however, to gratify the man, than as being myself an admirer of the study. And when he got me as his pupil, he began to teach me with all enthusiasm. And he said one thing, which has proved to me the truest of all his sayings, to wit, that my education in the laws would be my greatest *viaticum*—for thus he phrased it—whether I aspired to be one of the public speakers who contend in the courts of justice, or preferred to belong to a different order. . . .

And from the very first day of his receiving us (which day was, in truth, the first day to me, and the most precious of all days, if I may so speak, since then for the first time the true Sun began to rise upon me), while we, like some wild creatures of the fields, or like fish, or some sort of birds that had fallen into the toils or nets, and were endeavouring to slip out again and escape, were bent on leaving him, and making off for Berytus or our native country, he studied by all means to associate us closely with him, contriving all kinds of arguments, and putting every rope in motion (as the proverb goes), and bringing all his powers to bear on that object. With that intent he lauded the lovers of philosophy with large laudations and many noble utterances, declaring that those only live a life truly worthy of reasonable creatures who aim at living an upright life, and who seek to know first of all themselves, what manner of persons they are, and then the things that are truly good, which man ought to strive after, and then the things that are really evil, from which man ought to flee. And then he reprehended ignorance and all the ignorant: and there are many such, who, like brute cattle, are blind in mind, and have no understanding even of what they are, and are as far astray as though they were wholly void of reason, and neither know themselves what is good and what is evil, nor care at all to learn it from others, but toil feverishly in quest of wealth, and glory, and such honours as belong to the crowd, and bodily comforts, and go distraught about things like these, as if they were the real good. And as though such objects were worth much, yea, worth all else, they prize the things themselves, and the arts by which they can acquire them, and the different lines of life which give scope for their attainment—the military profession, to wit, and the juridical, and the study of the laws. And with earnest and sagacious words he told us that these are the objects that enervate us, when we despise that reason which ought to be the true master within us. I cannot recount at present all the addresses of this kind which he delivered to us, with the view of persuading us to take up the pursuit of philosophy. Nor was it only for a single day that he thus dealt with us, but for many days, and, in fact, as often as we were in the habit of going to him at the outset; and we were pierced by his argumentation as with an arrow, from the very first occasion of our hearing him (for he was possessed of a rare combination of a certain sweet grace and persuasiveness, along with a strange power of constraint), though we still wavered and debated the matter undecidedly with ourselves, holding so far by the pursuit of philosophy, without however being brought thoroughly over to it, while somehow or other we found ourselves quite unable to withdraw from it conclusively, and thus were always drawn towards him by the power of his reasonings, as by the force of some superior necessity. For he asserted further that there could be no genuine piety towards the Lord of all in the man who despised this gift of philosophy—a gift which man alone of all the creatures of the earth has been deemed honourable and worthy enough to possess, and one which every man whatsoever, be he wise or be he ignorant, reasonably embraces, who has not utterly lost the power of thought by some mad distraction of mind. He asserted, then, as I have said, that it was not possible (to speak correctly) for any one to be truly pious who did not philosophize. And thus he continued to do with us, until, by pouring in upon us many such argumentations, one after the other, he at last carried us fairly off somehow or other by a kind of divine power, like people with his reasonings, and established us in the practice of philosophy, and set us down without the power of movement, as it were, beside himself by his arts. Moreover, the stimulus of friendship was also brought to bear upon us, a stimulus, indeed, not easily withstood, but keen and most effective—the argument of a kind and affectionate disposition, which showed itself benignantly in his words when he spoke to us and associated with us. For he did not aim merely at getting round us by any kind of reasoning; but his desire was, with a benignant, and affectionate, and most benevolent mind, to save us, and make us partakers in the blessings that flow from philosophy, and most especially also in those other gifts which the Deity has bestowed on him above most men, or, as we may perhaps say, above all men of our own time. I mean the power that teaches us piety, the word of salvation, that comes to many, and subdues to itself all whom it visits: for there is nothing that shall resist it, inasmuch as it is and shall be itself the king of all; although as yet it is hidden, and is not recognized, whether with ease or with difficulty, by the common crowd, in such wise that, when interrogated respecting it, they should be able to speak intelligently about it. And thus, like some spark lighting upon our inmost soul, love was kindled and burst into flame within us—a love at once to the Holy Word, the most lovely object of all, who attracts all irresistibly towards Himself by His unutterable beauty, and to this man, His friend and advocate. And being most mightily smitten by this love, I was persuaded to give up all those objects or pursuits which seem to us befitting, and among others even my boasted jurisprudence—yea, my very fatherland and friends, both those who were present with me then, and those from whom I had parted. And in my estimation there arose but one object dear and worth desire—to wit, philosophy, and that master of philosophy, this inspired man. . . .

And besides all his other patient and laborious efforts, how shall I in words give any account of what he did for us, in instructing us in theology and the devout character? and how shall I enter into the real disposition of the man, and show with what judiciousness and careful preparation he would have us familiarized with all discourse about the Divinity, guarding sedulously against our being in any peril with respect to what is the most needful thing of all, namely, the knowledge of the Cause of all things? For he deemed it right for us to study philosophy in such wise, that we should read with utmost diligence all that has been written, both by the philosophers and by the poets of old, rejecting nothing, and repudiating nothing (for, indeed, we did not yet possess the power of critical discernment), except only the productions of the atheists, who, in their conceits, lapse from the general intelligence of man, and deny that there is either a God or a providence. From these he would have us abstain, because they are not worthy of being read, and because it might chance that the soul within us that is meant for piety might be defiled by listening to words that are contrary to the worship of God. For even those who frequent the temples of piety, as they think them to be, are careful not to touch anything that is profane. He held, therefore, that the books of such men did not merit to be taken at all into the consideration of men who have assumed the practice of piety. He thought, however, that we should obtain and make ourselves familiar with all other writings, neither preferring nor repudiating any one kind, whether it be philosophical discourse or not, whether Greek or foreign, but hearing what all of them have to convey. And it was with great wisdom and sagacity that he acted on this principle, lest any single saying given by the one class or the other should be heard and valued above others as alone true, even though it might not be true, and lest it might thus enter our mind and deceive us, and, in being lodged there by itself alone, might make us its own, so that we should no more have the power to withdraw from it, or wash ourselves clear of it, as one washes out a little wool that has got some colour ingrained in it. For a mighty thing and an energetic is the discourse of man, and subtle with its sophisms, and quick to find its way into the ears, and mould the mind, and impress us with what it conveys; and when once it has taken possession of us, it can win us over to love it as truth; and it holds its place within us even though it be false and deceitful, overmastering us like some enchanter, and retaining as its champion the very man it has deluded. And, on the other hand, the mind of man is withal a thing easily deceived by speech, and very facile in yielding its assent; and, indeed, before it discriminates and inquires into matters in any proper way, it is easily won over, either through its own obtuseness and imbecility, or through the subtlety of the discourse, to give itself up, at random often, all weary of accurate examination, to crafty reasonings and judgments, which are erroneous themselves, and which lead into error those who receive them. And not only so; but if another mode of discourse aims at correcting it, it will neither give it admittance, nor suffer itself to be altered in opinion, because it is held fast by any notion which has previously got possession of it, as though some inexorable tyrant were lording over it . . .

Here, truly, is the paradise of comfort; here are true gladness and pleasure, as we have enjoyed them during this period which is now at its end—no short space indeed in itself and yet all too short if this is really to be its conclusion, when we depart and leave this place behind us. For I know not what has possessed me, or what offence has been committed by me, that I should now be going away—that I should now be put away. I know not what I should say, unless it be that I am like a second Adam and have begun to talk, outside of paradise. How excellent might my life be, were I but a listener to the addresses of my teacher, and silent myself! Would that even now I could have learned to be mute and speechless, rather than to present this new spectacle of making the teacher the hearer! For what concern had I with such a harangue as this? and what obligation was there upon me to make such an address, when it became me not to depart, but to cleave fast to the place? But these things seem like the transgressions that sprung from the pristine deceit, and the penalties of these primeval offences still await me here. Do I not appear to myself to be disobedient in daring thus to overpass the words of God, when I ought to abide in them, and hold by them? And in that I withdraw, I flee from this blessed life, even as the primeval man fled from the face of God, and I return to the soil from which I was taken. Therefore shall I have to eat of the soil all the days of my life there, and I shall have to till the soil—the very soil which produces thorns and thistles for me, that is to say, pains and reproachful anxieties—set loose as I shall be from cares that are good and noble. And what I left behind me before, to that I now return—to the soil, as it were, from which I came, and to my common relationships here below, and to my father's house—leaving the good soil, where of old I knew not that the good fatherland lay; leaving also the relations in whom at a later period I began to recognize the true kinsmen of my soul, and the house, too, of him who is in truth our father, in which the father abides, and is piously honoured and revered by the genuine sons, whose desire it also is to abide therein. But I, destitute alike of all piety and worthiness, am going forth from the number of these, and am turning back to what is behind, and am retracing my steps. . . . And would that, in going away, I only went away against my will, as a captive is wont to do; but I go away also of my own will, and not by constraint of another; and by my own act I am dispossessed of this city, when it is in my option to remain in it. Perchance, too, in leaving this place, I may be going to prosecute no safe journey, as it sometimes fares with one who quits some safe and peaceful city; and it is indeed but too likely that, in journeying, I may fall into the hands of robbers, and be taken prisoner, and be stripped and wounded with many strokes, and be cast forth to lie half-dead somewhere. . . .

But why should I utter such lamentations? There lives still the Saviour of all men, even of the half-dead and the despoiled, the Protector and Physician for all, the Word, that sleepless Keeper of all. We have also seeds of truth which thou hast made us know as our possession, and all that we have received from thee—those noble deposits of instruction, with which we take our course; and though we weep, indeed, as those who go forth from home, we yet carry those seeds with us. It may be, then, that the Keeper who presides over us will bear us in safety through all that shall befall us; and it may be that we shall come yet again to thee, bringing with us the fruits and handfuls yielded by these seeds, far from perfect truly, for how could they be so? but still such as a life spent in civil business makes it possible for us to rear, though marred indeed by a kind of faculty that is either unapt to bear fruit altogether, or prone to bear bad fruit, but which, I trust, is one not destined to be further misused by us, if God grants us grace. . . .

But, O dear soul, arise thou and offer prayer, and now dismiss us; and as by thy holy instructions thou hast been our rescuer when we enjoyed thy fellowship, so save us still by thy prayers in our separation. Commend us and set us constantly before thee in prayer. Or rather commend us continually to that God who brought us to thee, giving thanks for all that has been granted us in the past, and imploring Him still to lead us by the hand in the future, and to stand ever by us, filling our mind with the understanding of His precepts, inspiring us with the godly fear of Himself, and vouchsafing us henceforward His choicest guidance. For when we are gone from thee, we shall not have the same liberty for obeying Him as was ours when we were with thee. Pray, therefore, that some encouragement may be conveyed to us from Him when we lose thy presence, and that He may send us a good conductor, some angel to be our comrade on the way. And entreat Him also to turn our course, for that is the one thing which above all else will effectually comfort us, and bring us back to thee again.

# LACTANTIUS FIRMIANUS

260?–?340

Lucius Caecilius Lactantius was born into a pagan family about 260 at Cirta, in Numidia, Africa. He studied under Arnobius, then in turn became a teacher of rhetoric, first in Africa, then in Nicomedia, where he was converted to Christianity in 300. He survived the Diocletian persecution untouched, and in 317 was named by Constantine the tutor of his son Crispus. He died at Trèves. His theology is mediocre; indeed, he almost confounds Christianity with theism. His style has been rated "bland and insipid."

## FROM The Divine Institutes

. . . I come now to the pleasure of touch, a sense which is indeed common to the whole body. But I do not think that I need speak here of ornaments or of fine clothes; my subject rather is wantonness, a vice which must be sternly repressed inasmuch as it is capable of doing prodigious mischief. When God devised the plan of having two sexes He gave them as attributes mutual desire and delight in union. And so of all living creatures He put the most burning passions in men's bodies, so that they might most eagerly rush into love of this kind, and their races thereby be propagated and multiplied. This passion and this impulse is found in man to be more vehement and more intense than in any other animal; either because God wished that mankind should surpass all other creatures in number, or else, having given virtue to man alone, He meant him in checking his pleasures to win the praise and glory of self-restraint. Our great adversary, therefore, knows how powerful is the strength of this passion, which, indeed, some people prefer to call a natural necessity, and tries to move it from the straight and honest path into ways of evil and perversity. He inspires men with illicit desires, so that love for other men's wives sullies the heart of those who might love their own wives without sin. He puts suggestive shapes before their eyes, he adds fuel to fire, and gives food to vice. Deep in the flesh he plunges his restless spur, inciting and inflaming a man's natural ardour, until he has him bound fast in his toils. And lest there should be any who from fear of punishment might refrain from what is not theirs, he has even established public brothels, publishing the shame of unfortunate women and making a mock both of those who do the deed and those who are compelled to suffer it.

The soul that was born for holiness he plunges in obscenities of this kind, as though in a pool of mud; he destroys all modesty, he overwhelms all shame. He even joins male with male and devises abominable unions contrary to nature and contrary to God's law: so does he train men and equip them for every crime. What can be sacred to those men who take a poor helpless child and make him a victim to their foul lust? No language can match the enormity of crimes like these. The only name that fits such folk is that of impious parricide; the sex that God gave them for pleasure is not enough for them, they must indulge in profane wantonness with their own kind. But with them these are but trivial diversions and have a sort of respectability. What shall I say of those who pursue the abominations of their lust even to madness? I shrink from describing such deeds; but what are we to think of those men who do not shrink from doing them? Speak I must, for these things happen; there are some accursed madmen from whose disgusting caprices even the mouth is not immune. What words can indignation find fit to stigmatize such wickedness? The greatness of the crime surpasses all that our tongues could say. Since then these are the works of lust, and these the misdeeds it produces, we must arm ourselves against it with the shield of virtue. Whosoever cannot bridle his carnal affections, let him keep them within the bounds of lawful wedlock, and then he will obtain that which he eagerly desires without falling into sin. What do these sons of perdition want? Pleasure is the fruit of decent living; if it is pleasure only that they crave, here is a just and lawful pleasure which no one forbids them.

If necessity constrains us to a bachelor's life, we must call in the help of virtue and let continence wrestle against desire. God has bidden us to refrain not only from other men's wives, but also from the common women of the town; when two bodies are joined together, He says, they are made into one. So the man who plunges into filth must of necessity with filthiness be stained. The body, indeed, can be quickly washed clean: but the soul cannot escape the contagion of the body's shame, and only long years and many good works can purge it from that adhering foulness. Everyone then should remember that the union of the two sexes is meant only for the purpose of procreation in a man's lifetime, and that the carnal affections are rendered legitimate by the production of children. We received our eyes from God not that we might enjoy the pleasure of fine spectacles, but that we might see to do the acts necessary for life; and in the same way our genital organs were given us, as their name implies, in order that we might beget the next generation. This divine law we must devoutly obey. Let all who profess themselves to be God's disciples so order their ways and mode of life that they gain the power of self-mastery. For those who indulge in pleasure and give way to lust hand their soul over to their body and condemn it to death; inasmuch as they make themselves their body's slaves, and over the body death has power. Let each and every one, then, to the best of his ability, mould his life to the ways of virtue, let him honour modesty, let him guard his chastity with all the strength of heart and soul: let him not merely obey the laws of the state; let him be above all laws, as one who follows the law of God. If once he has accustomed himself to these good things he will be ashamed to turn aside to what is worse; let him find his pleasure in things right and honourable, for they give to the good more delight than things perverse and dishonourable give to the evil.

I have not yet finished the tale of duties which chastity imposes on us. God has fixed the bounds of lawful desire not only within the walls of one house but also within the narrow limits of one bed. A man who has a wife must not want another woman in addition, slave or free; he must be faithful to his marriage vow. The law of the state imputes adultery to the wife alone, if she has another man: the husband, even if he has several women, is held free of guilt. With us it is not so. The divine law, when it joins two people in marriage and makes of them one body, gives them both equal rights: whosoever of the twain shall break and sunder that union of bodies is held guilty of adultery. For no other reason than this has God decreed that all other creatures when pregnant should refuse the male, but that a woman should still submit to her husband's embrace. God saw that if women were unwilling, a man's desires would drive him elsewhere, and he would lose thereby the glory of chastity. Moreover, if a woman were not able to do wrong she could not possess the virtue of modesty. For who would say that a dumb creature is modest because when pregnant it refuses the male? It does so because if it allowed his approach it would bring upon itself pain and danger. It is no credit therefore not to do that which you cannot do. Modesty in human beings is praised because it is not a matter of nature but of will. So both spouses should keep their vows one to the other: nay, more, the wife should be taught to behave herself chastely by the example of continence that her husband gives. It is unfair to demand something which you yourself cannot guarantee; and unfairness like this affords an obvious reason for adultery, since wives are unwilling to keep their marriage vows when husbands do not show them mutual affection. Never was there a wanton so lost to all sense of shame that she did not make this a reason for her faults. "I am doing no wrong," she will say, "by leaving the straight path: I am merely paying my husband back." Quintilian expressed the exact truth when he declared: "A fellow who does not keep away from other men's wives will never be able to guard his own: the two things are naturally connected." A husband who is busy seducing other women has no time to give to the purity of his own house; and a wife who comes across such a partner as this is roused to action by his example and thinks either that she is merely taking pattern by him or that she is avenging the wrongs he has done her.

Beware, then, of giving occasion for wrongdoing by our own intemperance. Let husband and wife get used to one another's ways and bear the yoke of marriage equally. Let us see ourselves in our partner. For the law of justice may be summed up in one rule: "Never do to another what you would not have him do to you." . . . Even if the body be free from stain, no credit for modesty can be given, if the heart is impure: nor must we think that chastity is really pure when the conscience is sullied by fleshly desires. Let no one think it hard to put a bridle on pleasure and to confine its roving fancies within the bounds of modesty and chaste living. It is our business to do more, and win over it a complete victory. . . . God's precepts in this matter do not lay any binding command upon us; for the generation of human kind is a necessity: they are merely permissive. For He knows the compelling strength of carnal affection: it was His own endowment. If any man can do this, He says, he will have a glorious and incomparable reward. Continence is the pinnacle, as it were, and the consummation of all the virtues. . . .

# ST BASIL

330?–?379

St Basil, St Gregory of Nazianzus, and St Gregory of Nyssa form a group which is called the "Great Cappadocians." They were very different; as Cardinal Newman pointed out, "It often happens that men of very dissimilar talent and tastes are attracted together by their very dissimilitude." This was the case with Basil and Gregory of Nazianzus. Gregory of Nyssa, Basil's brother, was always close to them both. Of the three, Basil was the most gifted, a man firm in resolve and deed; Gregory of Nazianzus was gentle, affectionate, an eloquent preacher; Gregory of Nyssa, a philosopher.

Basil was born about 330 at Caesarea, in Cappadocia, into a pious family. His maternal grandmother, St Macrina, was a disciple of St Gregory Thaumaturgus; his maternal grandfather had been a martyr. Basil was the eldest of ten children, of whom three sons became bishops—Basil, Gregory, and Peter—and the eldest daughter became a nun. Basil studied at Caesarea and then at Constantinople and Athens, where he continued the friendship begun in childhood with Gregory of Nazianzus. They were both about twenty-one when they made the acquaintance of Julian the Apostate, at Athens. After they left Athens, both Basil and Gregory decided on the religious life. Cardinal Newman has translated some verses by Gregory of Nazianzus describing their friendship and their joint search for a satisfactory way of life.

Basil visited the most famous ascetics of Egypt, Palestine, and Mesopotamia. On his return to Europe he established a colony of monks on the river Iris, but was forced from this retreat by his local bishop, Dianius, who made him a priest. Later he became bishop of Caesarea. In this capacity he had to oppose the Arian Emperor Valens, pacify the church of Antioch, confirm his flock in its adherence to the Nicene Creed, and try to persuade the Latins of the West to help him. He wrote much and well, and was the founder of the Rule for monks which bears his name and which is still followed by Greek monastics both Orthodox and Catholic.

## Letters

### TO ATHANASIUS, BISHOP OF ALEXANDRIA

. . . I suppose there is no one feels such pain at the present condition, or rather want of condition, of the Churches, as your Grace;

comparing, as you naturally must, the present with the past, and considering the difference between them, and the certainty there is, if the evil proceeds at its present pace, that in a short time the Churches will altogether lose their present constitution. I have often thought with myself, if the corruption of the Churches seems so sad to me, what must be the feelings of one who has witnessed their former stability and unanimity in the faith. And as your Perfectness has more abundant grief, so one must suppose you have greater anxiety for their welfare. For myself, I have been long of opinion, according to my imperfect understanding of ecclesiastical matters, that there was one way of succouring our Churches—viz., the cooperation of the bishops of the West. If they would but show, as regards our part of Christendom, the zeal which they manifested in the case of one or two heretics among themselves, there would be some chance of benefit to our common interests; the civil power would be persuaded by the argument derived from numbers, and the people in each place would follow their lead without hesitation. Now there is no one more able to accomplish this than yourself, from sagacity in counsel, and energy in action, and sympathy for the troubles of the brethren, and the reverence felt by the West for your hoary head. Most Reverend Father, leave the world some memorial worthy of your former deeds. Crown your former numberless combats for religion with this one additional achievement. Send to the bishops of the West, from your Holy Church, men powerful in sound doctrine: relate to them our present calamities; suggest to them the mode of relieving us. Be a Samuel to the Churches; condole with flocks harassed by war; offer prayers of peace; ask grace of the Lord, that He may give some token of peace to the Churches. I know letters are but feeble instruments to persuade so great a thing; but while you need not to be urged on by others, more than generous combatants by the acclamation of boys, I, on the other hand, am not as if lecturing the ignorant, but adding speed to the earnest.

As to the remaining matters of the East, you would perhaps wish the assistance of others, and think it necessary to wait for the arrival of the Western bishops. However, there is one Church the prosperity of which depends entirely on yourself—Antioch. It is in your power so to manage the one party, and to moderate the other, as at length to restore strength to the Church by the union. You know, better than anyone can tell you, that, as wise physicians prescribe, it is necessary to begin with treating the more vital matters. Now what can be more vital to Christendom than the welfare of Antioch? If we could but settle the differences there, the head being restored, the whole body would regain health. . . .

### TO GREGORY OF NAZIANZUS

. . . My brother Gregory writes me word that he has long been wishing to be with me, and adds that you are of the same mind; however, I could not wait, partly as being hard of belief, considering I have been so often disappointed, and partly because I find myself pulled all ways with business. I must at once make for Pontus, where, perhaps, God willing, I may make an end of wandering. After renouncing, with trouble, the idle hopes which I once had, or rather the dreams (for it is well said that hopes are waking dreams), I departed into Pontus in quest of a place to live in. There God has opened on me a spot exactly answering to my taste, so that I actually see before my eyes what I have often pictured to my mind in idle fancy.

There is a lofty mountain, covered with thick woods, watered towards the north with cool and transparent streams. A plain lies beneath, enriched by the waters which are ever draining off upon it; and skirted by a spontaneous profusion of trees almost thick enough to be a fence; so as even to surpass Calypso's Island, which Homer seems to have considered the most beautiful spot on earth. Indeed, it is like an island, enclosed as it is on all sides; for deep hollows cut it off in two directions; the river, which has lately fallen down a precipice, runs all along one side, and is impassable as a wall; while the mountain, extending itself behind, and meeting the hollows in a crescent, stops up the path at its roots. There is but one pass, and I am master of it. Behind my abode there is another gorge, rising to a ledge up above, so as to command the extent of the plain and the stream which bounds it, which is not less beautiful to my taste than the Strymon as seen from Amphipolis. For while the latter flows leisurely, and swells into a lake almost, and is too still to be a river, the former is the most rapid stream I know, and somewhat turbid, too, by reason of the rock which closes on it above; from which, shooting down, and eddying in a deep pool, it forms a most pleasant scene for myself or anyone else; and is an inexhaustible resource to the country people, in the countless fish which its depths contain. What need to tell of the exhalations from the earth, or the breezes from the river? Another might admire the multitude of flowers, and singing birds; but leisure I have none for such thoughts. However, the chief praise of the place is, that being happily disposed for produce of every kind, it nurtures what to me is the sweetest produce of all, quietness; indeed, it is not only rid of the bustle of the city, but is even unfrequented by travellers, except a chance hunter. It abounds indeed in game, as well as other things, but not, I am glad to say, in bears or wolves, such as you have, but in deer, and wild goats, and hares, and the like. Does it not strike you what a foolish mistake I was near making when I was eager to change this spot for your Tiberina, the very pit of the whole earth? Pardon me, then, if I am now set upon it; for not Alcmæon himself, I suppose, would endure to wander further when he had found the Echinades. . . .

### TO ANTIPATER, GOVERNOR OF CAPPADOCIA

. . . How excellent is philosophy, if only for this reason, that it cures even its disciples at a modest cost; for in philosophy the one and the same dish serves both for a dainty and for a sick man's diet. I hear you have recovered your lost appetite by eating pickled cabbage. At one time I used to dislike it both on account of the proverb, and of its reminder of the poverty that is generally its companion. Now I must alter my views and laugh at the proverb, and regard cabbage as a splendid nourisher of men, since it has restored our Governor to health. In future I shall think there is nothing like cabbage, not even Homer's lotus, nor the celebrated ambrosia, whatever it was, that the Olympians had for their salad. . . .

FROM ANTIPATER TO BASIL

. . . "Cabbage twice is death," says the unkind proverb. As for me, I can die but once, whether I order cabbage many times, and even if I never have it at all. So, as you have to die in any case, do not be afraid to eat a delicious relish, which the proverb quite unjustifiably condemns. . . .

# ST GREGORY OF NAZIANZUS

329?–?389

Gregory was born at Arianzus, in Cappadocia. His father, a convert from paganism, had become bishop of Nazianzus. Gregory attended school both in Caesarea in Cappadocia and Caesarea in Palestine, and also studied in Athens and Alexandria. About 360, he and his friend Basil (see page 84) withdrew to take up monastic life, and compiled a "collection of select passages from Origen called Philokalia." He was ordained by his father in 361, and in November 380 was installed as archbishop of Constantinople. He resigned in 381 and returned to Nazianzus. He was a born orator, but hypersensitive and unsuited to active life. He wrote forty-five discourses, many panegyrics and funeral orations, a good deal of bad poetry (interspersed with a few good personal poems), and wonderful letters, of which 243 are extant.

## Letters

### TO BASIL

. . . Since you take my castigation well, I will now give you more of it; and, to set off with Homer, let us

Pass on, and sing thy garniture within,

to wit, the dwelling without roof and without door, the hearth without fire and smoke—walls, however, baked enough, lest the mud should trickle on us, while we suffer Tantalus's penalty, thirst in the midst of wet—that sad and hungry banquet, for which you called me from Cappadocia, not as for the frugal fare of the Lotophagi, but as if for Alcinous's board for one lately shipwrecked and wretched. I have remembrance of the bread and of the broth—so they were named—and shall remember them: how my teeth got stuck in your hunches, and next lifted and heaved themselves as out of paste. You, indeed, will set it out in tragic style yourself, taking a sublime tone from your own sufferings. But for me, unless that true Lady Bountiful, your mother, had rescued me quickly, showing herself in need, like a haven to the tempest-tossed, I had been dead long ago, getting myself little honour, though much pity, from Pontic hospitality. How shall I omit those ungardenlike gardens, void of pot-herbs? or the Augean store, which we cleared out and spread over them; what time we worked the hillside plough, vine-planter I, and awful you, with this neck and hands, which still bear the marks of the toil (O earth and sun, air and virtue! for I will rant a bit), not the Hellespont to yoke, but to level the steep? If you are not annoyed at this description, nor am I; but if you are, much more I at the reality. Yet I pass over the greater part, for tender remembrance of those other many things which I have shared with you. . . .

. . . What I wrote before, concerning your Pontic abode, was in jest, not in earnest; but now I write very much in earnest. "Who shall make me, as in months past, as in the days" when I had had the luxury of suffering hardship with you? since voluntary pain is a higher thing than involuntary comfort. Who shall restore me to those psalmodies, and vigils, and departures to God through prayer, and that (as it were) immaterial and incorporeal life? or to that union of brethren, in nature and soul, who are made gods by you, and carried on high? or to that rivalry in virtue and sharpening of heart, which we consigned to written decrees and canons? or to that loving study of divine oracles, and the light we found in them, with the guidance of the Spirit? or, to speak of lesser and lower things, to the bodily labours of the day, the wood-drawing and the stone-hewing, the planting and the draining? or that golden plane, more honourable than that of Xerxes, under which, not a jaded king, but a weary monk did sit?—planted by me, watered by Apollos (that is, your honourable self), increased by God, unto my honour; that there should be preserved with you a memorial of my loving toil, as Aaron's rod that budded, as Scripture says and we believe, was kept in the ark. It is very easy to wish all this, not easy to gain. Do you, however, come to me, and revive my virtue, and work with me; and whatever benefit we once gained together, preserve for me by your prayers, lest otherwise I fade away by little and little, as a shadow, while the day declines. For you are my breath, more than the air, and so far only do I live, as I am in your company, either present, or, if absent, by your image. . . .

### TO AMPHILOCHIUS

. . . I did not ask you for bread, any more than I would look for water from the people of Ostracine. But it is not extraordinary, nor contrary to friendship, to ask you, a man of Ozizala, for vegetables, of which you have enormous abundance, and we a great dearth. So make up your mind to send me some, and plenty of them, and of the best quality, or, at any rate, as many as you can spare (for even small quantities are great to those who lack utterly), for I am about to receive the great Basil, and you who know him when he is full, and philosophical, would not like to see him hungry, and cross. . . .

. . . What a very small quantity of vegetables you sent! They must be made of gold. But really, your whole wealth is in gardens, rivers, groves and orchards, and your land is rich in vegetables, as is that of others in gold, and you dwell by verdant meads. Corn, on the other hand, is a fairy-tale to you, and bread with you is *panis angelicus,* as they say, so precious and precarious is it. So either send us a more generous supply of vegetables, or I will threaten you with nothing less than a cessation of your corn supply. And I shall find out whether it is true that "cicalas live on dew." . . .

. . . You're making fun. Well can I picture an Ozizalean in danger of starvation, when he has taken especial pains with his gardening! This, however, can be said of them, that even when dead of hunger, they smell sweet, and have a splendid funeral. Why? Because they are covered with quantities of all sorts of flowers. . . .

### TO BASIL

. . . You accuse me of indolence and sloth because I would not accept your See of Sasima, nor bestirred myself, in episcopal fashion, to become an occasion for your controversies, like a bone thrown to dogs. My principal business is always to keep clear of business, and to give you some conception of my good qualities—I take such a pride in peace and quiet that I regard myself as a pattern to all men of this sort of virtue. If only the world would copy me in this, the Church would be free from broils, and the Faith, which is used by all as a weapon in their private differences, would not be torn in sunder. . . .

## The Divinity of the Holy Spirit a Case of Development in Doctrine

. . . You see lights breaking upon us gradually; and the order of Theology, which it is better for us to keep, neither proclaiming things too suddenly, nor yet keeping them hidden to the end. For the former course would be unscientific, the latter atheistical; and the former would be calculated to startle outsiders, the latter to alienate our own people. I will add another point to what I have said; one which may readily have come into the mind of some others, but which I think a fruit of my own thought. Our Saviour had some things which He said could not be borne at that time by His disciples (though perhaps they were filled with many teachings), perhaps for the reasons I have mentioned; and therefore they were hidden. And again He said that all things should be taught us by the Spirit when He should come to dwell amongst us. Of these things one, I take it, was the Deity of the Spirit himself, made clear later on when such knowledge should be seasonable and capable of being received after our Saviour's restoration, when it would no longer be received with incredulity because of its marvellous character. For what greater thing than this did either He promise, or the Spirit teach? If indeed anything is to be considered great and worthy of the Majesty of God, which was either promised or taught.

# The Lordliness of Prelates

381

. . . Perhaps we may be reproached, as we have been before, with the exquisite character of our table, the splendour of our apparel, the officers who precede us, our haughtiness to those who meet us. I was not aware that we ought to rival the consuls, the governors, the most illustrious generals, who have no opportunity of lavishing their incomes; or that our belly ought to hunger for the enjoyment of the goods of the poor, and to expend their necessaries on superfluities, and belch forth over the altars. I did not know that we ought to ride on splendid horses, and drive in magnificent carriages, and be preceded by a procession and surrounded by applause, and have everyone make way for us, as if we were wild beasts, and open out a passage so that our approach might be seen afar. If these sufferings have been endured, they have now passed away: "Forgive me this wrong." Elect another who will please the majority; and give me my desert, my country life, and my God, whom alone I may have to please, and shall please by my simple life. . . .

# ST JEROME

340?–420

Eusebius Hieronymus, born of Christian parents at Stridon, in Dalmatia, went to Rome when he was twenty, to study under the grammarian Donatus. In 360 he was baptized by Pope Liberius. He went to Trèves, where he decided to become a monk. About 373 he set out for the East, and, after a brief stay at Antioch, plunged into the desert of Chalcis, where he led a hermit's life. After five years he returned to Antioch and was ordained priest by Bishop Paulinus, whom he accompanied to Rome for the synod of 382. Jerome lived three years in Rome, commissioned by Pope Damasus to translate the Psalms and the New Testament; later he translated the Old Testament, except the deutero-canonical books, from the original Hebrew into Latin. In 384, when Pope Damasus died, Jerome was obliged to leave Rome because of the objections of the Roman clergy to the boldness of his scriptural criticism. He set out for the East again; after a stay in Alexandria he settled in Bethlehem in 386, in a grotto near the monastery of his friend Paula. He spent a comparatively happy and very busy old age. He was the greatest scholar among the Latin Fathers. He knew Latin, Greek, and Hebrew really well, and also Aramaic; he was a careful historian and a good geographer.

## To Pope Damasus, on the Revision of the Latin Bible

383

. . . You urge me to revise the old Latin version and, as it were, to sit in judgment on the copies of the Scriptures which are now scattered throughout the whole world; and, inasmuch as they differ from one another, you would have me decide which of them agree with the Greek original. The labour is one of love, but at the same time both perilous and presumptuous; for, in judging others, I must be content to be judged by all; and how can I dare to change the language of the world in its hoary old age, and carry it back to the early days of its infancy? Is there a man, learned or unlearned, who will not, when he takes the volume into his hands, and perceives that what he reads does not suit his settled tastes, break out immediately into violent language, and call me a forger and a profane person for having the audacity to add anything to the ancient books, or to make any changes or corrections therein? Now there are two consoling reflections which enable me to bear the odium—in the first place, the command is given by you who are the supreme bishop; and, secondly, even on the showing of those who revile us, readings at variance with the early copies cannot be right. For if we are to pin our faith to the Latin texts, it is for our opponents to tell us *which;* for there are almost as many forms of texts as there are copies. If, on the other hand, we are to glean the truth from a comparison of many, why not go back to the original Greek and correct the mistakes introduced by inaccurate translators, and the blundering alterations of confident but ignorant critics, and further all that has been inserted or changed by copyists more asleep than awake? . . . I am now speaking of the New Testament. This was undoubtedly composed in Greek, with the exception of the work of Matthew the Apostle, who was the first to commit to writing the Gospel of Christ, and who published his work in Judæa in Hebrew characters. We must confess that as we have it in our language it is marked by discrepancies, and now that the stream is distributed into different channels we must go back to the fountainhead. . . . I promise in this short Preface the four Gospels only, which are to be taken in the following order, Matthew, Mark, Luke, John, as they have been revised by the comparison of Greek manuscripts. Only early ones have been used. But to avoid any great divergences from the Latin which we are accustomed to read, I have used my pen with some restraint: and while I have corrected only such passages as seemed to convey a different meaning, I have allowed the rest to remain as they are. . . .

## Account of His Conversion

373

. . . Many years ago when, for the kingdom of heaven's sake, I had cut myself off from home, parents, sister, relatives and—harder still

—from the dainty food to which I had been accustomed, and when I was on my way to Jerusalem to wage my warfare, I still could not bring myself to forgo the library which I had formed for myself at Rome with great care and toil. And so, miserable man that I was, I would fast only that I might afterwards read Cicero. After many nights spent in vigil, after floods of tears called from my inmost heart, after the recollection of my past sins, I would once more take up Plautus. And when at times I returned to my right mind and began to read the prophets, their style seemed rude and repellent. I failed to see the light with my blinded eyes; but I attributed the fault not to them, but to the sun. While the old serpent was thus making me his plaything, about the middle of Lent a deep-seated fever fell upon my weakened body, and while it destroyed my rest completely—the story seems hardly credible—it so wasted my unhappy frame that scarcely anything was left of me but skin and bone. Meantime, preparations for my funeral went on; my body grew gradually colder, and the warmth of life lingered only in my throbbing breast. Suddenly I was caught up in the spirit and dragged before the judgment-seat of the Judge; and here the light was so bright, and those who stood around were so radiant, that I cast myself upon the ground and did not dare to look up. Asked who and what I was, I replied: "I am a Christian." But He who presided said: "Thou liest, thou art a follower of Cicero, not of Christ. For 'where thy treasure is, there will thy heart be also.' " Instantly, I became dumb, and amid the strokes of the lash—for He had ordered me to be scourged—I was tortured most severely still by the fire of conscience, considering with myself that verse: "In the grave who shall give thee thanks?" Yet, for all that, I began to cry and to bewail myself, saying: "Have mercy upon me, O Lord: have mercy upon me." Amid the sound of the scourges this cry still made itself heard. At last the bystanders, falling down before the knees of Him who presided, prayed that He would have pity on my youth, and that He would give me space to repent of my error. He might still, they urged, inflict torture on me, should I ever again read the works of the Gentiles. Under the stress of that awful moment, I should have been ready to make even still larger promises than these. Accordingly I made oath and called upon His name, saying: "Lord, if ever again I possess worldly books, or if ever again I read such, I have denied Thee." Dismissed then, on taking this oath, I returned to the upper world. . . . Thenceforth I read the books of God with a zeal greater than I had previously given to the books of men. . . .

## The Roman Psalter and the Gallican Psalter

. . . Long ago, when I was living at Rome, I revised the Psalter and corrected it in a great measure, though but cursorily, in accordance with the Septuagint version. You now find it, Paula and Eustochium, again corrupted through the faults of copyists, and realize the fact that ancient error is more powerful than modern correction; and you therefore urge me, as it were, to cross plough the land which has already been broken up, and, by means of the transverse furrows, to root out the thorns which are beginning to spring again; it is only right, you say, that rank and noxious growths should be cut down as often as they appear. And so I issue my customary admonition by way of preface both to you, for whom it happens that I am undertaking the labour, and to those persons who desire to have copies such as I describe. Pray see that what I have carefully revised be transcribed with similar painstaking care. Every reader can observe for himself where there is placed either a horizontal line, or a mark issuing from the centre, that is, either an obelus (÷) or an asterisk (*). And wherever he sees the former, he is to understand that between this mark and the two stops (:) which I have introduced, the Septuagint translation contains superfluous matter. But wherever he sees the asterisk, an addition from the Hebrew books is indicated, which also goes as far as the two stops. . . .

## The Avarice of Clergy and Religious

c. 370

. . . Shameful to say, idol-priests, play-actors, jockeys, and prostitutes can inherit property: clergymen and monks alone lie under a legal disability, a disability enacted not by persecutors, but by Christian emperors. I do not complain of the law, but I grieve that we have deserved a statute so harsh. Cauterizing is a good thing, no doubt; but how is it that I have a wound which makes me need it? The law is strict and far-seeing, yet even so rapacity goes on unchecked. By a fiction of trusteeship we set the statute at defiance: and, as if Imperial decrees outweigh the mandates of Christ, we fear the laws and despise the Gospels. . . .

## Letters

TO MARCELLA

. . . Ambrose, whose generous supplies of paper, money and copyists enabled that iron man, that *Robot,* our Origen, to write his innumerable books, records in a letter to Origen from Athens that they never sat down to a meal together without something being read aloud to them, and that they never went to bed without one of the brethren to read the Scriptures aloud. Thus it was both day and night, prayer followed reading, and reading, prayer. Have we ever done the like? Brute beasts that we are, slaves of the flesh. A couple of hours' reading finds us beginning to yawn, we pass a hand over the face, we try to repress our languor, and as if wearied with much toil, betake ourselves again to worldly pursuits.

I pass over those meals which burden and oppress the mind. I am ashamed to mention the habit of morning calls, which day by day we either receive ourselves, or pay to others. The conversation gradually gets under way, becomes a regular gossip, the absent are torn to pieces, other people's lives are discussed, there is mutual rending and devouring till no one has a shred of character left. Such is the meal that regales us. Then when the guests are gone, we make up our accounts, and these are sure to make us either anxious or angry. At one time we are like raging lions, at another we are striving vainly to make provision for years to come, unmindful of the words of the Gospel—"Fool, this night thy soul shall be required of thee."

Clothing is less for necessity than for elegant display. Wherever our interest lies, our foot is swift, our tongue apt, our ears attentive. If, as often happens in a household, news comes of some loss, our faces are downcast. The gain of a penny fills us with joy, the loss of a halfpenny with sorrow. Made in God's image, what divers characters, in the corruption of our hearts, do we assume! As in the theatre a single actor can impersonate sometimes a robust Hercules, at others a melting Venus, or a trembling Cybele, so we whom the world would hate if we were not of the world, can play as many roles as there are sins to commit.

Wherefore, since we have accomplished a large part of our life's voyage, rolled this way and that by the waves, our ship tossed by the storm's whirlwinds, so that it has sprung leaks by striking on the rocks, now that the opportunity is ours for the first time, let us enter into these rural retreats as into a haven. Here rustic dainties, coarse bread, humble but unoffending, salads watered by our own hands, and milk, afford us sustenance. With such a diet sleep does not interrupt prayer, nor over-eating interfere with reading. In summer, a leafy bower will afford shade. In autumn, the very mildness of the air, and a couch spread beneath the boughs, invite repose. In spring-time, flowers enamel the vale, and our pious psalms will rise more sweetly to the accompaniment of the feathered choir. When winter comes with his snows, I shall not purchase fuel; watching or sleeping, I shall be warm; at any rate, I shall not for this be cold.

Let Rome keep her din, the arena its atrocities, the circus its follies, the theatre its revels, and to use a word in favour with our friends, may the House of Ladies hold its daily sessions. For us it is good to cleave unto the Lord, and to place our hope in Him. And one day, when Heaven has transmuted this poverty of ours, we shall declare, "what does Heaven hold for me, and what have I required on earth, save only Thee, O Lord?" When Heaven promises us such good, shall we grieve over the trivial and paltry things of earth? . . .

### FROM AUGUSTINE TO JEROME

402

To my lord most beloved and longed for, my honoured brother in Christ, and fellow-presbyter, Jerome, Augustine sends greeting in the Lord.

I have heard that my letter has come to your hand. I have not yet received a reply, but I do not on this account question your affection; doubtless something has hitherto prevented you. Wherefore I know and avow that my prayer should be, that God would put it in your power to forward your reply, for He has already given you power to prepare it, seeing that you can do so with the utmost ease if you feel disposed.

I have hesitated whether to give credence or not to a certain report which has reached me; but I felt that I ought not to hesitate as to writing a few lines to you regarding the matter. To be brief, I have heard that some brethren have told your Charity that I have written a book against you and have sent it to Rome. Be assured that this is false: I call God to witness that I have not done this. But if perchance there be some things in some of my writings in which I have been found to be of a different opinion from you, I think you ought to know, or if it cannot be certainly known, at least to believe, that such things have been written not with a view of contradicting you, but only of stating my own views. In saying this, however, let me assure you that not only am I most ready to hear in a brotherly spirit the objections which you may entertain to anything in my writings which has displeased you, but I entreat, nay implore you, to acquaint me with them; and thus I shall be made glad either by the correction of my mistake, or at least by the expression of your goodwill.

Oh that it were in my power, by our living near each other, if not under the same roof, to enjoy frequent and sweet conference with you in the Lord! Since, however, this is not granted, I beg you to take pains that this one way in which we can be together in the Lord be kept up; nay, more improved and perfected. Do not refuse to write me in return, however seldom.

Greet with my respects our holy brother Paulinianus, and all the brethren who with you, and because of you, rejoice in the Lord. May you, remembering us, be heard by the Lord in regard to all your holy desires, my lord most beloved and longed for, my honoured brother in Christ.

## TO AUGUSTINE

402

To Augustine, my lord, truly holy and most blessed father, Jerome sends greetings in Christ.

When my kinsman, our holy son Asterius, subdeacon, was just on the point of beginning his journey, the letter of your Grace arrived, in which you clear yourself of the charge of having sent to Rome a book written against your humble servant. I had not heard that charge; but by our brother Sysinnius, deacon, copies of a letter addressed by someone apparently to me have come hither. In the said letter I am exhorted to sing the *παλινωδία*, confessing mistake in regard to a paragraph of the Apostle's writing, and to imitate Stesichorus, who, vacillating between disparagement and praises of Helen, recovered, by praising her, the eyesight which he had forfeited by speaking against her. Although the style and the method of argument appeared to be yours, I must frankly confess to your Excellency that I did not think it right to assume without examination the authenticity of a letter of which I had only seen copies, lest perchance, if offended by my reply, you should with justice complain that it was my duty first to have made sure that you were the author, and only after that was ascertained, to address you in reply. Another reason for my delay was the protracted illness of the pious and venerable Paula. For, while occupied long in attending upon her in severe illness, I had almost forgotten your letter, or more correctly, the letter written in your name, remembering the verse, "Like music in the day of mourning is an unseasonable discourse." Therefore, if it is your letter, write me frankly that it is so, or send me a more accurate copy, in order that without any passionate rancour we may devote ourselves to discuss scriptural truth; and I may either correct my own mistake, or show that another has without good reason found fault with me.

Far be it from me to presume to attack anything which your Grace has written. For it is enough for me to prove my own views without controverting what others hold. But it is well known to one of your wisdom, that everyone is satisfied with his own opinion, and that it is puerile self-sufficiency to seek, as young men have of old been wont to do, to gain glory to one's own name by assailing men who have become renowned. I am not so foolish as to think myself insulted by the fact that you give an explanation different from mine; since you, on the other hand, are not wronged by my views being contrary to those which you maintain. But that is the kind of reproof by which friends may truly benefit each other, when each, not seeing his own bag of faults, observes, as Persius has it, the wallet borne by the other. Let me say further, love one who loves you, and do not because you are young challenge a veteran in the field of Scripture. I have had my time, and have run my course to the utmost of my strength. It is but fair that I should rest, while you in your turn run and accomplish great distances; at the same time (with your leave, and without intending any disrespect), lest it should seem that to quote from the poets is a thing which you alone can do, let me remind you of the encounter between Dares and Entellus, and of the proverb, "The tired ox treads with a firmer step." With sorrow I have dictated these words. Would that I could receive your embrace, and that by converse we might aid each other in learning!

With his usual effrontery, Calphurnius, surnamed Lanarius, has sent me his execrable writings, which I understand that he has been at pains to disseminate in Africa also. To these I have replied in part, and shortly; and I have sent you a copy of my treatise, intending by the first opportunity to send you a larger work, when I have leisure to prepare it. In this treatise I have been careful not to offend Christian feeling in any, but only to confute the lies and hallucinations arising from his ignorance and madness.

Remember me, holy and venerable father. See how sincerely I love thee, in that I am unwilling, even when challenged, to reply, and refuse to believe you to be the author of that which in another I would sharply rebuke. Our brother Communis sends his respectful salutation.

## FROM AUGUSTINE TO JEROME

403

To my venerable lord Jerome, my esteemed and holy brother and fellow-presbyter, Augustine sends greeting in the Lord.

Never since I began to write you, and to long for your writing in return, have I met with a better opportunity for our exchanging communications than now, when my letter is to be carried to you by a most faithful servant and minister of God, who is also a very dear friend of mine, namely, our son Cyprian, deacon. Through him I expect to receive a letter from you with all the certainty which is in a matter of this kind possible. For the son whom I have named will not be found wanting in respect of zeal in asking, or persuasive influence in obtaining a reply from you; nor will he fail in diligently keeping, promptly bearing, and faithfully delivering the same. I only pray that if I be in any way worthy of this, the Lord may give His help and favour to your heart and to my desire, so that no higher will may hinder that which your brotherly goodwill inclines you to do.

As I have sent you two letters already to which I have received no reply, I have resolved to send you at this time copies of both of them, for I suppose that they never reached you. If they did reach you, and your replies have failed, as may be the case, to reach me, send me a second time the same as you sent before, if you have copies of them preserved: if you have not, dictate again what I may read, and do not refuse to send to these former letters the answer for which I have been waiting so long. My first letter to you, which I had prepared while I was a presbyter, was to be delivered to you by a brother of ours, Profuturus, who afterwards became my colleague in the episcopate, and has since then departed from this life; but he could not then bear it to you in person, because at the very time when he intended to begin his journey, he was prevented by his ordination to the weighty office of bishop, and shortly afterwards he died. This letter I have resolved also to send at this time, that you may know how long I have cherished a burning desire for conversation with you, and with what reluctance I submit to the remote separation which prevents my mind from having access to yours through our bodily senses, my brother, most amiable and honoured among the members of the Lord.

In this letter I have further to say, that I have since heard that you have translated Job out of the original Hebrew, although in your own translation of the same prophet from the Greek tongue we had already a version of that book. In that earlier version you marked with asterisks the words found in the Hebrew but wanting in the Greek, and with obelisks the words found in the Greek but wanting in the Hebrew; and this was done with such astonishing exactness, that in some places we have every word distinguished by a separate asterisk, as a sign that these words are in the Hebrew, but not in the Greek. Now, however, in this more recent version from the Hebrew, there is not the same scrupulous fidelity as to the words; and it perplexes any thoughtful reader to understand either what was the reason for marking the asterisks in the former version with so much care that they indicate the absence from the Greek version of even the smallest grammatical particles which have not been rendered from the Hebrew, or what is the reason for so much less care having been taken in this recent version from the Hebrew to secure that these same particles be found in their own places. I would have put down here an extract or two in illustration of this criticism; but at present I have not access to the MS. of the translation from the Hebrew. Since, however, your quick discernment anticipates and goes beyond not only what I have said, but also what I meant to say, you already understand, I think, enough to be able, by giving the reason for the plan which you have adopted, to explain what perplexes me.

For my part, I would much rather that you would furnish us with a translation of the Greek version of the canonical Scriptures known as the work of the Seventy Translators. For if your translation begins to be more generally read in many churches, it will be a grievous thing that, in the reading of Scripture, differences must arise between the Latin Churches and the Greek Churches, especially seeing that the discrepancy is easily condemned in a Latin version by the production of the original in Greek, which is a language very widely known; whereas, if anyone has been disturbed by the occurrence of something to which he was not accustomed in the translation taken from the Hebrew, and alleges that the new translation is wrong, it will be found difficult, if not impossible, to get at the Hebrew documents by which the version to which exception is taken may be defended. And when they are obtained, who will submit to have so many Latin and Greek authorities pronounced to be in the wrong? Besides all this, Jews, if consulted as to the meaning of the Hebrew text, may give a different opinion from yours: in which case it will seem as if your presence were indispensable, as being the only one who could refute their view; and it would be a miracle if one could be found capable of acting as arbiter between you and them.

A certain bishop, one of our brethren, having introduced in the church over which he presides the reading of your version, came upon a word in the book of the prophet Jonah, of which you have given a very different rendering from that which had been of old familiar to the senses and memory of all the worshippers, and had been chanted for so many generations in the church. Thereupon arose such a tumult in the congregation, especially among the Greeks, correcting what had been read, and denouncing the translation as false, that the bishop was compelled to ask the testimony of the Jewish residents (it was in the town of Oea). These, whether from ignorance or from spite, answered that the words in the Hebrew MSS. were correctly rendered in the Greek version, and in the Latin one taken from it. What further need I say? The man was compelled to correct your version in that passage as if it had been falsely translated, as he desired not to be left without a congregation—a calamity which he narrowly escaped. From this case we also are led to think that you may be occasionally mistaken. You will also observe how great must have been the difficulty if this had occurred in those writings which cannot be explained by comparing the testimony of languages now in use.

At the same time, we are in no small measure thankful to God for the work in which you have translated the Gospels from the original Greek, because in almost every passage we have found nothing to object to, when we compared it with the Greek Scriptures. By this work, any disputant who supports an old false translation is either convinced or confuted with the utmost ease by the production and collation of MSS. And if, as indeed very rarely happens, something be found to which exception may be taken, who would be so unreasonable as not to excuse it readily in a work so useful that it cannot be too highly praised? I wish you would have the kindness to open up to me what you think to be the reason of the frequent discrepancies between the text supported by the Hebrew codices and the Greek Septuagint version. For the latter has no mean authority, seeing that it has obtained so wide circulation, and was the one which the Apostles used, as is not only proved by looking to the text itself, but has also been, as I remember, affirmed by yourself. You would therefore confer upon us a much greater boon if you gave an exact Latin translation of the Greek Septuagint version: for the variations found in the different codices of the Latin text are intolerably numerous; and it is so justly open to suspicion as possibly different from what is to be found in the Greek, that one has no confidence in either quoting it or proving anything by its help.

I thought that this letter was to be a short one, but it has somehow been as pleasant to me to go on with it as if I were talking with you. I conclude with entreating you by the Lord kindly to send me a full reply, and thus give me, so far as is in your power, the pleasure of your presence.

### TO AUGUSTINE

404

To Augustine, my lord truly holy, and most blessed father, Jerome sends greeting in the Lord.

You are sending me letter upon letter, and often urging me to answer a certain letter of yours, a copy of which, without your signature, had reached me through our brother Sysinnius, deacon, as I have already written, which letter you tell me that you entrusted first to our brother Profuturus, and afterwards to someone else; but that Profuturus was prevented from finishing his intended journey, and, having been ordained a bishop, was removed by sudden death; and the second messenger, whose name you do not give, was afraid of the perils of the sea, and gave up the voyage which he had intended. These things being so, I am at a loss to express my surprise that the same letter is reported to be in the possession of most of the Christians in Rome, and throughout Italy, and has come to everyone but myself, to whom alone it was ostensibly sent. I wonder at this all the more, because the brother Sysinnius aforesaid tells me that he found it among the rest of your published works, not in Africa, not in your possession, but in an island of the Adriatic some five years ago.

True friendship can harbour no suspicion; a friend must speak to his friend as freely as to his second self. Some of my acquaintances, vessels of Christ, of whom there is a very large number in Jerusalem and in the holy places, suggested to me that this had not been done by you in a guileless spirit, but through desire for praise and celebrity, and *éclat* in the eyes of the people, intending to become famous at my expense; that many might know that you challenged me, and I feared to meet you; that you had written as a man of learning, and I had by silence confessed my ignorance, and had at last found one who knew how to stop my garrulous tongue. I, however, let me say it frankly, refused at first to answer your Excellency, because I did not believe that the letter, or as I may call it (using a proverbial expression), the honeyed sword, was sent from you. Moreover, I was cautious lest I should seem to answer uncourteously a bishop of my own communion, and to censure anything in the letter of one who censured me, especially as I judged some of its statements to be tainted with heresy. Lastly, I was afraid lest you should have reason to remonstrate with me, saying, "What! had you seen the letter to be mine—had you discovered in the signature attached to it the autograph of a hand well known to you, when you so carelessly wounded the feelings of your friend, and reproached me with that which the malice of another had conceived?"

Wherefore, as I have already written, either send me the identical letter in question subscribed with your own hand, or desist from annoying an old man, who seeks retirement in his monastic cell. If you wish to exercise or display your learning, choose as your antagonists young, eloquent, and illustrious men, of whom it is said that many are found in Rome, who may be neither unable nor afraid to meet you, and to enter the lists with a bishop in debates concerning the Sacred Scriptures. As for me, a soldier once, but a retired veteran now, it becomes me rather to applaud the victories won by you and others, than with my worn-out body to take part in the conflict; beware lest, if you persist in demanding a reply, I call to mind the history of the way in which Quintus Maximus by his patience defeated Hannibal, who was, in the pride of youth, confident of success.

*Omnia fert ætas, animum quoque. Sæpe ego longos*
*Cantando puerum memini me condere soles:*

*Nunc oblita mihi tot carmina: vox quoque Mœrin*
*Jam fugit ipsa.*

Or rather, to quote an instance from Scripture: Barzillai of Gilead, when he declined in favour of his youthful son the kindnesses of King David and all the charms of his court, taught us that old age ought neither to desire these things, nor to accept them when offered.

As to your calling God to witness that you had not written a book against me, and of course had not sent to Rome what you had never written, adding that, if perchance some things were found in your works in which a different opinion from mine was advanced, no wrong had thereby been done to me, because you had, without any intention of offending me, written only what you believed to be right; I beg you to hear me with patience. You never wrote a book against me: how then has there been brought to me a copy, written by another hand, of a treatise containing a rebuke administered to me by you? How comes Italy to possess a treatise of yours which you did not write? Nay, how can you reasonably ask me to reply to that which you solemnly assure me was never written by you? Nor am I so foolish as to think that I am insulted by you, if in anything your opinion differs from mine. But if, challenging me as it were to single combat, you take exception to my views, and demand a reason for what I have written, and insist upon my correcting what you judge to be an error, and call upon me to recant it in a humble *παλινῳδία*, and speak of your curing me of blindness; in this I maintain that friendship is wounded, and the laws of brotherly union are set at nought. Let not the world see us quarrelling like children, and giving material for angry contention between those who may become our respective supporters or adversaries. I write what I have now written, because I desire to cherish towards you pure and Christian love, and not to hide in my heart anything which does not agree with the utterance of my lips. For it does not become me, who have spent my life from youth until now, sharing the arduous labours of pious brethren in an obscure monastery, to presume to write anything against a bishop of my own communion, especially against one whom I had begun to love before I knew him, who also sought my friendship before I sought his, and whom I rejoiced to see rising as a successor to myself in the careful study of the Scriptures. Wherefore either disown that book, if you are not its author, and give over urging me to reply to that which you never wrote; or if the book is yours, admit it frankly; so that if I write anything in self-defence, the responsibility may lie on you who gave, not on me who am forced to accept, the challenge.

You say also that if there be anything in your writings which has displeased me, and which I would wish to correct, you are ready to receive my criticism as a brother; and you not only assure me that you would rejoice in such proof of my goodwill toward you, but you earnestly ask me to do this. I tell you again, without reserve, what I feel: you are challenging an old man, disturbing the peace of one who asks only to be allowed to be silent, and you seem to desire to display your learning. It is not for one of my years to give the impression of enviously disparaging one whom I ought rather to encourage by approbation. And if the ingenuity of perverse men finds something which they may plausibly censure in the writings even of evangelists and prophets, are you amazed if, in your books, especially in your exposition of passages in Scripture which are exceedingly difficult of interpretation, some things be found which are not perfectly correct? This I say, however, not because I can at this time pronounce anything in your works to merit censure. For, in the first place, I have never read them with attention; and in the second place, we have not beside us a supply of copies of what you have written, excepting the books of Soliloquies and Commentaries on some of the Psalms; which, if I were disposed to criticize them, I could prove to be at variance, I shall not say with my own opinion, for I am nobody, but with the interpretations of the older Greek commentators.

Farewell, my very dear friend, my son in years, my father in ecclesiastical dignity; and to this I most particularly request your attention, that henceforth you make sure that I be the first to receive whatever you may write to me.

# ST AMBROSE

340?–397

Ambrose, governor of Aemilia and Liguria, was living at Milan when in 374 the Christians assembled to elect a successor to Bishop Auxentius, newly dead. The assembly, which included both Catholics and Arians, was divided, and Ambrose interposed to try to calm the dissidents. Suddenly a child's voice piped, "Ambrose, bishop." The crowd took up the cry, and Ambrose, not even baptized, was unanimously elected.

Ambrose was born at Trèves where his father was prefect of southern Gaul. His sister Marcellina became a nun in 353. Before his ordination, Ambrose had studied to be a lawyer. He was the confidant of emperors Gratian, Valentinian II, and Theodosius, all of whom lived in Milan. Ambrose drew up the statute which for centuries regulated the relations of Church and state. He wrote many scriptural and dogmatic works, moral and ascetical treatises, letters, of which ninety-one survive, and hymns, some of which are still in use.

## On the Death of Theodosius

Translated by Sister Mary D. Mannix, in *Patristic Studies.*

Recently we lamented the death of our most merciful Emperor Theodosius. Now we are celebrating the fortieth day, with the prince Honorius assisting at the holy altar. . . .

Theodosius of august memory thought he had received a kindness when asked to pardon, and he was more disposed to forgiveness at the time when the emotions of his wrath had been greatest. The token of forgiveness was that he had been angry, and what was feared in others was desired in him, that he be moved to wrath. And so because Theodosius, the Emperor, showed himself humble, and, when sin had stolen upon him, asked pardon, his soul has turned to its rest, as the Scripture holds, which says, "Turn my soul unto thy rest, for the Lord hath been bountiful to thee." Beautifully it says to the soul, "Turn," that the soul as it were, tired out with the continued sweat of each work, may turn from labour to rest. The horse is turned toward the stable when it has finished its course, the ship to its port, where it is drawn up to safe mooring from the force of the waves. But what does it mean by saying "to thy rest" unless you understand it according to the words of the Lord Jesus: "Come, ye blessed of my Father, possess the kingdom prepared for you by inheritance from the foundation of the world"?

See, O man, the grace of Christ about you; as yet you are harassed on earth, but in heaven you possess. There, then let your heart be where your possession is. This is the rest which is due the just, and is denied the unworthy. . . .

Theodosius, now at peace, rejoices that he has been snatched away from the cares of this world, and lifts up his soul, and directs it to that perpetual rest. . . .

I have loved the man who esteemed an admonitor more than a flatterer. He threw on the ground all the royal attire which he was wearing; he wept publicly in the church, for his sin which had stolen upon him by the deceit of others; he prayed for pardon with groans and with tears. That which brings a blush to private citizens, the Emperor did not blush to do—that is, to perform penance publicly, nor did a day pass afterwards on which he did not grieve for that mistake of his. What of the fact that when he had gained an illustrious victory, still because the enemy had fallen in battle he abstained from a participation of the sacraments, until he experienced the grace of God around him by the arrival of his children?

I have loved the man who in his dying hour kept asking for me with his last breath. I have loved the man who at the moment he was being released from the body was more concerned about the condition of the Church than about his own trials. I have loved, therefore I confess it, and for that reason I have suffered my sorrow in the depths of my heart and I thought solace should be obtained by the delivery of this too lengthy discourse. I have loved and I trust that God is receiving the voice of my prayer, with which I accompany his pious soul.

Now Theodosius of august memory acknowledges that he reigns, since he is in the kingdom of our Lord Jesus Christ. Now indeed in his own eyes he is a king as he receives his son Gratian and Pulcheria, his sweetest children whom he had lost here; when his Flacilla, a soul faithful to God, clings to him, when he rejoices that his father has been restored to him, when he greets Constantine, who, though resolved in his last hour, was freed by the grace of baptism from all sin, and because he was the first of the emperors to believe and left after him a heritage of faith to princes, has found a place of great merit.

Happy Constantine, because of such a mother, who at her son's command sought the aid of divine favor by which in battle he might both engage safely and not fear danger. Noble woman, who found something much greater to give to the emperor than she could receive from the emperor.

They claim that at first she was hostess of an inn, and known as such to the elder Constantine, who afterwards secured the realm. Good hostess, who so diligently sought for the manger of the Lord. Good hostess, who did not ignore that host who cared for the wounds of the man wounded by robbers. Good hostess, who preferred to be considered dung, to gain Christ.

Helen, then, came and commenced to look about the sacred places. The Spirit inspired her to search for the wood of the Cross. She drew near to Golgotha and said, "Behold the place of combat. Where is the victory? I seek the standard of salvation, and I do not find it. I," she said, "among kings, and the Cross of my Lord in the dust? I in golden ornaments, and the triumph of Christ among ruins?"

And so she opens the ground; she casts off the dust. She finds three fork-shaped gibbets thrown together which the debris had covered; which the enemy had hidden. But the triumph of Christ could not be obliterated. She hesitates, uncertain; she hesitates as a woman, but the Holy Spirit inspires a careful investigation, with the thought that two robbers had been crucified with the Lord. Therefore she seeks the middle wood, but it could have happened that the debris mixed up the crosses with one another and by chance had interchanged them. She returned to the text of the Gospel, and found that on the middle gibbet a title had been displayed: "Jesus of Nazareth, King of the Jews." Hence a sequence of truth was formulated; the saving Cross was disclosed by its titles.

She discovered, then, the title; she adored the King; not the wood, indeed, because this is an error of the Gentiles, and a vanity of the wicked; but she adored Him who hung on the wood, who was described in the title. The woman eagerly hastened to reach the remedy of immortality. She was afraid to trample underfoot the mystery of salvation.

She sought the nails with which the Lord was crucified, and found them. From one nail she ordered reins to be made, from another she wove a diadem. She turned one to an ornamental use, the other to a devotional use. Therefore she sent to her son Constantine a diadem remarkable for its jewels in which the more precious gem of divine redemption was interwoven as the jewels were inlaid in the iron of the Cross. She also sent the bridle.

Helen has done wisely who has placed the Cross on the head of sovereigns, in order that the Cross of Christ may be adored among kings. That is not presumption but piety, since it was consecrated to our holy redemption. Therefore, honorable is the nail of the Roman Empire, which rules the whole world and adorns the forehead of princes, in order that they may be preachers who were accustomed to be persecutors. Rightly is the nail on the head, that where the intelligence is, there a guard may be. On the forehead a crown; in the hands, reins. A crown made from the Cross, that faith may shine forth; reins likewise from the Cross, that power may rule, and that there may be just moderation and not unjust caprice.

But I ask, Why is the holy relic upon the bridle, unless to curb the insolence of emperors, to check the wantonness of tyrants, who as horses neigh after lust, that they may be allowed to commit adultery unpunished?

Lazarus, the poor man, bore the heavy yoke from his youth, therefore he rests apart in Abraham's bosom, according to the testimony of the divine text. Theodosius bore the heavy yoke from youth, since those who killed his father, the conqueror, were plotting against his safety. He bore the heavy yoke since he endured an exile of filial devotion, since he assumed the imperial power in the Roman Empire when it was overrun by barbarians. He bore the heavy yoke that he might remove tyrants from the Roman Empire. But because here he laboured, there he rests.

# ST JOHN CHRYSOSTOM

345?–407

John Chrysostom was born at Antioch of a noble and wealthy family. His mother, Anthusa, left a widow, refused to remarry, in order to devote herself to the education of her son. Libanius, a famous rhetorician, and a philosopher named Andragatius were his teachers. After practicing law for a short time, he lived at home, leading an ascetic life, until his mother died in 374. He then withdrew to a monastery on a local mountainside, and after four years withdrew still further, to a cave where he lived alone until his health gave way, about 380. He then returned to Antioch. In 386 he was ordained priest, and became a noted preacher. In 397 he was made archbishop of Constantinople, at the suggestion of Emperor Arcadius. At this time morals were lax in monasteries, at court, and among the people. Because of John Chrysostom's stand against this laxity, a few bishops, led by the Patriarch of Alexandria and abetted by the Empress Eudoxia, deposed him at the so-called Synod at the Oak, near Chalcedon; but after he had been in exile a few days the people demanded the recall of their bishop. In 404 he was exiled again, to Cucusus, in the valley of the Taurus. In 407 he was transferred to Arabissus at the foot of the Caucasus, but died during the journey, near Comana, in Pontus.

St John was primarily a moralist; he was also the greatest orator among the Greek Fathers. He left about 240 letters, mostly brief, all dating from his second exile. *On the Priesthood* was written between 381 and 385.

## FROM On the Priesthood

Among the many and intimate friends I possessed, who felt for me the emotions, and practised in my behalf all the offices of friendship, there was one who in the zeal of his attachment excelled all the rest as much as they did my common acquaintance. He was my constant companion—we pursued the same branches of science, and studied under the same masters. There was in both the same zeal and ardor in the paths of learning in which we labored; our inclinations were the same, and excited by the same subjects. For not only while we frequented the same teachers, but afterward, when it became necessary for us to choose our respective walks in life, our minds appeared to take a similar bent. There were other circumstances also which contributed to preserve our intimacy unshaken and continued. Neither of us had any advantage over the other in the reputation of his native land; I had no excess of wealth, and he was exceedingly poor; so that the measure of our fortunes resembled the coincidence of our pursuits. Our families were equal in rank, and everything about us bore a happy similarity. But when the time had arrived for choosing the happy life of seclusion, and pursuing the path of true philosophy, the balance between us remained no longer the same. His scale was borne aloft, whilst I, impeded by worldly desires, drew mine along, and was obliged to remain beneath him, borne down by the weight of youthful follies and thoughts. Our friendship, however, continued unbroken as before, though our intimacy became less; for it was hardly possible that they whose attention was directed to different objects could be constantly together. Whenever, indeed, I could lift my head, for a time, above the waves of worldly occupation, he received me with open arms: but neither thus was I able to maintain our former equality. Having the start of me in point of time, and manifesting an exceeding zeal, he still towered above me, and attained to an extraordinary height of excellence; yet would this excellent man so far honor my friendship, as to separate himself from everyone else, and afford me his society as often as he possibly could, desirous that we might always be together, but prevented, as I said, by my dullness of soul. Nor was it to be supposed that I, who was constantly engaged in attendance on the forum, and was engrossed with the pleasures of the scene, could often be in company with one who was wholly wedded to his books, and scarce ever threw himself in the way of public observation. When therefore I at last devoted myself to the same mode of life as his (a thing he had striven to effect), he put into execution what had long been his desire, and was hardly to be found absent from me during any part of the day, soliciting me at the same time to leave our respective homes, and take up our abode in common. This plan was on the point of being carried into operation at his desire, when the earnest entreaties of my mother prevented my yielding to his wishes, or rather, I should say, receiving from him so great a blessing. For when my mother perceived I was meditating such a step, taking me by the hand, she led me into the apartments appropriated to herself; and seating me by her side upon the very couch on which I first saw the light, poured forth a torrent of tears, and in words more moving than even her tears, thus affectionately but sorrowfully addressed me:

"I was not long permitted, my son," she said, "to enjoy the virtues of your excellent father. It pleased God to remove him. His death occurring shortly after I had given you birth, made you an orphan, and brought upon me an untimely widowhood, and all the calamities attendant upon widowhood, which those only can properly estimate who have actually experienced them. No language can sufficiently express the storm and tempest of perplexities which a young woman has to sustain, when, leaving for the first time her paternal home, and entirely ignorant of the world, she is suddenly thrown into the midst of anxieties, and is obliged to undergo a multitude of cares beyond her strength and nature. She is necessitated for the most part to awaken the indolence and guard against the treachery of servants, to repel the arts of her relations, to encounter the malpractices of traders, and to endure with fortitude and resolution the unfeelingness of creditors and tax-gatherers. But should her husband die and leave behind him a child, that child, if a girl, becomes a source of anxiety to her mother, though how to support her be no subject of fear, and her education be but little expense; while if that child be a boy, he fills the bosom of his mother with a thousand daily fears and alarms. I forbear to mention the great expense she must incur if she wishes to educate him liberally. Yet now, my son, none of these considerations have induced me to enter a second time upon marriage, or to lead another bridegroom into the house of your father: rather have I preferred to endure the storm and the tempest, and to pass through the iron furnace of widowhood. I have been chiefly supported by grace from above, but it has afforded me no small consolation in all my afflictions to contemplate frequently your countenance, and trace in it the living and perfectly defined image of him who is no more. On this account it was that even while you were an infant, and not yet able to speak, when other children are a trouble to their parents, you were a source of great consolation to me. Nor can you lay to my charge, or say that I have spent my widowhood in splendor, or that your patrimony has suffered by the difficulties of my situation; a misfortune of which I know many orphans have had to complain. On the contrary, I have preserved your fortune untouched, and for whatever was necessary or conducive to your advantage, have spared nothing of what was my own, or of that property which I brought with me when I left the parental roof. Think not I mention these circumstances because I wish to reproach you, but because, in recompense for them all, I would ask you one favour, that you will not render me doubly a widow, nor awaken again the grief which had slept. Wait rather the day of my death. It is a period which cannot be far off. The hope of living to old age may belong to the young; the old like myself have nothing else to look forward to than death. When therefore you commit me to the ground and mingle my bones with those of your father, then prepare for your journey, and leave if you will even the ocean behind you. There will then be none to prevent you. But until I breathe my last continue to endure the same residence with me, nor rashly and causelessly provoke God, by bringing so much evil upon me who have not deserved it at your hands. . . ."

This, and more, which my mother said to me, I repeated to my friend, but he not only remained unpersuaded by what I told him, but only pressed me the more, repeating the arguments he had previously used. While things were in this state between us, he pressing the subject upon me, and I scarcely able to refuse, a report suddenly arose which gave disturbance to us both. This report was no other than that we were about to be elevated to the episcopacy. . . .

My excellent friend having taken me aside, and communicated the circumstance to me, as to one yet unacquainted with it, besought me that in this instance, as heretofore, our councils and our actions should appear to be directed by the same mind; that for his own part he was prepared to follow me, whichever path I pursued, whether I thought proper to decline or accept the honour intended us. Perceiving then from this what was the state of his inclinations, and reflecting how great would be the loss to the church at large if, from any infirmity of mine, I were to deprive the flock of Christ of so worthy a young man, and so fitted for the charge and oversight of others, I concealed from him my own intentions on the subject; though never had I suffered myself before to keep any of my purposes a secret from him. Observing therefore that it were better to defer the consideration of the subject to another time (for there was no urgency at present) I persuaded him not to think of it any further, concluding with myself that he would count upon my concurrence whenever the event under contemplation should occur. A short time only had elapsed, when, the period for our appointment having arrived, I took the precaution to conceal myself. He, upon the other hand, being ignorant of this, and fully hoping, from what had passed between us, that I would follow in his steps, or rather would precede him, is artfully drawn into the measure, and receives the weight of the episcopal charge. . . .

But when he observed my satisfaction, and for the first time perceived that I was an accomplice in the scheme, he became more troubled and distressed, and after recovering a little from the tumult of his mind—

*Basilius.* If you disclaim my friendship, and refuse any farther connection with me (for what reason I know not) you ought surely to have advertised me of your resolution. You have now opened everybody's mouth, and all men agree in saying that from a vainglorious feeling you have declined this office, while there is no one who can properly defend you from the charge. To me indeed it has become intolerable to go abroad, such is the number of those who, whenever they meet me, assail me with reproaches. Those who can claim any sort of acquaintance, no sooner observe me in any part of the city, than they take me privately aside, and charge me with being a party to your offence. You ought not, say they, when you well knew his purpose—for he never hid anything from you—you ought not to have concealed it from us, but have given us timely notice, and in that case we should have fully prepared a plan to prevent his escape. To this I am ashamed, and blush to reply that I knew not of this your long-formed purpose, lest they should think that our friendship was nothing but hypocrisy. Yet if it be only pretence as it seems, and as you cannot deny, from the manner in which you have treated me, still it were well to hide our failings from those that are without, and those who are not favorably inclined toward us. Reluctant to tell them the true state of the case, and as it really stands between us, the only method I have left is to be silent, to hang my head to the earth, and turn from and avoid those who meet me. Should I escape their former charge by disavowing any knowledge of your intention, they will accuse me of falsehood, since they will not believe that you rank Basilius among those to whom you were under no obligation to impart your designs. On that subject, however, I have nothing further to say, since such has been your pleasure; but how shall I support this additional disgrace? Some condemn you as contumacious, others as vainglorious, and those who are most severe in their judgment lay both to your account, and express their indignation against those who have conferred this honor upon us; declaring that they have justly suffered, and deserved to suffer still more, because, to the neglect of many and deserving men, they have suddenly elevated to so exalted an office, and such as they never dreamed of receiving, two very young men, hardly yet disengaged from the cares of the world (for it is only lately, it is observed, they have contracted a supercilious demeanor, clothed themselves in black, and affected to move with their eyes bent upon the ground); while those who have spent their whole lives, from childhood to old age, in the exercises of religion, are to be subjected to mere boys, entirely unacquainted with the laws by which this office should be administered. These sarcastic expressions, and more such, they raise against us. For my own part I have nothing to answer to it all; and am therefore obliged to apply myself to you, since I cannot suppose that you fled as you have done inconsiderately and without thought, or would offer an affront of that kind to such estimable men, without some settled purpose, and upon mature reflection, from whence I presume you can furnish a reasonable apology. Tell me then what just plea we can offer to those who complain of us. . . . In the face of all this, and without its producing any effect upon your mind, you have left me like an unarmed and unprepared vessel on the ocean, suspecting nothing of the rough billows you have compelled me to encounter. To whom shall I now have it in my power to fly, when, as must often occur, I am overpowered by calumny, by ridicule, by reproaches, or any other evil of a similar kind? To whom can I communicate my sorrows? who will be willing to aid me, to answer my detractors, to hush up my griefs, to comfort me in affliction, and arm me to bear with patience the follies which I meet with. Alas! there is not one, if you stand aloof from me in this terrible war, and cannot even hear me complain. Do you now see how great an injury you have done me? do you now know, after the blow has been struck, how deadly a wound has been inflicted? . . .

*Chrysostom*. Take courage, I am ready not only to answer their complaints on these accounts, but will endeavour, as well as I can, to render you a reason upon those points also in which you have left me without blame. . . . Unreasonable and inconsistent would I be, if, regardful only of my reputation with those that are without, and to silence their reproaches, I should not convince my best friend (who uses such consideration towards me as to forbear charging me with his own wrongs, and be concerned principally on my account) that I have not treated him unjustly, but have used more foresight with respect to him than he in his zeal with respect to me. How then have I been unjust to you, since here I have professed to launch forth upon the ocean of apologies? Is it that I have circumvented you, and hidden from you my intentions? The art which I have used is at once for your good, whom I have deceived, and for theirs into whose hands I have delivered you up. If every species of art be altogether sinful, and it be not lawful under any circumstances to employ it, I am ready to undergo any punishment you choose, or rather, since you would not bear to inflict it, I will pronounce the same sentence on myself which judges are wont to pronounce upon criminals when convicted of what their accusers lay to their charge; but if the thing is not always injurious, and becomes criminal or otherwise according to the intentions of those who practise it, cease to blame me for having deceived you, and show that I have done it with an evil intent or in an improper way; for where these do not appear, it should seem that they who would decide equitably, should not only forbear reproaches and complaints, but bestow their approbation. Such is the advantage arising from a policy when properly employed, and with a good intent, that many have suffered from carrying on their purposes without it. If you contemplate, from the earliest period, the military commanders who have rendered themselves illustrious, you will find the greater part of the trophies they have acquired to be the result of happily devised schemes, and that those who have acquired honor in this way have been in greater estimation than those who have succeeded by open violence. The latter we find terminate their wars with great expense both of men and money, so that there is scarce any other result even of victory than to leave the conquerors under not much fewer disadvantages than the vanquished, both from the destruction of their troops and the exhaustion of their treasury. Besides, they are not even permitted to enjoy all the glory of victory, since no small part of it belongs to those who have fallen, as to men whose souls have been victorious though their bodies have been overcome, and who, had they not fallen, or had not death intervened between them and their object, had not ceased to exhibit proofs of their valor. The use of policy and foresight not only gives success, but gives it to the confusion and at the expense of the adversary. Not as in the former case, where both parties divide the praise of valour, do they here divide the honor of wisdom; but the whole is secured to the victors; and what is of no less consequence, they secure to their country a lasting benefit from their victory. It is not with the powers of the mind, as it is with men and money; the latter of which when freely used in war are necessarily spent, and fail those who make use of them; while it is the nature of the former, the more they are made use of, the more to be strengthened and increased. And not only in war, but in peace also, you will find the employment of foresight and caution highly necessary; and not in public matters only, but in domestic, from a wife to her husband, from a husband to his wife, from a father to his son, from one friend to another, and even from sons to their father. Without them the daughter of Saul had been unable to rescue her husband from the hands of her father, which by circumventing her father she was able to do. To the same means did her brother resort, when he labored to save the life of the same man once already preserved by the wife.

*Basilius*. This has no reference to me, for I am no enemy or adversary, nor among the number of those who would injure you, but entirely otherwise; for I have ever submitted myself in every respect to your guidance and followed in the path you prescribed.

*Chrysostom*. My admirable and dear Basilius, it was on this account, anticipating your remark, I said that not in war only, nor to our enemies, but in peace, and towards our dearest friends, the employment of a judicious management was beneficial: it is so indeed, not to those only who employ it, but to those on whom it is employed. Inquire of medical men, how they relieve the sick of their complaints, and you will learn that their science is not always sufficient, but that there are cases in which they resort to the aid of stratagem, for the purpose of restoring their patient to health. When the peevishness of the sick, and the obstinacy of the disease, resist the efforts of the physicians, then are they obliged to put on the appearance of deception, so as to hide under cover, as it were, the real nature of what they do. I will give you an instance out of many which I have heard practised among physicians. A certain individual lay under a burning and constant fever, and the fever was daily gaining ground; but the sick man rejected all the remedies capable of quenching its fire, and entreated his attendants to give him a draught of wine, to quench his fatal thirst. Now had his wish been gratified, not only would the fever have been increased, but the miserable man driven to madness. Here then, where science was at fault, the use of a little management proved its efficaciousness, as you shall hear; for the doctor, taking an earthen vessel from the fireplace, and dipping it in wine and then emptying it again, and filling it with water, ordered a domestic to carefully draw the curtains where the sick man lay, that the light might not discover the deceit, and give him to drink as if the vessel had been filled with wine. The patient, deceived by the smell, which reached him before he took it into his hands, suffered not himself to examine what was given him, but depending on the smell, and deceived by the darkness, and urged by desire, drank with eagerness, and, thus satisfied, got rid of his fever and escaped the impending danger. You discern the utility of such a stratagem. And were I to collect together instances of all the arts which physicians practise, the description would run into endless prolixity. You will find that not only those whose attention is directed to the cure of the body, but those also who are concerned in the diseases of the soul, make free use of this instrument of cure. . . .

*Basilius*. And what advantage is derived to me from this economy, or wisdom, or whatever else you please to call it, sufficient to persuade me that I have not been wronged by you?

*Chrysostom*. And what greater gain can there be than to be engaged in the performance of those very things, which Christ Himself has pronounced to be the marks of love to Christ? For, addressing himself to the chief of the Apostles, Peter, He says, "Lovest thou me?" and adds, on his confessing that he did so, "if thou lovest me feed my lambs." The Master asked His disciple if he loved Him, not to learn whether he did so (for how could He be ignorant of it, who enters into the very hearts of all men?) but that He might teach us how precious to Him is the oversight of His flock. This then being evident, it will be manifest that a great and unspeakable reward is laid up for him who watches over that which Christ so highly esteems. If when we see anyone take an interest in our domestics, or our cattle, we look on it as a mark of their affection for us (though such things are purchasable with money), what reward will not be rendered him who watches over the flock which Christ purchased, not with earthly possessions, or any such thing, but by His own death, and giving His own blood a ransom for the sheep? On this account it was, that when the disciple said, "Thou knowest, Lord, I love thee," and called on Him he loved as a witness of his love, the Saviour stopped not upon that, but enjoined on him a proof of his love. He wanted not at the time to test how much Peter loved Him (for of that we have many indications) but wished Peter and us to learn how much He loved His own Church; so that we also might exhibit an earnest zeal for it. Wherefore did

God not spare His only begotten Son, but yield him? That He might reconcile us even when we were enemies to Himself, and make us His peculiar people. Wherefore did He pour out His blood? Surely that He might gain those very sheep which He committed to Peter and those who should come after him. . . . Contemplate now the magnitude of the reward. He will make him ruler, He says, over all His goods. Will you then contend that the policy I have used towards you has not been for your advantage, when I was desirous for you to be placed over the goods of God, and for doing which He permitted Peter to be eminent, and to excel the other Apostles. "Peter," he says, "lovest thou me more than these? Feed my lambs." He might have said, Peter, if thou lovest Me, exercise thyself in fasting, in penitential sorrow, in frequent watchings; protect the injured, be as a father to the orphan, and as a husband to their mother. But passing by all this, what does He say? "Feed my lambs." The former things are what many of the flock themselves might easily perform, not only of the men, but even of the women.

But when it becomes necessary to appoint someone over the church, and to put in trust the care of so many souls, the nature of the female, and indeed of the majority of the male sex, must be deemed inferior to the weight of such a charge. Let those be then brought forward who are eminent above others to as great a degree in all spiritual excellence, as Saul excelled the whole Hebrew nation in the size of his body. The point here to be determined is not a superiority in height. As great as is the difference between the rational and irrational part of the creation, should be the superiority of the pastor over the flock, if I ought not to say greater, when we consider of what infinite consequence are the things in which his labours are exerted. Should a shepherd lose one of his brute flock by the attack of prowling wolves, by the incursion of robbers, by any species of disease, or by other such misfortune, he may possibly be excused by the owner of the flock; or if the owner demand compensation, his loss is only that of temporal possessions. But he who is entrusted with the care of men, the rational flock of Christ, subjects himself, for any injury sustained by the flock, not to the loss of temporal possessions, but to the loss of his own soul, while he has to undergo a greater and severer conflict. He has to encounter no contest with wolves, no terror of robbers, no fear of diseases making inroads on his flock. With what then is his conflict, and with what is he to wrestle? Hear the language of St. Paul. "We wrestle not against flesh and blood, but against principalities, against powers, against the rulers of the darkness of this world, against spiritual wickedness in high places." You see then the terrible number of our adversaries, the fierce phalanx they compose, not armed for the contest with steel, but supplied by their own nature with the whole panoply of war. . . . I know also the magnitude of the ministerial office, and the great difficulties which attend it. More are the tempests which assail the soul of a bishop, than those storms which agitate the ocean. . . .

# ST AUGUSTINE

354–430

Augustine, described as "the richest mind in Christendom," was born on November 13, 354, at Tagaste, in Numidia. His father, Patricius, was a heathen, but his mother, Monica, was a Christian. He studied first at Tagaste, then at Madaura and at Carthage, where he took a mistress with whom he lived for sixteen years and who bore him a son, Adeodatus. In 373 he became a Manichaean. In 383 he went to Italy, where, thanks to the prefect Symmachus, he obtained the chair of rhetoric at Milan. He attended Ambrose's sermons, and in September 386 was converted to Catholicism, receiving baptism on Easter Sunday, 387. In 388, after his mother's death, he returned to Africa, and in 391 was ordained priest at Hippo. He received episcopal ordination in 395 and was made coadjutor to Bishop Valerius, whom he succeeded as bishop of Hippo the following year. On August 28, 430, while the Vandals were laying siege to the city, Augustine died.

St Augustine was the greatest genius and the most voluminous writer of the Western Church. His most famous works are the *Confessions* (issued as a Pocket Book in 1952), *The City of God,* the *De Trinitate,* and the *Enchiridion.* Two hundred and twenty of his letters survive.

Samples of his correspondence with Jerome (no two men ever maddened each other more, except, perhaps, Augustine and Ambrose) are given on pages 100–110, 376–78; some letters to and from Publicola, who seems to have been the scrupulous type, follow; and excerpts from a letter to a group of nuns appear on pages 494–504.

# Letters

### FROM PUBLICOLA TO AUGUSTINE

398

It is written: "Ask thy father, and he will show thee; thy elders, and they will tell thee." I have therefore judged it right to "seek the law at the mouth of the priest" in regard to a certain case which I shall state in this letter, desiring at the same time to be instructed in regard to several other matters. I have distinguished the several questions by stating each in a separate paragraph, and I beg you kindly to give an answer to each in order.

I. In the country of the Arzuges it is customary, as I have heard, for the barbarians to take an oath, swearing by their false gods, in the presence of the decurion stationed on the frontier, or of the tribune, when they have come under engagement to carry baggage to any part, or to protect the crops from depredation; and when the decurion certifies in writing that this oath has been taken, the owners or farmers of land employ them as watchmen of their crops; or travellers who have occasion to pass through their country hire them, as if assured of their now being trustworthy. Now a doubt has arisen in my mind whether the landowner who thus employs a barbarian, of whose fidelity he is persuaded in consequence of such an oath, does not make himself and the crops committed to that man's charge to share the defilement of that sinful oath; and so also with the traveller who may employ his services. I should mention, however, that in both cases the barbarian is rewarded for his services with money. Nevertheless in both transactions there comes in, besides the pecuniary remuneration, this oath before the decurion or tribune involving mortal sin. I am concerned as to whether this sin does not defile either him who accepts the oath of the barbarian, or at least the things which are committed to the barbarian's keeping. For whatever other terms be in the arrangement, even such as the payment of gold, and giving of hostages in security, nevertheless this sinful oath has been a real part of the transaction. Be pleased to resolve my doubts definitely and positively. For if your answer indicate that you are in doubt yourself, I may fall into greater perplexity than before.

II. I have also heard that my own land-stewards receive from the barbarians hired to protect the crops an oath in which they appeal to their false gods. Does not this oath so defile these crops that if a Christian uses them or takes the money realized by their sale, he is himself defiled? Do answer this.

III. Again, I have heard from one person that no oath was taken by the barbarian in making agreement with my steward, but another has said to me that such an oath was taken. Suppose now that the latter statement were false, tell me if I am bound to forbear from using these crops, or the money obtained for them, merely because I have heard the statement made, according to the scriptural rule: "If any man say unto you, This is offered in sacrifice unto idols, eat not, for his sake that showed it." Is this case parallel to the case of meat offered to idols; and if it is, what am I to do with the crops, or with the price of them?

IV. In this case ought I to examine both him who said that no oath was taken before my steward, and the other who said that the oath was taken, and bring witnesses to prove which of the two spoke truly, leaving the crops or their price untouched so long as there is uncertainty in the matter?

V. If the barbarian who swears this sinful oath were to require of the steward, or of the tribune stationed on the frontier, that he, being a Christian, should give him assurance of his faithfulness to his part of the engagement about watching the crops, by the same oath which he himself has taken, involving mortal sin, does the oath pollute only that Christian man? Does it not also pollute the things regarding which he took the oath? Or if a pagan who has authority on the frontier thus give to a barbarian this oath in token of acting faithfully to him, does he not involve in the defilement of his own sin those in whose interest he swears? If I send a man to the Arzuges, is it lawful for him to take from a barbarian that sinful oath? Is not the Christian who takes such an oath from him also defiled by his sin?

VI. Is it lawful for a Christian to use wheat or beans from the threshing-floor, wine or oil from the press, if, with his knowledge, some part of what has been taken thence was offered in sacrifice to a false god?

VII. May a Christian use for any purpose wood which he knows to have been taken from one of their idols' groves?

VIII. If a Christian buy in the market meat which has not been offered to idols, and have in his mind conflicting doubts as to whether it has been offered to idols or not, but eventually adopt the opinion that it was not, does he sin if he partake of this meat?

IX. If a man does an action good in itself, about which he has some misgivings as to whether it is good or bad, can it be reckoned as a sin to him if he does it believing it to be good, although formerly he may have thought it bad?

x. If anyone has falsely said that some meat has been offered to idols, and afterwards confess that it was a falsehood, and this confession is believed, may a Christian use the meat regarding which he heard that statement, or sell it, and use the price obtained?

xi. If a Christian on a journey, overpowered by want, having fasted for one, two, or several days, so that he can no longer endure the privation, should by chance, when in the last extremity of hunger, and when he sees death close at hand, find food placed in an idol's temple, where there is no man near him, and no other food to be found; whether should he die or partake of that food?

xii. If a Christian is on the point of being killed by a barbarian or a Roman, ought he to kill the aggressor to save his own life? or ought he even, without killing the assailant, to drive him back and fight with him, seeing it has been said, "Resist not evil"?

xiii. May a Christian put a wall for defence against an enemy round his property? and if some use that wall as a place from which to fight and kill the enemy, is the Christian the cause of the homicide?

xiv. May a Christian drink at a fountain or well into which anything from a sacrifice has been cast? May he drink from a well found in a deserted temple? If there be in a temple where an idol is worshipped a well or fountain which nothing has defiled, may he draw water thence, and drink of it?

xv. May a Christian use baths in places in which sacrifice is offered to images? May he use baths which are used by pagans on a feast-day, either while they are there or after they have left?

xvi. May a Christian use the same sedan-chair as has been used by pagans coming down from their idols on a feast-day, if in that chair they have performed any part of their idolatrous service, and the Christian is aware of this?

xvii. If a Christian, being the guest of another, has forborne from using meat set before him, concerning which it was said to him that it had been offered in sacrifice, but afterwards by some accident finds the same meat for sale and buys it, or has it presented to him at another man's table, and then eat of it, without knowing that it is the same, is he guilty of sin?

XVIII. May a Christian buy and use vegetables or fruit which he knows to have been brought from the garden of a temple or of the priests of an idol?

That you may not be put to trouble in searching the Scriptures concerning the oath of which I have spoken and the idols, I resolved to set before you those texts which, by the Lord's help, I have found; but if you have found anything better or more to the purpose in Scripture, be so good as let me know. For example, when Laban said to Jacob, "The God of Abraham and the God of Nahor judge betwixt us," Scripture does not declare which god is meant. Again, when Abimelech came to Isaac, and he and those who were with him sware to Isaac, we are not told what kind of oath it was. As to the idols, Gideon was commanded by the Lord to make a whole burnt-offering of the bullock which he killed. And in the book of Joshua the son of Nun, it is said of Jericho that all the silver, and gold, and brass should be brought into the treasures of the Lord, and the things found in the accursed city were called sacred. Also we read in Deuteronomy: "Neither shalt thou bring an abomination into thine house, lest thou be a cursed thing like it."

May the Lord preserve thee. I salute thee. Pray for me.

### TO PUBLICOLA

398

Your perplexities have, since I learned them by your letter, become mine also, not because all those things by which you tell me that you are disturbed disturb my mind: but I have been much perplexed, I confess, by the question how your perplexities were to be removed; especially since you require me to give a conclusive answer, lest you should fall into greater doubts than you had before you applied to me to have them resolved. For I see that I cannot give this, since, though I may write things which appear to me most certain, if I do not convince you, you must be beyond question more at a loss than before; and though it is in my power to use arguments which weigh with myself, I may fail of convincing another by these. However, lest I should refuse the small service which your love claims, I have resolved after some consideration to write in reply.

One of your doubts is as to using the services of a man who has guaranteed his fidelity by swearing by his false gods. In this matter I beg you to consider whether, in the event of a man failing to keep his word after having pledged himself by such an oath, you would not regard him as guilty of a twofold sin. For if he kept the engagement which he had confirmed by this oath, he would be pronounced guilty in this only, that he swore by such deities; but no one would justly blame him for keeping his engagement. But in the case supposed, seeing that he both swore by those whom he should not worship, and did, notwithstanding his promise, what he should not have done, he was guilty of two sins: whence it is obvious that in using, not for an evil work, but for some good and lawful end, the service of a man whose fidelity is known to have been confirmed by an oath in the name of false gods, one participates, not in the sin of swearing by the false gods, but in the good faith with which he keeps his promise. The faith which I here speak of as kept is not that on account of which those who are baptized in Christ are called faithful: that is entirely different and far removed from the faith desiderated in regard to the arrangements and compacts of men. Nevertheless it is, beyond all doubt, worse to swear falsely by the true God than to swear truly by the false gods; for the greater the holiness of that by which we swear, the greater is the sin of perjury. It is therefore a different question whether he is not guilty who requires another to pledge himself by taking an oath in the name of his gods, seeing that he worships false gods. In answering this question, we may accept as decisive those examples which you yourself quoted of Laban and of Abimelech (if Abimelech did swear by his gods, as Laban swore by the god of Nahor). This is, as I have said, another question, and one which would perchance perplex me, were it not for those examples of Isaac and Jacob, to which, for aught I know, others might be added. It may be that some scruple might yet be suggested by the precept in the New Testament, "Swear not at all"; words which were in my opinion spoken, not because it is a sin to swear a true oath, but because it is a heinous sin to forswear oneself: from which crime our Lord would have us keep at a great distance, when He charged us not to swear at all. I know, however, that your opinion is different: wherefore it should not be discussed at present; let us rather treat of that about which you have thought of asking my advice. On the same ground on which you forbear from swearing yourself, you may, if such be your opinion, regard it as forbidden to exact an oath from another, although it is expressly said, "Swear not"; but I do not remember reading anywhere in Holy Scripture that we are not to take another's oath. The question whether we ought to take advantage of the concord which is established between other parties by their exchange of oaths is entirely different. If we answer this in the negative, I know not whether we could find any place on earth in which we could live. For not only on the frontier, but throughout all the provinces, the security of peace rests on the oaths of barbarians. And from this it would follow, that not only the crops which are guarded by men who have sworn fidelity in the name of their false gods, but all things which enjoy the protection secured by the peace which a similar oath has ratified, are defiled. If this be admitted by you to be a complete absurdity, dismiss with it your doubts on the cases which you named.

Again, if from the threshing-floor or wine-press of a Christian anything be taken, with his knowledge, to be offered to false gods, he is guilty in permitting this to be done, if it be in his power to prevent it. If he finds that it has been done, or has not the power to prevent it, he uses without scruple the rest of the grain or wine, as uncontaminated, just as we use fountains from which we know that water has been taken to be used in idol-worship. The same principle decides the question about baths. For we have no scruple about inhaling the air into which we know that the smoke from all the altars and incense of idolaters ascends. From which it is manifest that the thing forbidden is our devoting anything to the honour of the false gods, or appearing to do this by so acting as to encourage in such worship those who do not know our mind, although in our heart we despise their idols. And when temples, idols, groves, etc., are thrown down by permission from the authorities, although our taking part in this work is a clear proof of our not honouring, but rather abhorring, these things, we must nevertheless forbear from appropriating any of them to our own personal and private use; so that it may be manifest that in overthrowing these we are influenced, not by greed, but by piety. When, however, the spoils of these places are applied to the benefit of the community or devoted to the service of God, they are dealt with in the same manner as the men themselves when they are turned from impiety and sacrilege to the true religion. We understand this to be the will of God from the examples quoted by yourself: the grove of the false gods from which He commanded wood to be taken for the burnt-offering; and Jericho, of which all the gold, silver, and brass was to be brought into the Lord's treasury. Hence also the precept in Deuteronomy: "Thou shalt not desire the silver or gold that is on them, nor take it unto thee, lest thou be snared therein; for it is an abomination to the Lord thy God. Neither shalt thou bring an abomination into thine house, lest thou become a cursed thing like it: but thou shalt utterly detest it, and thou shalt utterly abhor it; for it is a cursed thing." From which it appears plainly, that either the appropriation of such spoils to their own private use was absolutely forbidden, or they were forbidden to carry anything of that kind into their own houses with the intention of giving to it honour; for then this would be an abomination and accursed in the sight of God; whereas the honour impiously given to such idols is, by their public destruction, utterly abolished.

As to meats offered to idols, I assure you we have no duty beyond observing what the Apostle taught concerning them. Study, therefore, his words on the subject, which, if they were obscure to you, I would explain as well as I could. He does not sin who, unwittingly, afterwards partakes of food which he formerly refused because it had been offered to an idol. A kitchen-herb, or any other fruit of the ground, belongs to Him who created it; for "the earth is the Lord's, and the fulness thereof," and "every creature of God is good." But if that which the earth has borne is consecrated or offered to an idol, then we must reckon it among the things offered to idols. We must beware lest, in pronouncing that we ought not to eat the fruits of a garden belonging to an idol-temple, we be involved in the inference that it was wrong for the Apostle to take food in Athens, since that city belonged to Minerva, and was consecrated to her as the guardian deity. The same answer I would give as to the well or fountain enclosed in a temple, though my scruples would be somewhat more awakened if some part of the sacrifices be thrown into the said well or fountain. But the case is, as I have said before, exactly parallel to our using of the air which receives the smoke of these sacrifices; or, if this be thought to make a difference, that the sacrifice, the smoke whereof mingles with the air, is not offered to the air itself, but to some idol or false god, whereas sometimes offerings are cast into the water with the intention of sacrificing to the waters themselves, it is enough to say that the same principle would preclude us from using the light of the sun, because wicked men continually worship that luminary wherever they are tolerated in doing so. Sacrifices are offered to the winds, which we nevertheless use for our convenience, although they seem, as it were, to inhale and swallow greedily the smoke of these sacrifices. If anyone be in doubt regarding meat, whether it has been offered to an idol or not, and the fact be that it has not, when he eats that meat under the impression that it has not been offered to an idol, he by no means does wrong; because neither in fact, nor now in his judgment, is it food offered to an idol, although he formerly thought it was. For surely it is lawful to correct false impressions by others that are true. But if anyone believes that to be good which is evil, and acts accordingly, he sins in entertaining that belief; and these are all sins of ignorance, in which one thinks that to be right which it is wrong for him to do.

As to killing others in order to defend one's own life, I do not approve of this, unless one happen to be a soldier or public functionary acting, not for himself, but in defence of others or of the city in which he resides, if he act according to the commission lawfully given him, and in the manner becoming his office. When, however, men are prevented, by being alarmed, from doing wrong, it may be said that a real service is done to themselves. The precept, "Resist not evil," was given to prevent us from taking pleasure in revenge, in which the mind is gratified by the sufferings of others, but not to make us neglect the duty of restraining men from sin. From this it follows that one is not guilty of homicide, because he has put up a wall round his estate, if anyone is killed by the wall falling upon him when he is throwing it down. For a Christian is not guilty of homicide though his ox may gore or his horse kick a man, so that he dies. On such a principle, the oxen of a Christian should have no horns, and his horses no hoofs, and his dogs no teeth. On such a principle, when the Apostle Paul took care to inform the chief captain that an ambush was laid for him by certain desperadoes, and received in consequence an armed escort, if the villains who plotted his death had thrown themselves on the weapons of the soldiers, Paul would have had to acknowledge the shedding of their blood as a crime with which he was chargeable. God forbid that we should be blamed for accidents which, without our desire, happen to others through things done by us or found in our possession, which are in themselves good and lawful. In that event, we ought to have no iron implements for the house or the field, lest someone should by them lose his own life or take another's; no tree or rope on our premises, lest someone hang himself; no window in our house, lest someone throw himself down from it. But why mention more in a list which must be interminable? For what good and lawful thing is there in use among men which may not become chargeable with being an instrument of destruction?

I have now only to notice (unless I am mistaken) the case which you mentioned of a Christian on a journey overcome by the extremity of hunger; whether, if he could find nothing to eat but meat placed in an idol's temple, and there was no man near to relieve him, it would be better for him to die of starvation than to take that food for his nourishment? Since in this question it is not assumed that the food thus found was offered to the idol (for it might have been left by mistake or designedly by persons who, on a journey, had turned aside there to take refreshment; or it might have been put there for some other purpose), I answer briefly thus: Either it is certain that this food was offered to the idol, or it is certain that it was not, or neither of these things is known. If it is certain, it is better to reject it with Christian fortitude. In either of the other alternatives, it may be used for his necessity without any conscientious scruple.

. . . All is contained in these brief sentences: "Love the Lord thy God with all thy heart, and with all thy soul, and with all thy strength: and love thy neighbour as thyself"; for these are the words in which the Lord, when on earth, gave an epitome of religion, saying in the Gospel, "On these two commandments hang all the law and the prophets." Daily advance, then, in this love, both by praying and by well-doing, that through the help of Him who enjoined it on you, and whose gift it is, it may be nourished and increased, until, being perfected, it render you perfect. "For this is the love which," as the Apostle says, "is shed abroad in our hearts by the Holy Ghost, which is given unto us." This is "the fulfilling of the law"; this is the same love by which faith works, of which he says again, "Neither circumcision availeth anything, nor uncircumcision; but faith, which worketh by love."

In this love, then, all our holy fathers, patriarchs, prophets, and apostles pleased God. In this all true martyrs contended against the devil even to the shedding of blood, and because in them it neither waxed cold nor failed, they became conquerors. In this all true believers daily make progress, seeking to acquire not an earthly kingdom, but the kingdom of heaven; not a temporal, but an eternal inheritance; not gold and silver, but the incorruptible riches of the angels; not the good things of this life, which are enjoyed with trembling, and which no one can take with him when he dies, but the vision of God, whose grace and power of imparting felicity transcend all beauty of form in bodies not only on earth but also in heaven, transcend all spiritual loveliness in men, however just and holy, transcend all the glory of the angels and powers of the world above, transcend not only all that language can express, but all that thought can imagine concerning Him. And let us not despair of the fulfilment of such a great promise because it is exceeding great, but rather believe that we shall receive it because He who has promised it is exceeding great, as the blessed Apostle John says: "Now are we the sons of God; and it doth not yet appear what we shall be: but we know that, when He shall appear, we shall be like Him; for we shall see Him as He is."

Do not think that it is impossible for anyone to please God while engaged in active military service. Among such persons was the holy David, to whom God gave so great a testimony; among them also were many righteous men of that time; among them was also that centurion who said to the Lord: "I am not worthy that Thou shouldest come under my roof, but speak the word only, and my servant shall be healed: for I am a man under authority, having soldiers under me: and I say to this man, Go, and he goeth; and to another, Come, and he cometh; and to my servant, Do this, and he doeth it"; and concerning whom the Lord said: "Verily, I say unto you, I have not found so great faith, no, not in Israel." Among them was that Cornelius to whom an angel said: "Cornelius, thine alms are accepted, and thy prayers are heard," when he directed him to send to the blessed Apostle Peter, and to hear from him what he ought to do, to which apostle he sent a devout soldier, requesting him to come to him. Among them were also the soldiers who, when they had come to be baptized by John—the sacred forerunner of the Lord, and the friend of the Bridegroom, of whom the Lord says: "Among them that are born of women there hath not risen a greater than John the Baptist"—and had inquired of him what they should do, received the answer, "Do violence to no man, neither accuse any falsely; and be content with your wages." Certainly he did not prohibit them to serve as soldiers when he commanded them to be content with their pay for the service.

They occupy indeed a higher place before God who, abandoning all these secular employments, serve Him with the strictest chastity; but "everyone," as the Apostle says, "hath his proper gift of God, one after this manner, and another after that." Some, then, in praying for you, fight against your invisible enemies; you, in fighting for them, contend against the barbarians, their visible enemies. Would that one faith existed in all, for then there would be less weary struggling, and the devil with his angels would be more easily conquered; but since it is necessary in this life that the citizens of the kingdom of heaven should be subjected to temptations among erring and impious men, that they may be exercised, and "tried as gold in the furnace," we ought not before the appointed time to desire to live with those alone who are holy and righteous, so that, by patience, we may deserve to receive this blessedness in its proper time.

Think, then, of this first of all, when you are arming for the battle, that even your bodily strength is a gift of God; for, considering this, you will not employ the gift of God against God. For, when faith is pledged, it is to be kept even with the enemy against whom the war is waged, how much more with the friend for whom the battle is fought! Peace should be the object of your desire; war should be waged only as a necessity, and waged only that God may by it deliver men from the necessity and preserve them in peace. For peace is not sought in order to the kindling of war, but war is waged in order that peace may be obtained. Therefore, even in waging war, cherish the spirit of a peace-maker, that, by conquering those whom you attack, you may lead them back to the advantages of peace; for our Lord says: "Blessed are the peace-makers; for they shall be called the children of God." If, however, peace among men be so sweet as procuring temporal safety, how much sweeter is that peace with God which procures for men the eternal felicity of the angels! Let necessity, therefore, and not your will, slay the enemy who fights against you. As violence is used towards him who rebels and resists, so mercy is due to the vanquished or to the captive, especially in the case in which future troubling of the peace is not to be feared.

Let the manner of your life be adorned by chastity, sobriety, and moderation; for it is exceedingly disgraceful that lust should subdue him whom man finds invincible, and that wine should overpower him whom the sword assails in vain. As to worldly riches, if you do not possess them, let them not be sought after on earth by doing evil; and if you possess them, let them by good works be laid up in heaven. The manly and Christian spirit ought neither to be elated by the accession, nor crushed by the loss of this world's treasures. Let us rather think of what the Lord says: "Where your treasure is, there will your heart be also"; and certainly, when we hear the exhortation to lift up our hearts, it is our duty to give unfeignedly the response which you know that we are accustomed to give.

In these things, indeed, I know that you are very careful, and the good report which I hear of you fills me with great delight, and moves me to congratulate you on account of it in the Lord. This letter, therefore, may serve rather as a mirror in which you may see what you are, than as a directory from which to learn what you ought to be: nevertheless, whatever you may discover, either from this letter or from the Holy Scriptures, to be still wanting to you in regard to a holy life, persevere in urgently seeking it both by effort and by prayer; and for the things which you have, give thanks to God as the Fountain of goodness, whence you have received them; in every good action let the glory be given to God, and humility be exercised by you, for, as it is written, "Every good gift and every perfect gift is from above, and cometh down from the Father of lights." But however much you may advance in the love of God and of your neighbour, and in true piety, do not imagine, as long as you are in this life, that you are without sin, for concerning this we read in Holy Scripture: "Is not the life of man upon earth a life of temptation?" Wherefore, since always, as long as you are in this body, it is necessary for you to say in prayer, as the Lord taught us: "Forgive us our debts, as we forgive our debtors," remember quickly to forgive, if anyone shall do you wrong and shall ask pardon from you, that you may be able to pray sincerely, and may prevail in seeking pardon for your own sins.

These things, my beloved friend, I have written to you in haste, as the anxiety of the bearer to depart urged me not to detain him; but I thank God that I have in some measure complied with your pious wish. May the mercy of God ever protect you, my noble lord and justly distinguished son.

# SYNESIUS

373?–?414

Synesius, a native of Cyrene, was bishop of Ptolemais. He was a friend and follower of Hypatia, the Neoplatonic woman philosopher (see page 379).

## Letter to His Brother

Translated by Augustine FitzGerald.

I should be altogether lacking in sense if I did not show myself very grateful to the inhabitants of Ptolemais, who consider me worthy of an honour to which I should never have dared to aspire. At the same time I ought to examine, not the importance of the duties which they desire to entrust to me, but my own capacity to fulfil them. For one that is but common clay, to behold himself called to a vocation almost divine, is a matter of great joy, if he truly deserve it. If, on the other hand, he be most unworthy, the future is but dark. This fear in me is by no means new, rather, of long standing, that I should win honour from men at the price of sinning against God.

When I examine myself, I fail to find the strength needful to raise me to the sanctity of such a priesthood as this. I will now tell you of the emotions of my soul: for to no one can I rather speak than to you who are so dear to me, and have been brought up with me. It is quite natural that you should share my anxieties, that you should watch with me by night, and that by day we should seek together whatever may bring me joy, or turn away sorrow from me. Let me then tell you how I am situated, although you know beforehand most of what I am about to say.

I took up a light burden, and till this moment I think that I have borne it well. It is, in a word, philosophy. Inasmuch as I have never fallen short of the duties it imposed upon me, I have been praised for my work. And I am regarded as capable of yet better things, by those who do not well estimate the direction of my talents. Now, if I frivolously accept the dignity of the position which has been offered to me, I fear that I may fail in both causes, slighting the one, without at the same time attaining the high level of the other. Consider my situation. All my days are divided between study and recreation. In my hours of work, above all, when I am occupied with divine matters, I withdraw into myself. In my leisure hours I give myself up to my friends. For you know that when I look up from my books I like to enter into every form of sport. I have no part in the political turn of mind, either by nature, or in my pursuits.

But the priest should be a man above human weaknesses. He should be a stranger to every diversion, even as God Himself. All eyes keep watch upon him to see that he fulfils his mission. He is of little use or none, unless he has made himself austere, unyielding to any form of pleasure. In carrying out his holy office, he should belong to himself no more, but to all men. He is a teacher of the law, and should utter that which is approved by law. Over and above all this, he has as many calls upon him as all the rest of the world put together, for he alone must attend to the affairs of all, or incur the reproaches of all. Now, unless he has a great and noble soul, how can he sustain the weight of so many cares, without his intellect being submerged? How can he keep the divine flame alive within him when such varied duties claim him on every side? I know well that there are such men, I have every admiration for their character, and I regard them as really divine whom intercourse with man's affairs does not separate from God. But I know myself also. I go down to the town, and from the town I come up again, always enveloped in thoughts that drag me down to earth, and covered with more stains than anybody could imagine. In a word, I have so many personal defilements of old date, that the slightest addition fills up my measure. My strength fails me. I have no strength, and there is no health in me. I am not equal to confronting what is without me, and within, I am far from being able to bear the distress of my own conscience. If anybody asks me what my idea of a bishop is, I have no hesitation in saying explicitly that he ought to be spotless, more than spotless, in all things—he to whom is allotted the purification of others.

In writing to you, my brother, I have still another thing to say. You will not be by any means the only one to read this letter. In addressing it to you I wish above all things to make known to everyone what I feel, so that whatever happens hereafter, no one will have a right to accuse me before God, or before man, nor, above all, before the venerable Theophilus. In publishing my thoughts, and in giving myself up entirely to his decision, how can I be in the wrong? God Himself, the law of the land, and the blessed hand of Theophilus himself gave me a wife. I, therefore, proclaim to all, and call them to witness once for all, that I will not be separated from her, nor shall I associate with her in secret, like an adulterer; for of these two acts, one is impious, the other is unlawful. I shall desire and pray to have many virtuous children. This is what I must inform the man upon whom depends my consecration. Let him learn from his comrades, Paul and Dionysius, for I understand they have become his deputies by the will of the people.

There is one point, however, which is not new to Theophilus, but of which I must remind him. I must press my point here a little more, for beside his difficulty, all the others are as nothing. It is difficult, if not impossible, that convictions should be shaken, which have entered the soul through knowledge to the point of demonstration. Now you know that philosophy rejects many of those convictions which are cherished by the common people. For my own part, I can never persuade myself that the soul is of more recent origin than the body. Never would I admit that the world and the parts that make it up must perish. This resurrection, which is an object of common belief, is nothing for me but a sacred and mysterious allegory, and I am far from sharing the views of the vulgar crowd thereon. The philosophic mind, albeit the discerner of truth, admits the employment of falsehood, for light is to truth what the eye is to the mind. Just as the eye would be injured by excess of light, and just as darkness is more helpful to those of weak eyesight, even so do I consider that the false may be beneficial to the populace, and the truth injurious to those not strong enough to gaze steadfastly on the radiance of Reality. If the laws of the priesthood current with us permit me these views, I can undertake the holy office on condition that I may prosecute philosophy at home, and publish legends abroad, so that if I teach no doctrine, at all events, I undo no teaching, and allow men to remain in their already acquired convictions. But if anybody tells me that he must be under this influence, that the bishop must belong to the people in his convictions, then I shall betray myself very quickly. What can there be in common between the ordinary man and philosophy? Divine truth should remain hidden, but the vulgar need a different system. I shall never cease repeating that I think the wise man, as far as necessity allows him, should not force his opinions upon others, nor allow others to force theirs upon him.

No, if I am called to the priesthood, I declare before God and man that I refuse to preach dogmas in which I do not believe. Truth is an attribute of God, and I wish in all things to be blameless before him. This one thing I will not dissimulate, I feel that I have a good deal of inclination for amusements. Even as a child I was charged with a mania for arms and horses. I shall be grieved, indeed greatly shall I suffer, at seeing my beloved dogs deprived of their hunting, and my bow eaten up by worms. Nevertheless, I shall resign myself to this, if it is the will of God. Again, I hate all care; nevertheless, whatever it costs, I will endure lawsuits and quarrels so long as I can fulfil this mission, heavy though it be, according to God's will; but never will I consent to conceal my beliefs, nor shall my opinions be at war with my tongue. I believe that I am pleasing God in thinking and speaking thus. I do not wish to give anyone the opportunity of saying that I, an unknown man, grasped at the appointment. But let the beloved of God, the right reverend Theophilus, knowing the situation and giving me clear evidence that he understands it, decide on this issue concerning me. He will then either leave me by myself to lead my own life—to philosophize—or he will not leave any grounds on which hereafter to sit in judgment over me, and to turn me out of the priesthood. In comparison with these truths, every opinion is insignificant, for I know well that Truth is dearest to God. I swear it by your sacred head, nay, better still, I swear by God, the Guardian of Truth, that I suffer. How can I fail to suffer, when I must, as it were, remove from one life to another? But if after that has been made clear which I least desire to conceal, if the man who holds this power from Heaven insists in putting me in the hierarchy of bishops, I will submit to the inevitable, and accept the token as divine. For I reason thus, that if the Emperor or some ill-fated Augustus had given an order, I should have been punished if I disobeyed, but that God must be obeyed with a willing heart. But even at the cost of God's not admitting me to His service, I must place first my love of Truth, the most divine thing of all. And I must not slip into His service through ways most opposed to it—through falsehood. See, then, that the scholastics know well my sentiments, and that they inform Theophilus.

# ST LEO I (THE GREAT)

390?–461

Leo I succeeded Sixtus III as Pope. He was born in Rome, and under Pope Celestine was consecrated deacon. He visited France in order to arbitrate between two generals, Aëtius and Albinus. While there, he was chosen Pope by both clergy and people, and he was recalled in September 440 to fill the chair of St Peter. In the East the situation was complicated by the struggle between Flavian and Eutyches, two rival bishops; Pope Leo annulled the decisions of the Synod of Ephesus of 449, and condemned Monophysitism at the Council of Chalcedon (451). In the West, he checked the Manichaean and Priscillian heresies. In 452 he persuaded Attila, who was threatening Rome, to withdraw, and in 455 he prevailed upon Genseric to spare the lives of the Romans, as well as the city's monuments. He died after a pontificate of twenty-one years, leaving discourses and letters; ninety-six of the former and one hundred forty-three of the latter have been preserved.

## Letters

### TO DIOSCORUS, BISHOP OF ALEXANDRIA

How much of the divine love we feel for you, beloved, you will be able to estimate from this, that we are anxious to establish your beginnings on a surer basis, lest anything should seem lacking to the perfection of your love, since your meritorious acts of spiritual grace, as we have proved, are already in your favour. Fatherly and brotherly conference, therefore, ought to be most grateful to you, holy brother, and received by you in the same spirit as you know it is offered by us. For you and we ought to be at one in thought and act, so that as we read, in us also there may be proved to be one heart and one mind. For since the most blessed Peter received the headship of the Apostles from the Lord, and the Church of Rome still abides by His institutions, it is wicked to believe that His holy disciple Mark, who was the first to govern the church of Alexandria, formed his decrees on a different line of tradition: seeing that without doubt both disciple and Master drew but one

Spirit from the same fount of grace, and the ordained could not hand on aught else than what he had received from his ordainer. We do not therefore allow it that we should differ in anything, since we confess ourselves to be of one body and faith, nor that the institutions of the teacher should seem different to those of the taught. . . .

### TO THE BISHOPS OF THE PROVINCE OF VIENNE

Our Lord Jesus Christ, Saviour of mankind, instituted the observance of the divine religion which He wished by the grace of God to shed its brightness upon all nations and all peoples in such a way that the Truth, which before was confined to the announcements of the Law and the Prophets, might through the Apostles' trumpet blast go out for the salvation of all men, as it is written: "Their sound has gone out into every land, and their words into the ends of the world." But this mysterious function the Lord wished to be indeed the concern of all the Apostles, but in such a way that He has placed the principal charge on the blessed Peter, chief of all the Apostles: and from him as from the Head wishes His gifts to flow to all the body: so that anyone who dares to secede from Peter's solid rock may understand that he has no part or lot in the divine mystery. For He wished him who had been received into partnership in His undivided unity to be named what He Himself was, when He said: "Thou art Peter, and upon this rock I will build My Church": that the building of the eternal temple by the wondrous gift of God's grace might rest on Peter's solid rock: strengthening His Church so surely that neither could human rashness assail it nor the gates of hell prevail against it. But this most holy firmness of the rock, reared, as we have said, by the building hand of God, a man must wish to destroy in overweening wickedness when he tries to break down its power, by favouring his own desires, and not following what he received from men of old: for he believes himself subject to no law, and held in check by no rules of God's ordinances, and breaks away, in his eagerness for novelty, from your use and ours, by adopting illegal practices, and letting what he ought to keep fall into abeyance. . . .

### TO THE SYNOD OF EPHESUS

449

The devout faith of our most clement prince, knowing that it especially concerns his glory to prevent any seed of error from springing up within the Catholic Church, has paid such deference to the divine institutions as to apply to the authority of the Apostolic See for a proper settlement: as if he wished it to be declared by the most blessed Peter himself what was praised in his confession, when the Lord said, "whom do men say that I, the Son of man, am?" and the Disciples mentioned various people's opinion: but, when He asked what they themselves believed, the chief of the Apostles, embracing the fullness of the Faith in one short sentence, said, "Thou art the Christ, the Son of the living God": that is, Thou who truly art Son of man art also truly Son of the living God: Thou, I say, true in Godhead, true in flesh and one altogether, the properties of the two natures being kept intact. And if Eutyches had believed this intelligently and thoroughly, he would never have retreated from the path of this Faith. For Peter received this answer from the Lord for his confession. "Blessed art thou, Simon Barjona; for flesh and blood hath not revealed it unto thee, but My Father which is in heaven. And I say unto thee, that thou art Peter, and upon this rock I will build My Church: and the gates of Hades shall not prevail against it." But he who both rejects the blessed Peter's confession, and gainsays Christ's Gospel, is far removed from union with this building; for he shows himself never to have had any zeal for understanding the Truth, and to have only the empty appearance of high esteem, who did not adorn the hoary hairs of old age with any ripe judgment of the heart.

But because the healing even of such men must not be neglected, and the most Christian Emperor has piously and devoutly desired a council of bishops to be held, that all error may be destroyed by a fuller judgment, I have sent our brothers Julius the bishop, Renatus the presbyter, and my son Hilary the deacon, and with them Dulcitius the notary, whose faith we have proved, to be present in my stead at your holy assembly, brethren, and settle in common with you what is in accordance with the Lord's will. To wit, that the pestilential error may be first condemned, and then the restitution of him, who has so unwisely erred, discussed, but only if embracing the true doctrine he fully and openly with his own voice and signature condemns those heretical opinions in which his ignorance has been ensnared: for this he has promised in the appeal which he sent to us, pledging himself to follow our judgment in all things. On receiving our brother and fellow-bishop Flavian's letter, we have replied to him at some length on the points which he seems to have referred to us: that when this error which seems to have arisen, has been destroyed, there may be one Faith and one and the same confession throughout the whole world to the praise and glory of God, and that "in the name of Jesus every knee should bow, of things in heaven, and things on earth, and things under the earth, and that every tongue should confess that the Lord Jesus Christ is in the glory of God the Father."

## TO FLAVIAN, BISHOP OF CONSTANTINOPLE

449

When our brethren had already started whom we despatched to you in the cause of the Faith, we received your letter, beloved, by our son Basil the deacon, in which you rightly said very little on the subject of our common anxiety, both because the accounts which had already arrived had given us full information on everything, and because for purposes of private inquiry it was easy to converse with the aforesaid Basil, by whom now through the grace of God, in whom we trust, we exhort you, beloved, in reply, using the Apostle's words, and saying: "Be ye in nothing affrighted by the adversaries; which is for them a cause of perdition, but to you of salvation." For what is so calamitous as to wish to destroy all hope of man's salvation by denying the reality of Christ's Incarnation, and to contradict the Apostle, who says distinctly: "great is the mystery of godliness which was manifest in the flesh"? What so glorious as to fight for the Faith of the Gospel against the enemies of Christ's Nativity and Cross? About whose most pure light and unconquered power we have already disclosed what was in our heart, in the letter which has been sent to you, beloved: lest anything might seem doubtful between us on those things which we have learnt, and teach in accordance with the Catholic doctrine. But seeing that the testimonies to the Truth are so clear and strong that a man must be reckoned thoroughly blind and stubborn, who does not at once shake himself free from the mists of falsehood in the bright light of reason; we desire you to use the remedy of long-suffering in curing the madness of ignorance that through your fatherly admonitions they who though old in years are infants in mind, may learn to obey their elders. And if they give up the vain conceits of their ignorance and come to their senses, and if they condemn all their errors and receive the one true Faith, do not deny them the mercifulness of a bishop's kind heart: although your judgment must remain, if their impiety which you have deservedly condemned persists in its depravity.

Our anxiety is increased by your silence, for it is long now since we received a letter from you, beloved: while we who bear a chief share in your cares, through our anxiety for the defence of the Faith, have several times, as occasion served, sent letters to you: that we might aid you with the comfort of our exhortations not to yield to the assaults of your adversaries in defence of the Faith, but to feel that we were the sharers in your labour. Some time since we believe our messengers have reached you, brother, through whom you find yourself fully instructed by our writings and injunctions, and we have ourselves sent back Basil to you as you desired. Now, lest you should think we had omitted any opportunity of communicating with you, we have sent this note by our son Eupsychius, a man whom we hold in great honour and affection, asking you to reply to our letter with all speed, and inform us at once about your own actions and those of our representatives, and about the completion of the whole matter: so that we may allay the anxiety which we now feel in defence of the Faith, by happier tidings.

# APOLLINARIS SIDONIUS

430?–?487

Gaius Sollius Apollinaris Sidonius, bishop of Clermont, was a poet and letter writer.

## Letters

Translated by O. M. Dalton.

### TO DONIDIUS

. . . To your question why, having got as far as Nîmes, I still leave your hospitality expectant, I reply by giving the reason for my delayed return. I will even dilate upon the causes of my dilatoriness, for I know that what I enjoy is your enjoyment too. The fact is, I have passed the most delightful time in the most beautiful country in the company of Tonantius Ferreolus and Apollinaris, the most charming hosts in the world. Their estates march together; their houses are not far apart; and the extent of intervening ground is just too far for a walk and just too short to make the ride worth while. The hills above the houses are under vines and olives; they might be Nysa and Aracynthus, famed in song. The view from one villa is over a wide flat country, that from the other over woodland; yet different though their situations are, the eye derives equal pleasure from both. But enough of sites; I have now to unfold the order of my entertainment.

Sharp scouts were posted to look out for our return; and not only were the roads patrolled by men from each estate, but even winding short-cuts and sheep-tracks were under observation, to make it quite impossible for us to elude the friendly ambush. Into this, of course, we fell, no unwilling prisoners; and our captors instantly made us swear to dismiss every idea of continuing our journey until a whole week had elapsed. And so every morning began with a flattering rivalry between the two hosts, as to which of their kitchens should first smoke for the refreshment of their guest; nor, though

I am personally related to one, and connected through my relatives with another, could I manage by alternation to give them quite equal measure, since age and dignity of praetorian rank gave Ferreolus a prior right of invitation over and above his other claims.

From the first moment we were hurried from one pleasure to another. Hardly had we entered the vestibule of either house when we saw two opposite pairs of partners in the ball game, repeating each other's movements as they turned in wheeling circles; in another place one heard the rattle of dice-boxes and the shouts of contending players; in yet another, were books in abundance ready to your hand; you might have imagined yourself among the shelves of some grammarian, or the tiers of the Athenaeum, or a bookseller's towering cases. They were so arranged that the devotional works were near the ladies' seats; where the master sat were those ennobled by the great style of Roman eloquence. The arrangement had this defect, that it separated certain books by certain authors in manner as near to each other as in matter they are far apart. Thus, Augustine writes like Varro, and Horace like Prudentius; but you had to consult them on different sides of the room. Turrianus Rufinus' interpretation of Adamantius Origen was eagerly examined by the readers of theology among us; according to our different points of view we had different reasons to give for the censure of this Father by certain of the clergy as too trenchant a controversialist and best avoided by the prudent. But the translation is so literal and yet renders the spirit of the work so well that neither Apuleius' version of Plato's *Phaedo* nor Cicero's of the *Ctesiphon* of Demosthenes is more admirably adapted to the use and rule of our Latin tongue.

While we were engaged in these discussions as fancy prompted each, appears an envoy from the cook to warn us that the hour of bodily refreshment is at hand. And, in fact, the fifth hour had just elapsed, proving that the man was punctual, and had properly marked the advance of the hours upon the water-clock. The dinner was short, but abundant, served in the fashion affected in senatorial houses where inveterate usage prescribes numerous courses of very few dishes, though, to afford variety, roast alternated with stew. Amusing and instructive anecdotes accompanied our potations; wit went with the one sort, learning with the other. To be brief, we were entertained with decorum, refinement, and good cheer. After dinner, if we were at Vorocingus (the name of one estate), we walked over to our quarters and our own belongings. If at Prusianum, as the other is called, the young Tonantius and his brother turned out of their beds for us because we could not be always dragging our gear about: they are surely the elect among the nobles of our own age.

The siesta over, we took a short ride to sharpen our jaded appetites for supper. Both of our hosts had baths in their houses, but in neither did they happen to be available; so I set my servants to work in the rare sober intervals which the convivial bowl, too often filled, allowed their sodden brains. I made them dig a pit at their best speed near a spring, or by the river; into this a heap of red-hot stones was thrown, and the glowing cavity covered over with an arched roof of wattled hazel. This still left interstices, and to exclude the light and keep in the steam given off when water was thrown on the hot stones, we laid coverings of Cilician goats' hair over all. In these vapour baths we passed whole hours with lively talk and repartee; all the time the cloud of hissing steam enveloping us induced the healthiest perspiration.

When we had perspired enough we were bathed in hot water; the treatment removed the feeling of repletion, but left us languid; we therefore finished off with a bracing douche from fountain, well or river. For the River Gardon runs between the two properties; except in time of flood, when the stream is swollen and clouded with melted snow, it looks red through its tawny gravels, and flows still and pellucid over its pebbly bed, teeming none the less with the most delicate fish. I could tell you of suppers fit for a king; it is not my sense of shame, but simply want of space which sets a limit to my revelations. You would have a great story if I turned the page and continued on the other side; but I am always ashamed to disfigure the back of a letter with an inky pen. Besides, I am on the point of leaving here, and hope, by Christ's grace, that we shall meet very shortly; the story of my friends' banquets will be better told at my own table or at yours—provided only that a good week's interval elapses to restore me the healthy appetite I long for. There is nothing like thin living to give tone to a system disordered by excess. Farewell.

### TO AMBROSE

. . . Your Holiness has interceded before Christ with effect on behalf of our well-beloved friend (I will not mention his name—you will know whom I mean), the laxity of whose youth you used sometimes to lament before a few chosen witnesses of your sorrow, sometimes to bemoan in silence and alone. For he has suddenly broken off his relations with the shameless slave-girl to whose low fascination he had utterly abandoned his life; by this prompt reformation he has taken a great step in the interests of his estate, of his descendants, and of himself. He dissipated his inheritance until his coffers were empty; but when he once began to consider his position, and understood how much of his patrimony the extravagance of his domestic Charybdis had swallowed up, not a moment too soon he took the bit in his teeth, shook his head, and stopping his ears, as one might say, with Ulysses' wax, he was deaf to the voice of evil, and escaped the shipwreck that follows meretricious lures. He has led to the altar a maid of high birth and ample fortune, and for that we must give him credit. It would, of course, have been a greater glory to have abandoned the voluptuous life without taking to himself a wife; but few of those who forsake error at the call of virtue can begin on the highest level, and after indulging themselves with everything, cut off all indulgence at one stroke.

It is now your part by assiduous prayer to obtain for the newly married couple good hope of issue; and then, when they have one or two children (perhaps even in that we concede too much), to see to it that this stealer of unlawful joys shall abstain thereafter even from lawful pleasures. At present, the conduct of this bride and bridegroom is so seemly that to see them once together is enough to reveal the gulf between the honourable love of a wife, and the feigned endearments of the concubine. Deign to hold me in remembrance, my Lord Bishop.

# ST GREGORY I (THE GREAT)

540?–604

Gregory belonged to a rich and noble family, and became praetor at the age of thirty. Gradually, however, he withdrew from the world, and about 574 he sold his goods, built seven monasteries with the proceeds, and became a monk in one of them. He was brought out of his retirement by Pope Benedict I, who made him a deacon about 577, and in 578 he was sent as papal nuncio, or ambassador, to the court of Constantinople. There he remained some six years; when his mission ended he returned to his monastery. But after the death of Pope Pelagius II (February 7, 590), the unanimous choice of the senate, clergy, and people fell upon Gregory. His papacy of fourteen years, fighting heresy, leading back to Catholic unity the schismatic bishops of Istria, and enforcing ecclesiastical discipline, was also remarkable for the reformation of official prayer, the organization of the liturgical chant (still called Gregorian), and the evangelization of Great Britain, through St Augustine. He is the link connecting Christian antiquity and the Middle Ages, and he seems to have lived up to his own portrait of the ideal shepherd given in his *Pastoral Care,* written in 591 and dedicated to John, bishop of Ravenna. The excerpts given here are from the West Saxon version, translated by King Alfred of England.

## FROM Pastoral Care

Thou dearest brother, very friendlily and very profitably thou blamedst me, and with humble spirit thou chidedst me, because I hid myself, and wished to flee the burdens of pastoral care. The heaviness of which burdens (all that I remember of it) I will write of in this present book, lest they seem to anyone easy to undertake; and I also advise no one to desire them who manages them rashly; and let him who desires them rashly and unrighteously fear ever undertaking them. Now I wish this discourse to rise in the mind of the learner as on a ladder, step by step, nearer and nearer, until it firmly stands on the floor of the mind which learns it; and therefore I divide it into four parts: one of the divisions is how he is to attain the dignity; the second how he is to live in it; the third is how he is to teach in it; the fourth is how he is to desire to perceive his own faults, and subdue them, lest, having attained it, he lose his humility, or, again, lest his life be unlike his ministration, or he be too presumptuous and severe because he has attained the post of instruction; but let the fear of his own faults moderate it, and let him confirm with the example of his life his teaching of those who do not believe his words; and when he has performed a good work, let him remember the evil he has done, that his contrition for his evil deeds may moderate his joy for his good works; lest he be puffed up in spirit before the eyes of the unseen Judge, and inflated with pride, and so through his egotism lose his good works. But there are many who seem to me to be very similar in want of learning, who, although they were never disciples, yet wish to be teachers, and think the burden of teaching very light, because they do not know the power of its greatness. From the very door of this book, that is, from the beginning of this discourse, the unwary are driven away and blamed, who arrogate to themselves the art of teaching which they never learned.

*That the unlearned are not to presume to undertake the office of teacher.*

Since no art can be taught by him who has not diligently learnt it before, why are the unlearned ever so rash as to undertake the care of teaching, when the art of teaching is the art of all arts? Who does not know that the wounds of the mind are more obscure than the wounds of the body? And yet worldly physicians are ashamed of undertaking to cure wounds which they cannot see, especially if they neither understand the disease nor the herbs which are to be employed. And sometimes those who are to be physicians of the mind, although they cannot understand anything of the spiritual precepts, are not ashamed of taking upon themselves to be physicians of the mind. But since now all the honour of this world is turned by the grace of God to the honour of the pious, so that now the most pious are in greatest estimation, many pretend to be pious teachers because they desire great worldly honour. On which subject Christ Himself exclaimed, and said thus: "They desire to be greeted first, and honoured in market-places and at banquets, and to recline first at suppers, and they seek the most honourable seat in assemblies." Since with pride and vainglory they thus arrive at the honour of pastoral care, they are unable properly to fulfil the duties of their ministration and to become teachers of humility; but their exhortation in teaching is disgraced, when they teach one thing, having learnt another. Such men God chided through the prophet, and reproached them with such doings, when he said: "They reigned, but not by My will; they were princes, and I knew them not." Those who so rule, rule through their own power, not through that of the highest Judge, since they are not supported on any foundation of the divine power, nor chosen for any excellence, but they are inflamed by their own desire, so as to seize on so high an office rather than obtain it by their deserts. And the eternal and unseen Judge exalts them as if he knew them not, and suffers it without interfering, as an example of patience. But though they perform many wonders in their office, when they come to him he says, "Depart from Me, ye evildoers; I know not what ye are." Again, he rebuked them through the prophet for their want of learning, when he said, "The shepherds had not understanding; they had My law, and knew Me not." He who knows not God's commands is not acknowledged by God. The same said St Paul: "He who knows not God, God knows not him." Foolish teachers come for the people's sins. Therefore often through the teacher's folly the disciples come to grief, and often through the teacher's wisdom foolish disciples are preserved. If, then, both are foolish, we must consider what Christ himself said in His Gospel, He said: "If the blind lead the blind, they will both fall into a pit." On the same subject the Psalmist spoke: "May their eyes be dimmed that they may not see, and their back always bent." He did not say this because he wished or desired it to befall any man, but he prophesied how it was to happen. For the eyes are the teachers, and the back the disciples; because the eyes are in the front and upper part of the body, and the back comes after everything; and in the same way the teachers go before the people, and the people after. When the eyes of the teacher's mind are dimmed, which ought to go before with good examples, the people bend their backs under many heavy burdens. . . .

*Of those who through humility avoid the burden of teaching, but if they are really humble, do not oppose the divine decree.*

And there are many who avoid it out of humility alone, because they do not wish to be raised above those whom they think better than themselves. There is no doubt that if such humility is enforced with other virtues, it is before God's eyes genuine humility, when he does not out of any obstinacy reject the useful works which are offered for his acceptance. It is not true humility, if a man perceives that it is God's will that he be above others, for him to refuse it, but to submit to God's will and decree, and relinquish the vice of obstinacy. When he is exalted and appointed that he may be useful to others in the post which is offered him, he should avoid it in spirit, and yet out of obedience accept it. . . .

*What kind of a man he is to be who is to rule.*

But every effort is to be made to induce him to undertake the office of bishop who mortifies his body with many hardships, and lives spiritually, and regards not the pleasures of this world, nor dreads any worldly trouble, but loves the will of God alone. It is befitting for such a disposition, not for weakness of body or mere worldly reproach to decline the supremacy, nor to be greedy of other men's property, but liberal with his own, and his heart is to be always inclined to forgiveness for piety's sake, yet never more so than is befitting for righteousness. He must not do anything unlawful, but he must bewail the unlawful deeds of others as if they were his own sins; and he must sympathize with their weakness in his heart, and rejoice in the prosperity of his neighbours as his own. His works must make him worthy of being imitated by other men. He must strive to live so as to moisten the dried-up hearts with the flowing waves of his instruction. He must learn to accustom himself to incessant prayer, until he sees he can obtain from God what he requires, as if it were said to him, "Thou hast called me; here I am." What thinkest thou, now, if a criminal comes to one of us, and prays him to lead him to a man in power who is angry with him, and intercede for him? If he is not known to me, or any man of his household, I shall very soon answer him and say: "I cannot undertake such an errand: I am not familiar enough with him." If we are ashamed to speak so to strangers, how dare we speak so to God? Or how can he presume to undertake the office of mediator between God and other men, who is not sure of being himself intimate with God through the merits of his life, or to intercede for other men while he knows not whether he himself has been interceded for? He has reason to fear arousing greater anger because of his own sins. We all know that among men he who prays a man to intercede for him with another, who is angry with the interceder also, irritates the angry mind and arouses worse anger. Let those consider this who still desire this world, and avoid arousing with their intercessions more violent anger of the severe Judge, lest, when they covet so great authority, they lead their disciples into destruction. But let everyone carefully examine himself, lest he presume to undertake the office of instruction whilst any vice prevail within him. Let him not desire to intercede for the sins of others who is disgraced with his own.

*What kind of man is not to attain thereto.*

About which the sublime voice commanded Moses to tell Aaron that no man of their kin or household was to offer to his God any bread, nor come to His ministration, if he had any blemish: if he were blind or lame, or had too big or too little a nose, or if he were crooked-nosed, or had broken hands or feet, or were humpbacked or blear-eyed, or afflicted with albugo or continual scabbiness, or eruptions or hydrocele. He is quite blind who has no conception of the light of sublime contemplation, and is enveloped in the darkness of this present life, when he never sees with his mind's eye the future light so as to love it, and knows not whither he is tending with the steps of his works. About which Anna prophesied, saying: "The Lord will direct the feet of His saints, and the unrighteous shall lament in darkness." He is altogether lame who knows whither he ought to go, and for the infirmity of his mind, although he see the way of life, cannot properly follow it, when he has accustomed himself to good works and then relaxes his vigour, and will not raise it to the state of perfect works; then the steps of the works cannot entirely arrive at the desired point. Of which Paul spoke: "Stretch out your relaxed hands and knees, and proceed rightly, and limp no longer, but be saved." The little nose is want of sagacity; for with the nose we distinguish odours, therefore the nose is put for sagacity. By sagacity we distinguish between good and bad, and choose the good and reject the bad. Of which it is said in the praise of the bride: "Thy nose resembles the tower on Mount Lebanon." For the holy assembly through sagacity sees and understands whence every temptation comes, and whence they are to expect the impending attack of vices. And there are many men who, not wishing to be thought fools, often try to speak and meditate more than is profitable for them to do, and are led astray in their meditation. The big and crooked nose is the desire of over-sagacity, when a man desires it more eagerly than he ought, he has too big and crooked a nose, for his sagacity shames itself by its excessive contemplation. The broken hand and foot is when a man knows the path of God's commands and will not follow it, but is deprived of every good work and frustrated, not at all like a lame or diseased man, who is sometimes in motion, sometimes at rest, while the broken foot is always entirely deprived of motion. He is humpbacked who is oppressed by the burden of earthly desire, and never contemplates exalted virtue, but ever pursues earthly things, and when they hear aught of the excellence of the kingdom of heaven, their hearts are oppressed by the burdens of their perverse habits, so that they cannot exalt the state of their mind. Of which the Psalmist spoke: "I am bowed and humiliated on all sides." And, again, Truth itself spoke about the same sins: "Their seed fell among thorns." That is those who hear the word of God, and by the cares and desires of this world and its wealth the seed of God's words is smothered, although they spring up, so that they cannot flourish or bear fruit. He is blear-eyed whose mind is clear enough to perceive the truth, but is obscured by fleshly works. The pupils of the bleared eyes are sound, but the eyelashes become bushy, being often dried because of the frequent flow of tears, until the sharpness of the pupil is dulled. Thus there are very many who wound their mind with the works of this fleshly life who could clearly and sharply perceive righteousness with their understanding, but with the habit of bad works the mind is dimmed. He is altogether blear-eyed who has a naturally good heart and understanding, and of himself disgraces it with his bad habits and perverse desires. Of which was well spoken through the angel: "Anoint your eyes with salve, that ye may see." We anoint the eyes of our heart to see better, when we aid our understanding with the medicine of good works, so that it is sharpened enough to perceive the brightness of true light. He has altogether albugo in his mind's eyes who can in no wise see righteousness, but is blinded with folly so that he does not understand celestial righteousness. A man can see with the pupil of the eye if it is not covered with albugo, but if it is entirely covered with albugo, he cannot see anything. So also it is said of the mind's eyes that if the understanding of human thought perceives that it is itself foolish and sinful, through that idea it grasps the conception of inner brightness; but if he himself thinks that he is wise and prudently righteous, he thereby deprives himself of the recognition of celestial light, and he understands so much the less of the brightness of true light by extolling himself in spirit with such pride and egotism; as is said of certain men: "They said they were wise, and therefore they became foolish." He is afflicted with chronic scabbiness who never refrains from wantonness. The scab of leprosy is a type of fornication. The body is leprous when the inflammation of the body spreads to the skin. Thus temptation is first in the mind and then spreads to the skin until it bursts forth in actions. Doubtlessly, unless the mind oppose the desire beforehand, the internal inflammation breaks forth and becomes scab, causing many external sores with the perverse actions. Hence Paul desired to wipe off the prurience of the flesh with the words he spoke: "Let no temptation seize on you unless human"; as if he had openly said: "It is only human for a man to suffer temptations in his mind from the desire of bad deeds, but it is devilish for him to carry out his desire." He suffers from ringworm on his body whose mind is filled with covetousness, which, unless soon checked, will increase enormously. Ringworm doubtlessly spreads over the body without pain, and yet disfigures the limb; scab is not at all painful, and itch is very mild, and yet if it is allowed to go too far, it wounds, and the wound pains. Thus covetousness wounds the mind that it enslaves with desires when it excites in the mind the desire of obtaining something. It promises him enough of everything, which, although it pleases and delights the mind, yet wounds it by causing enmity. Through the wound he loses the beauty of his limbs, when he through the evil work loses the beauty of other good works, as if he polluted his whole body by perverting his mind with every vice, which Paul confirmed by the remark that "covetousness is the root of all evil." He who is afflicted with hydrocele cannot carry out his shameful desires, and yet is excessively troubled with continually thinking of it, and yet can never accomplish the unrighteous deed, although the mind is altogether desirous of lasciviousness without any restraint or hesitation if he could accomplish it. Hydrocele is caused by the humours of the body collecting in the member, so that it swells and becomes heavy and disfigured. He is altogether hydrocelous whose whole mind is addicted to wantonness and folly, when he bears in his heart the burden of shame, and yet does not too perversely carry it out in evil deeds, although he cannot dismiss it from his mind, nor fully habituate himself to good works, for he is secretly oppressed by the burden of shame. Whoever, then, is subject to one of these vices is forbidden to offer bread to God, for it is to be expected that he will not be competent to wash away the sins of others while he is harassed by his own. We have briefly stated above what kind of man the proper pastor and teacher ought to be, and also he who has cause to fear being incompetent. We have said above what kind of man is to be appointed bishop; we will now say how he is to conduct himself when he has attained the dignity. . . .

*How the teacher is not to diminish his care of inner things for outer occupations, nor neglect outer things for the inner.*

Let not the ruler forsake the inner care of the divine ministration for the occupation of outer works, nor let him diminish his care of inner government for outward occupations; lest he be hampered by the outer or engaged exclusively in the inner occupations, so that he cannot accomplish the exterior duties which he owes to his neighbours. Many, however, will not consider that they are set over other brothers to superintend them in divine things; but with the desire of their entire heart exercise worldly care, and rejoice that they have it to exercise; and when they have it not, they strive day and night to obtain it, and are greatly grieved in spirit when they are without that which they would like to have. And when they happen to be again without authority they are more troubled in mind because of the want; since it was his desire to be allowed to toil therein, and it seems to him a hardship to be without worldly troubles. And so it happens, when he rejoices in being occupied with worldly matters, that he knows not how to teach the divine things which he ought to teach. Therefore the subjects become indifferent to righteous life when they wish to live spiritually, through the evil example set by their superior. Then they become rebellious, and thus are led astray. As when the head is unsound all the members are useless, even if they are sound, and as the army which is ready to attack another nation is useless if the general goes wrong; so also when the bishop is engaged in the ministrations which properly belong to earthly judges, no one incites or encourages the minds of the subjects to spiritual works, nor does anyone correct their faults, but the shepherd is useless who ought to watch over the flock. Therefore the subjects cannot obtain the light of truth, because the desire of earthly things occupies the understanding and blinds the mind's eyes of the people with temptation, as dust does the eyes of the body in summer in a high wind. Therefore the Redeemer of mankind spoke very rightly dissuading us from gluttony: "Beware dulling your hearts with gluttony and drunkenness and manifold worldly cares." He also added fear when he said: "Lest the terrible day of judgment come on you." He showed what was to be the coming of this day when he said: "It shall come as a snare on all dwellers on the earth." And again he said: "No man can obey two masters." Paul also said, wishing to divert the mind of pious men from the companionship of this world, and charged them very straitly when he said: "Let no servant of God be too much engaged in worldly matters, lest he offend Him to whom he formerly rendered himself." When he directed that the servants of the Church were to have quietness in their ministrations, he also directed that they were to keep themselves free from other occupations; he said: "If ye have to deliver judgment in worldly things, take those who are least esteemed in the household, and appoint them judges, that they may rule and arrange about earthly things who are not so greatly honoured with divine gifts." As if he had openly said: "Make them useful in the one pursuit if they cannot be so in the other." Therefore Moses, who was in such honour with God that he often spoke to him, was once reproved by his father-in-law Jethro, although he was a heathen and foreigner, who said that he occupied himself foolishly with the earthly service of the people, and advised him to appoint others to decide for him the differences among the people, that he might have the more leisure to understand secret and spiritual matters, so as to be able to teach the people more wisely and prudently; because lords and rulers ought to meditate on the loftiest subjects, and the subjects discharge humbler duties. The rulers ought to be before the people as a man's eye before his body, to see his path and steps. So it is necessary that the eye of the ruler be not obscured by the dust of earthly cares, because all those in authority are heads of the subjects, and the head has to guide the feet and make them step in the right path; the head above must take care not to let the feet slip in their course, for, if the feet fail, the whole body is inclined, and the head comes to the ground. How, then, can the bishop properly enjoy the pastoral dignity, if he is himself engaged in those earthly occupations which he ought to blame in others? Therefore God justly requited them by reproving them through the prophet when he said: "As the people are, such is the priest." The priest is the same as the people, when he does the same as they do, and has the same aspirations as they. Jeremiah the prophet perceived it, when he wept very sorely, and spoke as if the temple were altogether destroyed; he said: "Alas, why is the gold dimmed, and why is the noblest colour changed? The stones of the temple are scattered, and lie at the end of every street." What signifies the gold, which is so precious above all substances, but the excellence of holiness? Or what signifies the noble colour but the reverence of piety, which is to be loved by all? What signify also the stones of the holy edifice but the office of holy ordination? What also signifies the wide street but the wide road of this present life? Of the wide road Truth, that is Christ himself, spoke: "It is a very spacious and wide road which leads to destruction." The gold is blackened when the sanctity of a man's life is stained with earthly works. The noblest hue is changed when the possession of the good deeds he formerly accomplished is diminished, since he was formerly thought to live virtuously. When anyone, after obtaining the holy office, is busily engaged in earthly works, it is as if the fair hue of the gold were changed and it were dulled and despised in the eyes of men. And the gems of the sanctuaries lie scattered at the end of the streets. The gems of the sanctuaries lie scattered along the streets when the men, who ought to keep themselves unoccupied for the adornment of the church in the secret ministrations of the temple, desire the wide roads of this world outside. For the gems of the sanctuaries were made in order to shine on the robe of the highest priest among the holiest holinesses. But when the priests do not incite their subjects to virtue and reverence of our Redeemer with the merits of their life, their gems of the holiest holinesses are not in the ornaments of the bishop's robe, but lie scattered up and down the streets, when the offices of holy ordination are left to the wide roads of their own desires and are tied to earthly occupations. We must also know that he did not say that the gems were scattered along the streets, but at the ends of the streets; because although they live in a worldly manner they desire to be considered the best, and, although they go in the wide road of their own will and desires, they wish to be considered the best and holiest. And yet, in cases of need, earthly occupations are sometimes to be tolerated, yet never to be loved too much, lest they oppress the mind of the man who loves them too much, so that he is oppressed and overcome with the burden, and depressed from the highest to the lowest. Yet many undertake ministration, and wish to be free and unoccupied, so as to devote themselves to divine works, and would not concern themselves at all with earthly things. These, when they entirely neglect the care of worldly things, do not at all help their subjects in their need. Therefore their instruction is often despised when they blame and hate the faults of their subjects, and do them no other good in this world; for the word of instruction cannot penetrate the heart of the poor man unless he be encouraged with kindness. But the seed of words grows very well when the humanity of the teacher softens and moistens the breast of the hearer. Therefore it is necessary for the ruler to be able and know how to irrigate and water the minds of others, and also to provide for their outer wants. The pastors are to be fervidly zealous about the inner wants of their subjects, without neglecting the care of their outer wants. The spirit of the subjects is necessarily broken if the teacher and shepherd neglect helping them outwardly. About which the first shepherd, St Peter, earnestly admonished us, and said: "I, your fellow-servant and witness of Christ's suffering, entreat you to feed God's flock which is under your care." Soon after he showed whether he meant food of the mind or of the body, when he said: "Without compulsion, of your own free will, ye must provide for your flock for the love of God, not for base gain." With these words he fully warned and taught us, lest, after replenishing and bettering the wants of their subjects, they themselves should be slain with the sword of avarice, lest, while their neighbours are refreshed and aided by them, they themselves abstain from the bread of righteousness. This same zeal of the shepherds St Paul aroused, saying: "He who cares not for those that are his, and especially God's, servants, is an apostate and infidel." Yet, with all this, it is always to be feared and due care taken, lest, while they are to perform outer duties, they be not estranged from inner contemplation; because the minds of rulers, as we have remarked above, when occupied with these transitory things and inconsiderately devoted to them, often let the inner love grow cold, and are not afraid of forgetting that they have received the control of men's souls. But it is necessary that their solicitude about the outer wants of their subjects be kept within due bounds. Concerning which it was well said to the prophet Ezekiel that the priests were not to shave their heads with razors, nor, on the other hand, let their locks grow, but clip them with scissors. Priests are very properly called *sacerds,* that is in English "cleansers," because they are to act as guides of believers and govern them. The hair on their head signifies outer thoughts, for it grows and flourishes over the brain and yet no one feels it; which signifies the cares of this present life. Our thoughts often proceed from us so carelessly that we no more feel it than a man can feel his hair above the skin, because we often meditate on improper subjects. Yet all those who are to be above others must be careful of outer things, and yet must not be too much hampered by them. The priest was with good reason forbidden to shave his head, or let his hair grow; that is, that he is not to cut away from his mind all the thoughts which he ought to preserve for the benefit of his subjects, nor yet let them grow too rankly so as to be useless and evil. About which it was well said that the cutter was to cut his hair; in other words, that he is to be as zealous as is needful in the care of transitory things, and yet so as easily to be able to clip them without pain to prevent their growing too luxuriantly; lest, while the bodily life is protected, the thoughts of the heart be tied down through the excessive care of outer things; the priest must preserve his locks so as to cover the skin, and yet clip them before they fall into his eyes. . . .

*That men are to be admonished in one way, in another women.*

Men are to be admonished in one way, in another women. Men are to be taught more seriously and severely, women more lightly; that the men may aspire to a greater burden, and the women be brought on with flattery. . . .

*That those who are too silent are to be admonished in one way, in another those who are given to speaking too much that is useless and unprofitable.*

The very silent are to be admonished in one way, in another those who waste themselves with loquacity. The very silent are to be advised, when they avoid a vice incautiously, not to turn to a worse one and involve themselves therein, as it often happens to them that, when they excessively restrain their tongues, they are much more severely afflicted in their hearts than the loquacious, since their thoughts boil in their hearts because of their silence, since they compel themselves to preserve excessive silence, and are therefore greatly troubled. Therefore it often happens that they are so much the more distracted in their minds with vacillation, the quieter and securer they expect to be able to be with their silence. But since we cannot find anything in their outward demeanour to blame, because of their silence, they are often internally elated, so as to despise the loquacious and count them as nought, and do not understand how much they open up their heart with the vice of pride, although they keep their bodily mouth shut; though the tongue lies humbly still, the heart is greatly elated, and the less he notices his own vices the more freely he blames all other men in his heart. The very silent are also to be admonished eagerly to strive to understand that it is not only necessary for them to consider how they are to display themselves outwardly to men, but it is much more necessary for them to consider how they are to display themselves internally to God; and that they are more to dread the secret Judge who knows them all, on account of their thoughts, than the blame of their companions for their words and deeds. It is written in the Proverbs of Solomon: "My son, attend to my wisdom and prudence, and direct thine eyes and ears to being able to guard thy thoughts." For there is nothing in us more restless and changeable than the mind, for it departs from us as often as vain thoughts approach us, and is dissipated by each of them. Of which spoke the Psalmist: "My mind and wisdom have forsaken me." And afterwards he returned to himself, and regained his wits, and said: "Now Thy servant has found his wisdom, that is, praying to Thee." Therefore, when a man restrains his mind, it finds that which it formerly used to avoid. Often also the very silent, when they have many unprofitable thoughts internally, they cause them all the more internal pain if they do not speak them out; and sometimes it happens that, if they speak them out properly, they thus relieve their grief. We know that the hidden is more painful than the open wound, for when the matter which collects in it is allowed to escape, the wound is opened and the pain relieved. Those who are more silent than they ought to be must also know that they are not to increase their trouble by holding their tongue. They are also to be admonished, if they love their neighbours as themselves, not to conceal from them the reason of their blaming them in their mind, since speech is beneficial to both of them, because it both opens and lets out the inflammation in the one, and heals him, and teaches the other and restrains him from vices. He, then, who perceives any evil in his neighbour, and keeps silent about it, acts like the surgeon who looks at his friend's wound and will not cure it. How, is he not as it were his murderer, when he can cure him and will not? Therefore the tongue is to be moderately bridled, not to be bound immoderately. Of which it is written: "The wise man is silent, till he perceives that it is more profitable for him to speak." It is no wonder that he is silent, and waits his time; but when he perceives that it is a profitable time for speaking, he disregards silence and speaks all that he sees to be profitable to speak. And again, it is written in the books of Solomon which are called Ecclesiastes, that it is sometimes time for speech, sometimes for silence. Therefore he must sagaciously consider when it is profitable for him to speak, that, when he desires to speak, he may restrain his tongue, lest it be directed to unprofitable speeches, or, on the other hand, be idle when he can speak what is profitable. Of which the Psalmist spoke very well: "May the Lord put a guard over my mouth, and the door of constancy." He did not pray him to enclose him entirely with a whole wall, but he prayed that a door might be added, that he might sometimes open, sometimes shut. Thereby we must learn to arrange very cautiously a proper time, and when the voice is to open the mouth prudently, and also to arrange sagaciously the time when silence is to close it. On the contrary, the loquacious are to be taught to note carefully from how great virtue they have departed, when they slip about among many words. The human mind has the properties of water. When water is dammed up, it increases and rises and strives after its original place, when it cannot flow whither it would. But if the dam is thrown open or the weir bursts, it runs off, and is wasted, and becomes mud. So does the mind of man when it cannot preserve a rational silence, but bursts out into idle loquacity, and so is diverted various ways, as if it were all dispersed in little rivulets, and had flowed out of himself, so that it cannot return again into his own understanding and mind. That is because it is diverted into too manifold speeches, as if he had externally shut himself out from the meditation of his own mind, and so exposed himself naked to the wounds of his foes, because he is not enclosed in any defences of a fortress. As it is written in the Proverbs of Solomon, that the man who cannot restrain his tongue is most like an open city, which is not circumvallated. Therefore the city of the mind which is not enclosed in any silence must very often experience the spears of its foes, because it lays itself very open to its foes when it throws itself out of itself with useless words, and it is much the easier to overcome, because it fights against itself with loquacity, helping the adversary; therefore it is often overcome without any trouble. Often, then, the heavy mind slips down lower and lower by degrees in useless words, until it falls altogether, and becomes nought; because it would not formerly guard against useless words, it must therefore fall when it slips. At first a man takes pleasure in talking frivolity about others, and then after a time he likes to blame and backbite their lives without any fault of those he talks about, until at last it bursts forth from his tongue into open reviling of the others. Thus he sows the thorn of envy, until therefrom grows discord, and by discord the fire of hatred is kindled, and hatred extinguishes peace. Of which was very well said through the wise Solomon, that he who lets out the water is the cause of discord. He lets out the water, who allows the voice of his tongue to be dissipated in useless words. The wise Solomon said that a very deep pool is weired in the wise man's mind, and very little of what is useless flows out. He who breaks the weir and lets out the water is the cause of strife. That is, he who bridles not his tongue is he who destroys concord. Again, Solomon said: "He moderates anger who bids the fool be silent." Therefore he who is loquacious can never preserve virtue and wisdom. That the Psalmist showed when he said: "The loquacious man will never be corrected or taught in this world." Again, Solomon spoke of the same: "Loquacity is never without sin." Of which also Isaiah the prophet spoke, saying that silence is the support and helper of virtue. That signifies that the virtue of the mind which will never refrain from loquacity is dispersed. Of which the Apostle James spoke: "If any one thinks to be pious, and will not bridle his tongue, the mind deceives itself, because his piety is very useless." And again, he said: "Let every man be very ready and zealous to hear, and very slow to speak." Again, about the same he showed what the power of the tongue is, saying that it is restless, evil, and full of deadly poison. And again, Truth, that is Christ, of itself warned us, saying: "Every vain word that men speak they shall account for at the day of doom."

Those are evidently useless words, which wise men cannot perceive to belong to virtuous and useful necessity, either now or afterwards. If, then, we are to account for useless words, what punishment do we think that the loquacious ought to have, who is always sinning in loquacity? . . .

# Letters

### TO THEODELINDA, QUEEN OF THE LOMBARDS

. . . For they say that in the times of Justinian of pious memory, some things were ordained contrary to the Council of Chalcedon; and, while they neither read themselves nor believe those who do, they remain in the same error which they themselves feigned to themselves concerning us. For we, our conscience bearing witness, declare that nothing was altered, nothing violated, with respect to the faith of this same holy Council of Chalcedon; but that whatever was done in the times of the aforesaid Justinian was so done that the faith of the Council of Chalcedon should in no respect be disturbed. Further, if anyone presumes to speak or think anything contrary to the faith of the said synod, we detest his opinion, with interposition of anathema. Since then you know the integrity of our faith under the attestation of our conscience, it remains that you should never separate yourself from the communion of the Catholic Church, lest all those tears of yours, and all those good works should come to nothing, if they are found alien from the true faith. It therefore becomes your Glory to send a communication with all speed to my most reverend brother and fellow-bishop Constantius, of whose faith, as well as his life, I have long been well assured, and to signify by your letters addressed to him how kindly you have accepted his ordination, and that you are in no way separated from the communion of his Church; although I think that what I say on this subject is superfluous: for, though there has been some degree of doubtfulness in your mind, I think that it has been removed from your heart on the arrival of my son John the abbot, and Hippolytus the notary. . . .

. . . It has come to our knowledge from the report of certain persons that your Glory has been led on by some bishops even to the offence against holy Church of suspending yourself from the communion of Catholic unanimity. Now the more we sincerely love you, the more seriously are we distressed about you, that you believe unskilled and foolish men, who not only do not know what they talk about, but can hardly understand what they have heard; who, while they neither read themselves, nor believe those who do, remain in the same error which they have themselves feigned to themselves concerning us. For we venerate the four holy synods; the Nicene, in which Arius, the Constantinopolitan, in which Macedonius, the first Ephesine, in which Nestorius, and the Chalcedonians, in which Eutyches and Dioscorus, were condemned; declaring that whosoever thinks otherwise than these four synods did is alien from the true faith. We also condemn whomsoever they condemn, and absolve whomsoever they absolve, smiting, with interposition of anathema, anyone who presumes to add to or take away from the faith of the same four synods, and especially that of Chalcedon, with respect to which doubt and occasion of superstition has arisen in the minds of certain unskilled men.

Seeing, then, that you know the integrity of our faith from my plain utterance and profession, it is right that you should have no further scruple of doubt with respect to the Church of the blessed Peter, Prince of the Apostles: but persist ye in the true faith, and make your life firm on the rock of the Church; that is on the confession of the blessed Peter, Prince of the Apostles, lest all those tears of yours and all those good works should come to nothing, if they are found alien from the true faith. For as branches dry up without the virtue of the root, so works, to whatsoever degree they may seem good, are nothing, if they are disjoined from the solidity of the faith. . . .

### TO CONSTANTINA AUGUSTA

. . . Almighty God, who holds in His right hand the heart of your Piety, both protects us through you and prepares for you rewards of eternal remuneration for temporal deeds. For I have learnt from the letters of the deacon Sabinianus my *responsalis* with what justice your Serenity is interested in the cause of the blessed Prince of the Apostles Peter against certain persons who are proudly humble, and feignedly kind. And I trust in the bounty of our Redeemer that for these your good offices with the most serene Lord and his most pious sons you will receive retribution also in the heavenly country. Nor is there any doubt that you will receive eternal benefits, being loosed from the chains of your sins, if in the cause of his Church you have made him your debtor to whom the power of binding and of loosing has been given. Wherefore I still beg you to allow no man's hypocrisy to prevail against the truth, since there are some who, according to the saying of the excellent preacher, by sweet words and fair speeches seduce the hearts of the innocent—men who are vile in raiment, but puffed up in heart. And they affect to despise all things in this world, and yet seek to acquire for themselves all the things that are of this world. They confess themselves unworthy before all men, but cannot be content with private titles, since they covet that whereby they may seem to be more worthy than all. Let therefore your Piety, whom Almighty God has appointed with our most serene Lord to be over the whole world, through your favouring of justice render service to Him from whom you have received your right to so great a dominion, that you may rule over the world that is committed to you so much the more securely as you more truly serve the Author of all things in the execution of truth.

Furthermore, I inform you that I have received a letter from the most pious Lord desiring me to be pacific towards my brother and fellow-priest John. And indeed so it became the religious Lord to give injunctions to priests. But, when this my brother with new presumption and pride calls himself universal bishop, having caused himself in the time of our predecessor of holy memory to be designated in synod by this so proud a title, though all the acts of that synod were abrogated, being disallowed by the Apostolic See—the most serene Lord gives me a somewhat distressing intimation, in that he has not rebuked him who is acting proudly, but endeavours to bend me from my purpose, who in this cause of defending the truth of the Gospels and Canons, of humility and rectitude; whereas my aforesaid brother and fellow-priest is acting against evangelical principles and also against the blessed Apostle Peter, and against all the churches, and against the ordinances of the Canons. But the Lord, in whose hands are all things, is almighty; of Him it is written, "There is no wisdom nor prudence nor counsel against the Lord." And indeed my often before mentioned most holy brother endeavours to persuade my most serene Lord of many things: but well I know that all those prayers of his and all those tears will not allow my Lord to be in anything cajoled by anyone against reason or his own soul.

Still it is very distressing, and hard to be borne with patience, that my aforesaid brother and fellow-bishop, despising all others, should attempt to be called sole bishop. But in this pride of his what else is denoted than that the times of Antichrist are already near at hand? For in truth he is imitating him who, scorning social joy with the legions of angels, attempted to start up to a summit of singular eminence, saying, "I will exalt my throne above the stars of heaven, I will sit upon the mount of the testament, in the sides of the North, and will ascend above the heights of the clouds, and I will be like the Most High." Wherefore I beseech you by Almighty God not to allow the times of your Piety to be polluted by the elation of one man, nor in any way to give any assent to so perverse a title, and that in this case your Piety may by no means despise me; since, though the sins of Gregory are so great that he ought to suffer such things, yet there are no sins of the Apostle Peter that he should deserve in your times to suffer thus. Wherefore again and again I beseech you by Almighty God that, as the princes your ancestors have sought the favour of the holy Apostle Peter, so you also take heed both to seek it for yourselves and to keep it, and that his honour among you be in no degree lessened on account of our sins who unworthily serve him, seeing that he is able both to be your helper now in all things and hereafter to remit your sins.

Moreover, it is now even seven years that we have been living in this city among the swords of the Lombards. How much is expended on them daily by this Church, that we may be able to live among them, is not to be told. But I briefly indicate that, as in the regions of Ravenna the Piety of my Lords has for the first army of Italy a treasurer to defray the daily expenses for recurring needs, so I also in this city am their treasurer for such purposes. And yet this Church, which at one and the same time unceasingly expends so much on clergy, monasteries, the poor, the people, and in addition on the Lombards, lo it is still pressed down by the affliction of all the Churches, which groan much for this pride of one man, though they do not presume to say anything.

Further, a bishop of the city of Salona has been ordained without the knowledge of me and my *responsalis,* and a thing has been done which never happened under any former princes. When I heard of this, I at once sent word to that prevaricator, who had been irregularly ordained, that he must not presume by any means to celebrate the solemnities of mass, unless we should have first ascertained from our most serene Lords that they had ordered this to be done; and this I commanded him under pain of excommunication. And yet, scorning and despising me, supported by the audacity of certain secular persons, to whom he is said to give many bribes so as to impoverish his Church, he presumes up to this time to celebrate mass, and has refused to come to me according to the order of my Lords. Now I, obeying the injunction of their Piety, have from my heart forgiven this same Maximus, who had been ordained without my knowledge, his presumption in passing over me and my *responsalis* in his ordination, even as though he had been ordained with my authority. But his other wrongdoings—to wit his bodily transgressions, which I have heard of, and his having been elected through bribery, and his having presumed to celebrate mass while excommunicated—these things, for the sake of God, I cannot pass over without inquiry. But I hope, and implore the Lord, that no fault may be found in him with respect to these things that are reported, and that his case may be terminated without peril to my soul. Nevertheless, before this has been ascertained, my most serene Lord, in the order that has been despatched, has enjoined me to receive him with honour when he comes. And it is a very serious thing that a man of whom so many things of such a nature are reported should be honoured before such things have been inquired into and sifted, as they ought in the first place to be. And, if the causes of the bishops who are committed to me are settled before my most pious Lords under the patronage of others, what shall I do, unhappy that I am, in this Church? But that my bishops despise me, and have recourse to secular judges against me, I give thanks to Almighty God that I attribute it to my sins. This however I briefly intimate, because I am waiting for a little while; and, if he should long delay coming to me, I shall in no wise hesitate to exercise strict canonical discipline in his case. But I trust in Almighty God, that He will give long life to our most pious Lords, and order things for us under your hand, not according to our sins, but according to the gifts of His grace. These things, then, I suggest to my most tranquil lady, since I am not ignorant with how great zeal for rectitude the most pure conscience of her Serenity is moved. . . .

### TO CHILDEBERT, KING OF THE FRANKS

The letter of your Excellency has made us exceedingly glad, testifying as it does that you are careful, with pious affection, of the honour and reverence due to priests. For you thus show to all that you are faithful worshippers of God, while you love His priests with the acceptable veneration that is due to them, and hasten with Christian devotion to do whatever may advance their position. Whence also we have received with pleasure what you have written, and grant what you desire with willing mind; and accordingly we have committed, with the favour of God, our vicariate jurisdiction to our brother Virgilius, bishop of the city of Arelate, according to ancient custom and your Excellency's desire; and have also granted him the use of the pallium, as has been the custom of old.

But, inasmuch as some things have been reported to us which greatly offend Almighty God, and confound the honour and reverence due to the priesthood, we beg that they may be in every way amended with the support of the censure of your power, lest, while headstrong and perverse doings run counter to your devotion, your kingdom, or your soul (which God forbid) be burdened by the guilt of others.

Further, it has come to our knowledge that on the death of bishops some persons from being laymen are tonsured, and mount to the episcopate by a sudden leap. And thus one who has not been a disciple is in his inconsiderate ambition made a master. And, since he has not learned what to teach, he bears the office of priesthood only in name; for he continues to be a layman in speech and action as before. How, then, is he to intercede for the sins of others, not having in the first place bewailed his own? For such a shepherd does not defend, but deceives, the flock; since, while he cannot for very shame try to persuade others to do what he does not do himself, what else is it but that the Lord's people remains a prey to robbers, and catches destruction from the source whence it ought to have had a great support of wholesome protection? How bad and how perverse a proceeding this is let your Excellency's Highness consider even from your own administration of things. For it is certain that you do not put a leader over an army unless his work and his fidelity have first been apparent; unless the virtue and industry of his previous life have shown him to be a fit person. But, if the command of an army is not committed to any but men of this kind, it is easily gathered from this comparison of what sort a leader of souls ought to be. But it is a reproach to us, and we are ashamed to say it, that priests snatch at leadership who have not seen the very beginning of religious warfare.

But this also, a thing most execrable, has been reported to us as well: that sacred orders are conferred through simoniacal heresy, that is for bribes received. And, seeing that it is exceedingly pestiferous, and contrary to the Universal Church, that one be promoted to any sacred order not for merit but for a price, we exhort your Excellency to order so detestable a wickedness to be banished from your kingdom. For that man shows himself to be thoroughly unworthy of this office, who fears not to buy the gift of God with money, and presumes to try to get by payment what he deserves not to have through grace.

These things, then, most excellent son, I admonish you about for this reason, that I desire your soul to be saved. And I should have written about them before now, had not innumerable occupations stood in the way of my will. But now that a suitable time for answering your letter has offered itself, I have not omitted what it was my duty to do. Wherefore, greeting your Excellency with the affection of paternal charity, we beg that all things which we have enjoined on our above-named brother and fellow-bishop to be done and observed, may be carried out under the protection of your favour, and that you allow them not to be in any way upset by the elation or pride of anyone. But, as they were observed by his predecessor under the reign of your glorious father, so let them be observed now also, by your aid, with zealous devotion. It is right, then, that we should thus have a return made to us; and that, as we have not deferred fulfilling your will, so you too, for the sake of God and the blessed Peter, Prince of the Apostles, should cause our ordinances to be observed in all respects; that so your Excellency's reputation, praiseworthy and well-pleasing to God, may extend itself all around.

### TO BRUNICHILD, QUEEN OF THE FRANKS

The laudable and God-pleasing goodness of your Excellence is manifested both by your government of your kingdom and by your education of your son. To him you have not only with provident solicitude conserved intact the glory of temporal things, but have also seen to the rewards of eternal life, having planted his mind in the root of the true faith with maternal, as became you, and laudable care of his education. Whence not undeservedly it ensues that he should surpass all the kingdoms of the nations, in that he both worships purely and confesses truly the Creator of these nations. But that faith may shine forth in him the more laudably in his works, let the words of your exhortation kindle him, to the end that, as royal power shows him lofty among men, so goodness of conduct may make him great before God.

Now inasmuch as past experience in many instances gives us confidence in the Christianity of your Excellence, we beg of you, for the love of Peter, Prince of the Apostles, whom we know that you love with your whole heart, that you would cherish with the aid of your patronage our most beloved son the presbyter Candidus, who is the bearer of these presents, together with the little patrimony for the government of which we have sent him, to the end that, strengthened by the favour of your support, he may be able both to manage profitably this little patrimony, which is evidently beneficial towards the expenses of the poor, and also to recover into the possession of this little patrimony anything that may have been taken away from it. For it is not without increase of your praise that after so long a time a man belonging to Church has been sent for the management of this patrimony. Let your Excellency, then, deign so willingly to give your attention to what we request of you that the blessed Peter, Prince of the Apostles, to whom the power of binding and loosing has been given by the Lord Jesus Christ, may both grant to your Excellence to rejoice here in your offspring, and after courses of many years cause you to be found, absolved from all ills, before the face of the eternal Judge.

## TO THE BRETHREN GOING TO ENGLAND

Since it had been better not to have begun what is good than to return back from it when begun, you must, most beloved sons, fulfil the good work which with the help of the Lord you have begun. Let, then, neither the toil of the journey nor the tongues of evil-speaking men deter you; but with all instancy and all fervour go on with what under God's guidance you have commenced, knowing that great toil is followed by the glory of an eternal reward. Obey in all things humbly Augustine your provost (*præposito*), who is returning to you, whom we also appoint your abbot, knowing that whatever may be fulfilled in you through his admonition will in all ways profit your souls. May Almighty God protect you with His grace, and grant to me to see the fruit of your labour in the eternal country; that so, even though I cannot labour with you, I may be found together with you in the joy of the reward; for in truth I desire to labour. God keep you safe, most beloved sons.

### TO BRUNICHILD, QUEEN OF THE FRANKS

. . . The Christianity of your Excellence has been so truly known to us of old that we do not in the least doubt of your goodness, but rather hold it to be in all ways certain that you will devoutly and zealously concur with us in the cause of faith, and supply most abundantly the succour of your religious sincerity. Being for this reason well assured, and greeting you with paternal charity, we inform you that it has come to our knowledge how that the nation of the Angli, by God's permission, is desirous of becoming Christian, but that the priests who are in their neighbourhood have no pastoral solicitude with regard to them. And lest their souls should haply perish in eternal damnation, it has been our care to send to them the bearer of these presents, Augustine the servant of God, whose zeal and earnestness are well known to us, with other servants of God; that through them we might be able to learn their wishes, and, as far as is possible, you also striving with us, to take thought for their conversion. We have also charged them that for carrying out this design they should take with them presbyters from the neighbouring regions. Let, then, your Excellency, habitually prone to good works, on account as well of our requests as of regard to the fear of God, deign to hold him as in all ways commended to you, and earnestly bestow on him the favour of your protection, and lend the aid of your patronage to his labour; and, that he may have the fullest fruit thereof, provide for his going secure under your protection to the above-written nation of the Angli, to the end that our God, who has adorned you in this world with good qualities well-pleasing to Him, may cause you to give thanks here and in eternal rest with His saints.

Furthermore, commending to your Christianity our beloved son Candidus, presbyter and rector of the patrimony of our Church which is situated in your parts, we beg that he may in all things obtain the favour of your protection. . . .

# ST ISIDORE OF SEVILLE
## (Isidorus Hispalensis)

560?–636

Isidore's father fled from one Spanish province, Carthaginensis, to another, Baetica. The family escaped none too soon; their fatherland was destroyed by the Goths. The eldest son, Leander, already a priest when his parents died, assumed charge of the family, including Florentina, who became a nun, and Isidore, who later succeeded Leander as bishop of Seville. Leander was a close friend of Gregory the Great, and for Isidore, both were beloved examples. Arian Goths and Catholic Hispano-Romans formed Leander's far from homogeneous flock. Gregory, writing to congratulate Leander on the conversion of King Recared, warned him to "take care that he [Recared] complete the good work he has begun and by the merits of his life hold fast the faith he has adopted."

Isidore is the last of the Fathers in the West, as St John Damascene is in the East. Isidore even in his own time was revered as a saint and looked upon as the wonder of his age. He was "above all a compiler, perhaps the greatest compiler there has ever been." He undertook to compile a summary of all human knowledge available at his time and bequeathed to the Middle Ages a sort of encyclopedia containing a summary of the learning of pagan and Christian antiquity. His work is superficial, made up of documents and fragments gathered from all quarters, yet it bespeaks enormous research, extensive information, and a mind in thorough sympathy with the needs of his time. During his episcopate he wrote at least eight books, of which *On the Catholic Faith against the Jews,* the *History of the Visigothic Kings,* and the *Etymologies* are the best known. He served as president of two councils, at Seville in 619, and at Toledo in 633. After thirty-six years as archbishop of Seville, Isidore died on April 4, 636.

## FROM The Perfection of the Clergy

The man who desires to exhort others to virtue must first correct himself so as to present in every way a model life and lead all to good works by teaching and example. Knowledge of the Scriptures is also necessary for him, because if a bishop is merely a holy man he benefits only himself, but if he is learned in doctrine and in speech, he can instruct others. . . . He, beyond all others, should make it his special duty to read the Scriptures, to study the canons, to imitate the examples of the saints, to give himself up to watching, fasting and prayer, to preserve peace with his brethren, to despise no member of the Church, to condemn no one without proof, to excommunicate no one without consideration. He must show such humility and authority that he neither allows the vices of his subjects to increase because of excessive meekness nor through immoderate zeal exercises power with severity, but acts the more cautiously toward his subjects in proportion as he expects to be judged the more severely by Christ. He will maintain also the supereminent gift of charity, without which all virtue is nothing, for the guard of sanctity is charity, but the station of this guard is humility. Among all these things he will possess an eminent degree of chastity so that the mind which is to consecrate the body of Christ may be pure and free from all defilement of the flesh. It behooves him to care for the poor with solicitous dispensation, to feed the hungry, to clothe the naked, to receive strangers, to ransom captives, to protect widows and orphans, to exhibit in all things vigilant care, foresight, and prudent management. . . . Let him have also, according to the words of the Apostle, meekness, patience, sobriety, moderation, abstinence, and modesty, so that he abstain not only from sinful deeds but even from glances and evil thoughts, so that while he permits no vice to reign within him, he may be able to obtain from God pardon for the sins of his subjects. He who pursues these things will be a useful minister of God and will show forth the perfection of the priesthood. . . .

# THE MARTYRS

# The Martyrdom of St Polycarp

69?–?155

Polycarp was born in about 69 or 70. His parents were well off, and he was early a disciple of St John the Evangelist. He met and talked with people who had actually known Jesus, and he was made bishop of Smyrna while yet quite young. He received St Ignatius when he came in chains on his way to Rome. St Irenaeus praises him for his respect for tradition and his love of sound doctrine. Late in life, Polycarp visited Pope Anicetus in Rome to discuss with him the question of the celebration of Easter and to defend the custom in use in Smyrna. No agreement was reached, but the two men parted friends. A year or two later, Polycarp was martyred. The circumstances of his martyrdom are described in a letter written in the following year by one Marcion, in the name of the church of Smyrna, to the church of Philomelium.

The Church of God which dwells in Smyrna to the Church of God which dwells in Philomelium and to all the dioceses of the Holy Catholic Church in every place. May the mercy, peace, and love of God the Father and of our Lord Jesus Christ be multiplied.

We write unto you, brethren, the story of the martyrs and of blessed Polycarp, who put an end to the persecution, setting his seal thereto by his martyrdom. For almost all that went before so happened, that the Lord might show forth anew an example of martyrdom which is conformable to the Gospel. For he waited to be betrayed, as did also the Lord, that we also might be imitators of Him, looking not only on our own things, but also on the things of others. For it is a mark of true and steadfast love to desire not our own salvation only but that of all the brethren.

Blessed and noble are all martyrdoms that happen according to the will of God. For we should act with discretion, leaving the power over all events to God. For who can fail to admire their nobility and patience and love of their Master? Who being so torn with scourges that the framework of the flesh was laid bare to the veins and arteries within, showed such patience that the very bystanders felt pity and sorrow, while some reached so high a pitch of nobility that no sound or groan escaped them, making manifest to us all that in the hour of their torture the martyrs of Christ were absent from the flesh, or rather that the Lord was present and of their company. Fixing their thoughts on the grace of Christ they despised the torments of the world, redeeming in one hour eternal punishment. And the fire of their inhuman torturers was cold to them, for their eyes were set on escape from the eternal fire which is never quenched, and with the eyes of the heart they looked upon the good things reserved for them that endure, which ear hath not heard, nor eye seen, "neither have they entered into the heart of man," but they were revealed by the Lord unto them who were no longer men, but already angels. Likewise those who were condemned to the beasts endured terrible torments, having harrows laid beneath them, and being tormented with other kinds of manifold tortures, that the Devil, if he could, might through the continual torment turn them to deny their faith; for he devised many things against them.

But, thanks be to God, he did not prevail against all. For the noble Germanicus gave strength to their cowardice by his own fortitude, who made a notable fight with the beasts. For when the proconsul endeavoured to prevail upon him, bidding him take pity on his own youth, he with violence dragged the wild beasts towards him, wishing to be rid the sooner of their life of unrighteousness and sin.

At this all the multitude, wondering at the nobility of the people of Christ, who were beloved of God and honoured Him, cried out, "Away with the Atheists! Seek Polycarp!"

But one, Quintus by name, a Phrygian just arrived from Phrygia, lost heart when he saw the beasts. He it was who constrained himself and some others to come forward of their own motion. Him the proconsul after much entreaty persuaded to take the oath and offer sacrifice. Therefore, brethren, we do not commend those who give themselves up; for this is not the teaching of the Gospel.

The excellent Polycarp, on hearing the news, was not dismayed, but wished to remain in the city; but the greater number urged him to depart secretly. And so he did, to a little farm, not far from the city, and passed the time with a few companions, doing naught else but pray night and day for all and for the Churches throughout the world, as was his custom. And while praying he fell into a trance three days before he was taken, and saw his pillow being consumed by fire. And he turned and said to those with him, "I must be burned alive."

While his pursuers were still waiting for him, he went away to another farm, and immediately they followed close upon him. Not finding him, they laid hands on two young slaves, one of whom confessed under the torture. Now it was impossible Polycarp should escape, since his betrayers belonged to his own household. And the justice of the peace whose lot it was to bear the same name as Herod, was in a hurry to bring him into the stadium, that he, being made partner with Christ, might fulfil his lot, and his betrayers might meet the same punishment as Judas.

Taking the young slave with them, the constables and horsemen, armed in the usual way, went out on the Preparation about the dinner-hour "as against a thief" at a run. Coming up in a body late in the day, they found him lying in a cottage in an upper room; he could indeed have escaped from thence also elsewhere, but he refused, saying, "The will of the Lord be done." Hearing then that they were come, he went down and talked with them, those present marvelling at his great age and his constancy, and at their excessive eagerness to take a man so old. So he bade food and drink to be set before them at that hour, as much as they wanted; and besought them to give him an hour to pray undisturbed. On leave being given, he stood and prayed, being so full of the grace of God that for two hours he could not once be silent, and the hearers were astonished, and many repented for having assailed an old man so godlike.

When at length he ended his prayer after remembering all that ever had dealings with him, great and small, well-known and unknown, and the whole Catholic Church throughout the world, the time having now come for his departure, they set him on an ass and brought him to the city, it being a High Sabbath. He was met by Herodes, the High Sheriff, and by Herodes' father, Nicetes, who, having transferred him to the carriage, sat down beside him, and strove to persuade him with these words: "What is the harm of saying, 'Cæsar is Lord,' and offering incense"—with more to this effect—"and saving your life?" At first he made them no answer, but, when they persisted, he said: "I do not intend to do as you advise me." Failing to persuade him, they reviled him, and made him descend with so much haste that in getting down from the carriage he hurt his shin. He, as though nothing had happened, paid no heed, but went on quickly with much eagerness on his way to the stadium, where the din was so great that none could be so much as heard.

As Polycarp entered the stadium, there came a voice from heaven, saying, "Be strong, Polycarp, and play the man." None saw the speaker, but the voice was heard by those of our brethren who were present. When he was brought in, thereupon a great din arose as soon as they heard "Polycarp is taken."

So the proconsul asked him whether he were the man. And when he said "Yes," he tried to persuade him to deny his faith, saying: "Have respect to your age," and other such things as they were used to say: "Swear by the Fortune of Cæsar, repent, say, 'Away with the Atheists.'" Polycarp, gazing with a steadfast countenance on all the crowd of lawless heathen in the stadium, waved his hand to them, sighed, and, looking up to heaven, said: "Away with the Atheists."

When the proconsul pressed him further and said, "Swear and I set you free: Curse Christ," Polycarp answered, "Eighty and six years have I served Him, and He did me no wrong. How can I blaspheme my King, that saved me?"

When the proconsul persevered, saying: "Swear by the Fortune of Cæsar," Polycarp answered: "If you vainly imagine that I shall swear by the Fortune of Cæsar, as you say, and suppose that I know not what I am, hear a plain answer, 'I am a Christian.' If you wish to learn the Christian's reason, give me a day and listen." The proconsul said: "It is the people you must convince." Polycarp answered: "I would have counted you worthy to be reasoned with; for we have been taught to give honour as is fit, where we can without harm, to governments and powers ordained by God, but the people I do not deem worthy to hear any defence from me."

The proconsul said: "I have beasts, and to them I will throw you, unless you repent." "Bring them in," he answered. "For repentance from the better to the worse is no change to be desired, but it is good to change from cruelty to justice."

The other spake again to him: "If you despise the beasts, I will have you consumed by fire, unless you repent." "You threaten me," answered Polycarp, "with the fire that burns for an hour and is speedily quenched; for you know nothing of the fire of the judgment to come and of eternal punishment which is reserved for the wicked. Why delay? Bring what you will."

While speaking these and many other words, he grew full of confidence and joy, and his face was filled with grace, so that it fell out that not only was he not troubled by the things said to him, but on the contrary the proconsul was amazed and sent his own herald to proclaim thrice in the midst of the stadium, "Polycarp has confessed himself to be a Christian."

Upon this proclamation of the herald the whole multitude of heathen and Jews that dwelt in Smyrna cried aloud in ungovernable fury: "This is the teacher of Asia, the father of the Christians, the destroyer of our Gods, who teaches many not to sacrifice or worship." So saying, they shouted, beseeching Philip, the Asiarch, to let loose a lion on Polycarp. However, he said it was not lawful for him to do this, as he had concluded the wild beast combat. Then they thought good to cry with one voice that Polycarp should be burnt alive. For it must needs be that the vision revealed to him on his pillow be fulfilled, when in prayer he saw it aflame, and turning to the faithful who were with him said in prophecy: "I must be burned alive."

This then was brought about with great speed, more quickly than words can say, the crowd gathering together forthwith from the shops and baths wood and fuel, the Jews being particularly zealous in the work, as is their custom. When the pyre was ready, he put off all his upper garments and undid his girdle, and endeavoured to take off his shoes, which he had not been used to do before because all the faithful used to contend with one another who should first touch his body. For even before his martyrdom he was treated with all honour for the goodness of his life. So he was immediately girded with the things devised for his burning; but when they were about to nail him to the stake as well, he said: "Leave me as I am; for He that enabled me to abide the fire will also enable me to abide at the stake unflinching without your safeguard of nails."

So they bound him without nailing him. And he, with his hands bound behind him, like a choice ram taken from a great flock for sacrifice, an acceptable whole burnt-offering prepared for God, looked up to heaven and said: "Lord God Almighty, Father of Thy well-beloved and blessed Son, Jesus Christ, through whom we have received the knowledge of Thee, God of Angels and Powers and of the whole creation and of all the race of the righteous who live before Thee, I bless Thee that Thou didst deem me worthy of this day and hour, that I should take a part among the number of the martyrs in the cup of Thy Christ to the resurrection of life eternal of soul and body in incorruption of the Holy Spirit: among whom may I be accepted before Thee today, a rich and acceptable sacrifice, as Thou didst foreordain and foreshow and fulfil, God faithful and true. For this above all I praise Thee, I bless Thee, I glorify Thee through the Eternal and Heavenly High Priest Jesus Christ, Thy well-beloved Son, through whom to Thee with Him and the Holy Spirit be glory now and for evermore. Amen."

When he had offered up the Amen, and finished his prayer, those who had charge of the fire set light to it. And a great flame blazing forth, we to whom it was given to behold, who were indeed preserved to tell the story to the rest, beheld a marvel. For the fire forming a sort of arch, like a ship's sail bellying with the wind, made a wall about the body of the martyr, which was in the midst, not like burning flesh, but like bread in the baking, or like gold and silver burning in a furnace. For we caught a most sweet perfume, like the breath of frankincense or some other precious spice.

At last when the impious people saw that his body could not be consumed by the fire they gave orders that a slaughterer should go and thrust a dagger into him. This being done there came forth a dove and such a gush of blood that it put out the fire, and all the throng marvelled that there should be so great a difference between the unbelievers and the elect; one of whom was the most admirable martyr, Polycarp, an apostolic and prophetic teacher of our time, and bishop of the Catholic Church in Smyrna. For every word that he uttered from his mouth was fulfilled then and shall be fulfilled hereafter.

But the Adversary, the malicious and wicked one who is the enemy of the race of the just, seeing the greatness of his witness, and the blamelessness of his life from the beginning, and that he was crowned with the crown of immortality, and had won a prize beyond gainsaying, made it his business that we might not even recover his body, though many were eager so to do and to touch his sacred flesh. At any rate he suggested to Nicetas, the father of Herodes and brother of Alce, to entreat the proconsul not to give us his body, "Lest," said he, "they should abandon the Crucified, and begin to worship him." The Jews made the same suggestions with much vehemence, who also watched the body, when we were about to take it from the fire, not knowing that we can never abandon Christ, who suffered for the salvation of those who are being saved throughout the whole world, the sinless for sinners, nor can we worship any other. For Him, being the Son of God, we adore, but the martyrs we love as disciples and imitators of the Lord, and rightly for their unsurpassable loyalty to their own King and Master; may it be granted us to have partnership and fellow-discipleship with them.

So the centurion, seeing the contentiousness of the Jews, set him in the midst and burnt him according to their custom. So we later took up his bones, being of more value than precious stones and more esteemed than gold, and laid them apart in a convenient place. There the Lord will grant us to gather so far as may be and to celebrate with great gladness and joy the birthday of his martyrdom, in memory of those who have fought the good fight before us and for the training and preparation of those to come.

Such is the story of the blessed Polycarp, who with the eleven from Philadelphia was martyred in Smyrna, and is more particularly remembered by all, so that he is spoken of in every place even by the Gentiles, having been not only a famous teacher, but also an illustrious martyr, whose martyrdom all desire to imitate, as being after the pattern of the Gospel of Christ. Having vanquished by his patience the unjust ruler, and thus received the crown of immortality, he rejoices greatly with the Apostles and with all the just, and glorifies the Almighty God and Father, and praises our Lord Jesus Christ, the Saviour of our souls, the Pilot of our bodies, and the Shepherd of the Catholic Church throughout the world.

You indeed made request that the events might be described to you at greater length, but we for the present have declared them to you in brief by our brother Marcion. On receiving this, send on the letter to the more distant brethren that they may glorify the Lord who makes choice of his own servants.

To Him that is able to bring us all by His grace and bounty to His eternal kingdom through His only-begotten Son Jesus Christ be glory, honour, power, and majesty for ever and ever. Salute all the saints. Those with us, and Euarestus, the writer of this, with his whole house, salute you.

The blessed Polycarp was martyred on the second day of the first part of the month Xanthicus, on the seventh day before the Kalends of March, on a High Sabbath, at the eighth hour. He was taken by Herodes, when Philip of Tralles was chief priest, in the proconsulship of Statius Quadratus, in the everlasting reign of Jesus Christ; to whom be glory, honour, majesty, and a throne eternal, from generation to generation. Amen.

# The Martyrdom of St Justin

100?–?165

Justin was one of the earliest and best known of the Apologists. He was born between 100 and 110 in Syria, of pagan parents. His early inclinations to philosophy led him to become in turn a Stoic, a Peripatetic, and a Pythagorean, but all these left him unsatisfied. He was converted to Christianity in Ephesus, about 130, following a long discussion with an old man whom he met there. Crescens the Cynic, with whom he held public disputations, is said by Eusebius to have denounced him and caused his death. At all events, he was condemned to death by the prefect Rusticus and was beheaded, with six other Christians, in Rome.

In the time of the wicked defenders of idolatry impious decrees were issued in town and country against the pious Christian folk to compel them to offer libations to vain idols. So the saints were seized and brought before the prefect of Rome, by name Rusticus.

When they were brought before the judgment seat, Rusticus the prefect said to Justin: "First of all obey the gods, and make submission to the princes."

Justin said: "To obey the commands of our Saviour Jesus Christ is not worthy of blame or condemnation."

The prefect Rusticus said: "What doctrines do you hold?"

Justin said: "I have endeavoured to make myself acquainted with all doctrines, but I have given my assent to the true doctrines of the Christians, whether they please the holders of false beliefs or no."

The prefect Rusticus said: "Do those doctrines please you, miserable man?"

Justin said: "Yes, for the belief in accordance with which I follow them is right."

The prefect Rusticus said: "What belief do you mean?"

Justin said: "That which we religiously profess concerning the God of the Christians, in whom we believe, one God, existing from the beginning, Maker and Artificer of the whole creation, seen and unseen; and concerning our Lord Jesus Christ, the Son of God, who hath also been proclaimed aforetime by the prophets as about to come to the race of men for herald of salvation and for master of true disciples. And I, being but a man, regard what I say to be of little worth in comparison of His infinite Godhead, but there is a power in prophecy, and that I acknowledge; therein hath proclamation been made aforetime of Him of whom I just spoke as the Son of God. For I know that from the beginning the prophets foretold His coming among men."

The prefect Rusticus said: "Where do ye meet together?"

Justin said: "Where each wills and can. Do you really think that we all meet in the same place? Not so: for the God of the Christians is not confined by place, but being unseen fills heaven and earth, and is worshipped and glorified by the faithful everywhere."

The prefect Rusticus said: "Tell me, where do ye meet, or in what place do you gather your disciples?"

Justin said: "I lodge above in the house of Martin, near the baths of Timothy, and during all this time (this is my second visit to Rome) I have known no other place of meeting but his house. And if any wished to come to me, I imparted to him the word of truth."

Rusticus said: "To come to the point then, are you a Christian?"

Justin said: "Yes, I am a Christian."

The prefect Rusticus said to Chariton: "Tell me further, Chariton, are you also a Christian?"

Chariton said: "I am a Christian by God's command."

The prefect Rusticus said to Charito: "What do you say, Charito?"

Charito said: "I am a Christian by God's gift."

Rusticus said to Euelpistus: "And what are you?"

Euelpistus, a slave of Cæsar, answered: "I also am a Christian, freed by Christ, and share by the grace of Christ in the same hope."

The prefect Rusticus said to Hierax: "Are you also a Christian?"

Hierax said: "Yes, I am a Christian, for I worship and adore the same God."

The prefect Rusticus said: "Did Justin make you Christians?"

Hierax said: "I was, and shall ever be, a Christian."

A man called Pæon stood up and said: "I also am a Christian."

The prefect Rusticus said: "Who taught you?"

Pæon said: "I received from my parents this good confession."

Euelpistus said: "I listened indeed gladly to the words of Justin, but I too received Christianity from my parents."

The prefect Rusticus said: "Where are your parents?"

Euelpistus said: "In Cappadocia."

Rusticus said to Hierax: "Where are your parents?" He answered, saying: "Our true father is Christ, and our mother our faith in Him. My earthly parents are dead, and I was dragged away from Iconium in Phrygia before coming hither."

The prefect Rusticus said to Liberian: "And what do you say? Are you a Christian? Are you an unbeliever like the rest?"

Liberian said: "I also am a Christian; for I am a believer and adore the only true God."

The prefect said to Justin: "Listen, you that are said to be a learned man, and think that you are acquainted with true doctrine, if you shall be scourged and beheaded, are you persuaded that you will ascend to heaven?"

Justin said: "I hope if I endure these things to have His gifts. For I know that for all who so live there abides until the consummation of the whole world the free gift of God."

The prefect Rusticus said: "Do you then think that you will ascend to heaven, to receive certain rewards?"

Justin said: "I do not think, I know and am fully persuaded."

The prefect Rusticus said: "Let us now come to the pressing matter in hand. Agree together and sacrifice with one accord to the gods."

Justin said: "No one who is rightly minded turns from true belief to false."

The prefect Rusticus said: "If ye do not obey, ye shall be punished without mercy."

Justin said: "If we are punished for the sake of our Lord Jesus Christ we hope to be saved, for this shall be our salvation and confidence before the more terrible judgment-seat of our Lord and Saviour which shall judge the whole world." So also said the other martyrs: "Do what you will. For we are Christians and offer no sacrifice to idols."

Rusticus the prefect gave sentence: "Let those who will not sacrifice to the gods and yield to the command of the Emperor be scourged and led away to be beheaded in accordance with the laws."

The holy martyrs went out, glorifying God, to the customary place and were beheaded, and fulfilled their testimony by the confession of their Saviour. And some of the faithful took their bodies by stealth and laid them in a convenient place, the grace of our Lord Jesus Christ working with them, to Whom be glory for ever and ever. Amen.

# CLEMENT OF ALEXANDRIA

(See page 48.)

## In Praise of Martyrdom

FROM *The Miscellanies*

We call martyrdom perfection, not because the man comes to the end of his life as others, but because he has exhibited the perfect work of love. And the ancients laud the death of those among the Greeks who died in war, not that they advised people to die a violent death, but because he who ends his life in war is released without the dread of dying, severed from the body without experiencing previous suffering or being enfeebled in his soul, as the people that suffer in diseases. For they depart in a state of effeminacy and desiring to live, and therefore they do not yield up their soul pure, but bearing their lusts with it like weights of lead, all but those who have been conspicuous in virtue. Some die in battle with their lusts, these being in no respect different from what they would have been if they had wasted away by disease.

If the confession to God is martyrdom, each soul which has lived purely in the knowledge of God, which has obeyed the commandments, is a witness both by life and word, in whatever way it may be released from the body, shedding faith as blood along its whole life till its departure.

You see that martyrdom for love's sake is taught. And should you wish to be a martyr for the recompense of advantages, you shall hear again, "For we are saved by hope; but hope that is seen is not hope: for what a man seeth why doth he yet hope for? But if we hope for that we see not, then do we with patience wait for it." "But if we also suffer for righteousness' sake," says Peter, "blessed are we. Be not afraid of their fear, neither be troubled. But sanctify the Lord in your hearts: and be ready always to give an answer to him that asks a reason of the hope that is in you, but with meekness and fear, having a good conscience."

So the church is full of those, as well chaste women as men, who all their life have courted the death which raises up to Christ. For the individual whose life is framed as ours is may philosophize without learning, whether barbarian, whether Greek, whether slave, whether an old man, or a boy, or a woman. For self-control is common to all human beings who have made choice of it. And we admit that the same nature exists in every race, and the same virtue. As far as respects human nature, the woman does not possess one nature and the man exhibit another, but the same, so also with virtue. If, consequently, self-restraint and righteousness, and whatever qualities are regarded as following them, are the virtues of the male, it belongs to the male alone to be virtuous, and to the woman to be licentious and unjust. But it is offensive even to say this. Accordingly every woman is to practise self-restraint and righteousness, and every other virtue, as well as man, both bond and free; since it is a fit consequence that the same nature possesses one and the same virtue.

# Letter from the Churches of Lyons and Vienne

177

This letter, describing the martyrdom of St Pothinus and others, was possibly carried to Pope Eleutherius by St Irenaeus (see page 335), who succeeded Pothinus as bishop of Lyons. Certainly Irenaeus, a disciple of St Polycarp, carried a letter to the Pope, concerning the Montanistic troubles, from the martyrs of Lyons, most of whom were still in prison.

The servants of Christ dwelling in Vienne and Lyons to the brethren in Asia and Phrygia who have the same faith as we in redemption and the same hope, peace and grace and glory from God the Father and our Lord Christ Jesus. . . . The greatness of the tribulation here, and the exceeding wrath of the heathen against the saints, and all that the blessed martyrs suffered, neither are we capable of describing accurately, nor can it be compassed in writing.

For the Adversary fell upon us with all his strength, making already a prelude to his coming in full force hereafter, and went to all lengths, practising and training his own against the servants of God, so that not only were we banished from houses and baths and market-places, but it was forbidden for any of us to be seen at all in any place whatsoever. But the grace of God took the field against him, and protected the weak, and ranged on the other side steadfast pillars able through their endurance to draw on themselves all the onset of the Evil One; who also closed with him, bearing all kind of reproach and torment; who also, counting great things as small, made haste towards Christ, showing in very truth that "the sufferings of this present time are not worthy to be compared with the glory that shall be revealed in us."

And in the first place they endured nobly what the crowd in general heaped upon them, taunts, blows, halings, robberies, stone-throwings, beleaguerings, and all else that a furious multitude inflicts on private and public enemies. And then they were brought into the market-place by the tribune of the soldiers and the magistrates of the city, and after being examined in the presence of the whole multitude and making their confession were shut up in prison until the arrival of the governor. Afterwards they were brought before the governor, and he was showing all the usual cruelty towards us. Now among the brethren was Vettius Epagathus, one filled with the fullness of love towards God and his neighbour, whose conversation had been so rightly ordered that though young he did not fall below the witness borne to old Zacharias, he had indeed "walked in all the commandments and ordinances of the Lord blameless," and untiring in all service towards his neighbour, having great zeal for God and "fervent in the spirit." He being of this sort did not suffer the judgment so unreasonably being passed against us, but was indignant on our behalf, and claimed to be heard himself, pleading in defence of the brethren that there was nothing godless or impious about us. When those about the tribunal shouted him down (for he was a man of mark), and the governor did not allow the just claim he put forward, but asked no more than this, whether he too were a Christian, he confessed in a loud voice and was added to the company of the martyrs. And he was styled the advocate of the Christians, having indeed the Advocate in himself, even the Spirit of Zacharias, which he showed through the fullness of his love, being well pleased even to lay down his own life for the defence of the brethren. For he was and is a true disciple of Christ, "following the Lamb whithersoever He goeth."

After this the rest were divided: some were protomartyrs manifest and ready, who with all zeal fulfilled their confession even unto martyrdom; then too were manifested the unready, untrained, and still feeble, unable to bear the strain of a great contest. Of these about ten in number miscarried, who also wrought in us great sorrow and grief immeasurable, and checked the zeal of those that had not yet been taken, but, in spite of all sorts of dreadful sufferings, nevertheless accompanied the martyrs and refused to leave them. Then we were all greatly distraught from uncertainty about the confession, not from fear of the torments that were coming upon us, but from looking to the end and dreading lest some should fall away. There were taken, however, day by day, those who were worthy, and these filled up their number, so that there were gathered from the two Churches all persons of merit by whom more particularly affairs had been ordered here. There were taken, too, certain pagan slaves of ours, since the governor had given public orders for all of us to be sought out. These by the lying in wait of Satan, in fear of the tortures which they saw the saints suffering, and urged thereto by the soldiers, falsely charged us with Thyestean banquets and Oedipodean unions and with other crimes which we are not permitted to mention or imagine, nor even to believe that such things ever happened among men.

On the spread of these reports all were like wild beasts against us, so that some who had formerly behaved with moderation out of friendship were then greatly enraged and gnashed their teeth at us. Then was fulfilled what was spoken by our Lord, that there should come a time when "whosoever killeth you will think that he doeth God service."

After this the holy martyrs endured tortures beyond all telling, Satan being desirous that some blasphemous word should escape their lips also. Beyond measure all the fury of crowd and governor and soldiers fell on Sanctus, the deacon from Vienne, and on Maturus, newly baptized, but a noble combatant, and on Attalus, a native of Pergamus, who had always been "a pillar and stay" of the people here, and on Blandina, through whom Christ made manifest that what things appear paltry and uncomely and contemptible are accounted of great honour with God, for their love to Him, which does not glory in appearance but is shown in power.

For when we were all in fear, and her mistress according to the flesh, herself a combatant among the martyrs, was in agony lest Blandina should not be able from weakness of body even to make her confession boldly, she was filled with so much power that even those who tortured her in relays in every way from morning until evening were faint and weary. Indeed they themselves confessed that they were beaten, having no longer any more that they might do to her, wondering that she remained alive, all her body being broken and torn, and testifying that one kind of torture, let alone so many and so grievous, was enough to release her soul. But the blessed woman, as a noble athlete, renewed her strength in her confession, and it was refreshment and peace and freedom from pain amid her sufferings to repeat, "I am a Christian, and there is no evil done among us."

And Sanctus too endured nobly beyond all measure and all human patience all outrages at the hands of men, and, when the wicked hoped that because of the continuance and severity of the tortures something unseemly would be heard from him, with such constancy did he range himself against them that he uttered not his own name nor the name of the nation or city whence he came, nor whether he were bond or free; but to all questions answered in the Latin tongue, "I am a Christian." This he confessed repeatedly to serve for name and city and race and everything, and the heathen heard from him no other word.

Whence there arose great rivalry in the governor and the tormentors against him, so that when they had nothing more that they could do to him at the last they applied red-hot brazen plates to the most tender parts of his body. And these indeed were burned, but he himself continued unbent and unyielding, stout in his confession, bedewed and strengthened by the heavenly fountain of the water of life issuing from the belly of the Christ. His poor body was witness to his sufferings, for it was nothing but wound and weal, bent double, and robbed of the outward form of humanity, his body wherein Christ suffered and wrought great wonders, destroying the Adversary, and showing as a pattern to the rest that there is nothing terrible where is the love of the Father, nothing painful where the glory of Christ. For when the wicked some days later tortured the martyr again and thought that his body being swollen and inflamed, if they applied the same torments they would overcome him, since he could not bear even a touch of the hand, or that by dying under torture he would frighten the rest, nothing of the sort happened in his case. Nay more, beyond all human imagining his poor body revived and was restored in the later trial, and recovered its former appearance and the use of the limbs, so that the second torture became to him through the grace of Christ not a torment but a cure.

Moreover, there was a certain Biblias, one of those who had denied the faith, and the Devil, who thought that he had already devoured her, wishing to damn her by blasphemy as well, brought her to torture, that he might force her to say impious things about us, being to start with frail and timid.

But she, while she was being tortured returned to her sober mind and woke as it were from a deep slumber, being reminded by her temporal punishment of the eternal torment in hell, and directly contradicted the blasphemers, saying: "How can those eat children, who are forbidden to eat the blood even of brute beasts?" And from this moment she confessed herself a Christian and was added to the company of the martyrs.

When the tyrants' cruelties were made of none effect by Christ through the patience of the martyrs, the Devil set about contriving other devices, shutting them up in darkness in the foulest part of the prison, stretching their feet, strained to the fifth hole, in the stocks; with the other outrages which attendants angry, and full of the Devil besides, are wont to inflict on prisoners; so that most of them were suffocated in the prison, as many as the Lord, manifesting forth His glory, wished so to pass away. For some, after being so cruelly tormented that it did not seem as if they could live any longer even if every attention were given them, lingered on in prison, destitute of all human care, but confirmed by the Lord, and strengthened in body and soul, encouraging and consoling the rest. Others, young and lately taken, whose bodies had not been already inured to torture, were unable to bear the burden of confinement and died there.

Blessed Pothinus, who had been entrusted with the charge of the bishopric in Lyons, being over ninety years of age and very sick in body, scarcely breathing from the sickness aforesaid, but strengthened by zeal of the spirit from his vehement desire for martyrdom, was dragged with the others onto the tribunal, his body fainting with old age and disease, but his soul sustained within him, that thereby Christ might triumph. He was conveyed by the soldiers onto the tribunal, accompanied by the magistrates of the city and the whole multitude who cried this and that; accusing him of being also one of Christ's followers, and he "witnessed a good confession." Being questioned by the governor, who was the God of the Christians, he answered: "If you are worthy, you shall know." After this he was hustled without mercy, and suffered hurts of all kinds: for those who were close showed him all manner of insolence with hand and foot, not reverencing his years, and those at a distance hurled at him anything each might have ready, all deeming that anyone was guilty of great offence and impiety, who was behindhand in brutality towards him; for they thought in this way to avenge their gods. So he was cast scarcely breathing into the prison, and after two days expired.

And here took place a great dispensation of God, and there was manifested the immeasurable mercy of Christ, after a fashion rarely known among the brotherhood, but worthy of Christ's devising. For those who when first taken denied the faith were imprisoned like the rest and shared their sufferings; for their denial was of no profit to them at all at that time, since those who confessed to be what indeed they were were imprisoned as Christians, having no other charge brought against them, while the others were detained as murderers and villains, being punished twice as hardly as the rest. For those were comforted by the joy of their martyrdom, and the hope of the promises, and by love towards Christ, and the Spirit of the Father, whereas these were greatly tormented by their conscience, so that as they passed they were easily distinguished by their looks from all the rest. For those advanced full of joy, having in their looks a mingling of majesty and great beauty, so that even their chains were worn by them as a comely ornament, as for a bride adorned with fringed raiment of gold richly wrought, exhaling at the same time the "sweet savour of Christ," so that some thought they had been anointed with perfume of this world, but these, downcast, dejected, ill-favoured, full of all unseemliness, taunted beside by the heathen as base and cowardly, bearing the reproach of murderers, but having lost their universally honourable and glorious and life-giving name. The rest, seeing this, were strengthened, and those who were taken afterwards made their confession undoubtingly, giving not so much as a thought to the Devil's arguments. . . .

After this their martyrdoms were parcelled into deaths of all sorts. For, plaiting one crown of different colours and all kinds of flowers, they offered it to the Father; it was needful indeed that the noble athletes should endure a manifold conflict and win a great victory before they received the great crown of immortality.

Maturus, then, and Sanctus and Blandina and Attalus were taken into the amphitheatre to the beasts to give the heathen a public spectacle of cruelty, a special day being appointed because of our brothers for a fight with beasts. And Maturus and Sanctus again went in the amphitheatre through every form of torture, as though they had suffered nothing at all before; or rather, as having overcome the Adversary already in many bouts, and contending now for the final crown of victory, they bore the usual running of the gauntlet of whips, and the mauling by the beasts, and everything else that the maddened people, on this side or on that, clamoured for and demanded, and on the top of all the iron chair, whereon their bodies were roasted and filled with the savour the nostrils of the people. But they did not rest even so, but were more mad than ever, in their desire to overcome the martyrs' endurance, yet not even then did they hear from Sanctus aught else save the word of his confession he had been wont to utter from the beginning. These, then, after their spirits had long held out through a great contest, when in place of all the diversity of single combats they had been throughout that day a spectacle to the world, were offered up at last. But Blandina was exposed, hung on a stake, to be the food of the beasts let loose on her. Alike by the sight of her hanging in the form of a cross and by her earnest prayer she put much heart in the combatants; for they saw during the contest even with the eyes of flesh in the person of their sister Him who was crucified for them, to assure those who believed on Him that everyone who suffereth for the glory of Christ hath forever fellowship with the living God. And as none of the beasts at that time touched her, she was taken down from the stake and brought back again to the prison, to await another contest, that having won in many trials she might make that "crooked Serpent's" condemnation irreversible, and inspire her brethren—she, the little, the weak, the contemptible—who had put on Christ, the great and invincible athlete, and had worsted in many bouts the Adversary, and through conflict crowned herself with the crown of immortality.

Attalus, too, being loudly called for by the crowd (for he was a man of repute), entered the arena as a combatant well-prepared by his good conscience, for he was soundly trained in the Christian discipline, and had ever been a witness to truth amongst us. He was being led around the amphitheatre with a placard preceding him, on which was written in Latin: "This is Attalus the Christian," the people being violently inflamed against him, when the governor, learning that he was a Roman citizen, ordered him to be remanded with the rest that were in the prison, and, having written a dispatch to Cæsar concerning them, waited his sentence.

The interval was not idle nor unfruitful to them, but through their patience was made manifest the immeasurable mercy of Christ. For the dead were made alive through the living, and martyrs showed kindness to those who were not martyrs, and there was much joy in the heart of the Virgin Mother, in recovering alive those untimely births she had cast forth as dead. For through them the most part of those who had denied the faith entered again into their mother's womb, and were conceived again, and quickened again, and learned to make their confession, and, alive already and braced, came to the tribunal (for He who hath no pleasure in the death of the wicked made sweet their bitterness, and God was gracious to them unto repentance), that they might again be questioned by the governor. For the command of Cæsar was that these should be beheaded, but that those who denied the faith should be set free. So as it was the beginning of the festival here (it is thronged by an assemblage of all peoples), the governor brought the blessed ones to the tribunal, making a gazing-stock and a show of them to the multitude. Therefore he examined them again, and beheaded those who appeared to possess Roman citizenship, and sent the rest to the beasts.

And Christ was greatly glorified in those who had formerly denied the faith, but then contrary to the expectation of the heathen made their confession. For they were privately examined with the intent they should be set free, and, confessing, were added to the company of the martyrs. There remained outside those who had never had even a vestige of the faith, nor any knowledge of the wedding garment, nor any thought of the fear of God, but through their conversation blasphemed the Way, that is the sons of perdition.

All the rest were added to the Church. As they were being examined, a certain Alexander, Phrygian by birth, doctor by profession, who had spent many years in the Gauls, and was known to almost all for his love to God and his boldness in preaching the Word (for he was not without a share in the Apostolic gift), was standing by the tribunal and urging them by signs to confession, and so became manifest to those surrounding the tribunal as one in travail. The multitude, angered at the renewed confession of those who had formerly denied the faith, clamoured against Alexander as the cause of this. So when the governor had ordered him to be set before him, and asked him who he was, Alexander said: "A Christian." The governor in anger condemned him to the beasts, and on the next day he entered the arena with Attalus. For to gratify the people the governor had given Attalus also to the beasts, for the second time. And when they had gone through all the instruments devised for torture in the amphitheatre, and had endured a contest very great, they also were offered up at last. Alexander, indeed, neither groaned nor uttered any sound at all, but communed in his heart with God. But Attalus, when he had been placed in the iron chair, and was burning everywhere, as the savour from his body was rising upward, said to the multitude in the Latin tongue: "Lo! as for eating of men, this is what you yourselves do; but we neither eat men nor work any other wickedness." And being asked what was the name of God, he answered: "God hath no name as man hath."

After all these, on the last day of the single combats, Blandina was again brought in with Ponticus, a boy of about fifteen. They had also been led in daily to look upon the torture of the rest, and their enemies would fain have forced them to swear by their idols; but because they continued steadfast and made nought of them, the multitude was enraged against them, so that they neither pitied the age of the boy, nor reverenced the sex of the woman. They exposed them to every terror, they made them pass through every torment in turn, again and again constraining them to swear, but unable to achieve their purpose. For Ponticus, encouraged by his sister, so that even the heathen saw that she was exhorting and strengthening him, after nobly enduring every torment, gave up the ghost.

The blessed Blandina last of all, like a noble mother that has encouraged her children and sent them before her crowned with victory to the King, retracing herself also all her children's battles, hastened towards them, rejoicing and triumphing in her departure, as though she were called to a marriage supper, instead of being cast to the beasts. After the whips, after the beasts, after the frying-pan, she was thrown at last into a net, and cast before a bull. And after being tossed for some long time by the beast, having no further sense of what was happening because of her hope and hold on the things she had believed, and because of her communing with Christ, she was herself also offered up, the very heathen confessing that they had never known a woman endure so many and so great sufferings.

But not even so were their madness and savagery towards the saints appeased. For wild and barbarous people stirred up by that wild Beast were hard to satisfy, and their cruelty found another and peculiar outlet upon the bodies of the dead. For because they lacked human reason their defeat did not shame them, rather it fired their beast-like fury, both governor and people showing towards us the same undeserved hatred, that the Scripture might be fulfilled: "He that is wicked, let him do wickedly still, and he that is righteous let him do righteousness still." For those that were suffocated in the prison they threw to the dogs, watching carefully by night and day, lest we should give any of them burial. After that they exposed what the beasts and the fire had left, part torn, part charred, and the heads of the rest with the trunks; these likewise they left unburied, and watched them for many days with a guard of soldiers. Some raged and gnashed their teeth at the dead, seeking to take some more exquisite revenge upon them. Others laughed and mocked, magnifying at the same time their idols, and attributing to them the punishment of the martyrs. Others again who were more reasonable and seemed to have some degree of feeling for us reproached us, repeating: "Where is their God, and how did their religion which they preferred even to their lives profit them?" On their side such were the varieties of behaviour; on ours there was great sorrow because we could not bestow the bodies in the earth. For night did not help us towards this, nor money persuade, nor prayer shame, but they watched every way, as though they would derive some great profit from the martyrs' loss of burial. . . . So the bodies of the martyrs, after being subjected to all kinds of contumely and exposed for six days, were then burnt and reduced to ashes by the impious, and swept into the river Rhone which flows hard by, that not a fragment of them might be left on earth. And they planned this, as though they could get the better of God, and rob them of the other Life; that, in their own words, "They may have no hope of resurrection, trusting in which they introduce among us a strange and new religion, and despise tortures, going readily and with joy to death. Let us see now whether they will rise again and whether their God can help them and deliver them from our hands." . . .

So completely did they emulate and imitate Christ, who "being in the form of God thought it not a prize to be on an equality with God," that, though they had reached such a height of glory and had borne witness not once nor twice but often, and had been brought back alive from the beasts, bearing about them burns and weals and wounds, they neither proclaimed themselves to be martyrs, nor suffered us to address them by that name, but, if ever any one of us by letter or by word of mouth called them martyrs, they rebuked him sharply. For they gladly yielded the title of Martyr to Christ, the faithful and true Witness and first-begotten of the dead and Prince of the Life of God, and they remembered the martyrs already departed, and said: "They are already martyrs, whom Christ thought worthy to be taken up in the hour of their confession, having sealed their witness by their death, but we are ordinary humble confessors." And with tears they exhorted the brethren, beseeching them that earnest prayer might be offered for them to be made perfect.

And, though they showed the power of martyrdom in deed, speaking with much boldness to all the heathen, and made manifest their nobleness by their patience and fearlessness and fortitude, yet they begged not to be given the title of Martyr among the brethren, being filled with the fear of God. . . .

They humbled themselves under the mighty Hand, by which they have now been greatly exalted. Then, however, they gave a reason for their faith to all, but accused none; they loosed all, but bound none; and prayed for those who cruelly used them, as did Stephen, the perfect martyr: "Lord, lay not this sin to their charge." And if he prayed for those who stoned him, how much more for the brethren. . . .

This on account of the sincerity of their love was the greatest of all their contests with the Devil, that the Beast, being throttled, might disgorge alive those whom he at first thought to have devoured. For they did not boast themselves against the fallen, but wherein they themselves abounded gave to those that lacked, having a mother's tender mercy, and shedding many tears on their behalf unto the Father.

They asked for life, and He gave it them, which they shared with their neighbours, and departed to God all ways victorious. Having loved peace ever, and ever commended peace to us, they went in peace to God, leaving no sorrow to their Mother, nor strife and war to their brethren, but joy and peace and concord and love.

# The Acts of the Scillitan Saints

July 17, 180

Scillium was a see in Africa Proconsularis, suffragan of Carthage. The Acts of Martyrdom of the Christians condemned to death by the sword in that place are the most ancient Acts in existence for the Roman province of Africa. They, like the Acts of St Cyprian, are among the best examples of that class of Acts which is founded on official reports, but are even more perfect than those, in the sense that there is even less added by the editor. There are numerous versions; that from which the text is taken is from a manuscript in the British Museum discovered by the Dean of Wells.

In the consulship of Praesens, then consul for the second time, and Claudian, on the seventeenth of July, Speratus, Nartzalus and Cittinus, Donata, Secunda, Vestia were brought to trial at Carthage in the council-chamber. The proconsul Saturninus said to them: "You may merit the indulgence of our Lord the Emperor, if you return to a right mind."

Speratus said: "We have never done harm to any, we have never lent ourselves to wickedness; we have never spoken ill of any, but have given thanks when ill-treated, because we hold our own Emperor in honour."

The proconsul Saturninus said: "We also are religious people, and our religion is simple, and we swear by the genius of our Lord the Emperor, and pray for his safety, as you also ought to do."

Speratus said: "If you will give me a quiet hearing, I will tell you the mystery of simplicity."

Saturninus said: "If you begin to speak evil of our sacred rites, I will give you no hearing; but swear rather by the genius of our Lord the Emperor."

Speratus said: "I do not recognize the empire of this world; but rather I serve that God whom no man has seen nor can see. I have not stolen, but if I buy anything, I pay the tax, because I recognize my Lord, the King of kings and Emperor of all peoples."

The proconsul Saturninus said to the rest: "Cease to be of this persuasion."

Speratus said: "The persuasion that we should do murder, or bear false witness, that is evil."

The proconsul Saturninus said: "Have no part in this madness."

Cittinus said: "We have none other to fear save the Lord our God, who is in heaven."

Donata said: "Give honour to Cæsar as unto Cæsar, but fear to God."

Vestia said: "I am a Christian."

Secunda said: "I wish to be none other than what I am."

The proconsul Saturninus said to Speratus: "Do you persist in remaining a Christian?"

Speratus said: "I am a Christian." And all consented thereto.

The proconsul Saturninus said: "Do you desire any space for consideration?"

Speratus said: "When the right is so clear, there is nothing to consider."

The proconsul Saturninus said: "What have you in your case?"

Speratus said: "The Books, and the letters of a just man, one Paul."

The proconsul Saturninus said: "Take a reprieve of thirty days and think it over."

Speratus again said: "I am a Christian." And all were of one mind with him.

The proconsul Saturninus read out the sentence from his notebook: "Whereas Speratus, Nartzalus, Cittinus, Donata, Vestia, Secunda, and the rest have confessed that they live in accordance with the religious rites of the Christians, and, when an opportunity was given them of returning to the usage of the Romans, persevered in their obstinacy, it is our pleasure that they should suffer by the sword."

Speratus said: "Thanks be to God!"

Nartzalus said: "Today we are martyrs in heaven: thanks be to God!"

The proconsul Saturninus commanded that proclamation be made by the herald: "I have commanded that Speratus, Nartzalus, Cittinus, Veturius, Felix, Aquilinus, Laetantius, Januaria, Generosa, Vestia, Donata, Secunda be led forth to execution."

They all said: "Thanks be to God!"

And so all are crowned with martyrdom together, and reign with the Father and Son and Holy Spirit for ever and ever. Amen.

# ORIGEN

(See page 66.)

## FROM Exhortation to Martyrdom

The *Exhortation* was addressed to Origen's friend and patron, Ambrosius, and to Protoctetus, bishop of Caesarea, during the persecutions under Maximinus Thrax (emperor 235–38).

We must remember that we have sinned and that it is impossible to obtain forgiveness of sins without baptism, and that according to the evangelical laws it is impossible to be baptized a second time with water and the Spirit for the forgiveness of sins, and therefore the baptism of martyrdom is given us. For thus it has been called, as may be clearly gathered from the passage: "Can ye drink of the cup that I drink of, and be baptized with the baptism that I am baptized with?" And in another place it is said: "But I have a baptism to be baptized with; and how am I straightened until it be accomplished!" For be sure that just as the expiation of the Cross was for the whole world, it (the baptism of martyrdom) is for the cure of many who are thereby cleansed. For as according to the law of Moses those placed near the altar are seen to minister forgiveness of sins to others through the blood of bulls and goats, so the souls of those who have suffered on account of the testimony of Jesus are not in vain near that altar in heaven but minister forgiveness of sins to those who pray. And at the same time we know that just as the High Priest, Jesus Christ, offered Himself as a sacrifice, so the priests, of whom He is the High Priest, offer themselves as sacrifices, and on account of this sacrifice they are at the altar as in their proper place.

Just as we have been redeemed with the precious blood of Christ, who received the name that is above every name, so by the precious blood of the martyrs will others be redeemed.

# FROM Homilies on Numbers

. . . Concerning the martyrs, the Apostle John writes in the Apocalypse that the souls of those who have been slain for the name of the Lord Jesus are present at the altar; but he who is present at the altar is shown to perform the duties of priest. But the duty of a priest is to make intercession for the sins of the people. Wherefore I fear, lest, perchance, inasmuch as there are made no martyrs, and sacrifices of saints are not offered for our sins, we will not receive remission of our sins. And therefore I fear, lest our sins remaining in us, it may happen to us what the Jews said of themselves, that not having an altar, nor a temple, nor priesthood, and therefore not offering sacrifices, our sins remain in us, and so no forgiveness is obtained. . . . And therefore the Devil, knowing that remission of sins is obtained by the passion of martyrdom, is not willing to raise public persecutions against us by the heathen.

# The Martyrdom of Saints Perpetua and Felicitas

died 203

Among the first victims of the persecution of Septimius Severus at Carthage were five catechumens, among them Perpetua, a high-born young woman of pagan parentage, and a slave, Felicitas. Felicitas was eight months pregnant; Perpetua had a suckling baby. The two women were baptized between the time of their arrest and their imprisonment. The early chapters of this account were written by Perpetua, then follow several written by St Saturus, her teacher, while the remainder are by an unknown editor who, according to some authorities, might have been Tertullian.

If the ancient examples of faith, such as both testified to the grace of God, and wrought the edification of man, have for this cause been set out in writing that the reading of them may revive the past and so both God be glorified and man strengthened, why should not new examples be set out equally suitable to both those ends? For these in like manner will some day be old and needful for posterity, though in their own time because of the veneration secured to antiquity they are held in less esteem. But let them see to this who determine the one power of the one Spirit by times and seasons: since the more recent things should rather be deemed the greater, as being "later than the last." This follows from the pre-eminence of grace promised at the last lap of the world's race. For "In the last days, saith the Lord, I will pour forth of My Spirit upon all flesh, and their sons and their daughters shall prophesy: and on My servants and on My handmaidens will I pour forth of My Spirit: and their young men shall see visions, and their old men shall dream dreams." And so we who recognize and hold in honour not new prophecies only but new visions as alike promised, and count all the rest of the powers of the Holy Spirit as intended for the equipment of the Church, to which the same Spirit was sent bestowing all gifts upon all as the Lord dealt to each man, we cannot but set these out and make them famous by recital to the glory of God. So shall no weak or despairing faith suppose that supernatural grace, in excellency of martyrdoms or revelations, was found among the ancients only; for God ever works what He has promised, to unbelievers a witness, to believers a blessing. And so "what we have heard and handled declare we unto you also," brothers and little children, "that ye also" who were their eyewitnesses may be reminded of the glory of the Lord, and you who now learn by the ear "may have fellowship with" the holy martyrs, and through them with the Lord Jesus Christ, to whom belong splendour and honour for ever and ever. Amen.

Certain young catechumens were arrested, Revocatus and his fellow-slave Felicitas, Saturninus, and Secundulus. Among these also Vibia Perpetua, well-born, liberally educated, honourably married, having father and mother, and two brothers, one like herself a catechumen, and an infant son at the breast. She was about twenty-two years of age. The whole story of her martyrdom is from this point onwards told by herself, as she left it written, hand and conception being alike her own.

"When I was still," she says, "with my companions, and my father in his affection for me was endeavouring to upset me by arguments and overthrow my resolution, 'Father,' I said, 'do you see this vessel, for instance, lying here, waterpot or whatever it may be?' 'I see it,' he said. And I said to him, 'Can it be called by any other name than what it is?' And he answered, 'No.' 'So also I cannot call myself anything else than what I am, a Christian.'

"Then my father, furious at the word 'Christian,' threw himself upon me as though to pluck out my eyes; but he was satisfied with annoying me; he was in fact vanquished, he and his Devil's arguments. Then I thanked the Lord for being parted for a few days from my father, and was refreshed by his absence. During those few days we were baptized, and the Holy Spirit bade me make no other petition after the holy water save for bodily endurance. A few days after we were lodged in prison; and I was in great fear, because I had never known such darkness. What a day of horror! Terrible heat, thanks to the crowds! Rough handling by the soldiers! To crown all I was tormented there by anxiety for my baby. Then Tertius and Pomponius, those blessed deacons who were ministering to us, paid for us to be removed for a few hours to a better part of the prison and refresh ourselves. Then all went out of the prison and were left to themselves. My baby was brought to me, and I suckled him, for he was already faint for want of food. I spoke anxiously to my mother on his behalf, and strengthened my brother, and commended my son to their charge. I was pining because I saw them pine on my account. Such anxieties I suffered for many days; and I obtained leave for my baby to remain in the prison with me; and I at once recovered my health, and was relieved of my trouble and anxiety for my baby; and my prison suddenly became a palace to me, and I would rather have been there than anywhere else.

"Then my brother said to me: 'Lady sister, you are now in great honour, so great indeed that you may well pray for a vision and may well be shown whether suffering or release be in store for you.' And I who knew myself to have speech of the Lord, for whose sake I had gone through so much, gave confident promise in return, saying: 'Tomorrow I will bring you word.' And I made request, and this was shown me. I saw a brazen ladder of wondrous length reaching up to heaven, but so narrow that only one could ascend at once; and on the sides of the ladder were fastened all kinds of iron weapons. There were swords, lances, hooks, daggers, so that if anyone went up carelessly or without looking upwards he was mangled and his flesh caught on the weapons. And just beneath the ladder was a dragon crouching of wondrous size who lay in wait for those going up and sought to frighten them from going up. Now Saturus went up first, who had given himself up for our sakes of his own accord, because our faith had been of his own building, and he had not been present when we were seized. And he reached the top of the ladder, and turned, and said to me: 'Perpetua, I await you; but see that the dragon bite you not.' And I said: 'In the name of Jesus Christ he will not hurt me.' And he put out his head gently, as if afraid of me, just at the foot of the ladder; and as though I were treading on the first step, I trod on his head. And I went up, and saw a vast expanse of garden, and in the midst a man sitting with white hair, in the dress of a shepherd, a tall man, milking sheep; and round about were many thousands clad in white. And he raised his head, and looked upon me, and said: 'You have well come, my child.' And he called me, and gave me a morsel of the milk which he was milking and I received it in my joined hands, and ate; and all they that stood around said: 'Amen.' And at the sound of the word I woke, still eating something sweet. And at once I told my brother, and we understood that we must suffer, and henceforward began to have no hope in this world.

"After a few days a rumour ran that we were to be examined. Moreover, my father arrived from the city, worn with trouble, and came up the hill to see me, that he might overthrow my resolution, saying: 'Daughter, pity my white hairs! Pity your father, if I am worthy to be called father by you; if with these hands I have brought you up to this your prime of life, if I have preferred you to all your brothers! Give me not over to the reproach of men! Look upon your brothers, look upon your mother and your mother's sister, look upon your son who cannot live after you are gone! Lay aside your pride, do not ruin all of us, for none of us will ever speak freely again, if anything happen to you!' So spoke my father in his love for me, kissing my hands, and casting himself at my feet; and with tears called me by the name not of daughter but of lady. And I grieved for my father's sake, because he alone of all my kindred would not have joy in my suffering. And I comforted him, saying: 'It shall happen on that platform as God shall choose; for know well that we lie not in our own power but in the power of God.' And, full of sorrow, he left me.

"On another day when we were having our midday meal, we were suddenly hurried off to be examined; and we came to the market-place. Forthwith a rumour ran through the neighbouring parts of the market-place, and a vast crowd gathered. We went up onto the platform. The others, on being questioned, confessed their faith. So it came to my turn. And there was my father with my child, and he drew me down from the step, beseeching me: 'Have pity on your baby.' And the procurator Hilarian, who had then received the power of life and death in the room of the late proconsul Minucius Timinianus, said to me: 'Spare your father's white hairs; spare the tender years of your child. Offer a sacrifice for the safety of the Emperors.' And I answered: 'No.' 'Are you a Christian?' said Hilarian. And I answered: 'I am.' And when my father persisted in trying to overthrow my resolution, he was ordered by Hilarian to be thrown down, and the judge struck him with his rod. And I was grieved for my father's plight, as if I had been struck myself, so did I grieve for the sorrow that had come on his old age. Then he passed sentence on the whole of us, and condemned us to the beasts; and in great joy we went down into the prison. Then because my baby was accustomed to take the breast from me, and stay with me in prison, I sent at once the deacon Pomponius to my father to ask for my baby. But my father refused to give him. And as God willed, neither had he any further wish for my breasts, nor did they become inflamed; that I might not be tortured by anxiety for the baby and pain in my breasts.

"After a few days, while we were all praying, suddenly in the middle of the prayer I spoke, and uttered the name of Dinocrates; and I was astonished that he had never come into mind till then; and I grieved, thinking of what had befallen him. And I saw at once that I was entitled, and ought, to make request for him. And I began to pray much for him, and make lamentation to the Lord. At once on this very night this was shown me. I saw Dinocrates coming forth from a dark place, where there were many other dark places, very hot and thirsty, his countenance pale and squalid; and the wound which he had when he died was in his face still. This Dinocrates had been my brother according to the flesh, seven years old, who had died miserably of a gangrene in the face, so that his death moved all to loathing. For him then I had prayed; and there was a great gulf between me and him, so that neither of us could approach the other. There was besides in the very place where Dinocrates was a font full of water, the rim of which was above the head of the child; and Dinocrates stood on tiptoe to drink. I grieved that the font should have water in it and that nevertheless he could not drink because of the height of the rim. And I woke and recognized that my brother was in trouble. But I trusted that I could relieve his trouble, and I prayed for him every day until we were transferred to the garrison prison, for we were to fight with the beasts at the garrison games on the Cæsar Geta's birthday. And I prayed for him day and night with lamentations and tears that he might be given me.

"During the daytime, while we stayed in the stocks, this was shown me. I saw that same place which I had seen before, and Dinocrates clean in body, well clothed and refreshed; and where there had been a wound, I saw a scar; and the font which I had seen before had its rim lowered to the child's waist; and there poured water from it unceasingly; and on the rim a golden bowl full of water. And Dinocrates came forward and began to drink from it, and the bowl failed not. And when he had drunk enough of the water, he came forward, being glad to play as children will. And I awoke. Then I knew that he had been released from punishment.

"Then after a few days Pudens the adjutant, who was in charge of the prison, who began to show us honour, perceiving that there was some great power within us, began to admit many to see us, that both we and they might be refreshed by one another's company. Now when the day of the games approached, my father came in to me, worn with trouble, and began to pluck out his beard and cast it on the ground, and to throw himself on his face, and to curse his years, and to say such words as might have turned the world upside down. I sorrowed for the unhappiness of his old age.

"On the day before we were to fight, I saw in a vision Pomponius the deacon come hither to the door of the prison and knock loudly. And I went out to him, and opened to him. Now he was clad in a white robe without a girdle, wearing shoes curiously wrought. And he said to me: 'Perpetua, we are waiting for you; come.' And he took hold of my hand, and we began to pass through rough and broken country. Painfully and panting did we arrive at last at an amphitheatre, and he led me into the middle of the arena. And he said to me: 'Fear not; I am here with you, and I suffer with you.' And he departed. And I saw a huge crowd watching eagerly. And because I knew that I was condemned to the beasts, I marvelled that there were no beasts let loose on me. And there came out an Egyptian, foul of look, with his attendants to fight against me. And to me also there came goodly young men to be my attendants and supporters. And I was stripped and was changed into a man. And my supporters began to rub me down with oil, as they are wont to do before a combat; and I saw the Egyptian opposite rolling in the sand. And there came forth a man wondrously tall so that he rose above the top of the amphitheatre, clad in a purple robe without a girdle with two stripes, one on either side, running down the middle of the breast, and wearing shoes curiously wrought made of gold and silver; carrying a wand, like a trainer, and a green bough on which were golden apples. And he asked for silence, and said: 'This Egyptian, if he prevail over her, shall kill her with a sword; and, if she prevail over him, she shall receive this bough.' And he retired. And we came near to one another and began to use our fists. My adversary wished to catch hold of my feet, but I kept on striking his face with my heels. And I was lifted up into the air, and began to strike him in such fashion as would one that no longer trod on earth. But when I saw that the fight lagged, I joined my two hands, linking the fingers of the one with the fingers of the other. And I caught hold of his head, and he fell on his face; and I trod upon his head. And the people began to shout, and my supporters to sing psalms. And I came forward to the trainer, and received the bough. And he kissed me, and said to me: 'Peace be with thee, my daughter.' And I began to go in triumph to the Gate of Life. And I awoke. And I perceived that I should not fight with beasts but with the Devil; but I knew the victory to be mine. Such were my doings up to the day before the games. Of what was done in the games themselves let him write who will."

But the blessed Saturus also has made known this vision of his own, which he has written out with his own hand. "Methought we had suffered, and put off the flesh, and began to be borne toward the east by four angels whose hands touched us not. Now we moved not on our backs looking upward, but as though we were climbing a gentle slope. And when we were clear of the world below we saw a great light, and I said to Perpetua, for she was by my side: 'This is what the Lord promised us, we have received His promise.' And while we were carried by those four angels, we came upon a great open space, which was like as it might be a garden, having rose-trees and all kinds of flowers. The height of the trees was like the height of a cypress, whose leaves sang without ceasing. Now there in the garden were certain four angels, more glorious than the others, who when they saw us, gave us honour, and said to the other angels: 'Lo! they are come; lo! they are come,' being full of wonder. And those four angels which bare us trembled and set us down, and we crossed on foot a place strewn with violets, where we found Jucundus and Saturninus and Artaxius, who were burned alive in the same persecution, and Quintus who, being also a martyr, had died in the prison, and we asked of them where they were. The other angels said unto us: 'Come first and enter and greet the Lord.'

"And we came near to a place whose walls were built like as it might be of light, and before the gate of that place were four angels standing, who as we entered clothed us in white robes. And we entered, and heard a sound as of one voice saying: 'Holy, holy, holy,' without ceasing. And we saw sitting in the same place one like unto a man white-haired, having hair as white as snow, and with the face of a youth; whose feet we saw not. And on the right and on the left four elders; and behind them were many other elders standing. And, entering, we stood in wonder before the throne; and the four angels lifted us up, and we kissed Him, and He stroked our faces with His hand. And the other elders said to us: 'Let us stand.' And we stood and gave the Kiss of Peace. And the elders said to us: 'Go and play.' And I said to Perpetua: 'You have your wish.' And she said to me: 'Thanks be to God, that as I was merry in the flesh, so am I now still merrier here.'

"And we went forth and saw before the doors Optatus the bishop on the right, and Aspasius the priest-teacher on the left, severed and sad. And they cast themselves at our feet, and said: 'Make peace between us, for you have gone forth, and left us thus.' And we said to them: 'Are not you our father, and you our priest? Why should ye fall before our feet?' And we were moved, and embraced them. And Perpetua began to talk Greek with them, and we drew them aside into the garden under a rose-tree. And while we talked with them, the angels said to them: 'Let them refresh themselves; and if ye have any quarrels among yourselves, forgive one another.' And they put these to shame, and said to Optatus: 'Reform your people, for they come to you like men returning from the circus and contending about its factions.' And it seemed to us as though they wished to shut the gates. And we began to recognize many brethren there, martyrs too amongst them. We were all fed on a fragrance beyond telling, which contented us. Then in my joy I awoke."

Such are the famous visions of the blessed martyrs themselves, Saturus and Perpetua, which they wrote with their own hands. As for Secundulus, God called him to an earlier departure from this world, while still in prison, not without grace, that he might escape the beasts. Nevertheless his body, if not his soul, made acquaintance with the sword.

As for Felicitas indeed, she also was visited by the grace of God in this wise. Being eight months gone with child (for she was pregnant at the time of her arrest), as the day for the spectacle drew near she was in great sorrow for fear lest because of her pregnancy her martyrdom should be delayed, since it is against the law for women with child to be exposed for punishment, and lest she should shed her sacred and innocent blood among others afterwards who were malefactors. Her fellow-martyrs too were deeply grieved at the thought of leaving so good a comrade and fellow-traveller behind alone on the way to the same hope. So in one flood of common lamentation they poured forth a prayer to the Lord two days before the games. Immediately after the prayer her pains came upon her. And since from the natural difficulty of an eight-months' labour she suffered much in child-birth, one of the warders said to her: "You who so suffer now, what will you do when you are flung to the beasts which, when you refused to sacrifice, you despised?" And she answered: "Now I suffer what I suffer: but then Another will be in me who will suffer for me, because I too am to suffer for Him." So she gave birth to a girl, whom one of the sisters brought up as her own daughter.

Since, therefore, the Holy Spirit has permitted, and by permitting willed, the story of the games themselves to be written, we cannot choose but carry out, however unworthy to supplement so glorious a history, the injunction, or rather sacred bequest, of the most holy Perpetua, adding at the same time one example of her steadfastness and loftiness of soul. When they were treated with unusual rigour by the commanding officer because his fears were aroused through the warnings of certain foolish people that they might be carried off from prison by some magic spells, she challenged him to his face: "Why do you not at least suffer us to refresh ourselves, 'the most noble' among the condemned, belonging as we do to Cæsar and chosen to fight on his birthday? Or is it not to your credit that we should appear thereon in better trim?" The commanding officer trembled and blushed; and so ordered them to be used more kindly, giving her brothers and other persons leave to visit, that they might refresh themselves in their company. By this time the governor of the prison was himself a believer.

Moreover, on the day before the games when they celebrated that last supper, called "the free festivity," not as a "festivity," but, so far as they could make it so, a "love-feast," with the same steadfastness they flung words here and there among the people, threatening them with the judgment of God, calling to witness the happiness of their own passion, laughing at the inquisitiveness of the crowd. Said Saturus: "Tomorrow does not satisfy you, for what you hate you love to see. Friends today, foes tomorrow. Yet mark our faces well, that when the day comes you may know us again." So all left the place amazed, and many of them became believers.

The day of their victory dawned, and they proceeded from the prison to the amphitheatre, as if they were on their way to heaven, with gay and gracious looks; trembling, if at all, not with fear but joy. Perpetua followed with shining steps, as the true wife of Christ, as the darling of God, abashing with the high spirit in her eyes the gaze of all; Felicitas also, rejoicing that she had brought forth in safety that so she might fight the beasts, from blood to blood, from midwife to gladiator, to find in her Second Baptism her child-birth washing. And when they were led within the gate, and were on the point of being forced to put on the dress, the men of the priests of Saturn, the women of those dedicated to Ceres, the noble Perpetua resisted steadfastly to the last. For she said: "Therefore we came to this issue of our own free will, that our liberty might not be violated; therefore we pledged our lives, that we might do no such thing: this was our pact with you." Injustice acknowledged justice; the commanding officer gave permission that they should enter the arena in their ordinary dress as they were. Perpetua was singing a psalm of triumph, as already treading on the head of the Egyptian. Revocatus, Saturninus, and Saturus were threatening the onlookers with retribution; when they came within sight of Hilarian, they began to signify to him by nods and gestures: "Thou art judging us, but God shall judge thee." The people, infuriated thereat, demanded that they should be punished with scourging before a line of beast-fighters. And they for this at least gave one another joy, that they had moreover won some share in the sufferings of their Lord.

But He who had said: "Ask and ye shall receive" had granted to those who asked Him that death which each had craved. For, whenever they talked amongst themselves about their hopes of martyrdom, Saturninus declared that he wished to be cast to all the beasts; so indeed would he wear a more glorious crown. Accordingly at the outset of the show he was matched with the leopard and recalled from him; he was also (later) mauled on the platform by the bear. Saturus on the other hand had a peculiar dread of the bear, but counted beforehand on being dispatched by one bite of the leopard. And so when he was offered to the wild boar, the fighter with beasts, who had bound him to the boar, was gored from beneath by the same beast, and died after the days of the games were over, whereas Saturus was only dragged. And when he was tied up on the bridge before the bear, the bear refused to come out of his den. So Saturus for the second time was recalled unhurt.

For the young women the Devil made ready a mad heifer, an unusual animal selected for this reason, that he wished to match their sex with that of the beast. And so after being stripped and enclosed in nets they were brought into the arena. The people were horrified, beholding in the one a tender girl, in the other a woman fresh from child-birth, with milk dripping from her breasts. So they were recalled and dressed in tunics without girdles. Perpetua was tossed first, and fell on her loins. Sitting down, she drew back her torn tunic from her side to cover her thighs, more mindful of her modesty than of her suffering. Then, having asked for a pin, she further fastened her disordered hair. For it was not seemly that a martyr should suffer with her hair dishevelled, lest she should seem to mourn in the hour of her glory. Then she rose, and seeing that Felicitas was bruised, approached, gave a hand to her, and lifted her up. And the two stood side by side, and the cruelty of the people being now appeased, they were recalled to the Gate of Life. There Perpetua was supported by a certain Rusticus, then a catechumen, who kept close to her; and being roused from what seemed like sleep, so completely had she been in the Spirit and in ecstasy, began to look about her, and said to the amazement of all: "When we are to be thrown to that heifer, I cannot tell." When she heard what had already taken place, she refused to believe it till she had observed certain marks of ill-usage on her body and dress. Then she summoned her brother and spoke to him and the catechumen, saying: "Stand ye all fast in the faith, and love one another; and be not offended by our sufferings."

Saturus also at another gate was encouraging the soldier Pudens: "In a word," said he, "what I counted on and foretold has come to pass, not a beast so far has touched me. And now, that you may trust me wholeheartedly, see, I go forth yonder, and with one bite of the leopard all is over." And forthwith, as the show was ending, the leopard was let loose, and with one bite Saturus was so drenched in blood that the people as he came back shouted in attestation of his Second Baptism, "Bless you, well bathed! Bless you, well bathed!" Blessed indeed was he who had bathed after this fashion. Then he said to the soldier Pudens: "Farewell! Keep my faith and me in mind! And let these things not confound, but confirm you." And with that he asked for the ring from Pudens's finger, plunged it in his own wound, and gave it back as a legacy, bequeathing it for a pledge and memorial of his blood. Then, by this time lifeless, he was flung with the rest onto the place allotted to the throat-cutting. And when the people asked for them to be brought into the open, that, when the sword pierced their bodies, these might lend their eyes for partners in the murder, they rose unbidden and made their way whither the people willed, after first kissing one another, that they might perfect their martyrdom with the rite of the Pax. The rest without a movement in silence received the sword, Saturus in deeper silence, who, as he had been the first to climb the ladder, was the first to give up the ghost; for now as then he awaited Perpetua. Perpetua, however, that she might taste something of the pain, was struck on the bone and cried out, and herself guided to her throat the wavering hand of the young untried gladiator. Perhaps so great a woman, who was feared by the unclean spirit, could not otherwise be slain except she willed.

O valiant and blessed martyrs! O truly called and chosen to the glory of Jesus Christ our Lord! He who magnifies, honours, and adores that glory should recite to the edification of the Church these examples also, not less precious at least than those of old; that so new instances of virtue may testify that one and the self-same Spirit is working to this day with the Father, God Almighty, and with His Son Jesus Christ our Lord, to whom belong splendour and power immeasurable for ever and ever. Amen.

# The Martyrdom of St Cyprian

200?–258

Thascius Caecilius Cyprianus, a native of North Africa, was a rich man well known in Carthage as an orator and pleader. He was converted to Christianity in 245, after which he gave up his profitable law practice, and three years later he was made bishop of Carthage. Having escaped the persecution of Decius by going into hiding, he was summoned before the proconsul of Carthage after the edict of Valerian, in 257, announcing further persecutions. He was banished to Curubis and on September 14, 258, was beheaded at Carthage.

During the consulship of the Emperors Valerian and Gallienus, Valerian being consul for the fourth and Gallienus for the third time, on August 30 at Carthage in his private room Paternus the proconsul said to Cyprian the bishop: "The most sacred Emperors Valerian and Gallienus have thought fit to send me a letter, in which they have commanded that those who do not observe the Roman religion must recognize the Roman rites. I have therefore made inquiries concerning yourself. What answer have you to give me?"

Cyprian the bishop said: "I am a Christian and a bishop. I know no other God but the One True God, who 'made heaven and earth, the sea, and all that in them is.' This God we Christians serve, to Him we pray day and night for ourselves, and for all men, and for the safety of the Emperors themselves."

The proconsul Paternus said: "Is your will constant in this?"

Cyprian the bishop answered: "A good will, which knows God, cannot be altered."

The proconsul Paternus said: "Can you then in accordance with the order of Valerius and Gallienus go into exile to the city of Curubis?"

Cyprian the bishop said: "I will go."

The proconsul Paternus said: "They have thought fit to write to me not about bishops only, but also about priests. I would know therefore from you who the priests are, who reside in this city."

Cyprian the bishop answered: "It is an excellent and beneficial provision of your laws that informers are forbidden. They cannot therefore be revealed and reported by me. They will be found in their own cities."

The proconsul Paternus said: "I will seek them out here today."

Cyprian the bishop said: "Since our discipline forbids anyone to offer himself unsought, and this is also at variance with your principles, they cannot offer themselves any more than I can report them; but if sought out by you they will be found."

The proconsul Paternus said: "They shall be found by me." And added: "The Emperors have also given instructions that in no place shall meetings be held, nor shall any enter the cemeteries. If therefore any fail to observe these beneficial instructions, he shall suffer death."

Cyprian the bishop answered: "Do as you are instructed."

Then the proconsul Paternus ordered the blessed Cyprian to be banished. And as he stayed long time in exile, the proconsul Aspasius Paternus was succeeded in the proconsulship by Galerius Maximus, who ordered the holy bishop Cyprian to be recalled from banishment and brought before him.

When Cyprian, the holy martyr chosen by God, had returned from the city Curubis, which had been assigned as his place of banishment by command of Aspasius, then proconsul, by divine command he remained in his own gardens, whence he daily expected to be summoned, as had been shown him. While he still lingered in that place, suddenly on September 13 in the consulship of Tuscus and Bassus there came to him two high officials, one an equerry of the staff of the proconsul Galerius Maximus, and the other a member of the same staff, an equerry of the bodyguard. These lifted him into a carriage, placed him between them, and conveyed him to the house of Sextus, whither the proconsul Galerius Maximus had retired to recover his health.

And so the same Galerius Maximus the proconsul ordered Cyprian to be remanded till the morrow. For the time being, blessed Cyprian withdrew under guard to the house of a high official, equerry on the same staff of the illustrious Galerius Maximus the proconsul, and remained with him at his house in the street which is called Saturn's between the temple of Venus and the temple of Public Welfare. There the whole congregation of the brethren gathered: when this came to holy Cyprian's knowledge he gave orders that charge should be kept of the young women, for all had remained in the street before the door of the official's house.

On the morrow, being September 14, a great crowd gathered in the morning to the house of Sextus in accordance with the command of Galerius Maximus the proconsul. And so the same Galerius Maximus the proconsul ordered that Cyprian the bishop should be brought before him on the morrow where he sat in the Hall Sauciolum. When he had been brought before him, Galerius Maximus the proconsul said to Cyprian the bishop: "Are you Thascius Cyprianus?"

Cyprian the bishop answered: "I am."

Galerius Maximus the proconsul said: "Have you taken on yourself to be Pope of persons holding sacrilegious opinions?"

Cyprian the bishop answered: "Yes."

Galerius Maximus the proconsul said: "The most sacred Emperors have commanded you to perform the rite."

Cyprian the bishop answered: "I refuse."

Galerius Maximus the proconsul said: "Consider your own interest."

Cyprian the bishop answered: "Do as you are bid. In so clear a case there is no need for consideration."

Galerius Maximus, having conferred with the council, gave sentence hardly and reluctantly in these terms: "You have long lived in the holding of sacrilegious opinions, and have joined with yourself very many members of an abominable conspiracy, and have set yourself up as an enemy of the gods of Rome and religious ordinances, nor have the pious and most sacred Emperors Valerian and Gallienus, the Augusti, and Valerian, the most noble Cæsar, been able to recall you to the observance of their rites. And therefore since you have been convicted as the contriver and standard-bearer in most atrocious crimes, you shall be an example to those whom by your wickedness you have joined with you: discipline shall be vindicated in your blood." With these words he read from his tablets the sentence: "It is our pleasure that Thascius Cyprianus should be executed by the sword."

Cyprian the bishop said: "Thanks be to God!"

After this sentence the crowd of brethren cried: "Let us also be beheaded with him." Hence arose an uproar among the brethren, and a great crowd accompanied him. So the same Cyprian was led forth onto the land of Sextus, and there he divested himself of his mantle, and kneeled upon the ground, and bowed in prayer to the Lord. And when he had divested himself of his dalmatic and handed it to the deacons, he stood clad in his linen garment, and prepared to await the executioner. When the executioner arrived he charged his friends that they should give to the same executioner twenty-five golden pieces. Napkins and handkerchiefs were strewn before him by the brethren. Thereafter blessed Cyprian bound his eyes with his own hand, but, as he could not fasten the ends of the handkerchief for himself, the priest Julianus and Julianus the sub-deacon fastened them for him.

So the blessed Cyprian suffered, and his body was laid out hard by to content the curiosity of the heathen. Thence it was removed by night, and, accompanied by tapers and torches, was conducted with prayers in great triumph to the burial-ground of Macrobius Candidianus the procurator, which lies on the Mappalian way near the fishponds. A few days later Galerius Maximus the proconsul died.

The most blessed martyr Cyprian suffered on the fourteenth day of September under the Emperors Valerian and Gallienus, in the reign of our Lord Jesus Christ, to whom belong honour and glory for ever and ever. Amen.

# The Martyrdom of Saints Marcellus and Cassian

died 298

Marcellus was a native of Tingis (now Tangier), and a centurion during the reign of Diocletian. He cast away his arms and declared himself a Christian, for which he was sentenced by the governor Fortunatus to be beheaded. At the time of Marcellus's trial Cassian was a shorthand writer in the court. He declared that the sentence of Marcellus was unjust, for which heresy he himself was imprisoned and a little later suffered the same martyrdom.

In the city of Tingis, during the administration of Fortunatus as governor, the time came for the birthday of the Emperor. When all in that place were feasting at banquets and sacrificing, a certain Marcellus, one of the centurions of the Trajan legion, deeming those banquets to be heathen, cast away his soldier's belt in front of the standards of the legion which were then in camp, and testified in a loud voice, saying: "I serve Jesus Christ the Eternal King." He also threw away his vine-switch and arms, and added: "Henceforward I cease to serve your Emperors, and I scorn to worship your gods of wood and stone, which are deaf and dumb idols. If such be the terms of service that men are forced to offer sacrifice to gods and Emperors, behold I cast away my vine-switch and belt, I renounce the standards, and refuse to serve."

The soldiers were dumbfounded at hearing such things; they laid hold on him, and reported the matter to Anastasius Fortunatus the commander of the legion, who ordered him to be thrown into prison. When the feasting was over, he gave orders, sitting in council, that the centurion Marcellus should be brought in. When Marcellus, one of the centurions of Asta, was brought in, Anastasius Fortunatus the governor said: "What did you mean by ungirding yourself in violation of military discipline, and casting away your belt and vine-switch?"

Marcellus answered: "On the twenty-first of July, in presence of the standards of your legion, when you celebrated the festival of the Emperor, I made answer openly and in a loud voice that I was a Christian and that I could not serve under this allegiance, but only under the allegiance of Jesus Christ the Son of God the Father Almighty."

Anastasius Fortunatus the governor said: "I cannot pass over your rash conduct, and therefore I will report this matter to the Emperors and Cæsar. You yourself shall be referred unhurt to my lord, Aurelius Agricolan, Deputy for the Prefects of the Guard." [The shorthand writer who took down the official proceedings was Caecilius.]

On the 30th of October at Tingis, Marcellus, one of the centurions of Asta, having been brought into court, it was officially reported: "Fortunatus the governor has referred Marcellus, a centurion, to your authority. There is in court a letter dealing with his case, which at your command I will read."

Agricolan said: "Let it be read."

The official report was as follows: "From Fortunatus to you, my lord, and so forth. This soldier, having cast away his soldier's belt, and having testified that he was a Christian, spoke in the presence of all the people many blasphemous things against the gods and against Cæsar. We have therefore sent him on to you, that you may order such action to be taken as your Eminence may ordain in regard to the same."

After the letter had been read, Agricolan said: "Did you say these things as appear in the official report of the governor?"

Marcellus answered: "I did."

Agricolan said: "Did you hold the rank of a centurion of the first class?"

Marcellus answered: "I did."

Agricolan said: "What madness possessed you to cast away the signs of your allegiance, and to speak as you did?"

Marcellus answered: "There is no madness in those who fear the Lord."

Agricolan said: "Did you make each of these speeches contained in the official report of the governor?"

Marcellus answered: "I did."

Agricolan said: "Did you cast away your arms?"

Marcellus answered: "I did. For it was not right for a Christian, who serves the Lord Christ, to serve the cares of the world."

Agricolan said: "The acts of Marcellus are such as must be visited with disciplinary punishment." And he pronounced sentence as follows: "Marcellus, who held the rank of centurion of the first class, having admitted that he has degraded himself by openly throwing off his allegiance, and having besides put on record, as appears in the official report of the governor, other insane expressions, it is our pleasure that he be put to death by the sword."

When he was being led to execution, he said to Agricolan: "May God bless thee! For so ought a martyr to depart out of this world."

And when he had said these words he was beheaded, dying for the name of our Lord Jesus Christ, who is glorious for ever and ever. Amen.

When Aurelius Agricolan was acting as deputy for the Prefects of the Praetorian Guard, at the time when he was preparing to hear the case of the holy martyr Marcellus, the blessed Cassian was a shorthand writer under the orders of his staff. So when Marcellus, one of the centurions of Asta, was brought into court at Tingis on the 30th of October, Aurelius Agricolan by his power as judge strove with many threats to seduce him from perseverance in his confession. But the blessed Marcellus by the power of his constancy, so that all henceforward considered him his judge's judge, proclaimed that he was the soldier of Christ, and could not serve the cares of the world, while Aurelius Agricolan on the other hand poured forth words full of fury. Cassian was taking down these statements, but, when he saw Aurelius Agricolan, beaten by the devotion of so great a martyr, pronounce sentence of death, he vowed with an imprecation he would go no farther, and threw on the ground his pen and note book. So, amid the astonishment of the staff and the laughter of Marcellus, Aurelius Agricolan trembling leapt from the bench and demanded why he had thrown down his note books with an oath. Blessed Cassian answered that Agricolan had dictated an unjust sentence. To avoid further contradiction, Agricolan ordered him to be at once removed and cast into prison.

Now the blessed martyr Marcellus had laughed because, having knowledge of the future through the Holy Spirit, he rejoiced that Cassian would be his companion in martyrdom. On that very day, amid the eager expectation of the city, blessed Marcellus obtained his desire. After no long interval, namely, on the 3rd of December, the worshipful Cassian was brought into the same court in which Marcellus had been tried, and by almost the same replies, the same statement as holy Marcellus had made, merited to obtain the victory of martyrdom, through the help of our Lord Jesus Christ, to whom belong honour and glory, excellency and power for ever and ever. Amen.

# The Passion of St Alban and His Fellows Which Did Shed Their Blood for Christ's Sake

died c. 304

Alban of Verulamium was the first martyr of Britain, during the Diocletian persecution. Though a pagan, he gave shelter to a cleric, and, moved by the man's example, Alban was baptized. When the hiding place was discovered, Alban gave himself up in the cleric's place. He refused to deny his Christian faith, and was beheaded. A church and monastery were afterward erected at the spot, and the town of St Albans grew up around it.

This account of the martyrdom is from *The Ecclesiastical History* by the Venerable Bede (673?–735), translated by Thomas Stapleton in 1565.

Among other suffered Saint Alban: of whom Fortunatus priest in the book he wrote in the praise of virgins, speaking of the martyrs which from all coasts of the world came unto God, saith, *Albanum egregium fœcunda Britannia profert.*

> The fertile land of batfull Brittany
> Bringeth forth Alban a martyr right worthy.

This Alban being yet but a pagan, when the cruel commandments of the wicked Princes were set forth against the Christians, received into his house one of the clergy which had fled from the persecutors: whom he perceiving both night and day to continue in praying and watching, being suddenly touched with the grace of God, began to follow the example of his faith and virtue, and by little and little instructed by his wholesome exhortations, forsaking his blind idolatry, became Christian with his whole heart. At length after the said person of the clergy had certain days tarried with him, it came to the ears of the Prince that this holy confessor of Christ (whose time was not yet come that God appointed for him to suffer martyrdom) lay hid in *Alban's* house. Whereupon he commanded his soldiers to search his house with all diligence. Whither when they were come, Saint Alban, apparelled in his guest's and master's garments, offered himself to the soldiers, and so was brought bound unto the judge. It chanced that the judge the same time was doing sacrifice unto the devils before the altars. And when he had seen Alban, being all chafed with anger for that he feared not voluntarily to offer himself unto the soldiers and peril of death, for his guest, whom he had harboured, he commanded him to be brought before the idols of the devils, before whom he there stood. "And for so much," quoth he, "as thou hadst rather to convey away the rebel and traitor to our gods, than deliver him up unto the soldiers that he might sustain due punishment for his blasphemous despising of the gods, look what pains he should have suffered if he had been taken, the same shalt thou suffer, if thou refuse to practise the rites of our religion." But Saint Alban, which wilfully had before discovered himself to the persecutors to be a Christian, little heeded the menaces of the Prince. But being thoroughly fenced with spiritual armour of grace, told him plainly to his face, that he would not obey his commandment. Then said the judge, "Of what house or stock art thou?" Alban answered: "What is that to thee of what house I am? but if thou be desirous to know of what religion I am, be it known unto thee that I am a Christian, and that I employ myself to Christian manners and exercises." Then the judge demanded him his name. "My parents," quoth he, "named me Alban: and I honour and worship the true and living God, which made all thing of naught." Then the judge, being very wroth, said, "If thou wilt enjoy long life, come off, and do sacrifice unto the great god." Alban answered: "These sacrifices which you offer up unto the devils, neither help the offerers nor obtain them their desires, but rather purchase them for their reward eternal pains in hell fire." The judge, hearing this, being in a rage, commanded the holy confessor of God to be all beaten of the tormentors, thinking his constancy would relent at stripes, which refused to yield to words: but he showed himself not only patient, but also joyful in the middle of all his torments. The judge, when he saw he could be neither won with words, nor turned with torments from the religion of Christ's faith, commanded that he should be beheaded. In the way as he was led to his death, he came to a flood which, with a very swift course, ran betwixt him and the place where he should suffer. Now he saw a great company of all sexes, degrees, and ages going with him to the place of his execution, in so much that it seemed the judge was left alone at home without any to attend upon him. This company was so great, and the bridge they had to pass over so little, that it would be toward night ere they all could get over. Alban, longing much for his blessed death, and hasting to his martyrdom, coming to the river's side and making there his prayer with lifting up his eyes and heart to heaven, saw forthwith the bottom to have been dried up, and the water give place for him and the people to pass over dryshod as it were upon even ground. Which when among other the executioner which should have beheaded him did see, he made haste to meet him at the place appointed for his death, and there (not without the holy inspiration of God) he fell down flat before his feet, and casting from him the sword which he held in his hand ready drawn, desired rather that he might be executioned either for him or with him, rather than to do execution upon him. Whereupon this man being now made a fellow of that faith whereof before he was persecutor, and the sword lying in the ground before them, the other officers staggering and doubting all who might take it up and do the execution, the holy confessor of God with the people there assembled went unto a hill almost half a mile off from that place, beautifully garnished with divers herbs and flowers, nor rough or uneasy to climb, but smooth, plain and delectable, worthy and meet to be sanctified with the blood of the blessed martyr, unto the top whereof when he was ascended, he required of God to give him water: and straight there arose a spring of fair water before his feet whereby all might perceive that the river before was by his means dried. For he which left no water in the river would not have required it in the top of the mountain, but that it was so expedient, for the glory of God in his holy martyr. For behold, the river, having obeyed the martyr, and served his devotion, leaving behind a testimony of duty and obedience, returned to its nature again. Here therefore this most valiant martyr, being beheaded, received the crown of life which God promiseth to them that love him. But he which there took upon him to do that wicked execution had short joy of his naughty deed: for his eyes fell upon the ground with the head of the holy martyr. There also was beheaded the soldier which, being called of God, refused to strike the holy confessor of God: of whom it is open and plain, that though he was not christened in the fount, yet he was baptized in the bath of his own blood and so made worthy to enter into the kingdom of heaven. Now the judge, seeing so many strange and heavenly miracles wrought by this holy martyr, gave commandment that the persecution should cease, beginning to honour in the saints of God the constant and patient suffering of death, by the which he thought at first to bring them from the devotion of their faith. Saint Alban suffered his martyrdom the 22nd day of June, nigh unto the city of Verolamium. Whereafter the Christian Church being quietly calmed and settled again, there was a temple builded of a marvellous rich work, and worthy for such a martyrdom. In the which place truly even unto this day are sick persons cured, and many miracles wrought. There suffered also about that time Aaron and Julius, town dwellers of the city of the Legions, and many other both men and women in sundry places, which after divers fell and cruel torments sustained in all parts of their bodies, by perfect victory achieved by patience, yielded their souls unto the joys of heaven.

# ST GREGORY OF NAZIANZUS

(See page 89.)

## Dialogue between Basil and Modestus

St Gregory of Nazianzus preserved the Dialogue between St Basil (see page 84) and Modestus, the praetorian prefect.

. . . "What is the meaning of this, you Basil," said the prefect, a bitter Arian, not deigning to style him bishop, "that you stand out against so great a prince, and are self-willed when others yield?"

*Basil.* What would you? and what is my extravagance? I have not yet learned it.

*Modestus:* Your not worshipping after the Emperor's manner, when the rest of your party have given way and been overcome.

*Basil.* I have a Sovereign whose will is otherwise, nor can I bring myself to worship any creature—I a creature of God, and commanded to be a god.

*Modestus.* For whom do you take me?

*Basil.* For a thing of nought, while such are your commands.

*Modestus.* Is it, then, a mere nothing for one like you to have rank like myself, and to have my fellowship?

*Basil.* You are prefect, and in noble place: I own it. Yet God's majesty is greater; and it is much for me to have your fellowship, for we are both God's creatures. But it is as great to be fellow to any other of my flock, for Christianity lies not in distinction of persons, but in faith.

The prefect was angered at this, and rose from his chair, and abruptly asked Basil if he did not fear his power.

*Basil.* Fear what consequences? what sufferings?

*Modestus.* One of those many pains which a prefect can inflict.

*Basil.* Let me know them.

*Modestus*. Confiscation, exile, tortures, death.

*Basil*. Think of some other threat. These have no influence upon me. He runs no risk of confiscation who has nothing to lose, except these mean garments and a few books. Nor does he care for exile who is not circumscribed by place, who does not make a home of the spot he dwells in, but everywhere a home whithersoever he be cast, or rather everywhere God's home, whose pilgrim he is and wanderer. Nor can tortures harm a frame so frail as to break under the first blow. You could but strike once, and death would be gain. It would but send me the sooner to Him for whom I live and labour, for whom I am dead rather than alive, to whom I have long been journeying.

*Modestus*. No one yet ever spoke to Modestus with such freedom.

*Basil*. Peradventure Modestus never yet fell in with a bishop; or surely in a like trial you would have heard like language. O Prefect, in other things we are gentle, and more humble than all men living, for such is the commandment; so as not to raise our brow, I say not against "so great a prince," but even against one of least account. But when God's honour is at stake, we think of nothing else, looking simply to Him. Fire and the sword, beasts of prey, irons to rend the flesh, are an indulgence rather than a terror to a Christian. Therefore insult, threaten, do your worst, make the most of your power. Let the Emperor be informed of my purpose. Me you gain not, yet persuade not, to an impious creed, by menaces even more frightful.

# The Testament of the Forty Martyrs of Sebaste

320

Licinius, after the year 316, persecuted the Christians of the East. Among these, according to St Basil (who wrote their eulogy only some fifty years after their death) were a party of forty Christian soldiers who were condemned by the prefect to be exposed naked on a bitterly cold night on a frozen pond near Sebaste, in Lesser Armenia.

Meletius and Aëtius and Eutychius, the prisoners of Christ, to the holy bishops and priests, deacons and confessors, in every city, and to all others who belong to the Church, greeting in Christ.

When we by the grace of God and the common prayers of all shall finish the strife that is set before us, and come to the rewards of the high calling, we desire that then this will of ours may be respected, to wit, that our relics be conveyed to our father the presbyter Proïdus, and our brethren Crispin and Gordius, and the zealous laity who are with them, to Cyril and Mark and Sapricius the son of Ammonius, in order that our relics may be deposited near the city of Zela, at the spot called Sarin. For although we all come from different localities, we have chosen one and the same resting-place. Since we have set before ourselves one common strife for the prize, we have agreed to make also one common resting-place in the aforesaid spot. These things have seemed good to the Holy Ghost and have pleased us. Therefore we which are with Aëtius and Eutychius and the rest of our brethren in Christ beseech our honoured parents and brethren to have no grief or distress, but to respect the decision of our brotherly fellowship, and to consent heartily to our wishes, in order that you may receive from our common Father the great recompense of obedience and of sharing in our sufferings. Moreover, we entreat all men that no one will secure for himself any single fragment of our relics gathered out of the furnace, but will give them up to the persons aforenamed with a view to their being gathered together in the same place, in order that by such a proof of earnest determination, and of disinterested goodwill, he may receive the gain of a share in our sufferings themselves; even as Mary, abiding steadfastly by the tomb of Christ, saw the Lord before the rest and was the first to obtain the grace of joy and blessing. If, on the other hand, anyone shall go counter to our wish, let him have no part in the sacred gain, but incur the penalty of the entire disobedience, for depriving us of our right by his petty self-will, by compelling us as far as lay in his power to be sundered from one another, when our Holy Saviour by His special grace and providence has united us together in faith. And if the boy Eunoïcus, by the favour of the gracious God, shall be brought to the same end of strife, he has requested to have the same dwelling-place with us. But if he shall be preserved unhurt by the grace of God and should be further proved in the world, we charge him to look liberally to our chapel; and we beseech him to keep the commandments of Christ, that in the great day of Resurrection he may obtain part in our felicity, because while he was in the world he endured the same afflictions with us. . . .

So, honoured friends, we all greet you all—forty brethren and fellow-prisoners, Meletius, Aëtius, etc. . . . We then, the forty prisoners of the Lord Jesus Christ, have subscribed with our hand by one of our number, Meletius, and have confirmed all that is above written, and it has pleased us all. We pray with our souls, and with the Divine Spirit, that we may all obtain the eternal good things of God and His Kingdom, now and for ever and ever. Amen.

# ST GREGORY I (THE GREAT)

(See page 155.)

## Dialogues Concerning Martyrdom

### PRISONERS MARTYRED BY THE LOMBARDS

*Gregory.* There be, Peter, two kinds of martyrdoms, the one secret, the other open: for if a man hath a burning zeal in his mind to suffer death for Christ, although he endureth not any external persecution, yet hath he in secret the merit of martyrdom. For that one may be a martyr without suffering death openly, our Lord doth teach us in the Gospel: Who said unto the sons of Zebedee, desiring as then through infirmity of soul, the principal places to sit upon in His kingdom: "Can you drink the chalice which I shall drink?" and when they answered that they could, He said to them both: "My chalice verily shall you drink: but to sit at My right hand or left, is not Mine to give you": in which words what is signified else by the name of chalice, but the cup of passion and death? And seeing we know that James was put to death for Christ, and that John died when the Church enjoyed peace, undoubtedly we do gather that one may be a martyr without open suffering: forasmuch as he is said to have drunk our Lord's chalice, who yet in persecution was not put to death. . . .

For about fifteen years since, as they report who might very well have been present, forty husbandmen of the country were taken prisoners by the Lombards, whom they would needs have enforced to eat of that which was sacrificed to idols: but when they utterly refused so to do, or so much as once to touch that wicked meat, then they threatened to kill them, unless they would eat it: but they, loving more eternal than transitory life, continued constant, and so they were all slain. What then were these men? What else but true martyrs, that made choice rather to die than by eating of that which was unlawful to offend their Creator?

At the same time, the Lombards, having almost four hundred

prisoners in their hands, did, after their manner, sacrifice a goat's head to the Devil, running round about with it in a circle, and by singing a most blasphemous song did dedicate it to his service. And when they had themselves with bowed heads adored it, then would they also have enforced their prisoners to do the like. But a very great number of them, choosing rather by death to pass unto immortal life than by such abominable adoration to preserve their mortal bodies, refused utterly to do what they commanded them; and so would not by any means bow down their heads to a creature, having always done that service to their Creator: whereat their enemies, in whose hands they were, fell into such an extreme rage, that they slew all them with their swords which would not join with them in that sacrilegious fact. What marvel then is it, that those notable men before mentioned might have come to martyrdom, had they lived in the days of persecution, who in the time of peace by continual mortification walked the strait way of martyrdom, when as we see that in the storm of persecution they merited to obtain the crown of martyrdom who, the Church being quiet, seemed to walk the broad way of this world? Yet that which we say concerning the elect servants of God is not to be holden for a general rule in all. For when open persecution afflicteth the Church, as most true it is that many may arrive to martyrdom, who, when no such tempest did blow, seemed contemptible, and of no account: so likewise sometimes they fall away for fear, who before persecution, and when all was quiet, seemed to stand very constant; but such holy men as have before been mentioned, I dare boldly say that they might have been martyrs, because we gather so much by their happy deaths: for they could not have fallen in open persecution, of whom it is certain, that to the very end of their lives they did continue in the profession of piety and virtue.

*Peter*. It is as you say: but I much wonder at the singular providence of God's mercy, which He showeth to us unworthy wretches, in that He doth so moderate and temper the cruelty of the Lombards, that He suffereth not their wicked priests to persecute the faith of Christians, when as they see themselves, as it were, the conquerors and rulers of Christian people.

### KING HERMENEGILD THE VISIGOTH

*Gregory*. Not long since, as I have learned of many which came from Spain, King Hermenegild, son of Leovigild, King of the Visigoths, was from the Arian heresy lately converted to the Catholic Faith by the most reverend man, Leander, Bishop of Seville, with whom I was not long since familiarly acquainted; which young prince, upon his conversion, his father, being an Arian, laboured both by large promises and terrible threats to draw again to his former errors: but when most constantly his son answered that he would never forsake the true Faith which he had once embraced, his father in great anger took away his kingdom, and besides deprived him of all wealth and riches; and perceiving that with all this his mind was nothing moved, he committed him to strait prison, laying irons both upon his neck and hands. Upon this, the young King Hermenegild began now to contemn his earthly kingdom, and to seek with great desire after the kingdom of heaven; and lying in prison fast bound, he prayed to Almighty God in hair-cloth to send him heavenly comfort; and so much the more did he despise the glory of this transitory world, by how much he knew himself in that case that he had now nothing that could be taken from him.

When the solemn feast of Easter was come, his wicked father sent unto him in the dead of the night an Arian bishop, to give him the communion of a sacrilegious consecration, that he might thereby again recover his father's grace and favour; but the man of God, as he ought, sharply reprehended that Arian bishop, which came unto him, and giving him such entertainment as his deserts required, utterly rejected him; for albeit outwardly he lay there in bands, yet inwardly to himself he stood secure in the height of his own soul. The father, at the return of the Arian prelate, understanding these news, fell into such a rage that forthwith he sent his officers of execution to put to death that most constant confessor in the very prison where he lay: which unnatural and bloody commandment was performed accordingly; for so soon as they came into the prison they clave his brains with an hatchet, and so bereaved him of mortal life, having only power to take that from him which the holy martyr made small account of. Afterwards, for the publishing of his true glory to the world, there wanted not miracles from heaven: for in the nighttime singing was heard at his body; some also report that in the night burning lamps were seen in that place, by reason whereof his body . . . was worthily worshipped of all Christian people. But the wicked father and murderer of his own son, albeit he was sorry that he had put him to death, yet was not his grief of that quality that it brought him to the state of salvation. For although he knew very well that the Catholic Faith was the truth, yet for fear of his people he never deserved to be a professor thereof.

At length, falling sick, a little before his death he commended his son Recarede, who was to succeed him in the kingdom, and was yet an heretic, unto Bishop Leander, whom before he had greatly persecuted, that by his counsel and exhortation he might likewise make him a member of the Catholic Church, as he had before made his brother Hermenegild; and when he had thus done, he departed this life. After whose death, Recarede the King, not following the steps of his wicked father, but his brother the martyr, utterly renounced Arianism, and laboured so earnestly for the restoring of religion that he brought the whole nation of the Visigoths to the true Faith of Christ, and would not suffer any that was an heretic in his country to bear arms and serve in the wars. And it is not to be admired that he became thus to be a preacher of the true Faith, seeing that he was the brother of a martyr, whose merits did help him to bring so many into the lap of God's Church: wherein we have to consider that he could never have effected all this if King Hermenegild had not died for the testimony of true religion; for as it is written: "Unless the grain of wheat falling into the earth doth die, itself remaineth alone; but if it die it bringeth forth much fruit." This we see to prove true in the members which before was verified in the Head; for one died amongst the Visigoths that many might live; and of one grain that was sown for the faith a great crop of faithful people sprang up.

*Peter*. A wonderful thing, and much to be admired in these our days.

# THE ARGUMENTS: ATTACKS AND APOLOGIES

# The Testimony of the Pagans

The event that changed our times, and substituted the letters A.D.—*Anno Domini,* the year of the Lord—for the letters A.U.C.—*Ab Urbe Condita,* from the founding of the city—at first affected the city in question—Rome and her colonies—very little. There is no contemporary pagan evidence for the events the four Evangelists said took place in Palestine, though soon the historians, in brief sentences, mention the Christians.

The first authentic written evidence of the new faith and its founder comes from Gaius Suetonius Tranquillus. Himself a great writer and one of the outstanding biographers of his age, Suetonius was the contemporary of the greatest historian of the Roman world, Cornelius Tacitus, and also a friend of the younger Pliny. Suetonius wrote the biographies of the twelve Caesars from Julius to Domitian. Commenting on Emperor Claudius (reigned 41–54 A.D.), Suetonius wrote: "He expelled from Rome the Jews who were continually agitated, at the instigation of a certain Chrestus"; and, writing about Nero: "The Christians, a kind of people addicted to a new and nasty superstition, were tortured."

## CORNELIUS TACITUS

55?–?120

Tacitus, one of the greatest historians who ever lived, survived the reigns of Nero, Galba, Otho, Vitellius, Vespasian, Titus, Domitian, Nerva, and Trajan. He was an eminent pleader at the Roman bar and an eyewitness of the terror under Domitian. Our only sources of information about his personal life are references found in his own writings and in eleven letters addressed to him by the younger Pliny. His most famous works are *Germany,* written in 98; the *Histories,* completed about 116; and the *Annals.* He also wrote a biography of Julius Agricola, his father-in-law.

### FROM The Annals

No human means, no donations made by the Prince [Nero], no expiatory sacrifices, availed to check the suspicion that the fire had been started at Nero's orders. So to silence this rumor Nero substituted as the accused, and inflicted on them the most refined tortures, men detested because of their superstition, men commonly called Christians. He from whom they derived their name, Christ, suffered under Pontius Pilate, during the reign of Tiberius. Arrested for a moment, this execrable superstition spread again, not only in Judea, birthplace of this pest, but even in Rome itself, where everything horrible and infamous congregates from all parts and finds a place. A number who confessed were seized, then, on their indications, a large number were convicted, not of arson but of hatred of the human race. To their agonies contempt was added. Men in beasts' skins were torn to death by dogs or attached to crosses or, at nightfall, lit as living torches. Nero lent his garden for this spectacle, and there gave circus games, mixing with the crowd, disguised as a groom, or riding on a chariot. Although these men were guilty and worthy of final punishment, pity for them arose in men's hearts, because they seemed to be sacrificed, not in the general interest, but to the cruelty of one man.

# PLINY THE YOUNGER

62–113

Pliny the Younger, nephew of the distinguished naturalist and writer the elder Pliny, was asked by the Emperor Trajan, about 111, to accept a mission to Bithynia, in northern Asia Minor, as legate and governor. Pliny devoted himself to reorganizing the somewhat run-to-seed province with a touching, if somewhat timorous, zeal. The only manuscript of his famous letters was lost some time later than 1508, after it had been edited by Jerome Avantius in 1502 and by Aldus Manutius in 1508. Pliny's correspondence was famous as early as 197, when Tertullian quoted from it.

## Letters

### TO TRAJAN

. . . It is my custom, my lord, to refer to you all questions about which I have doubts. Who, indeed, can better direct me in hesitation, or enlighten me in ignorance? In the examination of Christians I have never taken part; therefore I do not know what crime is usually punished or investigated or to what extent. So I have no little uncertainty whether there is any distinction of age, or whether the weaker offenders fare in no respect otherwise than the stronger; whether pardon is granted on repentance, or whether when one has been a Christian there is no gain to him in that he has ceased to be such; whether the mere name, if it is without crimes, or crimes connected with the name are punished. Meanwhile I have taken this course with those who were accused before me as Christians: I have asked them whether they were Christians. Those who confessed I asked a second and a third time, threatening punishment. Those who persisted I ordered led away to execution. For I did not doubt that, whatever it was they admitted, obstinacy and unbending perversity certainly deserve to be punished. There were others of the like insanity, but because they were Roman citizens I noted them down to be sent to Rome. Soon after this, as it often happens, because the matter was taken notice of, the crime became wide-spread and many cases arose. An unsigned paper was presented containing the names of many. But these denied that they were or had been Christians, and I thought it right to let them go, since at my dictation they prayed to the gods and made supplication with incense and wine to your statue, which I had ordered to be brought into the court for the purpose, together with the images of the gods, and in addition to this they cursed Christ, none of which things, it is said, those who are really Christians can be made to do. Others who were named by an informer said that they were Christians, and soon afterward denied it, saying, indeed, that they had been, but had ceased to be Christians, some three years ago, some many years, and one even twenty years ago. All these also not only worshipped your statue and the images of the gods, but also cursed Christ. They asserted, however, that the amount of their fault or error was this: that they had been accustomed to assemble on a fixed day before daylight and sing by turns [*i. e.,* antiphonally] a hymn to Christ as a god; and that they bound themselves with an oath, not for any crime, but to commit neither theft, nor robbery, nor adultery, not to break their word and not to deny a deposit when demanded; after these things were done, it was their custom to depart and meet together again to take food, but ordinary and harmless food; and they said that even this had ceased after my edict was issued, by which, according to your commands, I had forbidden the existence of clubs. On this account I believed it the more necessary to find out from two maid-servants, who were called deaconesses [*ministræ*], and that by torture, what was the truth. I found nothing else than a perverse and excessive superstition. I therefore adjourned the examination and hastened to consult you. The matter seemed to me to be worth deliberation, especially on account of the number of those in danger. For many of every age, every rank, and even of both sexes, are brought into danger; and will be in the future. The contagion of that superstition has penetrated not only the cities but also the villages and country places; and yet it seems possible to stop it and set it right. At any rate, it is certain enough that the temples, deserted until quite recently, begin to be frequented, that the ceremonies of religion, long disused, are restored, and that fodder for the victims comes to market, whereas buyers of it were until now very few. From this it may easily be supposed what a multitude of men can be reclaimed if there be a place of repentance. . . .

FROM TRAJAN TO PLINY THE YOUNGER

. . . You have followed, my dear Secundus, the proper course of procedure in examining the cases of those who were accused to you as Christians. For, indeed, nothing can be laid down as a general law which contains anything like a definite rule of action. They are not to be sought out. If they are accused and convicted, they are to be punished, yet on this condition, that he who denies that he is a Christian and makes the fact evident by an act, that is, by worshipping our gods, shall obtain pardon on his repentance, however much suspected as to the past. Papers, however, which are presented anonymously ought not to be admitted in any accusation. For they are a very bad example and unworthy of our times. . . .

# LUCIAN

125?–?190

Lucian, born at Samosata on the Euphrates in northern Syria, traveled widely in his youth. In 165 he settled in Athens, where he remained for some twenty years. He had first been apprenticed to a sculptor uncle, but after being beaten for breaking a marble slab he turned to literature. He wrote of Christ as "the Galilean who had ascended to the third heaven." Among his numerous works are *The Lover of Lying,* a witty dialogue; *The True History,* a novel about a voyage to the moon, from which countless subsequent writers have borrowed; and *The Death of Peregrinus,* one of his best pieces. Peregrinus was a real person who in 165 committed suicide very dramatically. Lucian's description of Peregrinus's adventures with the Christians follows.

## FROM The Death of Peregrinus

About this time, Peregrinus became a disciple of that extraordinary philosophy of the Christians, having met with some of their priests and scribes in Palestine. He soon convinced them that they were all mere children to him, becoming their prophet and choir-leader and chief of their synagogue, and, in short, everything to them. Several of their sacred books he annotated and interpreted, and some he wrote himself. They held him almost as a god, and made him their lawgiver and bishop. You know they still reverence that great man, him that was crucified in Palestine, for introducing these new doctrines into the world. On this account Proteus [Peregrinus] was apprehended and thrown into prison, which very thing brought him no small renown for the future, and the admiration and notoriety which he was so fond of. For, during the time that he was in prison, the Christians, looking upon it as a general misfortune, tried every means to get him released. Then, when this was found impossible, their attention to him in all other ways was zealous and unremitting. From early dawn you might see widows and orphans waiting at the prison doors; and the men of rank among them even bribed the jailers to allow them to pass the night with him inside the walls.

Then they brought in to him there sumptuous meals, and read their sacred books together; and this good Peregrinus (for he was then called so) was termed by them a second Socrates. There came certain Christians, too, from some of the cities in Asia, deputed by their community to bring him aid, and to counsel and encourage him. For they are wonderfully ready whenever their public interest is concerned—in short, they grudge nothing; and so much money came in to Peregrinus at that time, by reason of his imprisonment, that he made a considerable income by it. For these poor wretches persuade themselves that they shall be immortal, and live for everlasting; so that they despise death, and some of them offer themselves to it voluntarily. Again, their first lawgiver taught them that they were all brothers, when once they had committed themselves so far as to renounce the gods of the Greeks, and worship that crucified sophist, and live according to his laws. So they hold all things alike in contempt, and consider all property common, trusting each other in such matters without any valid security. If, therefore, any clever impostor came among them, who knew how to manage matters, he very soon made himself a rich man, by practising on the credulity of these simple people.

[Having served his term, Peregrinus is let out of prison.] A troop of Christians served Peregrinus as satellites, saw to his needs and kept him in abundant comfort. But after some time, he violated certain of their precepts (he had, I think, eaten meats which are forbidden to them) and the Christians abandoned him.

# JULIAN THE APOSTATE

c. 331–363

Flavius Claudius Julianus, son of Julius Constantius and nephew of Constantine the great, was born in Constantinople c. 331. He lost his father and eldest brother in a massacre by which the three sons of Constantine—Constantius, Constantine II, and Constans—secured the empire for themselves when their father died in 337. During Constantius's reign Julian and his elder half-brother, Gallus, spent much of their childhood in prison and exile. Julian, although raised a Christian, became an adherent of the pagan religion at the age of twenty. In 355 Constantius summoned him to the court at Milan and gave Julian his sister, Helena, in marriage. Julian was then sent to govern Gaul. On the death of Constantius in December 361 he became emperor. He at once proclaimed the pagan gods and restored pagan worship, but he tolerated Christianity, and there were no persecutions during his brief reign. He was mortally wounded in a battle with the Persians at Maranga, and died June 27, 363. That his dying words were *"Vicisti, Galilæe"* was first stated in the fifth century by the Christian historian Theodoret. Julian's treatise *Against the Galileans,* which survives only in fragments, is an explanation of his apostasy.

## FROM Against the Galileans

It is, I think, expedient to set forth to all mankind the reasons by which I was convinced that the fabrication of the Galileans is a fiction of men composed by wickedness. Though it has in it nothing divine, by making full use of that part of the soul which loves fable and is childish and foolish, it has induced men to believe that the monstrous tale is truth. . . .

It is worth while to recall in a few words whence and how we first arrived at a conception of God; next to compare what is said about the divine among the Hellenes and Hebrews; and finally to inquire of those who are neither Hellenes nor Jews, but belong to the sect of the Galileans, why they preferred the belief of the Jews to ours; and what, further, can be the reason why they do not even adhere to the Jewish beliefs but have abandoned them also and followed a way of their own. For they have not accepted a single admirable or important doctrine of those that are held either by us Hellenes or by the Hebrews who derived them from Moses; but from both religions they have gathered what has been engrafted like powers of evil, as it were, on these nations—atheism from the Jewish levity, and a sordid and slovenly way of living from our indolence and vulgarity; and they desire that this should be called the noblest worship of the gods.

Now that the human race possesses its knowledge of God by nature and not from teaching is proved to us first of all by the universal yearning for the divine that is in all men, whether private persons or communities, whether considered as individuals or as races. For all of us, without being taught, have attained to a belief in some sort of divinity, though it is not easy for all men to know the precise truth about it, nor is it possible for those who do know it to tell it to all men. . . . Surely, besides this conception which is common to all men, there is another also. I mean that we are all by nature so closely dependent on the heavens and the gods that are visible therein, that even if any man conceives of another god besides these, he in every case assigns to him the heavens as his dwelling-place; not that he thereby separates him from the earth, but he so to speak establishes the King of the All in the heavens as in the most honourable place of all, and conceives of him as overseeing from there the affairs of this world.

What need have I to summon Hellenes and Hebrews as witnesses of this? There exists no man who does not stretch out his hands towards the heavens when he prays; and whether he swears by one god or several, if he has any notion at all of the divine, he turns heavenward. . . .

But that from the beginning God cared only for the Jews and that He chose them out as his portion, has been clearly asserted not only by Moses and Jesus but by Paul as well; though in Paul's case this is strange. For according to circumstances he keeps changing his views about God, as the polypus changes its colours to match the rocks, and now he insists that the Jews alone are God's portion, and then again, when he is trying to persuade the Hellenes to take sides with him, he says: "Do not think that He is the God of Jews only, but also of Gentiles: yea of Gentiles also." Therefore it is fair to ask of Paul why God, if he was not the God of the Jews only but also of the Gentiles, sent the blessed gift of prophecy to the Jews in abundance and gave them Moses and the oil of anointing, and the prophets and the law and the incredible and monstrous elements in their myths? For you hear them crying aloud: "Man did eat angels' food." And finally God sent unto them Jesus also, but unto us no prophet, no oil of anointing, no teacher, no herald to announce his love for man which should one day, though late, reach even unto us also. Nay he even looked on for myriads, or, if you prefer, for thousands of years, while men in extreme ignorance served idols, as you call them, from where the sun rises to where he sets, yes and from North to South, save only that little tribe which less than two thousand years before had settled in one part of Palestine. For if he is the God of all of us alike, and the creator of all, why did he neglect us? Wherefore it is natural to think that the God of the Hebrews was not the begetter of the whole universe with lordship over the whole, but rather, as I said before, that he is confined within limits, and that since his empire has bounds we must conceive of him as only one of the crowd of other gods. Then are we to pay further heed to you because you or one of your stock imagined the God of the universe, though in any case you attained only to a bare conception of Him? Is not all this partiality? God, you say, is a jealous God. But why is he so jealous, even avenging the sins of the fathers on the children? . . .

But what great gift of this sort do the Hebrews boast of as bestowed on them by God, the Hebrews who have persuaded you to desert to them? If you had at any rate paid heed to their teachings, you would not have fared altogether ill, and though worse than you did before, when you were with us, still your condition would have been bearable and supportable. For you would be worshipping one god instead of many, not a man, or rather many wretched men. And though you would be following a law that is harsh and stern and contains much that is savage and barbarous, instead of our mild and humane laws, and would in other respects be inferior to us, yet you would be more holy and purer than now in your forms of worship. But now it has come to pass that like leeches you have sucked the worst blood from that source and left the purer. Yet Jesus, who won over the least worthy of you, has been known by name for but little more than three hundred years: and during his lifetime he accomplished nothing worth hearing of, unless anyone thinks that to heal crooked and blind men and to exorcise those who were possessed by evil demons in the villages of Bethsaida and Bethany can be classed as a mighty achievement. As for purity of life you do not know whether he so much as mentioned it; but you emulate the rages and the bitterness of the Jews, overturning temples and altars, and you slaughtered not only those of us who remained true to the teachings of their fathers, but also men who were as much astray as yourselves, heretics, because they did not wail over the corpse in the same fashion as yourselves. But these are rather your own doings; for nowhere did either Jesus or Paul hand down to you such commands. The reason for this is that they never even hoped that you would one day attain to such power as you have; for they were content if they could delude maidservants and slaves, and through them the women, and men like Cornelius and Sergius. But if you can show me that one of these men is mentioned by the well-known writers of that time—these events happened in the reign of Tiberius or Claudius—then you may consider that I speak falsely about all matters. . . .

But you are so misguided that you have not even remained faithful to the teachings that were handed down to you by the Apostles. And these also have been altered, so as to be worse and more impious, by those who came after. At any rate neither Paul nor Matthew nor Luke nor Mark ventured to call Jesus God. But the worthy John, since he perceived that a great number of people in many of the towns of Greece and Italy had already been infected by this disease, and because he heard, I suppose, that even the tombs of Peter and Paul were being worshipped—secretly, it is true, but still he did hear this—he, I say, was the first to venture to call Jesus God. And after he had spoken briefly about John the Baptist he referred again to the Word which he was proclaiming, and said, "And the Word was made flesh, and dwelt among us." But how, he does not say, because he was ashamed. Nowhere, however, does he call him either Jesus or Christ, so long as he calls him God and the Word, but as it were insensibly and secretly he steals away our ears, and says that John the Baptist bore this witness on behalf of Jesus Christ, that in very truth he it is whom we must believe to be God the Word. But that John says this concerning Jesus Christ I for my part do not deny. And yet certain of the impious think that Jesus Christ is quite distinct from the Word that was proclaimed by John. That, however, is not the case. For he whom John himself calls God the Word, this is he who, says he, was recognized by John the Baptist to be Jesus Christ. Observe accordingly how cautiously, how quietly and insensibly he introduces into the drama the crowning word of his impiety; and he is so rascally and deceitful that he rears his head once more to add, "No man hath seen God at any time; the only begotten Son which is in the bosom of the Father, He hath declared him." Then is this only begotten Son which is in the bosom of the Father the God who is the Word and became flesh? And if, as I think, it is indeed He, you also have certainly beheld God. For "He dwelt among you, and ye beheld his glory." Why then do you add to this that "No man hath seen God at any time"? For ye have indeed seen, if not God the Father, still God who is the Word. But if the only begotten Son is one person and the God who is the Word another, as I have heard from certain of your sect, then it appears that not even John made that rash statement.

However, this evil doctrine did originate with John; but who could detest as they deserve all those doctrines that you have invented as a sequel, while you keep adding many corpses newly dead to the corpse of long ago? You have filled the whole world with tombs and sepulchres, and yet in your Scriptures it is nowhere said that you must grovel among tombs and pay them honour. But you have gone so far in iniquity that you think you need not listen even to the words of Jesus of Nazareth on this matter. Listen then to what he says about sepulchres: "Woe unto you, scribes and Pharisees, hypocrites! for ye are like unto whited sepulchres; outward the tomb appears beautiful, but within it is full of dead men's bones, and of all uncleanness." If, then, Jesus said that sepulchres are full of uncleanness, how can you invoke God at them? . . .

# The Testimony of the Christians

Early Christian literature is only literature when it is not—or when, like Molière's bourgeois, its authors are unaware that they are writing prose. So long as the writers are purely practical and unselfconscious, writing only to remember, to reprove, to convince, and to refute, the early Christian writings *are* literature, and of the best. But from the moment when the authors roll the words around their tongues, when they seek to astonish, to impress, or even merely to emulate their pagan or worldly rivals, they fall into platitude, into bombast, or into sterile rhetoric.

At first, there were no Christian writings, for the traditions were oral, the teaching by exhortation, precept, and example. Unlike Judaism before it, and even more unlike Islam that followed, Christianity has never been the religion of *a* book, and even less of *the* Book. In Christianity the witness is the person; in Judaism, it is the scroll, the writing; in Islam the holy language. In Judaism, the bridge between God and man is a written record; in Christianity it is a man "of a reasonable soul and human flesh subsisting"; in Islam, it is *the* book, Al Quran.

So Christian literature begins in spite of itself; first-hand, sometimes even first-person, accounts of the life of Jesus Christ; letters from His friends. Only gradually do the arguments begin, apologetics, creeds, statements of faith, definitions of dogma. And these first Christian writings are naive, full of grammatical errors; they lack in taste, in polish, what they make up in sincerity, in immediacy. But they show the whole Christian life, the thought, the behavior; the arguments are honest, direct, courageous.

They begin with St Justin's argument with a Jew; they end—for this volume—with St John Damascene's argument with a Saracen. But they do not cease with the Age of the Fathers; they will cease only with the end of the world.

# ST JUSTIN MARTYR

(See page 193.)

## Dialogue with Trypho the Jew

This dialogue was dedicated to one Marcus Pompeius. Trypho was a learned rabbi, with whom St Justin argued in order to convince the Jews of the Messiahship of Jesus Christ. According to the author, the dialogue lasted two days. It took place—if it really did—at Ephesus during the war of Bar Cocheba, between 132 and 135.

As I was one morning pacing the walks of the Xystus, a person in company with others met me and, addressing me, said, "Good morrow, philosopher." He then turned about and walked with me, as also did his friends; whilst I in my turn accosted him. "What would you have with me, sir?" I said.

"I was instructed," he replied, "by Corinthus the Socratic at Argos, not to pass by or neglect those who wear your dress, but rather to show them every attention in my power, and to hold conversation with them, if haply they or myself might thus gain some improvement from our intercourse, for it would be well for both if either should thus be benefited. And for this reason, when I see anyone in such a dress, I gladly accost him; and was accordingly just now much pleased to be able to introduce myself to you, and these other persons come along with me, with the same hope of hearing something of value from you."

"Who are you then, excellent sir?" I replied with a smile.

He told me frankly who and what he was. "My name," he said, "is Trypho. I am a Hebrew of the circumcision, who have made my escape from the late war, and I live at present in Greece, and chiefly at Corinth."

"How then," said I, "can you derive so great benefit from philosophy as from your own lawgiver and prophets?"

"Why not?" he answered. "Are not all the discourses of the philosophers about God, and their disquisitions, inquiries into His unity and providence? Or is it not the very employment of philosophy to inquire into the nature of the Deity?"

"Yes," I said, "these are our principles also; but most of the philosophers are entirely indifferent as to whether there be one or many Gods, and whether their providential care is exercised over each of us or not; regarding this knowledge as in no way conducive to happiness. They even endeavour to prove to us that God regards indeed the universal, and the genus and species, but that of me and you and the individual He takes no care; or there would be no need for us to pray to Him night and day. It is easy to perceive to what end this reasoning conducts them. It confers a fearlessness and freedom both on the teachers and on the disciples, allowing all to do and to say whatever they please, without dreading any punishment or expecting any reward at the hand of God. How indeed can it be otherwise with those who assert that things will ever continue as they are now, and that you and I shall live in the next life just as we do in this, without being either better or worse? But others, who maintain the soul to be immortal and incorporeal, think it impossible that they should be punished even if they commit sin; because if the soul is incorporeal, it is incapable of suffering; and if immortal, they hold that they have no need of anything further from God."

"Tell us," he then said, politely smiling, "what is your opinion of these things, and what you think about God, and what is your philosophy."

"I will tell you," I replied, "what is my own conviction on the subject. Philosophy is indeed the greatest of treasures, and most precious in the sight of God, to whom it alone introduces and unites man; and they who have applied their minds to it are the really holy; but the many have not divined what this philosophy is, and for what end it is sent down to man, otherwise there would not be at the same time such persons as Platonists, Stoics, Peripatetics, Theoretics, and Pythagoreans, this knowledge being always one and the same; but I will now tell you how it eventually became thus many-headed; they who first applied themselves to philosophy, and became celebrated in consequence, happened to be followed by some who paid no regard to truth, but being struck merely by the fortitude and temperance of their teachers, with the novelty of their doctrines, considered that to be truth which they had learnt each from his own master; and they in their turn delivered to their successors some such and other like notions, so that they became known each by the name of the first author of their doctrine.

"And when I was at first desirous, for my own part, of holding converse with one of them, I put myself under the tuition of a Stoic. After I had lived a long time with him and had gained no certain knowledge of God (for this he knew not himself, nor did he consider such knowledge necessary), I left him, and went to a Peripatetic, a shrewd teacher as he thought himself. He endured my presence for some days, but then requested me to fix a remuneration, that our intercourse might not be without profit. On this account I left him, not thinking him worthy of the name of a philosopher; but my mind still hankering after whatever was peculiar and valuable in philosophy, I joined a very celebrated Pythagorean, a man who prided himself greatly upon his wisdom; but when I informed him of my wish to become his hearer and disciple, 'Are you then familiar,' he asked, 'with music, astronomy, and geometry? or how can you hope to comprehend any of the things which tend to happiness, unless you are first grounded in such studies as wean the mind from the objects of sense, and render it capable of entertaining those of the intellect, so that it may be enabled to discern the beautiful and the very essential of good?'

"When he had spoken much in favour of these sciences, and of the necessity of their attainment, he sent me away, as I confessed my ignorance of them. I was naturally much cast down at having my hopes thus disappointed, and the more so, as I really thought him a man of some knowledge. But when I considered, on the other hand, how long a time one must spend on these subjects, I could not endure the delay, and whilst I was in this difficulty, it occurred to me to try the Platonists too; for they also enjoyed a high reputation; I accordingly devoted as much time as possible to a sage who had lately arrived at our city, and who was distinguished among that school; with him I improved, and made rapid advances daily. The Platonic conception of incorporeals greatly captivated me, and their theory of ideas 'added wings to my thoughts,' so that within a short time I considered myself to have become a wise man, and in my vanity I hoped shortly to see God, for this is the object of the philosophy of Plato.

"In this disposition, thinking it right to accustom myself to extreme quietness, and absence from the haunts of men, I was in the habit of going to a spot not far from the sea, which as I one day approached, intending to spend some time there by myself, an aged person of a reverend aspect, and mild and venerable carriage, followed me at a little distance; but when I turned and looked at him somewhat keenly, 'Do you know me?' he asked. I replied, that I did not. 'Why then,' said he, 'do you look at me so closely?' 'I am surprised,' I answered, 'at your being in the same place with me, for I did not expect to see any one here.' 'I am anxious,' he replied, 'about some absent members of my family, and I came to look out whether they will come in sight from any quarter. But you yourself, why are you here?'

" 'I take pleasure,' I replied, 'in such walks as these, in which there is nothing to distract my attention, and where I can converse with myself without fear of interruption; for it is in such places that a lover of arguments can make most improvement.' 'Are you a lover of mere arguments,' he said, 'and not of deeds and of truth; and do you not endeavour to become a master of practice, rather than of sophistry?'

" 'What can one do better,' I answered, 'than thus prove, that reason beareth rule over all things, and that a man who hath taken hold of it and is supported by it can look down on the wanderings and the pursuits of others, and see that they do nothing that is sane, nothing that is pleasing to God; for without philosophy and right reason none can possess prudence. Every man should therefore give himself up to philosophy, and account it the greatest and most precious of gains, all other things being in comparison of second- or third-rate value; and if taken in connection with it, they should be held in moderate estimation, as worthy to be received; but if deprived of it and separated from it, even hurtful and degrading to those who take them in hand.'

" 'Does philosophy then confer happiness?' he inquired.

" 'It does indeed,' I said, 'and it alone.'

" 'But what is philosophy?' he said; 'and tell me, if you have no objection, what is the happiness which it bestows?'

" 'Philosophy,' I said, 'is the knowledge of *that which is,* and the discernment of truth; and happiness is the reward of this knowledge, and of wisdom.'

" 'What do you define God to be?' he inquired.

" 'That which is ever one and the same, and the cause of being to all creatures, such without doubt is God.' This was my reply, and he heard it with pleasure.

" 'Then,' he asked again, 'is not knowledge a term common to different things? for whoever is skilled in any of the arts, in that of strategy for instance, or of navigation, or of medicine, is said to have knowledge of it. But this cannot be asserted equally well of things divine and human: is there any science, for instance, which gives us the knowledge of things divine and human, and likewise of the divinity and righteousness in them?'

" 'Certainly there is,' I answered.

" 'What, then,' he exclaimed, 'can we know God and man, in the same way as we may know music, arithmetic, astronomy, and the like?'

" 'By no means,' I replied.

" 'You have not answered me correctly then,' he said, 'for of some things we have knowledge by study or application, of others by sight. If anyone were to tell you that in India there is a living creature unlike all others, of such or such a shape, multiform, and of various colours, you would have no positive knowledge of it until you had seen it, nor could you give any description of it, except you had heard from an eye-witness.'

" 'True,' I replied.

" 'How then,' he inquired, 'can philosophers think rightly, or speak with truth, of God, when they have no knowledge of Him, Whom they have neither seen nor heard?'

" 'The Deity, father,' I answered, 'is not to be viewed by the organs of sight, like other creatures, but He is to be comprehended by the mind alone, as Plato declares, and I believe him.'

" 'Have our minds then,' he asked, 'any power of such nature and extent, as can conceive that which has not first been communicated to them by the senses? Or will the mind of man ever see God, if it be not instructed by the Holy Spirit?'

" 'Plato tells us,' I answered, 'that the eye of the mind is of such a nature, and was given us to such an end, as to enable us to see with it by itself, when pure, that very Being Who is the source of whatever is an object of the mind itself, Who has neither colour, nor shape, nor size, nor anything which the eye can see, but Who is above all essence, Who is ineffable, and undefinable, Who is alone beautiful and good, and Who is at once implanted into those souls who are naturally well born, through their relationship to and desire of seeing Him.'

" 'What relationship then,' he inquired, 'have we with God? or is the soul divine and immortal, and a part of that very supreme Mind? And as It sees God, so can we in like manner with our mind comprehend Him, and thus obtain happiness even now?'

" 'Certainly it is so,' I returned.

" 'Do all the souls then,' he asked, 'of all animals comprehend Him? or is the soul of man of one kind, and that of a horse or ass of another?'

" 'Not so,' I replied, 'but the souls of all creatures are alike.'

" 'Shall horses and asses see God then?' he said, 'or have they done so at any time?'

" 'No,' I answered, 'for not many men see Him, but only those who have lived uprightly, and who are made pure by righteousness, and the practice of every virtue.'

" 'Man does not see God then,' he answered, 'through his relationship with Him, nor because he has mind, but because he is temperate and just.'

" 'Yes,' I answered, 'and because he is endowed with that by which he is able to think of Him.'

" 'What then,' he answered, 'do goats or sheep injure anyone?'

" 'No one,' I said, 'in any way.'

" 'Shall these animals then, according to your reasoning, see God?'

" 'No, for their bodies being such as they are prevent them.'

" 'If these animals could speak,' he said, 'be assured that they would with much more justice find fault with our bodies. But let us leave this for the present; and granting it to be as you say, tell me, does the soul see God whilst it is in the body, or when it is delivered from it?'

" 'Even whilst it is in a human form, it is able to rest upon God, through its mind, but especially when freed from the body, and existing by itself, does it possess that which it loved wholly and for ever.'

" 'Does it remember this when again united to a human body?'

" 'I suppose not,' was my answer.

" 'What good then accrues to those souls who have seen God? or what advantage has the man who has seen Him over him who has not, if he cannot remember even so much as that he has seen Him?'

" 'I cannot tell,' I replied.

" 'But what do they suffer who are judged unworthy of this sight?'

" 'Their punishment is to be imprisoned in the bodies of certain beasts.'

" 'Do they know, then, that it is for this reason, namely, their having committed sin, that they are enclosed in such bodies?'

" 'I think not.'

" 'As it appears, then, they gain no advantage from such punishment, and, in fact, cannot be said to be punished at all, if they are not conscious of it.'

" 'Assuredly not.'

" 'Souls then do not see God, nor do they pass into other bodies, or they would have known that they were thus punished; and have feared thereafter to commit even the least sin; but I grant you,' he continued, 'that souls are able to comprehend that there is a God, and that righteousness and piety are good.'

" 'You speak truly,' I replied.

" 'These philosophers then,' he continued, 'know nothing of such points, for they cannot even tell what the soul is.'

" 'It appears not.'

" 'Nor can the soul be termed immortal; for if it were, it must have been ingenerate as well.' 'It is both ingenerate and immortal,' I replied, 'according to some who are termed Platonists.'

" 'Do you then,' he asked, 'consider the world ingenerate?'

" 'There are some who do,' I said, 'but for myself I do not agree with them.'

" 'You are right; for what reason is there to suppose that a body possessed of such solidity and of the power of resistance, which is of a compound nature, is mutable, decays, and is renewed every day, did not derive its origin from some first cause? And if the world was generated, souls were of necessity generated also, and perhaps there was a time when they did not exist; for they were generated for the sake of men and other animals, even if you say that they were generated separately by themselves, and not with their own bodies.'

" 'This opinion appears to be correct. They are not immortal then?'

" 'No, for we have seen that the world itself was generated.'

" 'But at the same time I affirm that souls never perish, for this would be indeed a godsend to the wicked. What then befalls them? The souls of the good are consigned to a better place, and those of the evil and unjust to a worse, there to await the day of judgment. Thus such as are worthy to see God die no more, but others shall undergo punishment as long as it may please Him that they shall exist and be punished.' . . .

" 'I pay no regard,' he answered, 'to Plato, or Pythagoras, or anyone else who holds such opinions, but that the truth is so you may learn from hence. The soul either is life or receives life. If it is life, it would cause something else to live and not itself, as motion is the source of moving to something extraneous rather than to itself; now, that the soul lives, no one will deny; and if it does live, it lives not as being itself life, but as partaking of life; but that which partakes is different from that of which it does partake. The soul partakes of life, since God wills it to live; and hence it will cease to have life whenever He may please that it shall live no longer, for it is not the property of the soul to have life in itself as it is the property of God, but as man exists not for ever, nor is his body always united to his soul; but whenever it is expedient that this conjunction should be dissolved, the soul leaves the body, and the man exists no longer; so also when the soul is to live no more, the spirit of life is taken from it, and the soul exists no more, but itself returns again to whence it came.'

" 'Whom then,' I asked, 'shall a man take as his master, or whence shall he derive any instruction, if the truth is not with these philosophers?'

" 'There once lived men,' he replied, 'called prophets, who were anterior to any of those who are considered philosophers, and who were blessed, just, and beloved by God. These spoke by the Holy Ghost, and foretold what should happen thereafter, and what is now taking place. And they alone knew and taught the truth, neither regarding nor fearing any man, nor being themselves carried away by the love of glory, but declaring those things alone which they saw and heard when filled with the Holy Ghost. And their writings still remain to us, and whoever reads them will derive much instruction about the first principles and the end of things, together with all that a philosopher ought to know when he believes them.' . . .

"When he had said this, and much more which we have not now time to repeat, he left me, bidding me attend to what he had said, and I saw him no more.

"But a flame was immediately kindled in my mind, and I was seized with an ardent love of the prophets, and of those men who are the friends of Christ; and reflecting with myself on what I had heard, I saw that theirs was the only sure and valuable philosophy: thus it was that I became a philosopher, and I could wish that all men were of the same mind as myself, not to turn from the doctrines of the Saviour; for they inspire a certain dread, and possess a power to overawe those who are turned from the right way; but they become the most pleasant resting-place to such as fully practise them. If therefore you have any regard for your own welfare, and desire of salvation, and trust in God, you may now have an opportunity, if you are not averse to the task, of attaining happiness by knowledge of the Christ of God, and by being made a perfect disciple."

At these words, my dearest Pompey, Trypho's companions laughed aloud, and he himself smiled. "I approve," he answered, "the rest of what you have said, and I much admire your zeal of obtaining divine knowledge; but it were better for you to follow Plato or any other philosopher, and live in the practice of fortitude, self-control, and moderation, than to suffer yourself to be led away by lying doctrines, and to listen to worthless teachers; for whilst you pursued that school of philosophy and lived unblameably, there was some hope of your attaining a better state. But now that you have deserted God and based your hopes on man, what means of salvation are left for you? If you will therefore listen to me (for I already regard you as a friend), first be circumcised, and then, as commanded, observe the sabbath, and the feasts, and the new moons of God, with all that is written in the Law, in which case you may perhaps find mercy with Him. But as for Christ, if He be born and is to be found anywhere, He is both unknown to others, and He knows not Himself, nor has He any power until Elias comes to anoint and proclaim Him to all. But you Christians have all received an idle report, and have formed a Christ for yourselves, for whose sake you inconsiderately throw away your lives."

"You are excusable, man!" I replied, "and may it be forgiven you; for you speak you know not what, but you follow your teachers, who understand not the Scriptures, and utter at random whatever comes into your mind. If you will receive proof that we have not been deluded, and shall not cease to confess Christ, even though we thereby incur the reproaches of men, and the most cruel tyrant should endeavour to compel us to renounce Him, I will prove to you, where you stand, that we do not confide in baseless fables nor in empty words, but in doctrines which are full of Divine Spirit, and overflowing with power, and abounding in grace."

On this Trypho's companions laughed again, and exclaimed in so disorderly a way that I rose from my seat and was on the point of leaving them; but Trypho seized my gown, and said he would not let me go until I had performed my promise.

"Then do not permit your companions," I answered, "to create this disturbance, and conduct themselves so improperly; but either let them listen in silence, or leave us if they have business of more importance, whilst we ourselves will go and sit down where we may continue our discourse." To this proposal Trypho consented; whereupon we agreed to go aside, and came to the middle stadium of the Xystus, where two of his followers left us, laughing at our earnestness. For ourselves, when we reached the spot where there were some stone seats on each side, Trypho and his companions held some conversation about the war that had been recently carried on against Judea, and to which one of them had chanced to make allusion.

When they had finished their observations, I thus resumed, "Is there any other objection which you have to make to us, sirs, than this; that we do not live according to the Law, nor circumcise the flesh like your fathers, nor keep the sabbaths like yourselves? or do you also object to our lives and manners? What I mean is, do you believe of us, like others, that we devour men, and when we meet together after our banquet put out the lights, and wallow in promiscuous concubinage; or do you only blame us for adhering to doctrines and opinions which are as you think void of truth?"

"It is this last which surprises me," replied Trypho; "for as to those other accusations which so many urge against you, I do not think them worthy of credit, as they are too revolting to human nature; but the precepts in what you term your Gospel, and which I happen to have read, are so great and admirable, as in my opinion to be beyond the power of anyone to observe them. But it is this that chiefly perplexes us, that you who make a profession of piety, and consider yourselves better than others, do in no respect excel the heathen in your lives; for you do not keep the feasts nor observe the sabbaths, nor practise circumcision. . . . If therefore you . . . can show us on what you base your hopes, since you do not keep the Law, we will gladly hear you, and we can then in the same manner investigate the other points between us."

"There never will be any other God, Trypho, nor has there ever been any from eternity," I said, "but the One who created and ordered everything that we see; nor do we hold your God to be one and our own to be another, but we acknowledge one and the same, even Him who brought up your forefathers from the land of Egypt with a mighty hand and a stretched-out arm, nor do we put our trust in any other—for there is no other—but only in Him whom you also adore, the God of Abraham, the God of Isaac, and the God of Jacob. Our hope is, however, not through Moses, nor though the Law, or there would be no difference between you and ourselves; but I have read that there should hereafter be a final law, and a covenant more mighty than all others, which everyone who hopes for the inheritance of God should henceforth observe. The law given at Horeb has become obsolete, and was for you Jews only, but the one of which I speak is for all men alike. A new law passed upon a law abrogates that which is old, and in like manner does a subsequent covenant annul a former one. An everlasting and perfect law, and a faithful covenant, is given to us, even Christ, after which there shall be no other law, or ordinance, or command. . . .

"This very law you have despised, and His new and holy covenant have you set at nought, and even now you receive it not, nor do you repent of your evil deeds, for still 'your ears are stopped, and your eyes are blinded, and your heart is waxed gross.' And Jeremiah has cried, but you have not listened to him. The Lawgiver is come, but you discern Him not; 'the poor have the Gospel preached to them, the blind see,' but you understand not. You need a second circumcision, and yet you think much of that of the flesh. The new law commands you to keep a perpetual sabbath, and you rest on one day and think that you are religious, not considering why that commandment was given you. Again, if you eat unleavened bread, you say that you have fulfilled the will of God; but it is not by such means that the Lord our God is pleased. If any one of you is guilty of perjury or theft, let him sin no more. If any be an adulterer, let him repent, and then he will have kept a true and pleasant sabbath of God. If any has unclean hands, let him wash, and he will be pure. . . .

"But that you may have no pretence for saying that Christ *must* have been crucified, or that the transgression must have been in your nation, and it was impossible to be otherwise, I said briefly before, that God, wishing angels and men to follow His will, was pleased to create them with free power to practise righteousness, with reason to know Him by whom they were created, and through whom they, who were not previously in existence, derive their being; and with a law that they should be judged by Him if they act contrarily to right reason. And it is through our own fault that we, both men and angels, shall be convicted of sin, unless we hasten to repent. And if the word of God foretells that some, both angels and men, shall certainly be punished, it does so because God foreknew that they would become unchangeably wicked, and not because He made them so. Wherefore if they repent, all who wish can obtain mercy from God; and the Scripture pronounces them blessed, saying, 'Blessed is the man to whom the Lord will not impute sin,' that is, that having repented of his sins, he may obtain remission of them from God; but not, as you, and some others who resemble you in this particular, deceive yourselves, and say that even if they be sinners and know God, the Lord will not impute sin to them. . . .

Having said this, dearest Marcus Pompeius, I ceased speaking.

Trypho, after pausing for a time, said, "You see that it was not from design that we entered on a conversation with you on these subjects, and I confess that I have been exceedingly gratified by our meeting, and I think that these friends of mine will feel like myself; for we have found more than we expected, or than it was possible for us ever to have expected. But if we could do this more frequently, we should derive more profit, examining the very words of Scripture: but since," he said, "you are on the point of leaving, and daily expect to sail, do not think it a trouble to remember us as your friends when you go away."

"For my part," I replied, "if I had to remain, I would have wished to do this same thing every day: but expecting now, God willing and aiding, to set sail, I exhort you to apply yourselves to this very great struggle for your own salvation, and to be careful to prefer the Christ of Almighty God to your teachers."

After this they left me, praying that I might be preserved both from the dangers of my voyage, and from every calamity. And I prayed for them, and said, "I cannot wish you, sirs, any greater benefit than that, knowing that through this way wisdom is given to every man, you may assuredly believe with us that ours is the Christ of God."

# TERTULLIAN

(See page 59.)

## FROM The Christian Defence

. . . As regards infanticide, however, although child-murder differs from homicide, it makes no difference whether it is done wilfully or as part of a sacred rite. I will turn to you now as a nation. How many of the crowd standing round us, open-mouthed for Christian blood, how many of you gentlemen, magistrates most just and strict against us, shall I not prick in your inner consciousness as being the slayers of your own offspring? There is, indeed, a difference in the manner of death; but assuredly it is more cruel to drown an infant or to expose it to cold and starvation and the dogs; even an adult would prefer to die by the sword. But for us, to whom homicide has been once for all forbidden, it is not permitted to break up even what has been conceived in the womb, while the blood is still being drawn from the mother's body to make a new creature. Prevention of birth is premature murder, and it makes no difference whether it is a life already born that one snatches away or a life that is coming to birth that one destroys. The future man is a man already: the whole fruit is present in the seed. . . .

Today and here you may know the votaries of Bellona by the blood from a slit thigh, caught in the palm of the hand and given them to drink. Again, what of those who as a cure for epilepsy drain with eager thirst the blood of criminals slain at the gladiatorial shows, while it is still running fresh from their throats? What of those who dine on bits of wild beast from the arena, and seek a slice of boar or stag? Your boar in the struggle wiped off the blood which he himself had drawn from a man; your stag lay wallowing in gladiators' gore. The paunches of the very bears are eagerly sought while they are still full of undigested human flesh. Men belch the meat that has been fed on man.

How far removed are you who eat such things, from the Christians' feasts. And are those of you less guilty who with savage lust gloat over human bodies and take living members within your lips? Are they the less dedicated to filthiness by human blood, because they only lick that which may become blood? They make a meal, not of infants, but of well-grown lads. Your perversities may well blush before us Christians, who do not reckon the blood even of animals as an article of food, and abstain from things strangled and from such as die of themselves, lest we should be polluted in any way by the blood that is buried in their flesh. When you are putting Christians to the test you offer them sausages filled with blood, being, of course, quite sure that the means whereby you would have them deviate from their faith is to them a thing impermissible. How absurd it is for you to believe that they are panting for the blood of man, when to your own knowledge they abhor the blood of beasts—unless indeed you have found by experience that human blood is the more palatable of the two! This thirst for blood should have been used, like the little altar and the incense box, as a method of testing Christians. They could then have been discovered by their craving for human blood in the same way as by their refusal to sacrifice: if they refused to taste blood, or if they sacrificed, the charge against them would be disproved. And in any case you would have no lack of human blood at the hearing and condemnation of prisoners.

Again, who are more incestuous than those whom Jupiter himself has taught. Etesias tells us that the Persians have intercourse with their own mothers. The Macedonians also are suspect. On their first hearing the tragedy *Oedipus* they merely smiled at the guilty man's agony and said to each other: "He married his mother." Consider now how easily possible incest becomes owing to the mistakes for which promiscuous lust gives opportunity. In the first place you expose your children, to be brought up out of pity by some passing stranger; or you surrender them for adoption by parents better than yourselves. The memory of a family thus cast off must of necessity some time or other be lost, and when once the possibility of mistake has established itself, incest will begin to shoot out its tendrils, and as the family increases the chances of crime increase with it. Furthermore, everywhere at home, abroad, across the seas, lust walks by your side, whose indiscriminate fury can easily beget you children unawares in some place or other from the smallest portion of seed, so that a family thus scattered may in the ordinary intercourse of life meet its own past and yet fail to recognize the mixture of incestuous blood.

We, for our part, are protected from these accidents by a scrupulous and faithful chastity, and we are as safe from the chance of incest as we are from debauchery, and every post-matrimonial excess. Some gain an even greater security, since they repel all the assaults of sin by a virgin continence, old men and yet children. If you realized these faults in yourselves, you would see that among the Christians they have no existence. The same eyes would have reported both facts. The two kinds of blindness easily combine; those who fail to see what really is, fancy that they see what is not. . . .

# MARCUS MINUCIUS FELIX

fl. 3rd century

Marcus Minucius Felix was a distinguished lawyer, probably of African origin, who lived in Rome and who, in his later years, became a convert to Christianity from Stoicism. The hero of his dialogue, Octavius Januarius, was also a convert, but he had died before the book was written. As to the pagan, Caecilius Natalis, he also lived in Rome, although probably he was a native of Cirta. He is thought to have been a triumvir under Caracalla.

## FROM Octavius

. . . Octavius had come to Rome on business and also to see me; he had left home, wife, and children: the latter still in the age of innocence, when their broken utterances are so charming—the childish prattle, to which the halting accents of their faltering tongue lend additional sweetness. Words cannot express how eagerly and with what transports of joy I welcomed his arrival, a joy increased by the suddenness of this visit of my bosom friend.

After two days' uninterrupted enjoyment of his company, when the eager longings of our hearts were satisfied, and we had told each other of matters of mutual interest, unknown to us in consequence of our separation, we decided to pay a visit to Ostia. This is a delightful town, where I hoped to find in sea-bathing an agreeable and beneficial treatment for certain humours from which I suffered. Owing to the vacation, legal work was slack and had made way for the vintage; and just then, after the heat of summer, the weather had turned cooler with the coming of autumn.

One morning at dawn we happened to be walking along the bank of the Tiber towards the sea; the gentle breeze invigorated our limbs, and the walk over the sand, as it yielded beneath our soft tread, was especially delightful. Cæcilius noticed an image of Serapis and, after the custom of the superstitious vulgar, put his hand to his mouth and kissed it.

Thereupon Octavius said: "Brother Marcus, it is unworthy of an honest man to leave one who in and out of the house is your constant companion, in such blind and vulgar ignorance. On a fine day like this, how can you allow him to do homage to stones, even though they are fashioned in the likeness of the gods, anointed with oil, and crowned with garlands? You must be aware that the shame of his error will recoil as much upon you as upon him."

While Octavius was speaking, we were halfway between Ostia and the sea, and were already nearing the open beach, where the gentle waves, which laved the furthest stretch of sands, extended and as it were laid it out for a promenade. The sea is always restless, even when the winds are still, and although it did not reach the shore in white, foaming waves, we were highly delighted to see it curling and winding round and about our feet, when we dipped them at the water's edge. Alternately it dashed against our feet and sported with the waves, and then, as it retired and retraced its course, sucked them back into itself.

In this manner we walked on slowly and quietly along the shore of the gently winding beach, beguiling the way with conversation, which turned upon Octavius's account of his voyage. After we had gone on for a considerable distance during the course of our conversation, we turned back and went over the same ground again. When we reached a spot where some small vessels, hauled up on land, had been placed on oak supports, high and dry above the mud, we saw some boys thoroughly enjoying themselves in a game of "ducks and drakes." This game is played as follows. A shell, rounded and polished by the constant movements of the waves, is picked up from the beach, and firmly grasped between the fingers on the flat side. The player then stoops and, bending down, throws it as far as he can along the top of the water. The missile either skims the surface, or cutting through the crest of the waves darts along, springing in the air. The boy whose shell goes farthest and oftenest jumps out of the water, claims the victory.

While we were all enjoying the sight, Cæcilius alone was indifferent, and did not even smile at the eagerness of the contest. Silent, anxious, holding aloof, he showed clearly by the expression of his face the signs of some secret grief. "What does this mean?" I said to him; "what has become of your usual vivacity? I miss the cheerfulness natural to you even on serious occasions." He replied: "I have for some time felt keenly distressed and hurt by the manner in which Octavius attacked and reproached you with carelessness, in order to support his charges of ignorance against me more strongly, though indirectly. So I will go further; the whole matter shall be thrashed out between Octavius and myself. If he wishes me to argue with him, as a member of the sect which he attacks, he will see at once that it is easier to argue as among friends than to engage in a scientific discussion. Let us sit down on that rocky mole projecting into the sea, which has been made to protect the baths; we shall be able to rest after our walk and discuss matters more earnestly." We sat down as he proposed, myself between my two friends, with one of them on each side of me. This was not a mark of respect, rank, or honour, for friends are always equal or become so; the object of the arrangement was that I, as arbitrator, should be next to both, in order to hear them better and to keep the disputants apart.

Then Cæcilius began as follows: "My dear Marcus, you cannot be in doubt as to the matter which we are now to investigate, since, having carefully tested both systems, you have abandoned the one and chosen the other. Nevertheless, for the present occasion your mind should be so trained that you can hold the balance evenly as an upright judge, without inclining to one side more than the other. Otherwise, your verdict will appear to be the expression of your own feelings rather than the result of our arguments. If, then, you will take your seat as an entire stranger who knows nothing of either party, it will be easy for me to show that everything in human affairs is doubtful, uncertain, undecided, and probable rather than true. For this reason it is the more surprising that some, weary of a thorough search after truth, should blindly give in to any opinion whatever, rather than steadfastly and diligently persevere in their investigations. Surely all must feel grieved and indignant at the thought that certain people—people, too, ignorant of learning, unlettered, and unacquainted even with the meanest arts—should pronounce definitely upon the universe and the supreme power, which, after all these ages, still forms the subject of the deliberations of the philosophers and their numerous schools. And this is only natural, since human insignificance is quite incapable of investigating things divine. It is not given us to know, and we are forbidden to examine what is suspended above our heads in the heavens or buried deep down in the earth. We should rightly consider ourselves tolerably happy and wise, if we had a more intimate knowledge of ourselves in accordance with the maxim of the wise man of old. But inasmuch as, abandoning ourselves to idle and senseless efforts, we overstep the limits of our insignificance and, though thrown upon earth, in our bold ambition transcend heaven and the stars themselves, at least let us not complicate our mistake by idle and terrifying fancies. Granted that, in the beginning, the germs of everything were condensed by the self-fructifying action of nature, what god is the author of this? Granted that the members of the body of the universe have been united, arranged, and formed by a fortuitous concourse of atoms, what god is the architect? Let us admit that the stars have been lighted by fire, that the sky has been suspended aloft by the nature of its material, that the earth has been similarly secured by its own weight, and that the sea was formed from moisture, how does this explain this new religion, this dread, which is nothing but superstition? Man and every living creature which is born, lives, and grows, is formed by a haphazard union of elements, into which they are again separated, dissolved, and dispersed; and in like manner all things in the universe flow back to their source and return to themselves. There is no artificer, no judge, no creator of the world. Thus, when the elements of fire have united, new and ever new suns are always shining; when the vapours of earth have been given off, the mists are continually increasing. When these mists are compressed and gathered together, the clouds rise higher; when they fall, the rain pours down, the winds blow, the hail rattles; if the thunder-clouds collide, the thunder roars, the lightning glows, the thunderbolts flash and fall at random, hurl themselves upon the mountains, attack the trees, strike without distinction places sacred and profane, smite the guilty and oftentimes the pious. What need to speak of the shifting and uncertain storms, by which all things are violently whirled along, promiscuously and in disorder? In shipwrecks, are not the destinies of good and bad mixed up, with no distinction of their merits and defects? In fires, does not death come upon innocent and guilty alike? When an expanse of the sky is tainted by plague and pestilence, do not all perish indiscriminately? In the heat and fury of battle, is it not the best and bravest that fall? Even in peaceful times, not only is vice put on a level with virtue, but is even respected, so that often one does not know whether to detest a man's depravity or to envy his good fortune. But if the world were ruled by a divine providence and by the authority of some divinity, Phalaris and Dionysius would never have deserved a throne, Rutilius and Camillus banishment, Socrates the draught of hemlock. Look how the fruit-trees, the corn white for harvest, and the ripe grapes are spoilt by the rain and beaten down by the hail. So either the truth, being uncertain, is hidden from us and concealed, or more probably fortune, not restrained by any laws, exercises its power in various dangerous emergencies. . . .

"Accordingly, since all peoples are firmly convinced that there are immortal gods, although their nature and origin are undecided, I cannot think there is anyone so audacious and so swollen with impious pretensions to wisdom as to endeavour to destroy or weaken so ancient, useful, and salutary a religion . . . Is it not then deplorable that an attack should be made upon the gods by certain fellows —you must excuse my expressing with some freedom how strongly I feel in regard to the cause I have taken up—certain fellows, I repeat, belonging to a party whose case is hopeless, proscribed, and desperate? Having gathered together from the lowest dregs of the people a number of ignorant men and credulous women always ready to believe anything, they have formed a rabble of impious conspirators; at their nocturnal gatherings, solemn fasts, and barbarous meals the bond of union is not any sacred rite but crime. It is a people that lurks in darkness and shuns the light, silent in public, talkative in corners; they despise our temples as tombs, insult our gods, ridicule our ceremonies, and, in need of pity themselves, profess (if allowed) to pity our priests; half-naked themselves, they contemptuously refuse offices and dignities. Marvellous folly and incredible audacity!

They despise the torments that are before their eyes, but they fear those that are uncertain and in the future; they are afraid of dying after death, but have no fear of death itself. Thus treacherous hope quiets their alarm by the comforting assurance of a life hereafter.

"Ill weeds grow apace, and these vicious habits are spreading day by day, and these abominable secret haunts where these impious wretches hold their meetings are increasing in number all over the world. These execrable conspirators must be utterly rooted out. They recognize one another by secret signs and marks; they love one another after the briefest acquaintance; a kind of religion of sensuality prevails amongst them; they call themselves promiscuously brothers and sisters, and under the cloak of these names are guilty of the most horrible offences. Thus their vain and foolish superstition glories in its crimes. Were these charges untrue, rumour, which is ever shrewd, would never spread such scandalous reports about them, such as I should be ashamed to mention. I am told that, under the influence of some foolish belief, they worship as sacred the head of the lowest of animals—the ass. A religion worthy of the morality from which it sprang! . . . Again, to say that a man who had suffered capital punishment for a crime and the death-dealing wood of the cross are objects of their veneration, is to assign fitting altars to abandoned wretches, and to assert that they worship what they deserve to worship. The details of the initiation of novices are as horrible as they are well known. An infant, covered with dough to deceive the unwary, is brought to the would-be novice, who, misled by the coating of dough and encouraged to deal what are apparently harmless blows, secretly stabs it to death. Then—shame on them!—they thirstily lick up the child's blood and eagerly divide his limbs; this victim is their bond of union, complicity in the crime is their pledge of mutual silence. Such rites are more abominable than any acts of sacrilege. What takes place at their banquets is also well known; it is everywhere talked about, as is attested by a speech of our countryman of Cirta. On a fixed day they assemble together, children, sisters, mothers, people of both sexes and of all ages. After much feasting, a dog, fastened to the lamp, is encouraged by some pieces of meat thrown to it to spring violently beyond the length of its chain. The lamp, which would have been an inconvenient witness, is overturned and extinguished; after this riot and indecency reign supreme.

"I purposely omit much; what I have already said is too much, and all or most of it is shown to be true by the very atmosphere of secrecy which surrounds this impious religion. Why do they make such efforts to hide and conceal whatever it is that they worship? honourable acts always welcome publicity, only crimes delight in secrecy. Why have they no altars, no temples, no well-known images? Why do they never speak in public, never meet freely, unless it be that the hidden object of their worship is either criminal or disgraceful? But whence, who, or where is that one god, solitary, forsaken, whom no free people or kingdom, nor even Roman superstition has acknowledged? Only the miserable race of the Jews also worships one god, but at least openly, with temples, altars, victims and ceremonies. Yet their god is so weak and powerless that he and his people are prisoners of the Romans. And what monstrous absurdities the Christians invent! According to them, that god of theirs, whom they can neither see nor show to others, carefully investigates all men's characters, acts, even their words and secret thoughts, since he is present everywhere and always on the move. According to them, he is a nuisance, restless, shamelessly curious, being present at man's every act and wandering from place to place. But if he is occupied with the whole he cannot attend to details, and if he is engaged with details he cannot do his duty to the whole.

"Further, Christians threaten the whole world and the universe, together with the hosts of heaven, with destruction by fire, and profess to believe in its future ruin. As if the eternal order of things, established by the divine laws of nature, could be disturbed, the bond of all the elements broken, the framework of heaven taken to pieces, and that mass, by which it is enclosed and surrounded, undermined! Not content with this insane idea, they improve on it by adding certain old wives' fables. They assert that they are born again after death when they are nothing but dust and ashes, and, strangely confiding, believe each other's lies; you would think that they had already come to life again. A twofold evil and a double folly! While threatening the heavens and the stars with destruction, whereas we leave them as we found them, they promise themselves, on the other hand, eternal life when dead and extinct, the inevitable sequel of birth! Hence it is easy to understand why they curse our funeral pyres and condemn cremation; just as if every body, although withdrawn from the flames, were not reduced to dust as the years and ages roll on, just as if it makes any difference whether our bodies are torn to pieces by wild beasts, swallowed up in the sea, covered with earth, or destroyed by fire. Any kind of burial must be a punishment to them, if they have any feeling after death; if they have not, cremation must be regarded as a beneficent remedy in the rapidity of its effect. Self-deceived, they promise themselves, as the elect, the blessings of eternal life after death; the rest of the world, as evil-doers, are doomed to eternal punishment. I could say much more on this, but I am in a hurry to conclude my speech. I need not labour the point that it is they themselves who are the evil-doers, I have already proved it; although, even if I were to admit that they are good and honest men, I know that most people are of opinion—and in this you agree—that guilt or innocence is the work of fate. While some consider fate responsible for all our actions, you attribute them to God; so that the members of your sect do not favour it of their own accord, but as the elect of God. Thus you imagine an unjust judge who, while punishing men for an action which is due to fate, spares those who follow their own will.

"However, I should like to ask whether we are to rise again with or without bodies? If the former, with what bodies—with the old or new ones? Without bodies? but this, so far as I can judge, would mean no life, no mind, no soul. With the old bodies? but these would have been dissolved long ago. With new ones?—then it is a case of the birth of a new man, not of the renovation of the old. And yet, although so much time has elapsed and countless ages have passed, is there a single trustworthy instance of a man having returned from the dead like Protesilaus, if only for a few hours? All these figments of a disordered brain, these senseless consolations invented by lying poets to lend a charm to their verse, to your shame you have hashed up in your excessive credulity in honour of your god. . . ."

Having finished his speech, Cæcilius, beaming with joy (for the vehemence of his outburst had soothed his indignant excitement), turned to Octavius and asked: "Has Octavius, one of the tribe of Plautus, the best of bakers but the worst of philosophers, anything to say in reply to this?"

"Stop jeering at him," I interrupted; "you have no right to vaunt your carefully arranged speech, before the matter has been more fully discussed on both sides, especially as the aim of your argument is not glory, but truth. Every matter is capable of discussion from two points of view. On the one side is truth, though generally difficult to find; on the other a wonderful acuteness, which sometimes by its copious language apes the certainty of an undisputed proof. We must therefore consider each point by itself as carefully as we can, so that while duly appreciating subtlety of argument, we may at the same time be able to pick up, approve, and adopt what is right."

"You are deviating from the duty of a conscientious judge," said Cæcilius; "it is very wrong of you to weaken the force of my pleading by interposing so weighty an argument, since it is for Octavius to refute each point, at present untouched and not yet mooted, if he can."

"As for your charge," I answered, "unless I am mistaken, my words were spoken in the general interest. My idea was that we should examine everything most carefully and base our judgment not on bombastic eloquence but on the solid foundation of facts. But, as you justly complain, our attention must no longer be diverted; let us hear the answer of our friend Januarius, who is eager to speak, in perfect silence."

Then said Octavius: "I will reply to the best of my ability; at the same time you must help me to wash away bitter and disgraceful abuse with the water of truth. . . .

"Since there is no doubt about the existence of a providence, you think you ought to inquire whether the heavenly kingdom is governed by a single ruler or according to the will of several. The solution of the question presents little difficulty to one who considers the earthly kingdoms, which are modelled on the celestial. When has an imperial partnership ever begun in good faith or been dissolved without bloodshed? I say nothing about the Persians, who selected their ruler by omens drawn from the neighing of horses; I pass over the story of the Theban pair, now long forgotten. The story of the twins, fighting for a kingdom of shepherds and huts, is well known. The wars between father-in-law and son-in-law spread all over the world, and the fortunes of so mighty an empire had not room for two rulers.

"Consider other instances. The bees have only one king, the flocks only one head, the herds only one leader. Can you believe that in heaven the supreme power is divided, and that the entire majesty of that true, divine Authority is broken up? It is obvious that God, the Father of all, has neither beginning nor end; He who gives existence to all has given Himself eternal life; before the world was created He was a world in Himself. Whatsoever things there are He calls into being by His word, arranges them by His wisdom, and perfects them by His might.

"He is invisible, for He is too bright for us to look upon. He is impalpable, for He is too pure for us to touch. He is incomprehensible, for He is beyond our ken—infinite, immense, and His real greatness is known to Himself alone. Our mind is too limited to understand Him; therefore we can only form a just estimate of Him by calling him 'inestimable.' I will frankly state my opinion: the man who thinks that he knows the greatness of God, depreciates it; he who does not desire to depreciate it, is ignorant of it. Nor need you seek a name for God; God is His name. Names are only necessary where a large number of persons have to be distinguished individually by special marks and designations; for God, who is alone, the name God is all-sufficient. If I should speak of Him as Father, you would think of him as an earthly father; if as King, you would imagine his as a king of this world; if as Lord, you would certainly understand Him to be mortal. Take away all additional names and you will behold His splendour. On this point all agree with me. When the common people stretch out their hands to heaven, they say nothing but 'God' and 'God is great,' or 'God is true,' 'if God grant.' Is that the natural language of the people or a form of words used by the

Christian in confessing his faith? Even those who are in favour of Jupiter as their supreme lord are only mistaken in the name; they agree with us that there is a single undivided authority.

"I also find the poets proclaiming one Father of gods and men, and that the mind of man varies according to the day which the Father of all has appointed for him. What can be clearer, truer, or more apposite than what Maro of Mantua says? 'In the beginning heaven and earth' and the other parts of the world 'are nourished by a spirit within and moved by a pervading mind, whence come the race of man, flocks and herds,' and all other living things. In another passage he calls that mind and breath God. These are his words: 'God pervades all lands, the tracts of the sea, and high heaven, whence come the race of man, flocks and herds, fire and water.' What else do we also declare God to be but mind, intelligence, and spirit? . . .

"How unfair it is to pass judgment, as you do, upon what is unknown and unexamined, you can judge from our own confession. For we were once the same as you; blind and ignorant, our opinions were once the same as yours. We believed that the Christians worshipped monsters, ate the flesh of infants, and practised incest at their feasts. We did not understand that these tales were always being spread abroad by the demons, without examination or proof; we did not remember that, during all this time, no one came forward to betray the secret, although he would not only have been forgiven but also rewarded for his information. Christianity is so far from being an evil, that its followers, when accused, show neither shame nor fear; their one regret is that they have not become Christians sooner. We, however, when undertaking the defence and advocacy of certain sacrilegious and incestuous persons, even of parricides, did not think that Christians ought to be given a hearing at all. Sometimes, out of pity for them, we treated them with even greater cruelty, torturing them to force them to deny their faith, so as to save their lives. In their case the practice of torture was reversed; it was employed not to elicit the truth, but to compel people to lie. If any one, weaker than his neighbours, crushed and overwhelmed by suffering, abjured his faith, we looked upon him with favour, as if in renouncing the name he had atoned for all his crimes. Do you understand that we once thought and acted as you do now? whereas, if reason and not the prompting of a demon had controlled our decision, Christians should rather have been forced, not to disavow their faith, but to confess their incests, their sinful rites, their sacrifice of children. It is with these and such-like fables that these same demons have filled the ears of the ignorant to our prejudice, to excite horror and indignation against us. And no wonder; since rumour, which ever feeds on the lies that are spread about but is put an end to by the manifestation of the truth, is equally the work of demons; it is they who propagate and keep alive false reports.

"This is the origin of the story which you say you have heard—our deification of an ass's head. Who would be so foolish as to worship such a thing? or even still more foolish and believe it—except yourselves, who keep whole asses as sacred in your stables together with your or their Epona, and piously decorate them in company with Isis, who sacrifice oxen and sheep and worship their heads, and set up as gods being half goats, half men, or with dogs' and lions' faces? Do you not, like the Egyptians, worship and feed the bull Apis? Nor do you condemn their rites instituted in honour of serpents, crocodiles, and other beasts, birds, and fishes, the penalty for killing any one of which gods is death. Again, like these same Egyptians, you are guilty of certain shameful acts of which you accuse us. These and the like infamous practices we may not even hear described; many of us think it a disgrace to speak of them even in our own defence. You falsely allege that acts are committed by modest, clean-living persons, such as we should deem incredible, if your own acts did not demonstrate their possibility.

"As to the worship of a criminal and His Cross with which you charge our religion, you are far from the truth in thinking either that a criminal deserved, or that a mortal had the power, to be believed to be a god. Truly, the man deserves pity who rests all his hopes on a mere mortal, with whose death all his power of rendering assistance is at an end! The Egyptians certainly select one of themselves as an object of worship, court his favour alone, consult him about everything, sacrifice victims to him. But this man, whom others regard as a god, is certainly only a man in his own eyes, whether he will or no; for even if he can dupe another person's conscience he cannot deceive his own. Even kings and princes are not only hailed as great and elect, names to which they have a right, but are falsely called gods by disgraceful flatterers; whereas honour would be the truest homage to a famous man, and affection the most agreeable tribute that could be offered to the worthiest. Thus they invoke the godhead of these men, offer up supplication at their images, implore the aid of their genius (that is, their demon), and it is more dangerous to swear falsely by the genius of the Emperor than by that of Jupiter.

"We neither worship crosses nor wish for them. Certainly, you, who consecrate gods of wood, may perhaps worship wooden crosses as parts of your gods. For what are your standards, banners, and ensigns but gilded and decorated crosses? Your trophies of victory not only present the appearance of a simple cross but also that of one crucified. Certainly, we see the sign of the cross represented in a natural manner on a ship, when it rides over the waves with swelling sails or glides along gently with outspread oars: again, when a yoke is set up, it is like the sign of the cross, and in like manner when a man with outstretched hands worships God with a pure heart. Thus, there is either some natural explanation of the sign of the cross or it embodies the form of your religion.

"I should like to meet the man who says or believes that initiation into Christianity is accompanied by the murder of an infant and the drinking of its blood. Do you think it possible that so tender, so small a body could receive such fatal wounds, that anyone could have the heart to kill one just born, hardly entered upon life, and shed and drink its fresh young blood? No one can believe this unless he himself were capable of doing so. I see your newly born sons exposed by you to wild beasts and birds of prey, or cruelly strangled to death. There are also women among you who, by taking certain drugs, destroy the beginnings of the future human being while it is still in the womb and are guilty of infanticide before they are mothers. . . .

"The story of our incestuous banquet is a monstrous lie, invented by a league of demons to injure us, in order that our reputation for chastity might be sullied by charges of infamous and disgusting practices, and that, before they had learnt the truth, men might be driven to shun us owing to the terror inspired by unutterable suggestions. Thus also your friend Fronto has not given evidence as one who affirms a thing, but has scattered abuse broadcast like a public speaker; for such practices rather originated amongst people like yourselves. In Persia, a man is allowed to marry his mother, in Egypt and Athens his sister. Your histories and tragedies, which you eagerly read and listen to, treat incest as something to be proud of; hence it is that you worship incestuous gods, united to mother, daughter, and sister. Not without reason, then, is incest often detected amongst you, but always permitted. We, on the other hand, show our modesty not only outwardly but inwardly; we willingly cleave to one marriage-tie; in the desire to have children, we have only one wife—or else none. Our banquets are conducted not only with modesty, but also with sobriety; we indulge in no luxurious feasts, nor spin out our meals in drinking, but temper our gaiety with seriousness. Our language is pure, our body even more so, and most of us practise perpetual virginity without boasting of it; so far from our having any desire for incest, even a chaste and legitimate union calls forth a blush of shame.

"Nor, again are we composed of the lowest dregs of the people, even if we refuse your offices and dignities; nor do we belong to any faction, if we recognize only one virtue, and are as quiet when assembled together as by ourselves; nor are we talkative in corners, if you are either ashamed or afraid to listen to us in public.

"The fact that our number is increasing daily is no proof of error, but evidence of merit; for when men live an honourable life, their own friends remain constant and are joined by others. Lastly, we easily recognize each other, not by external marks, as you imagine, but by the stamp of innocence and modesty; we love one another (which annoys you), since we do not know how to hate; we call ourselves brethren (which excites your ill-will), as being children of one and the same Father, God, as showing the same faith, as coheirs of the same hope. Whereas you, on the contrary, do not recognize each other, give way to outbursts of mutual hatred, and only acknowledge any ties of brotherhood when leagued together for murder.

"Further, do you think that we wish to conceal the objects of our worship, because we have neither temples nor altars? By what image am I to represent God, since, rightly considered, man himself is the image of God? What temple am I to erect to Him, since the whole of this world, which has been fashioned by Him, is unable to contain Him? Am I to confine such might and majesty within the limits of a small temple, while I myself, a mere man, have a more spacious dwelling-place? Is not the mind a better place of dedication, the heart a better place for His consecration? Am I to offer to God the sacrifices and victims which He has provided for our use, and reject His gifts? This would be ungrateful, since the most acceptable sacrifice is a good heart, a clean spirit. Therefore, the man who practises innocence offers prayer to God; he who practises justice offers libation to him; he who abstains from wrongdoing propitiates him; the man who rescues another from danger sacrifices the most excellent victim. These are our sacrifices, these are our rites; he who is most just amongst us is the most religious. . . .

"Consider again how, as a consolation for us, the entire kingdom of nature foreshadows the resurrection. The sun sinks and rises again, the stars disappear and return: flowers die and revive: trees decay and again put forth leaves: seeds do not come up again until they rot. The body in the grave is like a tree in winter; both conceal their new life under an apparent dryness. Why are you so anxious that it should revive and return during the cruel winter? The body also has its spring, for which we must wait.

"I am aware that most men, conscious of what they deserve, hope rather than believe that they will not exist after death; they prefer total annihilation to resurrection with punishments to follow. Their error is aggravated by the immunity enjoyed by them in the world and by the infinite patience of God, whose judgment the slower it is the juster it is. . . .

"Further, as to the charge that most of us are paupers, this is no shame, but our glory; for as the mind is enervated by luxury, so it is strengthened by frugality. And yet who can be poor if he wants nothing, if he does not long for what is another's, if he is rich in the sight of God? That man rather is poor who, though he has great possessions, desires more. But I will tell you what I think; no one can be as poor as he was born. Birds live without possessing anything of their own, cattle obtain pasture daily; and yet they are all created for our use, and we possess all if we do not desire it. Therefore, as a man, when walking, makes the greater progress the more lightly he is burdened, so in this journey of life the man who lightens his burden by poverty is happier than one who groans beneath the weight of riches. And yet, if we thought it useful, we might ask for wealth from God; certainly He to whom all belongs could grant us a share of it. But we prefer to despise wealth than to possess it; we rather desire innocence and demand patience; we would rather be virtuous than extravagant. . . .

"What a beautiful sight for God to see, when the Christian wrestles with pain, braves threats, punishment and torture, scornfully derides the din at his execution and the horrible sight of the executioner; when he uplifts the banner of freedom against kings and princes, yielding to God alone, to whom he belongs; when, in triumph and victorious, he mocks the judge who has pronounced sentence against him. For he is the conqueror who has obtained what he desires. Where is the soldier who does not face danger more boldly under the eyes of his commander? For no one obtains a reward before he has been tested. And yet a general cannot give what he does not possess; he cannot prolong life, although he can reward service. But the soldier of God is neither abandoned in trouble nor destroyed by death. Thus the Christian may appear miserable, but cannot be proved so. . . . And how many of our community have suffered, without a groan, the loss not only of their right hand but the destruction of their whole body by fire, although they had it in their power to obtain their release? Need I compare *men* with Mucius, Aquilius, and Regulus? Why, even our lads and women, in their inspired endurance of suffering, laugh to scorn crucifixion, tortures, wild beasts, and all the terrors of punishment. And you, poor wretches, you cannot understand that there is no one who would desire to undergo punishment without reason or could endure torture without the help of God.

"But perhaps you are deceived by the fact that many who know not God possess wealth in abundance, are full of honours, and enjoy great authority. These unhappy men are uplifted the higher, that their fall may be greater. They are like victims fattened for punishment or crowned for sacrifice. So it is that some are raised to the throne and absolute power, in order that their profligate minds, in the unrestrained exercise of their authority, may freely barter away their natural character. For without the knowledge of God what happiness can be lasting, since this is death? Like a dream it slips away, before we can grasp it. Are you a king? You yourself feel as much fear as you inspire in others; however numerous your bodyguard, you are left alone to face danger. Are you rich? It is dangerous to trust fortune, and great store of provisions for the brief journey of life is not a help, but a burden. Are you proud of your fasces and purple? It is a vain error of man and an empty show of rank to shine in purple, while the mind is vile. Are you blessed with noble ancestors? Do you boast of your parents? But we are all born equal; it is virtue alone that distinguishes us . . .

"Who doubts that we are fond of the flowers of spring, when we pluck the early rose, lily, and any other flower of delightful scent and colour? for we use them free and loose or wear them round our necks as delicate garlands. You must excuse us for not crowning our heads; we are in the habit of inhaling the sweet perfume of a flower, not of using the back of the head or the hair as a means of conveying it. Nor do we crown our dead. In regard to this, I am the more surprised at your applying a torch to one who still feels, or offering a garland to one who does not, since those who are happy need no flowers, while those who are unhappy take no pleasure in them. On the other hand, we arrange our funerals as simply as our lives; we place no fading garland upon the grave, but await from God an undying crown of immortal flowers; quiet, modest, confident in the generosity of our God, we enliven our hope of future happiness by faith in His ever-present majesty. Thus we feel assured of our resurrection in blessedness and live in contemplation of the future . . .

"Why should we be ungrateful, why should we be dissatisfied, seeing that the truth about the Godhead has attained maturity in our times? Let us enjoy our happiness and avoid excess in our opinions; let superstition be restrained, let impiety be driven out, let true religion be preserved."

After Octavius had finished, for some time we remained in amazed silence, with our eyes intently fixed upon him; as for myself, I was lost in overwhelming admiration at the skill with which he backed up his principles, which can be more easily felt than expressed in words, by a wealth of argument, examples, and quotation from authorities; at the manner in which he repelled the attacks of the ill-disposed with their own weapons, namely those of the philosophers, and demonstrated that the truth was not only easy to discover but also agreeable.

While I was silently turning over these things in my mind, Cæcilius burst out: "I congratulate my friend Octavius most heartily, but I also congratulate myself, nor need I wait for the verdict. I too, in like manner, am victorious: for even if it seems audacious, I also claim a victory. As he has gained the victory over me, so have I triumphed over error. As to the main questions, in regard to Providence and God I accept your belief; I recognize the purity of your sect, which is henceforth my own. Even now there remain certain points, which although no obstacle to the truth, must be discussed to make my instruction complete. But as the sun is already setting, we will deal with these points tomorrow; they will not detain us long, since we are agreed upon the general issues."

"As for myself," said I, "I rejoice the more heartily on behalf of all of us, that Octavius has also conquered for my benefit, since I am relieved of the very disagreeable duty of giving a verdict. I cannot, however, adequately reward his merits by praising him in words; the testimony of one man by himself carries little weight; Octavius possesses an excellent gift of God, which inspired him when he spoke and assisted him to win his case."

After this we retired, all three joyful and happy: Cæcilius because he believed, Octavius because he was victorious, and I myself because of the conversion of the one and the victory of the other.

# ST METHODIUS OF OLYMPUS

d. 311?

Methodius, also sometimes called Euboulios, was bishop simultaneously of Olympus and Patara, in Lycia. Later he was bishop of Tyre, in Phoenicia, and at the end of the Diocletian persecution he suffered martyrdom at Chalcis, according to St Jerome's testimony. He is known chiefly as the antagonist of Origen, but was not a little influenced by his doughty opponent, as is shown in the *Banquet* and in other fragments of his which have come down to us, such as his treatise *On the Resurrection.* He also wrote against the Neoplatonist philosopher Porphyrius.

## FROM The Banquet of the Ten Virgins, or, Concerning Chastity

*Euboulios.* You have arrived most seasonably, Gregorion, for I have just been looking for you, wanting to hear of the meeting of Marcella and Theopatra, and of the other virgins who were present at the banquet, and of the nature of their discourses on the subject of chastity; for it is said that they argued with such ability and power that there was nothing lacking to the full consideration of the subject. If, therefore, you have come here for any other purpose, put that off to another time, and do not delay to give us a complete and connected account of the matter of which we are inquiring.

*Gregorion.* I seem to be disappointed of my hope, as someone else has given you intelligence beforehand on the subject respecting which you ask me. For I thought that you had heard nothing of what had happened, and I was flattering myself greatly with the idea that I should be the first to tell you of it. And for this reason I made all haste to come here to you, fearing the very thing which has happened, that someone might anticipate me.

*Euboulios.* Be comforted, my excellent friend, for we have had no precise information respecting anything which happened; since the person who brought us the intelligence had nothing to tell us, except that there had been dialogues; but when he was asked what they were, and to what purpose, he did not know.

*Gregorion*. Well then, as I came here for this reason, do you want to hear all that was said from the beginning; or shall I pass by parts of it, and recall only those points which I consider worthy of mention?

*Euboulios*. By no means the latter; but first, Gregorion, relate to us from the very beginning where the meeting was, and about the setting forth of the viands, and about yourself, how you poured out the wine

They in golden cups
Each other pledged, while towards broad heaven they looked.

*Gregorion*. You are always skilful in discussions, and excessively powerful in argument—thoroughly confuting all your adversaries.

*Euboulios*. It is not worth while, Gregorion, to contend about these things at present; but do oblige us by simply telling us what happened from the beginning.

*Gregorion*. Well, I will try. But first answer me this: You know, I presume, Arete, the daughter of Philosophia?

*Euboulios*. Why do you ask?

*Gregorion*. "We went by invitation to a garden of hers with an eastern aspect, to enjoy the fruits of the season, myself, and Procilla, and Tusiane." I am repeating the words of Theopatra, for it was of her I obtained the information. "We went, Gregorion, by a very rough, steep, and arduous path: when we drew near to the place," said Theopatra, "we were met by a tall and beautiful woman walking along quietly and gracefully, clothed in a shining robe as white as snow. Her beauty was something altogether inconceivable and divine. Modesty, blended with majesty, bloomed on her countenance. It was a face," she said, "such as I know not that I had ever seen, awe-inspiring, yet tempered with gentleness and mirth; for it was wholly unadorned by art, and had nothing counterfeit. She came up to us, and, like a mother who sees her daughters after a long separation, she embraced and kissed each one of us with great joy, saying, 'O my daughters, you have come with toil and pain to me who am earnestly longing to conduct you to the pasture of immortality; toilsomely have you come by a way abounding with many frightful reptiles; for, as I looked, I saw you often stepping aside, and I was fearing lest you should turn back and slip over the precipices. But thanks to the Bridegroom to whom I have espoused you, my children, for having granted an effectual answer to all our prayers.' And, while she is thus speaking," said Theopatra, "we arrive at the enclosure, the doors not being shut as yet, and as we enter we come upon Thekla and Agathe and Marcella preparing to sup. And Arete immediately said, 'Do you also come hither, and sit down here in your place along with these your fellows.' Now," said she to me, "we who were there as guests were altogether, I think, ten in number; and the place was marvellously beautiful, and abounding in the means of recreation. The air was diffused in soft and regular currents, mingled with pure beams of light, and a stream flowing as gently as oil through the very middle of the garden, threw up a most delicious drink; and the water flowing from it, transparent and pure, formed itself into fountains, and these, overflowing like rivers, watered all the garden with their abundant streams; and there were different kinds of trees there, full of fresh fruits, and the fruits that hung joyfully from their branches were of equal beauty; and there were ever-blooming meadows strewn with variegated and sweet-scented flowers, from which came a gentle breeze laden with sweetest odour. And the agnos grew near, a lofty tree, under which we reposed, from its being exceedingly wide-spreading and shady."

*Euboulios*. You seem to me, my good friend, to be making a revelation of a second paradise.

*Gregorion*. You speak truly and wisely. "When there," she said, "we had all kinds of food and a variety of festivities, so that no delight was wanting. After this Arete, entering, gave utterance to these words: 'Young maidens, the glory of my greatness, beautiful virgins, who tend the undefiled meadows of Christ with unwedded hands, we have now had enough of food and feasting, for all things are abundant and plentiful with us. What is there, then, besides which I wish and expect? That each of you shall pronounce a discourse in praise of virginity. . . .'

*Euboulios.* Tell me, Gregorion, which shall we say are the better, those who without lust govern concupiscence, or those who under the assaults of concupiscence continue pure?

*Gregorion.* For my part, I think those who are free from lust, for they have their mind undefiled, and are altogether uncorrupted, sinning in no respect.

*Euboulios.* Well, I swear by chastity, and wisely, O Gregorion. But lest in any wise I hinder you, if I gainsay your words, it is that I may the better learn, and that no one hereafter may refute me.

*Gregorion.* Gainsay me as you will, you have my permission. For, Euboulios, I think that I know sufficient to teach you that he who is not concupiscent is better than he who is. If I cannot, then there is no one who can convince you.

*Euboulios.* Bless me! I am glad that you answer me so magnanimously, and show how wealthy you are as regards wisdom.

*Gregorion.* A mere chatterer, so you seem to be, O Euboulios.

*Euboulios.* Why so?

*Gregorion.* Because you ask rather for the sake of amusement than of truth.

*Euboulios.* Speak fair, I pray you, my good friend; for I greatly admire your wisdom and renown. I say this because, with reference to the things that many wise men often dispute among themselves, you say that you not only understand them, but also vaunt that you can teach another.

*Gregorion.* Now tell me truly whether it is a difficulty with you to receive the opinion that they who are not concupiscent excel those who are concupiscent, and yet restrain themselves? or are you joking?

*Euboulios.* How so, when I tell you that I do not know? But, come, tell me, O wisest lady, in what do the non-concupiscent and chaste excel the concupiscent who live chastely?

*Gregorion.* Because, in the first place, they have the soul itself pure, and the Holy Spirit always dwells in it, seeing that it is not distracted and disturbed by fancies and unrestrained thoughts, so as to pollute the mind. But they are in every way inaccessible to lust, both as to their flesh and to their heart, enjoying tranquillity from passions. But they who are allured from without, through the sense of sight, with fancies, and receiving lust flowing like a stream into the heart, are often not less polluted, even when they think that they contend and fight against pleasures, being vanquished in their mind.

*Euboulios.* Shall we then say that they who serenely live and are not disturbed by lusts are pure?

*Gregorion.* Certainly. For these are they whom God makes gods in the Beatitudes; they who believe in Him without doubt. And He says that they shall look upon God with confidence, because they bring in nothing that darkens or confuses the eye of the soul for the beholding of God; but all desire of things secular being eliminated, they not only, as I said, preserve the flesh pure from carnal connection, but even the heart, in which, especially, as in a temple, the Holy Spirit rests and dwells, is open to no unclean thoughts.

*Euboulios.* Stay now; for I think that from hence we shall the better go on to the discovery of what things are truly the best; and, tell me, do you call anyone a good pilot?

*Gregorion.* I certainly do.

*Euboulios.* Whether is it he that saves his vessel in great and perplexing storms, or is it he who does so in a breathless calm?

*Gregorion.* He that does so in a great and perplexing storm.

*Euboulios.* Shall we not then say that the soul which is deluged with the surging waves of the passions, and yet does not, on that account, weary or grow faint, but directs her vessel—that is, the flesh—nobly into the port of chastity, is better and more estimable than he that navigates in calm weather?

*Gregorion.* We will say so.

*Euboulios.* For to be prepared against the entrance of the gales of the Evil Spirit, and not to be cast away or overcome, but to refer all to Christ, and strongly to contend against pleasures, brings greater praise than he wins who lives a virgin life calmly and with ease.

*Gregorion.* It appears so.

*Euboulios.* And what saith the Lord? Does He not seem to show that he who retains continence, though concupiscent, excels him who, having no concupiscence, leads a virgin life?

*Gregorion*. Where does He say so?

*Euboulios*. Where, comparing a wise man to a house well founded, He declares him immovable because he cannot be overthrown by rains, and floods, and winds; likening, as it would seem, these storms to lusts, but the immovable and unshaken firmness of the soul in chastity to the rock.

*Gregorion*. You appear to speak what is true.

*Euboulios*. And what say you of the physician? Do you not call him the best who has been proved in great diseases, and has healed many patients?

*Gregorion*. I do.

*Euboulios*. But the one who has never at any time practised, nor ever had the sick in his hands, is he not still in all respects the inferior?

*Gregorion*. Yes.

*Euboulios*. Then we may certainly say that a soul which is contained by a concupiscent body, and which appeases with the medicaments of temperance the disorders arising from the heat of lusts, carries off the palm for healing, over one to whose lot it has fallen to govern aright a body which is free from lust.

*Gregorion*. It must be allowed.

*Euboulios*. And how is it in wrestling? Whether is the better wrestler he who has many and strong antagonists, and continually is contending without being worsted, or he who has no opponents?

*Gregorion*. Manifestly he who wrestles.

*Euboulios*. And, in wrestling, is not the athlete who contends the more experienced?

*Gregorion*. It must be granted.

*Euboulios*. Therefore it is clear that he whose soul contends against the impulses of lust, and is not borne down by it, but draws back and sets himself in array against it, appears stronger than he who does not lust.

*Gregorion*. True.

*Euboulios*. What then? Does it not appear to you, Gregorion, that there is more courage in being valiant against the assaults of base desires?

*Gregorion*. Yes, indeed.

*Euboulios*. Is not this courage the strength of virtue?

*Gregorion*. Plainly so.

*Euboulios*. Therefore, if endurance be the strength of virtue, is not the soul which is troubled by lusts, and yet perseveres against them, stronger than that which is not so troubled?

*Gregorion*. Yes.

*Euboulios*. And if stronger, then better?

*Gregorion*. Truly.

*Euboulios*. Therefore the soul which is concupiscent, and exercises self-control, as appears from what has been said, is better than that which is not concupiscent, and exercises self-control.

*Gregorion*. You speak truly, and I shall desire still more fully to discourse with you concerning these things. If, therefore, it pleases you, tomorrow I will come again to hear respecting them. Now, however, as you see, it is time to betake ourselves to the care of the outward man. . . .

# PROSPER OF AQUITAINE

d. 463

Prosper was a layman of southern Gaul, connected with the monasteries there. He was married, but he and his wife consecrated themselves entirely to the service of God. He left Aquitaine for Rome and the papal court shortly after Cassian's death in 435. He obtained from Pope Celestine a letter confirming the orthodoxy of St Augustine and begging the Gallican bishops to end their campaign against him. Prosper is thought to have been at some time St Leo's secretary. He is the author of a chronicle, of which the first two parts are merely repetitions of St Eusebius and St Jerome, but of which the last part, covering the period from 379 to 455, is original.

## FROM The Call of All Nations

Translated by P. De Letter, S.J., in *Ancient Christian Writers.*

. . . The Apostle Paul, teacher of the Gentiles, writing to Timothy, says, "For there is one God and one Mediator of God and men, the man Christ Jesus who gave Himself a redemption for all."

For the universal Church this constitutes a fundamental norm of the Apostles' teaching. . . . There is no part of the world in which Christian people do not offer up prayers "for all men." The Church, then, pleads before God everywhere not only for the saints, and those regenerated in Christ, but also for all infidels and all enemies of the Cross of Christ, for all worshippers of idols, for all who persecute Christ in His members, for the Jews whose blindness does not see the light of the Gospel, for heretics and schismatics who are alien to the unity of faith and charity. . . .

First, we must confess that God wills all men to be saved and to come to the knowledge of truth. Secondly, there can be no doubt that all who actually come to the knowledge of the truth and to salvation do so not in virtue of their own merits but of the efficacious help of divine Grace. Third, we must admit that human understanding is unable to fathom the depths of God's judgments and we ought not to inquire why He who wishes all men to be saved does not in fact save all. . . .

Everyone receives with no merit on his part the means of gaining merit, and before he has done any work whatever he is given the dignity thanks to which his work will deserve a reward. For it is one thing to be able to work and another to work, one thing to be able to have charity and another to have it, one thing to be capable of continence, justice, wisdom, and another to be continent, just, and wise. And so not every man that can be remade is actually remade, and not every man who can be healed is actually restored to health, for only the possibility of restoration or healing is given with nature, but it is Grace that actually remakes or heals. . . .

Charity itself is not always given in such a way that the one who receives it takes in at once all that belongs to its perfection. For charity is a love that can be overcome by another love, and often enough the love of God is stifled by the love of the world, unless, kindled by the Holy Spirit, it reaches such a state of fervor that no cold can extinguish it nor any tepidity slacken its ardor. Indeed, since the sum total of all God's bounty and the soul of all virtues is given with this ineffable gift, all other gifts are granted us to enable the yearning of the faithful soul to strive effectively after perfect charity. As this is not only from God but is God Himself, it makes steadfast, persevering and unconquerable all those whom it floods with its delight. But men who do not know the sweetness of these waters and still drink of the torrents of this world, men who even after touching with their lips and tasting of the fountain of life, still like to get drunk with the golden cup of Babylon, are completely deceived by their own judgment and fall through their own fault. . . . For without charity it is easy to lose all gifts, which same gifts are useless without charity. . . .

And of no man can the verdict be given before his death that he will share in the glory of the elect: rather, a salutary fear should make him persevere in humility. Let him that standeth, take heed lest he fall, and if he should happen to fall, overcome by a temptation, let him not be consumed by sadness, nor despair of the mercy of Him "who lifteth up all that fall, and setteth up all that are cast down." . . .

# BOETHIUS

480?–?524

Anicius Manlius Severinus Boethius was born in Rome, of good family. At the age of thirty he was made consul by Theodoric the Ostrogoth, Arian king of Rome. His two sons were given the same honor in 522, and all seemed serene. However, Theodoric was influenced by Boethius's enemies, who accused him of magical practices and of intriguing with the Byzantine court. He was thrown into prison at Pavia and put to death in 524, partly, at least, for his Catholic faith. While in prison he wrote the *Consolation of Philosophy,* the best known of his works and one widely read throughout the Middle Ages. Few books have been so often translated and commented upon.

## FROM The Consolation of Philosophy

Translated by Geoffrey Chaucer; spelling modernized by the editor.

Then said I thus, "Oh, I wonder that thou promisest me such great things. Not that I doubt that thou wilt perform that thou dost promise; but I pray thee only this, that thou tarry not to tell me the things that thou has accomplished."

"First," said she, "thou must needs know that good folk are always strong and mighty, and the wicked are feeble, and deserted and naked of all strengths. And of these things, indeed, every one of them is declared and shown by the other. For just as good and evil are two contraries, if it so be that good be steadfast, then the feebleness of evil is showed openly; and if thou knowest clearly the frailty of evil, the steadfastness of good is known. But for as much as the truth of my sentence shall be the more clear and abundant, I will go by the one way or by the other, and will confirm the things that be purposed, now on this side and now on that. Two things there are, in which the effect of all the deeds of mankind stand, that is to say, will and power. And if one of these two fail there is nothing that can be done. For if will is lacking, there is no one who will undertake what is against his inclination; and if power faileth, the will is but vain, and avails nothing. And so it happens that if you see someone who would get what he may not, you need not doubt it is power he lacks to accomplish that he will."

"This is open and clear," said I, "and may in no wise be denied."

"And if you see one," said she, "who has done what he wishes to do, you will not doubt that he had power to do it?"

"No," I said.

"And it is according to what each man can do, that he is judged strong (as who saith, in so much as a man is mighty to do a thing, in so much do men hold him to be strong; and in that he may not, in so much do men deem him feeble)."

"I confess I agree," I said.

"Dost remember," quoth she, "that I have gathered and shown by the aforesaid reasons that all the intention of the will of mankind, which is led by diverse studies, hastens to come to blissfulness."

"I remember well," said I, "that this has been shown."

"And dost thou not recall," said she, "that blissfulness is this same good that men require? So that when that blissfulness is required of all, that good also is required and desired of all?"

"I do not have to recall it," I said, "for I have it firmly always fixed in my memory."

"All folk then," she said, "good and also bad, strive without difference of intention to come to good?"

"This indeed follows," said I.

"And certain it is," said she, "that by the getting of good men are made good?"

"This is certain," said I.

"Then good men get what they desire?"

"So it seems," I said.

"But wicked folk," she said, "if they get the good that they desire, they no more would be so wicked?"

"So is it," quoth I.

"Then since the one and the other," quoth she, "desire good, and the good folk get good and not the wicked folk, then there is no doubt that the good folk are mighty and the wicked folk are feeble?"

"Whosoever," quoth I, "doubteth of this, he has never considered the nature of things nor the consequence of reasons."

"And moreover," quoth she, "if that there be two things that have the same purpose by nature, and one of them pursueth and promoteth the same things by natural office and the other may not do it by the natural office, but followeth a manner other than that which is natural, he that accomplisheth his purpose kindly, even if he does not accomplish his own purpose—which of these two deemest thou to be the more mighty?"

"I think I can guess," quoth I, "what you are saying, but all the same I desire to hear it more plainly from thee."

"Thou wilt not deny," quoth she, "that the movement of going is in men by nature?"

"No, forsooth," quoth I.

"Nor dost thou doubt," quoth she, "that this natural office of going be the office of the feet?"

"I do not doubt it," quoth I.

"Then," quoth she, "if a man is mighty to move and goeth upon his feet, and another, to whom this natural office of feet is lacking, is forced to go creeping upon his hands, which of these two should be held to be the more mighty by right?"

"Bring out the remainder of your argument," quoth I, "for no one doubts that he that can go by the natural office of feet is mightier than he that may not."

"But the sovereign good," quoth she, "that is equally proposed to the good and to the bad, the good folk seek it by the natural office of the virtues, and the wicked force themselves to get it by diverse covetings of earthly things, by which it is not natural to get this same sovereign good. Can you imagine that this can be otherwise?"

"No," quoth I, "for the consequence is open and plain of things that I have granted, that needs be that good folk are mighty, and bad folk feeble and unmighty."

"Thou runnest right before me," quoth she, "and this is the judgment [that is to say, I judge thus] of the right. . . . And for as much as thou understandest what is the strength of this power of evil men, I have defined a little heretofore that nothing is so mighty as sovereign good."

"That is so," quoth I.

"And this same sovereign good may not do evil?"

"Certainly not," quoth I.

"Is there anyone then," quoth she, "who thinks that men may do all things?"

"No man," quoth I, "unless he be out of his wits."

"But certain evil men do wrong?"

"Yes," quoth I, "would to God that they might do none."

"Then," quoth she, "since he that is mighty to do only good things may do all things, and he that is mighty to do evil things may not do all things, then it is an open and manifest thing that to do evil is to be of less power. And further to prove this conclusion there helps me this: I have already shown how all power is to be numbered among the things men ought to require, and I have shown that all things that ought to be desired be referred to as good, being right as to the manner of their nature. But for men to do evil and felony may not be referred to as good. Then is not evil of the number of things that ought to be desired. But all power ought to be desired and required. Then it is open and clear that the power of evil men is no power. And of all these things it showeth well that the good folk are certainly mighty and the wicked are certainly not mighty. And it is clear and open that this sentence of Plato is true, that saith that only wise men may do that which they desire, and the wicked may desire what they wish, but that they have no power to accomplish what they desire (that is to say, to come to sovereign good). For the wicked do that which they least want, by doing the very things which delight; they want to attain to that good that they desire, but they never get to attain thereto, for vices never come to blessedness."

# SALVIAN

5th century

Salvian's long life (he was possibly one hundred when he died) covers most of the fifth century. Early in life he married a pagan, Palladia, who was later converted. After the birth of a daughter, Auspiciola, Salvian became a monk at Lérins, and Palladia entered a convent. Salvian was ordained to the priesthood and taught rhetoric at Lérins, where he may have known St Patrick, who was studying there at the same time. Later he became a priest at Marseilles, and there wrote his most famous book, *The Governance of God.*

## FROM The Governance of God

. . . In all these commandments of which I have spoken, our Lord has ordered our obedience. Where are they who obey all God's commandments or even a very few of them? Where are they who love their enemies or do good to those who persecute them, or overcome evil by good? Where are they who turn their cheek to those who strike them, who yield their property without litigation to those who despoil them? Where is he who is completely free from detracting? Where is he who injures nobody by his reproaches? Where is he who imposes silence on his lips lest they burst forth into acrimonious curses. Who is it who keeps these little commandments, and I will not mention the greater ones. . . .

Since this is so, and since we fulfil none of God's commands, why do we complain about God, who has more reason to complain about all of us? What is our reason for saying in sorrow that God does not heed us, when we ourselves do not heed Him? What is our reason for muttering that God does not look down towards earth, when we ourselves do not look up towards Heaven? What is the reason for being annoyed that our prayers are disdained by God, when we ourselves disdain His commandments? . . .

What more can I say? I am about to speak on a grave and lamentable subject. The Church herself, which should be the appeaser of

God in all things, what is she but the exasperator of God? Beyond a very few individuals who shun evil, what else is the whole assemblage of Christians but the bilge water of vice? How many will you find in the Church who are not either a drunkard or a beast, or an adulterer, or a fornicator, or a robber, or a debauchee, or a brigand or a murderer? And, what is worse than all this, they do all these things almost unceasingly. . . .

As regards people in high places, of what does their dignity consist but in confiscating the property of the state? As regards some whose names I do not mention, what is a political position, but a kind of plunder? There is no greater pillaging of poor states than that done by those in power. For this, office is bought by the few to be paid for by ravaging the many. What can be more disgraceful and wicked than this? The poor pay the purchase price for positions which they themselves do not buy. They are ignorant of the bargain, but know the amount paid. The world is turned upside down that the light of a few may become illustrious. The elevation of one man is the downfall of all the others. . . .

Consider the remedies recently given to some cities. What have they done but make all the rich immune and pile more taxes on the wretched poor? In order that the old taxes should be remitted the former, they have imposed new taxes on the latter. . . . The rich have become richer by lessening the obligations which they bore lightly; the poor are dying from the multiplication of the burdens which they were already unable to bear. . . .

Whence comes this good fortune to the Christian people, that the number of evil-doers would be less or even the same as the number of good? O lamentable misery! O mournful misery! How unlike, today, is the Christian people itself, that is, to what it formerly was! At that time, because they lied, Peter the chief of the Apostles punished Ananias and Sapphira with death. The most blessed Paul also expelled one evil man from the church, lest he make many evil by his presence.

Today, we are even content with an equal number of good and evil men. Why do I say we are content? Rather, it would be right for us to exult and dance with joy if that parity should happen to us. Behold how much we have fallen back. Behold how much we have fallen behind that purity of the Christian people, that purity by which all were formerly untainted. Behold how much we have been reduced, when we think the Church would be happy if it had within it as many good as evil men. For how could we judge the Church not blessed if it had half its members guiltless, the Church which we today lament is almost all sinful?

Hence, since this is the case, it was unnecessary, unnecessary indeed for me to speak so at length about one evil man. It was unnecessary for me to weep over one man's crimes, for all men's crimes, or almost all, must be wept for and lamented. There are many such evil men. Certainly, what is not less sinful, they desire to be such and they labor by their performance of evil works not to appear otherwise. Thus, although they commit lesser evils because they are capable only of lesser evils, they are, however, not less evil because they would not want to be less evil if they could. . . .

In the first place, there is almost no crime or vice which is not to be found at the games. There it is the height of pleasure to see men die, or, what is worse and more cruel than death, to see them torn to shreds; to see the bellies of wild animals filled with human flesh; to see men eaten for the entertainment of those standing around; to see the pleasure of the onlookers, that is, to be devoured almost no less by the looks of men than by the teeth of beasts. And that this be done, there is a world of expense. With great care and pains are the preparations made. Hidden places are approached, impassable ravines are searched, impenetrable forests are wandered through, the cloudy Alps are climbed, the deep valleys are probed. In order that the bowels of men may be devoured by wild animals, nature is not allowed to hold anything in secret.

But, you say, these things are not done all the time. This is correct. That they are not always done is an excellent excuse for wrongdoing! As if, indeed, we should let acts which injure God be done constantly, or let acts which are bad be done well because they are not done all the time. Murderers do not always kill. Yet they are murderers even when they are not killing, because all the while they are stained with murder. Robbers do not always rob. Yet they do not cease to be robbers, because even when they are not actually committing robbery they do not put the thoughts of robbery from their minds. In like manner, all those who delight in games of this sort are not mentally blameless of the guilt involved in looking at the games even when they are not looking, because they would always look if they could.

Nor is this the only sin. There are others greater. What are they? Are not hens fed by the consuls according to the custom of the old pagan profanations? Are not the auguries of the flying bird sought? Almost all those sacrifices are performed which the pagans of old thought foolish and laughable. When the very consuls do all those things, those men who give their names to the years and from whom the years themselves take their beginning, are we to believe that those years can proceed well for us which are begun with such ceremonies? Would that just as these things are done only for the consuls, so they would infect those only on whose account they are done. . . .

Indeed, because it would take long to speak about all these snares now, namely the amphitheatres, music halls, public processions, jesters, athletes, tumblers, pantomimes and other monstrosities, which disgust me to talk about, and because it is disgusting to have knowledge of such evil, I will speak only about the impurities of the circuses and theatres. Such things are done there that nobody can speak about them, let alone think of them, without being tainted.

For the most part, other vices claim for themselves particular portions of us: filthy thoughts affect our minds; immodest glances, our eyes; evil language, our ears. When one of these functions has gone astray, the rest can be without sin. But in the theatres none of our senses is free from guilt, because our minds are tainted by evil desires, our ears by hearing, our eyes by seeing. Indeed, all these scenes are so disgraceful that a person cannot even describe them and talk about them without shame. Who can talk about these imitations of evil things, these obscene voices and words, these base motions and foul gestures, and retain his sense of modesty intact? Thus we can understand how criminal are these sights when they forbid description. Indeed, some of the greatest crimes, such as murder, robbery, adultery, sacrilege, and others in the same vein, can be mentioned and argued about and the character of the speaker remains unimpaired. The impurities of the theatres are singular in that they cannot be honestly denounced in public.

Thus, there comes something new for the prosecutor when he discusses the baseness of these crimes, so that, although without doubt he who wishes to bring the charge is upright, he cannot speak and denounce these obscenities and his character remain whole. All other evils taint those who perform them, not those who see or hear them. Though you hear someone blaspheme, you are not tainted by the sacrilege because you mentally disagree. And if you come upon a robbery, you are not made evil by the act, because you abhor it in your mind.

The impurities of the game are unique, because, in a way, they make the crime one, both for those who perform them and those who watch them. For, while the spectators approve and gladly watch them, all perform them through sight and consent. Truly, that saying of the Apostle particularly falls not only on those who perform them, but even on those who consent to the performances, that they are worthy of death. Therefore, in these representations of fornication the whole audience mentally commits fornication, and those who, perhaps, came in purity to the games, return from the theatres in adultery. For, not only do they commit fornication when they return home, but also when they come to the theatre, for, by the very fact that anyone desires an obscene thing he is unclean while he hastens to uncleanliness.

Since this is the case, behold what kind of acts either all, or almost all, Romans do. Yet we who do these things claim we are neglected by God. We say we are forsaken by our Lord, when we ourselves forsake the Lord. Let us suppose that our Lord is willing to watch over us, even though we do not deserve it. Let us see if He can. See the countless thousands of Christians daily tarrying at the games where base performances are enacted. Can God watch over people like this? Can He watch over those who revel in the circuses and who commit adultery in the theatres?

Or, perhaps, do we wish and think it becoming that, when God sees us in the circuses and theatres, He also looks at those performances at which we look and at that wickedness on which we gaze? That He gazes at them with us, one or the other of the following must happen. If He deigns to see us, it follows that He must see those things where we are, or, if He averts His eyes from them, which is doubtless what happens, so He must likewise avert them even from us who are there. Nevertheless, we unceasingly do these things about which I have spoken.

Or do we think, perhaps, according to the custom of the old pagans, that we have a God of theatres and circuses? They made their theatres and circuses long ago because they believed that these were the delights of their idols. Why do we do these things, we who are certain that our God hates them? Certainly, if we knew that this wickedness pleases God, I would not forbid that we do them unceasingly.

If, indeed, we firmly believe that God abhors and hates these places, because in them there is just as much food for the devil as there is offence to God, how do we say that we worship God in church? We ever serve the devil in the obscenity of the games, and do this knowingly, understandingly and with well-considered deliberation. I ask, what hope shall there be for us before God, we who injure Him, not by chance or ignorance, but after the manner of those former giants whom we read to have attempted in their insane endeavours the heights of heaven and to have, as it were, climbed into the clouds?

In like manner, we, by the injuries which we constantly inflict on God throughout the whole world, fight heaven as if by common agreement. To Christ, therefore (O monstrous madness), to Christ we offer circuses and mimes, and this in our day especially when we receive something good from Him, when some prosperity is granted by Him, or a victory is given by the Divinity over our enemies. . . .

To Christ, therefore (O monstrous madness), to Christ we offer circuses and mimes, to Christ for His favours we return the indecencies of the theatres, to Christ we offer as sacrificial victims the vilest of games. Is this the teaching of our Saviour who became incarnate for our sake? Did He or His Apostles preach this? Was it on this account that he underwent the humility of human birth and undertook the shameful beginnings of earthly origin? Was it on this account He lay in a manger, to whom angels ministered while He lay there? Was it for this He wished to be wrapped in swaddling clothes and ruled heaven while wearing them? Was it for this He hung on a gibbet, whom the world feared as He hung there? . . .

In the games there is a certain apostasy from the faith and a deadly deviation from the Creed and from the heavenly pledges. For what is the first confession of faith of Christians in the saving baptism? What is it except that they profess they are renouncing the Devil, his pomps and games and works? Therefore, according to our profession of faith, the games and pomps are the work of the Devil.

How, therefore, O Christians, do you frequent the games after baptism, the games which you confess to be the work of the Devil? You have once renounced the Devil and his games. You must know that when you return to the games you are returning knowingly and deliberately to the Devil. For you have renounced both things, and at the same time you have said one is both. If you return to one, you resort to both. You say, "I renounce the Devil, his pomps, spectacles and works." . . .

Again, therefore, I must return to what I have often said: What is there like this among the barbarians? Where among them are there circuses, where are there theatres, where the crime of different impurities; that is to say, the ruin of our hope and salvation? Even if they, being pagans, used these things, their sin and guilt would be less offensive to what is holy, because, although the sights would be impure, there would be no violation of the sacrament.

But we, what can we answer on our behalf? We hold and cast aside the faith, and we confess the gift of salvation equally as we deny it. Where, therefore, is our Christianity, we who receive the sacrament of salvation only for the purpose that we may sin afterwards with the greater crime of deviation from righteousness? We prefer stage plays to the churches of God. We spurn the altars and honor the theatres. We love things and worship things. God alone, in comparison with all other things, is vile to us.

Finally, besides other instances which prove it, one particular illustration establishes the point I am making. If, when it should happen --because it often does happen that on the same day on which an ecclesiastical feast occurs the public games are performed—I ask of everybody's conscience what place has greater crowds of Christian men: the spectators' benches at the public games or the entrance to the house of God? Do the crowds prefer the temple or the theatre? Do they love more the teachings of the Gospel or the theatrical musicians; the words of life or the words of death; the words of Christ or the words of the mime?

There is no doubt that we love more that which we prefer. For, on every day of the fatal games, whatever feast of the Church it may be, not only do those who say they are Christians not come to the church, but, if any come perhaps unwittingly, if they hear the games being performed, while they are already in the church, they leave the church. They spurn the temple of God in order that they may run to the theatre. They leave the church in order to fill the circus. We leave Christ at the altar and feed our adulterous eyes with the most impure visions and with the fornication of the vilest games. Very rightly, therefore, the Lord has said to us: "On account of your dirt you have been expelled into banishment." And again He says: "The altars of this laughter shall be banished."

But it can be answered that these performances are not enacted in all Roman cities. That is true. I also add that they are not now done in those places where they were done formerly. They are not now done in the city of Mainz, but that is because it is ruined and destroyed. They are not performed at Cologne, but that is because it is filled with the enemy. They are not done in the most excellent city of Trier, but that is because it is laid low by invasion, four times repeated. They are not done in most of the cities of Gaul and Spain.

Therefore, woe to us and our iniquities; woe to us and our impurities! What hope is there for the commonalty of Christians in the sight of God, when these evils cease to exist in Roman cities only from that time when they began to be under the law of the barbarians? Vice and impurity are, as it were, native characteristics of the Romans, and are, as it were, their mind and nature. Wherever there are Romans, there is much vice. . . .

But, of course, we who are corrupted by prosperity are corrected by adversity and we, whom a long peace has made profligate, strife makes us temperate. Have the peoples of the cities who were lewd in prosperity begun to be chaste in adversity? Has drunkenness, which increased with peaceful and abundant years, ceased immediately with the plundering done by the enemy? . . .

Lest any part of the world be immune from fatal evils, wars have begun to cross over the seas. . . . And then what? When the barbarians entered these lands, did the inhabitants cease in their vices, perhaps in fear? . . .

Who can judge the enormity of this evil? The barbarian peoples were sounding their arms around the walls of Cirta and Carthage and the Christian population of Carthage still went mad in the circuses and reveled in the theatres. Some were strangled outside the walls; others were committing fornication within. A portion of the people was captive of the enemy without the walls and a portion was captive of vice within the walls. . . .

The noise of battle outside the walls and of the games within, the voices of the dying outside and the voices of the reveling within, were mingled. Perhaps there scarcely could be distinguished the cries of the people who fell in battle and the yelling of the people who shouted in the circus. . . .

Why do I speak about things that are far away and are, so to say, removed into another world, when I know that in my own native country and in the cities of Gaul almost all the more excellent men have been made worse by their misfortunes? Indeed, I myself have seen at Trier men, noble in birth and elevated in dignity, who, though already despoiled and plundered, were actually less ruined in property than in morality. Though they were despoiled and stripped, something of their property still remained to them, but nothing of self-restraint. They were more dangerous enemies in themselves than the enemy outside, so that, though they were overthrown by the barbarians from without, they were still overthrown by themselves.

It is sad to refer to what I saw there. Honoured old men, tottering Christians, the ruin of their city already imminent, tended slavishly to their palates and lusts. What is the first accusation here? That they were honoured, that they were old, that they were Christians, or that they were in danger? . . .

The leading men in the city were lying down at banquets; they forgot honour; they forgot age; they forgot religion; they forgot the dignity of their name. They were stuffed with food, lax from wine-bibbing, frantic from shouting, frenzied with revelry. They were bereft of no less than their senses. . . . Not even the ruin of their cities put an end to this waywardness. The wealthiest city of Gaul was taken by storm four times. . . .

What followed? What I say is incredible. The continuance of calamities in that city caused an increase of crimes there. Like the serpentine monster which multiplied when killed . . . so even in the most excellent city of Gaul crimes increased by the very blows with which crimes were checked so that you would think that the punishment of crime was . . . the mother of vice. . . .

Among chaste barbarians, we are unchaste. I say further: the very barbarians are offended by our impurities. Fornication of Goths is not lawful among the Goths. Only the Romans living among them can afford to be impure by prerogative of nation and name. I ask: What hope is there for us before God? We love impurity; the Goths abominate it. We flee from purity; they seek it. Fornication among them is a crime; with us a distinction and an ornament. . . .

The Gothic nation is lying, but chaste. The Alani are unchaste, but they lie less. The Franks lie, but they are generous. The Saxons are savage in cruelty, but admirable in chastity. In short, all peoples have their own particular bad habits, just as they have certain good habits. . . .

I ask: What hope can there be for the Roman State when the barbarians are more chaste and more pure than the Romans? . . . I ask: What hope of pardon or of life can there be for us in the sight of God when we see chastity among the barbarians and are ourselves unchaste? I say: Let us be ashamed and confused. Among the Goths, the only impure ones are the Romans. There are no impure ones among the Vandals except the Romans. . . .

You, O Roman people, be ashamed; be ashamed of your lives. Almost no cities are free of evil dens, are altogether free of impurities, except these cities in which the barbarians have begun to live. . . .

# ST JOHN DAMASCENE

700?–?754

Very few details are known about the life of the last of the Greek Fathers. He was born at Damascus, of a Christian family which held an important hereditary position under the Saracens, then masters of the city. John's Arabic name was Mansur—the Ransomed. In 726 he became famous through the publication of his first *Apology* for the veneration of the images, against the edict of Emperor Leo the Isaurian. In 735 he entered the monastery of St Sabas, near Jerusalem, having previously been ordained to the priesthood. A philosopher, theologian, ascetical writer, orator, and hymn writer, John was also a historian. His most famous dogmatic writing is the *Fountain of Wisdom*.

## Dialogue between a Christian and a Saracen

Translated by J. Kritzeck from J. P. Migne's *Patrologia Graeca*.

*A Christian was asked by a Saracen:* Whom do you say is the cause of good and evil?

*The Christian replied:* We say that no one but God is the cause of all good, but not of evil.

*Saracen.* Then whom do you say is the cause of evil?

*Christian.* The Devil, who is such by his own decision, and also we men.

*Saracen.* By virtue of what?

*Christian.* By virtue of our free will.

*Saracen.* What? You mean to say you have free will and can do anything you wish?

*Christian.* I was created by God with a will that is free. I may act well or badly, that is, I may do good or evil; if I do evil, I am punished by the Law of God, but if I do good I do not fear the Law, but I am rewarded and obtain mercy from God. Adam, the first man, was likewise created by God with free will, but the Devil deceived him and he sinned, so God cast him down from his proper status. But perhaps you will ask, in an effort to thwart me, "What are the goods and evils of which you speak?" The goods are the glorification of

God, prayer, almsgiving, and the like, and the evils are fornication, robbery, murder, and the like. Now if you want to make God the cause of evil as well as good, He appears, in your view, unjust, which He is not. For if God enjoined the fornicator to fornicate, the robber to rob, and the murderer to murder, as you say, then they deserve a reward, for they have done the will of God, and your lawgivers seem to be liars and your books false when they command us to whip the fornicator and robber and kill the murderer.

*Then the Saracen asked:* Do you say that a Christian who does the will of God is good or evil?

*But the Christian, knowing his craftiness, replied:* I know what you are getting at.

*Saracen.* Then you may tell it to me.

*Christian.* You want to ask me, "Did Christ suffer by His will or not?" And if I answer you, "He suffered by His will," you will reply, "Be off! Then honour the Jews, for they did the will of your God."

*Saracen.* Yes, that is most assuredly what I wanted to ask you, and if you have anything to say on this matter I should like to hear it.

*Christian.* You use the word "will"; I would be inclined to say "permission," "subsistence," and "forbearance."

*Saracen.* How could you demonstrate this?

*Christian.* If you or I are sitting or standing, can either of us rise or be moved without the power and will of God?

*Saracen.* By no means.

*Christian.* And when God said, "Thou shalt not rob, fornicate, or murder," He clearly did not want us to rob, fornicate, or murder?

*Saracen.* Clearly not, for if He had wanted that, He certainly would not have said, "Thou shalt not rob, fornicate, or murder."

*Christian.* Glory be to God, for then you agree with me and are saying precisely what I want to say. We are in accord that none of us can rise or be moved without God, and that God does not want us to rob, fornicate, or murder. Therefore if I should rise up and go and rob or fornicate or murder, what do you call that? Is it God's "will," or would "permission," "subsistence," and "forbearance" be better words? The truth of the matter is that God, although He could have intervened, agreed to the Crucifixion, and used it, by permitting it, against sin. But when He wishes to cause repentance, He punishes; He did this against the Jews also, for after a little while He aroused Titus, Vespasian, and the Greeks against them, and put down their insolence.

*Saracen.* What do you call Christ?

*Christian.* He is called the Word of God and many other things in our Scripture. What does your Scripture call Him?

*Saracen.* The Spirit and Word of God.

*Christian.* Does your Scripture consider that the Word of God was created or uncreated?

*Saracen.* It was uncreated.

*Christian.* But whatever is not created but uncreated is God. And if you were to answer me, "Created," I should ask you further, "Then who created the Word and Spirit of God?"

*Saracen.* What if I should answer that God Himself created them?

*Christian.* Then you would be forced to say that before God created His Spirit and Word He had neither the Spirit nor the Word. I say that I believe in only one Word of God which is uncreated, namely Christ, but of course I do not mean the Scripture itself when I say the "Word of God" here.

*Saracen.* I would like to know how you can say that God came down into the womb of a woman.

*Christian.* Very well. Let us make use of your Scripture as well as mine. Your Scripture says that God cleansed Mary beforehand above all womankind, and that the Spirit and Word of God came down to her. And my Gospel says, "The Holy Spirit will come down upon thee and the power of the Most High will overshadow thee." Thus it seems that the two have one and the same meaning. But it should be noted that because of the state of our intellects the Scripture uses the words "come down upon" tropologically.

*Saracen.* What is the meaning of "tropologically"?

*Christian.* "Tropologically" means "figuratively," or "by analogy." . . .

*Saracen.* If Christ was God, how is it that He ate and drank and slept and was crucified and died, and all the rest?

*Christian.* Because the Word of God, who created all things, as both my Scripture and yours attest, created Him from the flesh of the Holy

Virgin, a perfect man, endowed with life and intellect. He ate, drank, and slept. But the Word of God itself did not eat, drink, or sleep, nor was it crucified, nor did it die, but it was the flesh which Christ took on from the Holy Virgin that was crucified. Christ had a dual nature united in one by the hypostatic union; a fourth person was not added to the Trinity after the ineffable union of the Incarnation.

*Saracen.* Suppose I were wounded in a part of my flesh, and the wounded flesh contracted, leaving a scar, and in the scar an infection developed; who would have created that?

*Christian.* All creatures were created during the first week. God created man also during these days, and ordered him to propagate and fill the earth. However, after the Original Sin, the earth was condemned to bring forth thorns and thistles; then also our flesh was condemned, and it brings forth lice and worms to this day.

*Saracen.* To turn to another matter, who is the greater among you, he who sanctifies or he who is sanctified?

*But the Christian, knowing his hostile questioning, replied:* I understand what it is you want to know.

*Saracen.* Well, if you do, answer me.

*Christian.* If I say to you, "He who sanctifies is greater than he who is sanctified," you will immediately respond, "Be off! Then worship John the Baptist, who certainly baptized and sanctified your Christ."

*Saracen.* That is obviously what I would have said to you.

*The Christian answered with an allegory.* Suppose you go out with your slave to the bath to wash, and he washes and cleans you; whom would you say is the greater, that poor and penniless slave of yours or you yourself, whom he has washed?

*Saracen.* I would say that I myself, who own, am greater than he whom I own.

*Christian.* I give thanks to God for your reply. You should know, then, that John the Baptist, ministering to Christ as a slave and servant in the holy baptism in the Jordan in which my Saviour was baptized, broke the heads of those dragons and bad demons who were lying in the caves there.

*At this the Saracen marvelled greatly, and, having nothing to answer the Christian, went away and debated with him no further.*

# THE DEFINITIONS

The affirmations of the Apostles were based on the last charge Jesus made to them: "Go ye therefore and teach all nations, baptizing them in the name of the Father and of the Son and of the Holy Ghost; teaching them to observe all things whatsoever I have commanded you: and lo, I am with you always, even unto the end of the world" (Matthew 28: 19, 20). But they, and their successors, with fear and trembling, defined in human words the deposit of the Faith. As St Hilary put it, "We are compelled to attempt what is unattainable, to climb where we cannot reach, to speak what we cannot utter. Instead of the bare adoration of faith, we are compelled to entrust the deep things of religion to the perils of human expression." Here, following the text of the three creeds and of one of the oldest variants, are some of the earliest definitions and descriptions of councils, dogma, and ritual.

# The Creeds

The oldest Greek text of the oldest of the creeds, the Apostles' Creed, is found in Marcellus of Ancyra's letter to Pope Julius I, about 340. The Latin text in its oldest form is given by Rufinus (c. 400) in his *Commentary on the Symbol of the Apostles*. This symbol is the one which the Roman Church required the catechumens to learn and to say by heart before receiving baptism. There is no doubt that the symbol embodies the doctrine of the Apostles, and all its elements are found in the New Testament. Most probably it was composed in Rome "towards the end of the first or the beginning of the second century." It antedates the heresies of the second century. Kattenbusch and Harnack date it around 100. The so-called Nicene Creed, in the form currently used by Catholics and Protestants alike, expresses the mind of the Church at the close of the struggle that followed upon the Council of Nicaea (325). Its form is that adopted by the Council of Chalcedon (451). In origin it may have been a creed locally in use either in Jerusalem or Constantinople, but it represents the whole Church's stand at the end of the Arian controversy (381). The Athanasian Creed is a fifth-century Latin compilation. It is certainly not the work of St Athanasius, but its place in the liturgy of both Catholics and Protestants has made it the third creed of Christendom.

The three creeds are given here in the versions used by the Church of England in the Book of Common Prayer. All are used by Catholics, Orthodox, and some Protestants.

## The Apostles' Creed

I believe in God the Father Almighty, Maker of heaven and earth, and in Jesus Christ, His only Son, our Lord, Who was conceived by the Holy Ghost, born of the Virgin Mary, suffered under Pontius Pilate, was crucified, died, and was buried: He descended into hell: the third day He rose again from the dead. He ascended into heaven. And sitteth on the right hand of God the Father Almighty: from thence He shall come to judge the quick and the dead.

I believe in the Holy Ghost, the holy Catholic Church: the Communion of saints, the forgiveness of sins: the resurrection of the body, and the life everlasting.

# The Nicene Creed

I believe in one God
The Father Almighty, Maker of heaven and earth, and all things visible and invisible:
And in one Lord Jesus Christ, the only-begotten Son of God;
Begotten of his Father before all worlds,
God of God, Light of Light,
Very God of very God;
Begotten, not made; being of one substance with the Father; by whom all things were made:
Who for us men and for our salvation came down from heaven,
And was incarnate by the Holy Ghost of the Virgin Mary, and was made man:
And was crucified also for us under Pontius Pilate; He suffered and was buried:
And the third day He rose according to the Scriptures:
And ascended into heaven, and sitteth on the right hand of the Father:
And He shall come again, with glory, to judge both the quick and the dead; whose kingdom shall have no end.
And I believe in the Holy Ghost, the Lord, and Giver of Life, who proceedeth from the Father *and the Son* *;
Who with the Father and the Son together is worshipped and glorified; who spake by the prophets:
And I believe in one Catholic and Apostolic Church:
I acknowledge one baptism for the remission of sins:
And I look for the resurrection of the dead:
And the life of the world to come.

* These words are omitted by the Orthodox Church.

# The Athanasian Creed

Whoever will be saved: before all things it is necessary that he hold the Catholic Faith.

Which Faith except everyone do keep whole and undefiled: without doubt he shall perish everlastingly.

And the Catholic Faith is this: that we worship one God in Trinity, and Trinity in Unity.

Neither confounding the Persons: nor dividing the Substance.

For there is one Person of the Father, another of the Son, another of the Holy Ghost.

But the Godhead of the Father, of the Son, and of the Holy Ghost, is all one: the Glory co-equal, the Majesty co-eternal.

Such as the Father is, such is the Son, and such is the Holy Ghost.

The Father uncreate, the Son uncreate, and the Holy Ghost uncreate.

The Father incomprehensible, the Son incomprehensible, and the Holy Ghost incomprehensible.

The Father eternal, the Son eternal, and the Holy Ghost eternal.

And yet they are not three eternals: but one Eternal.

As also there are not three incomprehensibles, nor three uncreated: but one Uncreated and one Incomprehensible.

So likewise the Father is almighty, the Son almighty: and the Holy Ghost almighty.

And yet they are not three almighties: but one Almighty.

So the Father is God, the Son is God, and the Holy Ghost is God.

And yet they are not three gods: but one God.

So likewise the Father is Lord, the Son Lord and the Holy Ghost Lord.

And yet not three lords: but one Lord.

For like as we are compelled by the Christian verity to acknowledge every Person by Himself to be God and Lord:

So are we forbidden by the Catholic religion to say, there be three gods, or three lords.

The Father is made of none: neither created, nor begotten.

The Son is of the Father alone, not made, nor created, but begotten.

The Holy Ghost is of the Father and of the Son, neither made, nor created nor begotten, but proceeding.

So there is one Father, not three Fathers, one Son, not three Sons, one Holy Ghost, not three Holy Ghosts.

And in this Trinity none is afore, or after other: none is the greater or less than another.

But the whole three Persons are co-eternal together, and co-equal.

So that in all things, as is aforesaid, the Unity in Trinity, and the Trinity in Unity is to be worshipped.

He therefore that will be saved: must thus think of the Trinity.

Furthermore, it is necessary to everlasting salvation: that he also believe rightly the Incarnation of our Lord Jesus Christ.

For the right Faith is, that we believe and confess: that our Lord Jesus Christ, the Son of God, is God and Man:

God, of the Substance of the Father, begotten before the worlds: and Man, of the Substance of His mother, born in the world:

Perfect God, and perfect Man: of a reasonable soul and human flesh subsisting:

Equal to the Father, as touching His Godhead, and inferior to the Father, as touching His Manhood.

Who although He be God and Man, yet He is not two, but one Christ.

One: not by conversion of the Godhead into flesh, but by the taking of the Manhood into God.

One altogether: not by confusion of Substance, but by unity of Person.

For as the reasonable soul and flesh is one man: so God and Man is one Christ.

Who suffered for our salvation: descended into hell, rose again the third day from the dead.

He ascended into heaven, He sitteth on the right hand of the Father, God Almighty, from whence He shall come to judge the quick and the dead.

At whose coming all men shall rise again with their bodies, and shall give account for their own works.
And they that have done good shall go into life everlasting, and they that have done evil into everlasting fire.
This is the Catholic Faith: which except a man believe faithfully, he cannot be saved.

# ST CYRIL OF JERUSALEM

315?–386

Cyril was in charge of the catechumens in Jerusalem for fifteen years, and composed catechisms for them. Originally his Creed was a statement required by him of all catechumens before baptism. In 350 he was made bishop of Jerusalem but was exiled in 357 and again in 360 and 367. Only in 378 was he able finally to return to his see. He was present at the Council of Constantinople, the second of the Ecumenical Councils, in 381, and there defended the Creed of Nicaea.

## The Creed of St Cyril

We believe in one God, the Father Almighty, Maker of heaven and earth, and of all things visible and invisible.
And in one Lord Jesus Christ, the Son of God the only begotten, begotten of the Father, true God, before all the ages, through whom all things were made;
Incarnate and made man; crucified and buried;
And rose again the third day;
And ascended into heaven;
And sat on the right hand of the Father;
And shall come again in glory to judge the quick and the dead, of whose kingdom there shall be no end.
And in one Holy Ghost, the Paraclete, who spake by the prophets;
And in one baptism of repentance for remission of sins;
And in one holy Catholic Church;
And in the resurrection of the flesh;
And in the life eternal.

# The Councils

## The Seven Ecumenical Councils

In 312 Constantine became sole emperor of the West. By his defeat of Licinius, in 324, he became sole ruler of the entire Roman Empire. During his reign he granted to his own religion—he had become a Catholic after his victory at the Milvian Bridge in 312—the same favors hitherto accorded to the pagans alone. These were not accorded to heretics.

Together with Pope Sylvester I, Constantine summoned the first of the seven Ecumenical Councils, that of Nicaea, which took place in 325 at Nicaea in Asia Minor.

*Council of Nicaea,* 325, held under Constantine the Great. At this council, by Canon 6, it was affirmed: "Concerning the Primacy of the Roman Church: The Roman Church has always had the primacy. Let the ancient customs in Egypt, Libya, and Pentapolis prevail, that the bishop of Alexandria shall have jurisdiction in all these, since the like is customary for the bishop of Rome also. Likewise in Antioch and the other provinces, let the churches retain their privileges. . . ."

*Council of Constantinople,* 381, summoned by Theodosius I. At this council the following three canons were of paramount importance:

"Canon 1. The faith of the three hundred and eighteen Fathers who were assembled at Nicaea in Bithynia shall not be set aside but shall remain dominant. And every heresy shall be anathematized, especially that of the Eunomians or Anomoeans, the Arians or Eudoxians, the semi-Arians or Pneumatomachians, the Sabellians, Marcellians, Photinians, and Apollinarians.

"Canon 2. The bishops are not to go beyond their dioceses to churches lying outside of their bounds, nor bring confusion on churches; but let the bishop of Alexandria, according to the canons, alone administer the affairs of Egypt; and let the bishops of the East manage the East alone, the privileges of the church in Antioch, which are mentioned in the canons of Nicaea, being preserved; and let the bishops of the Asian diocese administer the Asian affairs only, and the Pontic bishops only Pontic matters; and the Thracian bishops only Thracian matters. And let not the bishops go beyond their dioceses for ordination or any other ecclesiastical ministrations, unless they be invited. And the aforesaid canon concerning dioceses being the affairs of that particular province as was decreed at Nicaea. But the churches of God in heathen nations must be governed according to the custom which has prevailed from the time of the Fathers.

"Canon 3. The bishop of Constantinople, however, shall have the prerogative of honor after the bishop of Rome; because Constantinople is New Rome."

*Council of Ephesus,* 431, called by Theodosius II and Valentinian III. Here the papal legate, Philip, described St Peter as "the prince and head of the Apostles . . . who up to this time and always lives in his successors and gives judgments."

*Council of Chalcedon,* 451, called by Marcian and Valentinian III.

*Council of Constantinople,* 553, called by Justinian I.

*Council of Constantinople,* 680–81, called by Constantine IV. The Fathers at this Council wrote to Pope Agatho: "We commit to thee, as the chief ruler of the universal Church standing on the firm rock of the Faith, what is to be done."

*Council of Nicaea,* 787, summoned by Constantine VI and his mother Empress Irene.

Hastings * comments generally that "With the exception of the Second Council and the canons of the Fourth, the decrees of the seven Ecumenical Councils were (a) subscribed by the Papal legates, or (b) both so subscribed and subsequently approved by the Pope, or (c) eventually approved by the Pope."

* *Encyclopaedia of Religion and Ethics,* Vol. 4, pp. 188, 189.

# Development of Dogma

## ST IRENAEUS

130?–d. after 190

Irenaeus (see also page 199) was a native of Smyrna, and became bishop of Lyons after the martyrdom of St Pothinus. He was active as an evangelist and in combating the Gnostics. His most famous work is the *Adversus Haereses* (*Against the False Gnosis*); he mentions in it his fear that the habit of speaking Celtic may have vitiated his Greek. Late in his life he interceded with Pope Victor I on behalf of the Churches of Asia in the matter of Paschal observance. He is supposed to have died a martyr, but the date of his death is unknown.

### FROM Against the False Gnosis

. . . Since the Church has received this preaching and this faith, as we have said, the Church, although it is scattered throughout the whole world, diligently guards it as if it dwelt in one house; and likewise it believes these things as if it had one soul and one heart, and harmoniously it preaches, teaches, and believes these things as if possessing one mouth. For although the languages of the world are dissimilar, yet the import of the tradition is one and the same. For the churches which have been founded in Germany have not believed nor handed down anything different, nor have those among the Iberians, nor those among the Gauls, nor those in the East, nor those in Egypt, nor those in Libya, nor those which have been established in the central regions of the world. . . .

The tradition, therefore, of the Apostles, manifested throughout the world, is a thing which all who wish to see the facts can clearly perceive in every church; and we are able to count up those who were appointed bishops by the Apostles, and to show their successors to our own time, who neither taught nor knew anything resembling these men's ravings. For if the Apostles had known hidden mysteries which they used to teach the perfect, apart from and without the knowledge of the rest, they would have delivered them especially to those to whom they were also committing the churches themselves. For they desired them to be very perfect and blameless in all things, and were also leaving them as their successors, delivering over to them their own proper place of teaching; for if these should act rightly great advantage would result, but if they fell away the most disastrous calamity would occur.

But since it would be very long in such a volume as this to count up the successions [i. e., series of bishops] in all the churches, we confound all those who in any way, whether through self-pleasing or vainglory, or through blindness and evil opinion, gather together otherwise than they ought, by pointing out the tradition derived from the Apostles of the greatest, most ancient, and universally known Church, founded and established by the two most glorious Apostles, Peter and Paul, and also the faith declared to men which through the succession of bishops comes down to our times. For with this Church, on account of its more powerful leadership, every church, that is, the faithful, who are from everywhere, must needs agree; since in it that tradition which is from the Apostles has always been preserved by those who are from everywhere.

The blessed Apostles having founded and established the Church, entrusted the office of the episcopate to Linus. Paul speaks of this Linus in his Epistles to Timothy. Anacletus succeeded him, and after Anacletus, in the third place from the Apostles, Clement received the episcopate. He had seen and conversed with the blessed Apostles, and their preaching was still sounding in his ears and their tradition was still before his eyes. Nor was he alone in this, for many who had been taught by the Apostles yet survived. In the times of Clement, a serious dissension having arisen among the brethren in Corinth, the Church of Rome sent a suitable letter to the Corinthians, reconciling them in peace, renewing their faith, and proclaiming the doctrine lately received from the Apostles. . . .

Evaristus succeeded Clement, and Alexander, Evaristus. Then

Sixtus, the sixth from the Apostles, was appointed. After him Telesphorus, who suffered martyrdom gloriously, and then Hyginus; after him Pius, and after Pius, Anicetus; Soter succeeded Anicetus, and now, in the twelfth place from the Apostles, Eleutherus [174–189] holds the office of bishop. In the same order and succession the tradition and the preaching of the truth which is from the Apostles have continued unto us.

But Polycarp, too, was not only instructed by the Apostles, and acquainted with many that had seen Christ, but was also appointed by Apostles in Asia bishop of the church in Smyrna, whom we, too, saw in our early youth (for he lived a long time, and died, when a very old man, a glorious and most illustrious martyr's death); he always taught the things which he had learned from the Apostles, which the Church also hands down, and which alone are true. To these things all the Asiatic churches testify, as do also those who, down to the present time, have succeeded Polycarp, who was a much more trustworthy and certain witness of the truth than Valentinus and Marcion and the rest of the evil-minded. It was he who was also in Rome in the time of Anicetus and caused many to turn away from the above-mentioned heretics to the Church of God, proclaiming that he had received from the Apostles this one and only truth which has been transmitted by the Church. And there are those who heard from him that John, the disciple of the Lord, going to bathe in Ephesus, when he saw Cerinthus within, ran out of the bath-house without bathing, crying: "Let us flee, lest even the bath-house fall, because Cerinthus, the enemy of the truth, is within." And Polycarp himself, when Marcion once met him and said, "Knowest thou us?" replied, "I know the first-born of Satan." Such caution did the Apostles and their disciples exercise that they might not even converse with any of those who perverted the truth; as Paul, also, said, "A man that is a heretic after the first and second admonition, reject; knowing that he that is such subverteth and sinneth, being condemned by himself." There is also a very powerful Epistle of Polycarp written to the Philippians, from which those who wish to, and who are concerned for their own salvation, may learn the character of his faith and the preaching of the truth. . . .

The Church, though dispersed through the whole world to the ends of the earth, has received from the Apostles and their disciples the Faith: In one God, the Father Almighty, who made the heaven and the earth and the seas, and all that in them is; and in one Christ Jesus, the Son of God, who was incarnate for our salvation; and in the Holy Ghost, who through the prophets preached the dispensations and the advents, and the birth from the Virgin, and the Passion, and the resurrection from the dead, and the bodily assumption into the heavens of the beloved Christ Jesus our Lord, and His appearing from the heavens in the glory of the Father, in order to sum up all things under one head and to raise up all flesh of all mankind, that to Christ Jesus, our Lord and God and Saviour and King, every knee of those that are in heaven and on earth and under the earth should bow according to the good pleasure of the Father invisible, and that every tongue should confess Him, and that He may execute righteous judgment on all; sending into eternal fire the spiritual powers of wickedness and the angels who transgressed and apostatized, and the godless and unrighteous and lawless and blasphemous among men, but granting life and immortality and eternal glory to the righteous and holy, who have both kept the commandments and continued in His love, some from the beginning, some from their conversion. . . .

If the Apostles had not left us the Scriptures, would it not be necessary to follow the order of tradition which they handed down to those to whom they committed the churches? To this order many nations of the barbarians gave assent, of those who believe in Christ, having salvation written in their hearts by the Spirit without paper and ink, and guarding diligently the ancient tradition: Believing in one God, Maker of heaven and earth, and all that is in them; through Jesus Christ, the Son of God; who, because of His astounding love towards His creatures, sustained the birth of the Virgin, Himself uniting man to God, and suffered under Pontius Pilate, and rising again was received in brightness, and shall come again in glory as the Saviour of those who are saved and the judge of those who are judged, and sending into eternal fire the perverters of the truth and despisers of His Father and His coming.

# ST JUSTIN MARTYR

(See page 193.)

## FROM First Apology

(See page 391.)

How we dedicated ourselves to God, being new made through Christ, I will explain, lest, if I omit this, I appear to be cheating in my explanation. All then who are persuaded, and believe, that the things which are taught and affirmed by us are true; and who promise to be able to live accordingly; are taught to pray, and beg God with fasting, to grant them forgiveness of their former sins; and we pray and fast with them. Then we bring them where there is water; and after the same manner of regeneration as we also were regenerated ourselves, they are regenerated; for, in the Name of God, the Father and Lord of all things, and of our Saviour Jesus Christ, and of the Holy Ghost, they then receive the washing of water: for, indeed, Christ also said, "Except ye be born again, ye shall not enter into the kingdom of heaven." And that it is impossible for those who are once born to enter into their mothers' wombs, is plain to all. And it is declared by the prophet Isaiah, as I have already written, in what way those who have sinned, and who repent, shall escape their sins. . . .

And we have received the following reason from the Apostles for so doing; since we were ignorant of our first birth, and were born by necessity of the moist seed through the mutual union of our parents, and were brought up in evil customs and wicked training; in order that we might not remain the children of necessity and ignorance, but of choice, and of knowledge; and that we might obtain remission of the sins we had formerly committed; in the water, there is called over him who chooses the new birth, and repents of his sins, the name of God the Father and Lord of all things; and calling Him by this name alone, we bring the person to be washed to the laver: for no one can declare the name of the ineffable God, but if anyone presumes to say that He has any, he commits an act of incurable madness. Now this washing is called illumination, because they who learn the meaning of these things are enlightened in their mind. And in the name of Jesus Christ, who was crucified under Pontius Pilate; and in the name of the Holy Ghost, who foretold, by the prophets, all these things about Jesus, does he who is enlightened receive his washing. . . .

But after thus washing him who has professed, and given his assent, we bring him to those who are called brethren; where they are assembled together, to offer prayers in common both for ourselves, and for the person who has received illumination, and all others everywhere, with all our hearts, that we might be vouchsafed, now we have learnt the truth, by our works also to be found good citizens and keepers of the commandments, that we may obtain everlasting salvation. We salute one another with a kiss when we have concluded the prayers: then is brought to the president of the brethren, bread, and a cup of water and wine, which he receives; and offers up praise and glory to the Father of all things, through the Name of His Son, and of the Holy Ghost; and he returns thanks at length, for our being vouchsafed these things by Him. When he has concluded the prayers and thanksgiving, all the people who are present express their assent by saying Amen. This word, Amen, means in the Greek language, So be it; and when the President has celebrated the Eucharist, and all the people have assented, they whom we call deacons give to each of those who are present a portion of the Eucharistic bread, and wine, and water; and carry them to those who are absent.

And this food is called by us the Eucharist, of which no one is allowed to partake but he who believes the truth of our doctrines; and who has been washed in the laver for the forgiveness of sins, and to regeneration; and who so lives, as Christ has directed. For we do not receive them as ordinary food, or ordinary drink, but as by the Word of God, Jesus Christ our Saviour was made flesh, and had both flesh and blood for our salvation; so also, the food which was blessed by the prayer of the Word which proceeded from Him, and from which our flesh and blood, by assimilation, receive nourishment, is, we are taught, both the flesh and blood of that Jesus who was made flesh.

For the Apostles, in the records which they made, and which are called Gospels, have declared that Jesus commanded them to do as follows: "He took bread, and gave thanks, and said, 'This do in remembrance of Me, This is My body.' And in like manner He took the cup, and blessed it, and said, 'This is My blood' ": and gave it to them alone. The same thing in the mysteries of Mithra also, the evil demons imitated, and commanded to be done; for bread, and a cup of water, are placed in the mystic rites for one who is to be initiated, with the addition of certain words, as you know or may learn.

But we, after these things, henceforward always remind one another of them; and those of us who have the means, assist all who are in want; and we are always together; and in all our oblations we bless the Maker of all things, through His Son Jesus Christ, and through the Holy Ghost. And on the day which is called Sunday, there is an assembly in the same place of all who live in cities, or in country districts; and the records of the Apostles, or the writings of the prophets, are read as long as we have time. Then the reader concludes: and the president verbally instructs, and exhorts us, to the imitation of these excellent things: then we all together rise and offer up our prayers; and, as I said before, when we have concluded our prayer, bread is brought, and wine, and water; and the president, in like manner, offers up prayers, and thanksgivings, with all his strength; and the people give their assent by saying Amen: and there is a distribution, and a partaking by everyone, of the Eucharistic elements; and to those who are not present they are sent by the hands of the deacons; and such as are in prosperous circumstances, and wish to do so, give what they will, each according to his choice; and what is collected is placed in the hands of the president, who assists the orphans, and widows, and such as through sickness, or any other cause, are in want; and to those who are in bonds, and to strangers from afar, and, in a word, to all who are in need, he is a protector. But Sunday is the day on which we all hold our common assembly, because it is the first day on which God, when He changed the darkness and matter, made the world; and Jesus Christ our Saviour, on the same day, rose from the dead; for the day before that of Saturn, He was crucified; and on the day after it, which is Sunday, He appeared to His Apostles and disciples, and taught them these things, which we have given to you also, for your consideration.

If, then, these things appear to you to have reason and truth, respect them; but if they seem to be frivolous, hold them in contempt as frivolities; and do not decree death against those who have done no wrong, as if they were enemies: for we forewarn you, that you shall not escape the future judgment of God, if you continue in your injustice; and we will exclaim, "Let what is pleasing to God be done." . . .

# TERTULLIAN

(See page 59.)

## The Rule of Faith

. . . The Rule of Faith is . . . namely, that by which it is believed: That there is only one God, and no other besides the Maker of the world, who produced the universe out of nothing, through His Word, sent forth first of all; that this Word, called His Son, was seen in the name of God in various ways by the patriarchs, and always heard in the prophets, at last was sent down from the Spirit and power of God the Father, into the Virgin Mary, was made flesh in her womb, and born of her, lived as Jesus Christ; that thereupon He preached the new law and the new promise of the kingdom of the heavens; wrought miracles; was fastened to the Cross; rose again the third day; was caught up into the heavens; and sat down at the right hand of the Father; He sent in His place the power of the Holy Ghost, to lead the believers; He will come again with glory to take the saints into the enjoyment of eternal life and the celestial promises, and to judge the wicked with perpetual fire, with the restoration of the flesh. . . .

The Apostles founded in the several cities churches from which the other churches have henceforth borrowed the shoot of faith and seeds of teaching and do daily borrow that they may become churches; and it is from this fact that they also will be counted as apostolic, being the offspring of apostolic churches. Every kind of thing must be judged by reference to its origin. Therefore so many and so great churches are all one, being from that first Church which is from the Apostles. Thus they are all primitive and all apostolic, since they altogether are approved by their unity, and they have the communion of peace, the title of brotherhood, and the interchange of hospitality, and they are governed by no other rule than the single tradition of the same mystery. . . .

Here, then, we enter our demurrer, that if the Lord Jesus Christ sent Apostles to preach, others than those whom Christ appointed ought not to be received as preachers. For no man knoweth the Father save the Son and he to whom the Son has revealed Him; nor does it appear that the Son has revealed Him unto any others than the Apostles, whom He sent forth to preach what, of course, He had revealed to them. Now, what they should preach, that is, what Christ revealed to them, can, as I must likewise here enter as a demurrer, properly be proved in no other way than by those very churches which the Apostles themselves founded by preaching to them, both *viva voce,* as the phrase is, and subsequently by epistles. If this is so, it is evident that all doctrine which agrees with those apostolic churches, the wombs and origins of the faith, must be reckoned for truth, as undoubtedly containing what the churches received from the Apostles, the Apostles from Christ, Christ from God. There remains, therefore, for us to show whether our doctrine, the rule of which we have given above, agrees with the tradition of the Apostles, and likewise whether the others come from deceit. We hold fast to the apostolic churches, because in none is there a different doctrine; this is the witness of the truth. . . .

Come, now, you who would indulge a better curiosity, if you would apply it to the business of your salvation, run over the apostolic churches, in which the very thrones of the Apostles are still pre-eminent in their places, in which their own authentic writings are read, uttering the voice and representing the face of each of them severally. Achaia is very near you, in which you find Corinth. Since you are not far from Macedonia, you have Philippi; there, too, you have the Thessalonians. Since you are able to cross to Asia, you get Ephesus. Since, moreover, you are close upon Italy, you have Rome, from which there comes even into our own hands the very authority of Apostles themselves. How happy is that church, on which Apostles poured forth all their doctrine along with their blood! Where Peter endures a passion like his Lord's; where Paul wins a crown in a death like John's; where the Apostle John was first plunged, unhurt, into boiling oil, and thence remitted to his island exile! See what she has learned, what taught; what fellowship she has had with even our churches in Africa! One Lord God does she acknowledge, the

Creator of the universe, and Christ Jesus born of the Virgin Mary, the Son of God the Creator; and the resurrection of the flesh; the law and the prophets she unites in one volume with the writings of Evangelists and Apostles, from which she drinks in her faith. This she seals with the water of baptism, arrays with the Holy Ghost, feeds with the eucharist, cheers with martyrdom, and against such a discipline thus maintained she admits no gainsayer. . . .

## FROM Against Praxeas

. . . We believe one God; but under this dispensation which we call the economy there is the Son of the only God, his Word who proceeded from Him, through whom all things were made, and without whom nothing was made. This One was sent by the Father into the Virgin, and was born of her, Man and God, the Son of Man and the Son of God, and called Jesus Christ; He suffered, He died and was buried according to the Scriptures; and raised again by the Father, and taken up into the heavens, and He sits at the right hand of the Father; He shall come again to judge the quick and the dead: and He thence did send, according to His promise, from the Father, the Holy Ghost, the Paraclete, the Sanctifier of the faith of those who believe in the Father and the Son and the Holy Ghost. That this rule has come down from the beginning, even before any of the earlier heresies, much more before Praxeas, who is of yesterday, the lateness of date of all heresies proves, as also the novelties of Praxeas, a pretender of yesterday. . . .

# BARDESANES

154–?223

Bardesanes, the son of noble parents, was born at Edessa on July 11, 154, and was reared with the future oparch of Edessa, Abgar IX (179–214). After the conquest of Edessa by Caracalla in 216, he retired to Armenia. He composed hymns and was a famous astrologer.

## FROM Concerning Fate

. . . In Syria and Edessa men used to part with their manhood in honor of Tharatha, but when King Abgar became a believer he commanded that everyone that did so should have his hand cut off, and from that day until now no one does so in the country of Edessa.

And what shall we say of the new race of us Christians, whom Christ at His advent planted in every country and in every region? For, lo, wherever we are, we are called after the one name of Christ—namely, Christians. On one day, the first day of the week, we assemble ourselves together, and on the days of the readings we abstain from sustenance. The brethren who are in Gaul do not take males for wives, nor those in Parthia two wives; nor do those in Judea circumcise themselves; nor do those of our sisters who are among the Geli consort with strangers; nor do those of our brethren who are in Persia take their daughters for wives; nor do those who are in Media abandon their dead or bury them alive or give them as food to the dogs; nor do those who are in Edessa kill their wives who commit adultery, nor their sisters, but they withdraw from them, and give them over to the judgment of God; nor do those who are in Hatra stone thieves to death; but wherever they are, and in whatever place they are found, the laws of the several countries do not hinder them from obeying the law of their Christ; nor does the Fate of the celestial governors compel them to make use of the things which they regard as impure. . . .

# ORIGEN

(See page 66.)

## On the Soul: An Interview with Heraclidius and the Bishops

This work was one of the papyri discovered by British workmen at Towra, near Cairo, in August 1941. It was edited and translated into French by Jean Scherer; the English translation is by the editor.

As the bishops present had raised the problem of the faith of Bishop Heraclidus, in order that he should make his confession of faith before them all, after everyone had said what they wished to say and asked their questions, Bishop Heraclidus said:

"I, too, believe exactly what the Holy Scriptures declare: 'In the beginning was the Word, and the word was with God, and the Word was God. He was in the beginning with God. All things were made by Him, and without Him was not anything made that was made.' Thus we share the same faith on this point, and moreover, we believe that Christ took flesh, that He was born, that He ascended to heaven in the flesh in which He was resurrected, and that He is seated at the right hand of God, from whence He shall come to judge the quick and the dead, simultaneously God and man."

*Origen.* Since the debate has now begun, and that the subject of the debate should be kept before us, I will speak. The whole Church is here, listening. There must not be any difference of belief between the churches, for there cannot be a church of lies. I beg of you, Father Heraclidus, there is one God, the Almighty, the uncreated, the Supreme God who has made all things—you agree?

*Heraclidus.* I agree; that is what I also believe.

*Origen.* Christ Jesus, existing in the form of God, whilst remaining distinct from God in the Whose form He existed, was God before He became incarnate, yes or no?

*Heraclidus.* He was God before.

*Origen.* God distinct from this God in whose form He Himself existed?

*Heraclidus.* Obviously distinct from another, and, since He was in His form, distinct from the Creator.

*Origen.* Is it not true that there was a God, Son of God, who is the only Son of God, the firstborn of every creature, and that we have no scruples in affirming, in one sense, two Gods, and to affirm, in another sense, one single God?

*Heraclidus.* Doubtless what you say there is clear. But for us, we say that there is one God who is the Almighty God who has no beginning and will have no end, Who contains all and is contained by nothing, and His Word, Son of the living God, God and man, by Whom all things are realized, God by the Spirit, and man in that he was born of Mary.

*Origen.* You do not seem to have answered my question. Explain yourself better, for perhaps I have not quite understood. The Father is God?

*Heraclidus.* Certainly.

*Origen.* The Son is distinct from the Father?

*Heraclidus.* Without doubt—how can He be the Son at the same time as being Father?

*Origen.* Whilst being distinct from the Father, is the Son also God?

*Heraclidus.* He also is God.

*Origen.* And the unity which exists is that of two Gods?

*Heraclidus.* Yes.

*Origen.* We confess two Gods?

*Heraclidus.* Yes, the power is one.

*Origen.* Yet since our brothers are shocked by the affirmation that there are two Gods, the subject should be treated with care, and it must be made clear in what respect they are two, and in what respect the two are one only God. Indeed, the Scriptures have shown us many cases where two things make a single unity and not merely two things, and not only in cases where there are two things but in cases where there are more than two, and even in cases where there are many things, they have taught us that there is a "unity." Our task, at this moment, is not to tackle the subject and just to glance over it and touch upon it lightly, but to chew it well like a meat, because of the beginners among us, and little by little to persuade the listeners to understand our reasoning. In many cases, then, in the Scriptures, it is said of two beings that they are "one." In what passages in the Scriptures? Adam, the woman, are two separate beings; Adam is separate from the woman, the woman is separate from the man. Now it is expressly stated, in Genesis, that the two are "one": "for they shall be one flesh." Thus it is sometimes possible that two beings should be a single flesh. But notice carefully that in the case of Adam and Eve it is not said that they twain shall be a single spirit, nor a single soul, but that these twain shall be one flesh. Elsewhere, the just man, while remaining distinct from Christ, is said by the Apostle to be "one" in his relation with Christ: "for he that is joined unto the Lord is one spirit with Him." Is it not true, nevertheless, that the one is of a less perfect, or of a corrupt and inferior essence, whilst Christ is of a more divine essence, more glorious and blessed? In these conditions, are they not two? No, for the man and the woman are no longer twain, but one flesh, and, in the same way, the just man and Christ are one spirit. And for his part, our Saviour and Lord, in his relationship with the Father and the God of the universe, is not one flesh, nor one spirit, but, which is superior to flesh and to spirit, one God. It was right, indeed, in the case of human beings attached to each other, to use the word flesh; in the case of the just man attached to Christ, to use the word spirit, and in the case of Christ united to the Father, to use neither the word flesh nor the word spirit, but a more significant word than those: the word God. It follows that the sentence: "My Father and I are one" must be understood in that sense. In our prayers, now, let us, as some do, introduce the duality, and at the same time, as others do, let us introduce the unity; and thus on the one hand we do not fall into the opinion of those who are separated from the Church because they have fallen into the error of the monarchy, suppressing the Son by withdrawing Him from the Father and at the same time actually suppressing the Father; nor do we fall into another impious doctrine, that which denies the divinity of Christ. What then do the Holy Scriptures mean, for example, in the passage: "Before me there was no God, neither shall there be after me," and in this other one: "Even I, am He, and there is no God with me"? In these formulae, it must not be believed that the unity belongs to the God of the universe separated from Christ, nor to Christ distinct from God. Let us say that it is as it is in the prayer of Jesus: "My Father and I are one." This is the language we should use, for there has been much agitation in this church. Often people write and ask that everyone sign, that the bishops sign, and also any suspected persons, and that everyone sign in the presence of all the faithful so that there may be no more dissensions or investigations into this subject. So, with God's consent, and in the second place with the consent of the bishop, and in the third place with the consent of the priests and of the faithful, I shall make my position on this question once more clear: The offering is always made to Almighty God, through the intercession of Jesus Christ, in so far as he is in communication with the Father by His divinity; that the offering is not to be made twice, but to God by the intermediary of God. I am going to appear to express myself very boldly: we must, in our prayers, respect the conventions, or the word: "Thou shalt not respect the person of the poor, nor honour the person of the mighty" will not be true. And if this is not true, then these conventions are merely an opportunity for new investigations: although a man is a bishop or a priest, he is not bishop, he is not priest; he may be a deacon, but is not a deacon, nor a layman either; he is not a layman, and he takes no part in the assemblies. If you agree, let these conventions be established. Some make this objection: that, when the problem of the divinity is in question, I thus attribute to Jesus Christ a substantial divinity, and that at the same time I confess before the church the resurrection of the dead body. Well, now, since our Saviour and Lord took to Himself a body, let us examine what this body was. Only the Church, faced with all the heresies which deny the resurrection, professed the resurrection of the dead body, for from the fact that the first fruits have arisen from the dead, it follows that the dead arise. Christ, the first fruits, that is why

His body became a corpse. For if His body had not become a corpse, capable of being wrapped in a winding sheet, of receiving the aromatics and all that corpses usually receive, and of being buried in a tomb (things which a spiritual body would not endure, for it is absolutely impossible that the spiritual become a corpse, nor can the spiritual become insensible)—if, indeed, it were possible that the spiritual became a corpse, then we would be afraid lest after the resurrection of the dead, when our body will be raised, according to the word of the Apostle, "It is sown a natural body, it is raised a spiritual body," we would all die. Actually, "Christ, being raised from the dead, dieth no more." And not only Christ, but those who belong to Christ, risen from the dead, die no more. If you agree on these points, they also, with the solemn consent of the faithful, shall be codified and definitely established.

What else, while we are on the subject of faith? Do you agree with us, Maximus?

*Maximus*. May everyone agree with me! Before God and the Church, I approve and I condemn. However, in order that I may no longer retain any shadow of doubt or uncertainty, I have a question to ask. Indeed, my friends know what it is, for I said: I need the help of my brother in order to obtain information on this point. Since the Spirit had been given back to the Father, as the words convey: "Father, into Thy hands I commend My spirit," and since, separated from the Spirit, the body was dead and lying in the tomb, how did this latter open and how do the dead arise?

*Origen*. We know from Holy Scripture that man is a complete being. In effect, the Apostle says: ". . . the very God of peace sanctify you wholly, and I pray God your whole spirit and soul and body be preserved blameless unto the coming of our Lord Jesus Christ!" This spirit is not the Holy Spirit but a part of the human amalgam, as the same Apostle teaches when he said: "The Spirit itself beareth witness with our spirit." If he was speaking of the Holy Spirit he could not say, "The Spirit beareth witness with our spirit." Thus then our Saviour and Lord, by His will to save man as He willed to save him (just as He wished equally the soul and the body), wished also to save what was left of man, the spirit. Now, man would not have been wholly saved had He not taken upon Himself the whole man. He who declares the body of the Saviour to be spiritual does away with the salvation of the human body. And thus does away with the salvation of the human spirit, about which the Apostle said: "What man knoweth the things of a man, save the spirit of man which is in him?" Wishing to save the spirit of man, the Saviour took it also upon Himself. At the Passion these three elements were separated; after the Resurrection, were reunited. At the Passion they were separated. How? The body in the tomb, the soul in hell; the spirit, He commended it into His Father's hands. The soul to hell: "for Thou wilt not leave my soul in hell." If it is true that He commended His soul into His Father's hands, it was as a deposit with the intention of recovering His deposit. This being so, why had He to confide this deposit, His spirit, to the Father? This question is beyond me, beyond my competence, beyond my intelligence. For I am not sufficiently sure of myself to affirm that in the same way that His body could not descend into hell (in spite of the assertions of those who declare the body of Jesus to have been spiritual), in the same way His spirit could not descend into hell, and because of that, until the resurrection from the dead, He confided His spirit as a deposit to His Father. This deposit He had left with His Father, He takes it back. When? Not immediately after the Resurrection. Witness, the Gospel text. Our Lord Jesus Christ was risen from the dead; Mary meets him, and He says to her, "Touch me not." He wished, in fact, that anyone who touched Him, touched Him in His integrity, in order that, having touched Him in His integrity, anyone who touched Him should receive the beneficient influence of His body in his body, or of His soul in his soul, of His spirit in his spirit. "For I am not yet ascended to My Father." He ascends to the Father, then He goes to find His disciples. With what intention? To withdraw His deposit.

Thus all the problems of faith which were troubling us have been examined. But we must know that we are not judged at the divine tribunal by faith alone, as though we did not have to answer for our conduct, nor on our conduct alone, as though our faith was not under examination. The rectitude of the one and the other will be our justification; the lack of rectitude of the one and the other will be the reason that we are punished for the one and for the other. There are also people who will be punished not for both, but for one; some for their faith, for its lapses, but not for the lack of rectitude in their conduct; the others, on the contrary, will not be punished for their faith, but for their conduct for not having acted according to the dictates of right reason. So, if we wish to be saved, let us not, clinging to faith, neglect our conduct, nor, on the other hand, do not let us be too sure of our conduct: it is by both—let us know this, understand this, believe this—that we shall receive acquittal or beatitude, or the contrary. Now, the punishable things are not only the atrocious and horrible faults in either field whose very names should not be mentioned, but also those which usually are regarded as being of little importance. It is for this, it seems, the Apostle has set alongside these abominable, infamous, and criminal acts (as one might call them) faults which are generally considered negligible. What, in effect, does he say? "Be not deceived: neither fornicators, nor idolators, nor adulterers, nor effeminate, nor abusers of themselves with mankind, nor thieves, nor the covetous, nor drunkards, nor revilers, nor extortioners shall inherit the kingdom of God." You see, alongside these enormous crimes—pederasty, effeminate morals, adultery, fornication—he has placed drunkenness, calumny, vices we think negligible, in order to teach us that it is not only the first which exclude us from the kingdom of God, but also the second, which ordinarily are regarded as less serious. Thus, let us not be calumniators, nor drunkards, nor avaricious, nor thieves, and do not let us commit abominable acts, even if we are in error. If there remains some doubtful point on the rule of faith, mention it: we will continue to comment on the Scriptures.

*Denys.* Is the soul the blood?

*Origen.* It has come to my ears, and I am speaking of what I know, that here, and in this locality, there are people who believe that after having left this life, the soul is deprived of sensibility and stays in the tomb with the body. This is an ineluctable question that our dear Denys is asking. First, we will quote all the passages which trouble people's spirits, so as not to leave any out, and to each one of them, if

God permits, we will reply according to your wish. The disquieting passage is: "For the life of the flesh is in the blood." This has terribly troubled those who have not understood it. Then also: "Only be sure that thou eat not the blood, for the blood is the life, and thou mayest not eat the life with the flesh." This is disturbing, for the other disturbing passages are far from being expressed so forcefully. For myself, in the measure of my capacities, and whilst praying to be assisted in the reading of the sacred texts (for we require assistance so that our thought does not stray from truth), I have noticed that the noncorporal things are designated by the homonyms of all corporal things, and that thus the corporal things have to do with exterior man, and the homonyms of corporal things with the interior man. Scripture says that there are two men in man: "For though our outward man perish, yet the inward man is renewed day by day," and, "For I delight in the law of God, after the inward man." . . .

Well, then, since we have to speak of man, and, dealing with the soul of man, to discover whether this is blood, and since this subject brings us to that of the two men, and that thus we have arrived at a mystical subject, I beg of you, don't let me suffer the reproach of "casting pearls before swine, or the sacred things to the dogs, or of throwing divine things to serpents, or of giving serpents a part of the tree of life." In order not to suffer this reproach, "transform yourselves, put off anger, wrath, malice, blasphemy, that there be no divisions among you, but be ye perfectly joined together in the same mind and in the same judgment."

I suffer an anguish if I speak, and anguish if I do not speak. Because of those who are worthy, I wish to speak, so that I be not reproached for having refused the word of truth to those who are capable of hearing it. Because of those who are not worthy, I hesitate to speak, for the reasons which I have given, being fearful of throwing sacred things to the dogs, and pearls before swine. Only Jesus can distinguish among His listeners those who are without from those who are within, and thus speak in parables to those from outside and to explain the parables to those who entered in His house. The outside, and the entry into the house, are of a mystical order. For what have I to do to judge them also that are without?

Whoever sins is "without"; that is why one must speak in parables to those outside, in case they may leave the outside to penetrate within. The entry into the house is the mystical order—enters into the house of Jesus His true disciple. He enters by thinking with the Church, living with the Church. "Without" and "within" are in the spiritual order.

Thus, at the creation of man, man was first created after the likeness: "And God said, Let us make man in Our image, after Our likeness, and let him command." And God created man, not of taking the dust of the earth, like the second time, but he created him after the image of God. Moses was not alone in knowing that this being after the likeness of God was immaterial, superior to any corporal hypostasis, but the Apostle also knew it, as he shows in his sentence when he says: "Having put off the old man with his deeds and having put on the new man, which is renewed in knowledge, after the image of Him that created him."

"There are thus two men in each one of us. How is it that it is said: "The soul of all flesh is the blood?" That is a great problem. As every exterior man has for homonym the interior man, so it is for all his members, and one can say that every member of the exterior man can be found under this name, in the interior man. . . .

Since you find all these elements of the material body in the interior man, do not doubt that the blood also, under the same name as the material blood, and just like all the other parts of the body, exists in the interior man. It is this blood which flows from the sinner's soul. "Indeed your blood of your lives will I require." He did not say, "of your blood" but "of the blood of your lives." And, "His blood will I require at the watchman's hand." What is this blood which God requires at the watchman's hand, other than that which the sinner sheds? In the same way the fool's heart perishes, and in the same way the blood and the vital force of his heart are shed. If one can imagine what the soul is, and if one can imagine it according to the interior man, and if one can imagine that in it dwells a being after the likeness, then it is evident that St. Paul is right to say: "To depart and be with Christ, which is far better." Before the resurrection, the just is with Christ, and in his soul he lives with Christ. Now, according to you, who say that the soul lies in the tomb with the body, the soul is not out of the body, it does not taste peace, it does not find itself in the paradise of God, it does not repose in the bosom of Abraham. So with you who maintain such enormities, it is not true that to depart and be with Christ is far better, for one is not with Christ as soon as one is gone, if the soul is the blood. If the soul is lying in the tomb, how can it be with Christ? But according to me, and according to the work of God, the soul which has gone far from suffering, gone far from sorrows, which has been freed from the body, which can say: "Now lettest Thou Thy servant, O Lord, depart in peace," this soul goes into peace and rests with Christ. It is of this soul that Abraham heard these words: "And thou shalt go to thy fathers in peace, thou shalt be buried in a good old age." He goes to his fathers. Which fathers? Those of whom St. Paul says: "I bow my knees unto the Father of our Lord Jesus Christ of whom the whole family in heaven and earth is named." Thus, according to us, Aaron was liberated. It is written, indeed in Ecclesiastes, anent the just man, he who has fought the good fight, who has come out from the prison of the body, for in Ecclesiastes it is written: "For out of prison he cometh to reign." Since, then, this is so, I am prepared to die for the truth; since it is thus, faced with what is called death, I despise it; since it is thus, let fierce animals, let crosses, let flames, let tortures, come; I know that as soon as I shall have expired, I leave my body and I rest with Christ. For that, let us fight; for that, let us struggle. Let us groan that we are in the body, persuaded that soon in our tomb we shall not be in the body, but that we shall leave it for a more spiritual condition. Destined to leave and to be with Christ, how much shall we groan, we who are in the body.

Bishop Philip having entered, another bishop said: "Here's our brother Demetrius, now, teaching that the soul is immortal."

*Origen*. By Father Demetrius's declaration, we are now plunged into another problem. According to him, we have said that the soul is immortal. To that affirmation I would answer that, on the one hand, the soul is immortal, on the other, the soul is not immortal. Let us begin by defining precisely the word death and all the meanings which arise from the term death. I will try to give all its meanings, not according to the Greeks, but all the meanings given in Scripture. Perhaps someone cleverer than I will find still more meanings, but as for me, at the moment, I know of three deaths. Which are these three deaths? One lives to God, and dies to sin, according to the Apostle: this death is blessed. One dies to sin. It is this death that died my Lord, for in that He died, He died unto sin once. I know yet another death, by which one dies to God, this death of which it is spoken in the word: "The soul that sinneth, it shall die." I know also a third death, according to which we commonly believe that all those who have left their bodies are dead: for example, Adam lived 930 years and died.

Since there are these three deaths, let us see if the human soul is immortal with regard to these three deaths or whether, although not with regard to all three, it is yet immortal with regard to some of them. With regard to death in the obvious sense, all men die; it is this death which we consider as a dissolution. Of this death, no human soul dies. For if it died, it would not be punished after death. "Men shall seek death," it is written, "and shall not find it." Souls in punishment will seek death. They prefer not to be, rather than to be punished. It is for this they shall seek death and not find it. In this sense, every human soul is immortal. As for the other meanings, according to one, the soul is mortal, and blessed if it dies to sin. It is of this death that Balaam made his astounding prophecy, and that, under the inspiration of God, he formulated this wish: "Let me die the death of the righteous and let my last end be like his." There exists another death in regard to which we are not immortal, whilst having the possibility of immortality, if we are vigilant. And perhaps that which is mortal in the soul is not always mortal. Indeed, in the measure in which it gives space in itself to a sin, which makes of it a sinful soul, which will die, the soul is mortal of real death. But if it finds itself confirmed in beatitude, so that it is inaccessible to death, possessing eternal life, it is no longer mortal, but in that sense also is immortal. How is it that the Apostle says, speaking of God, "Who alone has immortality"? I seek and I find that Christ Jesus died for all, except for God. This is how God alone possesses immortality.

Let us then seize upon eternal life, let us seize upon it with all our force. God does not give it, he proposes it to us: "See, I have set before thee this day life." It is in our power to stretch out our arms and, by doing good in our actions, to seize life and set it in our soul. This life of which Christ said, "I am the Life," this life which now is only present to us as a shadow but which one day we shall see face to face. "The breath of our nostrils, the anointed of the Lord, of whom we said, under His shadow we shall live among the heathen." If so many benefits are brought by the shadow you have of life—this shadow possessed by Moses when he prophesied, which Isaiah possessed when he saw the Lord Sabaoth sitting upon a throne high and lifted up, which Jeremiah possessed when he heard the words, "Before I formed thee in the belly I knew thee, and before thou camest forth out of the womb I sanctified thee," which Ezekiel possessed when he saw the wheels, the ineffable mysteries—what will our life not be when we shall no longer live in the shadow of life but will be in life itself? Now, our life is hid with Christ. But when Christ, who is our life, shall appear, then shall we also appear with Him in glory. Let us hasten toward that life, mourning and groaning that we are in this tent, that we remain in the body. For we that are in this tabernacle do groan. Let us have the desire to remove from our bodies and to go and dwell near the Lord, in order that, dwelling with Him, we may make one with the God of the Universe and His only Son, finding full salvation and blessedness in Jesus Christ, to whom be glory and power for ever and ever, Amen.

# ST CYPRIAN

(See page 229.)

## FROM On the Unity of the Catholic Church

Translated by F. A. Wright in *Fathers of the Church.*

. . . If you were to weigh and consider all this there would be no need of a long treatise or of arguments. For a convincing proof of the truth of this is easily found. The Lord saith unto Peter: "And I say unto thee that thou are Peter, and upon this rock I will build My church and the gates of hell shall not prevail against it. And I will give unto thee the keys of the kingdom of heaven and whatsoever thou shalt bind on earth shall be bound in heaven, and whatsoever thou shalt loose on earth shall be loosed in heaven." And again after His resurrection, He says: "Feed my sheep." Upon him alone He builds His church, and into his care He gives His sheep to be fed. And while after His resurrection He gives equal power to all the Apostles and says: "As my Father hath sent me even so I send you. . . . Receive ye the Holy Ghost. Whosesoever sins ye remit, they are remitted unto them; and whosesoever sins ye retain, they are retained." Still, in order to make clear the general unity, by His own authority He caused that same unity to be traced back to one man. It is granted that the other Apostles were even as Peter was, having an equal share with him of honour and power, but the beginning proceeds from unity. The primacy is given to Peter that it may be shown that the Church is one and the See of Christ is one. All are pastors, but the flock is one, and it is fed by all the pastors in perfect agreement, in order that the unity of Christ's Church may be demonstrated. It is this one Church to which the Holy Spirit refers in the Song of Songs, speaking with the voice of the Lord and saying: "My dove, my undefiled, is but one. She is the only one of her mother, elect of her that bore her." He that holds not this unity of the Church, does he think that he holds the true faith? He who resists the Church and contends with it, who abandons the throne of Peter on which the Church is founded, is he confident that he is within the Church? Does not the blessed Apostle Paul teach this and prove the doctrine of unity, when he says: "There is one body and one Spirit, one hope of your calling, one Lord, one faith, one baptism, one God."

It is our duty to hold fast this unity and to justify it, especially those of us who are bishops of the Church, that we may show that the episcopate itself also is one and indivisible. Let no man deceive the brethren with false doctrine or destroy faith in the truth by disloyally tampering with it. The episcopate is one, and a part of it is held by each of us, making a complete whole. The Church is one, but with rich exuberance it spreads far and wide among men. Even so there are many rays of the sun, but one sunlight; many branches of a tree, but one trunk firmly grounded in a sound root; and when many streams flow from one spring, although its unity seems to be scattered abroad in the very abundance of the water that flows, yet that unity is preserved in the source. Try to remove one ray of the sun from the whole: the unity of sunlight suffers no division. Break off a branch from a tree: the broken branch will not bud. Cut off a stream from its source: it will dry up. So also the Church of Christ pours forth its light and spreads its rays throughout the whole world; yet it is one light that is everywhere poured forth and the unity of the whole is not destroyed. Or, again, its inexhaustible fertility puts forth branches over the whole world; and like a mighty river it spreads its streams far and wide. But one is the head, one the source, one the mother of abundant and continuous fertility. From her womb we are sprung and reared on her milk, by her breath we are quickened.

The bride of Christ cannot admit of adultery, she is pure and chaste. She knows but one home, and with unbroken chastity she guards one sacred chamber. She it is who preserves us for God, who offers to the Kingdom of God the sons whom she has borne. He that separates himself from the Church and makes an adulterous union, he is cut off from the promises of the Church, nor shall he who has deserted the Church of Christ attain to the rewards of Christ; he is a stranger, an outsider, an enemy. He cannot have God as a father who has not the Church as his mother. There was no escape for any who remained outside the ark of Noah; and even so he who is outside the Church cannot escape. Our Lord Himself tells us: "He that is not with me is against me; and he that gathereth not with me scattereth abroad." He that breaketh the peace and harmony of Christ is an enemy of Christ. He that gathereth outside the Church, scattereth the Church of Christ. Our Lord says, "I and My Father are one." And again it is written of the Father, the Son, and the Holy Spirit, "And these three are one." How could anyone believe that this unity, coming as it does from the unchangeableness of God and bound together by the heavenly sacraments, could ever be sundered or split apart by the schism of conflicting opinions? He who holds not this unity holds not the law of God nor yet the faith of the Father and the Son, neither life nor salvation.

This sacrament of unity, this bond of concord inseparably cohering is set forth to us when in the Gospel the coat of the Lord Jesus Christ is not divided nor cut. The men draw lots for Christ's garment, as to who should put on Christ, and the winner receives the entire robe for his own, uninjured and undivided. Holy Scripture speaks, saying, "But as for his coat, because above it was not sewed but woven all in one piece, they said to each other 'Let us not rend but cast lots whose it shall be.' " That garment bore an unity coming from above, coming, that is, from heaven and from the Father; nor could it at all be rent by the receiver and possessor; it kept inseparably a whole and substantial integrity. He cannot possess the robe of Christ who rends and divides the Church of Christ. On the other hand, when at Solomon's death his kingdom and people were divided, the prophet Abijah, meeting King Jeroboam in the field, rent his mantle into twelve pieces and said: "Take ten parts for thyself; for thus saith the Lord, 'Behold I rend the kingdom from Solomon's hand and I will give thee ten sceptres; two sceptres shall be his for my servant David's sake and for Jerusalem, the city I have chosen that there I may set my name.' " When the twelve tribes of Israel were rent asunder, the prophet Abijah rent his mantle. But because Christ's people cannot be rent, His coat, woven and united throughout, is not divided by those who possess it. Undivided, closely fastened, firmly connected, it signifies the united concord of our people, we who put on Christ. By the sacrament and sign of His garment He has declared the unity of His church.

Who, then, is so wicked and faithless, so maddened by the frenzy of discord that he can believe it possible to rend the unity of God, the garment of the Lord, the Church of Christ? Who would dare to attempt it? He Himself in His Gospel warns us and teaches, saying, "And there shall be one flock and one shepherd." Do you suppose that in one place there can be many shepherds and many flocks? . . . The flesh of Christ and that which is holy of the Lord cannot be sent abroad, and there is no other house for believers save the one Church. This home, this resting place of concord, the Holy Spirit shows to us and announces in the Psalms, saying, "God who maketh men to dwell of one mind in a house." In the house of God, in the Church of Christ, the dwellers are of one mind and endure to the end in concord and simplicity.

Therefore it was that the Holy Spirit came in the form of a dove, a simple and joyous creature, not bitter with gall, not savage in its bite, not fierce with rending talons. Doves love to find a resting place with men; they cling to association with one house; when they have young they bring them forth together; when they go abroad they keep close in their flight; they spend their lives in mutual and friendly intercourse; they recognize the harmony of peace by the kisses of their beaks; in all things they fulfil the law of unanimity. This is the simplicity that we should know in our Church, this is the charity to which we should attain. The love of our brotherhood should take example from the doves; our gentleness and meekness should be like the lambs and sheep. What part in a Christian breast has the fierceness of wolves, the rage of dogs, the deadly poison of serpents, and the bloody cruelty of wild beasts? We may be thankful when such men as these are separated from the Church, so that they cannot prey upon Christ's doves and sheep, or infect them with the contagion of their cruelty and venom. Bitterness cannot combine or enter into union with sweetness, darkness with light, rain with fine weather, war with peace, barrenness with fertility, drought with running springs, tempest with tranquillity. Let no man think that the good can leave the church. The wind does not carry away the wheat, nor does the storm bring down the tree that has a firm solid root. It is the light stubble that is tossed by the tempest, the weak trees that are overthrown by the onrush of the hurricane. These are they whom the Apostle John smites with a curse, saying: "They went forth from us, but they were not of us. If they had been of us, with us they would have stayed."

Hence it is that heresies have arisen so often and still arise today. A perverted spirit has no peace, and faithless discord cannot maintain unity. Every man has freedom of choice and God allows and permits these things to be so that the test of truth may prove our hearts and understandings, and the faith of those that pass her test shine forth unharmed in the clear light. The Holy Spirit warns us by the Apostle's mouth, and says: "Heresies must be, that those who have been proved may be known among you." Thus the faithful are proved and the faithless are unmasked; thus even here, before the day of judgment, the souls of the just and the unjust are already divided, the straw is separated from the wheat. These are they who without divine order preside of their own accord at some convention of rash strangers, who appoint themselves prelates without any law of ordination, who take to themselves the name of bishop though no one has given them a bishopric. The Holy Spirit in the Psalms brands them as men who sit in the seat of pestilence, plague spots, and abominations of the faith, deceiving with a serpent's lips, crafty to corrupt the truth, vomiting deadly poisons from their pestiferous tongues, whose speech is as a creeping cancer and their conversation pours a mortal venom into each man's heart and breast.

Let not men deceive themselves by a vain interpretation, in that the Lord said: "Wherever two or three are gathered in My name, there am I with them." Corrupters of the Gospel and false interpreters take the last words and omit the previous ones, remembering one part and cunningly suppressing the other; and as they themselves are cut off from the Church, so they cut in twain the meaning of one passage. The Lord was urging his disciples to be peaceful and to be of one mind: "I tell you," He said, "that if two of you agree on earth on something you shall ask, it shall be given you by My Father who is in heaven. For wherever two or three are gathered in My name, there am I with them." Thereby He shows that most importance is attached not to the number of suppliants, but to their unanimity. "If two of you," He said, "agree on earth." Unanimity He put first; peaceful concord He made a prerequisite; He taught us faithfully and firmly to agree together. How can that man agree with anyone who does not agree with the body of the Church itself, and with our whole brotherhood? How can two or three be gathered in Christ's name, when it is certain that they are separated from Christ and from His Gospel? We did not leave them; they left us. Heresies and schisms have arisen by their setting up of other conventicles, and they have abandoned the one source and fountainhead of truth.

The word of the blessed Apostle John is this: "God," he says, "is love: he that dwelleth in love dwelleth in God, and God dwelleth in him." They cannot dwell with God who have refused to be of one mind in God's Church. Although they be burned, given up to flame and fire; although they lay down their lives, thrown to the wild beasts, their death will not be the crown of faith, but the punishment of faithlessness; it will not be the glorious end of religious courage, but the destruction of despair. Such an one may be killed, but he cannot be crowned. He professes himself to be a Christian in the same way as the Devil often feigns to be Christ. The Lord Himself has forewarned us, saying: "Many men will come in My name, saying, 'I am Christ,' and they will deceive many." As the Devil is not Christ, though he uses a false name; so that man cannot appear as a Christian who does not abide in His gospel and the truth of the faith.

To prophesy and cast out devils and perform great deeds upon earth is certainly a sublime and wonderful thing; but a man does not obtain the kingdom of heaven, though he be found doing all these things, unless he walks in the observance of the straight and just way. The Lord gives warning and says: "Many shall say to Me in that day, 'Lord, Lord, have we not prophesied in Thy name, cast out devils in Thy name, and in Thy name done great deeds?' And then I shall say to them, 'Depart from Me, ye who are workers of iniquity.'" There is need of righteousness that a man may deserve well of God the

Judge: we must obey His precepts and warnings that our services may receive their reward. The Lord in His Gospel, directing in a brief summary the way of our hope and faith, says: "The Lord thy God is one God: and thou shalt love the Lord thy God with all thy heart and with all thy soul and with all thy strength. This is the first commandment and the second is like unto it: thou shalt love thy neighbour as thyself. On these two commandments hang all the law and the prophets." By His instruction He taught us love and at the same time unity, including in two precepts the law and all the prophets. But what unity does that man observe, what love does he guard or consider who, mad with the frenzy of discord, divides the Church, destroys the faith, disturbs the peace, scatters charity, and profanes the sacrament? . . .

But let not the rash and excessive faithlessness of many move or disturb us. Let it rather strengthen our belief in the truth of what we have been told. As some men have begun to be of this kind, because this was predicted before, so let the rest of the brethren beware of them, because that, too, has been predicted and the Lord has instructed us, saying: "Beware: behold I have told you all things." Avoid, I beseech you, men of this kind and keep their mischievous talk from your side and from your ears, as if it were a deadly contagion. For it is written: "Hedge thine ears about with thorns and refuse to listen to a mischievous tongue." And again: "Evil communications corrupt good manners." From such men the Lord by His teaching warns us to depart. "They are blind," He says, "leaders of the blind, and if the blind lead the blind they shall both fall into the ditch." Such a man must be shunned and avoided, and so must all who have separated themselves from the Church. A man of this kind is perverse, a self-condemned sinner. Does he think that he has Christ who acts in opposition to Christ's priests and separates himself from the company of His clergy and people? He is carrying arms against the Church and fighting against God's appointment. An enemy of the altar, a rebel against Christ's sacrifice, faithless instead of having faith, profane instead of having religion, a disobedient servant, an undutiful son, an unfriendly brother, despising the bishops and deserting the priests of God, he dares to set up another altar, to make another and unlawful prayer and to profane the truth of the Lord's offering by false sacrifices, not knowing that he who strives against the ordinance of God is punished for his reckless temerity by the vengeance of heaven. . . .

## FROM Epistle to Caecilius

. . . Because Christ bore us all, in that He also bore our sins, we see that in the water is understood the people, but in the wine is showed the blood of Christ. But when in the cup the water is mingled with the wine the people is made one with Christ, and the assembly of believers is associated and conjoined with Him on whom it believes; which association and conjunction of water and wine is so mingled in the Lord's cup that that mixture cannot be separated any more. Whence, moreover, nothing can separate the Church—that is, the people established in the Church, faithfully and firmly continuing in that in which they have believed—from Christ in such a way as to prevent their undivided love from always abiding and adhering. Thus, therefore, in consecrating the cup water alone should not be offered to the Lord, even as wine alone should not be offered. For if wine only is offered, the blood of Christ begins to be without us. But if the water alone be offered, the people begin to be without Christ, but when both are mingled and are joined to each other by an intermixed union, then the spiritual and heavenly sacrament is completed. Thus the cup of the Lord is not, indeed, water alone, nor wine alone, nor unless each be mingled with the other; just as, on the other hand, the body of the Lord cannot be flour alone or water alone, nor unless both should be united and joined together and compacted into the mass of one bread: in which sacrament our people are shown to be one; so that in like manner as many grains are collected and ground and mixed together into one mass and made one bread, so in Christ, who is the heavenly bread, we may know that there is one body with which our number is joined and united.

There is, then, no reason, dearest brother, for anyone to think that the custom of certain persons is to be followed, who in times past have thought that water alone should be offered in the cup of the Lord. For we must inquire whom they themselves have followed. For if in the sacrifice which Christ offered none is to be followed but Christ, we ought certainly to obey and do what Christ did, and what He commanded to be done, since He himself says in the Gospel: "If ye do whatsoever I command you, henceforth I call you not servants, but friends." . . . If Jesus Christ, our Lord and God, is Himself the chief priest of God the Father, and has first offered Himself a sacrifice to the Father, and has commanded this to be done in commemoration of Himself, certainly that priest truly acts in the place of Christ who imitates what Christ did; and he then offers a true and full sacrifice in the Church of God to God the Father when he proceeds to offer it according to what he sees Christ himself to have offered. . . .

But the discipline of all religion and truth is overturned unless what is spiritually prescribed be faithfully observed; unless, indeed, anyone should fear in the morning sacrifices lest the taste of wine should be redolent of the blood of Christ. Therefore, thus the brotherhood is beginning to be kept back from the passion of Christ in persecutions by learning in the offerings to be disturbed concerning His blood and His blood-shedding. . . . But how can we shed our blood for Christ who blush to drink the blood of Christ? . . .

Does anyone perchance flatter himself with this reflection—that, although in the morning water alone is seen to be offered, yet when we come to supper we offer the mingled cup? But when we sup, we cannot call the people together for our banquet that we may celebrate the truth of the sacrament in the presence of the entire brotherhood. But still it was not in the morning, but after supper that the Lord offered the mingled cup. Ought we, then, to celebrate the Lord's cup after supper, that so by continual repetition of the Lord's Supper we may offer the mingled cup? It was necessary that Christ should offer about the evening of the day, that the very hour of sacrifice might show the setting and the evening of the world as it is written in Exodus: "And all the people of the synagogue of the children of

Israel shall kill it in the evening." And again in the Psalms: "Let the lifting up of my hands be an evening sacrifice." But we celebrate the Resurrection of the Lord in the morning.

And because we make mention of His Passion in all sacrifices (for the Lord's Passion is the sacrifice which we offer), we ought to do nothing else than what He did. For the Scripture says: "For as often as ye eat this bread and drink this cup, ye do show forth the Lord's death till He come." As often, therefore, as we offer the cup in commemoration of the Lord and His Passion, let us do what it is known the Lord did. . . .

# ST AUGUSTINE

(See page 127.)

## Letters

### TO JANUARIUS

400

In regard to the questions which you have asked me, I would like to have known what your own answers would have been; for thus I might have made my reply in fewer words, and might most easily confirm or correct your opinions, by approving or amending the answers which you had given. This I would have greatly preferred. But desiring to answer you at once, I think it better to write a long letter than incur loss of time. I desire you therefore, in the first place, to hold fast this as the fundamental principle in the present discussion, that our Lord Jesus Christ has appointed to us a "light yoke" and an "easy burden," as He declares in the Gospel: in accordance with which He has bound His people under the new dispensation together in fellowship by sacraments, which are in number very few, in observance most easy, and in significance most excellent, as baptism solemnized in the name of the Trinity, the communion of His body and blood, and such other things as are prescribed in the canonical Scriptures, with the exception of those enactments which were a yoke of bondage to God's ancient people, suited to their state of heart and to the times of the prophets, and which are found in the five books of Moses. As to those other things which we hold on the authority, not of Scripture, but of tradition, and which are observed throughout the whole world, it may be understood that they are held as approved and instituted either by the Apostles themselves, or by plenary councils, whose authority in the Church is most useful, e.g., the annual commemoration, by special solemnities, of the Lord's Passion, Resurrection, and Ascension, and of the descent of the

Holy Spirit from heaven, and whatever else is in like manner observed by the whole Church wherever it has been established.

There are other things, however, which are different in different places and countries: e.g., some fast on Saturday, others do not; some partake daily of the body and blood of Christ, others receive it on stated days: in some places no day passes without the sacrifice being offered; in others it is only on Saturday and the Lord's day, or it may be only on the Lord's day. In regard to these and all other variable observances which may be met anywhere, one is at liberty to comply with them or not as he chooses; and there is no better rule for the wise and serious Christian in this matter, than to conform to the practice which he finds prevailing in the Church to which it may be his lot to come. For such a custom, if it is clearly not contrary to the faith nor to sound morality, is to be held as a thing indifferent, and ought to be observed for the sake of fellowship with those among whom we live.

I think you may have heard me relate before, what I will nevertheless now mention. When my mother followed me to Milan, she found the Church there not fasting on Saturday. She began to be troubled, and to hesitate as to what she should do; upon which I, though not taking a personal interest then in such things, applied on her behalf to Ambrose, of most blessed memory, for his advice. He answered that he could not teach me anything but what he himself practised, because if he knew any better rule, he would observe it himself. When I supposed that he intended, on the ground of his authority alone, and without supporting it by any argument, to recommend us to give up fasting on Saturday, he followed me, and said: "When I visit Rome, I fast on Saturday; when I am here, I do not fast. On the same principle, do you observe the custom prevailing in whatever Church you come to, if you desire neither to give offence by your conduct, nor to find cause of offence in another's." When I reported this to my mother, she accepted it gladly; and for myself, after frequently reconsidering his decision, I have always esteemed it as if I had received it by an oracle from heaven. For often have I perceived, with extreme sorrow, many disquietudes caused to weak brethren by the contentious pertinacity or superstitious vacillation of some who, in matters of this kind, which do not admit of final decision by the authority of Holy Scripture, or by the tradition of the universal Church, or by their manifest good influence on manners, raise questions, it may be, from some crotchet of their own, or from attachment to the custom followed in one's own country, or from preference for that which one has seen abroad, supposing that wisdom is increased in proportion to the distance to which men travel from home, and agitate these questions with such keenness, that they think all is wrong except what they do themselves.

Someone may say, "The Eucharist ought not to be taken every day." You ask, "On what grounds?" He answers, "Because, in order that a man may approach worthily to so great a sacrament, he ought to choose those days upon which he lives in more special purity and self-restraint; for 'whosoever eateth and drinketh unworthily, eateth and drinketh judgment to himself.'" Another answers, "Certainly; if the wound inflicted by sin and the violence of the soul's distemper be such that the use of these remedies must be put off for a time, every man in this case should be, by the authority of the bishop, forbidden to approach the altar, and appointed to do penance, and should be afterwards restored to privileges by the same authority; for this would be partaking unworthily, if one should partake of it at a time when he ought to be doing penance; and it is not a matter to be left to one's own judgment to withdraw himself from the communion of the Church, or restore himself, as he pleases. If, however, his sins are not so great as to bring him justly under sentence of excommunication, he ought not to withdraw himself from the daily use of the Lord's body for the healing of his soul." Perhaps a third party interposes with a more just decision of the question, reminding them that the principal thing is to remain united in the peace of Christ, and that each should be free to do what, according to his belief, he conscientiously regards as his duty. For neither of them lightly esteems the body and blood of the Lord; on the contrary, both are contending who shall most highly honour the sacrament fraught with blessing. There was no controversy between those two mentioned in the Gospel, Zacchæus and the Centurion; nor did either of them think himself better than the other, though, whereas the former received the Lord joyfully into his house, the latter said, "I am not worthy that Thou shouldst come under my roof"—both honouring the Saviour, though in ways diverse and, as it were, mutually opposed; both miserable through sin, and both obtaining the mercy they required. We may further borrow an illustration here, from the fact that the manna given to the ancient people of God tasted in each man's mouth as he desired that it might. It is the same with this world-subduing sacrament in the heart of each Christian. For he that dares not take it every day, and he who dares not omit it any day, are both alike moved by a desire to do it honour. That sacred food will not submit to be despised, as the manna could not be loathed with impunity. Hence the Apostle says that it was unworthily partaken of by those who did not distinguish between this and all other meats, by yielding to it the special veneration which was due; for to the words quoted already, "eateth and drinketh judgment to himself," he has added these, "not discerning the Lord's body"; and this is apparent from the whole of that passage in the first Epistle to the Corinthians, if it be carefully studied. . . .

Suppose some foreigner visit a place in which during Lent it is customary to abstain from the use of the bath, and to continue fasting on Thursday. "I will not fast today," he says. The reason being asked, he says, "Such is not the custom in my own country." Is not he, by such conduct, attempting to assert the superiority of his custom over theirs? For he cannot quote a decisive passage on the subject from the Book of God; nor can he prove his opinion to be right by the unanimous voice of the universal Church, wherever spread abroad; nor can he demonstrate that they act contrary to the faith, and he according to it, or that they are doing what is prejudicial to sound morality, and he is defending its interests. Those men injure their own tranquillity and peace by quarrelling on an unnecessary question. I would rather recommend that, in matters of this kind, each man should, when sojourning in a country in which he finds a custom different from his own, consent to do as others do. If, on the other hand, a Christian, when travelling abroad in some region where the people of God are more numerous, and more easily assembled together, and more zealous in religion, has seen, e.g., the sacrifice twice offered, both morning and evening, on the Thursday of the last week in Lent, and therefore, on his coming back to his own country, where it is offered only at the close of the day, protests against this as wrong and unlawful, because he has himself seen another custom in another land, this would show a childish weakness of judgment against which we should guard ourselves, and which we must bear with in others, but correct in all who are under our influence.

Observe now to which of these three classes the first question in your letter is to be referred. You ask, "What ought to be done on the Thursday of the last week of Lent? Ought we to offer the sacrifice in the morning, and again after supper, on account of the words in the Gospel, 'Likewise also . . . after supper'? Or ought we to fast and offer the sacrifice only after supper? Or ought we to fast until the offering has been made, and then take supper as we are accustomed to do?" I answer, therefore, that if the authority of Scripture has decided which of these methods is right, there is no room for doubting that we should do according to that which is written; and our discussion must be occupied with a question, not of duty, but of interpretation as to the meaning of the divine institution. In like manner, if the universal Church follows any one of these methods, there is no room for doubt as to our duty; for it would be the height of arrogant madness to discuss whether or not we should comply with it. But the question which you propose is not decided either by Scripture or by universal practice. It must therefore be referred to the third class—as pertaining, namely, to things which are different in different places and countries. Let every man, therefore, conform himself to the usage prevailing in the Church to which he may come. For none of these methods is contrary to the Christian faith or the interests of morality, if favoured by the adoption of one custom more than the other. If this were the case, that either the faith or sound morality were at stake, it would be necessary either to change what was done amiss, or to appoint the doing of what had been neglected. But mere change of custom, even though it may be of advantage in some respects, unsettles men by reason of the novelty: therefore if it brings to advantage, it does much harm by unprofitably disturbing the Church.

Let me add, that it would be a mistake to suppose that the custom prevalent in many places, of offering the sacrifice on that day after partaking of food, is to be traced to the words, "Likewise after supper," etc. For the Lord might give the name of supper to what they had received, in already partaking of His body, so that it was after this that they partook of the cup: as the Apostle says in another place, "When ye come together into one place, this is not to *eat* the Lord's Supper," giving to the receiving of the Eucharist to that extent (i.e., the eating of the bread) the name of the Lord's Supper.

As to the question whether upon that day it is right to partake of food before either offering or partaking of the Eucharist, these words in the Gospel might go far to decide our minds, "As they were eating, Jesus took bread and blessed it," taken in connection with the words in the preceding context, "When the even was come, He sat down with the twelve: and as they did eat, He said, 'Verily I say unto you, that one of you shall betray Me.'" For it was after that He instituted the sacrament; and it is clear that when the disciples first received the body and blood of the Lord, they had not been fasting.

Must we therefore censure the universal Church because the sacrament is everywhere partaken of by persons fasting? Nay, verily, for from that time it pleased the Holy Spirit to appoint, for the honour of so great a sacrament, that the body of the Lord should take the precedence of all other food entering the mouth of a Christian; and it is for this reason that the custom referred to is universally observed. For the fact that the Lord instituted the sacrament after other food had been partaken of, does not prove that brethren should come together to partake of that sacrament after having dined or supped, or imitate those whom the Apostle reproved and corrected for not distinguishing between the Lord's Supper and an ordinary meal. The Saviour, indeed, in order to commend the depth of that mystery more affectingly to His disciples, was pleased to impress it on their hearts and memories by making its institution His last act before going from them to His Passion. And therefore He did not prescribe the order in which it was to be observed, reserving this to be done by the apostles, through whom He intended to arrange all things pertaining to the churches. Had He appointed that the sacrament should be always partaken of after other food, I believe that no one would have departed from that practice. But when the Apostle, speaking of this sacrament, says, "Wherefore, my brethren, when ye come together to eat, tarry one for another: and if any man hunger, let him eat at home; that ye come not together unto condemnation," he immediately adds, "and the rest will I set in order when I come." Whence we are given to understand that, since it was too much for him to prescribe completely in an epistle the method observed by the universal Church throughout the world, it was one of the things set in order by him in person, for we find its observance uniform amid all the variety of other customs.

There are, indeed, some to whom it has seemed right (and their view is not unreasonable), that it is lawful for the body and blood of the Lord to be offered and received after other food has been partaken of, on one fixed day of the year, the day on which the Lord instituted the Supper, in order to give special solemnity to the service on that anniversary. I think that, in this case, it would be more seemly to have it celebrated at such an hour as would leave it in the power of any who have fasted to attend the service before the repast which is customary at the ninth hour. Wherefore we neither compel nor do we dare to forbid anyone to break his fast before the Lord's Supper on that day. I believe, however, that the real ground upon which this custom rests is that many, nay, almost all, are accustomed in most places to use the bath on that day. And because some continue to fast, it is offered in the morning, for those who take food, because they cannot bear fasting and the use of the bath at the same time; and in the evening, for those who have fasted all day.

If you ask me whence originated the custom of using the bath on that day, nothing occurs to me, when I think of it, as more likely than that it was to avoid the offence to decency which must have been given at the baptismal font, if the bodies of those to whom that rite was to be administered were not washed on some preceding day from the uncleanness consequent upon their strict abstinence from ablutions during Lent; and that this particular day was chosen for the purpose because of its being the anniversary of the institution of the Supper. And this being granted to those who were about to receive baptism, many others desired to join them in the luxury of a bath, and in relaxation of their fast.

Having discussed these questions to the best of my ability, I exhort you to observe, in so far as you may be able, what I have laid down, as becomes a wise and peace-loving son of the Church. The remainder of your questions I purpose, if the Lord will, to answer at another time.

### TO JEROME

. . . But when we come to the penal sufferings of infants, I am embarrassed, believe me, by great difficulties, and am wholly at a loss to find an answer by which they are solved; and I speak here not only of those punishments in the life to come, which are involved in that perdition to which they must be drawn down if they depart from the body without the sacrament of Christian grace, but also of the sufferings which are to our sorrow endured by them before our eyes in this present life, and which are so various that time rather than examples would fail me if I were to attempt to enumerate them. They are liable to wasting disease, to racking pain, to the agonies of thirst and hunger, to feebleness of limbs, to privation of bodily senses, and to vexing assaults of unclean spirits. Surely it is incumbent on us to show how it is compatible with justice that infants suffer all these things without any evil of their own as the procuring cause. For it would be impious to say, either that these things take place without God's knowledge, or that He cannot resist those who cause them, or that He unrighteously does these things, or permits them to be done. We are warranted in saying that irrational animals are given by God to serve creatures possessing a higher nature, even though they be wicked, as we see most plainly in the Gospel that the swine of the Gadarenes were given to the legion of devils at their request; but could we ever be warranted in saying this of men? Certainly not. Man is, indeed, an animal, but an animal endowed with reason, though mortal. In his members dwells a reasonable soul, which in these severe afflictions is enduring a penalty. Now God is good, God is just, God is omnipotent—none but a madman would doubt that He is so; let the great sufferings, therefore, which infant children experience be accounted for by some reason compatible with justice. When older people suffer such trials, we are accustomed, certainly, to say, either that their worth is being proved, as in Job's case, or that their wickedness is being punished, as in Herod's; and from some examples, which it has pleased God to make perfectly clear, men are enabled to conjecture the nature of others which are more obscure; but this is in regard to persons of mature age. Tell me, therefore, what we must answer in regard to infant children; is it true that, although they suffer so great punishments, there are no sins in them deserving to be punished? for, of course, there is not in them at that age any righteousness requiring to be put to the proof.

What shall I say, moreover, as to the difficulty which besets the theory of the creation of each soul separately at the birth of the individual in connection with the diversity of talent in different souls, and especially the absolute privation of reason in some? This is, indeed, not apparent in the first stages of infancy, but being developed continuously from the beginning of life, it becomes manifest in children, of whom some are so slow and defective in memory that they cannot learn even the letters of the alphabet, and some (commonly called idiots) so imbecile that they differ very little from the beasts of the field. Perhaps I am told, in answer to this, that the bodies are the cause of these imperfections. But surely the opinion which we wish to see vindicated from objection does not require us to affirm that the soul chose for itself the body which so impairs it, and, being deceived in the choice, committed a blunder; or that the soul, when it was compelled, as a necessary consequence of being born, to enter into some body, was hindered from finding another by crowds of souls occupying the other bodies before it came, so that, like a man who takes whatever seat may remain vacant for him in a theatre, the soul was guided in taking possession of the imperfect body not by its choice, but by its circumstances. We, of course, cannot say and ought not to believe such things. Tell us, therefore, what we ought to believe and to say in order to vindicate from this difficulty the theory that for each individual body a new soul is specially created. . . .

In my books on *Free Will,* already referred to, I have said something, not in regard to the variety of capacities in different souls, but, at least, in regard to the pains which infant children suffer in this life. The nature of the opinion which I there expressed, and the reason why it is insufficient for the purposes of our present inquiry, I will now submit to you, and will put into this letter a copy of the passage in the third book to which I refer. It is as follows: "In connection with the bodily sufferings experienced by the little children who, by reason of their tender age, have no sins—if the souls which animate them did not exist before they were born into the human family—a more grievous and, as it were, compassionate complaint is very commonly made in the remark, 'What evil have they done that they should suffer these things?' as if there could be a meritorious innocence in anyone before the time at which it is possible for him to do anything wrong! Moreover, if God accomplishes, in any measure, the correction of the parents when they are chastised by the sufferings or by the death of the children that are dear to them, is there any reason why these things should not take place, seeing that, after they are past, they will be, to those who experienced them, as if they had never been, while the persons on whose account they were inflicted will either become better, being moved by the rod of temporal afflictions to choose a better mode of life, or be left without excuse under the punishment awarded at the coming judgment, if, notwithstanding the sorrows of this life, they have refused to turn their desires towards eternal life? Moreover, who knows what may be given to the little children by means of whose sufferings the parents have their obdurate hearts subdued, or their faith exercised, or their compassion proved? Who knows what good recompense God may, in the secret of His judgments, reserve for these little ones? For although they have done no righteous action, nevertheless, being free from any transgression of their own, they have suffered these trials. It is certainly not without reason that the Church exalts to the honourable rank of martyrs those children who were slain when Herod sought our Lord Jesus Christ to put Him to death."

# The Christian Reaction against Heretics

With the wheat, as was promised in the parable, grew the tares, and already by the second century, heresies were flourishing. The charm of heresy has always been threefold: the lure of the first temptation, to take instead of waiting to be given; the lure of being different, of knowing *more* and better than the ordinary fellow; and the lure of seeming better, more conscientious, nearer the mind of God. So Ebionites, Marcionites, Gnostics, Manichaeans, Pelagians, Semi-Pelagians, Donatists, Arians, Montanists, and literally hundreds of other sects pullulated, all starting out with emphasizing some part of the Christian truth, rather than the whole of it.

The Christian reaction was brutal. "If thine eye offend thee, pluck it out," Jesus had said. And the Church did just that.

## SOCRATES SCHOLASTICUS

5th century

Socrates, born about 380, was not a cleric but a *scholasticus,* or advocate. He depended largely on Rufinus for his Church history, but after he had studied Athanasius he revised his own writings and completely rewrote his own first and second books some time before 450. He had unlimited admiration for Origen and was very moderate in his judgments on dogmatic questions. As a source for the period in which he wrote, his work is of the greatest value, but as a history "it disappoints even the most modest expectations."

### The Murder of Hypatia

415

There was in Alexandria a woman whose name was Hypatia, the daughter of Theon the Philosopher, who profited so much in profound learning, that she excelled all the philosophers of that time: and not only succeeded in Plato his school, the which exercise Plotinus continued, but also expounded to as many as came to hear her the precepts and doctrine of all sorts of philosophers. Wherefore as many gave their study to the knowledge of philosophical discipline flocked unto her lessons from every country. Moreover for her grave courage of mind, the which she gathered out of the fountains and bowels of philosophical literature, for her modest and matronlike behaviour, she sticked not to present herself before princes and magistrates. Neither was she abashed to come into the open face of the assembly. All men did both reverence and had her in admiration for the singular modesty of her mind. Wherefore she had great spite and envy owed unto her, and because she conferred oft, and had great familiarity with Orestes, the people charged her that she was the cause why the bishop and Orestes were not become friends. To be short, certain heady and rash cockbrains whose guide and captain was Peter, a reader of that Church, watched this woman coming home from some place or other, they pull her out of her chariot: they hail her into the Church called Cæsarium: they stripped her stark naked: they raze the skin and rend the flesh of her body with sharp shells, until the breath departed out of her body: they quarter her body: they bring her quarters unto a place called Cinaron and burn them to ashes. This heinous offence was no small blemish both to Cyril and the Church of Alexandria. For the professors of Christian religion should be no fighters, they ought to be far from committing of murder and bloodshed with other such horrible offences. These things came thus to pass the fourth year of Cyril's consecration, the tenth consulship of Honorius, and the seventh of Theodosius, in the month of March, and on the Ember Days.

# SULPICIUS SEVERUS

360?–?410

Sulpicius Severus was of a distinguished Aquitanian family and was educated at Bordeaux. He married Bassula, well-born and wealthy, and became a lawyer. Following her early death, in 390 he and his friend Paulinus of Nola (see page 407) were baptized together. Sulpicius retired near Béziers, where he wrote the *Life of St. Martin* and the *Dialogues.*

## St Martin and the Condemnation of Priscillian

. . . When the victorious Maximus entered Trèves, [Ithacius] pressed upon him petitions directed against Priscillian and his adherents that were full of hatred and criminal intent. This action aroused the emperor. He sent letters to the prefect of the Gallic provinces and to the *vicarius* of the Spanish provinces, directing that absolutely everyone involved in the disgraceful affair should be brought for trial to a synod at Bordeaux.

When Instantius and Priscillian had been brought to trial in this way, Instantius was ordered to state his case first. He was unsuccessful in exculpating himself and was pronounced unworthy of the episcopate. Priscillian, however, was unwilling to be heard by the bishops and appealed his case to the emperor. The request was granted, because of the timidity of our bishops, who ought either to have pronounced their judgment even against a person who resisted their authority, or, if they were themselves under suspicion, to have reserved the case for a hearing before other bishops. In a matter involving such manifest crimes they ought not to have let the case pass to the emperor.

Thus, all who were compromised in the affair were brought before the emperor. Following after them came their accusers, the bishops Ydacius and Ithacius. I should not blame their zeal for condemning the heretics, if their efforts had not been fired by an excessive eagerness for victory. In my opinion there is as much fault to find with the accusers as with the accused. In any case, I find Ithacius to have been without principle and without scruple: he was audacious, excessively talkative, impudent, a spendthrift who bestowed most of his attention on his gullet and his belly. His foolishness went even so far that he denounced as accomplices and disciples of Priscillian all men, even holy ones, who had a taste for sacred reading or a firm disposition toward frequent fasting.

The wretched Ithacius even dared at this time to make an open charge of heresy against the bishop Martin, a man clearly to be compared with the Apostles. Martin was then at Trèves. He constantly upbraided Ithacius, so that he might give up the accusation; he constantly pleaded with Maximus not to shed the blood of the unfortunate defendants. It was enough and more, he urged, that these men should be declared heretics by the judgment of the bishops and dismissed from their sees; it would be a monstrosity and an unheard-of impiety for an ecclesiastical case to be tried by a secular judge. Finally, as long as Martin stayed at Trèves, the hearing was deferred. When he was about to leave, he used his exceptional authority to elicit from Maximus the promise that no capital punishment would be pronounced upon the accused.

But, later, the emperor was misled by the bishops Magnus and Rufus. Abandoning his counsel of clemency, he turned the case over to the prefect Evodius, a man of passionate severity. Submitting Priscillian to a double interrogation, Evodius convicted him of sorcery. In fact, Priscillian did not deny that he had been given to obscene doctrines, that he also had conducted night-time gatherings of infamous women, that he had the habit of praying naked. When Evodius had declared Priscillian guilty, he had him imprisoned until he could refer the case to the emperor. The proceedings were brought to the palace, and the emperor decreed that Priscillian and his adherents should be condemned to death.

# ST VINCENT OF LÉRINS

d. 450?

Vincent was of Gallic nationality. Before he became a monk, he had perhaps been a soldier. He retired to the monastery of Lérins, where he wrote the *Commonitory* under the pseudonym of Peregrinus. He refers to the Council of Ephesus as having taken place three years before, which dates his book at 434. Today he is famous chiefly for references to him made by Cardinal Newman in 1845, by Pope Pius X, and in the proceedings of the Vatican Council.

## FROM A Commonitory

### A GENERAL RULE FOR DISTINGUISHING THE TRUTH OF THE CATHOLIC FAITH FROM THE FALSEHOOD OF HERETICAL PRAVITY

I have often then inquired earnestly and attentively of very many men eminent for sanctity and learning, how and by what sure and so to speak universal rule I may be able to distinguish the truth of the Catholic faith from the falsehood of heretical pravity; and I have always, and in almost every instance, received an answer to this effect: That whether I or anyone else should wish to detect the frauds and avoid the snares of heretics as they rise, and to continue sound and complete in the Catholic faith, we must, the Lord helping, fortify our own belief in two ways; first, by the authority of the Divine Law, and then, by the tradition of the Catholic Church.

But here someone perhaps will ask, Since the canon of Scripture is complete, and sufficient of itself for everything, and more than sufficient, what need is there to join with it the authority of the Church's interpretation? For this reason—because, owing to the depth of Holy Scripture, all do not accept it in one and the same sense, but one understands its words in one way, another in another; so that it seems to be capable of as many interpretations as there are interpreters. For Novatian expounds it one way, Sabellius another, Donatus another, Arius, Eunomius, Macedonius, another, Photinus, Apollinaris, Priscillian, another, Jovinian, Pelagius, Celestius, another, lastly, Nestorius another. Therefore, it is very necessary, on account of so great intricacies of such various error, that the rule for the right understanding of the prophets and Apostles should be framed in accordance with the standard of ecclesiastical and Catholic interpretation.

Moreover, in the Catholic Church itself, all possible care must be taken, that we hold that faith which has been believed everywhere, always, by all. For that is truly and in the strictest sense "Catholic," which, as the name itself and the reason of the thing declare, comprehends all universally. This rule we shall observe if we follow universality, antiquity, consent. We shall follow universality if we confess that one faith to be true which the whole Church throughout the world confesses; antiquity, if we in no wise depart from those interpretations which it is manifest were notoriously held by our holy ancestors and fathers; consent, in like manner, if in antiquity itself we adhere to the consentient definitions and determinations of all, or at the least of almost all priests and doctors. . . .

### WHAT IS TO BE DONE IF ONE OR MORE DISSENT FROM THE REST?

. . . What then will a Catholic Christian do, if a small portion of the Church have cut itself off from the communion of the universal faith? What, surely, but prefer the soundness of the whole body to the unsoundness of a pestilent and corrupt member? What, if some novel contagion seek to infect not merely an insignificant portion of the Church, but the whole? Then it will be his care to cleave to antiquity, which at this day cannot possibly be seduced by any fraud of novelty. . . .

### THE NOTES OF A TRUE CATHOLIC

This being the case, he is the true and genuine Catholic who loves the truth of God, who loves the Church, who loves the body of Christ, who esteems divine religion and the Catholic Faith above every thing, above the authority, above the regard, above the genius, above the eloquence, above the philosophy, of every man whatsoever; who sets light by all of these, and continuing steadfast and established in the faith, resolves that he will believe that, and that only, which he is sure the Catholic Church has held universally and from ancient time. . . . For therefore it is that outside the most secure harbour of the Catholic Faith, they are tossed about, beaten, and almost killed, by divers tempestuous cogitations, in order that they may take in the sails of self-conceit, which they had with ill advice unfurled to the blasts of novelty, and may betake themselves again to . . . the most secure harbour of their placid and good mother, and may begin by vomiting up those bitter and turbid floods of error which they had swallowed, that thenceforward they may be able to drink the streams of fresh and living water. Let them unlearn well what they had learnt not well, and let them receive so much of the entire doctrine of the Church as they can understand: what they cannot understand let them believe.

### ON DEVELOPMENT IN RELIGIOUS KNOWLEDGE

But someone will say perhaps, Shall there, then, be no progress in Christ's Church? Certainly; all possible progress. For what being is there, so envious of men, so full of hatred to God, who would seek to forbid it? Yet on condition that it be real progress, not alteration of the faith. For progress requires that the subject be enlarged in itself, alteration, that it be transformed into something else. The intelligence, then, the knowledge, the wisdom, as well of individuals as of all, as well of one man as of the whole Church, ought, in the course of ages and centuries, to increase and make much and vigorous progress; but yet only in its own kind; that is to say, in the same doctrine, in the same sense, and in the same meaning.

The growth of religion in the soul must be analogous to the growth of the body, which, though in process of years it is developed and attains its full size, yet remains still the same. There is a wide difference between the flower of youth and the maturity of age; yet they who were once young are still the same now that they have become old, insomuch that though the stature and outward form of the individual are changed, yet his nature is one and the same, his person is one and the same. . . . This, then, is undoubtedly the true and legitimate rule of progress, this the established and most beautiful order of growth, that mature age ever develops in the man those parts and forms which the wisdom of the Creator had already framed beforehand in the infant. . . .

In like manner, it behoves Christian doctrine to follow the same laws of progress, so as to be consolidated by years, enlarged by time, refined by age, and yet, withal, to continue uncorrupt and unadulterate, complete and perfect in all the measurement of its parts, and, so to speak, in all its proper members and senses, admitting no change, no waste of its distinctive property, no variation in its limits. . . .

To give an example. In ancient times, our forefathers sowed the seeds of the wheat of faith in that field which is the Church. It would be quite unjust and improper if we, their descendants, gathered, instead of the genuine truth of wheat, the false tares of error. On the contrary, it is logically correct that the beginning and the end be in agreement, that we reap from the planting of the wheat of doctrine the harvest of the wheat of dogma. In this way, none of the characteristics of the seed is changed, although something evolved in the course of time from those first seeds and has now expanded under careful cultivation. What may be added is merely appearance, beauty, and distinction, but the proper nature of each kind remains. May it never happen that the rose garden of the Catholic spirit be turned into a field of thistles and thorns. May it never happen that in this spiritual paradise darnel and poison ivy suddenly appear from growths of cinnamon and balsam. Whatever has been planted in the husbandry of God's Church by the faith of the fathers should, therefore, be cultivated and guarded by the zeal of their children; it should flourish and ripen; it should develop and become perfect. For it is right that those ancient dogmas of heavenly philosophy should in the course of time be thoroughly cared for, filed, and polished; but it is sinful to change them, sinful to behead them or mutilate them. They may take on more evidence, clarity, and distinctness, but it is absolutely necessary that they retain their plenitude, integrity, and basic character.

If such a license for impious fraud be granted only once, what terrible danger—I am afraid even to speak of it—would result, with religion being destroyed and abolished. If one tenet of Catholic dogma were renounced, another, then another, and finally one after the other would be abandoned, first by custom, and then as though by right. When one segment after the other had been rejected, what else would the final result be, except that the whole would be likewise rejected? On the other hand, once there is a beginning of mixing the new with the old, foreign ideas with genuine, and profane elements with sacred, this habit will creep in everywhere, without check. At the end, nothing in the Church will be left untouched, unimpaired, unhurt, and unstained. Where formerly there was the sanctuary of chaste and uncorrupted truth, there will be a brothel of impious and filthy errors. May divine compassion divert such shocking impiety from the minds of its children; instead, may the impious crowd itself be left in its madness!

The Church of Christ, zealous and cautious guardian of the dogmas deposited with it, never changes any phase of them. It does not diminish them or add to them; it neither trims what seems necessary nor grafts things superfluous; it neither gives up its own nor usurps what does not belong to it. But it devotes all its diligence to one aim: to treat tradition faithfully and wisely; to nurse and polish what from old times may have remained unshaped and unfinished; to consolidate and to strengthen what already was clear and plain; and to guard what already was confirmed and defined. After all, what have the councils brought forth in their decrees but that what before was believed plainly and simply might from now on be believed more diligently; that what before was preached rather unconcernedly might be preached from now on more eagerly; that what before was practised with less concern might from now on be cultivated with more care? This, I say, and nothing but this, has the Catholic Church, aroused over the novelties of the heretics, again and again accomplished by the decrees of its councils, i.e., what it earlier received from our forefathers by tradition alone, it has handed down to posterity by authoritative decisions, condensing weighty matters in a few words, and particularly for the enlightenment of the mind, by presenting in new words the old interpretation of the faith.

# ST GELASIUS I

Pope 492–496

Gelasius was the successor of Felix III. Little is known of his actual share in the *Decretum Gelasii de Libris Recipiendis et Non Recipiendis,* the decretals regarding the authoritative and apocryphal books of Scripture, which bear his name.

## FROM Of Books to Be Accepted and Rejected

. . . Although the one dwelling of the universal Catholic Church spread through the world is of Christ, the holy Roman Church, however, has been placed before the other churches by no synodical decrees, but has obtained the primacy by the evangelic voice of our Lord and Saviour, saying, "Thou art Peter, and upon this rock I will build My Church," etc. To it was given the fellowship of the most blessed Apostle Paul, that chosen vessel who not at a different time, as heretics prate, but at one time and on one and the same day by a glorious death, was crowned together with Peter in agony in the city of Rome under the Emperor Nero. And they equally consecrated the said holy Roman Church to Christ and placed it over all the others in the whole world by their presence and venerable triumph.

Therefore the first see of Peter the Apostle is the Roman Church, not having any spot or wrinkle or any such thing. The second see was consecrated at Alexandria in the name of the blessed Peter by Mark, his disciple and the evangelist. He himself, having been directed by the Apostle Peter to Egypt, preached the word of truth and consummated a glorious martyrdom. But as the third see of the same most blessed Apostle Peter is held the see of Antioch, since he held that before he came to Rome, and there the name of the new people, the name of Christians, arose. . . .

# THE LIFE OF PRAYER

# ST JUSTIN MARTYR

(See page 193.)

## FROM First Apology

The *Apology* is addressed to Antoninus Pius, Marcus Aurelius, and Lucius Verus. Antoninus Pius reigned from 138 to 161, but textual criticism of the address has placed it as having been written between 150 and 155. (See also pages 339–42.)

To the Emperor Titus Ælius Adrianus Antoninus Pius Augustus Cæsar, to his son Verissimus the philosopher, and Lucius the philosopher, the natural son of Cæsar, but the adopted son of Pius, and the lover of learning; and to the sacred Senate, and to the whole people of Rome, in favour of those men of all nations who are unjustly hated and oppressed, I, Justin, the son of Priscus, and grandson of Bacchius, natives of Flavia Neapolis, a city of Palestine, being one of them, have composed this address and petition.

Reason directs that all who are really pious, and truly philosophers, should love that alone which is true, and refuse to follow the opinions of the ancients, should they prove to be worthless; for sound reason requires that we should not only reject those who act, or teach, anything contrary to that which is right; but that by every means, and before his own life, the lover of truth ought, even if threatened with death, to choose to speak and to do what is right.

Since, then, you are universally termed pious, and philosophers, and guardians of justice, and lovers of learning; it shall now be seen whether you are indeed such. For we have not come to flatter you by these writings of ours, nor to seek to please by our address; but to make our claim to be judged after a strict and searching inquiry; so that neither by prejudice, nor desire of popularity from the superstitious, nor by any unthinking impulse of zeal, nor by that evil report which has so long kept possession of your minds, you may be urged to give a decision against yourselves. For it is our maxim that we can suffer harm from none, unless we be convicted as doers of evil, or proved to be wicked: you may indeed slay us, but hurt us you cannot. . . . For it is in our power when examined to deny our faith, but we are not desirous of living by the utterance of a falsehood; for, possessed with the desire of a life of eternal duration and purity, and striving for that abode which is above, with God the Father and Maker of all things, we even hasten to confess our faith, persuaded and convinced as we are that they who have shown before God by their works that they are followers of Him, and lovers of the life that is with Him, where there is no evil to oppose, may obtain these rewards. Briefly then, what we look for, and have learnt from Christ, and what we teach, is as follows; Plato said to the same effect, that Rhadamanthus and Minos would punish the wicked when they came to them; we say that the same thing will take place; but that the Judge will be Christ, and that their souls will be united to the same bodies, and will undergo an eternal punishment; and not, as he said, a period of a thousand years only. And if any tell us that this is incredible or impossible, it is an error of no consequence; as long as we are proved to have done nothing wrong in practice.

We worship not with frequent sacrifices, and garlands of flowers, those whom men have made, and placed in temples, and call gods; for we know that they are senseless, and inanimate, and have not the form of God (for we do not consider that God has such a form as that in which some say that they represent Him, for the sake of worship), but have the names, and forms, of those evil demons who have appeared to men; for why should I relate to you who know it, how the workmen manage their materials, carving, cutting, casting, and hammering them, and often from vessels of dishonour, by merely changing their shape through their craft, and giving them a form, they make what they call gods. This we consider not only senseless, but also an insult to God, who has both a form and a glory ineffable, but whose name is thus transferred to objects that are perishable, and require to be taken care of: and that the artificers of them are intemperate, and not to enter into particulars, practise every kind of wickedness, you well know; and that they corrupt their own women who help them in their work. Oh, fatuity as of one struck by thunder, that licentious men should be said to form and fashion gods for you to worship, and that such should be constituted the keepers of the temples in which they are enshrined, not seeing that it is unlawful even to think, or to say, that men are guardians of the gods.

And we have learned that God has no need of material offerings from men, seeing that He gives us all things, and we have been taught, and are convinced, and believe, that He only receives those who imitate Him in the virtues which are part of His attributes, temperance, namely, and justice, humanity, and all that is worthy of a God who is called by no proper name; and we are also taught that He in His goodness created all things in the beginning from shapeless matter, for the sake of men, who, if by their works they approve themselves worthy of His design, shall, we believe, be thought worthy of a dwelling with Him, there to reign with Him free henceforth from corruption and suffering. For as He created us at first when we were not, so also we believe that He will hold those who choose what is pleasing to Him worthy, because of their choice, of immortality and of dwelling with Himself. For though our birth was not originally our own doing, yet in order that we may choose to follow what is pleasing to Him, He, by the reasonable faculties which He has bestowed on us, both persuades us, and leads us, to faith; and we think that it is to the benefit of all men, that they are not prohibited from the knowledge of these things, but are even urged to turn their attention to them; for what human laws were incapable of doing, that the Word, which is Divine, would effect, were it not that the evil demons, aided by the wicked and varied inclination to evil, which is in the nature of every man, have scattered about so many false and godless accusations, of which none apply to us.

And, when you hear that we look for a kingdom, you rashly conclude that we mean a human one, although we declare that it is to be that which is with God, as is proved by the fact that, when examined by you, we own ourselves to be Christians; though we know that for everyone who confesses this, the punishment is death: for, if we expected a human kingdom, we should deny our name that we might escape destruction, and should endeavour to elude you, that we might obtain our expectations. But since we fix not our hopes on the present, we take no thought when men murder us, knowing that all must assuredly die.

We in fact are, above all men, your helpers and assistants in the promotion of peace, who hold these doctrines, that it is impossible for the worker of wickedness, or the covetous, or the treacherous, or again for the virtuous man, to escape the notice of God, and that everyone is advancing either to eternal torment, or to salvation, according to the quality of his actions; for if all were aware of this, no man would be found to prefer sin for a season, knowing that he was passing to eternal condemnation through fire, but he would by every means practise self-control, and adorn himself with virtue, that he might obtain the blessings of God, and escape His punishments; for it is not because of the laws and punishments which you have instituted that men try to hide their misdeeds, but they commit their offences, as knowing that since you are but men, it is possible to elude you; if however they knew, and were assured, that it is impossible to deceive God in anything, not only in their actions, but even in their thoughts, they would by every means be well conducted, if only on account of His threatened punishments, as even you yourselves will allow.

But you appear to dread lest all men should become doers of good, and you no longer have any left to punish; this might be a cause of concern to the hangman, but never to upright princes. I am persuaded, however, that these things also, as I have said, are the doing of wicked spirits, who exact sacrifices and worship even from those who live contrarily to reason; but I suppose that you who aim at piety and philosophy, will do nothing unreasonable, but if you, like the senseless, prefer custom to truth, do what you can; even princes who place popular opinion before truth are no better than robbers in a desert; and the Word declares that you shall not prosper in your doings; that Word no other than Whom, after God the Father, we know to be the most noble and just Prince. For as all wish to escape inheriting the poverty, or sufferings, or disgrace of their fathers, so, whatever the Word forbids us to choose, of that the man of sense will not make choice. That all these things should come to pass, our Teacher, I say, Jesus Christ, who is both the Son, and the Apostle, of God the Father, and Ruler of all things, foretold (from Whom also we are called Christians); hence we are confirmed in all that He has taught us, for everything that He foretold should come to pass is seen to be fulfilled in fact; for it is the work of God to foretell beforehand, as He has done, an event, and then to show it taking place as it was foretold. I might even now conclude, and add nothing more, under the supposition that we ask what is both just and true; but as I know that it is not easy to effect a sudden change in a mind wholly occupied by ignorance, I have determined, in order to persuade those who love truth, to add a little more, knowing that it is not impossible, by the production of truth, to dissipate ignorance.

That we are not atheists, therefore, what moderate person will not confess, from our worship of the Creator of this universe, Whom we assert, as we have been taught, to have no need of sacrifices of blood, and libations, and incense, but Whom we praise to the best of our power with the reasonable service of prayer, and thanksgiving, in all our oblations, having been instructed that the only service that is worthy of Him is, not to consume by fire what He has given us for our sustenance, but to apply it to our own benefit, and to that of those who are in need, and, showing ourselves grateful to Him, in speech to offer Him solemn acts of worship and hymns, for our creation, for all our means of health, for the qualities of things, and for the changes of seasons, and putting up prayers that we may have a resurrection to incorruptibility, through our faith in Him. Our Teacher of these things is Jesus Christ, who was even born for that purpose, and was crucified under Pontius Pilate, procurator of Judæa in the reign of Tiberius Cæsar; Whom, having learned Him to be the Son of the Very God, and holding Him to be in the second place, and the Spirit of Prophecy in the third, I will prove that we worship with reason. . . .

# ST MELITO

latter half of 2nd century

Melito, bishop of Sardis, was active during the reign of Marcus Aurelius, to whom he addressed an *Apology* for the Christians.

## FROM Homily on the Passion

. . . Hear ye, beloved; thus the mystery of the Passover is new and old, eternal and transient, corruptible and incorruptible, mortal and immortal. It is old according to the Law, but new according to the Word; transient according to the world, but eternal through grace. . . . Ancient is the Word. . . .

But neither was it a lamb; for the type passed and the truth was found. For in place of the lamb there came a Son, and in place of the sheep a man, and in the man, Christ who contains all things. . . . For the Law became Word, and the old became new, going forth together from Sion and Jerusalem, and the command became grace, and the type became truth, and the lamb became a Son, and the sheep of sacrifice became man and the man became God. For born as a Son, led forth as a lamb, sacrificed as a sheep, buried as a man, he rose from the dead as God, being by nature God and man. Who is all things: in that he judges, Law, in that he teaches, Word, in that he saves, Grace, in that he begets, Father, in that he is begotten, Son, in that he suffers, a sacrificial sheep, in that he is buried, Man, in that he arises, God. This is Jesus the Christ, to whom belongs the glory to the ages of ages. Amen. . . .

Because he healed their lame, and cleansed their lepers, and gave sight to their blind, and raised their dead. For this reason he died. Is it not written in Law and Prophets, "Ye have returned unto me evil for good"? . . .

Why, O Israel, has thou done this strange wrong? Thou hast dishonoured Him who honoured thee, thou hast held in contempt Him who glorified thee, thou hast denied Him who acknowledged thee, thou hast renounced Him who proclaimed thee His own, thou hast slain Him who gave thee life. . . . Come, He says, Israel, thou hast slain the Lord. Why? Because He must needs die? Thou errest, O Israel, in reasoning thus falsely upon the slaying of the Lord. He must needs suffer, but not through thee. He must needs be dishonoured, but not by thee. He must needs be judged, but not by thee. He must needs be hanged upon the cross, but not by thee and thy right hand. Thus, O Israel, thou shouldst have cried to God: "O Master, even though Thy son must suffer, and this is Thy will, let Him then suffer, but not at my hand; let Him suffer at the hand of the Gentiles, let Him be judged by the uncircumcised, let Him be nailed to the cross by the oppressor's hand, but not by me." . . . Scourgings and pain, and thirst and hunger and oppression, O Israel, all these punishments from Him thou hast brought upon thyself. . . . Thou didst bind the beautiful hands with which He shaped thee from the earth; and His beautiful mouth, the mouth that fed thee with life, thou hast fed with gall, and thou hast slain thy Lord in the great feast.

And thou wast of good cheer, while He was hungry; thou wast eating bread and drinking wine, while He drank vinegar and gall; thou wast glad of countenance, while He was sad; thou wast rejoicing, He was oppressed; thou wast singing, He was judged; thou gavest command, He was nailed to the cross; thou wast dancing, He was being laid in the tomb; thou wast lying on a soft cushion, He in the grave and the coffin. . . .

Thou hast slain thy Lord in the midst of Jerusalem. Hear, all ye families of mankind, and see the strange murder that has been committed in the midst of Jerusalem. . . . And who is slain, and who is it that slayeth? . . . I am ashamed to tell and yet tell I must. For if He had been slain at night or early in the morning or even during the day in a lonely place, it would have been well to hold our peace; but now in the midst of a public place and the midst of the city and in the sight of all men hath so wicked a murder been done.

And so He is raised upon a high cross, and a title is set upon it making known Him who was slain. Who was He? Painful it is to tell, more terrible not to tell. Hear ye, and tremble before Him who made heaven and earth tremble. He who hung the earth in its place is hanged, He who fixed the heavens is fixed upon the cross, He who made all things fast is made fast upon the tree, the Master has been insulted . . . the King of Israel has been slain by an Israelitish hand. O strange murder, strange crime! The Master has been treated in unseemly wise, with His body naked, and has not even been deemed worthy of a covering, that He might not be seen. For this reason the lights of heaven turned away, and the day darkened, that it might hide Him who was stripped upon the cross, shrouding not the body of the Lord, but the eyes of men. For though the people trembled not, the earth trembled; though the people feared not, the heavens were afraid; though the people rent not their garments, the angel rent his; though the people did not lament, the Lord thundered from heaven, and the Most High uttered His voice. Why thus, O Israel, didst thou not tremble for the Lord, why didst thou not fear for the Lord, didst not wail for the Lord . . . ? Why, when He hung on the cross didst thou not rend thy garments in pity? Pitiless He found thee . . . compassionate He found thee not.

# AUSONIUS

310?–?395

Ausonius, born and educated at Bordeaux, was a better poet than Christian. His *Idyllia* are truly Virgilian in rhyme and diction, coupled, J. W. Mackail says, "with the new romantic sense of the beauties of nature." His prayer, however, seems to be Christian in expression though classic in form.

## FROM The Daily Routine

### THE INTERLUDE

Come, boy, get up! Bring me my slippers and my tunic of linen; bring all the clothes you have ready now for my going out. Fetch me spring water to wash my face and hands and eyes. Get me the chapel opened, but with no outward display; holy words and innocent prayers are enough for worship. I do not call for incense to be burned nor for any slice of honey cake; hearths of green turf I leave for the altars of the vain gods. I must pray to God, and to the Son of God most high, that co-equal Majesty united in one fellowship with the Holy Spirit. And lo, now I begin my prayers; my heart feels heaven is near, and trembles. Have faith and hope then anything to fear?

### THE PRAYER

Omnipotent God, whom through the worship of my heart alone I know, to the wicked unknown, yet known to every devout soul, Thou art without beginning and without end, more ancient than time past and time to come; Thy fashion and extent no mind can ever grasp, no tongue express. He only may behold Thee and, face to face, hear thy bidding and sit at Thy fatherly right hand, who is Himself the Maker of all things, Himself the cause of all created things, Himself the Word of God, the Word which is God, who was before the world which He was to make; begotten at that time when time was not yet; who came into being before the sun's beams and the bright morning star enlightened the sky. Without Him was nothing made, and through Him were all things made. His throne is in heaven, and beneath His seat lie earth and the sea and the invincible chaos of the darkling night; unresting, He is the very mover of all things, the quickener of the lifeless. He is God, the begotten of the unbegotten, Who, being provoked by the guile of his scornful people, called the nations into His kingdom, the worthier offshoot of an ingrafted stock to worship Him. To our forefathers it was granted to behold Him; and whoso discerned His Godhead, to him it was given to have seen the Father also. He bore our sinful stains and suffered a death with mockery, thus teaching us that there is a road to lead back to eternal life, and that the soul returns not alone, but with the body complete enters the realms of heaven and leaves the secret chamber of the grave empty, covered with earth which cannot hold it.

Son of the All-highest, bringer of salvation to our race, Thou unto whom Thy Begetter has committed all the powers of His fatherhood, keeping none back in envy, but giving freely, open a way for these my prayers and safely waft them to Thy Father's ears.

Grant me a heart, O Father, to hold out against all deeds of wrong, and deliver me from the serpent's deadly venom, sin. Let it suffice that the serpent did beguile our old mother Eve and involved Adam, too, in his deceit; let us, their progeny, once foretold by soothsaying prophets, escape the snares which the death-dealing serpent weaves.

Prepare a road that I, being freed from the fetters of this frail body, may be led up on high, where in the clear heaven the Milky Way stretches above the wandering clouds of the wind-vexed moon—that road by which the holy men of old departed from the earth; by which Elias, caught up in the chariot, once made his way alive above our lower air; and Enoch, too, who went before his end without change of body.

Grant me, O Father, the effluence of everlasting light for which I yearn, if I swear not by gods of stone, and, looking up to one altar of awful sacrifice alone, bring there the offering of a stainless life; if Thee I recognize as Father of the Only-begotten, our Lord and God, and, joined with both, the Spirit who brooded over the waters' face.

Grant me Thy pardon, Father, and relieve my anguished breast, if I seek Thee not with the bodies of slain beasts nor with blood poured forth, nor divine heaven's will from the secrets of their entrails; if I, though prone to stray, hold off from wrong, and if I long, rather than trust, to be approved upright and pure. Accept a soul which makes its confession, if I abhor these my frail limbs, if I repent me inwardly, and if deep-seated dread racks all my nerves and foretastes the final torments of Gehenna, and the stricken mind suffers its own ghostly doom.

And when the hour of my last day shall come, grant that the conscience of a life well spent suffer me not to fear death, nor yet long for it. When, through Thy mercy, I shall appear cleansed from my secret faults, let me despise all else, and let my one delight be to await in hope Thy judgment. And if that season tarries and the day delays, keep far from me that fierce tempter, the serpent, with his false allurements.

These prayers of a soul devout, albeit trembling with dark sense of guilt, claim for thine own before the eternal Father, Thou Son of God who mayest be entreated, Saviour, God and Lord, Mind, Glory, Word and Son, very God of very God, Light of Light, who remainest with the eternal Father, reigning throughout all ages, whose praise the harmonious songs of tuneful David echo forth, until respondent voices rend the air with "Amen."

### GOING OUT

Now I have prayed enough to God, albeit we sinful men can never entreat heaven enough. Boy! Bring me my morning coat. I must exchange my "Hail" and "Farewell" with my friends. But since the sun for four full hours has urged on his steeds and now verges towards noon, I needs must speak a word with Sosias.

# NICETAS OF REMESIANA

335?–?414

Nicetas ("Niketes" in Greek) was born in Remesiana, a town located on the imperial highway connecting East and West. The first mention of his name occurs in a letter of a Bishop Germinius in 366. Nicetas was a friend of St Paulinus of Nola, who wrote two poems to him. (One begins: "Go, if you must, but leave your heart behind.") Nicetas, as missionary to the people of what is now Yugoslavia, evangelized Illyria, which during the reign of Theodosius passed from the control of the patriarchate of Rome to that of the Eastern Empire. Nicetas visited St Ambrose in 396 and St Paulinus of Nola in 398. The last mention of him occurs in a letter of Pope Innocent I in 414.

## The Names and Titles of Our Saviour

In the Holy Scriptures there are many names and titles which are applied to our Lord and Saviour, Jesus. He is said to be the Word; He is called Wisdom, Light and Power; right hand, arm and angel; man and lamb, sheep and priest. He is the Way, the Truth, the Life; a vine, Justice and Redemption; bread, a stone and doctor; a fount of living water; peace and judge and door. Yet, for all these names—which are to help us grasp the nature and range of His power—there is but one and the same Son of God who is our God.

These, then, are His names; but what are the meanings of these names? He is called the Word, first, to imply that He was begotten of the Father with no more passivity or substantial diminution in the Father than there is in a person who utters a spoken word; second, for the obvious reason that God the Father has always spoken through Him both to men and angels. The name Wisdom tells us that in the beginning all things, through Him, were ordered wisely. He is the Light, because it was He who brought light into the primordial darkness of the world and who, by His coming among men, dissipated the darkness of their minds. Power is one of His names, since no created thing can ever overcome Him. He is a right hand and arm, for through Him all things were made and by Him they are all sustained. He is called an angel of great counsel, because He is the announcer of His Father's will. He is said to be the Son of man, because on account of us men He deigned to be born a man. He is called a lamb, because of His perfect innocence; a sheep, to symbolize His Passion. For two reasons He is called a priest: first, because He offered up His body as an oblation and victim to God the Father for us; second, because, through us, He condescends day after day to be offered up. He is the Way along which we journey to our salvation; the Truth, because He rejects what is false; the Life, because He destroys death. He is a vine, because He spread out the branches of His arms that the world might pluck in clusters the grapes of consolation from the Cross. He is called Justice, because through faith in His name sinners are made just; and Redemption, because He paid the price in His blood to buy us back—we who had been so long lost. He is called bread, because by His Gospel He fed the hunger of our ignorance; and a stone, both because on Him the serpent left no trace and because He afforded us protection. He is the doctor who came to visit us and cured our weakness and our wounds; the fount of living water, because by the "bath of regeneration" He cleanses sinners and gives them life. He is peace, because He brought together those who lived apart, and reconciled us to God the Father. He is the Resurrection, because He will raise all bodies from their graves; and the judge because it is He who will judge both the living and the dead. He is the door, because it is by Him that those who believe enter the kingdom of heaven.

These many names and titles belong to one Lord. Take courage, therefore, O man of faith, and plant your hope firmly in Him. If you would learn of the Father, listen to this Word. If you would be wise, ask Him who is Wisdom. When it is too dark for you to see, seek Christ, for He is the Light. Are you sick? Have recourse to Him who is both doctor and health. Would you know by whom the world was made and all things are sustained? Believe in Him, for He is the arm and right hand. Are you afraid of this or that? Remember that on all occasions He will stand by your side like an angel. If you find it hard to meet face to face the high majesty of the Only-begotten, do not lose hope. Remember, He was made man to make it easy for men to approach Him. If you are innocent, like a lamb He will join your company. If you are saddened by pagan persecution, take courage. Remember that He Himself went like a lamb to the slaughter, and, priest that He is, He will offer you up as a victim to the Father. If you do not know the way of salvation, look for Christ, for He is the road for souls. If it is truth that you want, listen to Him, for He is the Truth. Have no fear whatever of death, for Christ is the Life of those who believe. Do the pleasures of the world seduce you? Turn all the more to the Cross of Christ to find solace in the sweetness of the vine that clustered there. Are you a lost sinner? Then you must hunger for justice and thirst for the Redeemer, for that is what Christ is. Because He is bread, He takes away all hunger. If you are stumbling, fix your foot firmly on Him, for He is a rock; and like a wall He will protect you. Are you weak and sick? Ask for a medicine from Him, because He is a doctor. Especially, if you are still unbaptized, you may suffer from the ardors of passion. Then hurry to the well of life to put out the flame and to gain for your soul eternal life. If anger is tormenting you and you are torn by dissension, appeal to Christ, who is peace, and you will be reconciled to the Father and will love everyone as you would like to be loved yourself. If you are afraid that your body is failing and have a dread of death, remember that He is the Resurrection, and can raise up what has fallen. When sinful pleasure tempts you and the flesh is weak, recall that you are in the presence of a just judge, severe in weighing the evidence and one who is making ready everlasting fire. Then, sinner as you are, you will lose your taste for sin. In your hour of death, brother, should you lose hope of obtaining a just reward in heavenly glory, be bold in faith to remember that He is the door, and through Him, once you are raised from the dead, you will enter the mysteries of heaven, join the company of angels, and hear the longed-for words: "Well done, good and faithful servant; because thou hast been faithful over a few things, I will set thee over many; enter the joy of thy master . . . take possession of the kingdom prepared for you from the foundation of the world." Amen.

# ST JEROME

(See page 94.)

## FROM Attack on Vigilantius

. . . Among other words of blasphemy he [Vigilantius] may be heard to say: "What need is there for you not only to reverence with so great honor but even to adore I know not what, which you carry about in a little vessel and worship?" And again in the same book, "Why do you adore by kissing a bit of powder wrapped up in a cloth?" and further on, "Under the cloak of religion we see really a heathen ceremony introduced into the churches; while the sun is shining heaps of tapers are lighted, and everywhere I know not what paltry bit of powder wrapped in a costly cloth is kissed and worshipped. Great honor do men of this sort pay to the blessed martyrs, who, as they think, are to be glorified by trumpery tapers, but to whom the Lamb who is in the midst of the throne, with all the brightness of His majesty gives light." . . .

Is the Emperor Arcadius guilty of sacrilege, who, after so long a time, conveyed the bones of the blessed Samuel from Judæa to Thrace? Are all the bishops to be considered not only sacrilegious but silly as well, who carried that most worthless thing, dust and ashes, wrapped in silk and in a golden vessel? Are the people of all the churches fools, who went to meet the sacred relics, and received them with as much joy as if they beheld the living prophet in the midst of them, so that there was one great swarm of people from Palestine to Chalcedon and with one voice the praises of Christ resounded? . . .

For you say that the souls of the Apostles and martyrs have their abode either in the bosom of Abraham, or in some place of refreshment, or under the altar of God, and that they cannot leave their own tombs and be present where they will. They are, it seems, of senatorial rank and are not in the worst sort of prison and among murderers, but are kept apart in liberal and honorable custody in the isles of the blessed and the Elysian fields. Do you lay down laws for God? Will you throw the Apostles in chains? So that to the day of judgment they are to be kept in confinement and are not with the Lord, although it is written concerning them, "They follow the Lamb whithersoever He goeth." If the Lamb is present everywhere, then they who are with the Lamb, it must be believed, are everywhere. And while the Devil and the demons wander through the whole world, and with only too great speed are present everywhere, the martyrs, after shedding their blood, are to be kept out of sight shut up in a coffin from whence they cannot go forth? You say in your pamphlet that so long as we are alive we can pray for one another; but after we are dead the prayer of no person for another can be heard, and especially because the martyrs, though they cry for the avenging of their blood, have never been able to obtain their request. If Apostles and martyrs, while still in the body, can pray for others, when they ought still to be anxious for themselves, how much more must they do so after they have their crowns and victories and triumphs? A single man, Moses, won pardon from God for six hundred thousand armed men; and Stephen, the follower of his Lord and the first martyr for Christ, entreats pardon for his persecutors; and after they have entered on their life with Christ, shall they have less power? The Apostle Paul says that two hundred and seventy-six souls were given him in the ship; and after his dissolution, when he began to be with Christ, must he then shut up his mouth and be unable to say a word for those who throughout the whole world have believed in his Gospel? Shall Vigilantius the live dog be better than Paul the dead lion? . . .

# ST PAULINUS OF NOLA

353–431

Pontius Meropius Anicius Paulinus, son of a wealthy family near Bordeaux, was a pupil of the poet Ausonius. He married Therasia, a Spanish lady, and retired to his estates. He was converted and baptized about 390. He distributed his goods among the poor and withdrew to Barcelona, where he was ordained priest, and then to Nola, in Campania, where he and his wife settled near the tomb of St Felix, to lead a life of poverty and asceticism. In 409, on the death of the bishop of Nola, Paulinus was chosen to succeed him. He wrote a great deal of poetry, delightful letters to his friends, among whom were Ambrose, Augustine, and Jerome, and some rather ornate and inferior prose. Some fifty of his letters survive, but his panegyric on the Emperor Theodosius, written in 394, is lost.

This prayer of a peasant to St Felix is in verse in the original. Its result, St Paulinus relates, was that the oxen were quickly restored to their stalls.

## Prayer of a Peasant to St Felix

Restore these same animals; I shall not accept any others. Nor shall I go to other districts in search of them—I have a right to get them back here: they must be restored at this threshold where I, as a suppliant, constrain you yourself and cling to you; why should I seek, and where should I seek, I who have no idea who the thieves are? My debtor is right here, I hold the guardian himself on account of the theft; and this guardian, O saint, is you—answerable to me, cognizant of them: it is you that I hold; you know where they are, you who by the light of Christ see all things, even those hidden, who discern what is far removed, and comprehend, God surrounding you, where all things are. And for this reason the hidden thieves and their retreats, wherever these may be, are not concealed from you, nor can these thieves evade you, because a Hand is on them already. God is one everywhere, Christ's right hand is gentle to the faithful, but punishes the wicked. Therefore restore my oxen to me and lay hold of the thieves. I do not demand them as defendants; let them go, for I am not, O Saint, ignorant of your methods: you do not requite evil deeds, you prefer to correct the wicked by forgiving rather than ruin them by chastisements. Let this, therefore, be our covenant: separate what is yours from what is mine in this way: through you what is useful to me shall be kept from harm; mercy shall rightly claim what is yours; and let your verdict be evenly balanced: for your part free the guilty, for mine restore my oxen. There you have the terms; let no subordinate of yours be a cause of delay; hasten to relieve me of so much anxiety. For I am determined not to give way in anything or leave this doorpost until you shall have come to my help; unless you hasten I shall die on this threshold. In that case, returning my oxen which you recovered too late, you will not find me.

# ST AUGUSTINE

(See page 127.)

## Letters

### TO NEBRIDIUS

389

Although you know my mind well, you are perhaps not aware how much I long to enjoy your society. This great blessing, however, God will some day bestow on me. I have read your letter, so genuine in its utterances, in which you complain of your being in solitude, and as it were, forsaken by your friends, in whose society you found the sweetest charm of life. But what else can I suggest to you than that which I am persuaded is already your exercise? Commune with your own soul, and raise it up, as far as you are able, unto God. For in Him you hold us also by a firmer bond, not by means of bodily images, which we must meanwhile be content to use in remembering each other, but by means of that faculty of thought through which we realize the fact of our separation from each other.

In considering your letters, in answering all of which I have certainly had to answer questions of no small difficulty and importance, I was not a little stunned by the one in which you ask me by what means certain thoughts and dreams are put into our minds by higher powers or by superhuman agents. The question is a great one, and, as your own prudence must convince you, would require, in order to its being satisfactorily answered, not a mere letter, but a full oral discussion or a whole treatise. I shall try, however, knowing as I do your talents, to throw out a few germs of thought which may shed light on this question, in order that you may either complete the exhaustive treatment of the subject by your own efforts, or at least not despair of the possibility of this important matter being investigated with satisfactory results.

It is my opinion that every movement of the mind affects in some degree the body. We know that this is patent even to our senses, dull and sluggish though they are, when the movements of the mind are somewhat vehement, as when we are angry, or sad, or joyful. Whence we may conjecture that, in like manner, when thought is busy, although no bodily effect of the mental act is discernible by us, there may be some such effect discernible by beings of aerial or ethereal essence whose perceptive faculty is in the highest degree acute—so much so that, in comparison with it, our faculties are scarcely worthy to be called perceptive. Therefore these footprints of its motion, so to speak, which the mind impresses on the body, may perchance not only remain, but remain as it were with the force of a habit; and it may be that, when these are secretly stirred and played upon, they bear thoughts and dreams into our minds, according to the pleasure of the person moving or touching them: and this is done with marvellous facility. For if, as is manifest, the attainments of our earth-born and sluggish bodies in the department of exercise, e.g., in the playing of musical instruments, dancing on the tight-rope, etc., are almost incredible, it is by no means unreasonable to suppose that beings which act with the powers of an aerial or ethereal body upon our bodies, and are by the constitution of their natures able to pass unhindered through these bodies, should be capable of much greater quickness in moving whatever they wish, while we, though not perceiving what they do, are nevertheless affected by the results of their activity. We have a somewhat parallel instance in the fact that we do not perceive how it is that superfluity of bile impels us to more frequent outbursts of passionate feeling; and yet it does produce this effect, while this superfluity of bile is itself an effect of our yielding to such passionate feelings.

If, however, you hesitate to accept this example as a parallel one, when it is thus cursorily stated by me, turn it over in your thoughts as fully as you can. The mind, if it be continually obstructed by some difficulty in the way of doing and accomplishing what it desires, is thereby made continually angry. For anger, so far as I can judge of its nature, seems to me to be a tumultuous eagerness to take out of the way those things which restrict our freedom of action. Hence it is that usually we vent our anger not only on men, but on such a thing, for example, as the pen with which we write, bruising or breaking it in our passion; and so does the gambler with his dice, the artist with his pencil, and every man with the instrument which he may be using, if he thinks that he is in some way thwarted by it. Now medical men themselves tell us that by these frequent fits of anger bile is increased. But, on the other hand, when the bile is increased, we are easily, and almost without any provocation whatever, made angry. Thus the effect which the mind has by its movement produced upon the body, is capable in its turn of moving the mind again.

These things might be treated at very great length, and our knowledge of the subject might be brought to greater certainty and fullness by a large induction from relevant facts. But take along with this letter the one which I sent you lately concerning images and memory, and study it somewhat more carefully; for it was manifest to me, from your reply, that it had not been fully understood. When, to the statements now before you, you add the portion of that letter in which I spoke of a certain natural faculty whereby the mind does in thought add to or take from any object as it pleases, you will see that it is possible for us both in dreams and in waking thoughts to conceive the images of bodily forms which we have never seen.

No question of yours ever kept me so disturbed while reflecting upon it, as the remark which I read in your last letter, in which you chide me for being indifferent as to making arrangements by which it may be possible for us to live together. A grave charge, and one which, were it not unfounded, would be most perilous. But since satisfactory reasons seem to prove that we can live as we would wish to do better here than at Carthage, or even in the country, I am wholly at a loss, my dear Nebridius, what to do with you. Shall such a conveyance as may best suit your state of health be sent from us to you? Our friend Lucinianus informs me that you can be carried without injury in a palanquin. But I consider, on the other hand, how your mother, who could not bear your absence from her when you were in health, will be much less able to bear it when you are ill. Shall I myself then come to you? This I cannot do, for there are some here who cannot accompany me, and whom I would think it a crime for me to leave. For you already can pass your time agreeably when left to the resources of your own mind; but in their case the object of present efforts is that they may attain to this. Shall I go and come frequently, and so be now with you, now with them? But this is neither to live together, nor to live as we would wish to do. For the journey is not a short one, but so great at least that the attempt to perform it frequently would prevent our gaining the wished-for leisure. To this is added the bodily weakness through which, as you know, I cannot accomplish what I wish, unless I cease wholly to wish what is beyond my strength.

To occupy one's thoughts throughout life with journeyings which you cannot perform tranquilly and easily, is not the part of a man whose thoughts are engaged with that last journey which is called death, and which alone, as you understand, really deserves serious consideration. God has indeed granted to some few men whom He has ordained to bear rule over churches, the capacity of not only awaiting calmly, but even desiring eagerly, that last journey, while at the same time they can meet without disquietude the toils of those other journeyings; but I do not believe that either to those who are urged to accept such duties through desire for worldly honour, or to those who, although occupying a private station, covet a busy life, so great a boon is given as that amid bustle and agitating meetings, and journeyings hither and thither, they should acquire that familiarity with death which we seek: for both of these classes had it in their power to seek edification in retirement. Or if this be not true, I am, I shall not say the most foolish of all men, but at least the most indolent, since I find it impossible, without the aid of such an interval of relief from care and toil, to taste and relish that only real good. Believe me, there is need of much withdrawal of oneself from the tumult of the things which are passing away, in order that there may be formed in man, not through insensibility, not through presumption, not through vainglory, not through superstitious blindness, the ability to say, "I fear naught." By this means also is attained that enduring joy with which no pleasurable excitement found elsewhere is in any degree to be compared.

But if such a life does not fall to the lot of man, how is it that calmness of spirit is our occasional experience? Wherefore is this experience more frequent, in proportion to the devotion with which anyone in his inmost soul worships God? Why does this tranquillity for the most part abide with one in the business of life, when he goes forth to its duties from that sanctuary? Why are there times in which, speaking, we do not fear death, and, silent, even desire it? I say to you—for I would not say it to everyone—to you whose visits to the upper world I know well, Will you, who have often felt how sweetly the soul lives when it dies to all mere bodily affections, deny that it is possible for the whole life of man to become at length so exempt from fear, that he may be justly called wise? Or will you venture to affirm that this state of mind on which reason leans has ever been your lot, except when you were shut up to commune with your own heart? Since these things are so, you see that it remains only for you to share with me the labour of devising how we may arrange to live together. You know much better than I do what is to be done in regard to your mother, whom your brother Victor, of course, does not leave alone. I will write no more, lest I turn your mind away from considering this proposal.

## TO PROBA

### 412

To Proba, a devoted handmaid of God, Bishop Augustine, a servant of Christ and of Christ's servants, sends greeting in the name of the Lord of Lords.

Recollecting your request and my promise, that as soon as time and opportunity should be given by Him to whom we pray, I would write you something on the subject of prayer to God, I feel it my duty now to discharge this debt, and in the love of Christ to minister to the satisfaction of your pious desire. I cannot express in words how greatly I rejoiced because of the request, in which I perceived how great is your solicitude about this supremely important matter. For what could be more suitably the business of your widowhood than to continue in supplications night and day, according to the Apostle's admonition, "She that is a widow indeed, and desolate, trusteth in

God, and continueth in supplications night and day"? It might, indeed, appear wonderful that solicitude about prayer should occupy your heart and claim the first place in it, when you are, so far as this world is concerned, noble and wealthy, and the mother of such an illustrious family, and, although a widow, not desolate, were it not that you wisely understand that in this world and in this life the soul has no sure portion.

Wherefore He who inspired you with this thought is assuredly doing what He promised to His disciples when they were grieved, not for themselves, but for the whole human family, and were despairing of the salvation of anyone, after they heard from Him that it was easier for a camel to go through the eye of a needle than for a rich man to enter into the kingdom of heaven. He gave them this marvellous and merciful reply: "The things which are impossible with men are possible with God." He, therefore, with Whom it is possible to make even the rich enter into the kingdom of heaven, inspired you with that devout anxiety which makes you think it necessary to ask my counsel on the question how you ought to pray. For while He was yet on earth, He brought Zaccheus, though rich, into the kingdom of heaven, and, after being glorified in His Resurrection and Ascension, He made many who were rich to despise this present world, and made them more truly rich by extinguishing their desire for riches through His imparting to them His Holy Spirit. For how could you desire so much to pray to God if you did not trust in Him? And how could you trust in Him if you were fixing your trust in uncertain riches, and neglecting the wholesome exhortation of the Apostle: "Charge them that are rich in this world that they be not high-minded, nor trust in uncertain riches, but in the living God, who giveth us richly all things to enjoy; that they do good, that they be rich in good works, ready to distribute, willing to communicate, laying up in store for themselves a good foundation, that they may lay hold on eternal life"?

It becomes you, therefore, out of love to this true life, to account yourself "desolate" in this world, however great the prosperity of your lot may be. For as that is the true life, in comparison with which the present life, which is much loved, is not worthy to be called life, however happy and prolonged it be, so is it also the true consolation promised by the Lord in the words of Isaiah, "I will give him the true consolation, peace upon peace," without which consolation men find themselves, in the midst of every mere earthly solace, rather desolate than comforted. For as for riches and high rank, and all other things in which men who are strangers to true felicity imagine that happiness exists, what comfort do they bring, seeing that it is better to be independent of such things than to enjoy abundance of them, because, when possessed, they occasion, through our fear of losing them, more vexation than was caused by the strength of desire with which their possession was coveted? Men are not made good by possessing these so-called good things, but, if men have become good otherwise, they make these things to be really good by using them well. Therefore true comfort is to be found not in them, but rather in those things in which true life is found. For a man can be made blessed only by the same power by which he is made good.

It is true, indeed, that good men are seen to be the sources of no small comfort to others in this world. For if we be harassed by poverty, or saddened by bereavement, or disquieted by bodily pain, or pining in exile, or vexed by any kind of calamity, let good men visit us—men who can not only rejoice with them that rejoice, but also weep with them that weep, and who know how to give profitable counsel, and win us to express our feelings in conversation: the effect is, that rough things become smooth, heavy burdens are lightened, and difficulties vanquished most wonderfully. But this is done in and through them by Him who has made them good by His Spirit. On the other hand, although riches may abound, and no bereavement befall us, and health of body be enjoyed, and we live in our own country in peace and safety, if, at the same time, we have as our neighbours wicked men, among whom there is not one who can be trusted, not one from whom we do not apprehend and experience treachery, deceit, outbursts of anger, dissensions, and snares—in such a case are not all these other things made bitter and vexatious, so that nothing sweet or pleasant is left in them? Whatever, therefore, be our circumstances in this world, there is nothing truly enjoyable without a friend. But how rarely is one found in this life about whose spirit and behaviour as a true friend there may be perfect confidence! For no one is known to another so intimately as he is known to himself, and yet no one is so well known even to himself that he can be sure as to his own conduct on the morrow; wherefore, although many are known by their fruits, and some gladden their neighbours by their good lives, while others grieve their neighbours by their evil lives, yet the minds of men are so unknown and so unstable, that there is the highest wisdom in the exhortation of the Apostle: "Judge nothing before the time until the Lord come, who both will bring to light the hidden things of darkness, and will make manifest the counsels of the hearts; and then shall every man have praise of God."

In the darkness, then, of this world, in which we are pilgrims absent from the Lord as long as "we walk by faith and not by sight," the Christian soul ought to feel itself desolate, and continue in prayer, and learn to fix the eye of faith on the word of the divine sacred Scriptures, as "on a light shining in a dark place, until the day dawn, and the day-star arise in our hearts." For the ineffable source from which this lamp borrows its light is the Light which shineth in darkness, but the darkness comprehendeth it not—the Light, in order to seeing which our hearts must be purified by faith; for "blessed are the pure in heart, for they shall see God"; and "we know that when He shall appear, we shall be like Him, for we shall see Him as He is." Then after death shall come the true life, and after desolation the true consolation, that life shall deliver our "souls from death"—that consolation shall deliver our "eyes from tears," and, as follows in the psalm, our feet shall be delivered from falling; for there shall be no temptation there. Moreover, if there be no temptation, there will be no prayer; for there we shall not be waiting for promised blessings, but contemplating the blessings actually bestowed; wherefore he adds, "I will walk before the Lord in the land of the living," where we shall then be—not in the wilderness of the dead, where we now are: "For ye are dead," says the Apostle, "and your life is hid with Christ in God; when Christ, who is our life, shall appear, then shall ye also appear with Him in glory." For that is the true life on which the rich are exhorted to lay hold by being rich in good works; and in it is the true consolation, for want of which, meanwhile, a widow is "desolate" indeed, even though she has sons and grandchildren, and conducts her household piously, entreating all dear to her to put their hope in God: and in the midst of all this, she says in her prayer, "My soul thirsteth for Thee; my flesh longeth in a dry and thirsty land, where no water is"; and this dying life is nothing else than such a land, however numerous our mortal comforts, however pleasant our companions in the pilgrimage, and however great the abundance of our possessions. You know how uncertain all these things are; and even if they were not uncertain, what would they be in comparison with the felicity which is promised in the life to come!

In saying these things to you, who, being a widow, rich and noble, and the mother of an illustrious family, have asked from me a discourse on prayer, my aim has been to make you feel that, even while your family are spared to you, and live as you would desire, you are desolate so long as you have not attained to that life in which is the true and abiding consolation, in which shall be fulfilled what is spoken in prophecy: "We are satisfied in the morning with Thy mercy, we rejoice and are glad all our days; we are made glad according to the days wherein Thou hast afflicted us, and the years wherein we have seen evil."

Wherefore, until that consolation come, remember, in order to your "continuing in prayers and supplications night and day," that, however great the temporal prosperity may be which flows around you, you are desolate. For the Apostle does not ascribe this gift to every widow, but to her who, being a widow indeed, and desolate, "trusteth in God, and continueth in supplication night and day." Observe, however, most vigilantly the warning which follows: "But she that liveth in pleasure is dead while she liveth"; for a person lives in those things which he loves, which he greatly desires, and in which he believes himself to be blessed. Wherefore, what Scripture has said of riches: "If riches increase, set not your heart upon them," I say to you concerning pleasures: "If pleasures increase, set not your heart upon them." Do not, therefore, think highly of yourself because these things are not wanting, but are yours abundantly, flowing, as it were, from a most copious fountain of earthly felicity. By all means look upon your possession of these things with indifference and contempt, and seek nothing from them beyond health of body. For this is a blessing not to be despised, because of its being necessary to the work of life until "this mortal shall have put on immortality"—in other words, the true, perfect, and everlasting health, which is neither reduced by earthly infirmities nor repaired by corruptible gratification, but, enduring with celestial vigour, is animated with a life eternally incorruptible. For the Apostle himself says, "Make not provision for the flesh, to fulfil the lusts thereof," because we must take care of the flesh, but only in so far as is necessary for health; "For no man ever yet hated his own flesh," as he himself likewise says. Hence, also, he admonished Timothy, who was, as it appears, too severe upon his body, that he should "use a little wine for his stomach's sake, and for his often infirmities."

Many holy men and women, using every precaution against those pleasures in which she that liveth, cleaving to them, and dwelling in them as her heart's delight, is dead while she liveth, have cast from them that which is as it were the mother of pleasures, by distributing their wealth among the poor, and so have stored it in the safer keeping of the treasury of heaven. If you are *hindered* from doing this by some consideration of duty to your family, you know yourself what account you can give to God of your use of riches. For no one knoweth what passeth within a man, "but the spirit of the man which is in him." We ought not to judge anything "before the time until the Lord come, who both will bring to light the hidden things of darkness, and will make manifest the counsels of the hearts, and then shall every man have praise of God." It pertains, therefore, to your care as a widow, to see to it that if pleasures increase you do not set your heart upon them, lest that which ought to rise that it may live, die through contact with their corrupting influence. Reckon yourself to be one of those of whom it is written, "Their hearts shall live for ever."

You have now heard what manner of person you should be if you would pray; hear, in the next place, what you ought to pray for.

This is the subject on which you have thought it most necessary to ask my opinion, because you were disturbed by the words of the Apostle: "We know not what we should pray for as we ought"; and you became alarmed lest it should do you more harm to pray otherwise than you ought, than to desist from praying altogether. A short solution of your difficulty may be given thus: "Pray for a happy life." This all men wish to have; for even those whose lives are worst and most abandoned would by no means live thus, unless they thought that in this way they either were made or might be made truly happy. Now what else ought we to pray for than that which both bad and good desire, but which only the good obtain?

You ask, perchance, What is this happy life? On this question the talents and leisure of many philosophers have been wasted, who, nevertheless, failed in their researches after it just in proportion as they failed to honour Him from whom it proceeds, and were unthankful to Him. In the first place, then, consider whether we should accept the opinion of those philosophers who pronounce that man happy who lives according to his own will. Far be it, surely, from us to believe this; for what if a man's will inclines him to live in wickedness? Is he not proved to be a miserable man in proportion to the facility with which his depraved will is carried out? Even philosophers who were strangers to the worship of God have rejected this sentiment with deserved abhorrence. One of them, a man of the greatest eloquence, says: "Behold, however, others, not philosophers indeed, but men of ready power in disputation, who affirm that all men are happy who live according to their own will. But this is certainly untrue, for to wish that which is unbecoming is itself a most miserable thing; nor is it so miserable a thing to fail in obtaining what you wish as to wish to obtain what you ought not to desire." What is your opinion? Are not these words, by whomsoever they are spoken, derived from the Truth itself? We may therefore here say what the Apostle said of a certain Cretan poet whose sentiment had pleased him: "This witness is true."

He, therefore, is truly happy who has all that he wishes to have, and wishes to have nothing which he ought not to wish. This being understood, let us now observe what things men may without impropriety wish to have. One desires marriage; another, having become a widower, chooses thereafter to live a life of continence; a third chooses to practise continence though he is married. And although of these three conditions one may be found better than another, we cannot say that any one of the three persons is wishing what he ought not: the same is true of the desire for children as the fruit of marriage, and for life and health to be enjoyed by the children who have been received—of which desires the latter is one with which widows remaining unmarried are for the most part occupied; for although, refusing a second marriage, they do not now wish to have children, they wish that the children that they have may live in health. From all such care those who preserve their virginity intact are free. Nevertheless, all have some dear to them whose temporal welfare they do without impropriety desire. But when men have obtained this health for themselves, and for those whom they love, are we at liberty to say that they are now happy? They have, it is true, something which it is quite becoming to desire; but if they have not other things which are greater, better, and more full both of utility and beauty, they are still far short of possessing a happy life.

Shall we then say that in addition to this health of body men may desire for themselves and for those dear to them honour and power? By all means, if they desire these in order that by obtaining them they may promote the interest of those who may be their dependants. If they seek these things not for the sake of the things themselves, but for some good thing which may through this means be accomplished, the wish is a proper one; but if it be merely for the empty gratification of pride and arrogance, and for a superfluous and pernicious triumph of vanity, the wish is improper. Wherefore, men do nothing wrong in desiring for themselves and for their kindred the competent portion of necessary things, of which the Apostle speaks when he says: "Godliness with a competency is great gain; for we brought nothing into this world, and it is certain we can carry nothing out: and having food and raiment, let us be therewith content. But they that will be rich fall into temptation, and a snare, and into many foolish and hurtful lusts, which drown men in destruction and perdition; for the love of money is the root of all evil, which while some coveted after, they have erred from the faith, and pierced themselves through with many sorrows." This competent portion he desires without impropriety who desires it and nothing beyond it; for if his desires go beyond it, he is not desiring it, and therefore his desire is improper. This was desired, and was prayed for by him who said: "Give me neither poverty nor riches: feed me with food convenient for me: lest I be full, and deny Thee, and say, Who is the Lord? or lest I be poor, and steal, and take the name of my God in vain." You see assuredly that this competency is desired not for its own sake, but to secure the health of the body, and such provision of house and clothing as is befitting the man's circumstances, that he may appear as he ought to do among those amongst whom he has to live, so as to retain their respect and discharge the duties of his position.

Among all these things, our own welfare and the benefits which friendship bids us ask for others are things to be desired on their own account; but a competency of the necessaries of life is usually sought, if it be sought in the proper way, not on its own account, but for the sake of the two higher benefits. Welfare consists in the possession of life itself, and health and soundness of mind and body. The claims of friendship, moreover, are not to be confined within *too* narrow range, for it embraces all to whom love and kindly affection are due, although the heart goes out to some of these more freely, to others more cautiously; yea, it even extends to our enemies, for whom also we are commanded to pray. There is accordingly no one in the whole human family to whom kindly affection is not due by reason of the bond of a common humanity, although it may not be due on the ground of reciprocal love; but in those by whom we are requited with a holy and pure love, we find great and reasonable pleasure.

For these things, therefore, it becomes us to pray: if we have them, that we may keep them; if we have them not, that we may get them.

Is this all? Are these the benefits in which exclusively the happy life is found? Or does truth reach us that something else is to be preferred to them all? We know that both the competency of things necessary, and the well-being of ourselves and of our friends, so long as these concern this present world alone, are to be cast aside as dross in comparison with the obtaining of eternal life; for although the body may be in health, the mind cannot be regarded as sound which does not prefer eternal to temporal things; yea, the life which we live in time is wasted, if it be not spent in obtaining that by which we may be worthy of eternal life. Therefore all things which are the objects of useful and becoming desire are unquestionably to be viewed with reference to that one life which is lived with God, and is derived from Him. In so doing, we love ourselves if we love God; and we truly love our neighbours as ourselves, according to the second great commandment, if, so far as is in our power, we persuade them to a similar love of God. We love God, therefore, for what He is in Himself, and ourselves and our neighbours for His sake. Even when living thus, let us not think that we are securely established in that happy life, as if there was nothing more for which we should still pray. For how could we be said to live a happy life now, while that which alone is the object of a well-directed life is still wanting to us?

Why, then, are our desires scattered over many things, and why, through fear of not praying as we ought, do we ask what we should pray for, and not rather say with the Psalmist: "One thing have I desired of the Lord, that will I seek after: that I may dwell in the house of the Lord all the days of my life, to behold the beauty of the Lord, and to inquire in His temple"? For in the house of the Lord "all the days of life" are not days distinguished by their successively coming and passing away: the beginning of one day is not the end of another; but they are all alike unending in that place where the life which is made up of them has itself no end. In order to our obtaining this true blessed life, He who is Himself the True Blessed Life has taught us to pray, not with much speaking, as if our being heard depended upon the fluency with which we express ourselves, seeing that we are praying to One who, as the Lord tells us, "knoweth what things we have need of before we ask Him." Whence it may seem surprising that, although He has forbidden "much speaking," He who knoweth before we ask Him what things we need has nevertheless given us exhortation to prayer in such words as these: "Men ought always to pray and not to faint"; setting before us the case of a widow, who, desiring to have justice done to her against her adversary, did by her persevering entreaties persuade an unjust judge to listen to her, not moved by a regard either to justice or to mercy, but overcome by her wearisome importunity; in order that we might be admonished how much more certainly the Lord God, who is merciful and just, gives ear to us praying continually to Him, when this widow, by her unremitting supplication, prevailed over the indifference of an unjust and wicked judge, and how willingly and benignantly He fulfils the good desires of those whom He knows to have forgiven others their trespasses, when this suppliant, though seeking vengeance upon her adversary, obtained her desire. A similar lesson the Lord gives in the parable of the man to whom a friend in his journey had come, and who, having nothing to set before him, desired to borrow from another friend three loaves (in which, perhaps, there is a figure of the Trinity of persons of one substance), and finding him already, along with his household, asleep, succeeded by very urgent and importunate entreaties in rousing him up, so that he gave him as many as he needed, being moved rather by a wish to avoid further annoyance than by benevolent thoughts: from which the Lord would have us understand that if even one who was asleep is constrained to give, even in spite of himself, after being disturbed in his sleep by the person who asks of him, how much more kindly will He give who never sleeps, and who rouses us from sleep that we may ask from Him.

With the same design He added: "Ask, and ye shall receive; seek, and ye shall find; knock, and it shall be opened unto you: for everyone that asketh receiveth; and he that seeketh findeth; and to him that knocketh it shall be opened. If a son shall ask bread of any of you that is a father, will he give him a stone? or if he ask a fish, will he for a fish give him a serpent? or if he shall ask an egg, will he offer him a scorpion? If ye then, being evil, know how to give good gifts unto your children, how much more shall your heavenly Father give good things to them that ask Him?" We have here what corresponds to those three things which the Apostle commends: *faith* is signified by the fish, either on account of the element of water used in baptism, or because it remains unharmed amid the tempestuous waves of this world—contrasted with which is the serpent, that with poisonous deceit persuaded man to disbelieve God; *hope* is signified by the egg, because the life of the young bird is not yet in it, but is to be—is not seen, but hoped for, because "hope which is seen is not hope"—contrasted with which is the scorpion, for the man who hopes for eternal life forgets the things which are behind, and reaches forth to the things which are before, for to him it is dangerous to look back; but the scorpion is to be guarded against on account of what it has in its tail, namely, a sharp and venomous sting; *charity* is signified by bread, for "the greatest of these is charity," and bread surpasses all other kinds of food in usefulness—contrasted with which is a stone, because hard hearts refuse to exercise charity. Whether this be the meaning of these symbols, or some other more suitable be found, it is at least certain that He who knoweth how to give good gifts to His children urges us to "ask and seek and knock."

Why this should be done by Him who "before we ask Him knoweth what things we have need of," might perplex our minds, if we did not understand that the Lord our God requires us to ask not that thereby our wish may be intimated to Him, for to Him, it cannot be unknown, but in order that by prayer there may be exercised in us by supplications that desire by which we may receive what He prepares to bestow. His gifts are very great, but we are small and straitened in our capacity of receiving. Wherefore it is said to us: "Be ye enlarged, not bearing the yoke along with unbelievers." For, in proportion to the simplicity of our faith, the firmness of our hope, and the ardour of our desire, will we more largely receive of that which is immensely great; which "eye hath not seen," for it is not colour; which "the ear hath not heard," for it is not sound; and which hath not ascended into the heart of man, for the heart of man must ascend to it.

When we cherish uninterrupted desire along with the exercise of faith and hope and charity, we "pray always." But at certain stated hours and seasons we also use words in prayer to God, that by these signs of things we may admonish ourselves, and may acquaint ourselves with the measure of progress which we have made in this desire, and may more warmly excite ourselves to obtain an increase of its strength. For the effect following upon prayer will be excellent in proportion to the fervour of the desire which precedes its utterance. And therefore, what else is intended by the words of the Apostle: "Pray without ceasing," than, "Desire without intermission, from Him who alone can give it, a happy life, which no life can be but that which is eternal"? This, therefore, let us desire continually from the Lord our God; and thus let us pray continually. But at certain hours we recall our minds from other cares and business, in which desire itself somehow is cooled down, to the business of prayer, admonishing ourselves by the words of our prayer to fix attention upon that which we desire, lest what had begun to lose heat become altogether cold, and be finally extinguished, if the flame be not more frequently fanned. Whence, also, when the same Apostle says, "Let your requests be made known unto God," this is not to be understood as if thereby they become known to God, who certainly knew them before they were uttered, but in this sense, that they are to be made known to ourselves in the presence of God by patient waiting upon Him, not in the presence of men by ostentatious worship. Or perhaps that they may be made known also to the angels that are in the presence of God, that these beings may in some way present them to God, and consult Him concerning them, and may bring to us, either manifestly or secretly, that which, hearkening to His commandment, they may have learned to be His will, and which must be fulfilled by them according to that which they have there learned to be their duty; for the angel said to Tobias: "Now, therefore, when thou didst pray, and Sara thy daughter-in-law, I did bring the remembrance of your prayers before the Holy One."

Wherefore it is neither wrong nor unprofitable to spend much time in praying, if there be leisure for this without hindering other good and necessary works to which duty calls us, although even in the doing of these, as I have said, we ought by cherishing holy desire to pray without ceasing. For to spend a long time in prayer is not, as some think, the same thing as to pray "with much speaking." Multiplied words are one thing, long-continued warmth of desire is another. For even of the Lord Himself it is written, that He continued all night in prayer, and that His prayer was more prolonged when He was in agony; and in this is not an example given to us by Him who is in time an Intercessor such as we need, and who is with the Father eternally the Hearer of prayer?

The brethren in Egypt are reported to have very frequent prayers, but these very brief, and, as it were, sudden and ejaculatory, lest the wakeful and aroused attention which is indispensable in prayer should by protracted exercises vanish or lose its keenness. And in this they themselves show plainly enough, that just as this attention is not to be allowed to become exhausted if it cannot continue long, so it is not to be suddenly suspended if it is sustained. Far be it from us either to use "much speaking" in prayer, or to refrain from prolonged prayer, if fervent attention of the soul continue. To use much speaking in prayer is to employ a superfluity of words in asking a necessary thing; but to prolong prayer is to have the heart throbbing with continued pious emotion towards Him to whom we pray. For in most cases prayer consists more in groaning than in speaking, in tears rather than in words. But He setteth our tears in His sight, and our groaning is not hidden from Him who made all things by the word, and does not need human words.

To us, therefore, words are necessary, that by them we may be assisted in considering and observing what we ask, not as means by which we expect that God is to be either informed or moved to compliance. When, therefore, we say: "Hallowed be Thy name," we admonish ourselves to desire that His name, which is always holy, may be also among men esteemed holy, that is to say, not despised; which is an advantage not to God, but to men. When we say: "Thy kingdom come," which shall certainly come whether we wish it or not, we do by these words stir up our own desires for that kingdom, that it may come to us, and that we may be found worthy to reign in it. When we say: "Thy will be done on earth as it is in Heaven," we pray for ourselves that He would give us the grace of obedience, that His will may be done by us in the same way as it is done in heavenly places by His angels. When we say: "Give us this day our daily bread," the words "this day" signify for the present time, in which we ask either for that competency of temporal blessings which I have spoken of before ("bread" being used to designate the whole of those blessings, because of its constituting so important a part of them), or the sacrament of believers, which is in this present time necessary, but necessary in order to obtain the felicity not of the present time, but of eternity. When we say: "Forgive us our debts as we forgive our debtors," we remind ourselves both what we should ask, and what we should do in order that we may be worthy to receive what we ask. When we say: "Lead us not into temptation," we admonish ourselves to seek that we may not, through being deprived of God's help, be either ensnared to consent or compelled to yield to temptation. When we say: "Deliver us from evil," we admonish ourselves to consider that we are not yet enjoying that good estate in which we shall experience no evil. And this petition, which stands last in the Lord's Prayer, is so comprehensive that a Christian, in whatsoever affliction he be placed, may in using it give utterance to his groans and find vent for his tears—may begin with this petition, go on with it, and with it conclude his prayer. For it was necessary that by the use of these words the things which they signify should be kept before our memory.

For whatever other words we may say—whether the desire of the persons praying go before the words, and employ them in order to give definite form to its requests, or come after them, and concentrate attention upon them, that it may increase in fervour—if we pray rightly, and as becomes our wants, we say nothing but what is already contained in the Lord's Prayer. And whoever says in prayer anything which cannot find its place in that Gospel prayer, is praying in a way which, if it be not unlawful, is at least not spiritual; and I know not how carnal prayers can be lawful, since it becomes those who are born again by the Spirit to pray in no other way than spiritually. For example, when one prays: "Be Thou glorified among all nations as Thou art glorified among us," and "Let Thy prophets be found faithful," what else does he ask than, "Hallowed be Thy name"? When one says: "Turn us again, O Lord God of hosts, cause Thy face to shine, and we shall be saved," what else is he saying than, "Let Thy kingdom come"? When one says: "Order my steps in Thy word, and let not any iniquity have dominion over me," what else is he saying than, "Thy will be done on earth as it is in heaven"? When one says: "Give me neither poverty nor riches," what else is this than, "Give us this day our daily bread"? When one says: "Lord, remember David, and all his compassion," or, "O Lord, if I have done this, if there be iniquity in my hands, if I have rewarded evil to them that did evil to me," what else is this than, "Forgive us our debts as we forgive our debtors"? When one says: "Take away from me the lusts of the appetite, and let not sensual desire take hold on me," what else is this than, "Lead us not into temptation"? When one says: "Deliver me from mine enemies, O my God; defend me from them that rise up against me," what else is this than, "Deliver us from evil"? And if you go over all the words of holy prayers, you will, I believe, find nothing which cannot be comprised and summed up in the petitions of the Lord's Prayer. Wherefore, in praying, we are free to use different words to any extent, but we must ask the same things; in this we have no choice.

These things it is our duty to ask without hesitation for ourselves and for our friends, and for strangers—yea, even for enemies; although in the heart of the person praying, desire for one and for another may arise, differing in nature or in strength according to the more immediate or more remote relationship. But he who says in prayer such words as, "O Lord, multiply my riches"; or, "Give me as much wealth as Thou hast given to this or that man"; or, "Increase my honours, make me eminent for power and fame in this world," or something else of this sort, and who asks merely from a desire for these things, and not in order through them to benefit men agreeably to God's will, I do not think that he will find any part of the Lord's Prayer in connection with which he could fit in these requests. Wherefore let us be ashamed at least to ask these things, if we be not ashamed to desire them. If, however, we are ashamed of even desiring them, but feel ourselves overcome by the desire, how much better would it be to ask to be freed from this plague of desire by Him to whom we say, "Deliver us from evil"!

You have now, if I am not mistaken, an answer to two questions —what kind of person you ought to be if you would pray, and what things you should ask in prayer; and the answer has been given not by my teaching, but by His who has condescended to teach us all. A happy life is to be sought after, and this is to be asked from the Lord God. Many different answers have been given by many in discussing wherein true happiness consists; but why should we go to many teachers, or consider many answers to this question? It has been briefly and truly stated in the divine Scriptures, "Blessed is the people whose God is the Lord." That we may be numbered among this people, and that we may attain to beholding Him and dwelling for ever with Him, "the end of the commandment is, charity out of a pure heart, and of a good conscience, and of faith unfeigned." In the same three, hope has been placed instead of a good conscience. Faith, hope, and charity, therefore, lead unto God the man who prays, i.e., who believes, hopes, and desires, and is guided as to what he should ask from the Lord by studying the Lord's Prayer. Fasting, and abstinence from gratifying carnal desire in other pleasures without injury to health, and especially frequent almsgiving, are a great assistance in prayer; so that we may be able to say, "In the day of my trouble I sought the Lord, with my hands in the night before Him, and I was not deceived." For how can God, who is a Spirit, and who cannot be touched, be sought with hands in any other sense than by good works?

## FROM The Confessions

. . . If to any man the tumult of the flesh were silenced—silenced the phantasies of earth, waters, and air—silenced, too, the poles; yea, the very soul be silenced to herself, and go beyond herself by not thinking of herself—silenced fancies and imaginary revelations, every tongue, and every sign, and whatsoever exists by passing away, since, if any could hearken, all these say, "We created not ourselves, but were created by Him who abideth for ever": if, having uttered this, they now should be silenced, having only quickened our ears to Him who created them, and He alone speak not by them, but by Himself, that we may hear His word, not by fleshly tongue, nor angelic voice, nor sound of thunder, nor the obscurity of a similitude, but might hear Him—Him whom in these we love—without these, as we two now strained ourselves, and with rapid thought touched on that Eternal Wisdom which remaineth over all. If this could be sustained, and other visions of a far different kind be withdrawn, and this one ravish, and absorb, and envelop its beholder amid these inward joys, so that his life might be eternally like that one moment of knowledge which we now sighed after, were not this "Enter thou into the joy of Thy Lord"? . . .

But what is it that I love in loving Thee? Not corporeal beauty, nor the splendour of time, nor the radiance of the light, so pleasant to our eyes, nor the sweet melodies of songs of all kinds, nor the fragrant smell of flowers, and ointments, and spices, not manna and honey, not limbs pleasant to the embracements of flesh. I love not these things when I love my God; and yet I love a certain kind of light, and sound, and fragrance, and food, and embracement in loving my God, who is the light, sound, fragrance, food, and embracement of my inner man—where that light shineth unto my soul which no place can contain, where that soundeth which time snatcheth not away, where there is a fragrance which no breeze disperseth, where there is a food which no eating can diminish, and where that clingeth which no satiety can sunder. This is what I love, when I love my God . . .

Where, then, did I find Thee, so as to be able to learn Thee? For Thou wert not in my memory before I learned Thee. Where, then, did I find Thee, so as to be able to learn Thee, but in Thee above me? Place there is none; we go both backward and forward, and there is no place. Everywhere, O Truth, dost Thou direct all who consult Thee, and dost at once answer all, though they consult Thee on divers things. Clearly dost Thou answer, though all do not with clearness hear. All consult Thee upon whatever they wish, though they hear not always that which they wish. He is Thy best servant who does not so much look to hear that from Thee which he himself wisheth, as to wish that which he heareth from Thee.

Too late did I love Thee, O Fairness, so ancient, and yet so new! Too late did I love Thee! For behold, Thou wert within, and I without, and there did I seek Thee; I, unlovely, rushed heedlessly among the things of beauty Thou madest. Thou wert with me, but I was not with Thee. Those things kept me far from Thee, which, unless they were in Thee, were not. Thou calledst, and criedst aloud, and forcedst open my deafness. Thou didst gleam and shine, and chase away my blindness. Thou didst exhale odors, and I drew in my breath and do pant after Thee. I tasted, and do hunger and thirst. Thou didst touch me, and I burned for Thy peace. . . .

# HESYCHIUS OF JERUSALEM

370?–?433

Hesychius, a pupil of St Gregory of Nazianzus, was born in Jerusalem and ordained there in 412 by Juvenal, Patriarch of Jerusalem.

## FROM Texts on Sobriety and Prayer for the Saving of the Soul

. . . Attention is unceasing silence of the heart, free of all thoughts. At all times, constantly and without ceasing, it breathes Christ Jesus, the Son of God and God, and Him alone, it calls upon Him, and with Him bravely fights against the enemies, and makes confession to Him who has power to forgive sins. Such a soul, through continual calling on Christ, embraces Him who alone searches the heart; and it seeks to hide its sweetness and its inner attainment from all men in every way, lest the evil one should have an easy entrance for his wickedness and destroy its excellent working.

Sobriety is the steadfast setting up of the thought of the mind and posting it at the door of the heart, so that it sees alien thoughts as they come, those thieves and robbers, and hears what these destroyers say and do; and sees what is the image inscribed and figured in them by the demons, who are trying thus to seduce the mind by fantasy. For this work, when it is done with loving effort, reveals to us very fundamentally and clearly, by experience, the art of mental war and brings skill in it. . . .

When the mind stands upright and calls upon Christ against its enemies, and runs to Him for refuge, it is like some wild animal, surrounded by many hounds, courageously facing them from the cover of its shelter. It discerns mentally from afar the mental ambushes of its unseen enemies, and remains unwounded by them, for it continually prays the peace-giving Jesus for His help. . . .

He who has no prayer free from thoughts has no weapon for

battle. By prayer I mean the prayer which is constantly active in the innermost secret places of the soul, so that the enemy in his secret onslaughts is invisibly flogged and scorched by calling on the name of our Lord Jesus Christ. . . .

If you wish to struggle as you ought, beloved, let that little creature the spider be a pattern to you, showing you the way and order of silence of the heart. The spider seizes and kills small flies; like the spider (sitting in the middle of its web) may you too keep silence in the soul with the utmost effort, and never cease killing the children of Babylon; for such slaughter you would be called happy by the Holy Spirit through the mouth of David. . . .

As he who holds a mirror in his hands, and is standing amongst others as he looks into it, sees his own face, and what it is like, and sees too the faces of the others looking in the same mirror; so he who is looking into his own heart with complete attention, sees his own state in it, and sees too the dark faces of the Ethiopians of the mind. . . .

As material salt gives a savour to bread and to all food, and keeps meat from rotting, even for a long time; so in this same way should you think of guarding the inner savour of the mind and the wonderful doing in the heart. For it sweetens divinely both the inner and the outer man, drives away the evil smell of wicked thoughts, and preserves us continually in what is good. . . .

Since every thought enters the heart through imagining something sensory (and the sensory hinders the mental), so the light of the Deity begins to illumine the mind only when it is freed of everything and is totally empty of form (without representation of shape or form). For this illumination is manifested in a mind already pure, on condition that it is free of all thoughts.

In so far as you have perfect attention in your mind, by so much will you pray to Jesus with warm desire. And again, in so far as you watch over your mind carelessly, by so much will you become distant from Jesus. And as perfect attention entirely fills the air of the mind with light, so too, to be without sobriety and without the sweet invocation of Jesus makes it wholly dark. And the matter is naturally such as we have said it to be and not otherwise. This you will find by experience, if you will test it in practice; since virtue and especially this light-giving and sweet work is naturally learned only by experience. . . .

As it is not possible to go into battle naked, or to swim over a great sea fully clothed, or to live without breathing, so without humility and constant supplication to Christ, it is not possible to learn the secret war of the mind; nor are we able skilfully to put to flight and strike down the enemies. . . .

The most wonderful fruit of silence of the mind is this, that sins which start merely as thoughts knocking at the door of the mind and would, if accepted by the mind, become coarse visible sins, are all cut off mentally in our inner man by the virtue of sobriety, which prevents them from coming in and becoming transformed into evil deeds, by a movement of the hand and the intercession of our Lord Jesus Christ. . . .

This is written to you, Theodulus, by him who is silent in name (that is Hesychius), though not silent in deed. Maybe I have not said everything relating to our subject, but I have put down all that was given me by God the Father, the Son and the Holy Ghost, praised and glorified by all creatures with reason: by angels and men and by every creature created by the ineffable Trinity, the Invisible God. May we be granted His radiant kingdom by the prayers of the Holy Mother of God and of our blessed fathers. To Him, God exceeding all comprehension, eternal glory. Amen.

# The Pilgrimage of Etheria

Pilgrimage is also prayer; and pilgrimages began with the holy women's visit to the Holy Sepulcher on the first Easter morning. The first recorded pilgrimage to the Holy Places was that of a Burgundian pilgrim in 333 A.D.; the second is that of Etheria. This manuscript was discovered in another of the eleventh century at Arezzo by Signor Gamurrini, and was first published in 1887; the first English translation was made by Dr. J. H. Bernard in 1891. The text used here is taken from *The Pilgrimage of Etheria* by M. L. McClure and C. L. Feltoe.

Dom Férotin, in the *Revue des questions historiques,* gives Etheria's date as about 395; Karl Meister places the pilgrimage in the reign of Justinian I (died 565).

### THE APPROACH TO SINAI

. . . We came on foot to a certain place where the mountains, through which we were journeying, opened out and formed an infinitely great valley, quite flat and extraordinarily beautiful, and across the valley appeared Sinai, the holy mountain of God. And this place, where the mountains opened out, lies next to the place where are the graves of lust. Now on reaching that spot, the holy guides who were with us told us, saying, "The custom is that prayer should be made by those who arrive here, when from this place the mount of God is first seen." And this we did. The whole distance from that place to the mount of God was about four miles across the aforesaid great valley.

For that valley is indeed very great, lying under the slope of the mount of God, and measuring, as far as we could judge by our sight, or as they told us, about sixteen miles in length, but they called its breadth four miles. We had, therefore, to cross that valley in order to reach the mountain. Now this is the great and flat valley wherein the children of Israel waited during those days when holy Moses went up into the mount of the Lord and remained there forty days and forty nights. This moreover is the valley in which the calf was made, and the spot is shown to this day, for a great stone stands fixed there on the very site. This also is the same valley at the head of which is the place where, while holy Moses was feeding his father-in-law's flocks, God spake to him twice out of the burning bush. And as our route was first to ascend the mount of God, which is in sight here—because the ascent was easier by the way we were coming—and then to descend to the head of the valley where the bush was, that being the easier descent, so we determined, having first seen all that we desired, to descend from the mount of God so as to arrive at the place of the bush, and thence to return on our journey throughout the whole length of the valley, together with the men of God, who there showed us each place which is mentioned in the Scriptures. And so it was done. Thus, going from that spot where we had prayed when we arrived from Faran, our route was to cross the middle of the head of that valley, and so turn to the mount of God.

Now the whole mountain group looks as if it were a single peak, but, as you enter the group, you see that there are more than one; the whole group however is called the mount of God. But that special peak which is crowned by the place where, as it is written, the Glory of God descended, is in the centre of them all. And though all the peaks in the group attain such a height as I think I never saw before, yet the central one, on which the Glory of God came down, is so much higher than them all, that when we had ascended it, all those mountains which we had thought to be high, were so much beneath us as if they were quite little hills. This is certainly very wonderful, and not, I think, without the favour of God, that while the central height, which is specially called Sinai, on which the Glory of the Lord descended, is higher than all the rest, yet it cannot be seen until you reach its very foot, though before you go up it. But after that you have fulfilled your desire and descend, you can see it from the other side, which you cannot do before you begin to ascend. This I had learned from information given by the brethren before we had arrived at the mount of God, and after I arrived I saw that it was manifestly so.

### THE ASCENT OF SINAI

We reached the mountain late on the sabbath, and arriving at a certain monastery, the monks who dwelt there received us very kindly, showing us every kindness; there is also a church and a priest there. We stayed there that night, and early on the Lord's Day, together with the priest and the monks who dwelt there, we began the ascent of the mountains one by one. These mountains are ascended with infinite toil, for you cannot go up gently by a spiral track, as we say snail-shell-wise, but you climb straight up the whole way, as if up a wall, and you must come straight down each mountain until you reach the very foot of the middle one, which is specially called Sinai. By this way, then, at the bidding of Christ our God, and helped by the prayers of the holy men who accompanied us, we arrived, at the fourth hour, at the summit of Sinai, the holy mountain of God, where the law was given, that is, at the place where the Glory of the Lord descended on the day when the mountain smoked. Thus the toil was great, for I had to go up on foot, the ascent being impossible in the saddle, and yet I did not feel the toil, on the side of the ascent, I say, I did not feel the toil, because I realized that the desire which I had was being fulfilled at God's bidding. In that place there is now a church, not great in size, for the place itself, that is the summit of the mountain, is not very great; nevertheless, the church itself is great in grace. When, therefore, at God's bidding, we had arrived at the summit, and had reached the door of the church, lo, the priest who was appointed to the church came from his cell and met us, a hale old man, a monk from early life, and an ascetic, as they say here, in short one worthy to be in that place; the other priests also met us, together with all the monks who dwelt on the mountain, that is, such as were not hindered by age or infirmity. No one, however, dwells on the very summit of the central mountain; there is nothing there excepting only the church and the cave where holy Moses was. . . .

### EPIPHANY AT THE CITY OF ARABIA; RETURN TO JERUSALEM

Now it fell out by a very happy chance that the day on which we came to the station of Arabia was the eve of the most blessed day of the Epiphany, and the vigils were to be kept in the church on the same day. Wherefore the holy bishop detained us there for some two days, a holy man and truly a man of God, well known to me from the time when I had been in the Thebaid. He became a holy bishop after being a monk, for he was brought up from a child in a cell, for which reason he is so learned in the Scriptures and chastened in his whole life, as I said above. From this place we sent back the soldiers who according to Roman discipline had given us the help of their escort as long as we had walked through suspected places. Now, however, as the public road—which passed by the city of Arabia and leads from the Thebaid to Pelusium—ran through Egypt, there was no need to trouble the soldiers further. Setting out thence, we pursued our journey continuously through the land of Goshen, among vines that yield wine and vines that yield balsam, among orchards, highly cultivated fields and very pleasant gardens, our whole route lying along the bank of the river Nile among oft-recurring estates, which were once the homesteads of the children of Israel. And why should I say more? for I think that I have never seen a more beautiful country than the land of Goshen. And travelling thus for two days from the city of Arabia through the land of Goshen continuously, we arrived at Tatnis, the city where holy Moses was born. This city of Tatnis was once Pharaoh's metropolis. Now although I had already known these places—as I said above . . . yet I wished to learn thoroughly all the places through which the children of Israel marched on their journey from Rameses to Sinai, the holy mountain of God; this made it necessary to return to the land of Goshen and thence to Tatnis. We set out from Tatnis and, walking along the route that was already known to me, I came to Pelusium. Thence I set out again, and journeying through all those stations in Egypt through which we had travelled before, I arrived at the boundary of Palestine. Thence in the name of Christ our God I passed through several stations in Palestine and returned to Aelia, that is Jerusalem.

## VISIT TO AUSITIS

Now after some time I wished to go to the region of Ausitis to visit the tomb of holy Job, for the sake of prayer. For I used to see many holy monks coming thence to Jerusalem to visit the holy places for the sake of prayer, who, giving information of everything concerning those places, increased my desire to undertake the toil of going to them also, if indeed that can be called toil by which a man sees his desire to be fulfilled. So I set out from Jerusalem with the holy men who deigned to give me their company on my journey—they themselves also going for the sake of prayer—making my journey from Jerusalem through eight stations to Carneas. The city of Job is now called Carneas, but it was formerly called Dennaba, in the land of Ausitis, on the confines of Idumea and Arabia. Travelling on this journey I saw on the bank of the river Jordan a very beautiful and pleasant valley abounding in vines and trees, for much excellent water was there, and in that valley there was a large village, which is now called Sedima. The village, which is situated in the middle of the level ground, has in its midst a little hill of no great size, shaped as large tombs are wont to be. There is a church on the summit and down below, around the little hill, great and ancient foundations appear, while in the village itself some grave-mounds still remain. When I saw this pleasant place I asked what it was, and it was told me: "This is the city of king Melchizedek, which was called Salem, but now, through the corruption of the language, the village is called Sedima. On the top of the little hill, which is situated in the midst of the village, the building that you see is a church, which is now called in the Greek language *opu Melchisedech*. For this is the place where Melchizedek offered pure sacrifices—that is bread and wine—to God, as it is written of him."

## THE CITY OF MELCHIZEDEK

Directly I heard this, we alighted from our beasts, and lo! the holy priest of the place and the clergy deigned to meet us, and straightway receiving us led us up to the church. When we had arrived there, prayer was first said according to custom, then the passage from the book of holy Moses was read, then one psalm suitable to the place was said, then, after prayer made, we came down. When we had come down the holy priest addressed us. He was an elderly man, well taught in the Scriptures, and he had presided over the place from the time he had been a monk, to whose life many bishops—as we learned afterwards—bore great testimony, saying that he was worthy to preside over the place where holy Melchizedek—when Abraham was coming to meet him—was the first to offer pure sacrifices to God. When we had come down from the church, as I said above, the holy priest said to us: "Behold, these foundations which you see around the little hill are those of the palace of king Melchizedek. For from this time to the present day if anyone wishes to build himself a house here, and so strikes on these foundations, he sometimes finds little fragments of silver and bronze. And this way which you see passing between the river Jordan and this village is the way by which holy Abraham returned to Sodom, after the slaughter of Chedorlaomer, king of nations, and where holy Melchizedek, the king of Salem, met him.

### AENON

Then, because I remembered that it was written that St John had baptized in Aenon near to Salem, I asked him how far off that place was. The holy priest answered: "It is near, two hundred paces off, and, if you wish, I will now lead you there on foot. This large and pure stream of water, which you see in this village, comes from that spring." Then I began to thank him and to ask him to lead us to the place, which was done. So we began to go with him on foot through the very pleasant valley, until we reached a most pleasant orchard, in the midst of which he showed us a spring of excellent and pure water, which sent out continuously a good stream. The spring had in front of it a sort of pool, where it appears that St John the Baptist fulfilled his ministry. Then the holy priest said to us: "This garden is called nothing else to this day than *cepos tu agiu iohannu* in the Greek language, or as you say in Latin, *hortus sancti Johannis*. Many brethren, holy monks, direct their steps hither from various places that they may wash there." So at the spring, as in every place, prayer was made, the proper lection was read and an appropriate psalm was said, and everything that it was customary for us to do whenever we came to the holy places, we did there also. The holy priest also told us that to this day, at Easter, all they who are to be baptized in the village, that is in the church which is called *opu Melchisedech,* are always baptized in this spring, returning early to vespers with the clergy and monks, saying psalms and antiphons, so that they who have been baptized are led back early from the fountain to the church of holy Melchizedek. Then, receiving *eulogiae* out of the orchard of St John the Baptist from the priest, as well as from the holy monks who had cells in the same orchard, and always giving thanks to God, we set out on the way we were going. . . .

### VISIT TO ST THECLA'S CHURCH; RETURN TO CONSTANTINOPLE

So, setting out from Tarsus, I came to a certain city on the sea, still in Cilicia, which is called Pompeiopolis. Thence I entered the borders of Hisauria and stayed in a city call Coricus, and on the third day I arrived at a city which is called Seleucia in Hisauria; on my arrival I went to the bishop, a truly holy man, formerly a monk, and in that city I saw a very beautiful church. And as the distance thence to St Thecla, which is situated outside the city on a low eminence, was about fifteen hundred paces, I chose rather to go there in order to make the stay that I intended. There is nothing at the holy church in that place except numberless cells of men and of women. I found there a very dear friend of mine, to whose manner of life all in the East bore testimony, a holy deaconess named Marthana, whom I had known at Jerusalem, whither she had come for the sake of prayer; she was ruling over the cells of *apotactitae* and virgins. And when she had seen me, how can I describe the extent of her joy or of mine? But to return to the matter in hand: there are very many cells on the hill and in the midst of it a great wall which encloses the church containing the very beautiful memorial. The wall was built to guard the church because of the Hisauri, who are very malicious and frequently commit acts of robbery, to prevent them from making an attempt on the monastery which is established there. When I had arrived in the Name of God, prayer was made at the memorial, and the whole of the acts of St Thecla having been read, I gave endless thanks to Christ our God, who deigned to fulfil my desires in all things, unworthy and undeserving as I am. Then, after a stay of two days, when I had seen the holy monks and *apotactitae* who were there, both men and women, and when I had prayed and made my communion, I returned to Tarsus and to my journey. From Tarsus, after a halt of three days, I set out on my journey in the Name of God, and arriving on the same day at a station called Mansocrenae, which is under Mount Taurus, I stayed there. On the next day, going under Mount Taurus, and travelling by the route that was already known to me, through each province that I had traversed on my way out, to wit, Cappadocia, Galatia, and Bithynia, I arrived at Chalcedon, where I stayed for the sake of the very famous martyr-memorial of St Euphemia, which was already known to me from a former time. On the next day, crossing the sea, I arrived at Constantinople, giving thanks to Christ our God who deigned to give me such grace, unworthy and undeserving as I am, for He had deigned to give me not only the will to go, but also the power of walking through the places that I desired, and of returning at last to Constantinople. When I had arrived there, I went through all the churches—that of the Apostles and all the martyr-memorials, of which there are very many—and I ceased not to give thanks to Jesus our God, who had thus deigned to bestow His mercy upon me. From which place, ladies, light of my eyes, while I send these letters to your affection, I have already purposed, in the Name of Christ our God, to go to Ephesus in Asia, for the sake of prayer, because of the memorial of the holy and blessed Apostle John. And if after this I am yet in the body, and am able to see any other places, I will either tell it to your affection in person, if God deigns to permit me this, or in anywise, if I have another project in mind, I will send you news of it in a letter. But do you, ladies, light of my eyes, deign to remember me, whether I am in the body or out of the body.

JERUSALEM

## *Daily Offices.*

*Matins.* Now that your affection may know what is the order of service (*operatio*) day by day in the holy places, I must inform you, for I know that you would willingly have this knowledge. Every day before cockcrow all the doors of the Anastasis are opened, and all the monks and virgins, as they call them here, go thither, and not they alone, but lay people also, both men and women, who desire to begin their vigil early. And from that hour to daybreak hymns are said and psalms are sung responsively, and antiphons in like manner; and prayer is made after each of the hymns. For priests, deacons, and monks in twos or threes take it in turn every day to say prayers after each of the hymns or antiphons. But when day breaks they begin to say the Matin hymns. Thereupon the bishop arrives with the clergy, and immediately enters into the cave, and from within the rails he first says a prayer for all, mentioning the names of those whom he wishes to commemorate; he then blesses the catechumens, afterwards he says a prayer and blesses the faithful. And when the bishop comes out from within the rails, everyone approaches his hand, and he blesses them one by one as he goes out, and the dismissal takes place, by daylight.

*Sext and None.* In like manner at the sixth hour all go again to the Anastasis, and psalms and antiphons are said, while the bishop is being summoned; then he comes as before, not taking his seat, but he enters at once within the rails in the Anastasis, that is in the cave, just as in the early morning, and as then, he again first says a prayer, then he blesses the faithful, and as he comes out from the rails everyone approaches his hand. And the same is done at the ninth hour as at the sixth.

*Vespers.* Now at the tenth hour, which they call here *licinicon,* or as we say *lucernare,* all the people assemble at the Anastasis in the same manner, and all the candles and tapers are lit, making a very great light. Now the light is not introduced from without, but it is brought forth from within the cave, that is from within the rails, where a lamp is always burning day and night, and the vesper psalms and antiphons are said, lasting for a considerable time. Then the bishop is summoned, and he comes and takes a raised seat, and likewise the priests sit in their proper places, and hymns and antiphons are said. And when all these have been recited according to custom, the bishop rises and stands before the rails, that is, before the cave, and one of the deacons makes the customary commemoration of individuals one by one. And as the deacon pronounces each name the many little boys who are always standing by answer with countless voices: *Kyrie eleyson,* or as we say *Miserere Domine.* And when the deacon has finished all that he has to say, first the bishop says a prayer and prays for all, then they all pray, both the faithful and catechumens together. Again the deacon raises his voice, bidding each catechumen to bow his head where he stands, and the bishop stands and says the blessing over the catechumens. Again prayer is made, and again the deacon raises his voice and bids the faithful, each where he stands, to bow the head, and the bishop likewise blesses the faithful. Thus the dismissal takes place at the Anastasis, and one by one all draw near to the bishop's hand. Afterwards the bishop is conducted from the Anastasis to the Cross with hymns, all the people accompanying him, and when he arrives he first says a prayer, then he blesses the catechumens, then another prayer is said and he blesses the faithful. Thereupon both the bishop and the whole multitude further proceed behind the Cross, where all that was done before the Cross is repeated, and they approach the hand of the bishop behind the Cross as they did at the Anastasis and before the Cross. Moreover, there are hanging everywhere a vast number of great glass chandeliers, and there are also a vast number of *cereofala,* before the Anastasis, before the Cross and behind the Cross, for the whole does not end until darkness has set in. This is the order of daily services at the Cross and at the Anastasis throughout the six days.

*Sunday Offices.*

*Vigil.* But on the seventh day, that is on the Lord's Day, the whole multitude assembles before cockcrow, in as great numbers as the place can hold, as at Easter, in the basilica which is near the

Anastasis, but outside the doors, where lights are hanging for the purpose. And for fear that they should not be there at cockcrow they come beforehand and sit down there. Hymns as well as antiphons are said, and prayers are made between the several hymns and antiphons, for at the vigils there are always both priests and deacons ready there for the assembling of the multitude, the custom being that the Holy Places are not opened before cockcrow. Now as soon as the first cock has crowed, the bishop arrives and enters the cave at the Anastasis; all the doors are opened and the whole multitude enters the Anastasis, where countless lights are already burning. And when the people have entered, one of the priests says a psalm to which all respond, and afterwards prayer is made; then one of the deacons says a psalm and prayer is again made, a third psalm is said by one of the clergy, prayer is made for the third time and there is a commemoration of all. After these three psalms and three prayers are ended, lo! censers are brought into the cave of the Anastasis so that the whole basilica of the Anastasis is filled with odours. And then the bishop, standing within the rails, takes the book of the Gospel, and proceeding to the door, himself reads the narrative of the Resurrection of the Lord. And when the reading is begun, there is so great a moaning and groaning among all, with so many tears, that the hardest of heart might be moved to tears for that the Lord had borne such things for us. After the reading of the Gospel the bishop goes out, and is accompanied to the Cross by all the people with hymns, there again a psalm is said and prayer is made, after which he blesses the faithful and the dismissal takes place, and as he comes out all approach to his hand. And forthwith the bishop betakes himself to his house, and from that hour all the monks return to the Anastasis, where psalms and antiphons, with prayer after each psalm or antiphon, are said until daylight; the priests and deacons also keep watch in turn daily at the Anastasis with the people, but of the lay people, whether men or women, those who are so minded, remain in the place until daybreak, and those who are not, return to their houses and betake themselves to sleep.

*Morning Services.* Now at daybreak because it is the Lord's Day everyone proceeds to the greater church, built by Constantine, which is situated in Golgotha behind the Cross, where all things are done which are customary everywhere on the Lord's Day. But the custom here is that of all the priests who take their seats, as many as are willing preach, and after them all the bishop preaches, and these sermons are always on the Lord's Day, in order that the people may always be instructed in the Scriptures and in the love of God. The delivery of these sermons greatly delays the dismissal from the church, so that the dismissal does not take place before the fourth or perhaps the fifth hour. But when the dismissal from the church is made in the manner that is customary everywhere, the monks accompany the bishop with hymns from the church to the Anastasis, and as he approaches with hymns all the doors of the basilica of the Anastasis are opened, and the people, that is the faithful, enter, but not the catechumens. And after the people the bishop enters, and goes at once within the rails of the cave of the martyrium. Thanks are first given to God, then prayer is made for all, after which the deacon bids all bow their heads, where they stand, and the bishop standing within the inner rails blesses them and goes out, each one drawing near to his hand as he makes his exit. Thus the dismissal is delayed until nearly the fifth or sixth hour. And in like manner it is done at *lucernare,* according to daily custom.

This then is the custom observed every day throughout the whole year except on solemn days, to the keeping of which we will refer later on. But among all things it is a special feature that they arrange that suitable psalms and antiphons are said on every occasion, both those said by night, or in the morning, as well as those throughout the day, at the sixth hour, the ninth hour, or at *lucernare,* all being so appropriate and so reasonable as to bear on the matter in hand. And they proceed to the greater church, which was built by Constantine, and which is situated in Golgotha, that is, behind the Cross, on every Lord's Day throughout the year except on the one Sunday of Pentecost, when they proceed to Sion, as you will find mentioned below; but even then they go to Sion before the third hour, the dismissal having been first made in the greater church.

# JULIANUS POMERIUS

450?–?500

Julianus Pomerius, born in Mauretania in North Africa, is known chiefly as the founder of a school of rhetoric in Arles, where he had amongst his pupils St Caesarius, later bishop of Arles. All his treatises have been lost except one, *The Contemplative Life*. For some eight hundred years following 766, this manuscript was ascribed to Prosper of Aquitaine (died after 455).

## FROM The Contemplative Life

### THE HAPPINESS OF THE CONTEMPLATIVE LIFE EVEN HERE BELOW DELIGHTS THOSE WHO CONTEMN THE THINGS OF THE WORLD

That man longs to merit this happiness who renounces all present things for the sake of the things to come, and, being lifted from domestic cares, which sometimes hinder the progress of those trying to live perfectly, to that sublimity of divine contemplation, overcomes even the very affections of his flesh. By despising all things below, which very often cast to earth souls that feel secure by reason of the sanctity of their past life, he even approaches things celestial; and he is carried as much nearer to divine things as he ascends above all things human through a desire of perfection. He is confident that if with uncompromising will he prefers the contemplative life here to uncertain honors, wealth with the anxiety that it brings, and ephemeral delights, he will find true honors, wealth without care, and eternal delights when he has arrived at the perfection of the contemplative virtue in that blessed life where he will be by God's reward. Indeed, who will be more honorable than he whom the divine mercy has blessed with dignity equal to the angels'? Who will be richer than he whom the ineffably abounding happiness of the heavenly kingdom has enriched? Or what even here is more delightful than divine contemplation, which fills those who truly yearn for it with the incorruptible sweetness of the future reward? For, in truth, the contemplative life even on earth delights its lovers by a consideration of future blessings and illumines with the gift of spiritual wisdom those who devote themselves to it with the whole bent of their minds, as far as can be done in this life; and by means of a certain incentive for reaching perfection it sets them aglow for that fullness of the divine vision of which they, intent upon their desire for heaven, have hope, so that what they now behold in obscurity and do not completely discern they may then see in that revelation. . . .

### THE DIFFERENCE BETWEEN THE CONTEMPLATIVE LIFE AND THE ACTIVE

Now let me briefly discuss what the difference is between the contemplative life and the active. In order that it may be quite clear, let me compare the two lives: the contemplative, that is, and the active, bringing out their virtues. It pertains to the active life to advance in the midst of human affairs and to restrain the rebellious movements of the body by the rule of reason; to the contemplative, to ascend above things human by the desire of perfection and constantly to devote oneself to the increase of virtues. The active life is the journeying; the contemplative is the summit. The former makes a man holy; the latter makes him perfect. It is characteristic of the active life to inflict injuries on no one; of the contemplative, to bear inflicted injuries calmly. Nay, to state this more precisely, one who fulfils the requirements of the active life is prompt to forgive the man who has sinned against him; one who follows the contemplative life is prepared rather not to notice than to pardon the offences by which he is attacked but not at all affected. The former controls anger by the virtue of patience; places the bridle of moderation on unrestrained passions; is touched by carnal desires but does not consent; is smitten by the curiosity of this world but is not carried away; is shaken by the attacks of the Devil but is not overcome; and, being subject to his God with a devoted mind, is not worn down but proved by diverse temptations. The follower of the contemplative life by holy virtues overcomes all the feelings which variously affect the life of mortals; free from all desires and disturbances, he enjoys blessed quiet; and, being made superior to his temptations and passions by reason of his untrammelled mind, he is raised on high by the indescribable joy of divine contemplation. The follower of the active life, by harbouring the stranger, clothing the naked, governing the subject, redeeming the captive, protecting him who is oppressed by violence, is continually cleansing himself from all his sins and enriching his life with the fruits of good works. The other, having given his possessions for the use of the poor, in one act divests himself of the world and raises himself to heaven with all his strength. He casts the things of the world upon the world and delivers himself up with a devoted mind to Christ, of whom he asks that immortal riches be given him as a poor man; begs daily to be protected as one weak; desires to be clothed with the garment of immortality as one naked; prays to be defended from the attacks of invisible enemies as one oppressed by the frailty of the flesh; and desires that the land of heaven be given him as one who is a stranger.

The active life has an anxious course; the contemplative, everlasting joy. In the former a kingdom is being acquired; in the latter it is received. The active life causes men to knock at the gate as though with the hands of good works; the contemplative life calls into their homeland those who have completed their course. . . .

# DIODICUS

5th century

Diodicus was bishop of Photike in Epirus in 458 A.D. The only detail of his life that has survived, apart from his writings, is the fact that he signed a letter of remonstrance to Emperor Leo I because one Proterius had been murdered by the Monophysites.

## FROM One Hundred Chapters on Spiritual Perfection

### THEOLOGY AND CONTEMPLATION

All the gifts of our God are admirable and procure every good thing, but none inflames and stirs our heart to love His goodness so much as theology. A first spring burgeoning of divine grace, it also bestows on the soul absolutely primary fruits. To begin with, indeed, it disposes us to despise happily all this life's friendships, by giving us the idea of replacing earthly desires with the ineffable riches of the word of God. Next, it illuminates our spirit with a transforming fire, and brings it into contact with those spirits who verily serve the Lord. So we, my dearly beloved, who worthily have been prepared for it, we desire this lovely, this contemplative virtue, which bestows detachment, which, in the brightness of an indescribable light, nourishes the spirit with the word of God; which, in a word, brings the reasonable soul near to Reason, who is God, by means of the holy prophets, in an indissoluble union, so that even among men, O marvel, this divine initiator makes our divinized accents clearly sing the grandeurs of God. . . .

Usually our intellect endures prayer impatiently, because of its narrow and straitened capacity for prayer, but gladly gives itself up to theology because of the freedom and the expanse of its speculation about God. Therefore, in order not to give free rein to its longing, and even to prevent it, in its enthusiasm, over-reaching itself unreasonably, let us give as much time as is possible to prayer, to the recitation of psalms, to reading the Scriptures, without, however, neglecting the speculations of scientific men whose faith is demonstrated by their word. By doing this, we shall prevent our intellect mistaking its own words for those of [Divine] Grace, and we shall prevent it from being led astray by vanity and dissipated by an excess of joy of words: we will hold it, at the moment of contemplation, free from all imagination, and by this we shall ensure that all its thoughts, or almost all, will lead to tears. Relaxed, indeed, at the time of its withdrawal, and above all penetrated by the sweetness of prayer, not only does it avoid the inconveniences mentioned above, but moreover it renews itself in order to devote itself gaily and without weariness to heavenly considerations, not to mention the fact that it makes great progress, through humility, in the theory of discernment. But it must be realized that there is a prayer higher than any dilatation: this belongs only to those who in all intimacy and fullness are filled with divine grace.

### VICISSITUDES OF CONTEMPLATION

Usually grace begins by illuminating the soul with a deep awareness, with its own light. As the struggles increase, it generally works its mysteries insensibly in the contemplative soul, in order now to send us out joyfully on the tracks of divine contemplation, as though called from ignorance to knowledge, now, in the midst of battle, to keep our knowledge from vainglory. On the one hand, therefore, we must be moderate in our affliction at feeling ourselves abandoned, in order the better to humble ourselves and the more completely to submit ourselves to God's glory; on the other, we must rejoice in timely fashion when hope buoys us up. Indeed, just as an excess of sadness plunges the soul into despair and lack of faith, so excess of joy invites it to presumption; I speak for those who still are children, because midway between illumination and dereliction there is trial; and midway between sorrow and joy there is hope. . . .

Just as, from standing perpetually open, the door of the bath lets all the heat out from within, so, too, when the soul yields to a wish to talk a lot, even when everything it says is good it dissipates its recollectedness through the door of its voice. Therefore, too, it is deprived of opportune thoughts and bares to the firstcomers crowding to it the flow of its reasonings, for it no longer has the Holy Ghost to keep it in ideas without images. The good always avoids loquacity, for it is always stranger to every kind of agitation and imagination. A properly kept silence is a beautiful thing; it is nothing less than the father of very wise thoughts.

# DIONYSIUS
# THE PSEUDO-AREOPAGITE

c. 500

The true name of the author of what have been called the "Dionysian writings" is unknown. That he was not who he pretended to be, the disciple of St Paul and the first bishop of Athens, has been established, since he reflects, and even quotes, the pagan philosopher Proclus, who began lecturing in Athens in 430 A.D. Hierotheus, to whom Dionysius constantly refers, is thought to have been the Syrian mystic Stephen Bar Sudaili, who taught about the middle of the fifth century. Also, he speaks of the practice of singing the Credo at Mass, which the Monophysites introduced at Antioch in 476. Four treatises and ten letters survive. They were first mentioned at a debate that took place at Constantinople in 533 between Catholics and Severians, or moderate Monophysites, who taught that Christ has a single, compound nature, whereas according to Catholic orthodoxy He has two distinct natures.

The author was possibly a Syrian and probably a monk. He introduced Neoplatonic thoughts and methods into Christian theology; however, his doctrine of the Trinity is substantially the same as that of St Augustine ". . . only it is expressed in more exact, if at first sight somewhat fantastic, terms." St Maximus the Confessor wrote commentaries on Dionysius, and throughout the Middle Ages the works of the Pseudo-Areopagite were accepted as genuine and enjoyed enormous success and prestige.

## FROM On the Divine Names

And first of all, if it like thee, let us consider the highest Name, even "Goodness," by which all the emanations of God are conjointly revealed. And let us begin with an invocation of the Trinity, the Which, as It surpasseth Goodness, and is the Source of all goodness, doth reveal all conjoined together Its own good providences. For we must first lift up our minds in prayer unto the Primal Goodness, and by drawing nearer thereunto, we must thus be initiated into the mystery of those good gifts which are rooted in Its being. For the Trinity is nigh unto all things, and yet not all things are nigh unto It. And when we call upon It with holy prayers and unspotted mind and with our souls prepared for union with God, then are we also nigh thereto; for It is not in space, so as to be absent from any spot, or to move from one position to another. Nay, to speak of It as omnipresent doth not express Its all-transcendent all-embracing Infinitude. Let us then press on in prayer, looking upwards to the Divine benignant Rays, even as if a resplendent cord were hanging from the height of heaven unto this world below, and we, by seizing it with alternate hands in one advance, appeared to pull it down; but in very truth instead of drawing down the rope (the same being already nigh us above and below), we were ourselves being drawn upwards to the higher refulgence of the resplendent Rays. Or even as, having embarked on a ship and clinging to the cables, the which being stretched out from some rock unto us, presented themselves (as it were) for us to lay hold upon them, we should not be drawing the rock towards ourselves, but should, in very truth, be drawing ourselves and the vessel towards the rock; as also, conversely, if anyone standing upon the vessel pushes away the rock that is on the shore, he will not affect the rock (which stands immovable) but will separate himself therefrom, and the more he pushes it so much the more will he be staving himself away. Hence, before every endeavour, more especially if the subject be Divinity, must we begin with prayer: not as though we would pull down to ourselves that Power which is nigh both everywhere and nowhere, but that, by these remembrances and invocations of God, we may commend and unite ourselves thereunto. . . .

But if It is greater than all reason and all knowledge, and hath Its firm abode altogether beyond mind and being, and circumscribes, compacts, embraces and anticipates all things while Itself is altogether beyond the grasp of them all, and cannot be reached by any perception, imagination, conjecture, name, discourse, apprehension, or understanding, how then is our discourse concerning the Divine Names to be accomplished, since we see that the Super-Essential Godhead is unutterable and nameless? Now, as we said when setting forth our outlines of Divinity, the One, the Unknowable, the Super-Essential, the Absolute Good (I mean the Trinal Unity of Persons possessing the same Deity and Goodness), 'tis impossible to describe or to conceive in Its ultimate Nature. . . .

And godlike minds, angelically entering (according to their powers) unto such states of union and being deified and united, through the ceasing of their natural activities, unto the Light which surpasseth Deity, can find no more fitting method to celebrate its praises than to deny It every manner of attribute. For by a true and supernatural illumination from their blessed union therewith, they learn that It is the Cause of all things and yet Itself is nothing, because It super-essentially transcends them all. Thus, as for the Super-Essence of the Supreme Godhead (if we would define the Transcendence of its Transcendent Goodness) it is not lawful to any lover of that Truth which is above all truth to celebrate It as Reason or Power or Mind or Life or Being, but rather as most utterly surpassing all condition, movement, life, imagination, conjecture, name, discourse, thought, conception, being, rest, dwelling, union, limit, infinity, everything that exists. And yet since, as the Subsistence of goodness, It, by the very fact of Its existence, is the Cause of all things, in celebrating the bountiful Providence of the Supreme Godhead we must draw upon the whole creation. For It is both the central Force of all things, and also their final Purpose, and *is* Itself before them all, and they all subsist in It; and through the fact of Its existence the world is brought into being and maintained; and It is that which all things desire—those which have intuitive or discursive reason seeking It through knowledge, the next rank of beings through perception, and the rest through vital movement or the property of mere existence belonging to their state. Conscious of this, the sacred writers celebrate It by every Name while yet they call It nameless.

For instance, they call It nameless when they say that the Supreme Godhead Itself, in one of the mystical visions whereby It was symbolically manifested, rebuked him who said: "What is thy name?" and, as though bidding him not seek by any means of any name to acquire a knowledge of God, made the answer: "Why askest thou thus after My Name, seeing it is secret?" Now is not the secret Name precisely that which is above all names and nameless, and is fixed beyond every name that is named, not only in this world but also in that which is to come? On the other hand, they attribute many names to It when, for instance, they speak of It as declaring: "I am that I am," or "I am the Life," or "the Light," or "God," or "the Truth," and when the Inspired Writers themselves celebrate the Universal Cause with many titles drawn from the whole created universe, such as "Good," and "Fair," and "Wise," as "Beloved," as "God of Gods" and "Lord of Lords" and "Holy of Holies," as "Eternal," as "Existent" and as "Creator of Ages," as "Giver of Life," as "Wisdom," as "Mind," as "Word," as "Knower," as "possessing beforehand all the treasures of knowledge," as "Power," as "Ruler," as "King of kings," as "Ancient of Days"; and as "Him that is the same and whose years shall not fail," as "Salvation," as "Righteousness," as "Sanctification," as "Redemption," as "Surpassing all things in greatness," and yet as being in "the still small breeze." Moreover, they say that He dwells within our minds, and in our souls and bodies, and in heaven and in earth, and that, while remaining Himself, He is at one and the same time within the world, around it and above it (yea, above the sky and above existence); and they call Him a Sun, a Star, and a Fire, and Water, a Wind or Spirit, a Dew, a cloud, an Archetypal Stone, and a Rock, and All Creation, Who yet (they declare) is no created thing.

# ST BARSANUPHIUS

died 563

Barsanuphius, born in Egypt, lived as a monk in Palestine during the reign of Emperor Justinian I. It is said that no one saw him for more than fifty years. A certain John lived in the same monastery and helped him write his book, putting down eight hundred and fifty answers to questions asked of Barsanuphius.

## FROM Directions in Spiritual Work

. . . About the measure of abstinence in food and drink, the fathers say that one should partake of the one and the other in a measure somewhat less than one's actual need, that is, not to fill the stomach completely. Everyone should establish a measure for himself, whether in cooked food or in wine. Moreover the measure of abstinence is not limited to food and drink but embraces also conversations, sleep, garments and all the senses. Each of these should have its own measure of abstinence. . . .

"What does it mean to abstain according to one's strength?"

To abstain according to one's strength means precisely to use food and drink as I said; namely, to take slightly less than one needs. The same applies to sleep. But if owing to hardship and exhaustion a man somewhat increases the measure, this will not mean an infringement of the rule: "according to one's strength." You will ask: What should be the measure of sleep? The fathers set it as half the night. As regards food—stop eating when you would like to have a little more, and in this way always take it in moderation. . . .

"When I am drawn into a conversation I am carried away and forget myself; and later I feel sad and ashamed."

In order that a weak man should not fall into this danger, and into vainglory, he must at all costs avoid much talk and break off conversation, excusing himself under some pretext and withdrawing from the discussion. When conversation is useful and does not interfere with more necessary work, stand by while it is going on. But if it is not useful, say: "Forgive me, I feel weak"; and withdraw. . . .

"How behave on meeting others?"

When you meet someone, limit yourself to a bare greeting; then say: "Pray for me, I am busy"—and withdraw. And if you are asked about something and you know it, say what you know, and pass on; if you do not know, say: "I do not know," and go your way. . . .

"I am busy the whole day long—and this prevents me from remembering God."

It happens sometimes that a man has heard much about a certain city, but when he comes thither he does not realize that it is the same city about which he had heard so much. It is the same with you, brother: all day long you remember God without being aware of it. The meaning of obedience and remembrance of God is precisely to have a commandment and to try to keep it, as coming from God. . . .

"Is it good for me to leave my wife in order to enter a monastery?"

You must not leave her of your own accord, for you will thus break the commandment of the Apostle, who says: "Art thou bound unto a wife? seek not to be loosed." If (after you leave her) she sins and begins to lead a bad life, the sin will be on you; unless you have left her by mutual consent, agreeing that it will be profitable. But leave this matter to God; in His loving kindness He will do what pleases Him. . . .

"Is it proper to strive to do a clean piece of work, for example, in building a house or doing something else?"

To see that the thing you make is clean and beautiful is not improper if it is done for the sake of the use it serves, without passionate attachment. For the Lord rejoices in all kinds of clean workmanship. But if you observe in yourself a passionate attachment to anything, remember the end which awaits it, since it is subject to rot and corruption, and you will find peace. For not a single thing remains constantly in the same state, but all are subject to change and corruption.

## ST ISIDORE OF SEVILLE

(See page 181.)

# A Dialogue between the Erring Soul and Reason

*Man*. My soul is in anguish, my spirit burns, my heart fails, anguish takes possession of my heart. . . . I am surrounded by all evils, hemmed in by tribulations, surrounded by adversities, beset by miseries, covered with unhappiness, oppressed with anguish. I find nowhere a refuge amid such evil, I find no means of defence amid such sorrow, I see no way of avoiding misfortune, I can discover no means of lessening my pain, I find no way of fleeing disaster. . . . I come upon no path of escape. Everywhere unhappiness follows me; at home, abroad, misfortune never leaves me. . . .

*Reason*. The misfortune of evils does not kill you but instructs you; the suffering of adversity does not degrade you but exalts you; human tribulation teaches you, it does not destroy you. The more we are afflicted in this world, the greater is our assurance for the next; the more we sorrow in the present, the greater will be our joy in the future. If we are wasted by scourges here, we shall be found purified in the judgment. . . . Do not murmur, therefore; do not blaspheme; do not say, "Why do I suffer evil, why am I afflicted, for what cause am I tormented?" But rather say, "I have sinned; I receive my just deserts; I do not suffer a punishment equal to my sins, I am less afflicted than I have deserved." . . . He who bears adversity with patience pleases God. If you wish to be purified, accuse yourself in tribulation and praise the justice of God; it is beneficial for your salvation to praise the justice of God and humbly glorify Him for the punishment inflicted upon you. For God corrects you with the scourge of loving chastisement, He disciplines you and calls out by punishment that you, whom He recalled by mercy, may return. . . .

*Man.* Alas, wretched and miserable that I am! I knew not that I was stricken for my own iniquity. I realized not that I was suffering for my own deserts. . . .

*Reason.* Thence, O man, is all this misfortune, all this bitterness, this suffering, this punishment, this distress. The cause is known to you: not by any chance, nor by any accident, not by casual circumstance, but because of your own sin and iniquity has this distress and anguish come upon you. . . . If you are convinced of this, cast vice from you, flee from sin, avoid the taint of evil. . . .

*Man.* Unhappy man! I willingly yielded to vice, and formerly embraced the occasion of sin; now I am bound by the habit of evil; pernicious custom has enthralled me; the practice of sin has bound me with the chains of necessity; I will to depart from sin, but I am not able to do so. . . .

*Reason.* Struggle with all your power against the habit of sin. . . . Oppose the flames of eternal punishment to the fire of concupiscence. . . . Have death always before your eyes. . . . Perhaps this night the coming of death will demand your soul. . . . While you are yet alive, seek your future remedy, before the day of death prevents you, before hell seizes you, where there is no room for pardon, no opportunity for penance, no chance for amendment, no recourse to confession, no admittance to pardon.

*Man.* Earnestly do I desire to know if there is hope in confession, if there is assurance, if there is remission, pardon, indulgence, if there is a chance to regain justice through penance?

*Reason.* Confession heals, confession justifies, confession grants pardon of sin, all hope consists in confession, in confession there is a chance for mercy. Believe it firmly, do not doubt, do not hesitate, never despair of the mercy of God. Hope in confession, have confidence. Do not doubt the healing remedy; do not despair of salvation, if you are converted to a better life. He who despairs of pardon for his sin, damns himself by despair rather than by the crime he has committed. . . . Bewail your guilt, realize your punishment in tears; let the lamentation of penance purify you, let a wave of sorrow inundate you, let a flood of tears compel you to weep. . . .

*Man.* Alas, unhappy soul! In the midst of such great sins, such enormous crimes, such manifold iniquities, what first shall I bewail? What first shall I lament? What shall be the first cause of my grief? With what tears shall I begin? My memory cannot recall the commission of such deeds. My sins have taken from me the sense of sorrow, my tears are choked by insensibility, my soul is hardened, I am overwhelmed by no sorrow. . . . Grant unto me a bitter lament, for I have sinned more grievously than all others, I have fallen more basely. By my sins I have surpassed the punishment of all the impious; the torments of hell scarcely correspond to my iniquities. . . . Where art Thou, O Saviour of men? Where art Thou, O Redeemer of souls? Where art Thou, my Shepherd? Why hast Thou spurned me? Why hast Thou turned Thy face away from me? Why hast Thou departed from me, Consoler of my spirit? Return, O my God; do not forget me unto the end; do not eternally desert me; . . . I have sinned, O my God, be merciful to me. I have sinned, O my God, be propitious to me. Spare my evil deeds, forgive my sins, pardon my crimes, let Thy grace wipe out my offences.

*Reason.* At your lamentation I have poured forth tears; at your mourning, I have wept. God grant you pardon, God forgive you and spare your faults. . . . Do not commit that which you will again regret, do not presume to repeat the fault for which you now seek pardon. Vain is the penance stained by subsequent sin; a re-opened wound heals more slowly; you will scarcely merit pardon, alternately weeping and sinning. Lament avails nothing if sins are repeated. It is of no use to ask pardon for sins and again to commit them. Persevere, therefore, in confession; be strongly confirmed in penance.

# ST MAXIMUS THE CONFESSOR
## (Maximus of Constantinople)

580?–662

Maximus, born about 580, belonged to the ancient Byzantine aristocracy. In 610, when barely thirty years old, he was private secretary to Emperor Heraclius. But this rapid success did not deter him from retiring a few years later to a monastery at Chrysopolis, from which he was forced to flee by the Persian invasions. The rest of his life is obscure. It is not even certain whether he ever received Holy Orders. He was in Rome in 649, and was the center of resistance to Monothelism. (The Monothelites believed that in the combined human and divine natures of Christ there was but a single will, half human, half divine.) The Monothelite emperor, Constans II, exiled Maximus first to Byzia, in Thrace, and finally, after his tongue and right hand had been cut off, to Colchis. He died on August 13, 662, in the fortress of Shemari.

## FROM The Centuries on Charity

c. 626

Who sincerely loves God also prays absolutely undistracted, and who prays absolutely undistracted also sincerely loves God. Now, a man who has his mind riveted to some earthly object does not pray without distractions; therefore whose spirit is riveted to some earthly object does not sincerely love God.

If the mind dwells long upon some sensible object, it is because a passion attaches to it: covetousness, or sadness, or anger, or resentment. And, in so far as it does not despise this object, it cannot free itself from this passion. Passions, which bring the spirit into subjection, bind it to material things and separate it from God by occupying it wholly with these objects. But if the love of God is victorious it frees a man from these bonds, and makes him not only despise sensible things but our temporal life itself. The effect of the commandments is to make simple the representation of objects. The effect of reading and of contemplation is to abstract the spirit from matter and from form. From this, undistracted prayer results. In order to deliver the spirit so perfectly from the passions that it can pray without distractions, the active way is not enough, unless it is followed by various spiritual contemplations.

Action, indeed, only frees the spirit from profligacy and from anger; contemplations remove also from forgetfulness and ignorance. Thus freed, a man can pray as he ought.

At the summit of pure prayer, two states can be distinguished, one for the active, one for the contemplative. The first is in the soul, the effect of the fear of God, and of good hope; and the second, of the fervor of divine love and of total purification. Indications of the first state: the spirit collects itself and abstracts itself from all thought of the world, and, in the thought that God is present, as He is, indeed, prays undistracted and untroubled. Indication of the second: the spirit, in the very upsurge of prayer, is ravished by the infinite light of God; it loses all consciousness of itself, or of any other being, except of Him who by charity works in it this illumination. Then too, drawn by the properties of God, it arrives at pure and penetrating ideas about Him.

To that he loves, a man attaches himself unreservedly, despising every obstacle, afraid only of losing it. Who loves God works at pure prayers and rejects every passion that is an obstacle to them.

Reject selfishness, mainspring of the passions, and, God helping you, you will have no trouble in rejecting the others: anger, grief, resentment, etc. But yield to the one and, in spite of yourself, you will be wounded by the others. By selfishness, I mean a passion whose object is the body.

Does the spirit begin to make progress in the love of God? The demon will try to drive it to blasphemy, suggesting to it thoughts it could not have found by itself, and which come only from the Devil, their father. If the latter acts so, it is because, jealous of God's friend, he wants him to despair when he is confronted with such thoughts, and not to dare take wing to God with his customary prayers. But the evil one gains not a single step thereby towards his goal: on the contrary, he confirms us the more, because, after attack and counterattack, we find our love for God more firm and more sincere.

The spirit, when it applies itself to visible objects, naturally apprehends them through the intermediary of the senses. The spirit is not of itself evil, nor is this natural perception, nor are the objects, nor are the senses: all are the work of God. Where, then, is the evil?

Passion is an unnatural movement of the soul that is the result of a love without reason, or of an irrational aversion for some concrete object. An unreasonable love of good food, for example, of a woman, of a fortune, of passing fame, or of any sensible object whatsoever, or of any other thing because of such an object itself; or aversion for any of these objects, or for some other because of them: these are passions.

Some men bridle their passions out of respect for public opinion, others from vanity, others from self-control; others have their passions removed for them by the judgments of God. The reward of self-control is interior freedom; that of faith, knowledge. Furthermore, from interior freedom comes discernment; and from knowledge, the love of God. . . .

Marching upright in the way of action, the spirit progresses toward prudence; in that of contemplation, toward knowledge. The first, indeed, leads the fighter to a discernment of good and evil; the second leads the initiate to grasp the reasons for corporal and incorporal beings. But to obtain the gift of divine science it is necessary to have passed through all the degrees just enumerated, to be in God; and then, as much as is possible for a human spirit, through the Holy Ghost, the spirit will penetrate to their depths the nature of His divine attributes. On the threshold of the knowledge of God, one does not seek to know His essence; no human being could arrive at it; no one knows it but God. But, if you can, ponder deeply His attributes: for example, His eternity, His infinity, His invisibility, His goodness, His wisdom, His power which creates, governs, and judges creatures. For he best merits the name of the theologian who seeks to discover, however little, the truth of his attributes. . . .

The man who joins action to knowledge is strong: by the first, he curbs covetousness and calms anger; by the second, he gives wings to his spirit and emigrates toward God. . . .

He who, having arrived at the peak of interior liberty, possesses perfect charity, makes no distinction between himself and others, slave and free, man and woman. The zone is passed where the passions reign; now he sees only in man his unique nature: he sees all men on the same level; for all, he feels the same.

The reward of virtue's hard struggle is interior freedom and knowledge. It is these that introduce into the kingdom of heaven, as the passions and ignorance lead to eternal punishment. But if anyone desires them for the sake of human glory and not for the sake of the good alone, let him listen to the Scripture: "Ye ask and receive not, because ye ask amiss." . . .

Many human actions, good in themselves, can cease to be so because of their motive. Fasting, vigils, prayer and the singing of psalms, almsgiving, hospitality, in themselves are good actions; performed in vanity, they cease to be so.

In all our actions, God considers the intention: whether we act for Him or for some other motive. . . .

The demon of pride has two tactics: either he suggests the attribution to oneself of good work, instead of attributing it to God, Master of all good, Help of all success. Or else, if the monk turn a deaf ear, the demon inspires him with contempt for his still imperfect brothers. And that temptation, though one is unaware of it, leads to a rejection of God's help, for to despise others for not having known how to do good, really adds up to attributing one's good actions to one's own efforts. A profound error, said the Master, "Without Me, ye can do nothing." Our weakness, indeed, even if we are oriented toward the good, prevents us from accomplishing good actions without the help of the Guide.

Who knows the feebleness of human nature has acquired an experience of the strength of God. With this, either he has done well or he has tried to do well, without ever despising anyone. For he knows well that the divine help which has delivered him from many and tenacious passions can just as well be loaned to others, when God wishes it—to those, above all, who are in the midst of battling for Him.

When the passions are dormant, pride awakens—now from unconscious causes, now from a sneak attack of the devils.

Almost all sins have pleasure for cause and are effaced by suffering and interior pains, voluntary or otherwise, by repentance, and by those punishments which, following its plans, Providence sends us.

When a trial comes upon you suddenly, do not react against him through whom it comes, but find out its object, and then you will find a way of profiting from it. From wherever it may have come, you would still have to empty the bitter cup of God's decrees!

Bad as you are, accept suffering without grumbling: it will humiliate you, and you will vomit your pride. . . .

The prudent man, seeing recovery in the divine decrees, receives with gratitude the misfortunes which they bring; they have, he tells himself, no other cause than his own sins. But the fool who knows nothing of the very wise providence of God, when he is punished for his sins, blames God or his neighbour for the ills he endures.

Certain remedies immobilize the passions, prevent them from getting into motion and becoming intensified; others weaken and reduce them. Thus, fasting, hard work, vigils, prevent covetousness from increasing; solitude, contemplation, prayer weaken it and lead to its destruction. It is the same way for anger: forbearance, the forgetting of insults, gentleness, immobilize it and prevent it from gaining force; charity, almsgiving, goodness, benevolence, reduce it little by little. . . .

In the man whose spirit is wholly turned toward God, even covetousness gives strength to his burning love for God, even the power of anger is completely turned toward divine charity. Because in the long run, participation in the divine illumination makes a man completely luminous himself, and, concentrating in himself the force of all his lower faculties, he turns it toward a burning, insatiable love of God, and a limitless charity, converting it wholly from terrestrial to divine.

To harbour no envy, no anger, no resentment against the offender is still not to have charity for him. It is possible, without any charity, to avoid rendering evil for evil, because it is the law; but to render, spontaneously, good for evil, such disposition to do good to those who hate us belongs to a perfect spiritual love.

Not to love someone is still not to hate him; just as not hating him is not loving. One can be towards him between the two: neither loving nor hating.

If your spirit occupies itself with pleasure, with material objects, and dallies with their representations, recognize that you prefer these objects to God: for where your treasure is, there will your heart be also.

A spirit united to God, in a habitual manner by prayer and charity, acquires wisdom, goodness, strength, benevolence, liberality, greatness of soul . . . in short, it bears in itself, so to speak, the attributes of God. But if it abandons these dispositions and orients itself towards material objects, if it seeks its pleasure, it will become a true animal, and even a savage animal, if to obtain these objects it enters upon disputes with others.

In the Gospel, the *world* is the complex of material and worldly objects, and the worldly are those whose spirit is taken up with such objects. . . .

The highest state of prayer, they say, is when the spirit leaves the body and the world, and, in the act of prayer, loses all matter and all form. To keep oneself without fail in this state, that is truly to pray without ceasing.

Just as, in dying, the body separates itself from all the good things of this life, so the spirit that dies at the summit of prayer also leaves all the representations it has of the world. For without dying of that death, it is not possible to find and live with God.

Night follows day; winter, summer; and, in this life or in the other, sorrows and sufferings follow vanity and sensuality. . . .

Beware of abusing your thought, or else you will inevitably come to abuse things also; one would never commit a sin in action had one not first sinned in thought.

The image of terrestrial man is made up of the fundamental vices, stupidity, cowardice, intemperance. The image of the celestial man is made up of the fundamental virtues, such as prudence, strength, temperance, justice. . . .

Three important stages can be distinguished in the moral development of the monk: not to commit any sin of action; not to parley with a passionate thought; to keep peace of soul when faced with impure representations or the memory of past insults which present themselves to his mind.

The poor man is he who has renounced all his belongings to keep nothing whatever on earth except his body, and who, having ceased to be attached even to this body, confides to God the government of his person. . . .

"Pasture" is active virtue. "The water of repose" is the knowledge of beings. "The shadow of death" is human life.

He is "with God" who learns to know the Blessed Trinity, Its works, Its providence, and who, in the depth of his soul, keeps his passions in complete calm.

The virtues free the spirit from the passions; spiritual contemplations, from simple representations; pure prayer finally establishes it near God.

At the moment of prayer, chase from your spirit even the simple representations of human realities and the images of all creatures. Or the imagination, being occupied with objects of less importance, will lose Him who is incomparably superior to them all.

Do you wish to gain knowledge while remaining modest, without being a slave to the passion of presumption? Then seek in creatures what escapes your knowledge. Thus you will learn a thousand details that escape you; astonished by your ignorance, you will abandon your pretension, and, knowing yourself, you will understand many deep and wonderful things. To believe that one knows is, indeed, an obstacle to the growth of knowledge. . . .

The spirit is perfect when, thanks to a real faith, it possesses in super-ignorance the super-knowledge of the supremely unknowable; when it discovers in creatures their universal reasons; when it has received from God the knowledge which comprehends everything in itself. All this, of course, to the extent possible for a man.

# THE MONKS

# PALLADIUS

368?–?431

Palladius, a Galatian monk, spent his life traveling from one monastery to another, and in 417 became bishop of Aspuna. His *Paradise of the Holy Fathers,* or *Lausiac History,* was written in 420, at the request of a certain Lausus.

## The Blessed Pachomius the Great

### FROM *The Paradise of the Holy Fathers*

St Pachomius (292?–?346), the founder of the first organized community of monks, was born about 292 of pagan parents. After his conversion he founded at Tabennisi a monastery to which he gave his Rule. St Jerome made a Latin translation of the Rule in 404.

In the country of Thebes, and in the district thereof which is called Tabenna, there was a certain blessed man whose name was Pachomius, and this man led a beautiful life of ascetic excellence, and he was crowned with the love of God and of man. Now therefore as this man was sitting in his cell, there appeared unto him an angel who said unto him, "Since thou hast completed thy discipleship it is unnecessary for thee to dwell here; but come, and go and gather together unto thyself those who are wandering, and be thou dwelling with them, and lay thou down for them such laws as I shall tell unto thee"; and the angel gave him a book wherein was written the following:

I. Let every man eat and drink whensoever he wisheth, and according to the strength of those who eat and drink impose work; and thou shalt restrain them neither from eating nor fasting. Furthermore, on those who are strong thou shalt impose severe labours; and upon those who are of inferior strength and upon those who fast thou shalt impose light labours.

II. And thou shalt make for them a cell, and they shall dwell together three by three.

III. And they shall partake of food all together in one chamber (or house).

IV. And they shall not take their sleep lying down, but thou shalt make for them seats so that when they are sitting down they shall be able to support their heads.

V. At night time they shall put on garments without sleeves, and their loins shall be girded up, and they shall be provided with skull-caps; and they shall partake of the Offering on the Sabbath and on the First Day of the Week, wearing skull-caps without any nap upon them, and each skull-cap shall have in the front thereof a cross worked in purple.

VI. And thou shalt establish the monks in four-and-twenty grades, and to each grade give a letter of the Greek alphabet from Âlâf to Tâw; every grade a letter.

And the blessed Pachomius performed and fulfilled these things according as he had been commanded by the angel; and when the head of the monastery asked him that was next to him concerning the affairs of the brethren, the man said unto him, "The voice of Alpha and the voice of Beta salute the head of the monastery." Thus the whole of that assembly of brethren had letters of the alphabet assigned to them, according to the designation of the four and twenty letters. To those who were upright and simple he assigned the letter Yodh [i.e., ι], and to those who were difficult and perverse he assigned the letter Ksi [i.e., ξ], and thus according to the dispositions and according to the habits and rules of life of the orders of monks did he assign letters unto them.

And he [i.e., the angel] commanded that "a monk who was a stranger and who had a different garb from theirs should not enter in with them to the table; the man who sought to be accepted as a monk in that monastery was obliged to labour there for three years, after which he was to receive the tonsure. When the monks were eating together they were to cover up their faces with their head-coverings, that they might not see each other eating, and might not hold converse together over the table, and might not gaze about from one side to the other." And he commanded that during each day they should repeat twelve sections of the Psalter, and during each evening twelve sections of the Psalter, and during each night twelve sections of the Psalter, and that when they came to eat they should repeat the Great Psalm.

And the blessed Pachomius said unto the angel, "The sections of the Psalter which thou hast appointed unto us for repetition are far too few"; and the angel said unto him, "The sections of the Psalter which I have appointed are indeed few, so that even the monks who are small [i.e., weak] may be able to fulfil the canons, and may not be distressed thereby. For unto the perfect no law whatsoever is laid down, because their mind is at all seasons occupied with God, but this law which I have laid down for those who have not a perfect mind is laid down for them, so that although they fulfil only such things as are prescribed by the canons they can acquire openness of face." Now very many nuns hold fast unto this law and canon.

And there were living in that mountain about seven thousand brethren, and in the monastery in which the blessed Pachomius himself lived there were living one thousand three hundred brethren; and besides these there were there also other monasteries, each containing about three hundred, or two hundred, or one hundred monks, who lived together; and they all toiled with their hands and lived thereby, and with whatsoever they possessed which was superfluous for them they provided the nunneries which were there. Each day those whose week of service it was rose up and attended to their work; and others attended to the cooking, and others set out the tables and laid upon them bread, and cheese, and vessels of vinegar and water. And there were some monks who went in to partake of food at the third hour of the day, and others at the sixth hour, and others at the ninth hour, and others in the evening, and others who ate once a day only; and there were some who ate only once a week; and according as each one of them knew the letter which had been laid upon him, so was his work. Some worked in the paradise [i.e., the orchard], and some in the gardens, and some in the blacksmith's shop, and some in the baker's shop, and some in the carpenter's shop, and some in the fuller's shop, and some wove baskets and mats of palm leaves, and one was a maker of nets, and one was a maker of sandals, and one was a scribe; now all these men as they were performing their work were repeating the Psalms and the Scriptures in order.

And there were there large numbers of women who were nuns, and who closely followed this rule of life, and they came from the other side of the river and beyond it, and there were also married women who came from the other side of the river close by; and whensoever any one of them died, the [other] women would bring her and lay her down on the bank of the river and go away. Then certain brethren would cross over in a boat and bring her over with the [singing of] psalms and with lighted candles, and with great ceremony and honour, and when they had brought her over they would lay her in their cemetery; without elder or deacon no man could go to that nunnery, and then only from one Sunday to the other [i.e., they could go only on Sundays]. . . .

# ST ATHANASIUS

298?–373

Athanasius, born of heathen parents in the city of Alexandria, was converted at an early age. In 318 he was deacon to Bishop Alexander, whom he accompanied to the Council of Nicaea in 325. On June 8, 328, Athanasius succeeded Alexander as bishop, and spent the rest of his life defending orthodoxy against the Arians. Five times exiled, he was deposed by the Synods of Arles and Milan. Emperor Valens allowed him to return in 366, and he died on May 2, 373. The creed that carries his name (see page 329) is a Latin compilation which probably originated in the fifth or sixth century. His "Life of St Anthony" is included in Palladius's *Paradise of the Holy Fathers* (see page 471).

## The Life of St Anthony

Marvellous care and the loving urging of your understanding for the monkish brethren who are in Egypt have moved me with solicitude to hope that by constant meditation on the following stories your mind may be drawn to perfection, so that you may not be repeating with your mouth[s] only the following triumphs, and others which are like unto them, but that also in your persons you may be preachers of the example of these lives and deeds. Now, your careful solicitude is seemly and is most acceptable, and in this respect you have become ministers of the Sublime Will, for it is right that this appearance should not depart from the mirror of your career, and that ye should know at once the craftiness of the enemy, that is to say, what form exactly it taketh, and what it actually is, and by what means it bringeth a monk to nought. And this thing hath been wrought at this time by God, for behold! monasteries which flourish like the flowers and sweet scents of the springtime have been scattered throughout the whole earth, and the sign of the solitary ascetics ruleth from one end thereof unto the other. It is then a beautiful thing for us to embrace and to lay hold upon this power of discernment which your mind hath conceived, and to be the ministers of the fervour of your love with joy and solicitude. For who could be negligent of this service and be blameless, inasmuch as those who have invited me to write the history of the triumphs of a righteous man are themselves righteous? And may the Giver of gifts (blessed be His honour!) Himself open the door of our entreaty, and may we draw into our net each one of the stories which we have been deputed by your love to write down, not for our own sake only, but for the sake of your most excellent entreaty, and for the sake of the courageous [thoughts] which are in you, so that we may fulfil your labour, and for the sake of the work of him who triumphed by these acts and deeds, in order that his triumphs may never die among his sons in our Lord; and finally for his name's sake, that in this history we may also magnify the glory of God and show forth how great is the might which He giveth unto those who fear Him.

Now we have been deputed through your affection to write down the triumphs of the blessed man Anthony, and to send by an envoy a history of them to you in writing which will show how it was that he began his discipleship, and what manner of life he led before this took place, and how he was living when he brought his days to a close, and whether all the words which have been spoken concerning him and have come to our hearing are true; and straightway with joy I have devoted myself to the fulfilment of your command. Now by merely writing a commemorative history of the blessed Anthony I also shall gain great benefit, for I am convinced, O my beloved, that by narrating these histories two things will be effected: we shall increase the renown of the man of God in honour and wonder, and we shall begin to instruct your minds step by step; for the acts of the blessed Anthony form a perfect example for the solitary ascetics. . . .

Now, by race the blessed Anthony was an Egyptian, and he was descended from a noble family, and was, indeed, an owner of slaves. His forefathers were believers, and from his earliest childhood he was brought up in the fear of our Lord; and when he was a child and was being reared among his own kinsfolk, he knew nothing of his father or of what went on among his own people. He was so silent in disposition, and his mind was so humble, that he did not even trouble his parents by asking them questions. He was exceedingly modest, and he was honest beyond measure. He was unable to read or write because he could not bear the rough behaviour of the boys in the school; his whole desire was to be even according to what is written about Jacob, "He was a simple man, and a dweller in tents." He clung closely to his parents, and when they came to church he would run before them in the flow of his affection; and he was not like an ordinary child, the course of whose customary attendance is broken by the amusements of childhood. He never neglected the observance of any of the seasons of the Church, and he neither neglected them in his childhood, nor held them lightly in his early manhood. And from the time when he was a child and knew how to distinguish between good and evil, his going to church was not a mere matter of custom, but was the result of discerning understanding. And, moreover, he did not wait for the members of his family to be admonishers unto him, because by his life and acts he became a teacher unto them. For they learned by the experience of his childhood that he did not live among them like an ordinary simple child, and they accepted the proof of the rectitude of his early manhood; he paid them honour after the manner of a full-grown man, and they regarded him as the master of the house.

Now when the time arrived and they brought their days to an end, and they departed from this world when he was about eighteen or twenty years old, he and one little sister were left behind, and it happened from sheer necessity that he had to rule the house and take care of his sister. And when as yet not six months had passed since the death of his parents, and when, according to his wont, he was continually in the church, it came to pass one day, when he was in the church, that a righteous idea entered his mind, and that he began to meditate within himself how the blessed Apostles forsook everything and followed after our Redeemer; and how the others who succeeded them and walked in their footsteps sold everything which they had possessed and laid the money which they received at the feet of the Apostles, that it might be spent upon the poor; and how great was the blessing of those who had in this wise obeyed the voice of our Redeemer. Now whilst he was meditating these and such-like things, the Lesson was being read, and when the Scriptures were ended the Gospel was read, and he heard the words of our Lord, who said unto the rich man, "If thou wishest to be perfect, go and sell everything which thou hast, and give to the poor, and take thy cross, and come after Me, and there shall be unto thee treasure in heaven." And the blessed Anthony received the word of the Gospel as a sign to himself, and he reflected that this reading had not taken place as a matter of chance, but in order that the righteous idea which had taken up its abode in him might be confirmed. And straightway he went out from the church, and departed and set in order his house and the possessions which he had inherited from his parents. Now he had three hundred fields, a great estate which produced abundant crops, and these he handed over to the people of his village, so that they might trouble neither himself nor his sister; but the remainder of his other possessions which were in the house he sold, and gathered in money not a little, which he distributed among the poor, but he laid by a little which was sufficient for his sister's wants . . .

Now unto his sister he spake words of love, and of truth, and of the fear of God, and he made her mind to be like his own; and he delivered her over to certain chaste nuns who were living there at that time. And when he had made an end of these things, he forthwith became a solitary monk, and he took no care for anything whatsoever except his soul, and he began to train himself in the habits of the strictest abstinence and self-denial. Now he dwelt alone in a house which was by the side of the village, for as yet there were no monasteries for ascetics in Egypt, and among the monks there was no man who had any knowledge of the inner desert; and everyone who wished to have a care for his soul used to seek out an habitation of this kind. Saint Anthony did not betake himself to the mountain at a great distance from the village, but only at a sufficient distance therefrom, so that he might be somewhat apart from the habitation of men.

And at that time there was in another village on their borders a certain blessed old man, who from his youth up had lived a life of solitary asceticism, and this man the blessed Anthony saw, and was wishful to emulate his fair deeds. First of all he also began to live by the side of the village, in places which were free from the feet of men, and whilst living in this abode his mind was rent with doubt about the fair works of the ascetic life and he gave his soul no rest, for he was constant in meditation about the truth. And he used to ponder within himself and say, "How did the righteous men of old live? With what manner of triumphs did they please God? And who can make me worthy of even a sight of these?" And as a result of this meditation which arose from love of the righteous men, he began to ask and inquire, "What was the condition of the righteous men? And who shall inform me concerning them?" And whilst asking questions that he might learn something about any of the righteous men who were in that place, in the fervour of his love he used to go forth strenuously to seek him; and he did not at first return to his own place, without first of all paying homage to the man of God. And he was like unto the wise bee which hovereth and resteth over plants of every kind which are filled with honey that it may fill its habitation with the goodness of the earth. In this manner he himself also received from the sight of each of the righteous men provision for the marvellous way; and this was his manner at the beginning of his ascetic career. And his thoughts were exceedingly well disciplined by him at the beginning of his life of righteousness, so that he might not in any wise be anxious about his family, or be fettered by the love of kinsfolk, or be held fast by the affairs of this temporary life; from all these he purged himself that he might be a pure offering unto God. Now he used also to labour with his hands, because he had heard, "If a man doth not work, he shall not eat"; with a very little of the wages of the work of his hands he used to provide himself with food, and the rest he spent upon the poor. And he prayed continually, for he had heard, "Pray, and let it not be tedious unto you"; and he was wont to listen to the reading of the Scriptures in such wise that not one word might fall to the ground, and henceforth he kept in his mind the remembrance of the commandments which he heard, and they became unto him even as the Scriptures . . .

Now Saint Anthony was the storehouse of fasting, and of prayer, and of ascetic labours, and of patient endurance, and of love, and of righteousness, which is the mother of them all, but towards those who were young monks like himself he was not envious, except in one matter only, that is to say, he would not be second to any of them in fair works. And he contrived in every possible manner not to give offence to the wicked man; on the contrary, he wished that those who were yoked together with him might be drawn to his opinion by his solicitude and by his graciousness, and that they might make progress in their career. And he toiled in his labours in such a manner that they were not only not envious of him, but they rejoiced in him and gave thanksgiving for him. Now by reason of these triumphs every man used to call him "Theophilus," which is, being interpreted, "God-loving," and all the righteous gave him this name; and some of them loved him like a brother, and some of them like a son.

And when the Enemy, the hater of the virtues and the lover of evil things, saw all this great perfection in the young man, he could not endure it, and he surrounded himself with his slaves, even as he is wont to do, and began to work on Anthony. At the beginning of his temptings of the saint he approached him with flattery, and cast into him anxiety as to his possessions, and solicitude and love for his sister, and for his family, and for his kinsfolk, and the love of money and lusts of various kinds, and the thought of the rest of the things of the life of this world, and finally of the hard and laborious life which he lived, and of the weakness of body which would come upon him with the lapse of time; and, in short, he stirred up in him the power of the thoughts so that by means of one or other of them he might be flattered, and might be made to possess shortcomings and be caught in the net through his instigation

Now when the Enemy saw that his craftiness in this matter was without profit, and that the more he brought temptation unto Saint Anthony, the more strenuous the saint was in protecting himself against him with the armour of righteousness, he attacked him by means of the vigour of early manhood which is bound up in the nature of our humanity. With the goadings of passion he used to trouble him by night, and in the daytime also he would vex him and pain him with the same to such an extent that even those who saw him knew from his appearance that he was waging war against the Adversary. But the more the Evil One brought unto him filthy and maddening thoughts, the more Saint Anthony took refuge in prayer and in abundant supplication, and amid them all he remained wholly chaste. And the Evil One was working upon him every shameful deed according to his wont, and at length he even appeared unto Saint Anthony in the form of a woman; and other things which resembled this he performed with ease, for such things are a subject for boasting to him.

But the blessed Anthony knelt down upon his knees on the ground, and prayed before Him who said, "Before thou criest unto Me, I will answer thee," and said, "O my Lord, this I entreat Thee: let not Thy love be blotted out from my mind, and behold, I am, by Thy grace, innocent before Thee." And again the Enemy multiplied in him the thoughts of lust, until Saint Anthony became as one who was being burned up, not through the Evil One, but through his own lusts; but he girded himself about with the threat of the thought of the Judgment, and of the torture of Gehenna, and of the worm which dieth not. And whilst meditating on the thoughts which could be directed against the Evil One, he prayed for thoughts which would be hostile to him. Thus, to the reproach and shame of the Enemy, these things could not be performed; for he who imagined that he could be God was made a mock of by a young man, and he who boasted over flesh and blood was vanquished by a man who was clothed with flesh . . .

And it came to pass that in the process of time his fame reached all the monks who were in Egypt, and all the other folk therein who did not lead the life of the ascetic and recluse, and men of distinction, and monks in Egypt began to come unto him in large numbers. The Egyptian monks came that they might copy the manner of his life and deeds, and the laity came that he might pray over them, and might heal certain of them of their sicknesses. One day, when a multitude of people had come there in a body to see him and they had besought him repeatedly to speak to them, and he had answered them never a word, they lifted the door out of its socket, and threw themselves down on their faces before him, and made supplication unto him and pacified him, and then each man among them stood up, and made known his request unto him. And having gone forth to them even like a man who goeth forth from the depths of the earth, they saw that his appearance was like unto that of an angel of light, and they marvelled why it was that his body had not been weakened by all his confinement, and why it was that his understanding had not become feeble, and why, on the contrary, his appearance, and his bodily stature, and his countenance were then as they had known them always to have been in the times which were past.

Now when he saw a large concourse of people he was not disturbed, and when they brought their petitions unto him, he was not moved to impatient anger, but he remained in a placid and thoughtful state, for the Living Word was unto him a guide. Among those who came unto him, there were many who were indeed very sorely afflicted, and our Lord healed them by the hand of the blessed man; and, moreover, God gave him such a measure of grace in his speech that every man was wholly gratified thereat, for those who were in affliction and distress were encouraged to endure thereby, those who were occupied with contention were quieted thereby, those who were afflicted sorely became long-suffering, the haughty were made humble thereby, and the arrogant were brought low thereby, in order that every man might learn the doctrine of righteousness. For he used to say, "That we should possess anything besides Christ is unnecessary, and we should not esteem anything of value besides the love of Christ, neither possessions nor kinsfolk, not even our soul itself. For if God did not spare His Son, but delivered Him up on account of our sins, how much the more is it right for us, having tasted and known Divine Grace, to give our souls not on His behalf, for such a thing is not required from us, but on behalf of our own lives!" By these words he used to persuade many to withdraw themselves from this world, and from the tribulation thereof, and to take refuge in a habitation of monks. . . .

Now when he saw that much people were gathered together to him, and that the trouble which men and women caused him increased, he became afraid either lest he should be unduly exalted in his mind by reason of the things which God had wrought by his hand, or lest others should esteem him beyond what was right and more than he deserved, and he determined to go away from that place and to enter the Thebaïd. Then he took a little bread and went and sat down by the side of the river, and waited until he should see a boat going to that district to which he was ready to go. And as he was pondering these things in his mind, suddenly a voice from heaven was heard by him, and it called him and said unto him, "Anthony, whither goest thou? Why art thou departing from this place?" Now he was not afraid of the voice which came to him, but like a man who was accustomed to do so he spake with it, and answered and said, "Because, O my Lord, the people will not permit me to enjoy a little silent contemplation; it is for this reason that I am wishing to go up to the Thebaïd, and especially do I desire it because the people are seeking at my hands that which is wholly beyond my powers."

Then again the voice came to him, saying, "If thou goest up it will not be to the Thebaïd only, and even if thou goest unto the Thebaïd as thou art thinking of doing, thou wilt have to endure toil greater than that which thou performest here; if, however, thou wishest to enjoy silent contemplation and to be at rest, get thee gone into the innermost desert." And Anthony the blessed answered and said, "O my Lord, who will show me the way to that difficult place? For neither do I myself know it, nor am I acquainted with or have knowledge of men who do." Now whilst he was standing up, there passed by certain Arabs who had made ready and set out on their way to go to that region, and the blessed man drew nigh unto them and entreated them to let him go with them, and they received him gladly because it was manifest that it was the commandment of God which was to be performed in this matter. And having travelled with them for three days and three nights, he arrived at a certain high mountain, and he found in the lower parts thereof water which was clear, and cool, and sweet, and a few palm-trees, for the land which was by the side of the mountain was a flat plain; and the place was pleasing to the blessed Anthony, and he loved it well, and he loved it especially because God had been his Governor and had led him to that spot. Therefore Anthony encamped there and dwelt in that place, and he was exalted there like a king in the courts of his palace. Now when those Arabs who had brought him to that place saw this, they wondered and marvelled, and they left with him a little bread which was found with them; and from that time forward whenever they were journeying into Egypt and returning therefrom, those Arabs, by reason of the wonderful things which they saw in the man, always passed by the place where he was, and also brought him bread. Now there were found in that region a few small birds which came from the palm-trees. . . .

And the blessed Anthony was alone in that desert, for the place wherein he had his habitation was waste and desolate; and his mind therefore dwelt the more upon exalted things, and it was content therewith. Now the brethren who used to go to visit him besought and entreated him to allow them to bring him there month by month a few garden herbs and olives and oil; and although he contended with them about it they overcame him with their entreaty, and compelled him to receive them, and they began to pay him visits, one at a time, according to their entreaty to him. And the blessed man was exceedingly old, and he was far advanced in years. And in that desert also he endured strife, not with flesh and blood, but with devils and with impure spirits, and we have learned this also from those who were going to visit him continually. They used to hear also there the sound of tumult and of outcry, and to see flashing spears, and at night time they would see the whole mountain filled with fiery phantoms, and those men were greatly terrified; but the blessed Anthony was trained in stratagems of war like a man of war, and he was prepared, and he stood up and rebuked the Evil One, who straightway ceased according to his wont; and he encouraged the brethren who were with him not to be terrified or to tremble at such visions as these. For, said he to them, "They are only empty phantoms which perish as if they had never existed at the Name of the Cross"; and wonder and admiration laid hold upon every man at the greatness and at the manner of the righteousness which was found in the blessed man.

He was not terrified at the devils, he was not wearied by the desert, and his soul had no fear of the wild beasts which were therein; but Satan suffered torture from all these things. And one day he came to the blessed man, who was singing the Psalms of David, and he gnashed his teeth upon him loudly; but the blessed Anthony ceased not to sing, and he was comforted and helped by the Grace of our Lord. One night whilst he was standing up and was watching in prayer, Satan gathered together all the wild beasts of the desert, and brought them against him, and they were so many in number that he can hardly have left one beast in its den; and as they compassed him about on every side, and with threatening looks were ready to leap upon him, he looked at them boldly and said unto them, "If ye have received power over me from the Lord, draw nigh, and delay not, for I am ready for you; but if ye have made ready and come at the command of Satan, get ye back to your places and tarry not, for I am a servant of Jesus the Conqueror." And when the blessed man had spoken these words, Satan was straightway driven away by the mention of the Name of Christ like a sparrow before a hawk.

And on another day, when he was weaving palm leaves—for such was his occupation, and he used to toil thereat so that he might not be a burden upon any man, and that he might make baskets to give as gifts to the people who were continually coming to visit him—suddenly he put up his hand over the door, and took hold of a rope of palm leaves to bring outside, and he leaped and stood up to look out. And as he looked out from the door, he saw an animal which had the following form: from its head to its side it was like a man, and its legs and feet were those of an ass. When the blessed Anthony saw it he only made the sign of the Cross over himself, and said, "How can anyone imagine that the Evil One is crafty? And how can anyone be agitated by him more than once or twice? Is it not within the scope of his cunning to know that these things are accounted by me merely empty phantasms? And now, if there be anything whatsoever in the power of him that sent thee, come hither and perform that which thou wast sent to do; but if Christ, who shall make an end of thee, and in whom I have my hope, liveth, and if He be true, let the destruction of thyself and of him that sent thee take place immediately." Thereupon, at the word of Christ, there fell upon the creature quaking and trembling, and he took to flight, and as he was going forth in haste and was running along terrified, he fell down and burst asunder at no great distance from Anthony's abode. Now the devils did all these things in order that they might drive the blessed man from the desert. . . .

It is meet that we should call to remembrance his death, and should relate how it took place, and in what manner he finished his life, for I know that ye will be exceedingly pleased therewith. Now he was accustomed to go out and visit the memorial stones of the brethren in the outer mountain. Now the matter of his death also was not hidden from him, and he went forth to visit them even when he knew that his departure was nigh. And after he had spoken to the brethren according to his wont, he said unto them, "This act which ye have just performed is the end of all acts; and I marvel at this world. Let each look for himself alone; for it is time for me to die." Now he was then about one hundred and five years old.

And when the brethren heard these things, they wept bitter tears, and each of them began to embrace and to kiss him, and the old man, like unto a man from a strange country who is about to depart thereto, with great gladness besought them to be quiet, and exhorted them, saying, "Be not ye in despair by reason of your tribulations, and be not lax in your lives and works, but even as men who are dying daily prepare ye for life, and, as I have already said, be watchful ever. Keep ye your souls from thoughts of iniquity, and strive ye for good gifts, and guard ye yourselves against associating yourselves with the Meletians, who are heretics, for ye know the cause of their schisms, and how cunning and bitter they are. And flee ye with all your might also from the doctrine of the Arians, for their wickedness is clearly manifest, and take good heed to avoid them, and be not like unto them for ever, neither if they be mighty in their help, nor if they be many in bearing burdens, for however often error raiseth up her nest it shall never be able to contend against the truth. Be ye, therefore, free from all intercourse with them, and thus shall ye be able to take good heed to the true doctrine of our fathers, and to the preaching of the truth of our Lord Jesus Christ, which ye have received from the Scriptures."

Now when the brethren heard concerning the matter of his departure, they entreated him that he would remain with them in order that his course might be ended there, but he would not accede to their request for many reasons which he had made known in his silence, but for the following reason especially. The Egyptians were in the habit of taking the dead bodies of righteous men, and especially those of the blessed martyrs, and of embalming them and placing them not in graves, but on biers in their houses, for they thought that by so doing they were doing them honour. And the blessed old man had on very many occasions besought the bishops to preach to the people and to command them to cease from this habit. And he himself used to entreat and exhort the multitudes who came to him, saying, "This work is neither seemly nor right. Moreover, the burial places of the early Fathers, and of the prophets, and of the Apostles are known unto this day, and even the grave of our Lord who rose on the third day." And by these words he showed forth that it was a transgression of a command for a man not to hide in the ground the bodies of those who were dead, even though they were righteous men. Therefore many hearkened and were persuaded not to do so, and they laid their dead in the ground, and buried them therein, and they thanked God because they had accepted his entreaty, which was seemly. And it was through fear of this thing that he would not grant the entreaty of the brethren and remain with them, but departed to his own place.

And after a few months he became sick, and he cried out to the brethren who were with him (now these were only two in number, and they had been with him from the time when his old age began, which was nearly fifteen years before, and they ministered unto him with the greatest care), and said unto them, even as it is written, "Behold, I go the way of my fathers, for I have felt within myself for some days past that I have been called by my Lord. Observe ye now how carefully ye can maintain this contest, and take good heed that ye lose not the long-suffering which ye have acquired, and that, like men who are just beginning the strife, ye increase it more and more and add to it day by day. Ye are well acquainted with the baneful devils and their craftiness, and ye know well this fact, that if ye please they shall be accounted as nothing by you. Be ye therefore not terrified by them, but always take refuge in Christ. And remember ye everything which ye have heard from me during all this time which ye have been with me, that ye have no intercourse whatsoever with the Arians, the heretics, for ye know how filthy they are in my sight because of their blasphemy of our Lord Jesus Christ. Take ye also heed then diligently at all times that ye cleave to the Spirit of Christ and agree therewith, and be ye, moreover, friends and associates of just men that they may receive you into their everlasting habitations as friends and men of whom they have good knowledge. Therefore meditate ye upon these things and keep them in your minds. And if your minds are set upon me, and ye remember me as a father, permit no man to take my body and carry it into Egypt, lest, according to the custom which they have, they embalm me and lay me up in their houses, for it was to avoid this that I came into this desert. And ye know that I have continually made exhortation concerning this thing and begged that it should not be done, and ye well know how much I have blamed those who observed this custom. Dig a grave then, and bury me therein, and hide my body under the earth, and let these my words be observed carefully by you, and tell ye no man where ye lay me; and there I shall be until the resurrection of the dead, when I shall receive again this body without corruption.

"And divide ye my garments into lots, and give one leather tunic to Bishop Athanasius, and the covering of this my bed which he gave unto me when it was new; but now it hath become old. And to Bishop Serapion do ye give the other leather coat; and this covering of my bed which is made of hair ye yourselves shall keep; now therefore, my children, abide in peace, for, behold, Anthony bringeth his journey to an end, and he goeth whither Divine Grace shall bring him." And when he had spoken these words, he straightway stretched out his legs, whereupon the brethren began to cry out to him, and to kiss him; now his face was full of joy unspeakable at the meeting of those who had come for him, and it resembled that of a man when he seeth a friend whom it rejoiceth him to meet. So the blessed man held his peace and died, and was gathered to his fathers. . . .

# ST BASIL

(See page 84.)

## FROM The Rule of St Basil

*Question.* Since your words have given us full assurance that the life [i. e., the cenobitic life] is dangerous with those who despise the commandments of the Lord, we wish accordingly to learn whether it is necessary that he who withdraws should remain alone or live with brothers of like mind who have placed before themselves the same goal of piety.

*Response.* I think that the life of several in the same place is much more profitable. First, because for bodily wants no one of us is sufficient for himself, but we need each other in providing what is necessary. For just as the foot has one ability, but is wanting another, and without the help of the other members it would find neither its own power strong nor sufficient of itself to continue, nor any supply for what it lacks, so it is in the case of the solitary life: what is of use to us and what is wanting we cannot provide for ourselves, for God, who created the world, has so ordered all things that we are dependent upon each other, as it is written that we may join ourselves to one another. But in addition to this, reverence to the love of Christ does not permit each one to have regard only to his own affairs, for love, he says, seeks not her own. The solitary life has only one goal, the service of its own interests. That clearly is opposed to the law of love, which the Apostle fulfilled, when he did not in his eyes seek his own advantage but the advantage of many, that they might be saved. Further, no one in solitude recognizes his own defects, since he has no one to correct him and in gentleness and mercy direct him on his way. For even if correction is from an enemy, it may often in the case of those who are well disposed rouse the desire for healing; but the healing of sin by him who sincerely loves is wisely accomplished. . . . Also the commands may be better fulfilled by a larger community, but not by one alone; for while this thing is being done another will be neglected; for example, by attendance upon the sick the reception of strangers is neglected; and in the bestowal and distribution of the necessities of life (especially when in these services much time is consumed) the care of the work is neglected, so that by this the greatest commandment and the one most helpful to salvation is neglected; neither the hungry are fed nor the naked clothed. Who would therefore value higher the idle, useless life than the fruitful which fulfils the commandments of God? . . .

Also in the preservation of the gifts bestowed by God the cenobitic life is preferable. . . . For him who falls into sin, the recovery of the right path is so much easier, for he is ashamed at the blame expressed by so many in common, so that it happens to him as it is written: It is enough that the same therefore be punished by many. . . . There are still other dangers which we say accompany the solitary life, the first and greatest is that of self-satisfaction. For he who has no one to test his work easily believes that he has completely fulfilled the commandments. . . .

For how shall he manifest his humility, when he has no one to whom he can show himself the inferior? How shall he manifest compassion, cut off from the society of many? How will he exercise himself in patience, if no one opposes his wishes? . . .

## Letter to Gregory of Nazianzus

. . . Your letter brought you before me, just as one recognizes a friend in his children. It is just like you, to tell me it was but little to describe the place, without mentioning my habits and method of life, if I wished to make you desirous to join me; it was worthy of a soul which counts all things of earth as nothing, compared with that blessedness which the promises reserve for us. Yet really I am ashamed to tell you how I pass night and day in this lonely nook.

Though I have left the city's haunts, as the source of innumerable ills, yet I have not yet learned to leave myself. I am like a man who, on account of seasickness, is angry with the size of his vessel as tossing overmuch, and leaves it for the pinnace or boat, and is seasick and miserable still, as carrying his delicacy of stomach along with him. So I have got no great good from this retirement. However, what follows is an account of what I proposed to do, with a view of tracking the footsteps of Him who is our guide unto salvation, and who has said: "If anyone will come after Me, let him deny himself, and take up his cross, and follow Me."

We must strive after a quiet mind. As well might the eye ascertain an object put before it, while it is wandering restless up and down, and sideways, without fixing a steady gaze upon it, as a mind, distracted by a thousand worldly cares, be able clearly to apprehend the truth. He who is not yet yoked in the bonds of matrimony is harassed by frenzied cravings, and rebellious impulses, and hopeless attachments; he who has found his mate is encompassed with his own tumult of cares: if he is childless, there is desire of children; has he children, anxiety about their education; attention to his wife, care of his house, oversight of his servants, misfortunes in trade, quarrels with his neighbours, lawsuits, the risks of the merchant, the toil of the farmer. Each day, as it comes, darkens the soul in its own way; and night after night takes up the day's anxieties, and cheats the mind with corresponding illusions. Now, one way of escaping all this is separation from the whole world; that is, not bodily separation, but the severance of the soul's sympathy with the body, and to live so without city, home, goods, society, possessions, means of life, business, engagements, human learning, that the heart may readily receive every impress of divine teaching. Preparation of heart is the unlearning the prejudices of evil converse. It is the smoothing the waxen tablet before attempting to write on it. Now, solitude is of the greatest use for this purpose, inasmuch as it stills our passions, and gives opportunity to cut them out of the soul. Let there, then, be a place such as ours, separate from intercourse with men, that the tenor of our exercises be not interrupted from without. Pious exercises nourish the soul with divine thoughts.

What state can be more blessed than to imitate on earth the choruses of angels?—to begin the day with prayer, and honour our Maker with hymns and songs?—as the day brightens, to betake ourselves, with prayer attending on it throughout, to our labours, and to sweeten our work with hymns, as if with salt? Soothing hymns compose the mind to a cheerful and calm state. Quiet, then, as I have said, is the first step in our sanctification; the tongue purified from the gossip of the world; the eyes unexcited by fair colour or comely shape; the ear not relaxing the tone of mind by voluptuous songs, nor by that especial mischief, the talk of light men and jesters. Thus the mind, saved from dissipation from without, nor, through the senses, thrown upon the world, falls back upon itself, and thereby ascends to the contemplation of God.

The study of inspired Scripture is the chief way of finding our duty; for in it we find both instruction about conduct, and the lives of blessed men delivered in writing, as some breathing images of godly living, for the imitation of their good works. Hence, in whatever respect each one feels himself deficient, devoting himself to this imitation, he finds, as from some dispensary, the due medicine for his ailment. He who is enamoured of chastity dwells upon the history of Joseph, and from him learns chaste actions, finding him not only able to master the assaults of pleasure, but virtuous by habit. He is taught endurance from Job. Or, should he be inquiring how to be at once meek and great-hearted, hearty against sin, meek towards men, he will find David noble in warlike exploits, meek and unruffled as regards revenge on enemies. Such, too, was Moses, rising up with great heart upon sinners against God, but with meek soul bearing their evil speaking against himself.

This, too, is a very principal point to attend to—knowledge how to converse; to interrogate without over-earnestness; to answer without desire of display; not to interrupt a profitable speaker, nor to desire ambitiously to put in a word of one's own; to be measured in speaking and hearing; not to be ashamed of receiving, or to be grudging in giving, information, nor to hide what one has learned from others, as depraved women practise with their children, but to refer it candidly to the true parent. The middle tone of voice is best, neither so low as to be inaudible, nor ill-bred from its high pitch. One should reflect first what one is going to say, and then give it utterance; be courteous when addressed, amiable in social intercourse; not aiming to be pleasant by facetiousness, but cultivating gentleness in kind admonitions. Harshness is ever to be put aside, even in censuring. . . .

---

## On the Devotional Exercises of His Community

375

Now as to the charge relating to the singing of psalms, whereby my calumniators specially scare the simple folk, my reply is this. The customs which now obtain are agreeable to those of all the churches of God. Among us the people go at night to the house of prayer and, in distress, affliction and continual tears, making confession to God, at last rise from their prayers and begin to sing psalms. And now, divided into two parts, they sing antiphonally with one another, thus at once confirming their study of the Gospels, and at the same time producing for themselves a heedful temper and a heart free from distraction. Afterwards they again commit the prelude of the strain to one, and the rest take it up; and so, after passing the night in various psalmody, praying at intervals as the day begins to dawn, all together, as with one voice and one heart, raise the psalm of confession to the Lord, each forming for himself his own expressions of penitence. If it is for these reasons that you renounce me, you will renounce the Egyptians; you will renounce both Libyans, Thebans, Palestinians, Arabians, Phœnicians, Syrians, the dwellers by the Euphrates; in a word, all those among whom vigils, prayers and common psalmody have been held in honour. . . .

# ST AUGUSTINE

(See page 127.)

## FROM Letter to the Nuns

. . . The rules which we lay down to be observed by you as persons settled in a monastery are these:

First of all, in order to fulfil the end for which you have been gathered into one community, dwell in the house with oneness of spirit, and let your hearts and minds be one in God. Also call not anything the property of anyone, but let all things be common property, and let distribution of food and raiment be made to each of you by the prioress—not equally to all, because you are not all equally strong, but to everyone according to her need. For you read in the Acts of the Apostles: "They had all things common: and distribution was made to every man according as he had need." Let those who had any worldly goods when they entered the monastery cheerfully desire that these become common property. Let those who had no worldly goods not ask within the monastery for luxuries which they could not have while they were outside of its walls; nevertheless, let the comforts which the infirmity of any of them may require be given to such, though their poverty before coming into the monastery may have been such that they could not have procured for themselves the bare necessaries of life; and let them in such case be careful not to reckon it the chief happiness of their present lot that they have found within the monastery food and raiment, such as was elsewhere beyond their reach.

Let them, moreover, not hold their heads high because they are associated on terms of equality with persons whom they durst not have approached in the outer world; but let them rather lift their hearts on high, and not seek after earthly possessions, lest, if the rich be made lowly but the poor puffed up with vanity in our monasteries, these institutions become useful only to the rich, and hurtful to the poor. On the other hand, however, let not those who seemed to hold some position in the world regard with contempt their sisters, who in coming into this sacred fellowship have left a condition of poverty; let them be careful to glory rather in the fellowship of their poor sisters, than in the rank of their wealthy parents. And let them not lift themselves up above the rest because of their having, perchance, contributed something from their own resources to the maintenance of the community, lest they find in their riches more occasion for pride, because they divide them with others in a monastery, than they might have found if they had spent them in their own enjoyment in the world. For every other kind of sin finds scope in evil works, so that by it they are done, but pride lurks even in good works, so that by it they are undone; and what avails it to lavish money on the poor, and become poor oneself, if the unhappy soul is rendered more proud by despising riches than it had been by possessing them? Live, then, all of you, in unanimity and concord, and in each other give honour to that God whose temples you have been made.

Be regular in prayers at the appointed hours and times. In the oratory let no one do anything else than the duty for which the place was made, and from which it has received its name; so that if any of you, having leisure, wish to pray at other hours than those appointed, they may not be hindered by others using the place for any other purpose. In the psalms and hymns used in your prayers to God, let that be pondered in the heart which is uttered by the voice; chant nothing but what you find prescribed to be chanted; whatever is not so prescribed is not to be chanted.

Keep the flesh under by fastings and by abstinence from meat and drink, so far as health allows. When anyone is not able to fast, let her not, unless she be ill, take any nourishment except at the customary hour of repast. From the time of your coming to table until you rise from it, listen without noise and wrangling to whatever may be in course read to you; let not your mouths alone be exercised in receiving food, let your ears be also occupied in receiving the word of God.

If those who are weak in consequence of their early training are treated somewhat differently in regard to food, this ought not to be vexatious or seem unjust to others whom a different training has made more robust. And let them not esteem these weaker ones more favoured than themselves, because they receive a fare somewhat less frugal than their own, but rather congratulate themselves on enjoying a vigour of constitution which the others do not possess. And if to those who have entered the monastery after a more delicate upbringing at home, there be given any food, clothing, couch, or covering which to others who are stronger, and in that respect more favourably circumstanced, is not given, the sisters to whom these indulgences are not given ought to consider how great a descent the others have made from their style of living in the world to that which they now have, although they may not have been able to come altogether down to the severe simplicity of others who have a more hardy constitution. And when those who were originally more wealthy see others receiving—not as mark of higher honour, but out of consideration for infirmity—more largely than they do themselves, they ought not to be disturbed by fear of any such detestable perversion of monastic discipline as this, that the poor are to be trained to luxury in a monastery in which the wealthy are, so far as they can bear it, trained to hardships. For, of course, as those who are ill must take less food, otherwise they would increase their disease, so after illness, those who are convalescent must, in order to their more rapid recovery, be so nursed—even though they may have come from the lowest poverty to the monastery—as if their recent illness had conferred on them the same claim for special treatment as their former style of living confers upon those who, before entering the monastery, were rich. So soon, however, as they regain their wonted health, let them return to their own happier mode of living, which, as involving fewer wants, is more suitable for those who are servants of God; and let not inclination detain them when they are strong in that amount of ease to which necessity had raised them when they were weak. Let those regard themselves as truly richer who are endowed with greater strength to bear hardships. For it is better to have fewer wants than to have larger resources.

Let your apparel be in no wise conspicuous; and aspire to please others by your behaviour rather than by your attire. Let your head-dresses not be so thin as to let the nets below them be seen. Let your hair be worn wholly covered, and let it neither be carelessly dishevelled nor too scrupulously arranged when you go beyond the monastery. When you go anywhere, walk together; when you come to the place to which you were going, stand together. In walking, in standing, in deportment, and in all your movements let nothing be done which might attract the improper desires of anyone, but rather let all be in keeping with your sacred character. Though a passing glance be directed towards any man, let your eyes look fixedly at none; for when you are walking you are not forbidden to see men, but you must neither let your desires go out to them, nor wish to be the objects of desire on their part. For it is not only by touch that a woman awakens in any man or cherishes towards him such desire, this may be done by inward feelings and by looks. And say not that you have chaste minds though you may have wanton eyes, for a wanton eye is the index of a wanton heart. And when wanton hearts exchange signals with each other in looks, though the tongue is silent, and are, by the force of sensual passion, pleased by the reciprocation of inflamed desire, their purity of character is gone, though their bodies are not defiled by any act of uncleanness. Nor let her who fixes her eyes upon one of the other sex, and takes pleasure in his eye being fixed on her, imagine that the act is not observed by others; she is seen assuredly by those by whom she supposes herself not to be remarked. But even though she should elude notice, and be seen by no human eye, what shall she do with that Witness above us from whom nothing can be concealed? Is He to be regarded as not seeing because His eye rests on all things with a long-suffering proportioned to His wisdom? Let every holy woman guard herself from desiring sinfully to please man by cherishing a fear of displeasing God; let her check the desire of sinfully looking upon man by remembering that God's eye is looking upon all things. For in this very matter we are exhorted to cherish fear of God by the words of Scripture: "He that looks with a fixed eye is an abomination to the Lord." When, therefore, you are together in the church, or in any other place where men also are present, guard your chastity by watching over one another, and God, who dwelleth in you, will thus guard you by means of yourselves.

And if you perceive in any one of your number this forwardness of eye, warn her at once, so that the evil which has begun may not go on, but be checked immediately. But if, after this admonition, you see her repeat the offence, or do the same thing on any other subsequent day, whoever may have had the opportunity of seeing this must now report her as one who has been wounded and requires to be healed, but not without pointing her out to another, and perhaps a third sister, so that she may be convicted by the testimony of two or three witnesses, and may be reprimanded with necessary severity. And do not think that in thus informing upon one another you are guilty of malevolence. For the truth rather is that you are not guiltless if by keeping silence you allow sisters to perish, whom you may correct by giving information of their faults. For if your sister had a wound on her person which she wished to conceal through fear of the surgeon's lance, would it not be cruel if you kept silence about it, and true compassion if you made it known? How much more, then, are you bound to make known her sin, that she may not suffer more fatally from a neglected spiritual wound. But before she is pointed out to others as witnesses by whom she may be convicted if she deny the charge, the offender ought to be brought before the prioress, if after admonition she has refused to be corrected, so that by her being in this way more privately rebuked, the fault which she has committed may not become known to all the others. If, however, she then deny the charge, then others must be employed to observe her conduct after the denial, so that now before the whole sisterhood she may not be accused by one witness, but convicted by two or three. When convicted of the fault, it is her duty to submit to the corrective discipline which may be appointed by the prioress or the prior. If she refuses to submit to this, and does not go away from you of her own accord, let her be expelled from your society. For this is not done cruelly but mercifully, to protect very many from perishing through infection of the plague with which one has been stricken. Moreover, what I have now said in regard to abstaining from wanton looks should be carefully observed, with due love for the persons and hatred of the sin, in observing, forbidding, reporting, proving, and punishing of all other faults. But if anyone among you has gone on into so great sin as to receive secretly from any man letters or gifts of any description, let her be pardoned and prayed for if she confess this of her own accord. If, however, she is found out and is convicted of such conduct, let her be more severely punished, according to the sentence of the prioress, or of the prior, or even of the bishop.

Keep your clothes in one place, under the care of one or two, or as many as may be required to shake them so as to keep them from being injured by moths; and as your food is supplied from one storeroom, let your clothes be provided from one wardrobe. And whatever may be brought out to you as wearing apparel suitable for the season, regard it, if possible, as a matter of no importance whether each of you receives the very same article of clothing which she had formerly laid aside, or one receive what another formerly wore, provided only that what is necessary be denied to no one. But if contentions and murmurings are occasioned among you by this, and some one of you complains that she has received some article of dress inferior to that which she formerly wore, and thinks it beneath her to be so clothed as her own sister was, by this prove your own selves, and judge how far deficient you must be in the inner holy dress of the heart, when you quarrel with each other about the clothing of the body. Nevertheless, if your infirmity is indulged by the concession that you are to receive again the identical article which you had laid aside, let whatever you put past be, nevertheless, kept in one place, and in charge of the ordinary keepers of the wardrobe; it being, of course, understood that no one is to work in making any article for clothing or for the couch, or any girdle, veil, or head-dress, for her own private comfort, but that all your works be done for the common good of all, with greater zeal and more cheerful perseverance than if you were each working for your individual interest. For the love concerning which it is written, "Charity seeketh not her own," is to be understood as that which prefers the common good to personal advantage, not personal advantage to the common good. Therefore the more fully that you give to the common good a preference above your personal and private interests, the more fully will you be sensible of progress in securing that, in regard to all those things which supply wants destined soon to pass away, the charity which abides may hold a conspicuous and influential place. An obvious corollary from these rules is, that when persons of either sex bring to their own daughters in the monastery, or to inmates belonging to them by any other relationship, presents of clothing or of other articles which are to be regarded as necessary, such gifts are not to be received privately, but must be under the control of the prioress, that, being added to the common stock, they may be placed at the service of any inmate to whom they may be necessary. If anyone conceal any gift bestowed on her, let sentence be passed on her as guilty of theft.

Let your clothes be washed, whether by yourselves or by washerwomen, at such intervals as are approved by the prioress, lest the indulgence of undue solicitude about spotless raiment produce inward stains upon your souls. Let the washing of the body and the use of baths be not constant, but at the usual interval assigned to it, i.e., once a month. In the case, however, of illness rendering necessary the washing of the person, let it not be unduly delayed; let it be done on the physician's recommendation without complaint; and even though the patient be reluctant, she must do at the order of the prioress what health demands. If, however, a patient desires the bath, and it happen to be not for her good, her desire must not be yielded to, for sometimes it is supposed to be beneficial because it gives pleasure, although in reality it may be doing harm. Finally, if a handmaid of God suffers from any hidden pain of body, let her statement as to her suffering be believed without hesitation; but if there be any uncertainty whether that which she finds agreeable be really of use in curing her pain, let the physician be consulted. To the baths, or to any place whither it may be necessary to go, let no fewer than three go at any time. Moreover, the sister requiring to go anywhere is not to go with those whom she may choose herself, but with those whom the prioress may order. The care of the sick, and of those who require attention as convalescents, and of those who, without any feverish symptoms, are labouring under debility, ought to be committed to some one of your number, who shall procure for them from the storeroom what she shall see to be necessary for each. Moreover, let those who have charge, whether in the storeroom, or in the wardrobe, or in the library, render service to their sisters without murmuring. Let manuscripts be applied for at a fixed hour every day, and let none who ask them at other hours receive them. But at whatever time clothes and shoes may be required by one in need of these, let not those in charge of this department delay supplying the want.

Quarrels should be unknown among you, or at least, if they arise, they should as quickly as possible be ended, lest anger grow into hatred, and convert "a mote into a beam," and make the soul chargeable with murder. For the saying of Scripture: "He that hateth his brother is a murderer," does not concern men only, but women also are bound by this law through its being enjoined on the other sex, which was prior in the order of creation. Let her, whoever she be, that shall have injured another by taunt or abusive language, or false accusation, remember to remedy the wrong by apology as promptly as possible, and let her who was injured grant forgiveness without further disputation. If the injury has been mutual, the duty of both parties will be mutual forgiveness, because of your prayers, which, as they are more frequent, ought to be all the more sacred in your esteem. But the sister who is prompt in asking another whom she confesses that she has wronged to grant her forgiveness is, though she may be more frequently betrayed by a hasty temper, better than another who, though less irascible, is with more difficulty persuaded to ask forgiveness. Let not her who refuses to forgive her sister expect to receive answers to prayer: as for any sister who never will ask forgiveness, or does not do it from the heart, it is no advantage to such an one to be in a monastery, even though, perchance, she may not be expelled. Wherefore abstain from hard words; but if they have escaped your lips, be not slow to bring words of healing from the same lips by which the wounds were inflicted. When, however, the necessity of discipline compels you to use hard words in restraining the younger inmates, even though you feel that in these you have gone too far, it is not imperative on you to ask their forgiveness, lest while undue humility is observed by you towards those who ought to be subject to you, the authority necessary for governing them be impaired; but pardon must nevertheless be sought from the Lord of all, who knows with what goodwill you love even those whom you reprove it may be with undue severity. The love which you bear to each other must be not carnal, but spiritual: for those things which are practised by immodest women in shameful frolic and sporting with one another ought not even to be done by those of your sex who are married, or are intending to marry, and much more ought not to be done by widows or chaste virgins dedicated to be handmaids of Christ by a holy vow.

Obey the prioress as a mother, giving her all due honour, that God may not be offended by your forgetting what you owe to her: still more is it incumbent on you to obey the presbyter who has charge of you all. To the prioress most specially belongs the responsibility of seeing that all these rules be observed, and that if any rule has been neglected, the offence be not passed over, but carefully corrected and punished; it being, of course, open to her to refer to the presbyter any matter that goes beyond her province or power. But let her count herself happy not in exercising the power which rules, but in practising the love which serves. In honour in the sight of men let her be raised above you, but in fear in the sight of God let her be as it were beneath your feet. Let her show herself before all a "pattern of good works." Let her "warn the unruly, comfort the feeble-minded, support the weak, be patient toward all." Let her cheerfully observe and cautiously impose rules. And, though both are necessary, let her be more anxious to be loved than to be feared by you; always reflecting that for you she must give account to God. For this reason yield obedience to her out of compassion not for yourselves only but also for her, because, as she occupies a higher position among you, her danger is proportionately greater than your own.

The Lord grant that you may yield loving submission to all these rules, as persons enamoured of spiritual beauty, and diffusing a sweet savour of Christ by means of a good conversation, not as bondwomen under the law, but as established in freedom under grace.

That you may, however, examine yourselves by this treatise as by a mirror, and may not through forgetfulness neglect anything, let it be read over by you once a week; and in so far as you find yourselves practising the things written here, give thanks for this to God, the Giver of all good; in so far, however, as any of you finds herself to be in some particular defective, let her lament the past and be on her guard in the time to come, praying both that her debt may be forgiven, and that she may not be led into temptation. . . .

## FROM The Confessions

. . . Upon a certain day . . . there came to the house to see Alypius and me, Pontitianus, a countryman of ours, in so far as he was an African, who held high office in the Emperor's court. What he wanted with us I know not. We sat down to talk together, and upon the table before us, used for games, he noticed by chance a book; he took it up, opened it, and, contrary to his expectations, found it to be the Apostle Paul, for he imagined it to be one of those books the teaching of which was wearing me out. At this he looked up at me smilingly, and expressed his delight and wonder that he so unexpectedly found this book, and this only, before my eyes. For he was both a Christian and baptized, and in constant and daily prayers he often prostrated himself before Thee our God in the church. When, then, I had told him that I bestowed much pains upon these writings, a conversation ensued on his speaking of Anthony, the Egyptian monk, whose name was in high repute among Thy servants, though up to that time unfamiliar to us. When he came to know this he lingered on that topic, imparting to us who were ignorant a knowledge of this man so eminent, and marvelling at our ignorance. But we were amazed, hearing Thy wonderful works most fully manifested in times so recent, and almost in our own, wrought in the true faith and the Catholic Church. We all wondered—we that they were so great, and he that we had never heard of them.

From this his conversation turned to the companies in the monasteries, and their manners so fragrant unto Thee, and of the fruitful deserts of the wilderness, of which we knew nothing. And there was a monastery at Milan full of good brethren, without the walls of the city, under the care of Ambrose, and we were ignorant of it. He went on with his relation, and we listened intently and in silence. He then related to us how on a certain afternoon, at Treves, when the Emperor was taken up with seeing the Circensian games, he and three others, his comrades, went out for a walk in the gardens close to the city walls, and there, as they chanced to walk two and two, one strolled away with him, while the other two went by themselves; and these in their ramblings came upon a certain cottage where dwelt some of Thy servants, "poor in spirit," of whom "is the kingdom of heaven," and they found there a book in which was written the life of Anthony. This one of them began to read, marvel at, and be inflamed by it; and in the reading to meditate on embracing such a life, and giving up his worldly employments to serve Thee. . . . Then Pontitianus, and he that had walked with him through other parts of the garden, came in search of them to the same place, and, having found them, advised them to return as the day had declined. . . . But the other two, setting their affections upon heavenly things, remained in the cottage. And both of them had affianced brides who also, when they heard of this, dedicated their virginity to God. . . .

# SULPICIUS SEVERUS

(See page 381.)

## FROM The First Dialogue

Gallus and I had met together. He was a man very dear to me, both because of Martin's memory—for he was one of his disciples—and because of his own good qualities. We were joined by my friend Postumianus, who had returned from the Orient to see me. (He had left his own country and gone there three years before.) I embraced my loving friend and kissed his knees and his feet. Together, with tears of joy in our eyes, we walked up and down a few times, almost carried away by delight. Then we spread haircloth on the ground and sat down.

Postumianus was the first to speak. He looked at me and said: "When I was in the remoter parts of Egypt, I decided to journey up to the sea. I found a merchant vessel there getting ready to set sail for Narbonne, laden with cargo. That night I seemed to see you in my sleep. You had grasped me with your hand and were forcing me to embark on that ship. When dawn dispelled the darkness, I rose from the place where I had slept. I reflected on my dream and was suddenly seized with such a longing for you that I embarked on the ship without delay. On the thirtieth day I reached Marseilles and have arrived here after a further trip of ten days. Such was the propitious journey which favoured the loving desire of my heart. Please, then, put everything aside, and let me have you to embrace and enjoy. For it was on your account that I sailed over so many seas and travelled so far on land."

"Even when you were staying in Egypt," I said, "I was always and wholly with you in mind and spirit. As I gave my thought to you day and night, your love then quite possessed me, so do not suppose that now I shall be absent from you for an instant. As I look at you, I shall hang on your lips, I shall listen to you, I shall talk with you. Absolutely no one will be admitted to the private retreat with which this isolated cell provides us. I suppose you will not mind if my friend here, Gallus, is present. As you see, he is as drunk with joy at your arrival as I am."

"Excellent," said Postumianus. "Your friend Gallus will remain in our company. Even if I do not know him well, the fact that he is very dear to you necessarily makes him dear to me, especially since he is a product of Martin's training. I am not at all averse to chatting with you, as you ask, at any length you please. The very reason why I came"—and here he put both his arms about me—"was to devote myself to the wishes of my friend Sulpicius, even if it meant that I should have to talk a lot."

"You surely have proved," I said, "how far loving affection will go. For my sake you have travelled here over so many seas and so much land, voyaging almost from the very rising of the sun to the place of its setting. We are all by ourselves here, with nothing to do, and we ought to be quite free to listen to you talk. So, please give us the full story of your travels. Tell us how the faith of Christ flourishes in the Orient, what peace reigns among the faithful, how monks are established there, what signs and wonders Christ works there among His servants. Here, in these parts, surely, given what we have to live through, we find life itself distasteful. So, we should be very glad to have you tell us whether in the desert at least one can live as a Christian."

"I shall do what I see you want," said Postumianus. "But, first, may I please hear from you whether all those bishops I left here are still such as I knew them before I went away."

"Do not ask about those things," I said. "Either you know them, I suppose, as I do, or, if you do not, it is better not to learn them. But there is one thing I cannot keep back. Those you ask about have not become any better than when you knew them. Not only that: the one who once loved me, in whom I would find relief from the attacks of the others, has been more unkind to me than he should have. But I shall not say anything harsh about him. I cultivated his friendship and I still loved him when he was thought to be my enemy. As I think about this in private, I experience a great grief that I have been all but deprived of the friendship of a wise and religious man. But this subject is full of sorrow. Let us leave it and listen to the story you just now promised us."

"Agreed," said Postumianus. When he had spoken, we all kept quiet for a little while. Then he moved the haircloth mat he was sitting on closer to me and began in this way.

"It was three years ago, Sulpicius, that I bade you farewell and went away. We weighed anchor at Narbonne and on the fifth day entered an African harbour. God had willed that the crossing be successful. I decided to go to Carthage, there to visit the places made holy by the saints, and, most of all, to pray at the tomb of the martyr Cyprian. On the fifteenth day we returned to the harbour and put to sea, making for Alexandria. With the south wind opposing us, we were almost driven into the Syrtis. The sailors foresaw the danger and took care to anchor the ship.

"The continent lay before our eyes. We put out in little boats and landed. When we found no trace anywhere of human habitation, I went on farther to make a more careful investigation of the region. Some three miles from the shore, I spied a hut in the middle of the sand. Its roof, shaped like those which Sallust says resemble the hulls of ships, touched the earth and was built of quite strong planks. This was not because of any fear of rain—people did not even so much as speak of any precipitation in those parts—but rather of the winds. These blow with such violence that the least breeze, setting in even when the sky is quite clear, is of greater consequence there than a shipwreck at sea. Neither grass nor crops grow there. There is no firmness to the soil, since the dry sands yield to every motion of the winds. There are occasional promontories, however, turned away from the sea, which resist the winds. Here, the soil is somewhat firmer and can produce occasional rough herbs. Such are quite useful for nourishing sheep. The inhabitants live on milk. Those who are more skilful—or, so to speak, richer—have barley-bread, for barley is the only crop there. The soil causes such quick growth that it usually escapes destruction by the ravaging winds. It is reported that it matures on the thirtieth day after sowing. The only reason the people have for staying there is that they are all exempt from tribute.

These are, in fact, the extreme parts of Cyrenaica, touching on the desert which lies between Egypt and Africa. It was through this desert that Cato once led his army, fleeing from Caesar.

"So I made for the hut I had seen from a distance. I there found an old man, dressed in skins and working a handmill. After our greetings, he gave us a kindly reception. We explained that we had been cast upon that shore and were prevented by the calm from being able at once to continue our course. Following the bent of human nature, we continued, we had landed in the hope of learning about the geography of the place and the manners of the inhabitants. We were, moreover, Christians, and especially eager to know whether there were any Christians in those lonely parts. Then, with tears of joy in his eyes, he cast himself at our knees. He kissed us again and again and invited us to pray. Then he spread his sheepskins on the ground and had us recline. He placed before us a truly sumptuous meal—half a loaf of barley-bread. We were four and he made a fifth. He added a little bunch of herbs. Its name has escaped me: it was similar to mint, exuberant in leaf, and had a taste like honey. We were delighted with its very sweet and pleasant taste and had our fill."

At this I smiled and turned to my friend Gallus: "What do you say, Gallus? Would you be happy lunching on a bunch of herbs and half a loaf of bread, with five men eating?"

Gallus, being very shy by nature, took my teasing with a bit of a blush. "You are true to form, Sulpicius," he said. "Whenever the occasion arises, you never fail to rail at our good appetites. But it is an inhuman thing you do, to force us who are Gauls to live like angels. Still, my interest in eating makes me believe that the angels also eat. As for that half-loaf of barley-bread, I should be afraid to touch it even alone. Let it serve to satisfy that Cyrenian, whose hunger comes by necessity or else by nature. Or again, let it go to those travellers: they had lost their appetites, I suppose, after being tossed about on the sea. But we here are far from the sea and, as I have said to you, we are Gauls. But, enough of that. Let Postumianus conclude the story about his Cyrenian."

"Very well," said Postumianus. "I shall be careful from now on to avoid praising anyone's abstinence. I do not wish any such strenuous example to offend our Gallic friends. To be sure, I had intended to speak of the dinner that Cyrenian offered us and of the banquets which followed, for it was seven days that we were with him. But I must refrain, so that Gallus will not think he is being teased. Well, the following day some of the inhabitants began to stream in to see us. We learned that our host was a priest, a fact he had been completely successful in hiding from us. Later, we went with him to the church, some two miles away and hidden from our view by an intervening mountain. It was constructed from the interlacing of rough branches, hardly surpassing in splendour the dwelling of our host, where you could not stand unless you bent over. By our inquiry into the customs of the inhabitants we learned one notable thing: they neither buy nor sell. What cheating or theft is they have no idea. And, as for gold and silver, which men value highest, they neither have them nor wish to. When I offered our priest ten pieces of silver, he recoiled in horror, declaring in his profound wisdom that with gold one does not build up the Church but, rather, destroys it. We presented him with various articles of clothing, which he kindly accepted. . . .

"So I left, and made for the town of Bethlehem. This lies six miles from Jerusalem and is separated from Alexandria by a journey of sixteen stages. The Church there is governed by the priest Jerome; it is a parish of the bishop who has his seat at Jerusalem. I had already become acquainted with Jerome on my earlier journey, and he had easily secured my promise not to let anything stand in the way of my revisiting him. Aside from the merit of his faith and the quality of his virtues, he has such a fine training in letters, not only Greek and Latin, but Hebrew as well, that there is no science in which anyone dares to challenge him. I should be surprised if he is not also known to you through the many books which he has written and which are read throughout the world."

"With us," said Gallus, "he is well known; indeed, too well known. Five years ago I read a book of his in which he violently maltreats and reviles our whole class of monks. In consequence, it sometimes happens that our Belgian friend gets very angry with him because he said that we stuff ourselves to the point of vomiting. For my part, I excuse him, believing that it was about the monks of the Orient rather than those of the West he was talking. For the Greeks, heavy eating is gluttony; for the Gauls, it is natural appetite."

"That defence of your race, Gallus," said I, "was in the true style of the scholar. But tell me: that book of Jerome's, it was not only that one vice that it condemned in the monks?"

"By no means," he said. "There was absolutely nothing he failed to attack, tear apart, and expose. His principal reproach was against avarice and, equally, against vanity. He had much to say about pride and not a little about superstition. To be quite frank, I thought he depicted the vices of a great many people.

"Again, when he dealt with the intimacies of virgins with monks and even with clerics, he spoke with truth and great power. That is why we hear that he is not loved by certain persons, whom I decline to name. Our Belgian gets angry because we were reprimanded for heavy eating. Similarly, those persons, it is said, are enraged when in the little book in question they read this:

" 'The virgin disdains her own brother, who is celibate, and for a brother seeks out a stranger.' "

"You go too far, Gallus," said I. "Be careful that someone who recognizes this does not hear you; he will put you with Jerome and begin to dislike you. Because you are a scholar, it will not be inappropriate for me to quote as a warning to you that verse of the comic writer: 'Compliance begets friends; truth, hatred.' But, Postumianus, continue as you began and resume your narrative of the Orient."

"As I had intended to state," he said, "I spent six months with Jerome. His continuous, unrelenting warfare against evil men has aroused them to hostility against him. He is hated by the heretics because he never stops assailing them. He is hated by the clerics because he censures their vicious mode of life. On the other hand, he has the admiration and affection of all good men. Those who think he is a heretic are mad. In all sincerity I assure you: his learning is Catholic, his doctrine is sound. He is always fully absorbed in reading and in books. Day and night he takes no rest. He is continually reading or writing something. Had my mind not been made up and my vow given to God to visit the desert as I had already planned, I should have been unwilling to leave the side of this great man for as much as an instant.

"I handed over and committed to him all my baggage and all my attendants. The latter had followed me against my wishes and their presence hampered me. As if a heavy burden had been lifted from my back, I was quite free. I returned to Alexandria and visited the brothers there. I then set off for the upper Thebaid, that is, the outer reaches of Egypt. There, in the broad-spreading desert wildernesses, a vast number of monks were said to live. It would take me a long time if I wished to relate all the things I saw. I shall deal briefly with only a few.

"Not far from the desert, on the banks of the Nile, there are many monasteries. The monks live together, most commonly in groups of a hundred. The chief point in their polity is to live under the rule of an abbot, to do nothing by their own will, to depend in everything on his command and authority. Some among them, determined to achieve greater perfection, move to the desert to live a life of solitude, but they do not leave without the abbot's permission. For all the monks the chief virtue is to obey the order of another. When they get to the desert, the abbot arranges for bread or some other food to be supplied.

"In the days immediately after my arrival in that region, the following incident occurred. One of the brothers had recently withdrawn to the desert and set up his dwelling not more than six miles from the monastery. The abbot had sent bread to him by two boys, the older fifteen years of age, the younger twelve. On their way back, they encountered a serpent of extraordinary size. The encounter brought them no alarm. When the serpent was in front of their feet, as if under a spell, it lowered its dark-blue neck to the ground. The younger of the boys took it in his hand, wrapped it in his mantle, and carried it off. He returned to the monastery like a victor to meet the brothers. When all were looking on, he opened his mantle and put down the captive beast, not without boastful pride. The brothers extolled the faith and miraculous power of the boys. But the abbot, with his deeper wisdom, was afraid that in the weakness of their youth they might become haughty. He beat them both with rods, reproving them for having revealed the deed the Lord had done through them. What had happened did not come from their faith, but from the divine power. They should learn to serve God in humility rather than pride themselves on signs and wonders; it was better to be conscious of one's weakness than to draw vainglory from miracles.

"The monk who had withdrawn heard all this: that the boys had been put in peril by encountering a serpent, and that, further, after their victory over the serpent, they had been soundly whipped. He pleaded with the abbot that from then on no bread or any food at all should be sent to him. Eight days had passed since the man of Christ had cut himself off, at the risk of dying through hunger. His limbs were dried up through fasting, but his mind was directed to heaven and could not tire. His body was faint from lack of nourishment, but his faith stood firm.

"Meanwhile, the abbot had been advised by the Spirit to visit his disciple. In his loving care he was eager to know what life-giving substance was nourishing the man of faith who had declined to have any fellow-man supply him with bread. So he set off himself to find him. The hermit saw from a distance the old man coming. He ran to meet him, gave thanks, and brought him to his cell. When the two entered together, they saw hanging from a door post a basket made of palm branches and filled with warm bread. They first sensed the odour—the odour of warm bread; then, from touching it, they received the impression that it had been taken from the oven only a little while before. Still, the loaf they saw was not of the Egyptian shape. In amazement, they both recognized a gift from heaven. The hermit declared the gift had been made for the abbot's arrival, while the abbot ascribed it rather to the faith and virtue of the hermit. And so, together, in great gladness, they broke the heavenly bread. When the old man returned to the monastery, he reported the incident to the brothers. They all experienced such a great longing that each tried to outstrip the other in hastening to the desert and its sacred solitudes. They said they would be unhappy if they stayed any longer in a large community, where they had to tolerate relations with other men.

"I had now come into the first stretches of the desert, about twelve miles from the Nile. As a guide, I had one of the brothers who had a good knowledge of the region. We arrived at the dwelling of an old man who lived at the foot of a mountain. Here we found something that is very rare in those parts, a well. The old man owned an ox, whose work consisted entirely in turning a wheel for drawing water. The garden there was full of vegetables, contrary to what is usually the case in the desert. There, everything is parched, burned by the heat of the sun. Nowhere can the least root of any plant draw nourishment. That holy man owned his crop to the joint labour of himself and the ox and to his own diligence. What gave fertility to the sands was the repeated irrigation. As we saw, this caused the vegetables in that garden to be remarkably vigorous and fruitful. These were what the ox, along with his master, lived on, and from this same abundant supply the holy man gave us dinner. I saw there something you Gauls will perhaps not believe: the pot was filled with the vegetables that were being prepared for dinner and was boiling without any fire. The sun's heat is so great that there is no cook who would not find it sufficient even for preparing Gallic specialties.

"After dinner, when evening was coming on, our host invited us to go and see a palm tree, whose fruit he would eat from time to time. It was about two miles away. In the desert, palms are the only trees, and these are rare. Was it the industry of antiquity which provided them, or do they come about from the force of the sun? I do not know. Perhaps God foresaw that the desert was one day to be inhabited by His saints and provided these trees in advance for His servants. Of the people who have settled in those solitudes where there are no other plants, the greater part feed themselves on palm fruit.

"When we came to the tree to which our kind host was leading us, we met a lion there. My guide and I trembled at the sight of him, but the old man approached without hesitation. In spite of our fear, we followed him. The beast discreetly withdrew a short distance, as if under orders from God. He stopped while the old man picked the fruit that hung from the lower branches. He held out a handful of dates. The beast came running up and took the fruit more gently than any domestic animal. When he had eaten, he went away. As we watched this, still trembling, it was not hard for us to measure the great strength of the old man's faith and the extreme weakness of our own.

"We saw another man equally remarkable. He lived in a tiny hut not big enough for more than one. It was told of him that a she-wolf regularly attended him at dinner. The beast almost never failed to come running up at the regular mealtime. She would wait outside the door until the hermit would hand out whatever bread was left over from his meal. She would lick his hand and, as if having performed the proper courtesies and extended her greetings, go away.

"It once happened that the holy man had had a brother visit him and was accompanying him on his way home. In consequence, he was away some little while and failed to return until nightfall. Meanwhile, the beast had presented herself at the customary mealtime. She sensed that the cell was empty and that her familiar patron was not at home. She went in, making a careful search where the master could be. By chance, a palm-leaf basket hung near by, containing five loaves of bread. The wolf took one of these and devoured it. After perpetrating this crime, she went away. On his return, the hermit saw that the basket was disarranged and did not contain the proper number of loaves. He realized there had been a theft from his supply and near the threshold found fragments of the loaf that had been eaten. He then had no uncertainty about the identity of the thief. In the following days, the beast did not come as usual. She was, no doubt, conscious of her presumptuous deed and was refraining from visiting the victim of her wrong-doing. On his part, the hermit was distressed at losing the comfort of the guest and companion of his meals. After seven days, recalled by the hermit's prayers, the wolf was there again, as before, for dinner. The embarrassment of the penitent was easy to see. The wolf did not presume to come close.

In deep shame, she would not lift her eyes from the ground. It was plain that she was imploring some act of pardon. The hermit had pity on her confusion. He ordered her to come near and with a caressing hand stroked her sorrowful head. Then he refreshed the culprit with a double ration of bread. The wolf had received her pardon. She put her grief aside and renewed her habitual visits.

"I visited two monasteries of the blessed Anthony, which are today occupied by his disciples. I even went to the place in which the very blessed Paul, the first hermit, used to live. I saw the Red Sea and the mountain chain in which Sinai lies. The peak of Mount Sinai itself reaches nearly to heaven and is inaccessible.

"It was reported that an anchorite lived in the recesses of Mount Sinai, but, even after a long and intensive search, I failed to see him. He had cut himself off from human intercourse some fifty years before. He used no clothing. Covered only by the hairs of his own body, he was enabled by divine grace to ignore his nakedness. Whenever pious men tried to visit him, he ran to some inaccessible place and thus avoided human contact. It was said that he had let himself be interviewed only once, five years before, and that, I suppose, by a man whose strong faith had merited the privilege. The two had a long talk together. When the anchorite was asked why he so resolutely avoided men, it is said he replied that whoever receives visits from men cannot receive visits from angels. This remark led, not unreasonably, to the very general and widely circulated belief that this holy man often had angels as visitors. . . .

"As for me, when I left Mount Sinai, I went back toward the Nile. I covered both its banks and found them thick with monasteries. I saw that, for the most part, as I said a while back, the monks live together in groups of a hundred. However, it is not unknown for two or three thousand to form a single community. You must not suppose that the monks who live together in large numbers are inferior in virtue to those men I have been speaking of, who have withdrawn themselves from human society. Among the former, the chief and outstanding virtue is obedience, as I have said. Of such as come to the monastery only those are admitted by the abbot who have undergone probation: they must give evidence that they will never disobey an order of the abbot, however trying or difficult or intolerable it be." . . .

"Tell me," I said, "are you not satisfied with the book I wrote about Martin? You know well that I published one on his life and miracles."

"I am familiar with that fact," said Postumianus. "Indeed, that book of yours has never left my hands. If you recognize it, look: here it is!" The book had been hidden under his clothing and he opened it. "It has been my companion on land and sea. In all my travels it has been my associate and my comforter. I shall tell you how far that book of yours has penetrated. There is almost no place in the whole world where the happy story it tells is not commonly known. First to bring the book to Rome was your great friend Paulinus. Copies were zealously snatched up all over the city. I saw the booksellers there carried away with joy. It was their most profitable item, they said; nothing sold more readily and nothing sold at a higher price. When I crossed over the sea, it had long before preceded me. When I arrived in Africa, it was already being read throughout Carthage. Alone in not knowing it was my Cyrenian priest, but I lent it to him and he copied it. What to say about Alexandria? There almost everybody knew it better than you do. It had traversed Egypt, Nitria, the Thebaid, and all the kingdom of Memphis. I once saw an old man in the desert reading it. When I told him I was a good friend of yours, he—and many of the brothers, too—charged me with this mission: if I should ever reach your country and find you safe and sound, I was to compel you to complete your book on the virtues of the blessed man, adding what you there said you had omitted. Come, then! What has already been written down is enough for the book. It is not that which I am eager to hear, but, rather, all that you left out, for fear, I suppose, of wearying your readers. Please tell us that, and so comply with a wish that many men join me in making."

# Letter to Paulinus of Nola

. . . I hear that all your cooks have given notice, because, I suspect, they disdained to minister to your unassuming commissariat, so I am sending you a lad from my own kitchen, able to cook the innocuous bean, to serve the modest beetroot dressed with vinegar and sauce, and to make the humble porridge palatable to hungry monks. He is innocent of the use of pepper, and of spices he knows nought; he is familiar with cummin, and is especially ready with the noisy pestle and mortar, to crush sweet herbs. He has one fault—he is no mean peril to all gardens; let him in, and he will cut down everything in reach, and for cutting mallows, he is insatiable. As for keeping himself in firewood, he won't swindle you, but he will burn everything he can get hold of, he will chop it up and will not even hesitate to lay hands on the roof, or the ancient timbers of the house.

With these virtues and foibles, I trust he will be a son to you, rather than a servant, since you do not disdain to call the very humblest your children. I would have liked to serve you myself in his stead, but if the wish is on the way to the deed, remember me at your dinners and your cheerful suppers, for it is better to be a servant to you than a master to others. Farewell.

# JOHN CASSIAN

360?–?435

Cassian is supposed to have been a Scythian, but his elegant style, his freedom from barbarisms, have led many to wonder whether this was indeed so. He early became a monk, traveled widely in Palestine and Egypt, then settled at Marseilles about 415, where he wrote his three great works: the *Institutes,* the *Conferences,* and *On the Incarnation*. Although Cassian was later overshadowed by the fame of St Benedict, the latter ordered that Cassian's *Conferences* be read daily by the monks of his order.

## FROM The Institutes

As we are going to speak of the . . . monasteries, how by God's grace can we better begin than with the actual dress of the monks, for we shall then be able to expound in due course their interior life when we have set their outward man before your eyes. A monk, then, as a soldier of Christ ever ready for battle, ought always to walk with his loins girded. . . .

Let the robe also of the monk be such as may merely cover the body and prevent the disgrace of nudity, and keep off harm from cold, not such as may foster the seeds of vanity and pride; for the same Apostle tells us: "Having food and covering, with these let us be content." "Covering," he says, not "raiment" . . . that is, what may merely cover the body, not what may please the fancy by the splendour of the attire; commonplace, so that it may not be thought remarkable for novelty of colour or fashion among other men of the same profession; and quite free from anxious carefulness, yet not discoloured by stains acquired through neglect. Lastly, let them be so far removed from this world's fashions as to remain altogether common property for the use of the servants of God . . . wherefore they utterly disapproved of a robe of sackcloth as being visible to all and conspicuous, and what from this very fact will not only confer no benefit on the soul but rather minister to vanity and pride, and as being inconvenient and unsuitable for the performance of necessary work for which a monk ought always to go ready and unimpeded. . . .

And therefore they supplement their prayer by the addition of labour, lest slumber might steal upon them as idlers. For as they scarcely enjoy any time of leisure, so there is no limit put to their spiritual meditations. For practising equally the virtues of the body and of the soul, they balance what is due to the outer by what is profitable to the inner man; steadying the slippery motions of the heart and the shifting fluctuations of the thoughts by the weight of *labour,* like some strong and immovable anchor, by which the changeableness and wanderings of the heart, fastened within the barriers of the cell, may be shut up in some perfectly secure harbour, and so, intent on only spiritual meditation and watchfulness over the thoughts, may not only forbid the watchful mind to give a hasty consent to any evil suggestions, but may also keep it safe from any unnecessary and idle thoughts: so that it is not easy to say which depends on the other—I mean, whether they practise their incessant manual labour for the sake of spiritual meditation, or whether it is for the sake of their continuous labours that they acquire such remarkable spiritual proficiency and light of knowledge. . . .

Wherefore each one on his admission is stripped of all his former possessions, so that he is not allowed any longer to keep even the clothes which he has on his back: but in the council of the brethren he is brought forward into the midst and stripped of his own clothes, and clad by the abbot's hands in the dress of the monastery, so that by this he may know not only that he has been despoiled of all his old things, but also that he has laid aside all worldly pride, and come down to the want and poverty of Christ, and that he is now to be supported not by wealth sought for by the world's arts, nor by anything reserved from his former state of unbelief, but that he is to receive out of the holy and sacred funds of the monastery his rations for his service; and that, as he knows that he is thence to be clothed and fed and that he has nothing of his own, he may learn, nevertheless, not to be anxious about the morrow, according to the saying of the Gospel, and may not be ashamed to be on a level with the poor, that is with the body of the brethren, with whom Christ was not ashamed to be numbered, and to call himself their brother, but that rather he may glory that he has been made to share the lot of his own servants. . . .

If then any one by accident breaks an earthenware jar (which they call "baucalis"), he can only expiate his carelessness by public penance; and when all the brethren are assembled for service he must lie on the ground and ask for absolution until the service of the prayers is finished; and will obtain it when by the abbot's command he is bidden to rise from the ground. The same satisfaction must be given by one who when summoned to some work or to the usual service comes rather late, or who when singing a Psalm hesitates ever so little. Similarly if he answers unnecessarily or roughly or impertinently, if he is careless in carrying out the services enjoined to him, if he makes a slight complaint, if, preferring reading to work or obedience, he is slow in performing his appointed duties, if when service is over he does not make haste to go back at once to his cell, if he stops for ever so short a time with someone else, if he goes anywhere else even for a moment, if he takes anyone else by the hand, if he ventures to discuss anything however small with one who is not the joint-occupant of his cell, if he prays with one who is suspended from prayer, if he sees any of his relations or friends in the world and talks with them without his senior, if he tries to receive a letter from anyone or to write back without his abbot's leave. To such an extent does spiritual censure proceed and in such matters and faults like these. But as for other things which when indiscriminately committed among us are treated by us too as blameworthy, viz.: open wrangling, manifest contempt, arrogant contradictions, going out from the monastery freely and without check, familiarity with women, wrath, quarrelling, jealousies, disputes, claiming something as one's own property, the infection of covetousness, the desire and acquisition of unnecessary things which are not possessed by the rest of the brethren, taking food between meals and by stealth, and things like these—they are dealt with not by that spiritual censure of which we spoke, but by stripes; or are atoned for by expulsion. . . .

When the aged John, who was superior of a large monastery and of a quantity of brethren, had come to visit the aged Paesius, who was living in a vast desert, and had been asked of him as of a very old friend, what he had done in all the forty years in which he had been separated from him and had scarcely ever been disturbed in his solitude by the brethren: "Never," said he, "has the sun seen me eating." "Nor me angry," said the other. . . .

We knew an old man, Machetes by name, who lived at a distance from the crowds of the brethren, and obtained by his daily prayers this grace from the Lord, that as often as a spiritual conference was held, whether by day or by night, he never was at all overcome by sleep: but if anyone tried to introduce a word of detraction, or idle talk, he dropped off to sleep at once as if the poison of slander could not possibly penetrate to pollute his ears. . . .

And so when we had come, while still beginners, from the monasteries of Palestine, to a city of Egypt called Diolcos, and were contemplating a large number of monks bound by discipline of the coenobium, and trained in that excellent system of monasteries, which is also the earliest, we were also eager to see with all wisdom of heart another system as well which is still better, viz.: that of the anchorites, as we were incited thereto by the praises of it by everybody. For these men, having first lived for a very long time in coenobia, and having diligently learnt all the rules of patience and discretion, and acquired the virtues of humility and renunciation, and having perfectly overcome all their faults, in order to engage in most fearful conflicts with devils, penetrate the deepest recesses of the desert. Finding then that men of this sort were living near the river Nile in a place which is surrounded on one side by the same river, on the other by the expanse of the sea, and forms an island, habitable by none but monks seeking such recesses, since the saltness of the soil and dryness of the sand make it unfit for any cultivation—to these men, I say, we eagerly hastened, and were beyond measure astonished at their labours which they endure in the contemplation of the virtues and their love of solitude. For they are hampered by such a scarcity even of water that the care and exactness with which they portion it out is such as no miser would bestow in preserving and hoarding the most precious kind of wine. For they carry it three miles or even further from the bed of the above-mentioned river, for all necessary purposes; and the distance, great as it is, with sandy mountains in between, is doubled by the very great difficulty of the task. . . .

Our sixth combat is with what the Greeks call *accidie,* which we may term weariness or distress of heart. This is akin to dejection, and is especially trying to solitaries, and a dangerous and frequent foe to dwellers in the desert; and especially disturbing to a monk about the sixth hour, like some fever which seizes him at stated times, bringing the burning heat of its attacks on the sick man at usual and regular hours. Lastly, there are some of the elders who declare that this is the "midday demon" spoken of in the ninetieth Psalm. . . .

And when this has taken possession of some unhappy soul, it produces dislike of the place, disgust with the cell, and disdain and contempt of the brethren who dwell with him or at a little distance, as if they were careless or unspiritual. It also makes the man lazy and sluggish about all manner of work which has to be done within the enclosure of his dormitory. It does not suffer him to stay in his cell, or to take any pains about reading, and he often groans because he can do no good while he stays there, and complains and sighs because he can bear no spiritual fruit so long as he is joined to that society; and he complains that he is cut off from spiritual gain, and is of no use in the place, as if he were one who, though he could govern others and be useful to a great number of people, yet was edifying none, nor profiting anyone by his teaching and doctrine. He cries up distant monasteries and those which are a long way off, and describes such places as more profitable and better suited for salvation; and besides this he paints the intercourse with the brethren there as sweet and full of spiritual life. On the other hand, he says that everything about him is rough, and not only that there is nothing edifying among the brethren who are stopping there, but also that even food for the body cannot be procured without great difficulty. Lastly he fancies that he will never be well while he stays in that place, unless he leaves his cell (in which he is sure to die if he stops in it any longer) and takes himself off from thence as quickly as possible. Then the fifth or sixth hour brings him such bodily weariness and longing for food that he seems to himself worn out and wearied as if with a long journey, or some very heavy work, or as if he had put off taking food during a fast of two or three days. Then besides this he looks about anxiously this way and that, and sighs that none of the brethren come to see him, and often goes in and out of his cell, and frequently gazes up at the sun, as if it was too slow in setting, and so a kind of unreasonable confusion of mind takes possession of him like some foul darkness, and makes him idle and useless for every spiritual work, so that he imagines that no cure for so terrible an attack can be found in anything except visiting some one of the brethren, or in the solace of sleep alone. Then the disease suggests that he ought to show courteous and friendly hospitalities to the brethren, and pay visits to the sick, whether near at hand or far off. He talks too about some dutiful and religious offices; that those kinsfolk ought to be inquired after, and that he ought to go and see them oftener; that it would be a real work of piety to go more frequently to visit that religious woman, devoted to the service of God, who is deprived of all support of kindred; and that it would be a most excellent thing to get what is needful for her who is neglected and despised by her own kinsfolk; and that he ought piously to devote his time to these things instead of staying uselessly and with no profit in his cell. . . .

And so taught by these examples the Fathers in Egypt never allow monks, and especially the younger ones, to be idle, estimating the purpose of their hearts and their growth in patience and humility by their diligence in work; and they not only do not allow them to receive anything from another to supply their own wants, but further, they not merely refresh pilgrims and brethren who come to visit them by means of their labours, but actually collect an enormous store of provisions and food, and distribute it in the parts of Libya which suffer from famine and barrenness, and also in the cities, to those who are pining away in the squalor of prison; as they believe that by such an offering of the fruit of their hands they offer a reasonable and true sacrifice to the Lord. . . .

Wherefore this is an old maxim of the Fathers that is still current—though I cannot produce it without shame on my part, since I could not avoid my own sister, nor escape the hands of the bishop—viz., that a man ought by all means to fly from women and bishops. For neither of them will allow him who has once been joined in close intercourse any longer to care for the quiet of his cell, or to continue with pure eyes in divine contemplation through his insight into holy things. . . .

## FROM Conferences

When I was in the desert of Scete, where are the most excellent monastic fathers and where all perfection flourishes, in company with the holy father Germanus (who had since the earliest days and commencement of our spiritual service been my closest companion both in the coenobium and in the desert, so that to show the harmony of our friendship and aims, everybody would say that a single heart and soul existed in our two bodies), I sought out Abbot Moses, who was eminent amid those splendid flowers, not only in practical but also in contemplative excellence, in my anxiety to be grounded by his instruction: and together we implored him to give us a discourse for our edification; not without tears, for we knew full well his determination never to consent to open the gate of perfection, except to those who desired it with all faithfulness, and sought it with all sorrow of heart; for fear lest if he showed it at random to those who cared nothing for it, or only desired it in a half-hearted way, by opening what is necessary, and what ought only to be discovered to those seeking perfection, to unworthy persons, and such as accepted it with scorn, he might appear to lay himself open either to the charge of bragging, or to the sin of betraying his trust; and at last, being overcome by our prayers, he thus began.

"All the arts and sciences," said he, "have some goal or mark; an end or aim of their own, on which the diligent pursuer of each art has his eye, and so endures all sorts of toils and dangers and losses, cheerfully and with equanimity, e.g., the farmer, shunning neither at one time the scorching heat of the sun, nor at another the frost and cold, cleaves the earth unweariedly, and again and again subjects the clods of his field to his ploughshare, while he keeps before him his goal; viz., by diligent labour to break it up small like fine sand, and to clear it of all briers, and free it from all weeds, as he believes that in no other way can he gain his ultimate end, which is to secure a good harvest, and a large crop; on which he can either live himself free from care, or can increase his possessions. Again, when his barn is well stocked he is quite ready to empty it, and with incessant labour to commit the seed to the crumbling furrow, thinking nothing of the present lessening of his stores in view of the future harvest. Those men too who are engaged in mercantile pursuits, have no dread of the uncertainties and chances of the ocean, and fear no risks, while an eager hope urges them forward to their aim of gain. Moreover those who are inflamed with the ambition of military life, while they look forward to their aim of honours and power take no notice of danger and destruction in their wanderings, and are not crushed by present losses and wars, while they are eager to obtain the end of some honour held out to them. And our profession too has its own goal and end, for which we undergo all sorts of toils not merely without weariness but actually with delight; on account of which the want of food in fasting is no trial to us, the weariness of our vigils becomes a delight; reading and constant meditation on the Scriptures does not pall upon us; and further incessant toil, and self-denial, and the privation of all things, and the horrors also of this vast desert have no terrors for us. And doubtless for this it was that you yourselves despised the love of kinsfolk, and scorned your fatherland, and the delights of this world, and passed through so many countries, in order that you might come to us, plain and simple folk as we are, living in this wretched state in the desert. Wherefore," said he, "answer and tell me what is the goal and end, which incite you to endure all these things so cheerfully." . . .

*Germanus.* Who then, while he is burdened with our frail flesh, can be always so intent on this contemplation as never to think about the arrival of a brother, or visiting the sick, or manual labour, or at least about showing kindness to strangers and visitors? And lastly, who is not interrupted by providing for the body, and looking after it? Or how and in what way can the mind cling to the invisible and incomprehensible God, this we should like to learn.

*Moses.* To cling to God continually, and as you say inseparably to hold fast to meditation on Him, is impossible for a man while still in this weak flesh of ours. But we ought to be aware on what we should have the purpose of our mind fixed, and to what goal we should ever recall the gaze of our soul: and when the mind can secure this it may rejoice; and grieve and sigh when it is withdrawn from this, and as often as it discovers itself to have fallen away from gazing on Him, it should admit that it has lapsed from the highest good, considering that even a momentary departure from gazing on Christ is fornication. And when our gaze has wandered ever so little from Him, let us turn the eyes of the soul back to Him, and recall our mental gaze as in a perfectly straight direction. . . .

*Germanus.* How is it then, that even against our will, aye and without our knowledge, idle thoughts steal upon us so subtilly and secretly that it is fearfully hard not merely to drive them away, but even to grasp and seize them? Can then a mind sometimes be found free from them, and never attacked by illusions of this kind?

*Moses.* It is impossible for the mind not to be approached by thoughts, but it is in the power of every earnest man either to admit them or to reject them. As then their rising up does not entirely depend on ourselves, so the rejection or admission of them lies in our own power. . . .

In that choir of saints who shine like brilliant stars in the night of this world, we have seen the holy Paphnutius, like some great luminary, shining with the brightness of knowledge. For he was a presbyter of our company, I mean of those whose abode was in the desert of Scete, where he lived to extreme old age, without ever moving from his cell, of which he had taken possession when still young, and which was five miles from the church, even to nearer districts; nor was he when worn out with years hindered by the distance from going to church on Saturday or Sunday. But not wanting to return from thence empty handed he would lay on his shoulders a bucket of water to last him all the week, and carry it back to his cell, and even when he was past ninety would not suffer it to be fetched by the labour of younger men. He then from his earliest youth threw himself into the monastic discipline with such fervour that when he had spent only a short time in it, he was endowed with the virtue of submission, as well as the knowledge of all good qualities. For by the practice of humility and obedience he mortified all his desires, and by this stamped out all his faults and acquired every virtue which the monastic system and the teaching of the ancient fathers produces, and, inflamed with desire for still further advances, he was eager to penetrate into the recesses of the desert, so that, with no human companions to disturb him, he might be more readily united to the Lord, to whom he longed to be inseparably joined, even while he still lived in the society of the brethren. And there once more in his excessive fervour he outstripped the virtues of the anchorites, and in his eager desire for continual divine meditation avoided the sight of them: and he plunged into solitary places yet wilder and more inaccessible, and hid himself for a long while in them, so that, as the anchorites themselves only with great difficulty caught a glimpse of him every now and then, the belief was that he enjoyed and delighted in the daily society of angels, and because of this remarkable characteristic of his he was surnamed by them the Buffalo.

### CASSIAN AND GERMANUS VISIT ABBOT DANIEL

. . . We asked this blessed Daniel why it was that as we sat in the cells we were sometimes filled with the utmost gladness of heart, together with inexpressible delight and abundance of the holiest feelings, so that I will not say *speech,* but even *feeling* could not follow it, and pure prayers were readily breathed, and the mind, being filled with spiritual fruits, praying to God even in sleep, could feel that its petitions rose lightly and powerfully to God: and again, why it was that for no reason we were suddenly filled with the utmost grief, and weighed down with unreasonable depression, so that we not only felt as if we ourselves were overcome with such feelings, but also our cell grew dreadful, reading palled upon us, aye and our very prayers were offered up unsteadily and vaguely, and almost as if we were intoxicated: so that while we were groaning and endeavouring to restore ourselves to our former disposition, our mind was unable to do this, and the more earnestly it sought to fix again its gaze upon God, so was it the more vehemently carried away to wandering thoughts by shifting aberrations and so utterly deprived of all spiritual fruits as not to be capable of being roused from this deadly slumber even by the desire of the kingdom of heaven, or by the fear of hell held out to it. To this he replied:

"A threefold account of this mental dryness of which you speak has been given by the Elders. For it comes either from carelessness on our part, or from the assaults of the Devil, or from the permission and allowance of the Lord. From carelessness on our part, when through our own faults coldness has come upon us, and we have behaved carelessly and hastily, and owing to slothful idleness have fed on bad thoughts, and so make the ground of our heart bring forth thorns and thistles; which spring up in it, and consequently make us sterile, and powerless as regards all spiritual fruit and meditation. From the assaults of the Devil when, sometimes, while we are actually intent on good desires, our enemy with crafty subtlety makes his way into our heart, and without our knowledge and against our will we are drawn away from the best intentions."

# PALLADIUS

(See page 471.)

## FROM The Paradise of the Holy Fathers

### THE BLESSED WOMAN THAIS

And now I desire to narrate unto you the excellent history and the great repentance of the blessed woman Thais or Thaisis, for speech concerning her is most excellent, and it is full of encouragement and penitence of soul unto those who love God. Now this woman had a mother who, because her daughter was beautiful of face, made her to take up a position in the market, and the rumour of her beauty travelled unto every place, and those who were living afar off desired greatly to see her; and no man who looked upon her was satisfied with the sight of her face, because she burned like a flame of fire into the hearts of those who saw her, and many by reason of their mad love for her sold whatever property they had to her parents that they might have commerce with her. Now when Bessarion, the servant of God, heard these things concerning this woman and that through her beauty she was dragging many to destruction, he arrayed himself in the apparel of a man who was in the world, and took with him one dinar and went unto her, and when he saw her he brought forth the dinar and gave it to her; and, having taken the dinar, she said unto him, "Let us go into a room," and he said unto her, "Yea, let us go in." And, having gone in, the blessed man Bessarion saw the couch which was laid out, now it was a very high one, and the woman said unto the old man, "Come, get up on this bed"; and he said unto her, "Hast thou not inside this chamber another room?" and she said unto him, "Yea." Then he said unto her, "Let us then go in there." And Thais answered and said unto him, "If it be that thou art ashamed of men seeing thee, know that no man can see us in this chamber; but if it be God of whom thou art afraid, He can see us in whatsoever place we enter." And the blessed man Bessarion, hearing these words, said unto her, "My daughter, dost thou know that God existeth?" And she said unto him, "Yea, I know that God existeth, and that there will be kingdom, and judgment." Then the old man said unto her, "If thou knowest that God is, and that there will be kingdom and judgment, why dost thou destroy men in this manner?" And straightway the woman cast herself at his feet, and said unto him, "I know that there is repentance for those who sin. But I beseech thee, master, to tarry with me for three hours, and whatsoever thou wishest to do unto me that do because of all the evil things which have been wrought by me"; and having told her in what place he would await her he left her and went away.

Then in that same hour the woman took everything which she had gained by fornication and burnt it with fire in the midst of the city, and she said, "Come, O all ye who have had commerce with me, and see that I am burning before your eyes every possession which I have gathered together by means of sin"; and the things which were burned were worth three hundred pounds of gold, and there were there also goods and apparel of all kinds; and after she had burned up everything she went to the blessed man Bessarion. And when Bessarion saw her he took her by her hand and led her along and brought her to a religious house of sisters, and he shut her in a little cell, leaving her only one small window in the wall through which a woman passed in food to her. And the blessed Bessarion said unto the head of the house, "Give her a pound of dry bread each day, and water according to her need." Then the blessed woman Thais said unto the venerable Bessarion, "With what petition dost thou command me to pray unto God? That He should forgive me my sins?" The blessed Bessarion said unto her, "Thou art neither worthy to pray unto God, nor to make mention of His Name with thy lips, nor to stretch out thy hands unto Him; for thy lips are unclean and polluted, and thy hands are contaminated with impurity; thou shalt only sit down and gaze towards the East, and thou shalt say nothing except, 'O Thou who didst create me, have mercy upon me.'" And having dwelt in that cell for a space of about three years, the blessed Bessarion had mercy upon her, and the blessed man went to Abbâ Anthony that he might learn from him whether God had forgiven her her sins or not. Then having spoken concerning her unto Anthony that blessed man called unto his disciples, and said unto them, "Let each one of you shut himself in his cell all night, and pray ye unto God that we may see unto whom shall be revealed the matter concerning which the blessed Bessarion hath come unto us this day."

And when they all had done as they had been commanded and when a long time had elapsed, the blessed Paul, the chief of the disciples of Mâr Anthony, looked into the heavens and saw a couch which had been spread with great splendour, and three angels who were carrying three lamps were standing before that couch, and a crown of glory was laid thereupon. And having seen all this glorious sight, he said, "This couch can only be for my father Anthony." Then a voice came unto him from heaven, saying, "This couch is not for Anthony, thy father, but for Thais the harlot"; and the blessed Paul rose up early in the morning and related the vision which he had seen. And the blessed Mâr Bessarion came back from Abbâ Anthony in great joy, and he went to the religious house of the sisterhood, and he opened the door that he might bring the woman out from the cell wherein she was secluded; but she made entreaty unto him, saying, "Leave me here until my death, for my sins are many." Then the blessed man said unto her, "Behold the merciful God hath had compassion upon thee, and He hath accepted thy repentance"; and then she wished to go forth from her cell. And she answered and said unto him, "Believe me, O Father, from the day wherein I entered this cell I have made all my sins a mighty burden and I have set it before my eyes, in suchwise that as the breath of my nostrils hath not separated itself from me, so my sins have not separated themselves from me until this hour."

And the blessed Bessarion answered and said unto her, "God hath not forgiven thee thy sins because of thy repentance, but because of the thought which thou hadst—that thou wouldst deliver thyself over unto Christ." Now this blessed woman Thais lived after her repentance fifteen days, and she departed unto our Lord in peace. Thus was the crowning of the blessed Thais, who was lost and was found, and was dead and who came to life by the grace of Christ, unto whom belong mercy, and compassion, and glory, and honour, for ever and ever. Amen.

### THE BLESSED MAN PAUL THE SIMPLE

Now there was a certain husbandman whose name was Paul, who was more simple and innocent in nature than are usually the children of men; and he had a wife who was beautiful in her appearance, and wicked in her deeds and actions, and she had wandered from him and had been committing adultery for a long time. And one day, suddenly Paul went into his house from the field, and he found her and another working impurity together; now this took place so that Divine Grace might incite Paul to follow that which was more excellent. And having gone in and seen them, he laughed chastely, and answered and said, "It is good, it is good, truly she is not accounted mine by me. By Jesus, henceforth I will not take her again. Get thee gone, and behold she is thine, she and her children: and as for me, I will go and become a monk." And saying nothing unto any man he went away a journey of eight stages, and he arrived at the cell of Mâr Anthony the Great. And having knocked at the door, the blessed man Mâr Anthony went out, and he said unto Paul, "What dost thou seek?" Paul said unto him, "I seek to become a monk." Mâr Anthony answered and said unto him, "Thou art an old man eighty years old, and it is impossible for thee to become a monk here; but depart to the village, and work in the fields for thy living, and give thanks unto God at the same time that thou art not able to endure the afflictions of the desert." And again Paul answered and said unto him, "Whatsoever thou wilt teach me, that will I do." Anthony said unto him, "I have told thee that thou art an old man, and thou canst not do it; but if thou wishest to become a monk, get thee gone to some monastic house, and abide where the brethren are many, and where they will be able to bear with thy sickness. As for me, I live by myself alone here, and I only eat once in five days, and even then I do not eat a full meal." With these and suchlike words did Anthony frighten Paul. And as he would not be persuaded to depart, Anthony went into his cell, and shut the door upon himself for three days, and because of him he did not go outside his cell for three whole days, not even for his need's sake. Nevertheless Paul did not go away; and on the fourth day, when his need compelled him, Anthony opened the door and went forth. And again he said unto Paul, "Get thee gone, O old man, why dost thou trouble me? It is impossible for thee to stay here." Paul said unto him, "It is impossible for me to die in any other place except this."

And the blessed Anthony, having looked carefully and seen that he was carrying no food with him, and no bread and no water, and that he had fasted during the four days which he had remained, said within himself, "Peradventure he will escape and die, and will plunge my soul in tribulation"; so he accepted him and brought him into his cell. And because of Paul during those days Anthony performed exceedingly severe ascetic labours, the like of which, even in his early manhood, he had never performed. And he soaked palm leaves in water, and gave them unto Paul, and said unto him, "Take these palm leaves, and weave a mat therefrom even as do I myself." And the old man Paul took them, and wove them into a mat fifteen cubits long, until at the ninth hour he was exhausted. And Anthony, seeing what he had woven, was angry with him, and said unto him, "Thou hast woven the leaves loosely, unweave them, and weave them over again neatly and closely." And Paul unwove what he had woven, and wove the leaves over again, but still he wove too loosely, because the leaves had become twisted through the former weaving and unweaving. Meanwhile Paul was fasting all these days, and Anthony laid these hard labours upon him while his soul was vexed with hunger, so that he might become disgusted and depart from him.

Now when Anthony saw that Paul was neither angry nor wrathful, and that he made no complaint, his mercy made itself manifest; and behold when Paul had lived there another day, he said unto him, "Dost thou wish to eat a piece of bread?" The old man Paul said unto him, "As it pleaseth thee, father." And this also especially shamed Mâr Anthony, that he did not hasten in his desire to the promise of food, but that he cast all his desire upon him. Thereupon

Anthony said unto him, "Set the table and bring bread." And Anthony placed on the table four loaves, each of which was of the weight of about six ounces, and he dipped them in water because they were dry, and he placed one before himself and three before Paul. And having placed them there he sang a psalm which he knew twelve times, and he recited twelve prayers that he might try Paul, but Paul prayed with him in gladness; and after the twelve prayers they sat down to eat in the late evening. Having eaten one loaf Anthony did not touch another, but the old man Paul ate slowly, and when Anthony had finished he had still some of his loaf to eat, and Anthony was waiting for him to finish it. And having finished it, he answered and said unto him, "Little father, wilt thou eat another loaf?" And Paul said unto him, "If thou wilt eat another I will also; but if thou wilt not, I will not." Anthony saith unto him, "I have had enough, for I am a monk." And Paul said unto him, "I also have had enough, for I also seek to become a monk." And after these things Anthony again stood up, and made twelve prayers, and when they had said together the psalms twelve times they slept for a little during the night, and then they sang and prayed until the morning.

And when Anthony saw that the old man was carrying out with gladness a rule of life similar unto his own in every respect, he said unto him, "If thou art able to bear every day passed in this wise, then stay with me." Paul said unto him, "Although I know nothing else, yet the things which I do know I can perform easily"; and on another day Anthony said unto him, "Behold, thou hast become a monk." And a few months afterward when Anthony saw that his soul was perfect before God, and that he was simple beyond measure, and that Divine Grace was helping him, he built him a cell at a distance of about three or four miles away, and said unto him, "Behold, thou art a monk, and henceforth thou must live by thyself so that thou mayest receive the temptation of devils." Now when Paul had lived by himself for a year, the gift of healing and of casting out devils was given unto him.

And in those times they brought unto Anthony a certain man who was vexed by a fierce devil, and that devil was one of the princes of the devils, and he was so fierce that he would even revile and blaspheme the heavens. And when Anthony saw the man he said, "I cannot heal this man, for over this race of princes neither the gift nor the power of healing hath been given unto me; unto Paul it belongeth to heal this man." And Anthony therefore took them with him and went unto him, and said unto him, "O Abbâ Paul, cast out this devil from this man, so that, being made whole, he may depart to his house." Then Paul said unto him, "And what wilt thou do?" And Anthony said unto him, "I am not able to do it, for I have other work to do"; and he left the man with Paul and went back to his cell. Then the old man Paul rose up and prayed a prayer with great feeling, and he began to speak unto that devil, saying, "Father Anthony saith, 'Go forth from this man.'" And the devil answered with blasphemies, saying, "I will not go forth, O thou who eatest white bread"; then the old man took his shoulder garment, and began to smite the devil on his back and sides, saying, "I tell thee that Abbâ Anthony saith, 'Get thee forth from him'"; whereupon the devil began to curse and revile Abbâ Anthony and the old man Paul. Finally Paul said unto him, "Wilt thou go forth, or must I go and tell Christ, yea Jesus? For if thou wilt not go forth I will go and tell Christ, and great woe shall come upon thee"; and again he blasphemed and said, "I will not go forth." Then was the blessed man Paul wroth with him, and he went out from his cell; now it was the season of noon, and the heat with the Egyptians at this time is so fierce that it is akin to the heat of the fiery furnace of the Babylonians. And he stood upon a stone and prayed, and spake thus, "Behold, O Jesus Christ, who wast crucified in the days of Pontius Pilate, I will not come down from this stone, and I will neither eat nor drink until I die unless Thou dost cast out that devil from this man, and dost set him free from him." And whilst these words were yet in his mouth the devil cried out by reason of his tribulations, and said, "By Hercules, by whom am I ruled, by Hercules, I am being persecuted with violence, for the simplicity of Paul pursueth me; whither shall I go?" Paul saith unto him, "To the uttermost depths of the abyss"; and straightway the devil went forth from the man, and he transformed himself and became like unto a mighty dragon seventy cubits long, and he wriggled along the ground and in this wise went down to the Red Sea, that might be fulfilled that which is written, "Perfect faith removeth mountains." This is the triumph of Paul, who was called the "Simple" by the whole brotherhood.

### A CERTAIN OLD MAN IN SCETE

There was a certain old man in Scete who, having become very sick indeed, was ministered to by the brethren, and he thought in his mind that they were tired of him, and he said, "I will go to Egypt, so that the brethren may not have to labour on my account." And Abbâ Moses said unto him, "Thou shalt not go, for if thou goest, thou wilt fall into fornication"; and the old man was grieved and said, "My body hath long been dead, and sayest thou these things unto me?" So he went up to Egypt, and men heard about him, and they brought many offerings unto him, and a certain believing virgin came in faith to minister unto him. And after a time, when the old man had been healed, the young woman lay with him, and she conceived, and folk asked her, saying, "Whence hadst thou that which thou hast conceived?" And she said unto them, "From the old man," and they believed her not. Now when the old man heard that they would not believe her, he said, "Yea, I have done this thing; but protect ye for me the child which shall be born." And when the child had been born and was weaned, there was a congregation in Scete, and the old man went down carrying the child on his shoulder, and he went into the church before all the people; and when they saw him they all wept. Then the old man said unto the brethren, "Observe ye, O my brethren, this is the child of disobedience; take heed, then, unto yourselves, for I have committed this act in my old age, and pray ye for me"; and the old man went to his cell, and dismissed the things wherewith he hath lived, and returned to his former deeds, and after a time he arrived once more at his old measure of ascetic excellence.

### THE HARLOT WHOM SERAPION CONVERTED

Abbâ Serapion once came and passed through a certain village in Egypt, and he saw a harlot standing in his cell, and the old man said unto her, "Remain here until the evening, for I wish to come with thee, and to pass this night with thee"; and the harlot said, "It is well, O father." Then she made ready, and prepared her bed, and she awaited the old man with that which he required. Now when it was evening, Abbâ Serapion came, but he brought nothing with him, and he went into her cell, and said unto her, "Is thy bed ready?" And she said unto him, "Yea, father"; and they shut themselves in. Then the old man answered and said unto her, "Wait a little, because I must perform a certain thing which is a law unto us." And he began to recite the Book of the Psalms of David from the beginning, and with every Psalm he offered up a prayer on her behalf, and he made supplication before God that she might repent and live, and God hearkened unto him. And the harlot stood up in fear by the side of the old man and prayed also, and when Abbâ Serapion had finished all the Psalms she fell down upon the ground, and he began to repeat many verses from the books of the Apostles. When he had finished his service, God having opened the heart of that woman, she knew that Abbâ Serapion had not come unto her for the purposes of sin, but that he might redeem her, and she fell on her face before him, and said unto him, "Perform an act of grace for me, O father, and take me to any place whatsoever wherein I can please God." And he took her to an abode of nuns and placed her therein and he said to the mistress of the convent, "Take this sister, O mother, and lay not upon her the rules and the yoke like the other sisters, but whatsoever she requireth, that give her; and in proportion as she findeth rest let her submit to be led." And when the woman had dwelt in the nunnery for a few days, she said, "I am a sinful woman, and I wish to eat only in the evening"; and after a few days more she said, "Many sins lie to my charge, and I therefore beg that I may eat once every four days," and she did so; and after a few days more she besought the mistress of the nunnery, saying, "Do an act of grace for me. Since I have made God exceedingly angry, take me into a cell and wall it up, and through a small opening therein give me a little bread and work for my hands to do." And the abbess of the nunnery hearkened unto her, and did thus, and in this wise that woman pleased God all the days of her life.

# The Life and Works of St Daniel the Stylite

409–93

Daniel of Maratha, a Syrian by birth, was one of the "solitaries" of the early Christian era. After his conversion he went to Constantinople, at the age of forty-two. There, following the example of penitential asceticism set by St Simeon the Stylite in the fifth century, he lived for thirty-three years on top of a pillar. A younger disciple, and eye-witness, was the author of the Life from which these passages are taken.

Before all things it is right that we should give glory to Jesus Christ our God, who for us was made man and for our salvation endured all things according to the Dispensation; for His sake, too, prophets were killed, and just men crucified themselves because of this faith in Him and by His grace, after having kept patience under their sufferings unswervingly unto the end, they received a crown of glory. These men our Master and Saviour Christ gave us as an example that we might know that it is possible for a man by the patient endurance of his sufferings to please God and be called His faithful servant.

For this reason I thought good to take in hand a recital of the labours of St. Daniel, yet I do so with fear; for this man's way of life was great and brilliant and marvellous, whereas I am but a witless and humble person. . . .

This father among saints was the son of a father named Elias and a mother Martha; he came from a small village called Meratha (which is, being interpreted, "the Caves") in the territory of Samosata in Mesopotamia. As his mother was barren and was reproached for this by her husband and kinsfolk, she went out one day secretly at midnight unbeknown to her husband and, stretching forth her hands to heaven, prayed, saying, "O Lord Jesus Christ, who art long-suffering towards the sins of men, Thou Who didst in the beginning create woman to increase the race of men, do Thou Thyself take my reproach from me and grant me fruit of my womb that I may dedicate him to Thee, the Lord of All." After weeping bitterly and afflicting her soul with many lamentations, she came in to her husband and whilst sleeping beside him saw in a vision of the night two great circular lights coming down from heaven and resting near her. Next morning she related the vision to her husband and kinsfolk and each one interpreted differently the things she had told them. But she sighed and said to herself, "My God to Whom I prayed will do what is best for my unhappy soul." And not many days later she conceived the holy man of whom we spoke.

So he was born; and when in course of time he had reached the age of five years his parents took him with offerings of fruit to a monastery near the village and the abbot asked them, "By what name is the child called?" And when the parents mentioned some other name, the old man said, "He shall not be called that, but whatever the Lord shall reveal to us, that shall his name be." And the archimandrite said to the child in the Syrian dialect, "Go, child, and fetch me a book from the table." For it is a custom in monasteries that many different books should be laid in front of the sanctuary, and whichever book a brother wants he takes and reads. So the child went and fetched the book of the prophet Daniel, and from this he got that name.

But when the parents besought the abbot to receive him in the monastery and let him stay with the brothers he could not be persuaded, because the child was still so very young; so they took him home again and he abode with his parents.

Now when he was twelve years old he heard his mother say, "My child, I have dedicated you to God." Thereupon one day, without saying anything to anybody, he went out of the village for a distance of about ten miles where there was a monastery containing fifty brethren. And entering the monastery he fell at the abbot's feet and begged to be received by him. But the abbot said to him, "Child, you are still very young in years and are not able to endure so hard a discipline; you know nothing of the monks' life; go home, stay with your parents and after some time when you are able both to fast and to sing and to endure discipline, then come back to us." But the child answered, "Father, I should prefer to die in these hardships than to quit the shelter of your flock!" And when, in spite of all he could do, the archimandrite was unable to persuade the child, he said to the brethren, "In truth, my children, let us receive this boy for he seems to me to be very much in earnest." And they all yielded to the abbot's counsel, and thus Daniel remained in the brotherhood.

And shortly afterwards his parents, who had sought him, found him in this monastery and rejoiced with great joy, and then besought the abbot to give him the tonsure. And he, having noticed his advancement in godliness and good disposition, sent for him and said, "Child, do you wish me to give you the tonsure?" Daniel immediately threw himself at his feet and said, "I beseech your Holiness, father, do it today!" But the abbot again said, "You are unable to endure the discipline." To this the boy replied, "I know well that I am young and weak, but I trust in God and your holy prayers, because the Lord who accepts our purpose gives us strength, for He is a God of purposes." Then, after blessing him and praying fervently over him, the archimandrite with the wisdom that had been given him by God instructed him in the things necessary for salvation. And afterwards, according to custom, he bade all the brethren gather together, and while they sang a hymn he bestowed upon him the holy robe of the monk. And, dismissing the parents with blessings, he bade them not to visit their son frequently.

While Daniel made progress in asceticism and in the splendour of his way of life he could not bear the scrutiny and the praise of the abbot and, still less, that of the whole brotherhood; so he planned to go to the Holy City, Jerusalem, and at the same time to visit the holy and thrice-blessed Simeon, the man on the pillar, in whose footsteps he felt constrained to follow.

Therefore he began to pray the abbot of the monastery to set him free to attain his desire, but he could not persuade him.

Soon after this, since our Master God in truth so willed it and the need of the church demanded it, the archbishop of that time commanded all the archimandrites of the East to assemble in the capital city of Antioch. And so it happened that this abbot together with some others went, too, and amongst them he allowed the holy man also to travel with him as his disciple.

As God granted that the matter for which they had suffered many vexations should be brought to a satisfactory settlement, they departed to their own monasteries; and on their way they lodged in a village called Telanissae where there was a very large monastery and monks pursuing a very noble and virtuous way of life; here, too, the afore-mentioned holy Simeon had received his training. And when the monks there began talking about the achievements of the holy Simeon, the monks from Mesopotamia withstood them, contending that it was but a vainglorious proceeding. "For," said they, "it is true that a man even if he were living in your midst might practise a mode of life hitherto unknown and please God, yet never has such a thing happened anywhere, that a man should go up and live on a pillar."

So the monks of that monastery persuaded them to go and see what hardships Simeon was enduring for the sake of the Lord. And they were persuaded and went, and the holy Daniel with them. When they arrived at the place and saw the wildness of the spot and the height of the pillar and the fiery heat of the scorching sun and the saint's endurance and his welcome to strangers and further, too, the love he showed towards them, they were amazed.

For Simeon gave direction that the ladder be placed in position and invited the old men to come up and kiss him. But they were afraid and declined the ascent of the ladder—one said he was too feeble from old age, another pleaded weakness after an illness, and another gout in his feet. For they said to each other, "How can we kiss with our mouth the man that we have just been slandering with our lips? Woe unto us for having mocked at such hardships as these and such endurance." Whilst they were conversing in this manner, Daniel entreated the archimandrite and the other abbots and Saint Simeon as well, begging to be allowed to go up to him. On receiving permission, he went up and the blessed man gave him his benediction and said to him, "What is your name?" and he answered, "Daniel." Then the holy Simeon said to him, "Play the man, Daniel, be strong and endure; for you have many hardships to endure for God. But I trust that the God whom I serve will Himself strengthen you and be your fellow-traveller." And, placing his hand upon Daniel's head, he prayed and blessed him and bade him go down the ladder. Then after the holy and blessed Simeon had prayed for the archimandrites he dismissed them all in peace.

After they had all by the will of God been restored to their own monasteries and some little time had passed, the holy man, Daniel, was deemed worthy to be raised to the post of abbot.

Thereupon he said to himself, "At last you are free, Daniel, start boldly and accomplish your purpose." When he had made trial of him who held the second place and found that he was able to undertake the duties of an archimandrite, he left everything and quitted the monastery; and when he had reached the enclosure of the holy Simeon he stayed there two weeks.

The blessed Simeon rejoiced exceedingly when he saw him and tried to persuade him to remain still longer, for he found great joy in his company. But Daniel would not consent thereto but pressed towards his goal, saying, "Father, I am ever with you in spirit." So Simeon blessed him and dismissed him with the words, "The Lord of glory will accompany you." Then Daniel went forth, wishing to travel to the holy places and to worship in the church of the Holy Resurrection and afterwards to retire to the inner desert. . . .

After a space of nine years had elapsed, the servant of God fell into an ecstasy, as it were, and saw a huge pillar of cloud standing opposite him and the holy and blessed Simeon standing above the head of the column and two men of goodly appearance, clad in white, standing near him in the heights. And he heard the voice of the holy and blessed Simeon saying to him, "Come here to me, Daniel." And he said, "Father, father, and how can I get up to that height?" Then the saint said to the young men standing near him, "Go down and bring him up to me." So the men came down and brought Daniel up to him and he stood there. Then Simeon took him in his arms and kissed him with a holy kiss, and then others called him away, and, escorted by them, he was borne up to heaven, leaving Daniel on the column with the two men. When holy Daniel saw him being carried up to heaven he heard the voice of Saint Simeon, "Stand firm and play the man." But he was confused by fear and by that fearful voice, for it was like thunder in his ears. When he came to himself again he declared the vision to those around him. Then they, too, said to the holy man, "You must mount on to a pillar and take up Saint Simeon's mode of life and be supported by the angels." The blessed one said, "Let the will of God, our Master, be done upon His servant." And, taking the holy Gospel into his hands and opening it with prayer, he found the place in which was written, "And thou, child, shalt be called the prophet of the Highest, for thou shalt go before the face of the Lord to prepare His ways." And he gave thanks and closed the book.

Not many days later a monk came from the East by name Sergius, a disciple of Saint Simeon, announcing the good end of the saint's life and carrying in his hands Saint Simeon's leather tunic in order to give it to the blessed Emperor Leo by way of benediction. But as the Emperor was busy with public affairs, the aforesaid Sergius could not get a hearing, or rather it was God who so arranged it in order that the new Elisha might receive the mantle of Elijah. When Sergius grew weary of waiting in the city because he could not obtain a hearing, he decided to go as far as the monastery of the Akoimetoi; now it was not possible for anyone to reach that monastery except by passing the church and the channel by it, as there was generally a north wind blowing. When he had entered into the boat with many others, men and women, they set sail. On reaching the spot where the demons used formerly to hurl stones at the passengers and continually sank their boats, those in the boat gave thanks to God and made mention of the holy man.

Sergius inquired who he was, for, said he, "I should like to be blessed by him." They answered, "Whilst the sailors tow the boat past, we can all land and go up to him." And this they did. And Sergius came and embraced the saint. And whilst they were talking and Daniel, the servant of God, was hearing about the end of the holy Simeon he related his vision to Sergius, who on hearing it said, "It is to thee rather than to the Emperor that God has sent me; for here am I, the disciple of thy father; here, too, is his benediction." And taking out the tunic he handed it in through the window. The saint took it and, kissing it with tears, said, "Blessed be Thou, O God, who dost all things after Thy will and hast deemed my humbleness worthy of the benediction which Thy servant has brought." Then some men from the ship upbraided Sergius for delaying and preventing them from sailing; to them Sergius answered, "Go on your ways and fare well; God has led me from one father to another." . . .

And indeed after two days men came back from the city carrying the pillar; there were with them two workmen sent by the guardsmen to fix the column in whatever place it was desired. So Sergius went up with them by night and they fixed the pillar and came back reporting that the pillar was erected. Daniel gave them his blessings and sent his blessing to the guardsmen, and then dismissed them. And the blessed Daniel said to Sergius, "We do not know the measure of the circumference of the pillar." But Sergius was unwilling to go up again and take the measurement of the column. However, the blessed man had another disciple dwelling near him, by name Daniel; him he bade go up and take the measurement of the column. So he went up and, as he was measuring the column, he was seen by the men who were guarding the vineyards in the neighbouring field which belonged to Gelanius, who at that time was steward of the sacred table to the most pious Emperor Leo. They ran up and held him and asked, "Whence are you and by whose authority are you taking the measurements of the column?" He answered them, "I am not a stranger, I belong to the father Daniel who lives in the church and I have come upon his business. And when I saw the column I was delighted." And when they heard his answer they let him go. And the brother went back to the city to a place called The Three Crosses, and ordered a balustrade, and took it with him. Afterwards he related to Daniel everything that had happened to him and the answer he had given to the men. The blessed man replied, "The will of the Lord be done!"

And it came to pass after three days when night had fallen they opened the church in which Daniel was shut up, and taking the brother he went up to the spot—for Sergius had departed to another place Thrace-wards—and they found a long plank lying there which the inhabitants of the suburb had prepared for knocking down the column. This they bound with a rope and stood it up against the column, and then went up and put the balustrade on the column, for that column was not really high, only about the height of two men. When they had fitted the balustrade and bound it firmly with a rope they knelt and prayed to God. And the blessed Daniel went up and stood on the column inside the balustrade and said, "Oh Lord Jesus Christ, in Thy holy name, I am entering upon this contest; do Thou approve my purpose and help me to accomplish my course." And he said to the brother, "Take away the plank and the rest of the rope and get away quickly so that if anybody comes he may not find you." And the brother did as he was told.

The next morning the husbandmen came and when they saw Daniel they were amazed; for the sight was a strange one, and they came near him, and when they looked on him they recognized him as the man who had formerly been in the church. After having received the saint's blessing they left him and went to the city to report to Gelanius, the owner of the property. On hearing their news he was very angry with them for not having guarded that part of his land; and he was also annoyed with the blessed Daniel for having done this without his consent. And he went and reported the matter to the blessed Emperor Leo and the Archbishop Gennadius, for the blessed Anatolius had already gone to his rest. The Emperor for his part said nothing. But the archbishop said to him, "As master of the property, fetch him down; for where he was he had no right to be, but he was not there on my authority."

Then Gelanius took several men with him and went up to the servant of God, and, although it was a calm day and the air was still, yet it came to pass that suddenly the clouds gathered and a storm arose accompanied with hail so that all the fruit of the vineyards was destroyed and the leaves were stripped from the vines, for it was the time of the vintage. And it was only with difficulty that the men who were with Gelanius got away and they muttered amongst themselves, for they were astonished at the strangeness of the sight.

Gelanius then approached the blessed man and said, "Who gave you permission to take up your stand on land belonging to me? Was it not better for you in the church?—but since you have shown contempt of me, the owner of the property, and have taken no account of the Emperor and the archbishop, let me tell you that I have been empowered by them to fetch you down."

But when he persisted and repeated his demands it seemed an unjust and illegal proceeding to his companions and they opposed its being done, "Because," said they, "the Emperor himself is a pious man and this man is orthodox and this spot lies at a distance from your field." When Gelanius perceived that there would be a disturbance he said to the saint in the Syrian language—for by birth he was a Syro-Persian from Mesopotamia—"Please pretend to come down for the sake of those who ordered you to descend, and then I will not allow you really to touch the ground." So then a ladder was brought and Daniel came down about six rungs from the column. There were still several rungs before he actually reached the ground, when Gelanius ran forward and prevented his coming down the last rungs, saying, "Return to your dwelling and your place and pray for me." For as Daniel was coming down he had noticed that sores and swellings had begun to appear on his feet, and he was distressed. And the blessed man went up the rungs of the ladder down which he had come, and stood inside the balustrade on the column; and after offering prayer, all received his blessing and went down from the hill in peace. . . .

In the following year a storm of unbearable violence took place and caused the saint's leather tunic to become like a bit of tow under the searing blast of the winds, and then the wind tore off even that wretched rag from the holy man and hurled it some distance away into a gully and the holy man was exposed to the snow all night long. And as the bitterest winds dashed against his face, he came to look like a pillar of salt. When morning broke the ladder could not be dragged along to him because of the tempest's violence, so he remained as he was and very nearly became a lifeless corpse.

But by God's mercy a calm followed, and they brought up the ladder. His disciples saw the hair of his head and beard glued to the skin by icicles, and his face was hidden by ice as though it were covered by glass and could not be seen and he was quite unable either to speak or to move. Then they made haste and brought cans of warm water and large sponges and gradually thawed him and with difficulty restored his power of speech. When they said, "You have been in great danger, father," he answered them as though he were just awakening from sleep and said at once, "Believe me, children, until you woke me, I was completely at rest. When the terrible storm broke and my garment was torn off me by the force of the winds, I was in great distress for about an hour, and then after a violent fainting fit I called upon the merciful God for help. And I was wafted, as it were, into sleep and I seemed to be resting on a magnificent couch and kept warm by rich coverings and I saw an old man sitting on a seat by my head, and I thought he was the man who met me on the road when I was coming away from the blessed Saint Simeon's enclosure. And he appeared to be talking with great love and sincerity and he pointed out to me a huge hawk coming from the East and entering this great city and finding an eagle's nest on the column in the Forum of the most pious Emperor Leo. And he came and settled down in the nest with the eagle's young and then no longer appeared to be a hawk but an eagle. And I inquired of the old man what that might mean. And he answered, 'There is no need for you to learn that now, but you shall know hereafter.' And whilst he held me in his arm and warmed me, the same old man said very pleasantly, 'I love you dearly; I wanted to be near you; many fruit-bearing branches are to blossom from your root.' And as we found pleasure in each other you did not do well in waking me; for I was delighted at meeting him." Then the disciples said to the holy man, "We pray your forgiveness, but truly we were in great despair; for we thought your Holiness had died. What do you think that vision means, father?" He said to them, "I do not understand it clearly, but God will do what is pleasing to Him and expedient for us." But his disciples tried to interpret the vision and said, "It behoves you with the help of the Emperor to bring the corpse of the holy and most blessed Simeon to this city. For it appears from the vision that this is the pleasure of the blessed Saint Simeon."

The servant of God said to them, "Fetch another leather tunic and wrap me in it." . . .

Seven days before his falling asleep he summoned the whole brotherhood, from chiefest to least, and some he bade stand quite near him on the top of the ladder and listen to his words. When he knew they were assembled, he said, "My brothers and children, behold, I am going to our Master and Lord, Jesus Christ. God who created all things by His word and wisdom, both the heaven and the earth and the sea and all that in them is, Who brought the race of men into being from that which was not, He Who is terrible to the angels but good to men, Who 'bowed the heavens and came down' upon the earth 'like rain upon the mown grass,' upon the Holy Virgin Mary, the mother of God, and was pleased to be incarnate of her, as He alone understands, and to be seen by men upon earth, Who 'took away the sins of the world' and suffered for us, and 'with His stripes' upon the Cross healed our spiritual wounds, and 'nailed the bond that was against us to the wood of the Cross,' He will strengthen you and will guard you safe from evil and will keep your faith in Him firm and immovable if you continue in unity with each other and perfect love until you draw your last breath. May He give you grace to serve him blamelessly and to be one body and one spirit continuing in humility and obedience. Do not neglect hospitality; never separate yourselves from your holy mother, the Church, turn away from all causes of offence and the tares of heretics, who are the enemies of Christ, in order that ye may become perfect even as also your heavenly Father is perfect. And now, I bid you farewell, my beloved children, and I embrace you all with the love of a father; the Lord will be with you." These words he ordered to be read aloud to the brethren by those who had stood nearest to him and caught the words, for he was lying down. When this had been done, and the brethren had heard the holy father's prayer and farewell, they burst into such weeping and wailing that the noise of their lamentation sounded like unto a clap of thunder. Once again the holy man prayed over us and then dismissed us, telling us not to be faint-hearted but bear up bravely, "and make mention of me in your prayers!" . . .

When they took down the railing they found his knees drawn up to his chest, and his heels and legs to his thighs. And whilst his body was being forcibly straightened, his bones creaked so loudly that we thought his body would be shattered; yet when he was laid out, he was quite entire except that his feet had been worn away by inflammation and the gnawing of worms. The weight of the hair of his head was divided into twelve plaits, each of which was four cubits long; likewise his beard was divided into two and each plait was three cubits long. Most of the Christ-loving men saw this.

They clad him, as was his wont, in a leather tunic, and a plank was brought up and laid on the column and he was placed on it. . . .

Next there was great anxiety about the manner of bringing it down for the funeral; for the Archbishop Euphemius was afraid the corpse might be torn asunder by the crowd, so he ordered it to be put into a case of lead, and this coffin the aforementioned *illustria,* the most pious Herais, also provided. This coffin was raised on the shoulders of the most holy Archbishop Euphemius and he bore it together with the noblest officials and pious men, and they brought down the corpse by way of the spiral stairway without its being hurt. But in order to receive a blessing the people rushed forward in front of the entry to the chapel and as the planks could not bear such a sudden rush they parted from each other and all the men who were carrying the coffin were thrown to the ground with the holy corpse. By the grace of the Lord the carriers did not suffer any injury nor did they give way, but they most marvellously withstood the onrush of the crowd so that among those countless thousands of men, women and children not a single one sustained any harm.

And Daniel was brought into the oratory and laid to rest underneath the holy martyrs as he had wished.

# CASSIODORUS

490?–?585

Magnus Aurelius Cassiodorus was born in Calabria. When only twenty years old he was named private secretary to Theodoric, the Ostrogoth ruler of Rome. In 507–11 he was quaestor, and later governor and senator. In 540 he retired to the monastery of Vivarium, which he had founded on his estates, became a monk, and devoted himself to reforms. He died at the age of ninety-five.

## FROM The Divine Letters

### THE ZEAL WITH WHICH THE HOLY SCRIPTURES SHOULD BE READ

In general, therefore, let the mind always be aware of the purposes of books, and let us fix our minds upon that attentive consideration which not only addresses itself to the ears but is also clear to the inner eye. Even if the narration seems simple, there is nothing empty and nothing idle in divine literature, but what is said is always said for some useful purpose in order that this purpose may be received in its proper meaning and may bring salvation. When, therefore, good deeds are related, let us be instantly aroused to imitation: when bad deeds which deserve punishment are set forth, let us dread to be engaged in the like. . . .

### COSMOGRAPHERS TO BE READ BY THE MONKS

Not without reason do we recommend that you ought to acquire some notion of cosmography, in order that you may clearly know in what part of the world the individual places about which you read in the sacred books are located.

. . . Read the brief *Picture of the World* of Dionysius, in order that you may contemplate almost as an eye-witness the things which you perceived with your ears. . . . Then if a noble concern for knowledge has set you on fire, you have the work of Ptolemy, who has described all places so clearly that you judge him to have been practically a resident in all regions, and as a result you, who are located in one spot, as is seemly for monks, traverse in your minds that which the travel of others has assembled with very great labour.

### ON FIGURES OF SPEECH AND THE LIBERAL ARTS

May the task of the ancients be our task . . . and may we with laudable devotion recall to the service of truth what they diverted for the practice of subtlety, in order that the learning which was thereby secretly removed may be honorably restored to the service of upright understanding.

But if certain simple-minded brothers cannot understand the excerpts which have been gathered in the following book, since practically all conciseness brings obscurity, let it be enough for them to examine briefly the divisions, usefulness, and excellence of these studies, in order that they may be seized with an eager striving of their minds to acquire a knowledge of the divine law. Through the various holy Fathers they will discover the source from which they can satisfy their ardent longing to the fullest extent. Let there be merely a genuine inclination to read and a sober wish to understand, and then may a suitable assiduity bring learning to those who were frightened at the start by the profundity of the text.

We know, however, that intelligence is not placed in letters alone, but that God gives perfect wisdom to everyone according as He will. . . . For if knowledge of good things were present in letters alone, surely unlettered men would not possess suitable wisdom.

### ON THE SITUATION OF THE MONASTERY OF VIVARIUM AND THAT OF CASTELLUM

The situation of the monastery of Vivarium invites you to prepare many things for strangers and those in need, since you have well-irrigated gardens, and, close beside them, the waters of the river Pellena, which abound in fish—a river which should not be considered dangerous because of the greatness of its waves or contemptible because of their smallness. It flows into your grounds skilfully directed wherever it is considered necessary, adequate for your gardens and your mills alike. It is indeed present when it is wanted, and when it has satisfied your wishes goes far away: thus, being dedicated to a definite service, neither is it dangerously rough nor can it be lacking when it is sought. Seas too are so near you that they are accessible for various kinds of fishing, and, when it pleases you, a fish once caught may be shut up in the fish ponds. For there, with the help of the Lord, we have made pleasant ponds, where a multitude of fish may drift beneath the faithful monastery: the situation so much resembles the caves in mountains that the fish in no way realizes that it is a captive, and it is free to acquire food and to hide itself in the solitary caverns. We have also ordered baths to be built of a sort suitable for sick bodies in a place where fitly flows limpid water, which is most pleasant for drinking and for bathing. Consequently, in all justice your monastery is sought by other people rather than other places by you. But these matters, as you see, are delights in present affairs, not a future hope of the faithful. The former are transitory, the latter will abide without end. But situated in the monastery as we are, let us be conveyed rather to the desires which make us reign with Christ.

Carefully read and willingly hear the priest Cassian, who has written about the instruction of faithful monks. He states in the very beginning of his holy argument that eight cardinal sins are to be avoided. He penetrates so competently into the harmful disturbances of minds that he makes men practically see their excesses in physical form and avoid them, though through confused and dull perception they had no previous knowledge of them. In the matter of free will, however, he has been most rightly blamed by the blessed Prosper, and we therefore admonish you that you ought to exercise caution in reading a man who oversteps the mark in topics of this sort. . . . But if through God's grace the monastic life should suitably instruct you at the monastery of Vivarium, as is proper to believe, and if purified souls should happen to desire something higher, you have the solitary sweetness of Castellum's hill, where, through the Lord's beneficence, you may live happily as anchorites. For there you will find places secluded and like a desert, since they are shut in and encompassed by ancient walls. It will therefore be appropriate for those of you who have already been trained and tested to choose this habitation, if the ascent has previously been made ready in your heart. For through reading you perceive one of two things—either what you can desire or what you can endure. It is a wonderful thing for an upright man who cannot teach others by precept to teach them by the piety of his conduct.

### AN ADMONITION FOR THE ABBOT AND THE COMMUNITY OF MONKS

Do, all of you, therefore, whom the walls of the monastery enclose, observe the rules of the Fathers, as well as the biddings of your own superior, and do you carry out willingly the orders which are given you for your salvation, because men are well rewarded for obeying without a single rebellious murmur commands which pertain to their salvation. And I beg you, most holy men, abbots Calchedonius and Gerontius, to arrange all matters in such a way as to lead the flock entrusted to you to the gifts of beatitude, with the help of the Lord. Before all things, therefore, receive the stranger, give alms, clothe the naked, break "thy bread for the hungry" since that man is truly to be called comforted who comforts the wretched.

Do you, moreover, instruct the peasants who belong to your monastery in good morals, and do not burden them with the weight of increased taxes. For it is written "My yoke is sweet and my burden is light." May they be ignorant of sly dealings, and may they be completely without knowledge of the worshipping of sacred groves—both matters which are generally acknowledged to be familiar to peasants—and may they live in innocence and happy simplicity. Let a subordinate manner of life of the purest sort be imposed upon them: may they come frequently to the holy monasteries in order that they may be ashamed to be called yours without being recognized by the members of your institution. May they also perceive that God in His kindness will impart fertility to their fields if they have been wont to call upon Him faithfully.

You have therefore been given a city of your own, O pious citizens, and if with the help of the Lord you spend your time concordantly and spiritually, you already enjoy a prefiguration of the heavenly home. Do not delight in slothfulness, which you know is hateful to the Lord. The authentic documents of the Sacred Scriptures together with their interpreters attend you, and they are truly the flowery fields, the sweet fruits of the heavenly paradise, with which faithful souls are imbued to their salvation, and by which your tongues are instructed in a diction not destined to die but to bear fruit. Therefore enter ardently upon the mysteries of the Lord, in order that you may be able to point out the way to those who follow, since it is a great shame to have books to read and to be unable to teach their meaning through ignorance.

And, in addition, the most merciful Redeemer has granted us the Communion of His body and blood, in order that thereby the compassion of the Creator may be understood in the highest degree, since by this great gift He has brought about our forgiveness, if only we seek Him with pure heart. And now may He also increase His gifts, may He light up our minds, may He purify our hearts, in order that we may deserve to understand the Sacred Scriptures with mind most pure and supported by His grace may fulfil His commands. . . .

### PRAYER

Grant, O Lord, spiritual progress to those who read Thy law, remission of all sins to those who seek Thy law, in order that we who desire with great longing to attain the light of Thy Scriptures may be blinded by no dark sins. Draw us towards Thee with the strength of Thy omnipotence, do not suffer those "whom Thou redeemest with Thy precious blood" to wander about of their own accord: do not allow Thy image to be covered with darkness in our minds, for if it is guarded by Thee it is always surpassing.

# ST BENEDICT OF NURSIA

480?–?543

Benedict was born at Nursia, in Umbria. Fearing when a student in Rome to fall into sin, like his fellow students, he fled to the mountains of Subiaco. There a monk named Romanus gave him the religious habit and showed him a cave, where he lived for three years. His fame reached the ears of some monks who had just lost their abbot. They asked Benedict to become his successor, but a minority party, fearing lest he be too strict, put poison in his wine. The glass broke when Benedict made the sign of the cross over his drink. Leaving them with the words, "I warned you we would not suit each other," he went back to his cave. However, disciples flocked to him and he built twelve monasteries, each with twelve monks presided over by an abbot. About 529 Benedict left with Maurus, Placidus, and other followers, and turned toward Monte Cassino. Having thrown down the pagan idols there, he set fire to the sacred grove, and later built an abbey which was being rebuilt in 1952 not for the first or even the fifth time. St. Benedict's *Rule,* with additions or subtractions, is that followed by most monks of the Western Church.

## FROM The Rule of St Benedict

### PROLOGUE

Hearken, O my son, to the precepts of thy master, and incline the ear of thy heart; willingly receive and faithfully comply with the admonition of thy loving father, that thou mayest return by the labour of obedience to Him from Whom thou hast departed by the sloth of disobedience.

To thee, therefore, my words are now addressed, whoever thou art, who, renouncing thy own will, takest up the most powerful and brilliant armour of obedience in order to fight for the Lord Christ, our true King.

First of all, when beginning any good work, beg of Him with most earnest prayer to perfect it, so that He who has now deigned to number us among His children may not at any time be grieved by our evil deeds. For we ought at all times so to serve Him by means of the gifts He has entrusted to us that He may neither, as an angry

Father, at any time disinherit His children, nor, as a dread Lord, provoked by our evil deeds, deliver us as most wicked servants to everlasting punishment for refusing to follow Him to glory.

Wherefore, let us at length arise, since the Scripture stirs us up, saying: "It is now the hour for us to rise from sleep." And our eyes being now open to the Divine Light, let us listen with reverent awe to what the Divine Voice admonishes us, as it cries out daily and says: "Today if you shall hear His voice, harden not your hearts." And again: "He who has an ear, let him hear what the Spirit says to the Churches." And what does He say? "Come, children, hearken to Me; I will teach you the fear of the Lord." "Walk while you have the light, that darkness may not overtake you."

And the Lord, seeking His own labourer in the multitude of the people to whom He addresses the foregoing admonitions, says again: "Who is the man that loves life, who desires length of days in order to enjoy good things?" Shouldst thou, hearing this, make answer, "I am he," God says to thee, "If thou wilt have true and everlasting life, keep thy tongue from evil and thy lips from words of deceit. Forsake evil and do good; seek after peace and pursue it. And when you shall have done these things, Mine eyes shall be upon you and Mine ears shall be open to your prayers. And before you shall call upon Me, I will say, Lo, here I am."

What can be sweeter to us, beloved brethren, than this voice of the Lord inviting us? Behold, in His loving kindness the Lord points out to us the way of life.

Having, therefore, our loins girt about with faith and the observance of good works, let us, with the Gospel as our guide, go forward on His paths, that we may deserve to see in His kingdom Him who hath called us. And if we wish to dwell in the tabernacle of His kingdom, we can never attain to it unless we run thither by the practice of good works. But let us ask the Lord with the prophet, saying to Him: "Lord, who shall dwell in Thy tabernacle; or who shall live on Thy holy mountain?" After this interrogation, brethren, let us hear the Lord making answer and saying: "He who walks without sin, who acts with justice, who thinks truth in his heart, and slanders not with his tongue; who does no evil to his neighbour, nor casts slurs upon his neighbour"; he who hath brought to naught the malignant evil one with all his temptations, and hath repelled him together with his suggestion from his heart, and hath taken hold of his evil thoughts in the very beginning and dashed them against the Rock, which is Christ. These are they who, fearing the Lord, are not puffed up with their own good works, but, knowing that the good that is in them is not of themselves, but from the Lord, they magnify the Lord working in them, saying with the prophet: "Not to us, O Lord, not to us, but to Thy name give glory." Thus it was that the Apostle Paul imputed nothing of his preaching to himself, saying: "By the grace of God I am what I am." And again he says: "He who boasts, let him boast in the Lord."

Hence also the Lord says in the Gospel: "Everyone, therefore, who hears these My words and acts upon them, shall be likened to a wise man who built his house on rock. And the floods came, and the winds blew and beat against that house, but it did not fall, because it was founded on rock." And the Lord, in fulfilment of these His words, daily waits for us to respond by our deeds to His holy admonitions. Therefore are the days of our life lengthened for the amendment of our evil deeds, according to that saying of the Apostle: "Dost thou not know that the goodness of God is meant to lead thee to repentance?" For the loving Lord says: "I desire not the death of the sinner, but that he should be converted and live."

Having then, brethren, asked the Lord who it is that shall dwell in His tabernacle, we have heard what He commands to those who wish to dwell there; and if we fulfil those commands, we shall be heirs of the kingdom of heaven.

Therefore, our hearts and our bodies must be prepared to fight under holy obedience to His commands; and let us beg of God to supply by the help of His grace that which by nature is lacking to us. And if we desire to escape the pains of hell and to attain to life everlasting, let us, whilst there is yet time, and we abide in this body, and are able to fulfil all these things by this way of light, let us, I say, do with speed now that which will profit us for all eternity.

We have, therefore, to establish a school of the Lord's service, in the institution of which we hope to ordain nothing that is harsh or difficult. But if anything somewhat severe be laid down, as reason may dictate, in order to amend faults or preserve charity, do not straightway depart full of fear from the way of salvation, which way cannot be entered upon except by beginnings which are difficult. But when one shall have advanced in this manner of life and in faith, he shall run with his heart enlarged and with an unspeakable sweetness of love on the way of God's commandments. Thus, never departing from His guidance, but persevering in His teaching in the monastery until death, we may by patience share in the sufferings of Christ, that we may merit to be partakers of His kingdom.

### OF THE VARIOUS KINDS OF MONKS

It is plain that there are four kinds of monks. The first are the cenobites, that is, those who live in a monastery, serving under a rule and an abbot. The second are the anchorites, that is, the hermits; those, namely, who not in the first fervour of their conversion, but after long probation in the monastery, have long since learned by the help of many others to fight against the Devil, and, being well armed, are able to go forth from the ranks of their brethren to the singlehanded combat of the desert, safe now, even without the consolation of another, to fight with their own strength against the weaknesses of the flesh and their own evil thoughts, God alone aiding them.

The third kind of monks, a most detestable class, is that of the Sarabaites, who, not having been tried by rule or by experience, as gold is tried in the furnace, but, being softened like lead, by their works showing loyalty rather to the world, publicly by means of the tonsure profess their infidelity to God. These in twos or threes, or even alone without a master, shut up in the sheepfolds of their own choosing, not in those of the Lord, have as their law the gratification of their desires; since whatsoever they consider agreeable to their own will and fancy, this they call holy, and unlawful whatever is not to their choice.

The fourth sort of monks, called vagabonds, spend all their lives wandering about through different provinces, dwelling three or four days now in one monastery then in another, always roaming about with no fixed abode, given up to their own pleasures and to the excesses of gluttony, and in all things more vicious even than the Sarabaites; of the most wretched manner of life of all these it is better to be silent than to speak. Omitting all reference to these, therefore, let us proceed with the help of the Lord to formulate a rule for the cenobites, who are the most steadfast kind of monks.

### HOW THE MONKS ARE TO SLEEP

Let each one sleep in a separate bed, receiving bedding suitable to monastic manner of life as the abbot shall appoint. If possible, let all sleep in one place; but if the number does not permit this, let them sleep in tens or twenties with the seniors who have charge of them. A lamp shall burn constantly in the cell until morning. Let them sleep clothed and girded with cinctures or cords; but let them not have knives at their sides while they sleep, lest perhaps they wound themselves in their sleep. Being thus always ready, the monks shall rise without delay when the signal is given, and vie with one another in hastening to the Work of God, yet with all gravity and modesty.

The junior brethren are not to have their beds near each other, but are to be intermingled with the seniors. And when the brethren rise for the Work of God, let them gently encourage one another because of the excuses of those who are given to sleep.

### OF THE MEASURE OF FOOD

We think it sufficient for the daily meal, whether at the sixth or the ninth hour, that there be at all the tables two dishes of cooked food because of the weaknesses of different persons; so that he who perhaps cannot eat of the one may make his meal of the other. Therefore, let two cooked dishes suffice for the brethren; and if there be any fruit or fresh vegetables, let a third dish be added. Let a full pound of bread suffice for each day, whether there be but one meal or both dinner and supper. If they are to take a second meal, let a third part of the pound be reserved by the cellarer, to be given to them at supper. But if the work has been rather heavy, it shall be in the discretion and power of the abbot to make some addition, if he think it expedient, provided that excess be avoided above all things, that no monk be ever guilty of surfeiting; for nothing is more unworthy of any Christian than gluttony, as our Lord says: "Take heed to yourselves, lest perhaps your hearts be overcharged with self-indulgence and drunkenness." Let not the same quantity be allowed to children of tender years, but a smaller amount than that allowed to their elders, so that frugality may be observed in all things. All, however, except the very weak and the sick, are to abstain from eating the flesh of four-footed animals.

### THAT THE OBSERVANCE OF ALL JUSTICE IS NOT LAID DOWN IN THIS RULE

We have written this Rule that, by observing it in monasteries, we may give proof of our having attained at least some degree of virtue and made a commencement of religious life. But for those who are desirous of advancing with rapid strides to the perfection of religious life, there are the teachings of the Holy Fathers, the observance of which will lead a man to the heights of perfection. For what page or what passage is there in the divinely inspired books of the Old and the New Testament that is not a most perfect rule of human life? Or what book of the Holy Catholic Fathers does not proclaim how we may by a direct course reach our Creator? And what are the Conferences of the Fathers, their Institutes and Lives? or the Rule of our holy Father Basil? What else are they but instruments of virtue for righteous and obedient monks? But to us who are slothful and sinful and negligent they bring the blush of shame.

Whoever thou mayest be, then, who art hastening to thy heavenly country, fulfil with the aid of Christ this least of rules which we have drawn up for beginners; and then thou shalt come with the help of God's Providence to those loftier summits of doctrine and virtue of which we have spoken above.

# St Columba

521–597

Columba, one of the great figures of Western monasticism, was born in 521 in County Donegal, Ireland, a member of the reigning family. After being ordained priest, he went to the island of Iona, off Scotland, where he established a church and monastery. During his thirty-four years' work among the Picts, he founded numerous churches and monasteries and converted the whole of northern Scotland. He died at Iona in 597.

### A SEVENTH-CENTURY PORTRAIT

This description is from the *Life of St Columba,* by Adamnan (679–704), who was also Abbot of Iona.

St Columba was born of noble parentage. . . . In the forty-second year of his age, desiring to make a pilgrimage from Ireland to Britain, he sailed forth. And he, who even from boyhood had been devoted to the school of Christ and the study of wisdom, preserving by the gift of God integrity of body and purity of soul, showed that although placed upon earth he was fitted for a heavenly life. For he was angelic of aspect, clean in speech, holy in deed, of excellent disposition, great in counsel, for thirty-four years trained as an island-soldier (of Christ). He could not pass the space even of a single hour without applying himself either to prayer, or reading, or writing, or to some manual labour. By day and by night he was so occupied, without any intermission, in unwearied exercises of fasts and vigils that the burden of any one of these particular labours might seem to be beyond human endurance. And, amid all, dear to all, ever showing a pleasant, holy countenance, he was gladdened in his inmost heart by the joy of the Holy Spirit.

### THE CONVERSION OF THE PICTS

This account is from Bede's *Ecclesiastical History* (see page 237).

For in the five hundredth three score and fifth year of our Lord's incarnation (at which time Justin the younger, succeeding Justinian, had received the governance of the Roman empire), a priest and abbot notable by his habit and religious life called Columba came from Ireland into Brittany to preach the word of God to the Redshanks that dwelt in the North, that is to say to those that by high and hideous ridges of hills were dissevered from such Redshanks as dwelt in the south quarters. For the southern Redshanks, who had their dwelling places in the same mountains, did long before (as they say) receive the true faith and abandoned idolatry, at which time the word was preached unto them by the right reverend bishop and blessed man, Ninian, a Briton born. Who was at Rome perfectly taught the faith, and mysteries of the truth. Whose see the English nation hath even now notable for the name and church of Saint Martin the bishop, where he also doth rest together with many holy men. Which place appertaining to the Bernicians' province is commonly called *Ad candidam casam,* at the white cottage, forasmuch as there he made a church of stone after another fashion than the Britons were wont to build. Columba came to Brittany when the most puissant king Bride, Meilchon's son, reigned over the Redshanks, in the ninth year of his reign, and did by his learning and example of life convert that nation to the faith of Christ. In consideration whereof the aforesaid isle was given him in possession, to make a monastery. For the isle is not great, but as though it were of five families by the estimation of the English. His successors kept it until this day, where also he lieth buried, dying at the age of seventy-seven years, about thirty-two years after that he came into Britain to preach. But before that he travelled to Brittany, he made a famous monastery in Ireland which for the great store of oaks is in the Scottish tongue called *Dearmach,* that is to say, a field of oaks: of both the which monasteries very many more religious houses were afterwards erected by his scholars both in Brittany, and also in Ireland. Of all the which the same abbey that is in the isle wherein his body lieth buried, is the head house. This isle is always wont to have an abbot that is a priest, to be the ruler: to whom both the whole country and also the bishops themselves ought after a strange and unaccustomed order to be subject, according to the example of the first teacher, who was no bishop, but a priest and a monk. The report is that some things are written by his scholars concerning his life and sayings: but yet what manner of man soever he was, we know this of him for a surety, that he left successors, men that excelled in great continence, in passing charity, and virtuous trade of religious life. In observing the high feast of Easter they trusted to uncertain compasses, and no marvel, considering that no man sent unto them the decrees made in general council for the keeping thereof. Yet they diligently observed all such works of devotion and chaste conversation as they could learn in the prophets, in the Gospels, and the Apostles' writings. This keeping of Easter continued no small time with them, that is, to wit, until the seven hundredth and sixteenth year of our Lord's incarnation, by the space of an hundred and fifty years after they received the faith. But when the right reverend and holy father and priest Egbert came to them from England, living in Christ's quarrel in exile in Ireland, being a man very well learned in the holy scripture and singular for the perfect life, which he had led many years together, they were reformed by him, and brought to keep Easter on the true, right and lawful day. . . .

### THE PASSING OF COLUMBA

From Adamnan's *Life of St Columba.*

One day in the month of May . . . the old man, weary with age, is borne on a wagon and goes to visit the brethren while at their work. And while they are busy in the western part of the isle of Iona, he began on that day to speak thus: "During the Easter festival just over in April, 'with desire I have desired' to pass away to Christ the Lord, as He had even granted to me if I liked. But, lest your festival of joy should be turned into sadness, I preferred that the day of my departure from the world should be put off a little longer."

The monks of his household were greatly afflicted whilst they heard these sad words of his, and he began to cheer them as far as he could with words of consolation. At the close of which, sitting just as he was in the wagon, turning his face eastward he blessed the island, with its islanders. . . . After those words of blessing the saint is carried back to his monastery.

. . . At the end of the same week, that is, on the sabbath day [Saturday], he and his dutiful attendant, Diormit, go to bless the granary which was near by. And on entering it, when the saint had blessed it and two heaps of corn stored up in it, he uttered these words with giving of thanks, saying: "Greatly do I congratulate the monks of my household that this year, also, if I should perchance have to depart from you, you will have enough for the year without stint." And hearing this word Diormit, the attendant, began to be sorrowful and to speak thus: "Often dost thou make us sad, Father, at this time of the year, because thou dost make mention so often of thy passing away." To whom the saint made this answer: "I have a certain little secret chat to hold with thee, and if thou wilt firmly promise me to disclose it to no one before my death, I shall be able to tell thee something more clearly as to my going hence." And when the attendant, on bended knees, had finished making this promise according to the saint's wish, the venerable man thereupon thus speaks: "In the Sacred Volumes this day is called the sabbath, which is, interpreted, rest. And this day is truly a sabbath day for me, because it is for me the last day of this present laborious life, on which I rest after the fatigues of my labours; and this night, at midnight, when begins the solemn day of the Lord, according to the saying of the Scriptures, I shall go the way of my fathers. For already my Lord Jesus Christ deigns to invite me, to Whom, I say, in the middle of this night, He Himself inviting me, I shall depart. For so it has been revealed to me by the Lord Himself." Hearing these sad words, the attendant began to weep bitterly. And the saint tried to console him as well as he could.

After this the saint goes out of the granary, and, returning to the monastery, sits down halfway at the place where afterwards a cross, fixed in a mill-stone, and standing to this day, is to be seen at the roadside. And while the saint, weary with age as I have said, rested there, sitting for a little while, behold the white horse, a faithful servant, runs up to him, the one which used to carry the milk pails to and fro between the byre and the monastery. He, coming up to the saint, wonderful to tell, lays his head against his breast—inspired, as I believe, by God, by whose dispensation every animal has sense to perceive things according as its Creator Himself has ordained—knowing that his master was soon about to leave him, and that he would see him no more, began to whinny and to shed copious tears into the lap of the saint. . . . And the attendant, seeing this, began to drive away the weeping mourner, but the saint forbade him, saying: "Let him alone, let him alone, for he loves me. . . ." And so saying, he blessed his servant the horse as it sadly turned to go away from him.

And then going and ascending the knoll that overlooks the monastery he stood for a little while on its top, and there, standing and raising both hands, he blessed his monastery, saying: "Upon this place, small though it be and mean, not only the kings of the Scotic people, with their peoples, but also the rulers of barbarous and foreign races, with the people subject to them, shall confer great and no common honour; by the saints also even of other churches shall no common reverence be accorded to it."

After these words, coming down from the knoll and returning to the monastery, he sat in his hut transcribing the Psalter; and, coming to that verse of the thirty-third Psalm, where it is written: "But they that seek the Lord shall not want any good thing," "Here," he says, "I must stop at the foot of this page, and what follows let Baithene write."

. . . After transcribing the verse at the end of the page, as above mentioned, the saint enters the church for the vesper mass of the vigil of the Lord's Day, and as soon as this is over, he returns to his cell and sits up throughout the night on his bed, where he had the bare rock for pallet and a stone for pillow, which to this day stands by his grave as his monumental pillar. And so, there sitting up, he gives his last commands to the brethren, his attendant alone hearing them, saying: "These my last words I commend to you, O my sons, that ye have mutual and unfeigned charity among yourselves, with peace: and if, according to the example of the holy Fathers, ye shall observe this, God, the Comforter of the good, will help you; and I, abiding with Him, will intercede for you; and not only will the necessaries of this present life be sufficiently supplied by Him, but the rewards of the good things of eternity, prepared for those who keep His Divine commandments, shall also be bestowed."

After which, as the happy last hour gradually approached, the saint was silent. Then, when the bell began to toll at midnight, rising in haste he goes to the church, and, running faster than the others, he enters it alone, and on bended knees falls down in prayer at the altar. At the same moment Diormit, his attendant, who followed more slowly, sees from a distance the whole church filled within with angelic light round about the saint. And as he drew near to the door, the same light which he had seen suddenly withdrew, and this light a few others of the brethren who stood afar off also saw. Diormit, therefore, entering the church, moans out with mournful voice, "Where art thou, Father?" And as the lights of the brethren had not yet been brought in, groping his way in the dark he finds the saint lying before the altar, and raising him up a little and sitting down by him he lays the holy head on his bosom. And meanwhile the community of monks, running up with lights, began to weep at the sight of their dying father. And as we have learned from some who were there present the saint, his soul not yet departing, with open eyes upturned, looked round about on either side with wonderful cheerfulness and joy of countenance on seeing the holy angels coming to meet him. Diormit then lifts up the holy right hand of the saint that he may bless the choir of monks. But the venerable father himself at the same time moved his hand as much as he was able, so that what was impossible for him to do with his voice at his soul's departure he might still do by the movement of his hand, namely, give his blessing to the brethren. And after thus signifying his holy benediction, immediately breathed forth his spirit. And it having left the tabernacle of the body, the face remained so ruddy and wonderfully gladdened by the vision of the angels that it seemed not to be that of one dead, but of one living and sleeping. . . .

# ST GREGORY I (THE GREAT)

(See page 155.)

## Introduction to the Dialogues

Being upon a certain day too much overcharged with the troubles of worldly business, in which oftentimes men are enforced to do more than of duty they are bound, I retired myself into a solitary place, very fit for a sad and melancholy disposition, where each discontentment and dislike concerning such secular affairs might plainly show themselves, and all things that usually bring grief, mustered together, might freely be presented before mine eyes. In which place, after that I had sat a long while in much silence and great sorrow of soul, at length Peter, my dear son and deacon, came unto me—a man whom, from his younger years, I had always loved most entirely, and used him for my companion in the study of Sacred Scripture: who, seeing me drowned in such a depth of sorrow, spake unto me in this manner:

"What is the matter? or what bad news have you heard? for certain I am that some extraordinary sadness doth now afflict your mind." To whom I returned this answer: "O Peter, the grief which I continually endure is unto me both old and new: old through common use, and new by daily increasing. For mine unhappy soul, wounded with worldly business, doth now call to mind in what state it was when I lived in mine abbey, and how then it was superior to all earthly matters, far above all transitory and corruptible pelf, how it did usually think upon nothing but heavenly things; and though it was enclosed in mortal body, yet did it by contemplation pass far beyond earthly bounds, and penetrate to the very height of heaven; and as for death, the memory whereof is almost to all men grievous, that it did love and desire as the end of all misery, the reward of her labours, and the very entrance to an everlasting and blessed life. But now, by reason of my pastoral charge, my poor soul is enforced to endure the burden of secular men's business, and after so excellent and sweet a kind of rest, defiled it is with the dust of worldly conversation: and when it doth, at the request of others, attend to outward affairs, no question but it returneth back far less fit to think upon those that be inward, spiritual, and heavenly. Wherefore, at this present, do I meditate what I suffer, and consider what my soul hath lost: and the memory of my former loss doth make that more grievous which I do now endure. For do you not behold at this present how I am tossed with the waves of this wicked world, and see the ship of my soul beaten with the storms of a terrible tempest? and therefore, when I remember my former state of life, I cannot but sigh to look back, and cast mine eyes upon the forsaken shore. . . .

"Sometimes also, my sorrow is increased by remembering the lives of certain notable men who with their whole soul did utterly forsake and abandon this wicked world: whose high perfection when I behold, I cannot also but see mine own infirmities and imperfections: very many of whom did, in a contemplative and retired kind of life, much please God: and lest by dealing with transitory business they might have decayed in virtue, God's goodness vouchsafed to free them from the troubles and affairs of this wretched world.

"But that which I have now said will be far more plain and the better perceived, if the residue of my speech be dialogue-wise, distinguished by setting down each of our names, you asking what you shall think convenient, and I by answer giving satisfaction to such questions as you shall demand at my hands."

*Peter*. I do not remember any in Italy that have been very famous for virtue; and therefore I am ignorant who they be, that, comparing your life to theirs, you should be so much inflamed to imitate their steps; for although I make no doubt but that there have been many good men, yet do I verily think that none of them wrought any miracles, or at least they have been hitherto so buried in silence that, whether any such thing hath been done or no, not any one man can tell.

*Gregory*. If I should, Peter, but report only those things which myself alone have understood by the relation of virtuous and credible persons, or else learned by myself concerning the life and miracles of perfect and holy men, I should sooner, in mine opinion, lack day to talk in, than matter to speak of.

*Peter*. I am desirous that you would vouchsafe to make me partaker of some of them: and not to think much if, upon so good an occasion, you interrupt your other study of interpreting the Scripture: because no less edification doth grow by the relating of miracles. For as, by the exposition of that, we learn how virtue is to be found and kept; so by recounting the miracles of holy men, we know how that which is found out and possessed is declared and made manifest to the world. And some there are that be sooner moved to the love of God by virtuous examples than by godly sermons: and oftentimes by the lives of holy Fathers the heart doth reap a double commodity; for if, by comparing of his own life with theirs, he findeth himself inflamed with the love of heaven, although before he had haply a good opinion of himself, yet seeing now how far others do excel him, he becometh also more humble, and is brought to have a more lowly conceit of his own actions and virtue.

*Gregory*. Such things as venerable and holy men have told me I will now, without any further delay, make you partaker of, and that, following the example of Sacred Scripture: for sure I am that St Luke and St Mark learned that Gospel which they wrote, not by sight, but by the relation of others. Yet lest any in reading should have occasion to doubt whether such things as I write be true or no, I will set down by what means and of whom I have learnt them: yet in some of them you have to know that I remember not all the particulars, but only the matter: in other some, both the matter and also the words. . . .

# FROM The Life and Miracles of St Bennet *

## INTRODUCTION

There was a man of venerable life, blessed by grace, and blessed in name—for he was called Benedictus, or Bennet—who, from his younger years, carried always the mind of an old man; for his age was inferior to his virtue. All vain pleasure he contemned; and though he were in the world, and might freely have enjoyed such commodities as it yieldeth, yet did he nothing esteem it, nor the vanities thereof. He was born in the province of Nursia, of honourable parentage, and brought up at Rome in the study of humanities. But, forasmuch as he saw many by reason of such learning to fall to dissolute and lewd life he drew back his foot, which he had, as it were, now set forth into the world, lest, entering too far in acquaintance therewith, he likewise might have fallen into that dangerous and godless gulf. Wherefore, giving over his books and forsaking his father's house and wealth, with a resolute mind only to serve God, he sought for some place where he might attain to the desire of his holy purpose: and in this sort he departed, instructed with learned ignorance, and furnished with unlearned wisdom. All the notable things and acts of his life I could not learn; but those few which I mind now to report, I had by the relation of four of his disciples, to wit, of Constantinus, a most rare and reverend man, who was next abbot after him; of Valentinianus, who many years had the charge of the Lateran Abbey; of Simplicius, who was the third General of his Order; and lastly, of Honoratus, who is now abbot of that monastery in which he first began his holy life.

## OF A MIRACLE WROUGHT BY HIS SISTER, SCHOLASTICA

*Gregory.* What man is there, Peter, in this world, that is in greater favour with God than St Paul was? who yet three times desired our

* St Benedict of Nursia; see page 555.

Lord to be delivered from the pricks of the flesh, and obtained not his petition. Concerning which point also, I must needs tell you how there was one thing which the venerable father Bennet would have done, and yet he could not. For his sister, called Scholastica, dedicated from her infancy to our Lord, used once a year to come and visit her brother. To whom the man of God went not far from the gate, to a place that did belong to the abbey, there to give her entertainment. And she coming thither on a time, according to her custom, her venerable brother with his monks went to meet her, where they spent the whole day in the praises of God and spiritual talk, and when it was almost night they supped together, and as they were yet sitting at the table, talking of devout matters, and darkness came on, the holy nun, his sister, entreated him to stay there all night, that they might spend it in discoursing of the joys of heaven. But by no persuasion would he agree unto that, saying that he might not by any means tarry all night out of his abbey. At that time the sky was so clear that no cloud was to be seen. The nun, receiving this denial of her brother, joining her hands together, laid them upon the table; and so, bowing down her head upon them, she made her prayers to Almighty God, and lifting her head from the table, there fell suddenly such a tempest of lightning and thundering, and such abundance of rain that neither venerable Bennet nor his monks that were with him could put their head out of the door: for the holy nun, resting her head upon her hands, poured forth such a flood of tears upon the table that she drew the clear air to a watery sky, so that after the end of her devotions, that storm of rain followed; and her prayer and the rain did so meet together that, as she lifted up her head from the table, the thunder began, so that in one and the very same instant she lifted up her head and brought down the rain. The man of God, seeing that he could not by reason of such thunder and lightning, and great abundance of rain, return back to his abbey, began to be heavy, and to complain of his sister, saying: "God forgive you, what have you done?" to whom she answered: "I desired you to stay, and you would not hear me, I have desired our good Lord, and He has vouchsafed to grant my petition: wherefore if you can now depart, in God's name return to your monastery, and leave me here alone." But the good father, not being able to go forth, tarried there against his will, where willingly before he would not stay. And so by that means they watched all night, and with spiritual and heavenly talk did mutually comfort one another: and therefore, by this we see, as I said before, that he would have that thing which yet he could not: for if we respect the venerable man's mind, no doubt question but he would have had the same fair weather to have continued as it was when he set forth, but he found that a miracle did prevent his desire, which by the power of Almighty God a woman's prayers had wrought. And it is not a thing to be marvelled at that a woman which of long time had not seen her brother might do more at that time than he could, seeing according to the saying of St John, "God is charity": and therefore of right she did more which loved more.

*Peter.* I confess that I am wonderfully pleased with that which you tell me.

### HOW BENNET SAW THE SOUL OF HIS SISTER ASCEND INTO HEAVEN

*Gregory.* The next day the venerable woman returned to her nunnery, and the man of God to his abbey: who three days after, standing in his cell, and lifting up his eyes to heaven, beheld the soul of his sister, which was departed from her body, in the likeness of a dove to ascend into heaven: who rejoicing much to see her great glory, with hymns and lauds gave thanks to Almighty God, and did impart the news of this her death to his monks whom also he sent presently to bring her corpse to his abbey, to have it buried in that grave which he had provided for himself. By means whereof it fell out, that as their souls were always one in God whilst they lived, so their bodies continued together after their death.

# JOHN MOSCHUS

550?–?634

John Moschus, surnamed Eucrates, or the Temperate, was born at Damascus about 550. He early became a monk, and entered the monastery of St Theodosius, near Jerusalem. Soon he retired into the desert of Judah, where he remained for ten years. About 578 he undertook a series of long journeys in order to visit as many monasteries as possible and collect their stories. He went first to Egypt, stopping at all the Thebaid monasteries as far as the Great Oasis. Then he went to Mount Sinai, and for ten years lived in the Laura of Aeliatae. He returned to Jerusalem in time for the enthronement of the Patriarch Amos in 594, but the assassination of Emperor Maurice by Phocas, in 602, and the threat of Persian invasions, drove Moschus from Palestine. He visited Syria and Cilicia and from there set sail for Alexandria, where he lived for twelve years. In 614 the Persians seized Jerusalem, destroyed the religious establishments of Palestine, and threatened Egypt. Moschus then left for Rome, visiting on the way the various religious establishments of Cyprus, Samos, and other Mediterranean islands. In Rome he wrote his *Spiritual Meadow,* and died there probably in 634. His friend and disciple Sophronius buried him at the monastery of St Theodosius, where he had begun his religious life.

There are 219 chapters in *The Spiritual Meadow,* describing happenings and people in the various monasteries visited by Moschus.

## FROM The Spiritual Meadow

. . . There was at Tarsus in Cilicia a buffoon named Babylas. He had two mistresses: one called Comito, the other Nicosa. He led a debauched life, doing everything worthy of the Devil and his legions. One day he entered a church, and by God's mercy the Gospel was being read in which is the verse: "Do penance, for the kingdom of heaven is at hand." He was moved and began to cry, calling himself a sinner because of all that he had done. Immediately on leaving the church he called his two mistresses and said to them, "You know how I have lived with you in debauchery, and that I have not preferred one of you more than the other. Well, then, take everything of mine, and divide it between you; as for me, I am going to set my affairs in order and become a monk." But they, with one voice, answered him weeping, "We were associated with you in sin, and in the loss of our souls; and now that you wish to do what pleases God, you leave us and wish to do it alone. In truth, you may not wish it, but we shall remain associated with you in virtue." Instantly he shut himself up in one of the towers in the city wall. The other two, having sold their goods and given them to the poor, and having themselves entered the ascetic life, made themselves a cell near the tower and shut themselves up. . . .

While we were in Alexandria, this story was told us. A nun was in her house, leading a solitary life, attending to her soul, fasting much, and attentive to prayer and vigil, and giving much in alms. But the Devil, who always is at war with the human race, did not approve of the virtues practised by this virgin, and he raised a tempest against her. In short, he inspired a young man with a satanic passion for her. The young man took up his stand outside her house. When the nun wished to come out, in order to go to the house of prayer and to pray, the young man did not leave her side, tormenting her and pestering her to reply to his advances; so that the nun was obliged to give up ever leaving her house because of the young man's importunity. So one day the nun sent her maid to say to the young man, "Come, my mistress needs you." The young man followed her happily, thinking he had reached his goal. The nun was sitting spinning. She said to the young man, "Sit down." Then, she herself being seated, she asked him, "Frankly, my lord brother, why do you torment me so that I cannot leave my house?" The young man replied, "Your eyes; it is they seduced me." When the nun heard that her eyes had seduced the young man, she took her spindle and with it put out both her eyes. Seeing that for his sake the nun had put out her eyes, the young man, full of sorrow, retired to Scete where he became an exemplary monk. . . .

We went into the Thebaid, and there we met the sophist Phibamon in the town of Antinöe. He told us this for our edification. There was, on the desert side of the town, a brigand called David who had robbed and killed many people and had done many crimes, more than anyone else, it would seem. One day, whilst he was in the mountain on a robbing expedition, having more than thirty companions with him, he withdrew into himself, penetrated with sorrow for the evil he had done. Abandoning all who were with him, he went off to a monastery. He knocked at the door; the porter came and said, "What do you want?" The brigand chief replied, "I want to become a monk." The porter came in and told the abbot. The abbot came, and seeing that the robber was old, he said, "You cannot stay here, for the brothers have a very tiring life, their asceticism is great; you have moreover quite another temperament, and you could not endure the monastic discipline." The other insisted, "Yes, I will do it all; only receive me." But the abbot remained firm. "You cannot," he replied. Then the brigand chief told him, "Know that I am David, the brigand chief. I have come here to weep for my sins. If you will not receive me, I swear, and I take Him who lives in heaven as my witness, that I will return to my first profession, and I will bring here all that were with me, and I will kill you all and destroy your monastery." On hearing this the abbot received him into the monastery, and, having cut his hair, gave him the holy habit. He began then to struggle, and in asceticism, obedience, and humility he surpassed everyone who was in the monastery. Now there were about seventy monks in this monastery, and the robber became the edification and model of them all. One day when he was sitting in his cell an angel of the Lord appeared and said to him, "David, David, the Lord God has pardoned all your sins, and in future you will work miracles." He answered the angel, "I cannot believe that in such a short time God has forgiven all my sin, heavier than the sands of the sea." The angel replied, "If I did not spare Zacharias the priest, when he doubted what I told him about his son, am I likely to spare you? That is why in future you shall not speak at all." The monk David prostrated himself and said, "When I was in the world, committing crimes and shedding blood, I spoke; now that I wish to serve God and to offer His praises, you lock up my tongue so that I may no longer speak?" Then the angel told him, "You will only be able to speak during the office; outside of the office you will not speak at all." And that is what happened. God worked many miracles through him. He recited the Psalms, but could speak no other word.

# POETRY

# Hail, Gladdening Light

This, from the second century, is the earliest Christian hymn that has survived, apart from biblical or apocryphal sources. It is still used in the Greek liturgy. This translation is by John Keble.

Hail, gladdening Light, of His pure glory pour'd
Who is the Immortal Father, Heavenly, Blest,
Holiest of Holies, Jesus Christ, our Lord.

Now we are come to the sun's hour of rest,
The lights of evening round us shine,
We hymn the Father, Son, and Holy Spirit Divine.

Worthiest art Thou at all times to be sung
With undefilèd tongue,
Son of our God, Giver of life, Alone!
Therefore in all the world Thy glories, Lord, they own.

# The Liturgy of St James

The exact date of this ancient liturgy is still in dispute, but it was appealed to by a council held in 692, which claimed apostolic origin for it. Some still claim it was at least in part derived from formulas composed by St James himself. It is still used on the Greek island of Zakynthos on St James' feast day, October 23, and is extant in Greek, Syriac, and Coptic versions.

Let all mortal flesh keep silence, and with fear and trembling stand;
Ponder nothing earthly minded, for with blessing in His hand
Christ our Lord to earth descendeth, our full homage to demand.

King of kings, yet born of Mary, as of old on earth He stood,
Lord of lords, in human vesture in the Body and the Blood
He will give to all the faithful His own self for heavenly food.

Rank on rank the host of heaven spreads its vanguard on the way
As the Light of light descendeth from the realms of endless day
That the pow'rs of hell may vanish as the darkness clears away.

At His feet the six-winged seraph; cherubim with sleepless eye,
Veil their faces to the Presence, as with ceaseless voice they cry,
Alleluia, Alleluia, Alleluia, Lord most High. Amen. Amen.

# CLEMENT OF ALEXANDRIA

(See page 48.)

## Curb for Wild Horses

Translated by Elizabeth Barrett Browning.

Curb for wild horses,
Wing for bird-courses
Never yet flown!
Helm, safe for weak ones,
Shepherd, bespeak once,
The young lambs Thine own.
Rouse up the youth,
Shepherd and Feeder,
So let them bless Thee,
Praise and confess Thee—
Pure words on pure mouth—
Christ, the child-leader!
Oh, the saints' Lord,
All-dominant Word!
Holding, by Christdom,
God's highest wisdom!
Column in place
When sorrows seize us—
Endless in grace
Unto man's race,
Saving one, Jesus!
Pastor and ploughman,
Helm, curb, together—
Pinion that now can
(Heavenly of feather)
Raise and release us!

# ST EPHRAEM SYRUS

306?–373

St Ephraem is the greatest of the exponents of orthodox Syrian Christianity. Born at Nisibis, of pagan parents, he felt drawn to the monastic life at an early age. His bishop, James of Nisibis, valued his assistance, especially during the years 338, 346, and 350, when Nisibis was besieged by the armies of Sapor II. In 363 Nisibis surrendered to the King of Persia, and Ephraem withdrew to the Roman city of Edessa. Here numerous disciples came to him, and, still in deacon's orders, he continued writing and teaching until his death, on June 9, 373. He wrote nearly all his dogmatic and moral works in metrical form, usually with a seven-syllable line. In the sermons and discourses the verses simply follow one another; in the hymns they are grouped together into strophes ranging from four to twelve verses in length.

Examples of his funeral hymns, of which eighty-five have survived, are given here. The translations are by Henry Burgess.

## On the Death of a Child

MOTIVES FOR RESTRAINING SORROW

Oh my son, tenderly beloved!
Whom grace fashioned
In his mother's womb,
And divine goodness completely formed.
He appeared in the world
Suffering like a flower,
And death put forth a heat
More fierce than the sun,
And scattered its leaves
And withered it, that it ceased to be.
I fear to weep for thee,
Because I am instructed
That the Son of the Kingdom hath removed thee
To His bright habitation.

Nature, in its fondness,
Disposes me to tears,
Because, my son, of thy departure.
But when I remember the bright abode
To which they have led thee,
I fear lest I should defile
The dwelling-place of the King
By weeping, which is adverse to it;
And lest I should be blamed,
By coming to the region of bliss
With tears which belong to sadness;
I will therefore rejoice,
Approaching with my pure offering.

The sound of thy sweet notes
Once moved me and caught mine ear,
And caused me much to wonder;
Again my memory listens to it,
And is affected by the tones
And harmonies of thy tenderness.
But when my spirit groans aloud
On account of these things,
My judgment recalls me,
And listens with admiration
To the voices of those who live on high;
To the song of the spiritual ones
Who cry aloud, Hosanna!
At thy marriage festival.

# The Parting of Body and Soul

The soul, having left the body,
Is in great suffering,
And feels much grief;
And she is distracted
Hither and thither,
As to her destination;
For the evil spirits desire
That she should go with them
Into the midst of Gehenna;
And the angels also,
That she should journey with them,
To the region of light.

In that moment,
The soul lightly esteems
Her beloved friends and brethren,
Those whom she held dear,
And her neighbours,
And those with whom she was familiar.
In that hour she despises
Whatsoever appertains to riches,
Or worldly possessions;
But respecting her trespasses
She has great anxiety,
They being so many.

Then the soul, standing separate
Above the body she hath left,
Speaks thus to it,
"Death hath dismissed me.

Remain thou here in peace
For I am going away."
Then the body replies,
"Depart thou in peace,
O soul tenderly loved!
The Lord who hath fashioned us,
He will procure our deliverance
From Gehenna!"

## Christ the Companion of the Disembodied Soul

As my provision for my journey I have taken Thee,
Oh Thou Son of God!
And when I am hungry I will eat of Thee,
Thou Saviour of the world!
The fire will keep far off from my members,
Perceiving in me the savour of Thy body and blood.
Baptism shall become to me
A ship which cannot sink,
And I shall see Thee there, O Lord,
In the day of the resurrection.

I was living in my place of sojourn
(Thus speaks the soul),
But the Master of the house sent to me,
And I am not permitted to continue.
The messenger thus addressed me:
"Depart from the house and vacate its chambers."
O my body, my temporary home,
Remain here in peace!
And in the day of the resurrection
I shall see thee rejoicing.

The lictors came with speed,
  But I was ignorant of it;
The messenger stood at the door,
  But I did not perceive him;
Deliver me, Lord, from the judgment of the Devil,
  Who hateth Thy renowned children;
And with Thy holy ones may I attain
  To the house of the kingdom;
That I may utter a song of praise,
  And with them glorify Thee.

How bitter is this cup
  Which death hath mingled!
And how terrible is the time,
  And how grievous the hour,
Which calleth for Thee!
  The soul saith to the body,
"Remain thou here in peace,
  O much loved habitation,
In which I once dwelt
  While the Lord was willing."

How saddened is the sinner
  In his heart at that hour,
When the King Messiah shall sit
  Upon His dreadful judgment-seat;
And all tribes shall stand before Him,
  And all secrets of the heart shall be revealed.

Terrible is the tribunal!
  Terrible is the Judge, and that season!
Blessed is he whom Thy favour
  Shall protect, O Lord!

# NICETAS OF REMESIANA

(See page 402.)

## Te Deum

The *Te Deum,* traditionally supposed to have been composed by Saints Ambrose and Augustine jointly, on the occasion of the latter's baptism, at the beginning of the twentieth century was proved from internal evidence, to have been written by Nicetas, who also composed many other hymns. This translation is by John Dryden.

Thee, Sovereign God, our grateful accents praise;
We own Thee Lord, and bless Thy wondrous ways;
To Thee, eternal Father, earth's whole frame,
With loudest trumpets sounds immortal fame.
Lord God of Hosts! For Thee the heavenly powers
With sounding anthems fill the vaulted towers.
Thy Cherubim thrice, Holy, Holy, Holy, cry;
Thrice, Holy, all the Seraphim reply,
And thrice returning echoes endless songs supply.
Both heaven and earth Thy majesty display;
They owe their beauty to Thy glorious ray.
Thy praises fill the loud Apostles' choir;
The train of prophets in the song conspire.
Legions of martyrs in the chorus shine,
And vocal blood with vocal music join.
By these Thy church, inspired by heavenly art,
Around the world maintains a second part;
And turns her sweetest notes, O God, to Thee,
The Father of unbounded majesty;
The Son adored co-partner of thy seat,
And equal everlasting Paraclete.

Thou King of Glory, Christ of the Most-High,
Thou co-eternal filial Deity;
Thou who to save the world's impending doom
Vouchsaf'st to dwell within a Virgin's womb.
Old tyrant death disarmed, before Thee flew
The bolts of heaven, and back the foldings drew,
To give access, and make Thy faithful way,
From God's right hand Thy filial beams display.
Thou art to judge the living and the dead;
Then spare those souls for whom Thy veins have bled.
O take us up among Thy blessed above,
To share with them Thy everlasting love.
Preserve, O Lord, Thy people and enhance
Thy blessing on Thine own inheritance.
Forever raise their hearts, and rule their ways;
Each day we bless Thee and proclaim Thy praise;
No age shall fail to celebrate Thy name,
No hour neglect Thy everlasting fame.
Preserve our souls, O Lord, this day from ill;
Have mercy, Lord, have mercy still;
As we have hoped, do Thou reward our pain;
We've hoped in Thee—let not our hope be vain.

## ST AMBROSE

St Ambrose (see page 111) has been called the "Father of Latin hymnody." The hymns of the Canonical hours which are given here were translated by J. H. Newman; translations of the other poems are by John Mason Neale.

# The Hymns of the Little Hours

### PRIME

The star of morn to night succeeds;
  We therefore meekly pray,
May God in all our words and deeds,
  Keep us from harm this day;
May He in love restrain us still
From tones of strife and words of ill,
And wrap around and close our eyes
To earth's absorbing vanities.
May wrath and thoughts that gender shame
  Ne'er in our breasts abide;
And cheerful abstinences tame
  Of wanton flesh the pride:
So, when the weary day is o'er,
And night and stillness come once more,
Strong in self-conquering purity,
We may proclaim, with choirs on high:

### TERCE

Come, Holy Ghost, who, ever one,
Reignest with Father and with Son,
It is the hour, our souls possess
With thy full flood of holiness.
Let flesh and heart, and lips and mind,
Sound forth our witness to mankind;

And love light up our mortal frame
Till others catch the living flame.
Now to the Father, to the Son,
And to the Spirit, three in one,
Be praise and thanks and glory given,
By men on earth, by saints in heaven.

### SEXT

O God, who cannot change nor fail,
  Guiding the hours as they roll by;
Brightening with beams the morning pale,
  And burning in the midday sky.

Quench Thou the fires of hate and strife,
  The wasting fever of the heart;
From perils guard our feeble life,
  And to our souls Thy peace impart.

### NONE

O God, unchangeable and true,
  Of all the Light and Power,
Dispensing light in silence through
  Every successive hour;

Lord, brighten our declining day,
  That it may never wane,
Till death, when all things round decay,
  Brings back the morn again.

### COMPLINE

Now that the daylight dies away,
  By all Thy grace and love,
Thee, Maker of the world, we pray
  To watch our bed above.

Let dreams depart and phantoms fly,
  The offspring of the night,

Keep us, like shrines, beneath Thine eye,
Pure in our foe's despite.

This grace on Thy redeemed confer,
Father, coequal Son,
And Holy Ghost, the Comforter,
Eternal, three in one.

## O Trinity of Blessed Light

O Trinity of blessed light,
O Unity of princely might,
The fiery sun now goes his way;
Shed Thou within our hearts Thy ray.

To Thee our morning song of praise,
To Thee our evening prayer we raise;
Thy glory suppliant we adore
For ever and for evermore.

## O God, Creation's Secret Force

O God, Creation's secret Force,
Thyself unmov'd, all motion's source,
Who from the morn till evening's ray,
Through all its changes guid'st the day:

Grant us, when this short life is past,
The glorious evening that shall last:
That by a holy death attain'd,
Eternal glory may be gain'd.

O Father, that we ask be done,
Through Jesus Christ, Thine Only Son;
Who, with the Holy Ghost and Thee,
Shall live and reign eternally.

## Before the Ending of the Day

Before the ending of the day,
Creator of the world, we pray
That with Thy wonted favour, Thou
Would'st be our Guard and Keeper now.

From all ill dreams defend our eyes,
From nightly fears and fantasies;
Tread under foot our ghostly Foe,
That no pollution we may know.

O Father, that we ask be done,
Through Jesus Christ, Thine Only Son;
Who, with the Holy Ghost and Thee,
Shall live and reign eternally.

# ST GREGORY OF NAZIANZUS

(See page 89.)

## Soul and Body

Translated by Elizabeth Barrett Browning.

What wilt thou possess or be?
O my soul, I ask of thee.
What of great or what of small,
Counted precious therewithal?
Be it only rare, and want it,
I am ready, soul, to grant it.
Wilt thou choose to have and hold
Lydian Gyges' charm of old,
So to rule us with a ring,
Turning round the jewelled thing,
Hidden by its face concealed,
And revealed by it's revealed?
Or preferrest Midas' fate—
He who died in golden state,
All things being changed to gold?
Of a golden hunger dying,
Through a surfeit of "would-I"-ing
Wilt have jewels brightly cold,
Or may fertile acres please?
Or the sheep of many a fold,
Camels, oxen, for the wold?
Nay! I will not give thee these!
These to take thou hast not will
These to give I have not skill;
Since I cast earth's cares abroad,
That day when I turned to God.

Wouldst a throne, a crown sublime
Bubble blown upon the time?
So thou mayest sit tomorrow
Looking downward in meek sorrow,
Someone walking by thee scorning,
Who adored thee yester morning,
Some malign one? Wilt be bound
Fast in marriage (joy unsound!)
And be turnèd round and round
As the time turns? Wilt thou catch
That sweet sickness? and to match it
Have babies by the hearth, bewildering
And if I tell thee the best children
Are none—what answer?
Wilt thou thunder
Thy rhetorics, move the people under?
Covetest to sell the laws
With no justice in thy cause,
And bear on, or else be borne,
Before tribunals worthy scorn?
Wilt thou shake a javelin rather
Breathing war? or wilt thou gather
Garlands from the wrestler's ring?
Or kill beasts for glorying?
Covetest the city's shout,
And to be in brass struck out?
Cravest thou that shade of dreaming,
Passing air of shifting seeming,
Rushing of a printless arrow,
Clapping echo of a hand?
What to those who understand
Are today's enjoyments narrow,
Which tomorrow go again,
Which are shared with evil men,
And of which no man in his dying

Taketh aught for softer lying?
What then wouldst thou, if thy mood
Choose not these? what wilt thou be
O my soul? a deity?
A God before the face of God,
Standing glorious in His glories,
Choral in His angels' chorus?

Go, upon thy wing arise,
Plumèd by quick energies,
Mount in circles up the skies:
And I will bless thy wingèd passion,
Help with words thine exaltation,
And, like a bird of rapid feather,
Outlaunch thee, Soul, upon the ether

But thou, O fleshly nature, say,
Thou with odours from the clay,
Since thy presence I must have
As a lady with a slave,
What wouldst thou possess or be,
That thy breath may stay with thee?
Nay, I owe thee nought beside,
Though thine hands be open wide.
Would a table suit thy wishes,
Fragrant with sweet oils and dishes
Wrought to subtle niceness? where
Stringèd music strokes the air,
And blithe hand-clappings, and the smooth
Fine postures of the tender youth
And virgins wheeling through the dance
With an unveiled countenance—
Joys for drinkers, who love shame,
And the maddening wine-cup's flame.
Wilt thou such, howe'er decried?
Take them—and a rope beside!

Nay! this boon I give instead
Unto friend insatiated—
May some rocky house receive thee,
Self-roofed, to conceal thee chiefly;
Or if labour there must lurk,
Be it by a short day's work!
And for garment, camel's hair,
As the righteous clothèd were,
Clothe thee! or the bestial skin,
Adam's bareness hid within—
Or some green thing from the way,
Leaf of herb, or branch of vine,
Swelling, purpling as it may,
Fearless to be drunk for wine!
Spread a table there beneath thee,
Which a sweetness shall up-breathe thee,
And which the dearest earth is giving,
Simple present to all living!
When that we have placed thee near it,
We will feed thee with glad spirit.
Wilt thou eat? soft, take the bread,
Oaten cake, if that bestead;
Salt will season all aright,
And thine own good appetite,
Which we measure not, nor fetter:
'Tis an uncooked condiment,
Famine's self the only better.
Wilt thou drink? Why, here doth bubble
Water from a cup unspent,
Followed by no tipsy trouble,
Pleasure sacred from the grape!
Wilt thou have it in some shape
More like luxury? we are
No grudgers of wine-vinegar!
But if all will not suffice thee,

And thou covetest to draw
In that pitcher with a flaw,
Brimful pleasures heaven denies thee!
Go, and seek out, by that sign,
Other help than this of mine!
For me, I have not leisure so
To warm thee, sweet, my household foe,
Until, like a serpent frozen,
New-maddened with the heat, thou loosen
Thy rescued fang within mine heart!
Wilt have measureless delights
Of gold-roofed palaces, and sights
From pictured or from sculptured art,
With motion near their life; and splendour
Of bas-relief, with tracery tender,
And varied and contrasted hues?
Wilt thou have, as nobles use,
Broidered robes to flow about thee?
Jewelled fingers? Need we doubt thee?
Gauds for which the wise will flout thee?
I most, who, of all beauty, know
It must be inward, to be so!

And thus I speak to mortals low,
Living for the hour, and o'er
Its shadow, seeing nothing more:
But for those of nobler bearing,
Who live more worthily of wearing
A portion of the heavenly nature—
To low estate of clayey creature,
See, I bring the beggar's meed,
Nutriment beyond the need!
O beholder of the Lord,
Prove on me the flaming sword!
Be mine husbandman, to nourish
Holy plants, that words may flourish

Of which mine enemy would spoil me,
Using pleasurehood to foil me!
Lead me closer to the tree
Of all life's eternity;
Which, as I have pondered, is
The knowledge of God's greatnesses:
Light of One, and shine of Three,
Unto whom all things that be
Flow and tend!

In such a guise
Whoever on the earth is wise
Will speak unto himself: and who
Such inner converse would eschew—
We say perforce of that poor wight,
"He lived in vain!" and if *aright,*
It is not the worst word we might.

## PRUDENTIUS

348–?410

Aurelius Clemens Prudentius was born at Saragossa of a presumably Christian family. After having received a good education, he was given a military post by Theodosius I. Although he rose rapidly, he came to despise honors, and at forty-five he turned to prayer and good works, and made a pilgrimage to Rome. In 405 he published a collection of his works: The translations used here are by John Mason Neale.

# The Winged Herald of the Day

The winged herald of the day
Proclaims the morn's approaching ray:
And Christ the Lord our souls excites,
And so to endless life invites.

"Take up thy bed," to each He cries,
Who sick or wrapped in slumber lies:
"And chaste and just and sober stand,
And watch: My coming is at hand."

With earnest cry, with tearful care,
Call we the Lord to hear our prayer;
While supplication, pure and deep,
Forbids each chastened heart to sleep.

Do Thou, O Christ, our slumbers wake:
Do Thou the chains of darkness break:
Purge Thou our former sins away,
And in our souls new light display.

All laud to God the Father be:
All laud, Eternal Son, to Thee:
All laud, as is for ever meet,
To God the Holy Paraclete.

# Of the Father Sole Begotten

Of the Father sole begotten,
Ere the worlds began to be,
He the Alpha and Omega,
He the source, the ending He,
Of the things that are, that have been,
And that future years shall see,
Evermore and evermore!

He is here, Whom seers in old time
Chanted of, while ages ran;
Whom the writings of the Prophets
Promised since the world began:
Then foretold, now manifested,
To receive the praise of man,
Evermore and evermore!

O that ever-blessed birthday,
When the Virgin, full of grace
Of the Holy Ghost incarnate;
Bare the Saviour of our race,
And that Child, the world's Redeemer,
First displayed His Sacred Face,
Evermore and evermore!

Praise Him, O ye Heav'ns of Heavens!
Praise Him, Angels in the height!
Every Power and every Virtue
Sing the praise of God aright:
Let no tongue of man be silent,
Let each heart and voice unite,
Evermore and evermore!

Thee let age, and Thee let manhood,
Thee let choirs of infants sing;
Thee the matrons and the virgins,
And the children answering:
Let their modest song re-echo,
And their heart its praises bring,
Evermore and evermore!

Laud and honour to the Father!
Laud and honour to the Son!
Laud and honour to the Spirit!
Ever Three and ever One:
Consubstantial, Co-eternal,
While unending ages run,
Evermore and evermore!

# All Hail! Ye Infant Martyr Flowers

All hail! ye infant martyr flowers,
Cut off in life's first dawning hours:
As rosebuds, snapped in tempest strife,
When Herod sought your Saviour's life.

You, tender flock of lambs, we sing,
First victim slain for Christ your King:
Beneath the Altar's heavenly ray,
With Martyr Palms and Crowns ye play.

For their redemption glory be,
O Jesu, Virgin-born, to Thee!
With Father, and with Holy Ghost,
For ever from the Martyr Host.

# ST PAULINUS OF NOLA

## FROM Farewell to Nicetas

St Paulinus and Nicetas of Remesiana (see pages 402, 587) were friends from early youth. Nicetas, after spending several weeks in Rome in 398 A.D., was on his way home to Dacia, where he had established a flourishing Christian community. In this poem St Paulinus praises his friend's heroic labors among the barbarians north of the Danube.

You are now hurrying away and departing from us; and yet, though distance may separate us, in heart and mind we shall ever be united.

Smoothly you glide over the unruffled sea; with the symbol of salvation protecting your ship, and with the arms of the cross as sailyards, you will be secure and safe in the midst of storm and billows.

Who will give me the wings of a dove, that I may with speed join the chorus that, led by thee, makes the welkin ring with the refrain, "Christ is God."

Joyfully the sailors sing their chanteys, changing their accustomed melodies to pious hymns; and with sacred song invite the favouring breezes to speed them over the deep.

Loud above the chorus, like a clear-toned trumpet, sounds the voice of Nicetas chanting the Messiah, and over the sea's expanse rings the eternal psalm of the poet David.

And the whales in wonder listen to the "Amen," while the deep sea monsters sport in playful frolic, as the priest worships his Lord in song.

With what joy will that land re-echo where you teach the haughty natives to bend their untamed necks to the mild yoke of Christ!

# ST PATRICK

389?–?461

The "Apostle of Ireland" was a pupil of St Germain of Auxerre. He was born at Banavem Taberniae (possibly in Monmouthshire, England), as he himself tells in his *Confession*. His father, Calpurnius, owned a small farm. At the age of sixteen Patrick was kidnaped by Irish marauders and carried into captivity in Ireland, where he was sold as a slave. After six years of tending flocks, he escaped, made his way to the sea two hundred miles away, and managed to return safely home. Some time between his return to Britain in 412, and 432, when he was consecrated bishop, he was ordained deacon by Bishop Amator in Auxerre, and also studied at Lérins, the great monastery recently founded by St Honoratus on an island off southern France. After his consecration as successor to St Palladius, who had been sent to Ireland by Pope Celestine in 431, Patrick spent the remainder of his life evangelizing among the Irish.

The Irish hymn called the "Lorica [or Breastplate] of St Patrick" is preserved in three ancient manuscripts, and most critics agree there is little doubt that it was written by St Patrick. In the *Book of Armagh,* a manuscript written between 807 and 846 by Ferdomnach, the scribe notes of ". . . the fourfold honour due to St Patrick in all the monasteries and churches throughout Ireland," that the fourth is: "Always sing his Scottish [i.e., Gaelic] song."

The ancient Irish preface states: "Patrick made his hymn: in the time of Loegaire macNeill it was made, and the cause of its composition was for the protection of himself and his monks against the deadly enemies that lay in ambush for the clerics. And it is a lorica of faith for the protection of body and soul against demons and men and vices. . . ."

The translation used here is by Atkinson.

## The Lorica

I

I arise today:
　in vast might, invocation of the Trinity;
　belief in a Threeness;
　confession of Oneness;
　towards the Creator.

II

I arise today:
in the might of Christ's Birth and His Baptism;
in the might of His Crucifixion and Burial;
in the might of His Resurrection and Ascension;
in the might of His Descent to the Judgment of Doom.

III

I arise today:
in the might of the order of Cherubim;
in obedience of Angels;
in ministration of Archangels;
in hope of resurrection for the sake of reward;
in prayers of Patriarchs;
in predictions of Prophets;
in preachings of Apostles;
in faiths of Confessors;
in innocence of holy Virgins;
in deeds of righteous men.

IV

I arise today:
in the might of Heaven;
brightness of Sun;
whiteness of Snow;
splendour of Fire;
speed of Lightning;
swiftness of Wind;
depth of Sea;
stability of Earth;
firmness of Rock.

V

I arise today:
in the might of God for my piloting;
Power of God for my upholding

Wisdom of God for my guidance;
Eye of God for my foresight;
Ear of God for my hearing;
Word of God for my utterance;
Hand of God for my guardianship;
Path of God for my precedence;
Shield of God for my protection;
Host of God for my salvation;
against snares of demons;
against allurements of vices;
against solicitations of nature;
against every person that wishes me ill, far and near;
alone and in a crowd.

VI

I invoke therefore all these forces:
against every fierce merciless force that may come upon my body and my soul;
against incantations of false prophets;
against black laws of paganism;
against false laws of heresy;
against encompassment of idolatry;
against spells of women and smiths and druids;
against all knowledge that is forbidden the human soul.

VII

Christ for my guardianship today:
against poison, against burning,
against drowning, against wounding,
that there may come to me a multitude of rewards;
Christ with me, Christ before me,
Christ behind me, Christ in me,
Christ under me, Christ over me,
Christ to right of me, Christ to left of me,
Christ in lying down, Christ in sitting, Christ in rising up,
Christ in the heart of every person who may think of me!

Christ in the mouth of everyone who may speak to me!
Christ in every eye which may look on me!
Christ in every ear which may hear me!

I arise today:
    in vast might, invocation of the Trinity
    belief in a Threeness;
    confession of Oneness;
    meeting in the Creator;
*Domini est salus, Domini est salus, Christi est salus;*
*Salus tua, Domine, sit semper nobiscum.*

# VENANTIUS FORTUNATUS

530?–?610

Fortunatus was born in northeastern Italy, near Treviso, and studied grammar, rhetoric, and jurisprudence at Ravenna. He was miraculously cured of an eye disease through the intercession of St Martin, and about 565 he set out for Tours to visit his patron's tomb. From Tours he went on to Poitiers, where Radegunde, the widow of Clotaire I, had founded a monastery and retired to it. Fortunatus settled at Poitiers, was ordained priest, and became the chaplain of Radegunde's community. Toward the end of his life he became bishop of Poitiers. He wrote some of the best-known hymns of the Church and eleven books of songs. The translations used here are by John Mason Neale.

## Sing, My Tongue, the Glorious Battle

Sing, my tongue, the glorious battle,
With completed victory rife:
And above the Cross's trophy
Tell the triumph of the strife,
How the world's Redeemer conquer'd
By surrendering of His Life.

God his Maker, sorely grieving
That the first-made Adam fell,
When he ate the fruit of sorrow,
Whose reward was death and hell,
Noted then this Wood, the ruin
Of the ancient wood to quell.

For the work of our Salvation
Needs would have His order so,
And the multiform deceiver's
Art by art would overthrow,
And from thence would bring the med'cine
Whence the insult of the foe.

Wherefore, when the sacred fullness
  Of th' appointed time was come,
This world's Maker left His Father,
  Sent the Heavenly Mansion from,
And proceeded, God Incarnate,
  Of the Virgin's Holy Womb.

Weeps the Infant in the manger
  That in Bethlehem's stable stands;
And His limbs the Virgin Mother
  Doth compose in swaddling bands,
Meetly thus in linen folding
  Of her God the feet and hands.

Thirty years among us dwelling,
  His appointed time fulfill'd,
Born for this, He meets His Passion,
  For that this He freely will'd:
On the Cross the Lamb is lifted,
  Where His life-blood shall be spilled.

He endured the nails, the spitting,
  Vinegar, and spear, and reed;
From that Holy Body broken
  Blood and water forth proceed:
Earth, and stars, and sky, and ocean,
  By that flood from stain are freed.

Faithful Cross! above all other,
  One and only noble tree!
None in foliage, none in blossom,
  None in fruit thy peers may be:
Sweetest Wood, and sweetest Iron!
  Sweetest Weight is hung on thee.

Bend thy boughs, O Tree of Glory!
  Thy relaxing sinews bend;
For a while the ancient rigour
  That thy birth bestowed, suspend;
And the King of Heavenly Beauty
  On thy bosom gently tend!

## The Royal Banners Forward Go

The Royal Banners forward go;
The Cross shines forth in mystic glow;
Where He in flesh, our flesh Who made,
Our sentence bore, our ransom paid.

Where deep for us the spear was dy'd,
Life's torrent rushing from His side,
To wash us in that precious flood
Where mingled Water flow'd, and Blood.

Fulfill'd is all that David told
In true Prophetic song of old;
Amidst the nations God, saith he,
Hath reign'd and triumph'd from the Tree.

O Tree of Beauty! Tree of Light!
O Tree with royal purple dight!
Elect on whose triumphal breast
Those holy limbs should find their rest!

On whose dear arms, so widely flung,
The weight of this world's ransom hung:
The price of human kind to pay,
And spoil the Spoiler of his prey.

# ST JOHN DAMASCENE

(See page 321.)

## Ode III

Δεῦτε πόμα πίωμεν.

Come, and let us drink of that New River,
  Not from barren rock divinely poured,
But the Fount of Life that is for ever
  From the Sepulchre of Christ the Lord.

All the world hath bright illumination—
  Heav'n and Earth and things beneath the earth:
'Tis the Festival of all Creation:
  Christ hath ris'n, Who gave Creation birth.

Yesterday with Thee in burial lying,
  Now today with Thee aris'n I rise;
Yesterday the partner of Thy dying,
  With Thyself upraise me to the skies.

## The Stichera of the Last Kiss

Δεῦτε τελευταῖον ἄσπασμον δῶμεν.

Take the last kiss—the last for ever!
  Yet render thanks amidst your gloom:
He, severed from his home and kindred,
  Is passing onwards to the tomb:
For earthly labours, earthly pleasures,
  And carnal joys, he cares no more:

Where are his kinsfolk and acquaintance?
They stand upon another shore.
Let us say, around him pressed,
Grant him, Lord, eternal rest!

The hour of woe and separation,
The hour of falling tears is this:
Him that so lately was among us
For the last time of all we kiss:
Up to the grave to be surrendered,
Sealed with the monumental stone,
A dweller in the house of darkness,
Amidst the dead to lie alone.
Let us say, around him pressed,
Grant him, Lord, eternal rest!

Life, and life's evil conversation,
And all its dreams, are passed away:
The soul hath left her tabernacle:
Black and unsightly grows the clay.
The golden vessel here lies broken:
The tongue no voice of answer knows:
Hushed is sensation, stilled is motion;
Towards the tomb the dead man goes.
Let us cry with heart's endeavour,
Grant him rest that is for ever!

What is our life? A fading flower;
A vapour, passing soon away;
The dewdrops of the early morning:
Come, gaze upon the tombs today.
Where now is youth? Where now is beauty,
And grace of form, and sparkling eye?
All, like the summer grass, are withered;
All are abolished utterly!

While our eyes with grief grow dim,
Let us weep to Christ for him!

Woe for that bitter, bitter moment,
The fearful start, the parting groan,
The wrench of anguish, from the body
When the poor soul goes forth alone!
Hell and destruction are before her;
Earth in its truest worth she sees;
A flickering shade; a dream of error;
A vanity of vanities.
Sin in this world let us flee,
That in heaven our place may be.

Draw nigh, ye sons of Adam; viewing
A likeness of yourselves in clay:
Its beauty gone; its grace disfigured;
Dissolving in the tomb's decay;
The prey of worms and of corruption,
In silent darkness mouldering on;
Earth gathers round the coffin, hiding
The brother, now for ever gone.
Yet we cry, around him pressed,
Grant him, Lord, eternal rest!

When, hurried forth by fearful angels,
The soul forsakes her earthly frame,
Then friends and kindred she forgetteth,
And this world's cares have no more claim;
Then passed are vanity and labour;
She hears the Judge's voice alone;
She sees the ineffable tribunal:
Where we, too, cry with suppliant moan,
For the sins that soul hath done,
Grant Thy pardon, Holy One!

# Idiomela for All Saints

**τὰς ἑδρὰς τὰς αἰωνίας.**

Those eternal bowers
  Man hath never trod,
Those unfading flowers
  Round the throne of God:
Who may hope to gain them
  After weary fight?
Who at length attain them
  Clad in robes of white?

He, who gladly barters
  All on earthly ground;
He who, like the martyrs,
  Says, "I *will* be crown'd":
He, whose one oblation
  Is a life of love;
Clinging to the nation
  Of the Blest above.

Shame upon you, legions
  Of the Heavenly King,
Denizens of regions
  Past imagining!
What! with pipe and tabor
  Fool away the light,
When He bids you labour;
  When He tells you, "Fight!"

While I do my duty,
  Struggling through the tide,

Whisper Thou of beauty
  On the other side!
Tell who will the story
  Of our *now* distress:
Oh, the future glory!
  Oh, the loveliness!

# ACKNOWLEDGMENTS
# BIBLIOGRAPHY
# INDEX

# Acknowledgments

The editor wishes to thank the following for their kind permission to reprint in this volume excerpts from the books listed below:

Ernest Benn, Limited, London, *Private Letters Pagan and Christian,* selected by Dorothy Lamb Brooke.

Basil Blackwell & Mott, Limited, Oxford, *Three Byzantine Saints,* translated by Elizabeth Dawes and Norman H. Baynes.

The Catholic University of America Press, Washington, *Patristic Studies,* translated by Sister Mary Dolorosa Mannix; and *The Spiritual Life According to Saint Isidore of Seville,* translated by Sister Patrick Jerome Mullins.

Chatto & Windus, London, *The Paradise or Garden of the Holy Fathers,* translated by Sir Ernest A. T. Wallis Budge.

The Clarendon Press, Oxford, *Some Authentic Acts of the Martyrs* by E. C. E. Owen; *Letters from Sidonius* by Augustine Fitzgerald; and *The Letters of Sidonius* by O. M. Dalton.

Columbia University Press, New York, *Cassiodorus Senator: An Introduction to Divine and Human Readings,* translated by Leslie Webber Jones.

E. P. Dutton & Co., Inc., New York, *Fathers of the Church* by F. A. Wright.

Faber and Faber, Limited, London, *Writings from the Philokalia on Prayer of the Heart,* translated by E. Kadloubovsky and G. E. H. Palmer.

Fathers of the Church, Inc., New York, *The Fathers of the Church.*

Harvard University Press, Cambridge, from volumes in the Loeb Classical Library: *Julian, Volume III,* translated by William Cave Wright; and *Ausonius, Volume I,* translated by Hugh G. Evelyn White.

Dr. James Kritzeck, Harvard University, *Patrologia Graeca* by J. P. Migne, translated by James Kritzeck.

Loyola University Press, Chicago, *Early Christian Latin Poets* by Otto J. Kuhnmuench.

The Newman Press, Westminster, Maryland, *The Call of All Nations* by St. Prosper of Aquitaine, translated by P. DeLetter, S.J.; and *The Contemplative Life* by Julianus Pomerius, translated by Sister Mary Josephine Suelzer.

Whitney J. Oates and Random House, Inc., New York, *The Basic Writings of St. Augustine,* edited by Whitney J. Oates.

Routledge and Kegan Paul, Ltd., London, *Fathers of the Church* by F. A. Wright; and *Life of St. Columba* by Adamnan, translated by Wentworth Huysshe.

Charles Scribner's Sons, New York, *A Source Book of Ancient Church History* by Joseph Cullen Ayer, copyright 1913 by Charles Scribner's Sons, 1941 by Joseph Cullen Ayer, Jr.

The Society for Promoting Christian Knowledge, London, *Documents Illustrative of the History of the Church,* edited by B. J. Kidd; *On the Divine Names and the*

*Mystical Theology* by Dionysius the Areopagite, translated by Clarence E. Rolt; *The "Octavius" of Minucius* by J. H. Freese; *The Pilgrimage of Etheria* by M. L. McClure and C. L. Feltoe; and Justin Martyr's *"The Dialogue with Trypho,"* translated by A. Lukyn Williams.

# Bibliography


Altaner, Berthold. *Patrologie*. Freiburg im Breisgau: Herder & Co., 1938.

*Ante-Nicene Christian Library,* edited by Alexander Roberts and James Donaldson. Edinburgh: T. & T. Clark, 1867–72. 24 vols.

*Ante-Nicene Fathers, The,* ed. by Alexander Roberts and James Donaldson. Buffalo: Christian Literature Publishing Co., 1885–96. 10 vols.

Augustine, Saint. *On the Spirit and the Letter,* trans. by W. J. Sparrow Simpson. (In *Translations of Christian Literature,* Series II.) London: Society for Promoting Christian Knowledge, 1925.

Ayer, Joseph C. *A Source Book for Ancient Church History*. New York: Charles Scribner's Sons, 1913.

Bardesanes. *De Fato,* trans. by Benjamin P. Pratten. In *Ante-Nicene Christian Library,* vol. 22, part 2. Edinburgh: T. & T. Clark, 1871.

Batiffol, Pierre. *Anciennes littératures chrétiennes. La littérature grecque*. Paris: V. Lecoffre, 1897.

Bede, the Venerable. *The History of the Church of Englande,* trans. by Thomas Stapleton (1565). Oxford: B. Blackwell, 1930.

Budge, Sir Ernest A. T. Wallis, ed., *The Paradise or Garden of the Holy Fathers*. London: Chatto & Windus, 1907. 2 vols.

Cabrol, Fernand. *Dictionnaire d'archéologie chrétienne et de liturgie*. Paris: Letouzey et Ané, 1903–37. 13 vols.

Cassiodorus Senator. *Letters of Cassiodorus,* ed. by Thomas Hodgkin. London: Henry Frowde, 1886.

Cayré, Fulbert. *Précis de patrologie*. Paris: Société de S. Jean l'Évangéliste, Desclée et cie., 1927–30. 2 vols.

Chrysostomus, Joannes. *On the Priesthood,* trans. by Henry M. Mason. Philadelphia: E. Littell, 1826.

Collins, W. Lucas. *Lucian*. Edinburgh and London: Blackwood, 1873.

Dawes, Elizabeth, and Baynes, Norman H., trans. *Three Byzantine Saints*. Oxford: B. Blackwell, 1948.

Diadoque de Photicé. *Cent chapitres sur la perfection spirituelle,* trans. by Édouard des Places. (In *Sources Chrétiennes.*) Paris: Éditions du Cerf, 1943.

Dionysius the Areopagite. *On the Divine Names and the Mystical Theology,* trans. by Clarence E. Rolt. London: Society for Promoting Christian Knowledge, 1940.

*Encyclopaedia of Religion and Ethics,* ed. by J. Hastings. New York: Charles Scribner's Sons, 1908–27. 13 vols.

Ephraem, Saint. *Select Metrical Hymns and Homilies of Ephraem Syrus,* trans. by Henry Burgess. London: Blackader, 1853.

Ghellinck, Joseph de. *Littérature latine au moyen âge*. Paris: Bloud & Gay, 1939.

Gregory the Great, Saint. *Dialogues of St. Gregory the Great, an Old English Version,* ed. by Henry J. Coleridge. London: Burns & Oates, 1874.

———. *King Alfred's West-Saxon Version of Gregory's Pastoral Care,* ed. by Henry Sweet. London: Oxford University Press, 1871.

Gregory of Nazianzus. *Five Theological Orations,* ed. by Arthur J. Mason. (In Cambridge Patristic Texts.) Cambridge: Cambridge University Press, 1899.

Justin Martyr. *The Dialogue with Trypho,* trans. by A. Lukyn Williams. (In *Translations of Christian Literature,* Series I.) New York and Toronto: The Macmillan Co., 1930.

Kadloubovsky, E., and Palmer, G. E. H., trans. *Writings from the Philokalia on Prayer of the Heart.* London: Faber & Faber, 1951.

Kidd, Beresford J., ed. *Documents Illustrative of the History of the Church.* London: Society for Promoting Christian Knowledge, 1920–41. 3 vols.

Kuhnmuench, Otto J., ed. *Early Christian Latin Poets from the Fourth to the Sixth Century.* Chicago: Loyola University Press, 1929.

Labriolle, Pierre de. *Histoire de la littérature latine chrétienne.* 2nd ed. Paris: Société d'édition "Les belles lettres," 1924.

———. *La réaction païenne.* Paris: L'Artisan du livre, 1934.

*Library of the Fathers of the Holy Catholic Church,* ed. by E. B. Pusey, J. H. Newman, J. Keble, and C. Marriott. Oxford: J. H. Parker, 1838–85. 50 vols.

Lightfoot, Joseph B., ed. and trans. *The Apostolic Fathers.* London and New York: Macmillan & Co., 1889–90. 5 vols.

Lightfoot, Joseph B., trans. *The Apostolic Fathers.* Revised texts ed. and completed by J. R. Harmer. London and New York: Macmillan & Co., 1907.

*Loeb Classical Library,* ed. by T. E. Page, E. Capps, and W. H. D. Rouse. London: W. Heinemann, 1912–49.

Marucchi, Orazio. *Christian Epigraphy.* Cambridge: Cambridge University Press, 1912.

Maxime le Confesseur. *Centuries sur la charité,* trans. by J. Pegon. (In *Sources Chrétiennes.*) Paris: Éditions du Cerf, 1943.

McClure, M. L., and Feltoe, C. L. *The Pilgrimage of Etheria.* London: Society for Promoting Christian Knowledge, 1919(?).

McGiffert, Arthur C. *A History of Christian Thought.* New York and London: Charles Scribner's Sons, 1932–33. 2 vols.

Melito. *The Homily on the Passion by Melito, Bishop of Sardis,* ed. by Campbell Bonner. Philadelphia: University of Pennsylvania Press, 1940.

Migne, Jacques Paul, ed. *Patrologiae Cursus Completus; Series Graeca.* Paris: 1857–80. 161 vols.

———. *Series Latinae.* Paris: 1842–92. 221 vols.

Moschos, Ioannes, *Le Pré spirituel,* trans. by Marie-J. Rouët de Journel, S.J. Paris: Éditions du Cerf, 1946.

Moschus, Jean. *Le Pré spirituel.* (In *Sources Chrétiennes.*) Paris: Éditions du Cerf, 1946.

Mullins, Sister Patrick Jerome. *The Spiritual Life According to Saint Isidore of Seville.* Washington, D.C.: Catholic University of America Press, 1940.

Neale, John Mason. *Collected Hymns, Sequences and Carols.* London: Hodder and Stoughton, 1914.

Newman, John Henry. *The Church of the Fathers.* 4th ed. London: Burns, Oates, & Co., 1868.

Nicholson, Dorothy Brooke. *Private Letters, Pagan and Christian.* London: E. Benn, Ltd., 1929.

Nicholson, Sir Sydney H., ed. *Hymns Ancient and Modern.* London: W. Clowes & Sons, Ltd., 1932.

Nunn, Henry P. V. *Christian Inscriptions.* London: Society for Promoting Christian Knowledge; New York: The Macmillan Co., 1920.

Oates, Whitney J., ed. *Basic Writings of St. Augustine.* New York: Random House, 1948. 2 vols.

Owen, Edward C. E., trans. *Some Authentic Acts of the Early Martyrs.* Oxford: Clarendon Press, 1927.

Photius. *The Library of Photius,* trans. by John H. Freese. Vol. 1. London: Society for Promoting Christian Knowledge, 1920.

Pickman, Edward M. *The Mind of Latin Christendom.* London, New York, etc.: Oxford University Press, 1937.

Pomerius, Julianus. *The Contemplative Life,* trans. by Sister Mary Josephine Suelzer (Ancient Christian Writers; Works of the Fathers in Translation, No. 4). Westminster, Md.: Newman Bookshop, 1947.

Ryelandt, Idesbald. *St. Benedict the Man,* trans. by Patrick Shaughnessy. St. Meinrad, Ind.: Grail Publication, 1950.

Salvian. *The Governance of God,* trans. by Jeremiah F. O'Sullivan. New York: Cima Publ. Co., 1947.

Schaff, Philip, ed. *A Select Library of the Nicene and Post-Nicene Fathers of the Christian Church.* New York: The Christian Literature Co., 1886–90. 14 vols.

Schaff, Philip, and Wace, Henry, eds. *A Select Library of Nicene and Post-Nicene Fathers of the Christian Church.* Second series. New York: The Christian Literature Co., 1890–1900. 14 vols.

Socrates Scholasticus. *Ecclesiasticall History,* trans. by Meredith Hanmer. London: Abraham Miller, 1649.

*Sources Chrétiennes,* ed. by H. de Lubac and J. Daniélou. Paris: Éditions du Cerf, 1943–52.

Sulpicius Severus. *Writings of Sulpicius Severus,* trans. by Bernard M. Peebles. New York: Fathers of the Church, Inc., 1949.

Tacitus, Cornelius. *The Histories,* with English trans. by Clifford H. Moore. (Loeb Classical Library) London: W. Heinemann; New York: G. P. Putnam's Sons, 1925–37. 4 vols.

Robinson, Joseph Armitage, ed. *Texts and Studies. Contributions to Biblical and Patristic Literature.* Cambridge: Cambridge University Press, 1893. 9 vols.

Tixeront, Joseph, trans. *A Handbook of Patrology;* trans. based on 4th French ed. by S. A. Raemers. St. Louis, Mo., and London: B. Herder, 1947.

White, Newport J. D., ed. *St. Patrick, His Writings and Life.* London: Society for Promoting Christian Knowledge; New York: The Macmillan Co., 1920.

Wright, Frederick A. *A History of Later Greek Literature.* London: G. Routledge & Sons, Ltd., 1932.

———, trans. *Fathers of the Church.* New York: E. P. Dutton, 1929.

Wright, William. *A Short History of Syriac Literature.* London: A. & C. Black, 1894.

# Index

*(Figures in italics indicate biographical references)*